THE DUAL MANDATE IN BRITISH TROPICAL AFRICA

THE DUAL MANDATE IN BRITISH TROPICAL AFRICA

LORD LUGARD

With a new introduction by

MARGERY PERHAM
C.B.E., D.Litt., F.B.A.

Routledge
Taylor & Francis Group
LONDON AND NEW YORK

First published by Frank Cass & Co. Ltd.,
by arrangement with
William Blackwood & Sons Ltd.

First edition	**1922**
Second edition	**1923**
Third edition	**1925**
Fourth edition	**1929**
Fifth edition	**1905**

Published 2005 by Routledge
2 Park Square, Milton Park, Abingdon, Oxfordshire OX14 4RN
711 Third Avenue, New York, NY 10017

First issued in paperback 2014

Routledge is an imprint of the Taylor and Francis Group, an informa business

ISBN 13: 978-0-714-61690-2 (hbk)
ISBN 13: 978-0-415-76070-6 (pbk)

TO

MY WIFE

Whose unfailing sympathy and understanding have ever helped me in my work.

"It will be the high task of all My Governments to superintend and assist the development of these countries . . . for the benefit of the inhabitants and the general welfare of mankind."—HIS MAJESTY THE KING.

"The wellbeing and development of peoples not yet able to stand by themselves, form a sacred Trust of Civilisation."—*Covenant of League, Art.* 22.

"We develop new territory as Trustees for Civilisation, for the Commerce of the World."—JOSEPH CHAMBERLAIN.

PREFACE TO THE FIRST EDITION

THE object which I have had in view in setting down these notes on administration in British tropical Africa is twofold. In the first place, I have hoped to put before those who are interested in the development of that part of the British Empire beyond the seas for which Great Britain is directly responsible, an outline of the system under which those responsibilities have originated and are being discharged, and some idea of the nature of the problems confronting the local administrator. In the second place, in discussing these problems I have ventured to make some few suggestions, as the result of experience, in the hope that they may be found worthy of consideration by the "men on the spot"—in so far as the varying circumstances of our Crown colonies and protectorates may render them in any degree applicable.

To Sir E. Speed, late Chief Justice of Nigeria, I am indebted for having kindly overlooked the chapters on "The Law and Courts of Justice," and those on the status of protectorates, &c.; to Colonel Amery, M.P. (late Under-Secretary for the Colonies), who has read the chapters on "Home Administration" and chapter xiii. ("Taxation"); and to Sir John Eaglesome, who has read the chapter on "Railways and Transport."

In the endeavour to present in a self-contained form each of the subjects with which the various chapters deal, it has been impossible to avoid frequent repetition, due to the different point of view presented, and for this I must ask my readers' indulgence.

I have made a point of citing authorities freely in the footnotes, with the object of indicating where fuller information may be found, should the reader desire to explore the subject further.

F. D. L.

ABINGER COMMON, SURREY,
December 1921.

PREFACE TO THE SECOND EDITION

THE exhaustion of the First Edition of this work has afforded me the opportunity to revise the pages referring to the Mandate System (pp. 50-58), and those referring to the "Kenya Question" (pp. 317-324) by the light of more recent events, and to make various other minor alterations and corrections in the first eighteen chapters (see Note *re* Abyssinian Slavery, p. 359, &c.).

F. D. L.

ABINGER COMMON,
15*th July* 1923.

CHAPTER VII.

THE BRITISH STAFF AND CONDITIONS OF LIFE IN THE TROPICS.

CHAPTER VIII.

THE HOME GOVERNMENT AND THE DEPENDENCIES.

CHAPTER IX.

THE HOME GOVERNMENT AND THE DEPENDENCIES (*continued*).

CONTENTS

INTRODUCTION.

PART I.

EUROPE AND TROPICAL AFRICA.

CHAPTER I.

THE ACQUISITION OF THE BRITISH AFRICAN TROPICS.

CHAPTER II.

THE STATUS AND CONDITIONS OF THE BRITISH TROPICS.

CHAPTER III.

PRINCIPLES GOVERNING CONTROL IN THE TROPICS.

CHAPTER IV.

THE PEOPLE OF BRITISH TROPICAL AFRICA.

CHAPTER V.

SOME GENERAL PRINCIPLES OF A

CHAPTER VI.

THE MACHINERY OF ADMIN

PART II.

SPECIAL PROBLEMS.

CHAPTER X.

METHODS OF RULING NATIVE RACES.

CHAPTER XI.

METHODS OF RULING NATIVE RACES (*continued*).

CHAPTER XII.

TAXATION.

APPENDIX.

CHAPTER XIII.

TAXATION (*continued*) AND METHODS OF RAISING REVENUE.

CONTENTS

INTRODUCTION.

PART I.

EUROPE AND TROPICAL AFRICA.

CHAPTER I.

THE ACQUISITION OF THE BRITISH AFRICAN TROPICS.

CHAPTER II.

THE STATUS AND CONDITIONS OF THE BRITISH TROPICS.

CHAPTER III.

PRINCIPLES GOVERNING CONTROL IN THE TROPICS.

CHAPTER IV.

THE PEOPLE OF BRITISH TROPICAL AFRICA.

PART II.

SPECIAL PROBLEMS.

CHAPTER X.

METHODS OF RULING NATIVE RACES.

CHAPTER XI.

METHODS OF RULING NATIVE RACES (*continued*).

CHAPTER XII.

TAXATION.

APPENDIX.

CHAPTER XIII.

TAXATION (*continued*) AND METHODS OF RAISING REVENUE.

CHAPTER V.

SOME GENERAL PRINCIPLES OF ADMINISTRATION.

CHAPTER VI.

THE MACHINERY OF ADMINISTRATION.

CHAPTER VII.

THE BRITISH STAFF AND CONDITIONS OF LIFE IN THE TROPICS.

CHAPTER VIII.

THE HOME GOVERNMENT AND THE DEPENDENCIES.

CHAPTER IX.

THE HOME GOVERNMENT AND THE DEPENDENCIES (*continued*).

CHAPTER XIV.

LAND TENURE AND TRANSFER.

CHAPTER XV.

LAND TENURE AND TRANSFER (*continued*).

CHAPTER XVI.

LAND TENURE AND TRANSFER (*continued*).

MINERALS.

CHAPTER XVII.

SLAVERY IN BRITISH AFRICA

CHAPTER XVIII.

SLAVERY IN BRITISH AFRICA (*continued*).

CHAPTER XIX.

LABOUR IN TROPICAL AFRICA.

CHAPTER XX.

LABOUR IN TROPICAL AFRICA (*continued*).

CHAPTER XXI.

EDUCATION.

CHAPTER XXV.

ECONOMIC DEVELOPMENT.

CHAPTER XXVI.

ECONOMIC DEVELOPMENT (*continued*).

CHAPTER XXVII.

THE LAW AND THE COURTS OF JUSTICE.

CHAPTER XXVIII.

COURTS OF JUSTICE (*continued*).

CHAPTER XXIX.

SOME OTHER PROBLEMS.

CHAPTER XXX.

SOME OTHER PROBLEMS (*continued*).

CHAPTER XXXI.

CONCLUSION. THE VALUE OF BRITISH RULE IN THE TROPICS TO THE BRITISH DEMOCRACY AND TO THE NATIVE RACES.

INTRODUCTION TO THE FIFTH EDITION

BY

Margery Perham

INTRODUCTION TO THE FIFTH EDITION

1. THE WRITING OF THE BOOK

SIR FREDERICK LUGARD, as he was then, retired from his last post under the Colonial Office, the Governor-Generalship of Nigeria, in 1919. In May of that year he wrote to the firm of Blackwoods, which in 1893 had published his earlier two-volume book, *The Rise of our East African Empire*, to offer "a book of no great size on problems of African *tropical* Administration". He had written his first book in six months. His second took him two years. But now he was a great man, with all the time-consuming responsibilities of that status. During the period, moreover, he was still concerned with tasks rounding off his long work in Nigeria. Moreover, a thrifty country having provided him with barely enough to live upon, he joined a new venture, the Abyssinia Corporation, and went out to that country on its behalf. The resultant book, while it does not balance the scales with Lord Hailey's weighty volumes on much the same subject, hardly fulfils Lugard's modest intention as to size. In view of its close-woven texture, and its load of footnotes, its production in two years was a triumph of concentrated energy such as he brought to all his tasks.

In this work he had the encouragement of his wife. He had brought his inability to do things by halves, or even by three-quarters, into his marriage and he felt for his wife a love passing that of the generality of men. In her he possessed Flora Shaw, a female phenonmenon of her period, former colonial correspondent of *The Times*, traveller, authoress, a woman of beauty and birth, who moved of right in the political and fashionable circles of the time.[1] They lived in the

[1] For her biography see Moberly Bell, *Flora Shaw*, 1947.

house which was an extension of the cottage of her unmarried days, high up amongst the beeches and pine trees of Leith Hill in Surrey. While he wrote at his desk in the business-like study planned for his work, she sat amongst the pink flowery chintzes of the drawing-room next door and read his chapters, or even his pages, as he brought them to her for comment. Her own writings had a structure, a grace and a sense of history beyond his capacity or ambition. Humble, too humble it might be thought, in his admiration for her, he was ready to defer to her even on their common ground of colonial affairs and to inscribe his gratitude in the dedication of this book. But, on internal evidence, it would not seem that she had done anything to decorate the solid structure of his work. She was confronted here with his immense experience in a continent where, to their great sorrow, she had never, after one brief attempt, been able to live. Yet, it must be noted, she had written, with impressive literary confidence, her own study of Nigerian history.[1]

Lugard's own book was widely and seriously reviewed, and was given the red ribbon of a classic. His name was now famous and the Nigeria where he had done his longest and most authoritative work, was, politically at least, Britain's most important dependency in Africa. The world war was over now and Britain was able to take up again her task, interrupted by hostilities in Africa as well as in Europe, of colonial development and administration. The task was generally seen to have been only just begun and its future had then no visible terminal point. At such a time the considered views of Britain's greatest colonial governor upon African administration naturally commanded great attention.

The book ran through four editions appearing in 1922, 1923, 1926 and 1929. The only important revision was in the 1929 edition in which the sections on the League of Nations Mandate system and the problems of East Africa were rewritten. In spite of the acclaim Lugard was disappointed in the sales, which reached 2,242. He was not much interested in literary fame, still less in royalties, but he was greatly disappointed that the price of two guineas put it out of the reach of the members of the Colonial Service whose instruction had been his main purpose in writing. It was not enough for him that the book was to be found in every British African

[1] F. Lugard, *A Tropical Dependency*, 1905.

headquarters, central and provincial. In all his correspondence with Mr. Blackwood—conducted upon a scale and with a personal flavour that would arouse the envy of most contemporary authors—Lugard continued to urge a price of ten shillings even if this required that he should sacrifice all royalties or even pay a subsidy.

The reviews, in their number, length and thoroughness, would also arouse nostalgia among modern authors. The cuttings fill a large volume. There are two points made in them which may be selected for discussion.

The first was the general recognition that the book was an authoritative justification of Britain's annexation and government of tropical Africa. It was especially regarded as an answer to an early Labour pamphlet which had recently appeared at the price of twopence, apparently inspired by Mr. Leonard Woolf, whose own denunciatory book, *Empire and Commerce in Africa*, had appeared in the previous year. The end of the war had seen the release of two contrary impulses in Britain. One was a hard business-like determination to make good the losses of war by pursuing, among other things, an energetic and self-regarding campaign to make the empire pay. The other was an idealistic fervour to establish a new order of international liberty and justice. In his book Lugard brought these two themes together in a compromise which was not one of soothing theory but of sustained administrative purpose.

This reconciliation of seeming opposites is his governing theme, expressed in the title Dual Mandate, and treated throughout almost entirely in a practical tone. On page 617 will be found one of the few passages of the book in which he deals with the controversy about imperialism in general terms. Here he shows his complete freedom from any delusions of that debate. He admits that European brains, capital and energy have not been applied to Africa from motives of pure philanthropy and never will be but that the benefit of the European effort "can be made reciprocal and that it is the aim and desire of civilised administration to fulfil this dual mandate." But, even concerning his own nation's capacity to carry out her side of the mandate, he did not make the comfortable assumption that this dualism would be easy to fulfil, Lugard was an enthusiast in his actions rather than in his ideas. There were contradictions in his make-up which did not accord with the conventional idea of the empire-builder of his period. He struggled to annex large parts of Africa because he shared the view of his one-time chief, Joseph Chamberlain, that the crowded millions of his own country needed the economic outlet provided by these virgin tropical lands. But he was no incarnation of economic imperialism: indeed, he fought long and hard against any suggestion of exploitation in Africa by business elements or of departure from the principles of freedom of trade even where the ex-enemy Germany was concerned. Again, though on both sides of Africa Lugard had been in conflict with Frenchmen to the very edge of open hostilities, and was intensely critical of some of the colonial methods of other powers, he believed in the need for a considerable measure of international co-operation in the interests of Africans. It was these veins of internationalism and liberalism in the intensely British marble of his character which made him in his later years such an effective member of the Mandates Commission and of other international organizations in which he participated vigorously until the very end of his life at the age of eighty-seven.

The second aspect of *The Dual Mandate* which struck reviewers was the comprehensiveness of the book. As one of them wrote, it seemed "to lead in endless directions." The general view of those who have not studied this well-known work is that it deals with native administration in the special and restricted sense that the term acquired partly as a result of Lugard's work in Nigeria. Yet this heading can be applied to no more than six out of the thirty-one chapters which follow. These cover a very wide range, including the historical and international aspects of colonial rule in Africa; the principles and total structure of the British colonial system, metropolitan, and territorial; native administration in the restricted special sense; either one or two chapters upon special problems, taxation, slavery, labour, education, law and justice; no less than three upon land; finally, two which give attention to municipal government, armed forces, missions and intoxicants. I have ventured to list items which any reader can see for himself by turning to the list of contents in order to emphasize an aspect of the book which gives it a special character. It is one that was in the mind of its reviewers when one of them said that "it has not only been written. It has been lived" while another stated that the book was in itself "almost a deed". These words point to what is unusual about such a comprehensive book; that the many subjects it covers are none of them activities which Lugard had merely studied, nor even ones which he had directed from the central eminence of a governor, though he certainly did this in his later years and learned the lessons belonging to that level. But long before that he had indeed *lived* most of these subjects, many of them in the hard way, close to the earth and to the tribes of nineteenth-century Africa and some, for extra comparative value, in Asia. One of the works of General Lyautey—who has, not quite appropriately, been regarded as the French version of Lugard—was called *Paroles d'Action.*[1] Certainly this description could be applied to Lugard's book in that it was based upon direct practical experience in the past and intended to govern action in the future.

To supply full meaning to this statement or, indeed, to the book, it is necessary to recall the main phases of his life up to the age of 63 when he finished its writing. Here I am in a difficulty. I have already written his biography in a full scale in two volumes and have also written biographical introductions to the three volumes of his East African diary and the volume of his Nigerian diary. Yet I can hardly assume that readers who take up *The Dual Mandate* will have read this material or, even if they have, will retain it in their memories as they read this book. For their convenience, and to help them to evaluate the deep and varied experience which informs these pages, I must offer them a summary of Lugard's life with emphasis upon those parts of his work which most directly underlie his chapters.

2. OUTLINE OF LUGARD'S LIFE.[2]

Lugard was born in India in 1858, the year of the Indian mutiny. He was, in the estimate of his time, and one which he cherished, a gentleman. Both sides of his family, without being aristocratic, were solidly placed both in social position and public service. His parents had met in India, both having

[1] Paris, 1927

[2] As references to my biography of Lugard and my other writings would be too numerous I have omitted them.

come there under the aegis of the Anglican Church, the father as a chaplain in the East India Company and the mother in the service of the Church Missionary Society. It was his mother, who brought him to England in 1863 and died in his sixth year, who moulded his character by implanting, more by love and example than by discipline, a very high sense of duty and of the rigorous self-mastery needed to perform it. At school, at Sandhurst, and in a regiment posted to India, Lugard's nature, so strongly formed in childhood, was further impelled by the double spur of poverty and the family tradition of service. In this lies the explanation of his sense of duty, of courage, of daily commitment to a discipline of unceasing work.

In India he came to terms with the tropics. He learned his soldiering, which was then, so much more than now, the management of men rather than of machines, in the Afghan war of 1879–80, in a diversion to Africa for the bloody and torrid Snakin Campaign, and in the second Burma war. He became a specialist upon that intricate and fundamental basis for frontier warfare, transport, which demanded a study of animals as well as of men. He also threw himself into every other activity of Kipling's India, including pony racing, tiger-shooting and pig-sticking. Further, he left India not unaware of the political and administrative meaning of British India and the princely states. He left because of a disastrous and dramatic love affair, in which the dementia of Burma fever was heightened by his pursuing his lady to Britain and finding, in the language of the period, that his love had been betrayed. On the edge of physical and mental breakdown he tried to escape from himself and his past by rushing almost penniless to East Africa. There he hoped to find oblivion and perhaps death by following Livingstone's footsteps into the campaign against the Arab slave-trade.

Lugard's course towards a successful and respectable career in the army was thus roughly broken and he found himself a friendless adventurer in a continent of which, at least south of the Red Sea, he knew nothing. Eastern Africa of the late 'eighties was still isolated, little known, unannexed except to the south by the lethargically oppressive Portuguese. From the Zambesi to the middle Nile most of the numerous tribes were becoming either the prey or the partners of the Arab and Swahili slave-traders. To confront them there were only the scattered Christian missionaries. Some of the British among these, appalled by the devastation and by the danger of European rivalries, were beginning to appeal to Britain for political support, and even for annexation. Lugard had hardly landed and ascended the Zambesi by native canoe, when he found himself on the shores of Lake Nyasa fighting Arab slavers in defence of ravaged tribes and endangered Scottish missionaries.[1] From that time until his death he not only fought slavery by every weapon, physical and political but he studied it until he became the leading expert of his time.

Lugard's succeeding African adventures, during the years 1888 to 1900 can be little more than itemized here. Desperately wounded in storming a slavers' stockade, he recovered to return to Britain and to press the needs of the missionaries, and of the tribes ravaged by the slave-trade, for the protection that only British rule could give. Though his private sorrow continued to deny him any inner calm or joy, he no longer wanted to die. He had found a continent and a cause to serve, enough even for his energies. Committed above all, not by sentiment, but by realistic knowledge, to the anti-slavery cause, he made friends with the greatest practical expert on the subject, Sir John Kirk. This famous ex-consul of Zanzibar, headquarters of the Arab slave trade, had coaxed and prodded its Sultan into a progressive limitation of the trade. Through his influence, since Britain was not yet prepared to annex in eastern Africa, Lugard took service with the Imperial British East African Company, a body of distinguished men more competent in patriotism and philanthropy than in commerce. He served this Company for the next four years, studying slavery on the Arabicised coast round Mombasa, exploring the Sabuki river line to the interior, and leading a caravan of African soldiers and porters 800 difficult miles inland to the main objective of the Company. This was the advanced, lonely kingdom of Buganda on the shores of Lake Victoria, torn by civil and religious wars and threatened by European rivalries. In the realm of sheer action these East African years of Lugard were perhaps the greatest in his life. All but cut off in an unexplored interior, with a handful of half-trained local soldiery, by force rather of character than of arms, he imposed his influence over the

[1] See his book *The Rise of our East African Empire*, chapters 1 to 8.

warring groups, explored and annexed along the western frontier of the future Uganda Protectorate, and dealt with African kings, as allies or enemies, with hostile French priests and difficult British missionaries. Throughout he was harassed by all kinds of the still uncontrolled tropical diseases and difficulties of Africa, while in far-away Britain his government seemed indifferent and his Company was trying to abandon the whole enterprise.

In 1892 the dangers on the home front seeming greater than those on Lake Victoria, Lugard hurried back to England. Here, for two years, he fought a double campaign, one to persuade British opinion of the need to annex Uganda and the other to defend his reputation against attacks upon his forceful handling of its affairs, and especially his dealings with the French missionaries who resented his intervention. He made speech-making tours to inform public opinion about East Africa: he wrote, as already stated, a two-volume book on the subject: he lobbied the politicians of both parties and became something of a lion in London society.

But British governments were not yet ready to employ a lion in Africa, especially one who attacked their policies in print and on the platform. So Lugard failed to obtain his heart's desire, to return to his beloved East Africa in the service of the Queen and establish the blessings, as he saw them, of peace, order and development. To his own deep regret, but certainly to the ultimate advantage of the future Nigeria, he felt obliged to accept the challenge of Sir George Goldie that he should lead an expedition to the Niger and outpace the French in drawing a boundary on the great westerly bend of that river. Here again there were trekking, animal transport, African soldiers and porters, diplomacy with chiefs, bush-fighting, wounds, malaria, a new picture of slave-raiding and slavery, another Chartered Company—the Royal Niger—for employer, and, in the background, the Foreign Office, concerned with the high politics of rivalry with France. But a brilliant and hazardous expedition brought Lugard no nearer the desired imperial employment. Again he had reluctantly to accept service under another Company, a mining enterprise which sent him down to the drought-stricken wilds of Bechuanaland. Here he had to parley once more with chiefs, including the famous Christian, Khama. He also saws omething of the political landscape of South Africa and the racial conflict out of which Southern Rhodesia came into being. He had little admiration for Cecil Rhodes and learned a distrust of white settlement in Africa which never left him.

From the shore of the inconstant Okavango Lake, if such it can be termed, Lugard was dramatically recalled by a new figure in the imperial field, Joseph Chamberlain, Secretary of State for the Colonies. Chamberlain was ready to take a bold forward move against France in West Africa. He wanted a man to create an imperial frontier force at high speed and command it in the disputed middle Niger region. To the masterful Chamberlain Lugard was his man. So at last Lugard gained his imperial appointment though he regretted that he had to become a soldier again, even though a general. From 1897 to 1899, stubbornly rather than gladly, he did all his resolute master asked of him. He created the West African Frontier Force, armed and trained it, and transported it some 800 miles up the Niger. He deployed it against the French in a perilous little campaign, part military, part political, one round in a game of international chess in Africa in which the stakes might be peace or war in Europe.

Lugard resented being a piece on a board, even though that piece were a king rather than a pawn. But his reward came in 1900 when he was given the official administrative post he had so long desired. He was appointed High Commissioner of Northern Nigeria and from that date held a governor's office for eighteen years. There was, however, nothing normal or peaceful about his first appointment. Northern Nigeria was vast, little known, populated by powerful Muslim emirs, some of them ready to fight for their independence, or by small defiant pagan tribes which had defied their rule. It had never been mastered by the Royal Niger Company. Most of the region had still to be conquered in daring campaigns or occupied in strength. Having created a military force Lugard had now to recruit, train and direct an administration, devise a system of government which could handle both large and historic Muslim emirates with their walled cities and naked pagans in their hills and forests. The whole range of government, law and order; communications by road, river and telegraph; finance; currency, trade, land, labour, health, had to be created *ab initio* with a skeleton staff in their apprenticeship, and in the absence of any revenue but a meagre annual grant-in-aid from Britain of some £300,000. Seldom can a man have been nearer to the measure of a task almost beyond the capacity of man. Lugard loved not only work, but overwork. He delighted to stretch his body in long marches in defiance of danger, distance, heat, flood, thirst, even fever, and to pit his mind in the same spirit of defiance against the stacks of files on his desk, signing off rapid and and vital decisions into the small hours. "I love to have more work than I can do," he wrote to his wife "and it exhilarates me sometimes to find useful and interesting work accumulating. . . ." Served by his scanty and still largely amateur staff, Lugard would have been forced, at least in the first years, to monopolize power even if he had not been, as one of his Residents called him, "a born centralizer."

As a man of action, as his devoted brother often told the writer, Lugard's finest hour was the time when he struggled first physically and then politically for Britain's annexation of Uganda. But his great creative period as an administrator was during the crowded seven years of his High Commissionership in Northern Nigeria. It was there, in addition to many other less remembered tasks, that he worked out, in action and on paper, the system known as "Indirect Rule", an achievement which will presently demand some discussion.

From his vast raw block of tropical Africa Lugard was transferred in 1907 to the minute, island emporium of Hong Kong, with subjects drawn from the ancient civilization of China. A relatively old and valuable colony, its picked colonial service had developed strong administrative traditions and a corporate sense which hardly promised co-operation with the pioneering "bush-whacker" Lugard was thought to be. He sympathized with them, and with himself, as he made the painful adjustment to the sophisticated and intimate affairs of what was little more than a city and a port. It stood on the fringe of the intense diplomatic and political activity concentrated upon China and was a favourite resort of globe-trotting celebrities of all kinds and nationalities. He dealt with the very big business of the small island, built a railway on the mainland, added to his study of the liquor traffic in Africa a knowledge of narcotics and of certain local practices which rounded out his deep knowledge of slavery. But most surprising as a bequest from African Lugard was the university which he founded in the teeth of opposition and even derision, local and metropolitan, in the hope that it would be a meeting-place for Chinese and western culture.

He made a quiet success of his difficult exercise in adaptation. He had gone there only in order to have his wife with him, a calculation defeated by her persistent ill-health. He was re-called from the East to undertake the immense task of bringing the whole of Nigeria under one administration. It would have been difficult enough, at least by his thorough standards, in normal conditions. But of his six years as Governor-General, four were years of war. This meant not only that his masters in Britain were distracted by the conflict in Europe, but also the threat of the submarine to African communications, the disruption of the economy, severe shortage of staff, and a local war to be fought, with Nigeria for base, across the 1,000-mile frontier of the German Cameroons.

The new structure he made had some faults. But it has at least held together for half a century, fifteen years of which have seen first a free and prolonged debate between the constituent regions, followed by the enactment of a formally democratic federation which in turn has endured, if not without stress, for five years. This degree of stability in the new Nigeria, even allowing for questions which overhang the future, is some proof of good workmanship on the foundations.

In 1919 Lugard resigned from the Colonial Service, of which he had been a late and unconventional member, as a result of a conflict with the Colonial Office. This demands mention here because it explains his discussion of the governor in relation to the Colonial Office in Chapter V of this book and also colours to some extent his treatment of the "Home Government" in Chapters VIII and IX. A personal issue lay behind his views. He was moved by the conflict between his two main devotions, the one to his work and the other to his wife. The first impelled him to work upon the administration of his colony with a concentration so complete that he could not bear to take his hands off the controls in order to rest during the statutory leave of a governor. Especially abhorrent to him was the transfer of the reins for a period of months into the hands of another man. Add to this his unhappiness and self-reproach at his long separations from his deeply loved and brilliant wife and—to them—the deduction was clear. He would return to England each year for some five months. But not to rest. He would remain in general control of Nigeria from a room in the Colonial Office. This meant, of course, that he would never have a holiday. But then he did not like holidays! There is no need to dwell here upon the prolonged conflict with the Colonial Office waged by Lugard in Africa, and his wife in London, in the attempt to achieve this strange combination of love and duty. I have described it fully in the biography. But it deserves mention as the only instance in which the steady pointing of Lugard's compass towards duty was distorted by the almost equally strong, aberrant force of love. The conflict was serious enough to result in Lugard's resignation and to a long continuing coolness, unfortunate for both sides, but especially, of course, for Lugard, between himself and the Colonial Office.

There is no space here, nor perhaps would it be appropriate to sketch even in outline what might be called Lugard's third life, that of the colonial expert and international figure. He continued to work some twelve hours a day in his Surrey home, a power-house for writing, planning, meeting and entertaining. There were frequent visits to London and also to Geneva and elsewhere upon international commissions and meetings concerned with the colonies and above all with Africa. One of the greatest ambitions of this later life, despite years of work, was never fulfilled. He wanted to bring out a fully revised edition of *The Dual Mandate* and wrote to Blackwoods in 1926 to offer the book. He worked upon it in every spare moment to the end of his life. But it was a circular and therefore an endless task. Africa was changing so quickly that by the time he reached the end of the last chapter he had to begin again at the first—revising, adding, correcting. The book grew longer and longer: his energy grew less, until at last, with a deep sense of failure and frustration, he had to acknowledge defeat. He died on April 11th, 1945, still working almost to the last hour.

INDIRECT RULE.

Lugard's name will always be connected with the two words of this heading. So much has been written about this subject, and there has been such a measure of misunderstanding about the term itself and about Lugard's connection with it, that some clearing of the issues it raises must preface its discussion.

While this book shows how wide was Lugard's contribution to colonial government in all its many aspects, it is true that his most individual contribution was in his development in Africa, and his rationalization in England, of the method of colonial government known as "indirect rule". Although, therefore, this subject is covered only in two chapters with some references in others, and especially in those upon taxation, law and courts of justice, it yet demands some introductory treatment.

A large literature has grown up since Lugard's day with "indirect rule" as its central theme and it continues to grow. In face of the sudden, unexpected rush of African states into independence, the philosophy and the practices of British colonial rule have been treated by nearly all African writers, and many British and American ones as a system, planned either upon a wholly mistaken interpretation of African society or as a deliberate policy to divert Africans from the true road to unity and self-government. The comment upon this is not simple. I have myself tried to make it more than once, and most fully in my biography of Lugard.[1]

Reduced to its briefest terms the comment is as follows. Throughout history there have been circumstances in the extension of imperial power when it suited the conquerors to preserve and utilize the institutions of the conquered and especially the kingships and chieftaincies which could be used as ready-made economical agencies of coherence and order. Several motives combined to make this policy especially acceptable to the British. Among these was the tradition of colonial self-government in the earlier "white" colonies; the extensiveness of the new "coloured" empire; its distant and scattered distribution; and the cost and difficulty of extending sufficient British staff to establish "direct" relations with tens of millions of new subjects. In tropical Africa especially the speed of advance inland from the coasts in the first two or three decades of the new century must be

[1] Parts of Lugard's *Political Memoranda*, which was printed privately for official use, have recently been reprinted with later relevant documents upon the administration of Northern Nigeria. This book will be published by the Oxford University Press in 1965, with introductions by A. H. M. Kirk-Greene and by myself, under the title, *The Principles of Native Administration in Nigeria.*

remembered, and also the variety and obscurity of the institutions of the new subjects with their diverse customs, economies and languages.

Using "indirect" in the widest sense, an important shift towards this principle was made when the policy was adopted of preserving the Indian states instead of extending the "direct" rule of British India. Other preservations, more modest in size and scope, could be found outside Africa, as in Malaya and Fiji, and in Africa, where Buganda, Basutoland, and Barotseland are examples. What Lugard did was to turn a rather widespread expedient into a carefully elaborated system, then to draw up a comprehensive code of laws with regulations and instructions, and finally to rationalize the system in his later writings.

This view of Lugard's work is not invalidated by the assertion that Lugard was making administrative virtue out of hard practical necessity. It is quite true that the Hausa and Bornu city-states were, by African standards, highly developed in their political structure their law and law-courts, and their system of taxation. True, also, that Lugard was so poor in staff, communications, finance, and knowledge of the immense new annexation, that a large measure of recognition was unavoidable. But there are different kinds of recognition. Lugard's form of decentralization was quite distinct from those employed in India or Malaya. Even in Africa, it was far more carefully worked out on paper and in practice than other similar systems; it was communicated more fully to the official staff, and was more evolutionary in intention. It is, however, possible to realize now that a danger lay in its astonishing practical success. Hausaland was unique. In comparison with the rest of black Africa the states which composed it had gone a long way towards a common culture. Tribalism had over the centuries been largely sublimated by Islam. Its peoples and rulers already acknowledged a suzerain in the holy ruler of Sokoto. The imposition of a still higher authority could therefore be accepted by emirs and people with little disturbance, political or administrative. There was not only a ruling class partially at least literate, but a rudimentary bureaucracy. The immediate practical success of Lugard's system, so readily accepted by rulers and people, so effective in action and so economical in staff and money, raised at least three large questions. Was it as sound in practice in Hausaland as appeared on the surface? Was it suitable for export to what may be called tribal pagan Africa? For how long would the system meet the needs of a changing Africa?

A full discussion of these three questions would take us beyond the proportions of an introduction. But a brief consideration of each should help readers of Lugard's book to form a judgment at some point between the enthusiasm with which his system was received in the two or three decades following its publication and the more recent tendency to regard it as an attempt to preserve and divide in order to prolong imperialist rule.

Regarding the first question, there was a tendency amongst the school of administrators which grew up under Lugard's strong influence to exalt the status of their emirates. A rather subtle rôle was presented to the Residents in which they had to strike their own discreet balance between two extremes. One was to interfere too much according to western standards of efficiency and humanity and so reduce in the eyes of his people that prestige of the ruler which was essential to the working of indirect rule. The other was to carry toleration too far in ignoring acts of oppression or corruption on the part of rulers, some of whom did not accept or even understand the ideology of their new masters. The tendency of some of the Residents, sharing in a measure the isolation of the region, was to exalt the status of the emirates and therefore of their own authority as the power behind the throne, and to expect a large degree of non-interference, even from the Governor-General.

When Lugard returned to West Africa as Governor-General of the whole of Nigeria he soon became aware of this tendency. The records show that he tried to restrain his Lieutenant Governor, Charles Temple, and some of the leading Residents from delegating too much power to the emirs and claiming too large a financial autonomy for them in the new Native Treasury system. Unfortunately, during his absence in Hong Kong, the Colonial Office had been won over to this policy and Lugard had to face this double opposition while he carried the burden of his main task, which was the unification of this vast region, and also deal with the distractions caused by the World War. He was therefore unable to correct the bias he deplored. What is strange is that he did not stress this danger that was enshrined in his system either in this book or in the Political Memoranda which he finalized after he left Nigeria in 1918. I discovered this issue only when all the documentation was available for writing the biography. I was therefore never able, to my great regret, to discuss this point with him. But there can be no doubt that he never intended the emirates to *grow* in autonomy. He was temperamentally not in sympathy with Sir Donald Cameron who administered Nigeria from 1931 to 1935, but he approved his emphasis upon the subordinate status of the emirs. Cameron's successor, Sir Bernard Bourdillon, was faced by a Lieutenant Governor of the Northern Provinces who wanted the emirates to grow towards something like independent statehood. Lugard's correspondence, which he and I discussed fully together, shows that he strongly supported Sir Bernard's rejection of this policy.

We pass now to the question of the suitability of his system for export outside Northern Nigeria. When Lugard wrote this book he had extended his northern indirect rule system to the chieftainships, mainly of the Yoruba group, in south-western Nigeria. This was the first extension of his principles which he believed were of general validity for tropical Africa. Perhaps even he could hardly have realized in the 'twenties how wide and deep their influence would be, especially during the 'thirties. I was travelling fairly widely in Africa at that time and almost everywhere our administrative staffs were using *The Dual Mandate* and the *Political Memoranda* as the canonical books of their profession. Yet the first extension of the system, originally tailored for the emirates of Northern Nigeria, should have revealed limits to its universality for Africa. Among many reasons for this two may be considered here. One was that in the north the system of rule was no longer bound up with tribal cultures, those close-knit structures of inter-locking beliefs in lineage, ancestor-worship, animism, status and magic. When British power and influence reached Northern Nigeria, the politico-social system, embedded in a stable world-religion, if only upon its fringe, remained largely unaffected by the contact. But in the south the cultures were far more vulnerable and were exposed to western influences from an earlier date and in much greater strength. Moreover, even in their pristine vigour the Yoruba pagan authorities differed from the emirates not only in their sanctions but also because in them power, instead of being concentrated, was dispersed widely and, to a western newcomer, obscurely, among a number of groups and persons. It was almost impossible for British administrators, most of whom had not mastered the difficult tonal language of the people, still less their complex and varying sociology, to find where to locate the executive agency which their newly imposed administrative system required. Lugard did not—perhaps in all his circumstances—could not, understand these hydra-headed obstacles to the successful transfer of his system. The marvel is that between the solidarity and sophistication of the Yoruba groups, the natural ambition of their rulers for promotion to emirate status, and the common sense of most of the officials, the administration of Yorubaland was conducted for some forty years after the amalgamation, if not without incidents of friction and failure, at least with some measure of efficacy.

Where indirect rule, on anything like northern lines, proved wholly inapplicable in Nigeria was in the south-east, the Ibo and Ibibio country. Here, in forests, lived a large population of what the anthropologists call acephalous groups, small independent clusters of pagans each bound only by ties of lineage. The complex distribution of duties according to seniority, sex and status, with ancestral and magical sanctions, offered, even less than among the Yoruba, any agency which an alien ruling power could use for the performance of administrative activities, most of which were too novel in kind and too large in scale to be within the capacity of these small forest groups.

As, during the 'thirties, the philosophy and practice of indirect rule spread over almost the whole of British Africa, adopted almost *in toto* in some dependencies and influencing the system in others, these kinds of obstacle to a success comparable with that in Northern Nigeria, were widely encountered. It may be, however, that in reaction against the dominance of Lugard's model, criticism of it has gone too far. As regards chieftainship, it must be remembered that during a period which varied from one state, and even one province, to another, this institution, with all the varying auxiliary structures which went with it, was a reality which an alien ruler had either to accept, or else to override, or even to destroy.

I found during the inter-war period, when I was travelling extensively in British dependencies in order to study native administration, that the general picture was one of close co-operation between officials, chiefs and their councils, with peaceful and economical administration and a considerable development of the social services and of agricultural production. The people were co-operating in campaigns against tsetse-fly, soil-erosion, famine and the major diseases: tax was collected: the native courts dealt with astronomical numbers of cases with few appeals or complaints. Everywhere on tour the administrative officers were well received: crowds would gather not only to listen but to discuss and to question.

We can see now that even in what may be called the golden age of indirect rule, and even in the most malleable types of society, there was some degree of distortion, perhaps some degree also of the pretence which Sir Donald Cameron castigated. African society did not, for example, endow chiefs with personal executive power to impose measures which sometimes offended or even destroyed tribal custom. Nor did it allow for young clerks or messengers to give orders to aged and, inevitably, conservative elders.

But the critics of indirect rule during this period should support their case by explaining how a constructive contact *should* have been made. It must not be forgotten that there could be no smooth or perfect articulation between the irresistible power of the twentieth century European state and the little isolated tribal societies of Africa over which it had been so suddenly imposed. Nor could the earlier generations of officials be expected to understand the complex and delicate structure of these small societies, each one of which had its own peculiarities. From what little I was able to see and to learn about the contrasting methods of the French, who did not share British respect for African social structure and tended to rule through the agency of subordinate French officials, African clerks and police, their results were no more impressive and were sometimes less humane in operation. It might be said that chieftainship acted as a shock absorber. It took the impact from the new rulers and, for periods which varied with its own structure and the local force of the impact, distributed its effects among the components of the tribal society. But too much was asked of this human agency. It was distorted in the using even before a revolutionary change in the total African situation made it obsolete.

The record is somewhat different for the acephalous societies. Lugard believed that this system, originally applicable to the emirates, could be adapted to all types of African society, down to the small pagan groups. But, as with south-eastern Nigeria, wherever in Africa British rule encountered this tribal situation of small-scale groupings it met almost insurmountable difficulties. Perhaps no system could have provided an activating nexus between two entities so immensely disproportionate in size and different in purpose. Sir Donald Cameron faced the problem frankly in Tanganyika when he laid down that such societies must be ruled directly through native agents such as the Germans had used. A long series of experiments and troubles in South-East Nigeria ended in the early 'forties in the acceptance of the African desire for something close to British forms of local government.

There is one further point to be remembered about indirect rule in the period of its domination. It was no rigid system devised by Europeans to be forced in uniform structure over the immense varieties of African society. Its principles demanded the utmost possible adaptation to these varieties, and the responsibility for devising and adjusting the structure of British authority to African chiefs and councils lay largely in the hands of the officials who were closest to the people, the District Commissioners.

In Chapter VII of this book Lugard lays down the high standard of selection and training he regarded as necessary for this administrative staff and in the following years the Colonial Office, in co-operation with the Universities of Oxford, Cambridge and London, and under the guidance of Sir Ralph Furse,[1] made the most determined efforts to raise the standard of entry and of training for the service. These administrators were originally chosen for their characters and initiative and were then given the degree of discretion which accorded with the British tradition of decentralization. This was often further reinforced by their isolated position. Moreover, under the indirect system they were obliged to study the societies they were administering and elicit the maximum

[1] In his book *Aucuparius*, 1960, Sir Ralph Furse gives an account of his life-work in the recruitment and training of the Colonial Services.

degree of co-operation from chiefs, elders and people. There was thus a bias—not of course always followed—towards a humane, sympathetic and evolutionary relationship with Africans whose leaders were treated as persons and not units, a relationship which tempered the hard impact of alien rule. It is to be remarked that an acute and critical American, who made a prolonged study of African government in 1925–26, recorded his general approval of indirect rule as contrasted with French methods.[1]

It is when we confront our third question as to the capacity of indirect rule to meet the changing needs of Africa that we may begin to question the fundamental validity of Lugard's ideas. It may, of course, be objected that constructing administration in the first two decades of the century, the foundation years of British rule in Africa, he could hardly be expected to provide for the fourth and fifth decades and for these in a rapidly changing continent and world. It must, however, be noticed that, although he could not have foreseen the nature, and still more, the pace, of change, his system was founded upon his belief, which in later years he never substantially changed, that African society was fundamentally and, so, permanently different from European. His views on this subject are expressed chiefly in Chapters IV and VI. From his knowledge of the Africa of 1897 to 1918—and few knew it better—he was impressed by the great differences in culture between the African and the European. The real Africa to him was tribal Africa. The inconsiderable numbers of Europeanized Africans whom he met in Lagos were an exception which could never for him prove the rule that Africans as a whole could fully and sucessfully assimilate western civilization. The growing points of Africa, he believed, lay in their own immemorial institutions. The educated class were a group which could find their expression in posts under government—and he promoted two or three to very high positions—and as members of councils dealing with municipal affairs. He saw them as being as little qualified to represent the vast population of Nigeria as were the white settlers in Kenya to represent their African majority. His own experience, and the views of many well known experts of his period, made

[1] R. L. Buell, *The Native Problem in Africa*, New York, 1928, 2 vol·s Second impression, London, 1965. See especially the chapters on Nigeria and Tanganyika.

him doubt the capacity of Africans to develop parliamentary institutions. Some of the few very highly educated Africans who had attached themselves to the Europeans, conscious of the vast cultural gulf between themselves and the masses, tended to share this view. When it is remembered that Lugard's idea of parliamentary government was the complete British model which the small educated minority were demanding—and which their successors continued to demand until the day of independence—there may be more understanding of his view. He was not thinking in terms of one-party states or veiled autocracies. What he did not foresee was that a small minority of westernized Africans would appeal successfully to the masses and lead them to independence across the ruins of chieftainship. But then most colonial experts failed to foresee this right up to the eve of the event.

How then, we may ask, did Lugard view the future? We are so conscious today not only of what has occurred in Africa in the last ten years but of the speed of African political change fostered by a world situation which was hardly imaginable in 1920, that we find it difficult to recapture the time-scale within which most British people foresaw development. Lugard's view was not static. He worked, with striking results, to improve the efficiency, humanity and prosperity of the emirates and he realized that this progress could be enhanced. But he could hardly imagine such continuing progress in the Africa he knew without the guiding control of British government, at least for some very long period which it seemed otiose to define. We must remember that most of those whose concern was with Africa retained this almost unlimited vista when they referred to African self-government, and even that term seldom meant the parliamentary independence which was actually achieved. Even Sir Donald Cameron, who certainly saw himself as more liberal and realistic than his old chief, took as his guiding aim the retention and development of indigenous institutions in order to make the native "a good African", not to "Westernize him and turn him into a bad imitation of a European." He believed that British administration should ensure that "the political energies and ability of the people are directed to the preservation and development of their own institutions."[1]

[1] *My Tanganyika Service and Some Nigeria*, 1939, p. 95.

In a pamphlet printed for private circulation in 1928 Lugard developed further his opinion, which is shown in this book, that there were forces at work inimical to the tribal foundations upon which, in his view, the future must be built. But he believed that tribal institutions could be developed and modernized, that chieftainship could be grafted even upon pagan groups, and that the chief of these evolving "native administrations" might be represented in a central council alongside the Legislative Council. He had, indeed, experimented with a council somewhat on these lines which met once a year in Nigeria. It was, however, abolished by the succeeding Governor.

CONCLUSION

It is no part of the Introduction to a book to try to forestall the general impression that it will make upon the reader's mind. But it is, perhaps, permissible to offer one warning to the contemporary African or non-African reader as he forms his final judgment upon a book written more than forty years ago, a judgment that must in large measure embrace also the life and work of a man during the thirty years before the date of publication.

The tendency today, not only among African writers, but many American experts upon Africa, is to condemn British administration of this period, especially indirect rule, as a deliberate and subtle attempt to retain power by suppressing African progress and unity. The counter-assumption seems to be that from the moment the British annexed parts of Africa they should have set to work with one main urgent objective, to create united, democratic, independent African nations. Such a concept must be based upon illusory views of the old Africa and of the impression it was bound to make upon men who had to deal with it as it was without the sociological skills or knowledge of recent years. The other cause for such a view must be the assumption, for which up to that date there had been no foundation, that nations—as distinct from private individuals or groups—would pursue a wholly altruistic policy in the interests of other peoples. But nations, even more than the men who compose them, enjoy power and tend to cling to it. The theme of this book, contained within its title and set out in sober terms in the last two pages, is that Britain had at last reached the point where she could make some advance from the unqualified national egotism of past human history and deliberately endeavour to make her occupation of partsof Africa of mutual benefit to rulers and ruled, thus fulfilling a "dual mandate." The question which confronts readers of this book, one which it may, indeed, be still too soon to answer with confidence, is how far Lugard's influence was calculated to help Britain to fulfil her side of the mandate.

November 1964 MARGERY PERHAM

THE DUAL MANDATE

IN

BRITISH TROPICAL AFRICA.

INTRODUCTION.

Contrast between Africa and the rest of the world—Its isolation—Causes which led to the penetration of Africa—Moral progress—The respective tasks of the eighteenth, nineteenth, and twentieth centuries—Object of this book.

AFRICA has been justly termed "the Dark Continent," for the secrets of its peoples, its lakes, and mountains and rivers, have remained undisclosed not merely to modern civilisation, but through all the ages of which history has any record. There are many regions in Asia—in Persia, Assyria, Arabia, and Western China—in which modern explorers have claimed to have made discoveries. But all these countries were the seats of ancient civilisations, some of them highly developed, and exploration was concerned rather with piecing together chapters of past history than in discovery. The penetration into the interior of Africa, on the other hand, may as truly be described as discovery as that of America by Columbus.

The Muscat Arabs from Zanzibar were pioneers in the exploration of the region of the great lakes and the Congo basin, while in Western Africa the zeal of the Moslem Arabs and Berbers led them across the Sahara. Here indeed a great empire, famed for its culture, boasted a fragmentary history dating back to the eighth or ninth centuries; but in this or any other part of tropical Africa, from the frontiers of Egypt to the Zambesi, there are no traces of antecedent civilisations—no monuments or buried cities—like those of the prehistoric civilisations of Asia and South America.

That portion of the north of Africa which is included in the temperate zone, and contiguous to Europe, had been the home of the most ancient civilisations, first of Egypt, dating back to perhaps 4000 B.C., and later of the Phœnicians. But Egypt had penetrated no further south than Ethiopia, while the Carthagenians (though they had trade routes with the interior) [1] for the most part confined their efforts to the establishment of colonies on the coast. We read of one or two expeditions to the interior both by Pharaoh Necho and by Carthage, but they were barren of results. So were the expeditions of the Greeks, who founded their first colony at Cyrene 1000 years before Christ, and of the Romans, who later incorporated all North Africa as a Roman province.

Accurate knowledge even of the coast-line, and the establishment of European settlements upon it, dates only from the fifteenth century—synchronising with the discovery of America. The outlet for commerce and the new fields which this great discovery—together with the development of India—afforded to adventurous pioneers, diverted for some three centuries or more the tide of exploration which might otherwise have set towards Africa. The voyages of Da Gama and others in the fifteenth century had, however, already produced one very notable result. Hitherto the gateway which led to the great unknown interior had been situated in the north. Access to Timbuktu was by caravan across the desert from Tripoli or Algeria. The sea route discovered by Da Gama disclosed a back door, which was henceforth to become the principal entrance. As modern railways have rendered the desert route obsolete, they may in the not distant future restore it.

Thus the interior of Africa remained unknown. It appeared on the map as a great blank space, with a fringe of names all round its coasts, till Livingstone, Barth, and others began its systematic exploration about seventy years ago. For thirty or forty years tropical Africa remained a field for adventurous and sensational exploration, and it was not till 1885—when the Berlin Act was passed—that the modern development of Africa began to assume definite and recognised form.

What, then, were the causes which led to the opening up

[1] Heeren's Historical Researches—vol. African Nations, p. 17 *et seq.*

of Africa, a continent which all the preceding ages of the world's history had left untouched, though it lay close to the homes of the early civilisations in Europe and Asia—a continent containing a fifth of the earth's land surface and a ninth of its population?

The dominant cause of Africa's isolation was, no doubt, that the world had not hitherto had urgent need of its products, and that its warlike tribes were able to repel unwelcome visitors armed but little better than themselves. Even when the economic pressure caused by the rapidly increasing population of Europe began to exert its inevitable influence, in driving men to seek for new markets and fresh supplies of food and raw material, the discovery of America, and the new fields for commerce in India, more than met the demand for several centuries. It was not until the great industrial revival which followed the Civil War in America that America began herself to compete in the world's markets, and to utilise her own resources primarily for the needs of her own industry.[1]

One of the more immediate causes which led to the opening up of Africa was the Franco-Prussian War of 1870. Crippled by her defeat, France proclaimed by the mouth of her principal statesmen and writers[2]—just as she is doing to-day—that it was to Greater France beyond the seas, and especially in West and North-West Africa, that she must look for rehabilitation. At that time, moreover, colonisation in tropical Africa was believed to be both possible and desirable. Germany, on the other hand, found herself with a great and

[1] It is interesting to note that it was the conquest of the ocean which directly led to the expansion of the peoples of Europe, and relieved them from the age-long pressure of Asia on their frontiers. In 1492 Columbus discovered America, and in 1494 Vasco da Gama rounded the Cape and opened up the way to India. At that time (A.D. 1500) the population of Europe was about 70 millions. At the end of the next three centuries (A.D. 1800) it is said to have been 150 millions, an additional 10 millions having migrated overseas. But at the close of the succeeding century—which witnessed the industrial revolution, and the advent of steam navigation—it is estimated (A.D. 1900) at nearly 450 millions, with 100 million additional emigrants. Thus while the population of Europe only doubled itself in the three centuries prior to 1800, it more than trebled itself in the following century. The figures for Great Britain are: population in 1600 (England only), 4,800,000; in 1800 about 16,000,000; and in 1900 about 42,000,000.—(Stoddard, 'The Rising Tide of Colour,' p. 155, Whittaker, &c.)

An additional reason for the demand for increased supplies of food and raw materials at the close of the nineteenth century was to be found in the immensely improved standard of living of the people. See pp. 614, 615.

[2] See M. Leroy Beaulieu, 'Histoire de la Colonisation chez les peuples modernes.'

increasing industrial population in urgent need of raw materials and additional food supplies. Not content with the wholly unrestricted market offered by British colonies, where Germans were welcomed, and exercised every privilege equally with their British rivals, she not unnaturally desired to have colonies of her own. We have since learnt that she had other motives—the creation of naval bases and world-wide wireless stations, and the raising of negro armies for world conquest.

Humanitarian motives—the desire to suppress the slave-trade, &c.—also played their part, but it was the rivalry of these two great Continental Powers which was the immediate cause of the modern "partition of Africa." By the Berlin Act of 1885, and the Brussels Act of 1892, Europe and America endeavoured in some feeble way to safeguard the interests of the natives—but these Acts were practically ineffective for their purpose. The one thing they did succeed in effecting was the restriction of the import of arms of precision to the natives, theoretically as a check to the slave-trade, but with the practical result of rendering the African more powerless than ever to resist conquest by Europeans.

England was unwillingly forced into the competition. On the one hand her colonies on the West Coast demanded some effort, to save them from being cut off from all access to the interior by hostile foreign tariffs, and becoming mere coast enclaves. Her vital interests in India, on the other hand, compelled her to protect her route thither—Egypt, the Suez Canal, and the eastern shores of Africa. The essential interests of Egypt, for which she had become responsible, demanded the protection of the Nile sources.

For a decade and more the "scramble" went on till it was brought to a close by the conventions with France of 1898 and 1899, and the Fashoda incident of the latter year. Germany had secured large colonies in East, West, and South Africa, at the expense of prior British claims, but we recognised her right to a place in the tropical sun. France added largely to her territory in West and Central Africa, and annexed the great island of Madagascar.

It was towards the close of this period of rivalry that Mr Joseph Chamberlain became Colonial Secretary, and for the first time in our history a policy of progress and development found favour at Whitehall. The colonies were encouraged to raise loans, supported if necessary by Imperial credit, for the development of their resources, and had it not been for the South African War this policy would, I know, have been carried much further. During the twelve years which elapsed between the South African and the recent world war, great progress was made in the construction of roads and railways, and the opening up of waterways,—for the material development of Africa may be summed up in the one word "transport."

Though we may perhaps at times entertain a lingering regret for the passing of the picturesque methods of the past, we must admit that the locomotive is a substantial improvement on head-borne transport, and the motor-van is more efficient than the camel. The advent of Europeans has brought the mind and methods of Europe to bear on the native of Africa for good or for ill, and the seclusion of ages must perforce give place to modern ideas. Material development is accompanied by education and progress.

The condition of Africa when Europe entered the continent, which Isaiah so graphically describes as "the land shadowing with wings, which is beyond the rivers of Ethiopia . . . a people scattered and peeled," was deplorable. On the East Coast, Arabs and half-castes were engaged in a lucrative trade in slaves for export to Arabia and to Turkish possessions. In the west, powerful armies of Moslem States depopulated large districts in their raids for slaves. Europe had failed to realise that throughout the length and breadth of Africa inter-tribal war was an ever-present condition of native life, and that extermination and slavery were practised by African tribes upon each other.

It was the task of civilisation to put an end to slavery, to establish Courts of Law, to inculcate in the natives a sense of individual responsibility, of liberty, and of justice, and to teach their rulers how to apply these principles; above all, to see to it that the system of education should be such as to produce happiness and progress. I am confident that the verdict of history will award high praise to the efforts and the achievements of Great Britain in the discharge of these great responsibilities. For, in my belief, under no other rule—be it of his own uncontrolled potentates, or of aliens—does the African enjoy such a measure of freedom and of impartial justice, or a more sympathetic treatment, and for that reason I am a profound believer in the British Empire and its mission in Africa.

In brief, we may say that the eighteenth century was chiefly remarkable for the acquisition of large and almost uninhabited portions of the earth, situated in the temperate zone. The nineteenth century saw the development of these great colonies into nations enjoying self-government. Its closing decade witnessed the dawning recognition of the vital importance of the tropics to civilisation, and the "discovery" and acquisition of large non-colonisable areas in tropical Africa—no longer regarded as picturesque appanages of Empire, but as essential to the very existence of the races of the temperate climes.

To the twentieth century belongs the heritage of the tropics and the task of their development. Two decades have already passed and wonderful progress has been made, not only in the improvement of the quality and quantity of the material output, by scientific research, by organised method, and by the expenditure of capital, but also in methods of administration for the welfare of the subject races, education, free labour, taxation, and other similar problems.

A comparative study of the methods by which these various problems—administrative and economic—have been approached in the several tropical dependencies of the Empire and by other nations would form a fascinating study and a useful guide,[1] but the racial differences between Asiatics and Africans are so great (as my own experience in India and China have taught me) that methods applicable to the one may be quite misplaced with the other. The tropical dependencies in Africa, on the other hand, offer almost identical problems.

"No serious attempt," says Mr Kidd, "has so far been made to set forth the principles which should underlie our future relations with the tropical regions of the world. . . . Nowhere is there to be found any whole-hearted or consistent attempt either to justify the political relations which already exist, or to define the principles of any relations which ought to exist in the future."[2] The following pages have been

[1] The great value of a bureau to collate and publish the results of administrative experience in various tropical countries was urged by Sir T. Morison in a letter to the 'Times' of 21st July 1920.

[2] 'Control of the Tropics,' pp. 15, 16. Compare the 'Times' (1st Oct. 1901). "No attempt has been made to ascertain what are the special conditions of the administrative problem in Equatorial Africa, no attempt has been made to formulate the general lines of a well-considered policy in dealing with that problem, and no machinery has been devised for maintaining continuity of administration."

written in the hope that an experience, with short intervals, of forty years in the tropics, and of over thirty in responsible positions in Africa, may enable me to make some useful contribution to the study of these subjects. During the first half of these thirty years it was my privilege to assist in some degree in bringing under British control portions of Nyasaland, East Africa, Uganda, and Nigeria, where the difficulties of the pioneer had to be encountered. During the second fifteen it has been my good fortune to be entrusted with the development of Nigeria, and with the aid of capable colleagues to lay the foundations of a system of administration upon which others may build. I shall endeavour to describe the difficulties encountered, the methods used, and the results obtained in administration—which forms the most important part of our task in Africa.

It is, moreover, also of great moment that the British democracy, faced with problems which portend great changes in our social organisation, should understand the relation which our overseas dependencies bear to the economic well-being of this country—how vital to our industrial life are the products of the tropics, and its markets for our manufactures. It is indeed essential that democracy should take an intelligent and well-informed interest in questions which affect the Empire of which it is the inheritor and trustee.

PART I.

EUROPE AND TROPICAL AFRICA.

CHAPTER I.

THE ACQUISITION OF THE BRITISH AFRICAN TROPICS.

Reason for acquisition—Restraint of Britain—British policy of Free Trade—The Berlin Conference and effective occupation—The Hinterland theory—Spheres of influence—The Government's dilemma—Creation of Chartered Companies—Treaties as valid titles—Method of obtaining treaties—The real sanction for intervention in Africa—Status of Chartered Companies — The Royal Niger Company's Charter—The Imperial British East African Company—The British South African Company—Advantages of the Agency of Chartered Companies—Liabilities of Government on revocation—Lessons from Chartered Company rule—Separation of administration and commerce—Disposal of lands and minerals—Contrast with the older Charters—Other methods of acquisition—British Consuls in Africa—India Office control—Foreign Office control.

The desire of France and Germany to acquire tropical possessions was due primarily to the idea that they were colonisable —an idea, as we shall presently see, not yet exploded in Germany, and at one time shared by Great Britain, who, however, having already acquired great tracts in the temperate zone, had no need to seek a tropical outlet for her emigrants.

The African possessions of Great Britain were not therefore acquired, as in the case of the Continental Powers, in pursuance of a definite policy, for which they were willing to risk war. The older "settlements" on the West Coast were originally maintained to assist in putting an end to the overseas slave trade, and so little were they valued that a Royal Commission in 1865 recommended their abandonment as soon as convenient. Missionaries—as in Uganda and Nyasaland—were often the pioneers, and it was in defence of their interests that the Government was forced to intervene. The desire to extend protection and to introduce justice and peace have from time to time led to the enlargement of frontiers, for law and order cannot exist side by side with barbarism. In the west traders such as the Niger Company took the lead as pioneers, but it was not till the close of the nineteenth century that the value of the produce of the tropics began to be realised in England.

When, however, the "scramble for Africa" followed the Berlin Act of 1885, the popular demand that Britain, as the foremost colonising Power, should not be backward in claiming her share was irresistible, and it was due to this popular demand to "peg out claims for futurity"—however little their value was understood at the time—that we owe our African Empire of to-day. It was, moreover, felt that whatever value our existing tropical possessions might have, would be lost if other nations with exclusive tariffs appropriated their hinterlands. Their value as coaling stations in the scheme of Empire was indeed recognised, but the great importance of these bases for attack and defence by submarines, and for wireless installations, was a lesson for the future to teach. The instinct of the nation recognised with Dr Pearson that "the permanency of Empire consists in its extension." The vital importance of the control of the tropics for their economic value had, however, already begun to be realised by the nations of Europe, and France, Germany, and Italy, laying aside their ambitions in Europe, emerged as claimants for large "colonies" in Africa.

When Great Britain took part in the scramble, she willingly recognised the claims of Germany—a Power newly consolidated, and with an increasing and industrial population. She stood aside in the Cameruns, where the chiefs had more than once formally asked for British protection. She renounced the territorial claims which she might have asserted in the Congo region in virtue of Cameron's treaties, and in East Africa she was contented with a fraction of the territory which the Sultan of Zanzibar offered. In South-West Africa, bordering the tropics, her delay and indifference made it easy for Germany to forestall her.

To the no less energetic action of France no opposition

was offered, until her encroachments affected the interests of our existing possessions so closely that national prestige and honour were involved.

In one very notable particular the policy of Great Britain differed from that of her rivals. The great territories which she controlled were entirely free to the trade and commerce of all nations. Not merely were there no discriminating tariffs, but the French and German merchants who established themselves in British territory were treated with precisely the same cordiality, and were afforded the same facilities for travel in the interior, and for acquiring land, as our own nationals. "Our rise," says the German writer, Emil Zimmermann, "depended essentially on the English policy of the open door." [1]

The Berlin Conference of 1885 limited the necessity for "effective occupation"—by which the validity of a claim to territorial acquisition should be tested—to coast lands, and defined it as "the necessity of securing the existence of a sufficient authority, in the territories occupied, to ensure respect for acquired rights, and if necessary for freedom of commerce and transit in the conditions in which it may have been stipulated." [2] The British delegate (Sir E. Mallet) had proposed that this rule should be made applicable to interior lands,[3] but the proposal was negatived, largely at the instance of the French delegate (Baron de Courcel). The Conference therefore laid down no definite rule as to the basis upon which the validity of claims to sovereignty in the interior should be recognised.

The principle of the "voluntary consent of the natives whose country is taken possession of in all cases where they have not provoked the aggression" was put forward by the American delegate (Mr Kasson),[4] and it may be assumed that it was tacitly accepted. For on 23rd February 1885 the president of the International Association of the Congo submitted to the Conference the various declarations and conventions concluded with each of the Powers represented there, under which they recognised "the formation of this new State," and the declarations with Great Britain, the United States, and Belgium set out that it was by virtue of treaties with

[1] 'The German Empire of Central Africa,' pp. 2 and 5.
[2] C. 4361/1885, Protocol 8, p. 219.
[3] Ibid., p. 214.
[4] Ibid., p. 209.

the legitimate sovereigns in the Congo basin that vast territories had been ceded to the State with all the rights of sovereignty.[1]

Since the Conference had refused to deal explicitly with the acquisition of territory other than coast lands, "the hinterland theory"—made in Germany—which had not the sanction of the Berlin Act or any precise definition, gradually received acceptance, in so far as the "rights" of the European Powers and their relations towards each other in the partition were concerned. By this dictum a Power in occupation of coast lands was entitled to claim the exclusive right to exercise political influence for an indefinite distance inland. Obviously in a very irregularly-shaped continent no method could be more calculated to create difficulties, and the climax seemed to have been reached when France claimed to restrict the frontiers of Nigeria, on the ground that they formed the hinterland of Algeria on the Mediterranean.

The Powers, in their haste to declare the "spheres of influence" which they claimed, had not in some cases time to go through the formality of making treaties with the natives, and considered it sufficient to notify that they claimed them as hinterlands, or because they had some special interest in them. They were vaguely demarcated by lines of longitude and latitude regardless of tribal limits, or by reference to physical features which later exploration sometimes proved to be scores of miles from their supposed position, or even non-existent.

The conception of a "sphere of influence" was a new departure in the vocabulary of diplomacy—already foreshadowed by Article 6 of the Act, in which the exercise of "sovereign rights *or influence*" is alluded to. It was, I think, invented by our Foreign Office, for Great Britain alone appeared to have scruples as to the legality or justice of assuming dominion based neither on conquest nor on the assent of the inhabitants. She would have preferred that effective occupation should be a matter of gradual and peaceful penetration. The term "sphere of influence" was thus used to designate those regions over which the right to exercise exclusive political influence was claimed, but in which no rights over the natives could be logically exercised, and no properly accredited representative of the suzerain Power

[1] Berlin Act, Protocol 9, pp. 253-278.

could be appointed until some legal claim had been established.

The success of the expedient was short-lived. Setting aside her former opposition to Sir E. Malet's proposal, France now insisted that effective occupation could alone confer title, and in 1887 this was fully admitted by the British Government. Lord Salisbury, in a despatch of 1887 to the Minister at Lisbon, writes: "It has now been admitted on principle by all parties to the Act of Berlin, that a claim of sovereignty in Africa can only be maintained by real occupation of the territory claimed. You will make a formal protest against any claims not founded on occupation, and you will say that H.M.'s Government cannot recognise Portuguese sovereignty in territories not occupied by her in sufficient strength to maintain order, protect foreigners, and control the natives." This passage is interesting, not only as stating the formal acquiescence of the British Government in the theory of effective occupation, but as containing a definition of what constituted it, and a frank admission that territorial acquisition, whether under the name of Protectorate or otherwise, meant nothing less than sovereignty and the control of the natives.

The rulers of Great Britain were strongly opposed to extension of our territory in Africa, but the popular demand left the Foreign Office no alternative.[1] The Government viewed with alarm the great cost of effective occupation, as that phrase was translated in England. But the British public never considers the cost of its demands, though it holds the Government to strict account for any disaster due to an inadequate staff and insufficient force to protect its officers. We had not yet learned to think in hundreds of millions. The staff, the troops, and the money were lacking,

[1] How clearly this was recognised abroad may be seen from the following passage in Baillaud's authoritative work: "Il faut, en effet, remarquer que, d'une manière coutume, jusque dans ces toutes dernières années, le Colonial Office, que représentait le gouvernment anglais dans ces affaires, ne cessa de manifester, sauf pendant le seul secrétariat de M. J. Chamberlain, une opposition constante à toute politique d'expansion et à tout accroissement des attributions des pouvoirs locaux; et Mary Kingsley ('West African Studies,' p. 305) est bien autorisée a dire, 'Jusqu'a nos jours le Colonial Office a été, excepté dans le detail des affaires interieures coloniales, une chaine d'entraves pour le développement de l'Angleterre en Afrique Occidentale. Il a été non pas indifférent, mais nettement opposé.'"—'La Politique indigene de l'Angleterre en Afrique Occidentale,' Introduction, p. xxvi. We need hardly recall Majuba, Gordon at Khartum, or Mr Gladstone's decision to evacuate Uganda.

and neither the Colonial nor the Foreign Office had any knowledge or experience of administration in the interior of tropical Africa, or of raising and commanding troops. Above all, the statesmen of Britain had not grasped the incalculable value of the claims which the instinct of the nation urged them to peg out. But something had to be done to prevent European rivalries developing into a war. The comfortable —albeit statesmanlike—expedient of a sphere of influence in which rival diplomacy would cease from troubling, and development might await the millenium, was repudiated by the Continental Powers, and found no favour at home. Our rivals were constantly encroaching on our shadowy boundaries.

The modern "Merchant Adventurer" was ready to employ his capital in the development of these regions, and to accept the responsibility which the Government shunned, provided that he was allowed to monopolise the trade, to exercise rights of taxation direct and indirect, and to acquire rights in lands and minerals, which would not only afford a revenue for administration and defence, but also a prospect of profit. The Government of the day, ignoring the dictum of Adam Smith that "the government of an exclusive company of merchants is perhaps the worst of all forms of government,"[1] found an escape from its dilemma. Royal Charters on the Elizabethan model were granted to three companies—the Royal Niger Company in the west, the Imperial British East African Company in the east, and the British South African in the south, with Mr (now Sir G.) Goldie, Sir W. Mackinnon, and Mr Cecil Rhodes as their founders. They were overwhelmed with volunteers eager for adventure. To protect them from foreign encroachments, the British Government soon found itself compelled to declare the greater part of its spheres of influence to be Protectorates, and the other nations did the same. In many of these Protectorates, no treaties had been made with outlying tribes, and regions as yet unexplored were included.

The Foreign Office had at first hesitated to declare Protectorates, because it had acquired no legal right to do so. How then could it grant charters which conferred powers of taxation and rights to lands and minerals? The difficulty was solved by a subterfuge unworthy of the high line hitherto taken by Great Britain. The precedent set by King Leopold

[1] 'Wealth of Nations,' vol. ii. p. 302.

of Belgium was, as we have seen, acclaimed by all the Powers, and more specifically by Britain, the United States, and Belgium, that "treaties" with the natives, by which they were supposed at short notice to have voluntarily ceded all their sovereign rights, were to be accepted as valid titles to the acquisition of the African tropics by the European nations. Alternatively by conquest, provided the natives were the aggressors—and this would not be difficult to demonstrate. It was easy to stipulate that the charter powers were based on the production of such treaties. The sensitive official conscience was salved by this expedient, the real significance of which it no doubt failed to appreciate.[1]

The civilised nations entered for the competition with avidity. Treaties were produced by the cartload in all the approved forms of legal verbiage—impossible of translation by ill-educated interpreters.[2] It mattered not that tribal chiefs had no power to dispose of communal rights, or that those few powerful potentates who might perhaps claim such authority looked on the white man's ambassador with contempt, and could hardly be expected to hand over their sovereignty and lands or other assets had they understood what was asked of them. The Sultan of Sokoto, for instance, regarded the subsidy promised to him by the chartered company as tribute from a vassal.

[1] Though the Congo treaties were, I think, the first to gain International recognition, treaty-making had been adopted elsewhere. Consul Hewitt made thirty-seven treaties in West Africa in 1884 and the National African Company had made others dating from 1879. Hewitt's treaties, however, differ very essentially from those upon which King Leopold and the Chartered Companies in east and west founded their claims to territorial sovereignty. They stipulated that the Queen should extend to the chiefs and their territories "Her gracious favour and protection," while the chiefs undertook "to refrain from entering into any correspondence, agreement, or treaty with any foreign nation or Power, except with the knowledge and sanction of Her Majesty." Jurisdiction over British subjects was ceded, and the chiefs engaged to act on the advice of the British Consuls. Under the East African Chartered Company's treaties, on the other hand, the chief declared that he placed himself and his people under the rule of the Company, and ceded to it all his sovereign rights and rights of government. The Nyasa treaties "give all sovereign rights and all and every other claim absolutely" over all their country to the Queen for all time.—See Herslet, 'Map of Africa by Treaty,' vol. i. p. 166, quoted by Ilbert, 'Government of India,' p. 430. Also Hall, 'Foreign Jurisdiction of British Crown,' p. 217. For the progressive steps in the creation of the Congo State, see Dr Horn, 'United Empire,' March 1922.

[2] In later and more advanced times, the best that an intelligent Mallam could make of the phrase "The Protectorate of N. Nigeria," was to render it as "The instruction of compassion of the Sudan,"—thereby making absolute nonsense of the context.

The treaties were duly attested by a cross, purporting to convey the assent of the African chief, and this was sufficient. In some cases, it is said, the assent had been obtained by the gift of a pair of boots, or a few bottles of gin—the Kaiser had sent a parcel of opera-hats working with a spring. Elsewhere, by a show of force, or by vague promises, which were unrecorded and later ignored. Each nation pursued the course it preferred, or which its representative found most convenient.

No sooner was "occupation" effected by virtue of these treaties, than the controlling Power usually found itself involved in hostilities with the people with whom these treaties of amity and friendship had been made. If, however, the treaty-maker were too honest, or the native chief too shrewd or too rapacious, it sufficed that the treaty should vest in the European all jurisdiction over aliens. Here is the description by Commandant Toutée, one of the most successful of French treaty-makers :—

"Quand un état ou une tribu nègre, peu importe, a commis l'imprudence grande de donner l'hospitalité à un voyageur blanc, ce dernier n'a rien de plus pressé que de sortir de sa poche un traité d'alliance tout imprimé, et de ses cantines un petit drapeau national. Le voyageur signe ce traité pour son propre compte et prie le roitelet, plus ou moins coloré, d'ajouter sa signature à la sienne.

"Si le potentat nègre ne sait pas signer, comme ce dernier cas se présente neuf fois sur dix, la haute partie contractante et civilisée signe pour la deuxième supposée sauvage et le tour est joué.

"Il est arrivé même quelquefois que le voyageur blanc, s'il est anglais surtout, a oublié de demander son nom au nègre signataire, mais ce vice de forme n'a jamais été considéré comme une cause sérieuse de nullité du contrat."

The 'Temps' (March 1903) thus summarises the process: "One can see what it means: it is moral annexation. The evolution of colonial empires of this kind follows a well-known *processus* of which the stages are in a measure inevitable: first, travellers, missionaries, and traders; then treaties of commerce and friendship; then a kind of protectorate half concealed under the form of an unequal alliance; afterwards the delimitation of spheres of influence and the declaration of a kind of right of priority; then a protectorate properly so called, the establishment of tutelage, the appointment of Residents and all that follows in their train; and finally, annexation pure and simple."

It was thus that the conscience of Europe found relief. Ignorance of African conditions, and perhaps a latent feeling that the end justified the means, induced the rulers of the nations of Europe to accept these treaties without too close a scrutiny, and to persuade themselves that the omelette had been made without breaking any eggs.[1]

The frank assertion of the inexorable law of progress, based on the power to enforce it if need be, was termed "filibustering." It shocked the moral sense of a civilisation content to accept the naked deception of "treaty-making," or to shut its eyes and ears and thank God for the results.

In some cases the native ruler was himself an alien conqueror, holding in subjection tribes with which he had no affinity; in others he was a despot (as in Benin, Uganda, Dahomey, or Zululand) exercising a bloody tyranny; in others again, pagan tribes carried on an internecine warfare, and were powerless to defend themselves against organised slave-raiders.

In such circumstances it was surely more justifiable for the European Powers frankly to found their title to intervention upon force, and to admit that the chiefs, whom they recognised or appointed, derived their administrative and judicial powers from them, and exercised it with such limitations as they chose to impose, instead of assuming that they themselves derived the right of intervention through cessions of sovereignty, under the guise of "treaties," which were either not understood, or which the ruler had no power to make, and which rarely provided an adequate legal sanction for the powers assumed.[2]

The institution of courts of justice, the supervision of native courts, the protection of the peasantry from oppression by their rulers, and the deposition of the latter when incorrigible, the reorganisation or imposition of taxation for revenue, the prohibition of slave-raiding or slave-dealing, the restraint on firearms, liquor, and the destruction of game, the disposal in some cases of unused lands or minerals—in a word, the

[1] For an alternative method of making treaties with natives, see "Treaty-making in Africa," 'Proceedings Royal Geographical Society,' January 1893, p. 54, and 'The Rise of Our East African Empire,' vol. ii. p. 579, by Captain Lugard.

[2] See note 4, p. 35.

arbitrary enforcement of justice and good government and the safeguarding of natural resources,—all these are acts of sovereignty which no African chief would willingly concede by treaty to an unknown stranger, but which fifty and more nations of the world have now formally recognised as the essential duty of the Mandatory Powers, who under the covenant of the League are to be nominated as the protectors and trustees of backward races. For the civilised nations have at last recognised that while on the one hand the abounding wealth of the tropical regions of the earth must be developed and used for the benefit of mankind, on the other hand an obligation rests on the controlling Power not only to safeguard the material rights of the natives, but to promote their moral and educational progress.

The recognition of these great principles does away with the "make believe" of the former illogical system, by which the controlling Power, basing its rights on treaty, arbitrarily exercised sovereign powers often incompatible with those treaties, while admitting (in particular cases) the right of a petty kinglet to deflect the course of a railway, to restrict trade by arbitrary taxes and tolls, and to oppress the peasantry at will.

The problem of the methods of acquisition was followed by the problem of the methods of exercising control. The first British experiment was, as I have said, that of chartered companies, whose powers, so far as they related to the exercise of sovereignty and jurisdiction over the natives, were based on treaties with the chiefs, and were circumscribed by the necessity of obtaining the assent of the home Government to their local regulations, and the visé of their accounts. Their status *vis-à-vis* foreign Powers was that of delegates of the British Crown. Their obligations were to establish that effective occupation and control which was called for by the Continental Powers, and by the Press and Public of England. It was immaterial whether the area of their operations was a sphere of influence or a Protectorate.

Before discussing the meaning of this latter term, it will be worth while to review very briefly the results of the chartered company experiment. The modern adaptation of the instrument by which the Hudson's Bay Company had added the Dominion of Canada, and the East India Company had secured India to the Empire, and to which some of our American colonies had owed their origin, cannot fail to be of interest, the more so that, with the exception of Borneo, the new experiment was confined to tropical Africa.

The three chartered companies differed greatly in their methods. The Royal Niger Company, which was the first to obtain its charter (July 1886), held it for thirteen years. It was conducted on business lines as an amalgamation of various existing commercial interests, with a lucrative trade. From the outset it incurred the bitter hostility of the Liverpool merchants, who complained that though the charter conferred no monopolistic rights, these had in practice been created. The company, while denying the charge, held that a measure of exclusive privilege was necessary to enable them to meet the cost of administration, which their rivals in trade had not to incur.

The charter included vast territories in the north, from Sokoto to Lake Chad, controlled by very powerful Moslem rulers, with most of whom the company had made treaties, but its resources were not sufficient to enable it to comply at once with the dictum of "effective occupation," and French aggression on its frontier was the primary cause which compelled the intervention of the Imperial Government. It was not, of course, easy to secure capital for interior development while the commercial possibilities of the regions nearer to the coast offered much more tempting returns for investment. The achievement of its founders lay in the fact that they had succeeded in amalgamating all European interests on the Niger, and were thus enabled at the Berlin Conference to claim on behalf of Great Britain the custodianship of its free navigation.

The inherent defect of all chartered government, where dividends to shareholders must inevitably compete with administrative expenditure, formed the chronic obstacle to the desires of its patriotic directors. But if the exigencies of the company's finance did not admit of effective administration, it may honourably claim that, unlike the Congo State of those days, the natives were not subjected to any form of forced labour, or even to any direct tax, while the introduction of spirits in the north, from which a large revenue would have accrued, was prohibited.[1] The baleful system of the "domain

[1] That spirits had already begun to penetrate is clear from the appeal of Maleki, Emir of Nupe, a Moslem state.—"United Liquor Committee" Report, November 1886, p. 31.

privé" of the Congo State—of leasing lands and forests for exploitation by private concessionaires—was unknown, and the right of the native to his land and produce was not interfered with. He received a fair price, albeit his market was practically restricted to the company's depots.[1]

Germany in the east was no less keen a competitor for the control of the tropics than France in the west. Not content with the vast regions comprised in German East Africa, she threatened to absorb Uganda and the Nile sources. Sir Wm. Mackinnon—a man of large fortune—obtained in 1888 a Royal Charter, with the patriotic object of securing for the Empire the area which had been declared a British sphere of influence. His co-directors were almost all men pre-eminent for their public services, including Lord Lorne, Lord Brassey, Sir J. Kirk, Sir A. Kemball, Sir L. Pelly, Sir F. Buxton, Sir D. Stewart, and Mr Burdett-Coutts. It was the great misfortune, however, of the company that at the crucial moment of its inauguration it was deprived of the unrivalled experience of Sir John Kirk, who alone of the directors had personal knowledge of East Africa, by his appointment as British Plenipotentiary at the Brussels Conference. The company did not enter into the heritage of a "going concern" as the Royal Niger Company had done. The country was entirely unexplored, and such little trade as existed was in the hands of the Zanzibar Arabs, who were already in revolt against the Germans, and bitterly resented the measures taken by Great Britain to put an end to their trade in slaves.

The company had only recently been inaugurated when the notorious Karl Peters by way of the Tana river, and Emin Pasha as a German emissary by the southern route, started with the object of annexing Uganda. The British public and the Foreign Office looked to the company to secure effective occupation of a country 800 miles from the coast—from which it was separated by the warlike Masai tribe—ere yet its headquarters had been fully established at its coast port. Already it had sent an exploring expedition thither in the hope of assisting Stanley in his quest for Emin. It was not slow to respond to the new call. The German projects were frustrated—Uganda and the Nile sources, so vital to Egypt, were secured.

But no revenue was coming in, and private funds could

[1] *Re* this monopoly see Sir J. Kirk's report, Africa, 3, 1896.

not indefinitely sustain the heavy cost incurred. Moreover, owing to the withdrawal by the Sultan of Zanzibar, acting on the advice of H.M.'s Government, of the reserves under which he had adhered to the Berlin Act, the company was deprived of the revenue from import and export duties, which were, it maintained, an integral part of the terms of the concession from the Sultan under which it had acquired its rights, and upon which it had based its fiscal policy.[1] The company's Board consisted chiefly of administrators, and its earliest efforts had been directed to administration rather than to commerce. It appealed to the home Government for assistance, on the grounds that it had gone to Uganda on the mandate of the nation. But Lord Rosebery was disinclined to assist, and the company was forced to surrender its charter in 1895, after an existence of only six and a half years.

In spite of its apparent failure it had, like the Niger Company, succeeded in its great purpose. It had secured East Africa and Uganda, when the Government of the day was unwilling to move. For a moment there had been misgivings lest Mr Gladstone should abandon the results which the company had achieved at such sacrifice. The edict went forth that Uganda should be evacuated, and with it a large part of East Africa. But the feeling of the nation was too strong for the Government, and supported the company's continued and disinterested efforts for the "retention of Uganda." A Protectorate was declared, and a new British flag replaced the company's tattered ensign. The salubrious highlands of East Africa, the kingdoms of Uganda and Unyoro, with boundaries co-terminous with the Congo State on the west, and with Abyssinia and the Egyptian Sudan in the north, the continuous control of the Nile from its sources in the great Victoria and Albert Lakes, were secured to the Empire.

The credit due to the Niger Company for its treatment of the natives, and its exclusion of the concessionaire, is shared by the Imperial British East African Company.

A great part of the territory covered by the third charter—that of the British South African Company—lay south of the Zambesi, within the temperate or sub-tropical zone, and

[1] See Memo. by Sir J. Kirk. 'British East Africa,' by P. L. M'Dermott, p. 446.

therefore colonisable by Europeans. It was contiguous to the colonies and Protectorates under the control of the Colonial Office, and it therefore (unlike the other two) came under the control of that office. The Duke of Fife was its chairman, but the dominating personality and the founder was Mr Cecil Rhodes. The charter was granted in October 1889, and still continues. By the Northern Rhodesia Order in Council of 4th May 1911 its powers were extended in respect of territories north of the Zambesi.

The South African Company had to deal with conditions for the most part very dissimilar to those which had confronted the other two. Its territories, with a population estimated at four to the square mile, had no access to the sea, and the construction of railways was the first necessity. It was believed to contain great mineral wealth, and its frontiers marched with territories already peopled by a considerable European population, largely concerned in the mining industry, who hastened to peg out claims in the company's territory. The ordinary trade in raw materials and foodstuffs was hampered by lack of transport and distance from a seaport. The wealth of the founders, Messrs Rhodes and Beit, and the patriotism and confidence in the future of its other shareholders, rendered it possible, as in East Africa, to dispense with immediate dividends. The company rapidly became the parent of many subsidiary corporations, which undertook the exploitation of its mineral wealth, the construction of its railways, and even the provision of the requirements of its principal cities. The chartered company, by virtue of its rights in lands and minerals, whether acquired by treaties or inherent in it as a government, retained a substantial interest in these concerns, whose shares, of course, became the subject of Stock Exchange dealings. As the European population increased, the inevitable demand for the revocation of the charter and the substitution of self-government in Southern Rhodesia arose—a matter which was, of course, complicated by the expenditure incurred by the company.

North of the Zambesi, the pressing demand for immediate effective occupation, which had overwhelmed the other two companies, did not arise in so acute a form, though Belgium succeeded in extending her frontiers to include the valuable mineral districts of Katanga, and Germany was anxious to encroach to the south of Tanganyika. Treaties were made and frontiers settled, and the company was free to open up the country gradually.

Germany had coveted these regions—especially south of the Zambesi—and it was due to the Chartered Company and its great founder, Cecil Rhodes, that the British flag now flies from the Cape to the Lakes Tanganyika and Nyasa.[1]

From this brief review of the causes which gave rise to the creation of chartered companies in the nineteenth century some interesting reflections arise. That they are at best an imperfect form of government was shown conclusively by Adam Smith one hundred and fifty years ago, and modern experience has only confirmed his arguments.[2] But it is due to their agency alone that over a million square miles of tropical Africa, with a population of over twenty-five millions, has been added to the British Empire. In contrast to foreign methods they afford a striking illustration of the way in which individual enterprise has ever in our history anticipated the action of government.[3] They came forward at a moment when the Government, compelled by the action of other Powers to take some decision, not unnaturally shirked the responsibility of directly administering great regions, at a cost of which no estimate could be made. They formed a buffer between the Imperial Government and foreign States, which reduced the risks of international friction and of war, and their temporary reverses did not involve Imperial prestige. Alike from their successes and their failures the Government was enabled to obtain most valuable experience, so that when

[1] "In 1890," said the chairman at the last annual meeting, "Rhodesia, a country as large as Central Europe, was sparsely inhabited by uncivilised and barbarous peoples, who were hunted and raided by the strongest amongst them. After thirty years of Chartered administration we see them immensely advanced in numbers, order, contentment, and wealth. . . . Should His Majesty's Government decide that Southern Rhodesia is fit for self-government, we shall cordially concur in their decision. What higher tribute could possibly be paid to a corporation such as ours, than to pronounce that in thirty years it had brought a great territory from a state of primitive savagery to a condition in which it is fit to take its place among the self-governing dominions of the Crown."—Report, 28th October 1920.

[2] Mr Kidd, writing in 1897, says: "Government by chartered company is the oldest, the most indefensible, and in theory the most reprehensible of all forms of government in the tropics."—'Control of the Tropics,' p. 38.

[3] Compare Adam Smith: "In one way, and one way alone, has the policy of Europe contributed to the first establishment or the present grandeur of the colonies of America. It bred and formed the men who were capable of achieving such great actions, and of laying the foundations of so great an Empire."—'Wealth of Nations,' Bk. iv. p. 400.

the time should come to substitute direct Imperial rule, a more or less adequate knowledge of the nature of the task was available.

On the other hand, the Government incurred unknown liabilities. Ill-advised action on the part of a chartered company might at any time involve the Government in serious controversy with a foreign Power. Moreover, the bill of costs on revocation of the charter could be checked by no satisfactory standard. Expensive mistakes must be paid for by the British taxpayer, or *bona-fide* expenditure by the company repudiated, with scant justice to shareholders who had subscribed their money from motives of patriotism. Supposed assets in land and minerals may prove untenable by Government. Plantations and plant suitable to an industrial or commercial company may find no purchasers. If rights in land or minerals acquired by the company have already been disposed of to third parties, a new difficulty arises.

The Judicial Committee of the Privy Council has recently ruled that if the Government cancels the charter of the British South African Company, it is liable for all its administrative deficits—a ruling which would have made much difference to the unfortunate shareholders of the East African Company. Over the company's expenditure the Government had exercised little or no practical control, and prior to the decision of the Privy Council it had been assumed that the land and minerals belonged to and would remain the property of the company if the charter were revoked.[1]

In the case of the Niger charter, Government compounded for its own advantage by giving the expropriated company a share in the minerals of the country. This forms a heavy and increasing burden on the local government which follows the company. It is short-sighted, because the minerals which an undeveloped country may contain are, of course, of un-

[1] The claim amounted to £8,800,000 plus accumulated interest on the yearly deficits, less receipts from lands—about a million. Lord Cave's Commission has since awarded the Company £4,400,000 plus £830,000 for public works, less the value of lands appropriated by the Company, or disposed of otherwise than for cash. Lord Milner, in his Memo. of December 1920, informed the elected members of the Rhodesian Legislative Council that responsible government would be granted if the demand was persisted in. The new government would be responsible for a sum of about $1\frac{1}{2}$ million, the remaining liability to the Company being met by sales of unalienated land.—See Cmd. 547 of 1920, pp. 40 and 52, Cd. 1129 (Privy Council award), Cd. 1273 of 1921 (Lord Milner's Memo.), and Cd. 7645, appendix i.

known value. A parallel may be found in the land rights retained by the Hudson's Bay Company when it agreed to the transfer of the North-West Territory to the Canadian Government. The value of these lands and minerals will, of course, increase in proportion to subsequent expenditure by the local government and private enterprise, bringing an automatic profit to the original shareholders, or more often to those who had subsequently acquired the shares. It would seem preferable that whatever compensation is paid for the revocation of a charter should accrue to those who risked their money in the original venture, rather than that a speculative benefit should be conferred on the changing holders of the shares of the commercial company which succeeds it. Whatever may be said for a bargain of this kind, if contracted with the natives of the country, whose descendants continue to benefit, it is inapplicable to the conditions of a trading corporation.

The chartered company experiment, even though it be a bad form of government, may be said to have been justified by its results for the Empire. The experience gained has taught us many lessons, among which I venture to think that the following may be included.

A chartered company should obtain its administrative revenue rather from funds raised by the ordinary methods of a government than from its commercial profits, and the latter should be strictly limited to sources equally open to its competitors. From customs and taxes, &c., paid equally by its commercial branch as by its rivals, it should be increasingly able to derive an adequate revenue for administrative purposes. In the early years, while they are still insufficient, they must be supplemented by loans from its commercial branch, or if need be from the Imperial Exchequer. Its dual functions of administration and commerce should in fact be kept wholly distinct. Though its administrative machinery need not be so elaborate and expensive as that of the Imperial Government, the officers engaged in administrative and judicial work should be separate from those engaged in commerce, for it is impossible to maintain the prestige of a Government (upon which so much depends in Africa) if its officers have at one moment to drive a trade bargain, and presently to act in a magisterial capacity towards the same parties. If in a distant and unimportant district a commercial agent should be called upon to act as an administrative officer, he should do so by virtue of a commission as Justice of the Peace.

The charter should not only preclude the possibility of monopolies, direct or indirect, or any form of preference in favour of the charter in the matter of customs dues, &c., but railways and river transport services should be provided and maintained from administrative funds, and the commercial branch should enjoy no privileges, either in rates or priority of despatch, over its competitors. Coinage must be guaranteed by an adequate reserve, and all the servants of the administration (including the troops and native employees) should be paid in the legal currency, and not in "barter goods" at values arbitrarily fixed by the employer.

In view of the dubious right of chiefs to alienate lands belonging to the community, and their total inability to estimate the value of such grants, the charter should lay down explicitly the principles to be observed in dealing with lands and minerals. These principles should be identical with those observed in colonies and protectorates administered by the Crown. The administrative branch of the company in its governmental capacity should alone be competent to acquire rights in perpetuity in lands and minerals, acting as trustee for the natives on the one hand, and as custodian for the development of the country for the needs of civilised mankind on the other. It would grant leases to private companies and individuals—including its commercial branch—on reasonable and proper terms, the proceeds by way of rents, royalties, &c., being spent as administrative revenue only. If the charter is revoked, the Government which succeeds it would inherit that revenue without compensation. Actions at law, to which the Imperial Government and the chartered company are parties—such as that recently before the Privy Council—indicate a lack of foresight and a looseness of conception in those responsible for drafting the charter. Finally, a chartered company's reports should fully explain its laws and general progress, and its administrative revenue and expenditure, in order that the nation may know how its delegated sovereignty over native races is being exercised.

It would be an interesting task to trace in some detail the fortunes of the earlier charters granted to the Hudson's Bay Company, the East India Company, and the Exeter Merchants in West Africa, but it lies outside the scope of my present work. The "Merchant Adventurers" of the sixteenth century sought a Royal Charter to secure a monopoly of trade. They fought their own battles against French, Spanish, Dutch, and Portuguese, and the East India Company was empowered to seize ships and goods of any traders not licensed by itself, and to inflict "imprisonment, or such punishment as for so high a contempt shall seem meet and convenient."[1] The Hudson's Bay Company complained of the "Free-Traders" who robbed it of its profits, and the West African merchants made the same complaint regarding their rivals, whom they called the "Interlopers."[2] But Parliament did not greatly favour these monopolies granted by the Crown, and in 1698 private traders were recognised on the West African coast.[3]

But to say that the East India Company's conquests and administrative successes were merely "a bye-product of trade, which was the real object aimed at,"[4] is to ignore the spirit of the resolution passed as early as 1689: "The increase of our revenue is the subject of our care as much as our trade; 'tis that must maintain our force when twenty accidents may interrupt our trade; 'tis that must make us a nation in India; without that we are but a great number of interlopers united by a Royal Charter, fit only to trade where nobody of power thinks it their interest to prevent us, and upon this ground it is that the wise Dutch in all their general advices that we have seen write ten paragraphs concerning their government, their civil and military policy, welfare and the increase of their revenue, for one paragraph they write concerning trade."[5]

Nearly a century later the East India Company's administration acquired legal sanction from the Moghul Emperor, and Parliament at once questioned the right of a trading company to acquire territorial sovereignty. For this privilege they were called upon to pay £400,000 per annum to the home Government till 1773, when the Regulating Acts, which culminated in Pitt's Act of 1784, brought the whole machinery of administration under the control of Whitehall.

[1] 'Government of India,' Ilbert, pp. 5, 6.
[2] 'A Tropical Dependency,' Lady Lugard, p. 239.
[3] Adam Smith, vol. iii. p. 125.
[4] 'German Colonies,' Sir H. Clifford, p. 28.
[5] Ilbert, *loc. cit.*, p. 25.

About the same time (1765) the whole coast of West Africa was declared to be exempt from the jurisdiction of the African Company (already deprived of monopoly, "regulated" and subsidised though it was), and vested in the Crown for the free trade of His Majesty's subjects.[1] Crippled by the abolition of the slave-trade, the company was finally dissolved in 1821.

Meanwhile monopoly rights (except as regards China) were withdrawn from the East India Company in 1813, and finally abolished in 1833. From this date it was required to wind up its commercial affairs, and was vested with administrative powers only, under the strict control of the home Government, by whom its Governor-General was appointed.[2] It continued to hold its territories "in trust for His Majesty" till superseded in 1858.

Even so brief an outline as this will serve to illustrate the growth of the conception of charters. Beginning with a trade monopoly, the older charters gradually acquired administrative powers, for the exercise of which the East India Company had actually to pay the British taxpayer. Towards the close of the eighteenth century, Parliament began to "regulate" them, to withdraw the monopoly, and to charge them with administrative functions only, till the Imperial Government was ready to supersede them. The modern charter, on the other hand, started as an administration, the expenses of which were to be met from commercial profits—in theory to be exercised without monopoly. For protection against foreign aggression, and even in case of serious internal trouble, it had to look to the home Government. Thus the old charters were in theory monopolistic trading companies, and when they assumed administrative functions, the monopolies were revoked and they became Governmental agencies, with no trading functions. The modern charter, on the other hand, was created for administration, and when the charter was withdrawn it was left as a trading company only, and without monopoly.

We have seen that the scramble for Africa and the demand for effective occupation hurried the Government of the day into the declaration of spheres of influence and the creation

[1] Adam Smith, vol. iii. p. 125.

[2] Ilbert, *loc. cit.*, p. 65, from whom the chief facts regarding the East India Company are taken.

of chartered companies, upon whom should fall the responsibility for the three largest areas acquired by Great Britain. There were, however, some smaller areas which were acquired by a different method. The West African "colonies" at this time (1889) consisted of small settlements on the coast. Little or no attempt to develop their hinterlands was made until in 1895-96, France, in pursuance of her policy of linking up her various possessions in West Africa, alleging with truth the absence of any effective occupation, seized the interior lands, and threatened the territory immediately contiguous to these colonies. Mr Hanotaux in 1896 claimed that she "thus gave effect to the hinterland policy before it had received a name," but her action was in fact a violation of the policy. Under Mr Chamberlain's energetic direction each of these colonies now bestirred itself to secure what was left of its hinterland. An epidemic of treaty-making and expeditions ensued, and eventually frontiers were fixed and delimited, but not without "incidents" at Waima (Sierra Leone), Wa (Gold Coast), and Meko, Kissi, and Borgu (Nigeria).

The limited areas thus secured were at once declared Protectorates. The hinterland of the Oil Rivers, which had now become the "Niger Coast Protectorate," was safe, for the chartered company formed a buffer between it and foreign aggression. British authority was represented by a Consul-General, with several Consuls and Vice-Consuls distributed along the coast. In its new rôle as an administrative department the Foreign Office now vested these officials with judicial and administrative authority over the natives of the country.

Consular officers in Africa had indeed played unusual parts for some time. Back in the 'sixties, in the early days of African exploration, Livingstone, accredited to the chiefs in the interior, with no jurisdiction or place of abode, had been granted consular rank to facilitate his work as a traveller. Later in 1878 Captain Foote, R.N., was appointed Consul in Nyasaland—at that time under the protection of no European Power—with instructions to watch and report on the slave trade, and accredited by letters from Her Majesty to the slave-trading chiefs. It did not enhance British prestige that he was necessarily without power or influence. Shortly before I reached Nyasa in 1888 his successor had been seized and stripped naked, and his life was only spared in consideration of a ransom; while British subjects, whom he was power-

CHAPTER II.

THE STATUS AND CONDITIONS OF THE BRITISH TROPICS.

Meaning of terms—The sphere of influence—Protectorates—In India—In Africa—Status of the people—Crown colonies—Suggested modification of status—Registration of British subjects—Tropics misnamed "colonies"—Self-governing colonies—Colonies on tropical plateaux—Asiatic colonisation—Contrast of temperate and tropical development—Value of tropical products—Area and population of British tropical Africa—The example of India.

THE "sphere of influence" had served its purpose, and the tropical African dependencies have now become "protectorates" and "Crown colonies." It is essential to an understanding of the evolution of these territories that we should have some clear conception of what these terms connote.

The sphere of influence, as we have seen from the circumstances in which it originated, "is a term to which no very definite meaning is attached. . . . It represents an understanding which enables a State to reserve to itself a right of excluding other European Powers from territories that are of importance to it politically or strategically. . . . No jurisdiction is assumed, no internal or external sovereign power is taken out of the hands of the tribal chiefs," says Hall.[1] While foreign interference would be regarded as an unfriendly act, it is understood that "within a reasonable time a more solid form will be imparted to the civilised authority." Jurisdiction is limited to British subjects, and would be exercised over foreigners only with their own consent, or that of their State, and over natives as a result of treaties.

"Protectorates" are difficult to define, but in all cases the

[1] See Hall's 'Foreign Jurisdiction of the British Crown,' on which these paragraphs are based, pp. 228-234. Sir C. Ilbert similarly describes it, 'Government of India,' p. 431, note.

protected State has parted with its freedom of action in foreign affairs. The control exercised over the protected native States of India varies according to their standing. The Nizam of Hydrabad, who rules over 83,000 square miles and a population of eleven millions, imposes taxes, coins money, inflicts capital punishment without appeal, and maintains a powerful contingent of troops; while Kathiwar, the lord of a few acres, exercises only a shadow of judicial authority, but is exempt from British taxation.[1]

Generally speaking, the Government of India controls the relations of the States towards each other, and since it guarantees a ruler against dethronement by his subjects, it accepts a limited responsibility for preventing misrule, as well as for the safety of British subjects and aliens. To ensure justice to these it may enforce extra-territorial jurisdiction. Land may be required for railways, and co-operation is expected against external aggression. To give effect to these obligations a Resident is appointed to the Court of the native ruler. His influence in a minor State, or over a weak or vicious ruler, may be very considerable.[2]

The African protectorates were for the most part declared over uncivilised territories, in which (since the native Governments were incapable of maintaining law and order) there were instituted courts of law and police for the benefit of both Europeans and natives. With some exceptions, therefore, such as Egypt and Zanzibar, they bear little resemblance to the protected States of India, though, as we shall see, the method of rule in the Moslem States of Nigeria has some analogies.

Great Britain for long held the view that the declaration of a protectorate conferred no power or obligation except towards British subjects, but it was evident that all the other signatories of the Berlin Act maintained that it conferred jurisdiction over the subjects of other civilised States as well as over the natives. The Act contemplated, and indeed prescribed (Arts. 30-32), extensive assumption of internal sovereignty by the protecting Power. It is true that the Act had reference to coast protectorates only, but, as Hall remarks, since these differ from interior protectorates only in that the difficulty of maintaining effective jurisdiction in the latter is greater, it may be assumed that the powers were not restricted to coast protectorates.

[1] Ilbert, p. 204.

[2] Ilbert, pp. 142-146, &c.

The Brussels Act carried these principles further, and enjoined progressive administration and judicial organisation—terms which amount to the recognition, as a principle of international law, that in an uncivilised country the protecting Power is charged with the duty of establishing administrative and judicial institutions. The British attitude, based on the exploded theory of the indivisibility of sovereignty, continued to be held tenaciously, even though, as we have seen (p. 13), Lord Salisbury had in 1887 clearly accepted the other view. In Zanzibar, therefore, jurisdiction was based on treaty,[1] and there and in Somaliland foreigners were only amenable by consent. The African Order in Council 1889, by which jurisdiction was assumed over foreigners and natives in those protectorates to which it was applied, was supplemented by the South African Order of 1891, and the Pacific Order of 1893, which asserts jurisdiction over both classes, irrespective of consent. The principles of the latter were applied to regions contiguous to the Gold Coast, to which neither the African Order nor the Berlin Act were applicable. The Matabeleland Order went even further. Already the South African Charter had conferred complete jurisdiction, and the High Commissioner of South Africa was similarly empowered in regard to the protectorates under his control. The Royal Niger Company also exercised a like jurisdiction, based so far as the natives were concerned on treaties.

However complicated and unnecessary this multiplicity of instruments may seem to a layman, it is clear that at the time when Hall wrote (1894), and still more when Ilbert published his book (1898), Great Britain had finally accepted the view that "exercise of jurisdiction over all persons within a protected country is necessary, where native administrative and judicial organisation is inadequate," both on behalf of foreigners who are deprived of the protection of their own

[1] Even as late as October 1907 it was considered necessary for the Sultan of Witu, whose petty state "forms part of the territories known as the British East African Protectorate," to announce by proclamation that the laws of British East Africa applied to and were in force in his territory. The administration of the Zanzibar Protectorate was transferred from the Foreign to the Colonial Office in April 1914, and an Advisory Council, without legislative power, to be convened at the discretion of the British Resident, with four official and three unofficial members, was set up, with the Sultan as president. The High Commissioner was hardly justified in describing this as "complete autonomy and independence."—Zanzibar Report, 1914, Cd. 7622 of 1915, pp. 28, 29.

State, and on behalf of natives against foreigners.[1] Such powers are, "so far as they go, identical with those which the Crown would have in a conquered country. . . . It can prescribe laws until Parliament chooses to legislate. It can subject to its administration all persons upon the protected soil."[2]

We arrive, then, at the general conclusion that "for purposes of municipal law an African Protectorate is not, but for purposes of international law must be treated as if it were, a part of British dominions."[3]

In some cases a community whose independence had been specifically recognised by treaty—as, for instance, the Egbas in Southern Nigeria—were nevertheless included in a protectorate—a contradiction of terms which involved so many anomalies that the treaty was denounced at last by mutual consent.[4]

Thus the term "protectorate" gradually changed its meaning from that of a pact with the ruler of a State, which maintained its internal but not its external sovereignty, to a declaration of the territorial status of a region included in the Empire, in which not only the external, but in varying degrees the internal sovereignty also, had passed to the controlling Power, in many cases (since unexplored regions were included) without even the "treaty" consent of the people. Powers of administration coequal with those of a colony have been assumed.

The inhabitants of a British protectorate are styled "British

[1] Ilbert, p. 433. Hall, p. 219.

[2] Hall, p. 225. Sir S. Olivier writes: "Effective occupation and the capacity to enforce the law of the sovereign power are a recognised condition of the right to assert sovereignty."—'Contemp. Review,' Jan. 1919.

[3] Ilbert, p. 431.

[4] International conventions relative to firearms and spirits were made applicable to African protectorates by the Crown. The convention enforcing the protection of wild animals, however, did not deal with imported articles, in the interests of the natives themselves, but curtailed rights hardly less jealously cherished than rights in land. Extra-territorial jurisdiction may be justified on behalf of foreigners, but the claim to exercise it on behalf of wild animals, birds, and fishes, and to make it an offence to kill an elephant though destroying crops, is an assumption of internal sovereignty hardly compatible with "independence." On the other hand, it has been suggested on high authority that the independence recognised by the treaty was only intended to mean "independence from other native control," and was in effect construed in that way. Prior to amalgamation in Nigeria I found that "neither the Colonial Office nor the Chief Justice had any clear idea as to what jurisdiction the Crown could legally exercise, or what executive powers were under the treaties vested in the Colonial Government" in the Lagos Protectorate.—Cmd. 468, 1920, sect. 17.

protected persons," and do not enjoy the status of British subjects, although, as Hall points out,[1] the term "British subject" is defined in the African Order 1889 as "including all persons enjoying His Majesty's protection." The "natives," however, are separately defined as "the subjects of any country within the limits of this Order not being British subjects." The wording is therefore ambiguous, but in practice the natives of a protectorate, who do not already enjoy the status of British subjects, have apparently no rights or privileges either within or beyond the limits of the protectorate. A "British protected" Somali complains in the 'Times' that although his people have been called on to fight for the Empire, they are ineligible for the Merchant Service because they are not British subjects.[2]

A Crown colony is annexed territory, and an integral part of the King's dominions, acquired either by conquest, settlement, or cession,[3] and since all inhabitants born in it have the status of British subjects, herein appeared to reside the chief distinction between it and a protectorate. The injustice of such a distinction may be seen, for example, in the case of the Lagos Colony, whose boundaries had never been defined, and were unknown to the judicial officers until the amalgamation of 1st January 1914. They intersect tribes, and include many who are still in the very lowest stage of primitive savagery.

[1] Hall, p. 128.

[2] 'Times,' 7th August 1920. Subjects of the Indian native states are not British subjects.—Ilbert, pp. 436-457. The judge of the High Court of Mombasa defined the status of a protectorate "which has never been acquired by settlement, or ceded to, or conquered, or annexed by His Majesty, or recognised by His Majesty as part of his dominions," and the status of the native inhabitants, in the following terms, relying on the case of the King *v.* the Earl of Crewe (2 K.B., 1900, p. 577): "East Africa, being a protectorate in which the Crown has jurisdiction, is in relation to the Crown a foreign country under its protection, and its native inhabitants are not subjects owing allegiance to the Crown, but protected foreigners, who, in return for that protection, owe obedience." —Cd. 6939 of 1913, p. 5.

[3] Taring, 'Law Relating to the Colonies,' p. 3. The Governor of the Gold Coast observed in a message to Council that "the colony was what it always had been, a collection of little states, each of which is self-contained and entirely independent of its neighbours," and adds that in none of the treaties or agreements with the British Government was any cession of territory made or contemplated. Yet the 'Colonial Office List' states that the greater part of the Gold Coast was acquired by cession (1921, p. lxii). If before annexation it was difficult to say which part was colony and which protectorate, it seems equally difficult to say now on what basis it was declared a colony, and how its status has been affected by the change.

On the creation of the Kenya Colony, the 'Times' correspondent informed us that "the white settlers are in a better position than as dwellers in a protectorate," but fails to explain in what way.[1] To say that the native laws and customs may be usefully retained in a protectorate as opposed to a colony, is to ignore the fact that in old-established colonies in West Africa the Supreme Court Ordinance enacts that no person shall be deprived of the benefit of any existing native law or custom which is not repugnant to natural justice. The grant of Crown colony status does not in itself "give the settlers a fuller voice in the control of public affairs" than they already possessed in the Legislative Council of the protectorate, the constitution of which does not depend on the status of the country.

The real reason for the annexation was that a loan could not be raised on the security of a protectorate, and for the same reason Nigeria could only raise a loan through the instrumentality of the small colony of Lagos, where only a microscopic portion of the revenue which formed the security originated. The tenure of British rule is, however, as secure in a protectorate as in a colony. That such a purely artificial and technical difficulty should be held to justify the grant of the status of British subjects to the hardly-explored tribes of the Kenya frontier demonstrates the absurdity alike of the distinction between colony and protectorate, and of the obligatory status conferred by the former.

It was at one time understood that the institution of slavery could not exist in a colony, as being part of the King's dominions, though it might be tolerated in a protectorate, which is not a "possession." That wholesome distinction has, however, been swept away by recent annexations, and indeed domestic slavery still exists in the Gold Coast Colony, the slaves being owned presumably by British subjects, though not under Mohamedan law. Sir C. Ilbert thought the line of demarcation between a colony and a protectorate "very thin." It has become attenuated almost to invisibility since he wrote.

Formerly colonies possessed Legislative and Executive Councils, while a protectorate had neither; but here again the distinction has become obliterated. Gibraltar and St Helena (both Crown colonies) and also Ashanti (which is

[1] 'Times,' 9th July 1920.

annexed territory) have none, while Cyprus, before it became a colony, had a Legislative Council of an advanced type—partly elected and with an unofficial majority,—and East Africa, while still a protectorate, had, and Nyasaland has, one of the ordinary type.[1] In Sierra Leone and the Gambia (as formerly in Southern Nigeria) the Council of the colony legislates for the protectorate.

The official distinction between colonies and protectorates led for a time to the adoption of such meticulous devices as the calling the officer administering the government of the former a "Governor," and of the latter a "High Commissioner," while the laws of the one were styled "Ordinances" and of the other "Proclamations," but these confusing differences have already disappeared.

The distinction between the two is now without practical difference, nor is there any apparent good reason why in Africa protectorates should not be accorded the status of possessions of the Crown, or why jurisdiction and the right of administration should not be based on the same prerogative as in a colony. The moment at which the civilised Powers of the world have asserted the unequivocal right and obligation of the more advanced races to assume responsibility for the backward races seems an appropriate one to brush aside these archaic and anomalous distinctions, and to abandon the farce of "acquiring" jurisdiction by treaties not understood by their signatories, and foreign to their modes of thought. The time would seem to be ripe to declare the annexation of the British African protectorates, and to merge them, including the Nile Sudan,[2] with the Crown colonies,

[1] Taring, *loc. cit.*, pp. 60-61, and 'Colonial Office List' Regulations, chapter i.

[2] The British and Egyptian flags at present fly side by side in the Anglo-Egyptian Sudan. This territory, won originally by conquest, chiefly by Gordon, was lost to Egypt by the Mahdist revolt, and Mr Hardinge, on behalf of the Egyptian Government, wrote that it "declined any responsibility with regard to the natives of those provinces *which it has abandoned.*"—Desp. of 7/8/92. The demoralised Egyptian troops, who had allowed themselves to be slaughtered like sheep at Suakim, in spite of the leadership of Sir Valentine Baker, and who dare not face the Dervishes, were reorganised by Kitchener, and some of them were employed in the reconquest of the Sudan; but it was British valour and British money which saved Egypt from being overrun by the Dervish hordes, and eventually overthrew the Mahdi. No impartial judge could maintain that Britain owes any debt to Egypt on behalf of the Sudan—it is Egypt which owes her salvation to the defence of her frontiers by British bayonets in the critical years of 1884-85. There is, however, a nominal claim, I believe, for about £10,000,000 for advances before the Sudan became self-supporting in 1912—from which must be deducted the customs, &c., retained by Egypt.—(Foreign Office Handbook 98,

under some designation more appropriate than the term "colonies," accepting for all alike an obligation before civilisation to promote their progress and welfare, and confirming to each according to its degree of advancement, and in fulfilment of all existing pledges, its present form of government.

From what I have said in a previous paragraph regarding the ambiguity of the status of the natives of a protectorate, it will, I think, be agreed that this question need form no obstacle to the course proposed. In the British African tropics it is only the educated class who would set any value on the status of a British subject. It should, I suggest, be made obligatory by Order in Council upon every person claiming or desiring to be a British subject to register his name within a prescribed period. The status would not be denied to any persons who now enjoy it, or to others whom the competent authority considered qualified. Failure to register would, of course, leave a native in the same position as at present, but any person born after the date of the Order, whose father was not registered, would by the terms of the Order cease to enjoy the status of a British subject, and thus persons still in a condition of savagery would in course of time cease to possess it automatically from the mere accident of birth in a colony. On the other hand, registration would not, of course, deprive a native of the benefit of the clauses in the Supreme Court Ordinance relating to the application of native law and custom. Registered British subjects would not be allowed to own slaves.

Such a system of registration of British subjects, as a means of identification, is provided for in Eastern countries.[1] Failure to register entails liability to non-recognition as a British subject, and to refusal of protection (the onus of proof resting on the claimant), but there is no co-relative immunity from the consequences of illegal acts, since even though unregistered he cannot divest himself of his nationality. In the African tropics, however, unregistered persons would eventually cease to have the legal status of subjects. They would remain protected persons, whose rights as such would be

p. 158.) This claim might be referred to the arbitration of the Judicial Court of the League of Nations. The independence of Egypt, subject to treaty conditions, has now been recognised. The question of the Sudan has been reserved for subsequent discussion, but so long as it remains under the control of Great Britain Egypt can have no fear lest her essential interests should be neglected.

[1] Hall, p. 129.

clearly defined in the Order. This principle has been adopted by the French, who allow natives of proved loyalty and good character, who can speak French, and have means of their own, to acquire the status of French citizens, with all the privileges of Europeans.[1]

The term "colony," as I observed, is as inappropriate in the tropics as that of "protectorate" is vague and indefinite. It originated in the idea—which, strange to say, was at one time common to all the nations of Europe—that the tropics were colonisable by the white races. That was the conception which prompted France after her reverses in Europe in 1871 to endeavour to create a greater France in Africa,[2] and caused Portugal to offer free domains (prazos) with the title of "Donna" to Portuguese women who would settle in Africa. It was this belief which caused England, according to Sir John Keltie, to send out a number of women of indifferent reputation to the freed negro settlement in Sierra Leone, together with a number of English, Dutch, and Swedish colonists.[3] That the belief is still held in Germany we learn from Zimmerman, himself an extensive traveller in the German tropical colonies, who argues that ill-health is not due to climate but to alcoholic excess, which the presence of white women would restrain.[4]

No thoughtful man contemplating the incredible triumphs of modern medical science would presume to assert that the problem of tropical colonisation is insoluble; but Great Britain, with the attractions offered to her surplus population in the Dominions, need never look for homesteads in the low-lying tropics of Africa.

The true colonies situated in the temperate zone, and possessing responsible government, are five in number, and have within recent years been christened "Dominions." They have nothing to do with the subject of this book, but a very brief word regarding them may not be out of place. The terms of their admission to the Peace Conference has involved the recognition, not by Great Britain alone, but by the whole civilised world, of their status as nations, and when revising the nomenclature of the component parts of

[1] Decree of 25/5/1915 and Arrete of 29/10/1912, F.O. Handbook, No. 100, 1920, p. 13.

[2] 'Control of the Tropics,' Kidd, pp. 28, 29.

[3] Keltie, 'Partition of Africa,' p. 78.

[4] 'The German Empire of Central Africa,' p. 78. See also Dr Horn, 'United Empire,' March 1922.

the Empire they might well be called the "United Nations of Great Britain." The change in their status is no mere matter of sentiment. Hitherto the Imperial Parliament has claimed the right to control their foreign relations, and to make treaties on their behalf. Now they claim, and the Mother Country admits their right, to have a voice in Britain's foreign relations and treaties, which may involve the Empire in war. The United Kingdom, by virtue of her tradition, her population, her wealth, her navy and army, must be the predominant partner, but claims only to be *prima inter pares*. When granting responsible government to the Cape and Natal, the Mother Country recognised her special responsibility as trustee for the welfare of the native races, and certain large tribal units were placed outside the jurisdiction of these Dominions. Over these the Governor of the Cape assumed the title of "High Commissioner," and the Governor of Natal that of "Paramount Chief."

Emphasis has been laid on the fact that the tropical dependencies in Africa cannot be colonised by British emigrants. Against this dictum the British settlements on the plateaux of East Africa, and the German colonies on the slopes of Kilimanjaro and the Camerun Mountain, like those in the Himalayas or the Nilgherries in India, and those in Ceylon, may be quoted. Here the altitude creates a sub-tropical or even a temperate climate, apparently well suited to the white races. It has not yet, however, been conclusively established that European children can grow to maturity in such conditions, and many consider that the altitude which creates the climate induces a tendency to nervous excitement and tension.[1] However this may be, the conditions of such colonies, owing to their close proximity to the tropics, differ very radically from those of a true colony. The presence of an indigenous native population, which is available for the unskilled and menial work, militates against true colonial development. The agricultural immigrant, instead of tilling his own fields, becomes the supervisor of native labour, and is apt to look on manual work as derogatory to his position.[2] "All of them,"

[1] See 'Official Handbook of Kenya,' I.D. 1216, p. 321.

[2] Sir Sidney Olivier expresses the view that "such settlements in Africa produce (as they have done in all ages and in all countries) first, slavery, predial or domestic; second, compulsory or indentured labour; third, the expropriation of the natives from the land in order to compel them to work for wages on the estates; fourth, pressure on the natives to labour for wages through direct or indirect taxation,—each of which has in turn given rise to reactions of the humanitarian conscience."—'Contemp. Review,' Jan. 1919.

say the bishops in their memorandum, "depend for their very existence as farmers on native labour."[1] Where European enterprise depends for its success—and the greater the success the greater the demand—not on the sole efforts of the colonists, not on climate and soil, but on the labour of a subject race, the elements of true colonisation are absent. With this aspect of the subject I shall deal in the chapter on labour.

White and coloured labour have not learned to work side by side on equal terms in our dependencies, and the attempt has hitherto resulted in the demoralisation of both.[2] It is essential to remember that whereas the settlers in the American colonies, in Canada, and in Australasia, found the indigenous races (with the exception of the Maoris) sparse, decadent, and rapidly tending to extinction, the settlers in Africa encounter a race, virile, increasing, and racially potent.

While climate, except at the higher altitudes, and the difficulties of labour supply, operate to some extent as deterrents to unrestricted white colonisation, they are not deterrent to colonisation by Asiatics. The claims of Indian British subjects to equal facilities with Europeans in this regard has of late become a matter of acute controversy, which I shall discuss at some length in a later chapter.

Turning from the questions of political status, and of different types of colonisation and settlement, let us consider for a moment what is the justification of the assertion that the custodian of these regions becomes a trustee for their development on behalf of civilisation.

In the temperate zones the surplus population of the white races can find new homes, create new wealth, and elaborate new forms of government, looking in their earlier years to the parent State for protection against foreign aggression, and later becoming sister nations. Such colonies as Canada and Australia, by reason of their vast area of productive land, are able to export great quantities of surplus produce—

[1] Cmd. 873 of 1920, p. 8.

[2] It is reported that in Alabama, in the Southern States, "white and black men work side by side in the mines, in the same gangs, and for the same pay" ('Times,' 1st June 1921), a statement in startling contrast to the frequent descriptions of lynchings of negroes in the Southern States.

cereals, meat, fruit, hides, and wool, as well as minerals—to supplement the insufficient output of the congested countries of Europe, and in the earlier years of their development are eager to exchange these for the manufactures of the parent country. Since some of them lie south and some north of the Equator, they are able—thanks to rapid ocean transport—to interchange their summer produce without competing with each other's markets. The exports of the temperate colonies are, however, of the same character, and in augmentation only of those produced in the parent country, while their demand for manufactured goods in payment is likely to decrease as they themselves become industrialised, and less dependent on the skill and the machinery of the older countries. Unless by a mutually agreed system of preferential tariffs they eventually differ little, from the economic and trade point of view, from foreign countries.

The tropics, on the other hand, consist for the most part of regions populated by backward races. Both for this reason and on account of their climate, they offer no inducement for permanent settlement by white races. The backward condition of the people, and their preference for agricultural pursuits, offer the prospect of continued markets for manufactured goods. The tropics produce in abundance a class of raw materials and of foodstuffs which cannot be grown in the temperate zones, and are so vital to the needs of civilised man that they have in very truth become essential to civilisation. It was the realisation of this fact (as I have said) which led the nations of Europe to compete for the control of the African tropics.

Consider, for instance, the uses of vegetable oils—palm-oil, kernel-oil, copra, beniseed, cotton-seed, shea, ground-nut, &c.—all of which come from the tropics. As food, soft nut-oils are now, by a process of hydrogenisation, being hardened, deodorised, and increasingly used as margarine, and the residues as cake for cattle food. Ground-nuts supply much of the "olive-oil" of commerce. As raw materials, only those who have an expert knowledge of the processes of many various manufactures can appreciate how essential they are to many of our staple industries. Palm-oil is, of course, used for the lubrication of rolling-stock and other machinery, and for the making of soap; it is also essential for the rolling of tin-plates, which in turn are required for all "tinned" provisions, roofing-sheets, &c.

The uses of rubber are endless, from the "waterproofing" of cloth to the making of tyres, and of many medical appliances. The number of hides and skins supplied by the temperate zones would be wholly inadequate for the provision of leather, whether for boots or for belting for machinery, &c., unless they were largely augmented by the output of the tropics. It is needless to point to the necessity for raw cotton,—add to these coffee, tea, cocoa, rice, sago, tobacco, sugar, jute and other fibres, gums, drugs, dye-stuffs, and hard-wood timbers, and we can realise how intimately our daily life is dependent on the produce of the tropics.

This subject was admirably dealt with by Mr Kidd in 1898.[1] He gives the trade of the United Kingdom with the British tropics in 1896 as £102,000,000. We may see how enormously the dependence of the civilised world on the tropics has increased since then by a comparison of the trade of British tropical Africa (with which alone I am here concerned) in the years 1899 and 1919. In the former year the value of the imports of the Western Group was calculated at £3,390,758, and the exports at £3,347,297—a total trade of £6,738,055. The imports of the Eastern Group were valued in that year at £2,600,000, and the exports at £1,900,000—a total trade of £4,500,000,[2] of which more than half was with the little island of Zanzibar. The value of the combined trade of British tropical Africa—which I have assumed to include the regions lying between the southern frontier of Egypt, lat. 22° N., and the Zambesi, lat. 16° S.—thus stood at £11,238,055 in 1899. Only twenty years later it had multiplied itself more than 6½ times, as may be seen from the following table —for the figures of which (as well as those I have quoted for 1899) I am indebted to the statistical branch of the Board of Trade, with the exception of those in italics [3]:—

[1] 'Control of the Tropics,' p. 10.

[2] The Board of Trade return indicates that the value of the imports and exports of the Sudan and Northern Rhodesia are not ascertainable for 1899. The former, in the year following the defeat of the Khalifa, may be regarded as negligible; for the latter I have added £41,094 and £30,789 respectively to make round figures.

[3] The census returns for 1921 (which are, however, still largely hypothetical) give the population of the Western Group as 23,166,519, and of the Eastern as 18,047,257, making a total of 41,213,776.

	Area (in sq. miles).	Population in 1919.	Density per sq. mile.	Trade (exclusive of specie) in 1919.			
				Imports.	Exports.	Total.	Per head.
THE WESTERN GROUP.				£	£	£	
Nigeria . . .	336,481	17,587,000	*52·2*	10,766,580	14,675,790	25,442,370	*28/11*
Brit. Cameruns	31,150	*a*650,000	*20·8*	...	...	...	...
Gold Coast .	79,506	*b*1,501,793	*19·8*	7,111,919	10,779,444	17,981,363	*238/3*
Brit. Togoland	*a*12,500	*344,000*	*27·5*	...	...	...	...
Sierra Leone .	24,908	1,500,000	*60·2*	2,047,577	2,047,577	4,082,447	*54/5*
The Gambia .	4,132	240,000	*58·*	1,229,924	1,229,924	2,403,916	*200/3*
Totals . . .	488,677	21,822,793	*44·6*	21,087,361	28,732,735	49,820,096	*45/7*
THE EASTERN GROUP.							
The Sudan (*f*)	1,014,600	4,000,000	*3·9*	4,930,874	3,108,464	8,039,338	*40/2*
Somaliland (*e*)	68,000	336,000	*4·9*	503,212	231,011	734,223	*43/8*
Kenya (*e*) . .	248,800	2,627,103	*10·5*	} *c*4,451,905	3,563,724	8,015,629	*28/8*
Uganda (*e*) . .	111,828	2,962,550	*26·4*				
Zanzibar . .	1,020	196,733	*192·8*	1,905,175	2,439,817	4,344,992	*441/8*
Tanganyika (*e*)	365,000	*a*4,000,000	*10·9*	*d*1,737,641	*d*1,994,016	3,731,657	*18/7*
Nyasaland (*e*).	39,573	1,203,758	*30·4*	591,505	413,062	1,004,567	*16/8*
N. Rhodesia .	291,000	823,502	*2·8*	434,354	454,366	888,720	*21/7*
Totals . . .	2,139,821	16,149,626	*7·5*	14,554,666	12,204,460	26,759,126	*33/1*
Western Group	488,677	21,822,793	*44·6*	21,087,361	28,732,735	49,820,096	*45/7*
Eastern Group	2,139,821	16,149,626	*7·5*	14,554,666	12,204,460	26,759,126	*33/1*
Grand totals .	2,628,498	37,972,419	*14·4*	35,642,027	40,937,195	76,579,222	*40/4*

(*a*) Approximate; (*b*) 1911; (*c*) Excluding a very small quantity of bullion; (*d*) Rs10 to £1; (*e*) Trade figures are for the 12 months ending March 1920; (*f*) £E1=£1, 0s. 6½d.

The trade statistics are somewhat abnormal. The year 1919 was still affected by war conditions, while the year 1920, in which several dependencies show enormous increases (Nigeria from 25½ millions to over 42 millions, the Gold Coast from 18 millions to 27½ millions), was affected by the "boom" and the succeeding "slump." Trade has not yet stabilised into normal conditions.

This Empire in the African tropics is nearly two and a half times the size of British India, and nearly half as large again as all India, including the Native States, and nearly twenty-two times the area of the United Kingdom.[1] Its population,

[1] The figures are: British India, area 1,093,074 sq. miles; all India, 1,802,629 sq. miles; population respectively 244¼ millions and 315 millions. Area of United Kingdom, 121,377 sq. miles.

though small for so vast an area—about 14·4 to the square mile—is double the density of French tropical Africa, if we exclude the Sahara, or nearly treble its density if we include it.[1] Its trade, which is rapidly expanding, is more than double that of India per head of population, and more than a quarter of its total volume, and is equal per head to that of Japan.[2]

The problems of British tropical Africa, with which I am concerned in this volume, have, of course, much in common both with those sub-tropical regions in the north and south of the continent, which are peopled by a large indigenous African population, and also with India, the greatest of British tropical dependencies. The Government of India has been described as a model of beneficent, bureaucratic rule. India's ancient civilisation and social organisation, based on and an integral part of its religions, and the culture and high intelligence of its educated classes, all combine to differentiate the problems of its vast population from those of other tropical regions of the Empire. Parliamentary debates, national congresses, and the Press have made them almost as familiar to us as our own. For a long series of years they have been handled by some of the ablest administrators whom Britain has produced.

Recently the decision has been taken to grant to India progressive self-government on Western models. It is a new departure in the world's history—for Japan lies outside the tropics—and only the event can show how far alien, democratic systems are adapted to the government of tropical races. But apart from questions such as these, there is a large range of subjects common alike to India and to Africa, including the details of provincial and village organisation, which are not beyond the region of useful discussion and suggestion. In many of these there is much to be learned

[1] French tropical Africa consists of "French West Africa" (including Togoland), area 1,822,459 sq. miles, population, 11,969,377; "French Equatorial Africa" (including Cameruns), area 1,037,131 sq. miles, population, 8,870,000; Somaliland, area 5790 sq. miles, population, 206,000; and Sahara, area 1,544,000 sq. miles; population, 800,000. Total area, 4,409,380 sq. miles; population, 21,840,377. Density, 4·95. Excluding the Sahara, the density would be 7·3 to the sq. mile.—'Statesman's Year-Book,' pp. 887, 891, and 895.

[2] Trade of all India, £287 millions—viz., 18s. per head; Japan, 40s.; British tropical Africa, 40s. The independent States which have the lowest in the world are Abyssinia 6s., and Liberia 4s. per head. Both are countries of enormous natural possibilities.—'Whittaker's Almanac.'

from Indian experience in spite of differences in social evolution, in religion, and in the intelligence of her people.

In the sphere of material development India is no longer solely a producer of raw materials and a consumer of imported manufactured goods, for her factories, manned by the cheap labour of a frugal and industrious race, now not only supply a great part of her own needs, but compete successfully with the manufactures of other nations. Alike in the early stages of industrialism, as in the methods and results of research and experiment, in transport, and in labour-saving devices, the results of India's experience should be of the greatest benefit to Africa.

It is one of the defects of our system of State departments that the invaluable lessons of Indian administration and economic progress—the result of much costly experience and research—and the history of its successes and failures, is not more readily accessible to other tropical dependencies, which are emerging from the stage in which India was many years ago.

CHAPTER III.

PRINCIPLES GOVERNING CONTROL IN THE TROPICS.

The Berlin and Brussels Acts—Unavoidable limitations of these Acts—Effect of the war and treaty of peace—The convention of September 1919—The Mandate system—Classes of Mandates—Obligations assumed by Mandatory—Objects of system—Precedents—Choice of Mandatory and boundaries—Equal opportunity—Uncertainty of tenure—National status—Alternatives—International control or annexation—Task of the Commission—Duties to subject races—Responsibility of suzerain to itself—French economic policy—British economic policy—Alleged infringements of the "open-door" policy—Contrast of French and British policy—Reciprocal obligations on the part of the natives—Appendix, Article 22 of Covenant.

THE principles which should guide the controlling Powers in Africa were first laid down with international sanction in the Berlin Act of 1885, which, in the words of Professor Keith,[1] "aimed at the extension of the benefits of civilisation to the natives, the promotion of trade and navigation on the basis of perfect equality for all nations, and the preservation of the territories affected from the ravages of war." The moral obligations towards the natives were dealt with more explicitly and amplified by the Brussels Act, which came into operation in 1892, and have lately received a wider and more practical sanction under the Treaty of Versailles and the Convention of September 1919, to which I shall presently refer more fully.

The Berlin Act was applicable in its entirety only to the "conventional basin of the Congo," and its results were largely nullified by the failure to provide any means of enforcing its terms. Though the Congo was ostensibly an "international State," the signatory Powers could not inter-

[1] 'Journal,' African Society, July 1918.

vene, without grave risk of international friction, when the provisions of the Act as regards the natives were set at naught, or even when the commercial interests of the subjects of any one of them were involved, or State monopolies contrary to its spirit created. Free trade was suppressed in the "Congo Free State," and France for a time adopted the same régime in her neighbouring colonies,—a situation which was only partially remedied by the Anglo-French Convention of 1898, in which reciprocity in certain British and French territories —outside the conventional basin of the Congo—was arranged for a period of thirty years, simultaneously with a territorial adjustment favourable to France.[1]

The Berlin Act originated in the desire of the signatory Powers to set up an international free State in the Congo basin. Some of its articles extended to the existing coast possessions of the Powers, but it was feared that its application in its entirety to all the African territories of individual nations would involve interference with sovereign rights. The Congo State has now become a Belgian colony, no longer under the Mandate of the Powers, and under the wise rule of King Albert has adopted a liberal régime.

The Brussels Act essayed to apply certain principles—especially in regard to the import of arms and trade spirits into Africa—to all the territories under European control. It was a notable advance towards the goal which the "Mandate system" hopes to attain in respect of ex-enemy colonies, but, like the Berlin Act, it provided no means of enforcing its stipulations, and even the periodical reports which were to show how far they were being carried out, were in practice neglected.

Some features of the era of aggressive acquisitiveness, which the completion of the partition of Africa had brought to a close, have been recalled by the allocation between the victorious Allies of the tropical colonies wrested from Germany. It was decreed by the Treaty of Versailles, which embodied the Covenant of the League of Nations, that Germany should forfeit these colonies on the grounds (as the

[1] The clause in the Convention runs as follows: "Within the Ivory Coast, Gold Coast, Dahomey, and Nigeria, the persons and goods of both countries and of their colonies shall for thirty years enjoy the same treatment in all matters of river navigation, of commerce, and of tariff, and fiscal treatment and taxes of all kinds, but each may fix in its own territory tariffs, fiscal treatment, and taxes."

Allies explained) of misrule,[1] and that they should be held by the respective Allies under Mandates, which should be based on Article 22 of the Covenant.

A new Convention abrogated, as between the parties to it, the Berlin and Brussels Acts, except as regards the matters dealt with in Article 1 of the Convention, which applied the principle of "complete commercial equality" in an area therein defined. It pledged the signatories to maintain in their respective African territories "an authority and police forces sufficient to ensure protection of persons and property, and if necessary of freedom of trade and transit," and it bound "the signatory Powers exercising sovereign rights or authority in African territories, to continue to watch over the preservation of the native populations, and to supervise the improvement of the conditions of their moral and material wellbeing." Finally, it endeavoured to remedy the defect of the previous Acts by agreeing that "if any dispute whatever should arise between the signatory Powers relating to the application of the Convention which cannot be settled by negotiation, this dispute shall be submitted to an arbitral tribunal in conformity with the provisions of the Covenant of the League of Nations." A separate Convention was drawn up to deal with the liquor traffic.[2]

These Conventions, which were applicable to the regions over which the signatories already held control, were supplemented by the Covenant of the League of Nations, which forms a part of the Treaty of Versailles. It dealt with the ex-enemy colonies now assigned under Mandate to various Powers. Article 22 embodies the latest expression of the conscience of Europe in regard to "peoples not yet able to stand by themselves," and constitutes not only a pledge in respect of Mandate territories, but a model and an aspiration for the conduct of those already under the control of one or other of the signatories (see Appendix). There was, however,

[1] Setting aside the atrocities exposed in Blue-books, one may judge of the nature of German methods of promoting the moral and material interests of the natives by the three regulations for S.W. Africa reported some years ago in the 'Times.' (1) Natives are prohibited from acquiring any rights in, or titles to land; (2) from possessing any big cattle or riding animals without special sanction; and (3) every native must have a passport. On the other hand, Herren Dernburg and Solf—Colonial Ministers—themselves visited Africa, and expressed enlightened views regarding the natives, in opposition to the local governors and the German colonists.

[2] Conventions of 10th September 1919. Cmd. 477 and 478 of 1919.

much unfortunate delay detrimental to the welfare of the countries concerned in issuing the Mandates.[1] This was due in part to the difficulty of harmonising the views of the Mandatories, and in part to the claim of the United States to be consulted as to their terms.[2]

The Mandates were conferred by the Supreme Council of the victorious Allies, and, after acceptance by each Mandatory, were submitted to the Council of the League of Nations, which was charged with the duty of seeing that their terms were in accordance with the Covenant. Thereafter the Powers which had accepted them became "Mandatories of the League," to which they must submit an annual report. A permanent Commission was set up consisting of nine members appointed by the Council, the majority being nationals of non-Mandatory Powers.[3] They are selected "for personal merit and competence," as private individuals holding no office under their Governments, and in no way representative of their nations. Their duty is to examine the annual reports in the presence of the representative of the Mandatory in order to see that the conditions of the Mandate are being observed, and to report to the Council, which alone communicates with the Powers.

The Mandates were of three types: *Class A.* includes the ex-Turkish colonies—Iraq, Palestine, and Syria,—whose independence "can be provisionally recognised subject to the rendering of administrative advice and assistance" until they are able to stand alone. Their wishes must be a principal consideration in the selection of the Mandatory. *Class B.* comprises the Central African ex-German colonies. The Mandatory in this case is responsible for the administration,

[1] The first batch of Mandates was not issued till August 1922. That for Iraq has not yet (June 1923) been issued. Until a Mandate becomes operative the terms of the Hague Convention (which precludes alteration of the civil law by the Power in military occupation) would appear to be applicable (Manual, 'Int. Law,' pp. 288-290).

[2] The United States took particular exception to the Japanese Mandate over the islands of the Pacific north of the Equator, and the matter was only settled by a separate treaty between the two Powers. Nor does she admit the validity of the other Mandates (G. H. Blakislee in 'Foreign Affairs,' U.S.A., Sept. 1922). Certain alterations were made in the Central African Mandates to meet her views (House of Commons debate, March 13, 1922). By this action she would seem to share responsibility for the supervision of the Mandates, but she is not represented on the Commission.

[3] The nationality of the present members is as follows: Belgian, British, Dutch, French, Italian (Chairman), Japanese, Portuguese, Spanish, and Swedish. There is a permanent Director, Mons. Rappard (Swiss), and a small staff.

and undertakes to maintain public order and to promote the moral and material welfare of the people. *Class C.* includes South-West Africa and the Pacific Islands. Here the Mandatory administers the territory under its own laws as an integral portion of its own territory, subject to the safeguards named for the interests of the natives.

The essential conditions and obligations in respect of Classes *B.* and *C.* are: (1) freedom of conscience and religion, subject only to the maintenance of public order and morals; (2) prohibition of abuses, such as the arms and liquor traffic and the slave trade; (3) prevention of fortifications, military and naval bases, or the military training of natives except for police and defence; and (in Class *B.*) equal commercial opportunity for all members of the League. "It is not in the power of the Council of the League or of the principal Powers to alter these. Amendments can only be made if the Covenant is revised." [1]

In the *A.* Class Great Britain holds Mandates for Iraq and Palestine. In the *B.* Class for less than one-sixth of the Cameruns, for nearly a third of Togo, and for the greater part of German East Africa (Tanganyika). In the *C.* Class she holds no Mandate, but those granted to the Union of South Africa for "German South-West Africa," to Australia for New Guinea and other Pacific islands south of the Equator, to New Zealand for Samoa, and to the British Empire for Nauru [2] are all conferred upon the King "on behalf of" the various Mandatories.

[1] Report by Mons. Hymans, adopted by the Council, Aug. 5, 1920.

[2] Nauru Island has an area of eight square miles, only with 1084 inhabitants. The Mandate is shared between Great Britain, Australia, and New Zealand, who "act on behalf of and are responsible to the Empire." Australia administers the island for five years. It contains vast quantities of phosphates of great commercial value, the monopoly of which was acquired by a British company from the Germans prior to the war. The three Governments bought out the company for £3,607,495, subscribed in proportions of 42, 42, and 16 respectively. An agreement was made between them under which 6 per cent is paid on the capital, and their requirements in phosphates are met in proportion to their share capital at cost price, any balance being sold in the open market. This transaction has given rise to some criticism, but it is clear that the pre-existing monopoly had nothing whatever to do with the Mandate. If the phosphates were all sold in the open market, as the United States claim that they should be, there would merely be a larger profit to distribute between the shareholders. A more pertinent criticism is that the taxation of the islanders appears to be unduly heavy (15s. poll-tax + 10 per cent *ad val.* import duty, and 10s. per ton export duty on copra), since the expenses of administration (police, &c.) are chiefly incurred on behalf of the indentured labour employed by the phosphates Commission. The new system by which £20 per acre is paid for the barren phosphate areas,

The Mandate system was an attempt to compose conflicting claims, pledges, and ideals. The Allies have loudly condemned the colonial methods of Germany and Turkey. Led by President Wilson, they had given currency to the catchwords "No Annexations," "Self-determination," and "The Open Door," and stood committed to the principles they implied. They sought, moreover, for a method which should remedy the defects of the Berlin and Brussels Acts by providing something in the way of a supervising authority to ensure the observance of the pledges given. The alternatives were annexation, or joint international administration, which would assuredly give rise to friction, would paralyse all initiative and progress by the dead hand of a super-bureaucracy devoid of national sentiment and stifling to all patriotism, and would be very disadvantageous to the countries concerned. Since this was admittedly impracticable, annexation was strongly advocated by the Japanese and the three Dominion Governments. It was, however, opposed to the principles proclaimed by the Allies, if not in some cases, to definite pre-Armistice pledges. A compromise was with difficulty reached by dividing the Mandates into the three classes described. The *C.* Mandates held by Japan and the Dominions "amount," as General Smuts observed, "to annexation in all but the name,"—save for the obligations imposed in regard to the natives, and the annual report to the League.

The Mandate system is a new departure in international law and policy, in that it confers sovereignty [1] under definite obligations, for the fulfilment of which the Mandatory is responsible to a constituted authority. Its closest analogies were the Mandate conferred on King Leopold of Belgium as sovereign of the Congo State—which, however, lacked a clear definition of the obligations and a supervising body,—and the proposal made by President Roosevelt in 1906 that France and Spain should hold a joint "Mandate" for Morocco, and that they should render to Italy, as the supervising

and a rental for any non-phosphate areas seems equitable, but it appears that the administrator is the sole judge as to the classification and the amount of rental of the land. (See Reports of the Australian Government, C. 5007 and 5291 of 1922; also the observations of the Mandates Commission, Aug. 1922; also Professor Charteris of Sydney University in 'Sydney Morning Herald,' Aug. 12 and 23, 1922; the Commonwealth debate of Sept. 8, 1922; and Blakislee, *loc. cit.*)

[1] See Mons. Hymans' report cited. On the other hand, the Chairman of the Mandates Commission observes that "the Mandatories administer not as sovereign masters, but as guardians on behalf of the League of Nations."

authority on behalf of all the Powers, with the right of inspection and verification, a complete report, so as to ensure that the claims of Germany and the United States to equal commercial opportunity were duly observed.[1] Though probably the best solution of a question which at the moment threatened to produce very serious difficulties, it is naturally open to criticisms, some of which may be briefly noted.

1. The Covenant lays down as regards the *A.* class of Mandates that "the wishes of the communities must be a principal consideration in the selection of the Mandatory." It is asserted that the Powers by the neglect of this proviso have disregarded a fundamental injunction of the Covenant. The paragraphs of Article 22, upon which the *B.* and *C.* Mandates are based, contain no similar injunction. These territories have been divided up in most cases as best suited the jealousies of the Powers, sometimes with scanty regard even to tribal boundaries. Great Britain and France even undertook to compensate Italy by cession of territory if they increased their possessions in Africa as a consequence of the war. It is to be hoped that this is the last occasion on which the conscience of Europe will permit the exchange of "possessions" in Africa, as though they and their inhabitants were mere chattels for barter regardless of the pledges of protection, for the fulfilment of which the protecting Power is individually responsible, and which it has no moral right to transfer to another. It is a notable proof of the one-sided character of the so-called treaties.[2]

2. The Mandate to France for Togo and the Cameruns differs in one respect from the British Mandate for those countries, in that it appears to permit the recruitment of troops for service in emergency outside the territory. It seems difficult to reconcile this clause with the terms of Article 22.

3. Though the Allies professed to proclaim the doctrine of "equal commercial opportunity," there is no stipulation to this effect in the paragraphs of Article 22, on which the

[1] See Article by Professor Potter in the (American) 'Political Science Review,' Nov. 1922.

[2] The exchange of the Gambia for French Dahomey was at one time the subject of prolonged discussion (see Cd. 244 of 1870 and Cd. 1409 and 1498 of 1876, &c.). It would surely be an immoral and indefensible transaction, unless with the consent of the people. A French writer in the 'Observer' (Nov. 11, 1917) endorses this view.

A. and *C*. Mandates are based. In the former, it is true that the principle is affirmed in the Mandates themselves, but, as in the *B*. class, it is restricted to members of the League, to the exclusion apparently of the United States and Germany. Dr Schnee (late Governor of German East Africa) would seem to be justified in asserting that this is a retrograde step,[1] while the United States maintains that the denial of the Open Door in the *C*. Mandates is contrary to the implied conditions of the Covenant, and refuses to recognise their validity with the exception of that held by Japan, with whom she has made a separate treaty securing equal opportunity. Great Britain has granted a reduction in Customs duties to imports from her Mandate territories, but since she asks for no reciprocity for this "Imperial preference," there is no violation of the Mandate obligations.

4. A serious drawback of the Mandate system lies at present in the fact that it constitutes only "un titre précaire" as M. Ryckmans calls it. The Mandatory, therefore, may be unwilling to expend large sums in economic development, and is only able to grant a conditional title or to enter into conditional contracts with any private firm which may be anxious to invest capital in the development of the country. Business men will not risk their capital when (*a*) the Mandate is (theoretically at least) revocable; (*b*) the Mandatory may at any time resign the Mandate without the loss of national prestige which would be involved if it were a part of the national possessions [2]; (*c*) the Mandatory may prematurely consider that the country is ripe for self-government, and may transfer control to a native authority unable or unwilling to grant adequate protection.[3] This is manifestly a serious drawback to the material progress of a mandated territory,

1 'The German Colonies under the Mandates' (Berlin, 1922), p. 40. It seems regrettable that the "open door" should be restricted to members of the League. Industrial Germany must have assured access to sources of supply of raw materials. It is in her late colonies that she should learn the application of the principles of the Covenant.

2 The acceptation by France of a Mandate for Cilesia and its abandonment before confirmation is a case in point. Moreover, the British Government has been urged to resign its Mandate for Iraq and Palestine by speakers in Parliament and by responsible organs of the Press like the 'Spectator.'

3 France demurred to the possibility of revocation because, as M. Sarraut (Colonial Minister) observed, it would be unfavourable to continuous effort and the liberal expenditure of capital. The auction of the Cameruns properties (Oct 11, 1922) was a fiasco because would-be buyers considered the title too precarious.

and it is essential that some form of guarantee by the League or the Mandatory should be given. Failing this, annexation, if conditioned by all the existing safeguards, would probably find many advocates.

5. The question of the national status of the inhabitants of a Mandated territory has recently been the subject of exhaustive examination by the Mandates Commission and the Council of the League. I do not here touch on that aspect which is concerned with the status of Germans in South-West Africa, nor yet with the legal position of natives who had acquired the status of German subjects prior to the war. It is proposed that the inhabitants shall have the status of "persons administered or protected under Mandate." This would appear to be merely descriptive of their condition, and a definition of the rights connoted by the term is desirable. Though the legal status of a "protected person" in a British protectorate may be vague, his condition, as we have seen (p. 35), differs little in practice from that of the inhabitant of a colony.[1] He has no divided or precarious allegiance. His loyalty and patriotism (which count for much in Africa) are enlisted on behalf of the suzerain Power. But the person "protected under Mandate" shares with the owner of an estate "un titre précaire" subject to the contingencies of revocation, rendition, or resignation of the Mandate, and has no definitely legalised status and rights.

6. Fears have been expressed lest the fact that the Powers who now control the former German and Turkish colonies and act in the capacity of "Mandatories of the League" may deter Germany and Turkey from joining the League, and so hamper its main purpose of preserving peace among the nations—a fear which has recently been shown to be groundless so far as Turkey is concerned.

Some of these difficulties can, it would seem, only be solved by annexation, or at least by the declaration of a protectorate by the present Mandatories. On the assumption that there is no intention of ever restoring these countries to their former rulers, the principal objection to such a course seems to be one of sentiment, *provided that the annexing Powers accept as a condition of annexation all the conditions imposed by the*

[1] Sir J. Salmond, Solicitor-General of Australia, 1920, observes that "protected persons" are entitled to diplomatic protection in a foreign country. Even in the *A*. Mandates it is difficult to confer a local nationality, since the territories include diverse and conflicting nationalities. It would not be easy to induce either an Arab or a Jew to regard himself primarily as a "Palestinian."

present Mandates (including the annual report to the League) in the form of an international Convention.[1]

The task of the Council and of the Mandates Commission of the League is a delicate and difficult one. The observance of the pledges undertaken by Mandatories must in the last resort depend on the public opinion of the Mandatory State, and this, if the Mandatory is at fault, would naturally be inclined to defend the action of its agents against adverse criticism, which independent States are apt to resent. A Mandatory may avoid reference in its report to a matter open to hostile comment, or may burke inquiry by neglecting to send a representative to reply to questions. The Commission has little or no means of verifying a report, or of ascertaining how far it is an exhaustive and impartial account. For this it must depend on outside agencies. Finally, it will obviously not be easy to secure continuity among the members of the Commission, who are debarred from holding any office under their Governments.

On the other hand, the Commission will gradually acquire a unique experience of the methods of administration and development adopted by the different Mandatories, and by placing this at the common service, it may become an invaluable instrument of international co-operation even beyond the limits of Mandated territories. To achieve this object it must earn for itself the character of a useful ally rather than that of a censorious critic.

It will be its task to conciliate opposing views, as, for instance, the natural protest of Japan to the application to New Guinea of the Australian law which excludes all Asiatic immigrants. Ambiguous terms which conduce to mistaken policies—such as "Liquor Traffic" and "Trade Spirits," or "Vacant Lands" and "Crown (or State) Property"—must be defined. Already one such question has been disposed of by the decision that petitions from natives must be sent through the Mandatory, and representations from third parties will be sent to the Mandatory for comments.

The Mandate system, as we have seen, presents many difficult problems. Even if satisfactory solutions have not in all cases as yet been found, we must not minimise the substantial step achieved by the international recognition of

[1] The present administration of the Congo under the sovereignty of Belgium forms a striking contrast to its condition under a Mandate, but in that case the Mandatory was an individual, not a State.

the principles embodied in Article 22, and the machinery set up to preserve them. The great principle of trusteeship for backward races, though limited in its context to ex-enemy colonies, must obviously in future be regarded as no less applicable to the " possessions " of the Allies. The camouflage described in the last chapter is swept away, and the Powers, instead of arguing over the theoretical basis of sovereignty in Africa, frankly recognise that " the tutelage of nations not yet able to stand by themselves must be intrusted to advanced nations." They accept control under the Covenant primarily in the interests of the subject races.

The responsibility is one which the advantages of an inherited civilisation and a superior intellectual culture, no less than the physical superiority conferred by the monopoly of firearms, imposes upon the controlling Power. To the backward races civilisation must be made to mean something higher than the aims and methods of the development syndicate or the assiduous cultivation of new wants. Where these principles have been neglected, history has taught us that failure has been the result.

Such have been the successive steps by which Europe has sought to fulfil the Dual Mandate in Africa. Without underrating the great work which France and Belgium are doing, it is to England that Beaulieu generously awards the palm in having led the way in the recognition of the responsibility which is inseparable from rule.[1] The moral obligations to the subject races include such matters as the training of native rulers ; the delegation to them of such responsibility as they are fit to exercise ; the constitution of Courts of Justice free from corruption and accessible to all ; the adoption of a system of education which will assist progress without creating false ideals ; the institution of free labour and of a just system of taxation ; the protection of the peasantry from oppression, and the preservation of their rights in land, &c.

The material obligations, on the other hand, are concerned with development of natural resources for the mutual benefit of the people and of mankind in general. They involve the examination of such questions as " equal opportunity " and " Imperial Preference," and other problems of economic policy. To these dual aspects of the Mandate of civilisation in Africa the following chapters are devoted.

[1] Beaulieu, *loc. cit.*, vol. i. p. 92, and vol. ii. p. 246. Quoted on p. 619.

Nor is the obligation which the controlling Powers owe to themselves and their race a lesser one. It has been well said that a nation, like an individual, must have some task higher than the pursuit of material gain, if it is to escape the benumbing influence of parochialism and to fulfil its higher destiny. If high standards are maintained, the control of subject races must have an effect on national character which is not measurable in terms of material profit and loss. And what is true for the nation is equally true for the individual officers employed. If lower standards are adopted—the arrogant display of power, or the selfish pursuit of profit—the result is equally fatal to the nation and to the individual. Misuse of opportunity carries with it a relentless Nemesis, deteriorating the moral fibre of the individual, and permeating the nation, as M. Leroy Beaulieu has shown in his masterly survey of the standards and principles which have guided the colonial policy of successive nations.

But if the standard which the white man must set before him when dealing with uncivilised races must be a high one for the sake of his own moral and spiritual balance, it is not less imperative for the sake of the influence which he exercises upon those over whom he is set in authority. The white man's prestige must stand high when a few score are responsible for the control and guidance of millions. His courage must be undoubted, his word and pledge absolutely inviolate, his sincerity transparent. There is no room for "mean whites" in tropical Africa. Nor is there room for those who, however high their motives, are content to place themselves on the same level as the uncivilised races. They lower the prestige by which alone the white races can hope to govern and to guide.

Turning now to questions of economic policy, we find that the two chief Powers have adopted radically different principles in Africa. The French, as M. de Caix expresses it, adopt "a sort of economic nationalism," which aims at preserving the products and markets of her colonies for the exclusive use of France by every means in her power.[1] It was, as I have pointed out, only in certain specified colonies, for a limited period, and as the price of territorial adjustments in her favour, that she agreed to break down the tariff wall.

[1] See "British and French Colonial Policy," by M. Devereux, 'Anglo-French Review,' Sept. 1920.

This principle is regarded as essential to the theory that her colonies form an integral part of France, mutually interdependent and sufficing. After the war of 1870, and again after the recent war, the doctrine was proclaimed that "France can only remain a great Power by knowing how to draw from her colonies all she requires." [1]

Dutch methods need not be discussed here, since they do not affect Africa, but a succinct and most interesting account may be found in Mr Elliott's work on the Philippines.[2]

The conception that overseas possessions should be a source of direct profit to their "owners" lost Spain her South American colonies. Turkey, the Congo under Leopold, Holland and Portugal,[3] have adhered to the principle, the disastrous results of which not even Adam Smith has described with more relentless logic than the great French writer, M. Beaulieu. France, however, while imposing no tribute, maintains the policy of monopoly and conscription.

When Great Britain undertook the control of great regions in tropical Africa, she not only gave to her commercial rivals the same opportunities as were enjoyed by her own nationals, but she assisted in the development of these territories from Imperial revenues—not as loans to be repaid when they grew rich, but as free gifts—and later by the use of Imperial credit to float loans for development, while her Navy, and on occasion her troops, ensured their protection. She secured to their inhabitants an unrestricted market for their produce, and to all engaged in their development, of whatever nationality, equality of commercial opportunity and uniform laws.

She recognised that the custodians of the tropics are, in the words of Mr Chamberlain, "trustees of civilisation for the commerce of the world"; that their raw materials and foodstuffs—without which civilisation cannot exist—must be developed alike in the interests of the natives and of the world at large, without any artificial restrictions. Here are his words spoken twenty-four years ago: "We, in our colonial policy, as fast as we acquire new territory and develop it, develop it as trustees of civilisation for the commerce of the world. We offer in all these markets over which our flag floats the same opportunities, the same open

[1] French Colonial Minister at Paris Conference of 1917.

[2] 'The Philippines,' C. B. Elliott, pp. 15-18, and Prefatory Note by Mr Root.

[3] See Admiralty Handbook, I.D. 1189, p. 136. Reforms were instituted by the law of August 1914.

field to foreigners that we offer to our own subjects, and upon the same terms. In that policy we stand alone, because all other nations, as fast as they acquire new territory—acting, as I believe, most mistakenly in their own interests, and above all, in the interests of the country they administer,—all other nations seek at once to secure the monopoly for their own products by preferential and artificial methods." Viewed from this standpoint, the tropics are the heritage of mankind, and neither, on the one hand, has the suzerain Power a right to their exclusive exploitation, nor, on the other hand, have the races which inhabit them a right to deny their bounties to those who need them. The responsibility for adequate development rests on the custodian on behalf of civilisation—and not on behalf of civilisation alone, for much of these products is returned to the tropics converted into articles for the use and comfort of its peoples.

The democracies of to-day claim the right to work, and the satisfaction of that claim is impossible without the raw materials of the tropics on the one hand and their markets on the other. Increased production is more than ever necessary now, to enable England to pay the debts she incurred in preserving the liberties of the world. The merchant, the miner, and the manufacturer do not enter the tropics on sufferance, or employ their technical skill, their energy, and their capital as "interlopers," or as "greedy capitalists," but in fulfilment of the Mandate of civilisation. America, since she became a world Power, has adopted the same standards in the Philippines.

The policy of "the open door" has two distinct though mutually dependent aspects—viz., equal opportunity to the commerce of other countries, and an unrestricted market to the native producer. The tropics can only be successfully developed if the interests of the controlling Power are identical with those of the natives of the country, and it seeks no individual advantage, and imposes no restriction for its own benefit.

It has been alleged that in the matter of certain export duties on palm kernels in West Africa, as also in regard to "Imperial Preference," these principles have been violated, while the policy of "Empire cotton-growing" would seem to depend for its success upon an arbitrary hypothecation of the crop. The principles at issue in each of these cases are of such importance that I propose to consider these allegations in some detail in a later chapter (see pp. 268-279).

French writers have pointed to these measures as a violation of our vaunted policy of the "open door," and asked how we can consistently condemn the exclusive tariffs of France while adopting such measures ourselves. The principle of Imperial Preference is that of voluntary sacrifice, and cannot be compared with obligatory and exclusive tariffs imposed on colonies in restriction of their markets; if in any case the latter have been imposed, it was, as we shall see, as a temporary war measure only. Whether the exclusive tariffs of other nations may compel us to adopt any other policy the future will show, but there is no burking the conclusion that unless it is adopted with the consent, or for the benefit, of the dependency concerned, it would be contrary to our declared policy of trusteeship.

The acceptance of this policy of trusteeship involves, it may be said, some reciprocal obligation on the part of the natives. Their lands, which Germany coveted, and their liberties were at stake no less than our own in the recent war. They owe it to their inclusion in the Empire that they have escaped. Is, then, the native of the tropics to bear no share of the economic burden which the war has left, or in the cost of defence for the future? The African is not by nature ungrateful, and would not shirk his share of the burden. I have no doubt as to the response he would make to such a suggestion if he understood. Would, then, a trustee be justified in demanding some reciprocity, or exacting some participation in the cost of defence, as an obligation properly due from his ward, after consulting the vocal minority and the more intelligent chiefs? These are questions which merit consideration in their proper context (see pp. 274, 275).

ARTICLE 22 OF THE COVENANT OF THE LEAGUE OF NATIONS.

To those colonies and territories which as a consequence of the late war have ceased to be under the sovereignty of the States which formerly governed them, and which are inhabited by peoples not yet able to stand by themselves under the strenuous conditions of the modern world, there should be applied the principle that the wellbeing and development of such peoples form a sacred trust of civilisation, and that securities for the performance of this trust should be embodied in this Covenant.

The best method of giving practical effect to this principle is that the tutelage of such peoples should be entrusted to advanced nations who, by reason of their resources, their experience, or their geographical position, can best undertake this responsibility and who are willing to accept it, and that this tutelage should be exercised by them as Mandatories on behalf of the League.

The character of the Mandate must differ according to the stage of the development of the people, the geographical situation of the territory, its economic conditions, and other similar circumstances.

Certain communities formerly belonging to the Turkish Empire have reached a stage of development where their existence as independent nations can be provisionally recognised subject to the rendering of administrative advice and assistance by a Mandatory, until such time as they are able to stand alone. The wishes of these communities must be a principal consideration in the selection of the Mandatory.

Other peoples, especially those of Central Africa, are at such a stage that the Mandatory must be responsible for the administration of the territory under conditions which will guarantee freedom of conscience and religion, subject only to the maintenance of public order and morals, the prohibition of abuses such as the slave trade, the arms traffic and the liquor traffic, and the prevention of the establishment of fortifications or military and naval bases, and of military training of the natives for other than police purposes and the defence of territory, and will also secure equal opportunities for the trade and commerce of other members of the League.

There are territories, such as South-West Africa and certain of the South Pacific Islands, which, owing to the sparseness of their population, or their small size, or their remoteness from the centres of civilisation, or their geographical contiguity to the territory of the Mandatory, and other circumstances, can be best administered under the laws of the Mandatory as integral portions of its territory, subject to the safeguards above mentioned in the interests of the indigenous population.

In every case of Mandate, the Mandatory shall render to the Council an annual report in reference to the territory committed to its charge.

The degree of authority, control, or administration to be exercised by the Mandatory shall, if not previously agreed upon by members of the League, be explicitly defined in each case by the Council.

A permanent Commission shall be constituted to receive and examine the annual reports of the Mandatories, and to advise the Council on all matters relating to the observance of the Mandates.

CHAPTER IV.

THE PEOPLE OF BRITISH TROPICAL AFRICA.

Units of administration—Climate and physical characteristics of the country—History—Paucity of population—Hamites and negroes—Physical characteristics of the people—Character of the typical African—Illustration of lack of apprehension—Of fidelity and friendship—Diversity in evolution—Administrative classification—Primitive races—Settled tribes—Pastorals—The refugees—Social organisation—Advanced communities—Pagan tribes—Alien conquerors—Influence of Islam—Influence of Christianity—Summary—The Europeanised African—Characteristics—Comparison with Indian Progressives—The negro in the United States—Claims for self-government—Scope in municipal work—The true path to self-government—Opportunities now enjoyed—Fitness for responsible positions—A native cadet service—Critics of the educated native—Future of the educated African—The debt of Africa to him—The Syrian—Is civilisation a benefit?—Some drawbacks and some benefits.

Before discussing the methods by which the controlling Power can promote the material development of the tropics and the welfare of the inhabitants, it will be of interest to consider what manner of people they are, and the physical characteristics of the country they inhabit.

British tropical Africa includes some of the most densely populated and most richly endowed regions of the continent, including Nigeria, which, in view of its area, population, and trade, occupies a very prominent place among the dependencies of the Empire. We have already seen (*vide* table, p. 45) that, unlike India and the Dominions, the African tropical empire is divided into a number of dependencies, in some cases coterminous with each other, in other cases separated by intervening territories under the control of foreign Powers, each under its own Government and separate laws, and all except the Sudan under the control of the Colonial Office, which alone forms the nexus which co-ordinates their policies.

In the sub-tropical regions south of the Zambesi there are other dependencies which have been permeated by European settlement—Southern Rhodesia, Bechuana, Basuto, and Swaziland, as well as the regions in the South African Union. The native peoples who inhabit them are still for the most part in the tribal stage, and the problems of administration discussed in this volume apply in great part to them.

The climate and physical characteristics of a country which extends over sixty-two degrees of longitude and thirty-eight of latitude (say 4200 by 2600 miles) must naturally be extremely diversified. In the northern hemisphere the heavy rains fall in the summer months (June-October), in the south from November to April, while on and near the Equator there is a double rainy season partaking of both characteristics.

Across the northern part of the continent, from the Red Sea to the Atlantic, stretches a zone of arid desert, waterless, in parts devoid of vegetation, a sea of shifting, wind-driven sands, whose billows form sand-dunes, and bury and baffle the toil of man. Throughout its breadth in the British tropics it is traversed by the wonderful Nile. In the east there are great mountains whose crests are crowned with eternal snow, and elevated plateaux on which the climate and rainfall invite the European colonist. Through the heart of the country, from the temperate latitudes in the south to those in the north—and beyond them across the Red Sea to Northern Palestine—runs the Great Rift Valley, 3500 miles long, forming the long and narrow lakes of Tanganyika and Nyasa, with a maximum depth of 4758 feet and 2316 feet respectively.

The equatorial belt in West Africa is a region of moist forests and profuse vegetation, with a rainfall of 150 inches on the coast, culminating on the western slopes of the Camerun mountain in upwards of 400 inches. Here was no inducement for the conquering pastoral tribes, for the grasslands of the northern savannahs with their vast herds of cattle cease. Animal and bird life, other than the elephant, the hippopotamus, the buffalo, the monkeys which live in the tree-tops, the great fish-eagle, and aquatic birds, is scarce. Man is at perpetual warfare with the vegetable and insect world, and in the deltas of the tropical rivers leads a semi-aquatic life, subsisting on sylvan produce and fish. The British tropics in Africa include a great part of those mighty rivers —the Niger and the Nile—and the great lakes, of which

Victoria Nyanza is the largest, with an area of 27,000 square miles, but little less than that of Ireland.

The history of these peoples of tropical Africa, except on the coast fringe, has during the ages prior to the advent of European explorers some sixty years ago been an impenetrable mystery. Attempts to solve it consist chiefly in conjectural migrations of tribes and of mythical legends, except in so far as the history of the West African empires of Ghana, Melle, and Songhay have been recorded by the Arabic historians of the Moorish Empire.[1] Unlike the ancient civilisations of Asia and South America, the former inhabitants of Africa have left no monuments and no records other than rude drawings on rocks like those of neolithic man.

The paucity of the population of tropical Africa, as contrasted with that of Europe and Asia, is shown by the table on page 45.[2] In the regions under British control it averages only 14·4 to the square mile, while in British and French tropical Africa, covering over seven million square miles, it does not exceed 8·5. It is, moreover, very unevenly distributed. Considerable districts in Nigeria have a density of over 300, while in vast areas in the Sudan, owing to the desert conditions, there is only one person to two square miles. Northern Rhodesia, more than twice the size of the United Kingdom, fertile and well-watered, has only three to the square mile. This astonishing lack of inhabitants, though the races of Africa are virile and prolific, has been due in the past to intertribal warfare, slave-raiding, and the ravages of unchecked epidemics—especially sleeping-sickness and smallpox,—in more recent times to the prevalence of venereal disease, with its attendant infant mortality, and to the dissemination of diseases by freedom of communications.

The fecundity of the women—apart from the effects of venereal—appears to vary greatly in different tribes, and while some are decadent, others are correspondingly prolific. The custom, which seems fairly general among the negro tribes, of suckling a child for two or three years, during which a woman lives apart from her husband, tends to decrease

[1] See the account in 'A Tropical Dependency,' by Lady Lugard, of El Bekri, Ibn Khaldun, Ibn Batuta, and others who wrote in the eleventh and fourteenth centuries.

[2] The density per square mile of England and Wales is 649, of Germany 319, of France 184, of Japan (mainland) 640, of China (proper) 197, and of British India 225.—'Statesman's Year-Book,' 1923.

population. Polygamy, in so far as it ensures that every female is mated, would seem to conduce to increase, but the accumulation of great numbers of women in the harems of despotic rulers would have a contrary tendency.

It is essential to realise that tropical Africa is inhabited by races which differ as widely from each other as do the nations of Europe, and that some of the principal racial types present even greater divergence than those of Europe and parts of Asia.[1] Broadly speaking, the coloured population of tropical Africa divides itself into the races of Asiatic origin which have penetrated the continent from the north-east and east, with their negroid descendants, who chiefly occupy the northern tropical zone, and the negro tribes which inhabit the greater part of the remainder.[2] The immigrant races, generally called Hamites, are supposed to have invaded North-East Africa "probably a good deal more than 4000 or 5000 B.C." There was a Semitic invasion some 2000 years later, but its elements have entirely disappeared, though it has left indelible traces on the language and racial characteristics of Abyssinia. The principal Hamite—or Hamitic negroid—tribes in East Africa are the Abyssinians, the Somalis, the Gallas, the Masai, the Wahima, and the Nandi; in West Africa the Fulani, supposed to be descended from the Berbers. All have been modified to a greater or less degree by admixture with negro blood, which has produced racial types differing from each other, and widely different from the negro type. They vary in their mental and physical characteristics according to the amount of negro blood in their veins, which has shown itself extremely potent in assimilating alien strains to its own type. Perhaps the most distinctive external characteristic—much more reliable than that of colour—by which the degree of negro blood may be gauged, is the hair growth on the head and face, varying from the woolly head and smooth face of the pure negro, to the straight hair and bearded face of the Asiatic.

[1] Sir H. Clifford in his address to the Nigerial Council (Dec. 1920), received since first these pages were written, gives a very striking description of the greater contrast between West African tribes than between European nations. "Even the Singalese of Ceylon as an Aryan people are more nearly allied to the English and Germans than are to one another many of the peoples of West Africa."

[2] The existence of non-negro tribes in the extreme south is regarded by some as evidence that in very ancient times the conquering Hamites traversed the whole continent.

The Hamites and Hamitic negroids are "slim and wiry in build, markedly dolichocephalous, with high narrow foreheads, good features, reddish complexions, plentiful frizzy hair, and small hands and feet."[1] They exhibit, as we shall see, powers of social organisation and intellectual development in advance of the pure negro stock.[2] They are capable of immense physical endurance, but do not possess the physique and strength of the negroes. They are generally nomadic and pastoral, and for the most part have embraced Islam.

The finer negro races, among whom are included the group of tribes known as the Bantus, have no doubt in prehistoric times assimilated alien blood, which has differentiated them from the aboriginal negro type. They may, however, be said to constitute the general negro race-type of to-day. The skull and forehead are better developed, and the thick lips, the bridgeless nose, and the prognathous jaw are less pronounced than in the more archaic type. Their intelligence is more developed, and many tribes have reached a degree of social organisation which, in some cases, has attained to the kingdom stage under a despot with provincial chiefs of the feudal type.

The negroes, and the negroids who approximate most closely in race-type to them, consist of innumerable tribes—in Northern Nigeria alone there are said to be about 380—which have each their own special traits, but they share in varying degrees the general characteristics of the negro. In colour they are very black, with woolly hair growing in little tufts on the scalp, and with practically none on the face. They are for the most part settled agriculturists, though the aboriginal types, such as the Pigmies, the Wanderobbo, and the Wasania are nomad hunters.

The Bantus, and most other negroes, are physically fine specimens of the human race. Powerfully built, they are capable of great feats of strength and endurance. Individuals will carry a load of 100 lbs. on their heads from morning till night, up hills and through swamps, with but brief intervals for rest. The King's messengers in Uganda, in Mtesa's time, were, I believe, expected to cover sixty miles in a day.

[1] See Admiralty manuals, 'Kenya,' 1216, pp. 236, 237, and 'Abyssinia,' pp. 104, 156, &c., and Eliot, 'The East African Protectorate,' pp. 119, 133.

[2] The Bahutu (Bantus) in Urundi-Ruanda constitute 90 per cent of the population, but are the serfs of their Batutsi overlords.—Belgian Administrative Report for 1921. (Parl. Paper 384 of July 1922, p. 27.)

In character and temperament the typical African of this race-type is a happy, thriftless, excitable person, lacking in self-control, discipline, and foresight, naturally courageous, and naturally courteous and polite, full of personal vanity, with little sense of veracity, fond of music, and "loving weapons as an oriental loves jewelry." His thoughts are concentrated on the events and feelings of the moment, and he suffers little from apprehension for the future, or grief for the past. "His mind," says Sir C. Eliot, "is far nearer to the animal world than that of the European or Asiatic, and exhibits something of the animal's placidity and want of desire to rise beyond the state he has reached,"—in proof of which he cites the lack of decency in the disposal of the dead, the state of complete nudity common to one or other, or to both sexes among so many tribes, the general (though not universal) absence of any feeling for art (other than music), and the nomadic habits of so large a section of the race.

Through the ages the African has evolved no organised religious creed, and though some tribes appear to believe in a deity, the religious sense seldom rises above pantheistic animism, and seems more often to take the form of a vague dread of the supernatural. It is curious that whereas in East Africa Sir C. Eliot observes that prayers are always addressed to a benevolent deity, in the West the prevalent idea seems to be the propitiation of a malevolent spirit. Belief in the power of the witch and wizard, and of the Juju-priest and witch-doctor, in charms and fetish, and in the ability of individuals to assume at will the form of wild beasts, are also common among many tribes. To these superstitions the Hamite is less prone.

The African negro is not naturally cruel, though his own insensibility to pain, and his disregard for life—whether his own or another's—cause him to appear callous to suffering. He sacrifices life freely under the influence of superstition, or in the lust and excitement of battle, or for ceremonial display. The wholesale executions of Mtesa of Uganda, or Behanzin of Dahomey, would seem to have been dictated rather by a desire for the ostentatious display of power, or even by a blood-lust, than by a love of witnessing pain. If mutilation and other inhuman punishments are inflicted, it is because nothing less would be deterrent.

He lacks power of organisation, and is conspicuously deficient in the management and control alike of men or of business. He loves the display of power, but fails to realise its responsibility. His most universal natural ability lies in eloquence and oratory. He is by no means lacking in industry, and will work hard with a less incentive than most races. He has the courage of the fighting animal—an instinct rather than a moral virtue. He is very prone to imitate anything new in dress or custom, whether it be the turban and flowing gown of the Moslem, or the straw hat and trousers of the European, however unsuited to his environment and conditions of life. He is an apt pupil, and a faithful and devoted friend.

In brief, the virtues and the defects of this race-type are those of attractive children, whose confidence when once it has been won is given ungrudgingly as to an older and wiser superior, without question and without envy. "Valiant, clever, and lovable, they bear no malice and nurse no grievance." [1]

To attempt to condense into a paragraph or two a subject which would provide material for as many chapters, is to court contradiction, and indeed there is hardly a single trait that I have named to which I cannot quote striking exceptions within my own experience. For the ability to evolve an organised system we may point to the Baganda, the Benis, and the Yorubas, no less than to the Abyssinians and the Fulani; for indigenous art to the bronzes and the wood-carving of the Benis, the cloths and leather-work of the Hausas and Yorubas, and the bead and straw work of Uganda; for natural religion to the ancestor-worship of the Bantus and other tribes; and so on. But, speaking generally, the characteristics of the predominantly negro races are, I think, as I have described them, and Sir Chas. Eliot from personal experience extends his description to the West Indies and the Southern States of America.[2]

Perhaps the two traits which have impressed me as those most characteristic of the African native are his lack of apprehension and inability to visualise the future, and the steadfastness of his loyalty and affection. In illustration of the former, I may recall two incidents, told elsewhere, which

[1] Sir F. Fuller (of the Ashantis), 'A Vanished Dynasty.'

[2] His description of the African is, I think, the best I have read.—*Loc. cit.*, chap. iv.

occurred in my earliest experience of Africa thirty odd years ago, and seemed to me to afford a clue to his character and modes of thought.

We were about to attack a powerfully-constructed stockade, defended by a band of well-armed, slave-raiding Arabs. It was a hazardous enterprise, and the event proved that it was beyond our ability. We could not but expect a heavy loss of life. We had made an all-night march to effect a surprise, and as I lined up the men in the dark in front of the stockade, which in a few minutes we were about to charge, they instantly fell asleep! Later our scouting parties caught a man with a cow. He was a Mkondé, one of the timid unwarlike tribe which had been wiped out by the slave-raiders, and to whose rescue we had come. Questioned as to how he had got the cow, he replied that he had stolen it from the Arab stockade. Crawling up in the dark of night he had slowly dug out one pole after another, and made a breach through the wall until he had effected an entrance. Did he not feel afraid when he heard the sentries of the Slavers chanting their challenge to each other from their watch-towers close by? He explained in reply that there was no ground for misgiving, since he himself was only worth as a slave a quarter part of the value of the cow. The risk was worth taking, for the prospective gain was 3 to 1 on his stake. That it should make any difference that his own life was the stake in question was outside his comprehension, and his apologies were abject for his presumption in having secured an article so much more valuable than himself. He implored me to take it and spare his life. When I praised him for his pluck, and sent him away the possessor of the cow, his delight was ludicrous, but both he and his captors thought me mad. Criminals condemned to death show the same lack of apprehension until the moment of execution arrives.

I can give no better illustration of the constancy and single-mindedness of the African's friendship than the letters I continue to receive from chiefs in Uganda and Toro, though it is over twenty-nine years since I left their country. They cannot be prompted by any possible self-interest, and the initiative was theirs.

The character in which the African presents himself depends very greatly on the personality of the officer with whom he has to deal. Continuity alike of personnel and policy is essential to gain his confidence and to effect progress. Each new step must be introduced with care, and above all there must be no vacillation or change of front, and no broken promises. These natural characteristics have been modified, and in many cases completely changed, by two very powerful agencies. The first, as we have seen, is the influence of Asiatic immigration; the second is the introduction of monotheistic religions and of European and Asiatic education.

Such in brief are the peoples for whose welfare we are responsible in British tropical Africa. They have a fascination of their own, for we are dealing with the child races of the world, and learning at first hand the habits and customs of primitive man; not of some derelict and decadent remnant such as the aborigines of Australia, the Todas of India, or the Ainus of the Japanese islands, but of a virile and expanding race whose men are often models of symmetry and strength—a race which illustrates every stage in the evolution of human society, from the hardly human bushman of the Kalahari and the lowest type of cannibal, to the organised despotism and barbaric display of a negro kingdom like that of Uganda as we found it, where royalty is hedged about with more observance than in a modern palace in Europe; or to the educated native community, a few at least of whose members boast a training in the English universities and medical schools, or who, on the other hand, have inherited a civilisation drawn from the East, and owing much to Arabic literature and the teaching of Islam. Manifestly the system of administration suited to such diverse conditions of social organisation must vary greatly if it is to command the co-operation and hearty acquiescence of the people themselves, and be effective in promoting the progress of each to a higher standard.

From the point of view of the administrator, it will be convenient to classify the people of tropical Africa into three groups, according to their social organisation—viz., the primitive tribes, the advanced communities, and the Europeanised Africans. Such a division connotes a more real and profound difference than that of racial affinities, for intermarriage and concubinage with alien captives and slaves have tended to obliterate tribal characteristics.

The primitive peoples are usually classed by the anthropologist as settled tribes and pastorals.[1] The latter are nomadic in their habits, following their flocks and herds according to the season of the year, and building no cities. The tendency persists even among some of the settled tribes, who, like the Kikuyu in East Africa, the Kanuri of Bornu, and some Congo tribes, constantly desert their villages and fields and migrate to new sites in search of fertile land.

The settled tribes are almost entirely agriculturists, though a small section is engaged in industrial crafts—weaving, dyeing, and the forging of implements of agriculture or of war. Exchange of such articles is conducted in well-attended markets. Those tribes, however, which inhabit the coastal regions intersected by innumerable salt-water creeks, and covered by the densest forest growth, or interspaced by dreary miles of mangrove-swamp, are precluded from engaging to any great extent in agriculture, and sustain life chiefly by fishing. Since flocks and herds will not survive, and animal life is scarce, they have no flesh diet, and often resort to cannibalism.[2] Here the exuberant vegetation is too much for man, and the lowest and most primitive tribes are to be found.

Thus before European intervention changed the conditions of life in Africa, it was the dweller in the plains and the fertile plateaux, and not, as in Europe, the dwellers in the mountains, who were the virile and fighting races. On the plains the cattle-owning nomads must graze their herds, and be prepared to defend them with their lives. The settled population must no less be able to repel assault on the village flocks and on their crops, and they built walled cities for protection. The natural wealth of the African consists of live stock, and it is the ambition of the labourer and the peasant to buy one or two head of cattle and several wives. The system of land-tenure (to which I shall refer later) does not encourage the acquisition of personal property in land, and it is held only as a means of satisfying the absolute necessities of life. Women and children assist in production, and no more land is desired than will produce these neces-

[1] To these may be added the primitive hunting tribes, who wander in search of game, like the Wanderobbo and the Pigmies (Batwa).

[2] It is the craving for flesh which drives the human animal to cannibalism—in Fiji the practice was abandoned on the introduction of swine.

sities. But cattle represent individual and communal wealth. The mountains, on the other hand, are the refuge of the conquered, where they may escape extermination and lead a precarious existence on the hill-tops.

Though as a rule the desires of the pastoral tribes are limited to the acquisition of grazing lands, and they were indifferent to territorial sovereignty, it would seem that small sections were otherwise minded. Thus in South-East Africa the cattle-owning Zulus (with their off-shoots, the Magwangwara and Mangoni) founded in Zululand the dynasty of Tchaka, and further north the Wahima became kings of Uganda, Unyoro, and Ankolé. In the west the Fulani pastorals in like manner became the dominant race. The Masai and the Somalis, on the other hand, though they held undisputed sway over the greater part of East Africa, founded no dynasties. But though in these instances the pastorals created the governing caste over the settled agriculturists, the bulk of the tribe remained as semi-nomad pastorals, completely out of touch with their aristocratic kinsmen, socially less advanced than the settled and urban population, but maintaining by rigorous ordeals and tests a high standard of personal courage and endurance.[1] The ruling classes, on the other hand, became enervated by luxury. The offspring of their innumerable negro concubines lost the distinctive characteristics of their pastoral ancestors, and in Mwanga of Uganda, Kabarega of Unyoro, and many of the Fulani Emirs of Nigeria, we see the negro type markedly asserting itself. Probably most of these pastoral tribes were of Asiatic origin, and migrated slowly from north to south.

The aboriginal negroes, driven by the advancing migrations from the plains and plateaux, found refuge in the mountains, or in the dense forests or the interminable swamps of the equatorial belt, such as surround the upper reaches of the Nile and Zambesi, and the delta of the Niger. In such regions—including the coast lands of West Africa—may therefore be found the purest negro types. Where detached mountain masses afforded a refuge from pursuit, we find a confusing number of remnants of tribes, so that in the single

[1] Fulani youths voluntarily subject themselves to a merciless flogging before they are allowed the privileges of manhood. If the youth flinches or cries out he is degraded for a year. The scars of this flogging are generally visible all his life.

mountainous province of Bauchi (Nigeria) it has been estimated that no fewer than sixty-four different languages are spoken.

These primitive tribes vary in social status from those who recognise no chief and are still in the patriarchal stage, lacking any but the most rudimentary communal organisation,[1] up to those with well-defined tribal institutions, till they merge into the second class of more "advanced communities." Every phase of human evolution may be studied as a living force. Among the most primitive the family is the unit, and even the village head has but little authority. Among many both sexes are entirely nude. They are usually industrious agriculturists or fishermen, but, especially in West Africa, are generally the victims of gross and cruel superstitions and of degrading practices, such as cannibalism, human sacrifice, and the murder of twins, &c.[2]

Among those who have reached the tribal stage, with recognised chiefs and some cohesion for attack and defence, a few have evolved systems of government more or less efficient under paramount rulers, with an elaborate subdivision of authority and ceremonial observance. They have, however, been unable to evolve a written language, or any approach to culture.[3]

Where these institutions were of indigenous growth, or fell under the rule of dynasties preponderantly negro, they appear to have become despotisms marked by a ruthless disregard for human life. Holocausts of victims were sacrificed to appease the deity, or at the whim of the despot.

[1] It is in the lowest stages of human intercourse that men and women herd together, and individual effort and aspiration is effaced in the communal principle. Yet in such communities, I believe, some bond, however fragile, exists between a man and the mother of his child. It is to a still lower plane which the cannibal savage—nay, the anthropoid apes—have left behind them,—the level of mere gregarious mammals, that Bolshevist theorists aspire to drag western civilisation.

[2] Among the Baganda and Banyoro in East Africa, the birth of twins is, on the contrary, an occasion of great rejoicing.—'Notes on Waganda and Wanyoro Tribes,' Felkin, pp. 62 and 82. It is interesting to note that the moral sense finds expression even in the cannibal. Asked if he would eat his mother, a cannibal expressed horror at the thought. Only "bad men," he said, would so degrade themselves.

[3] The very remarkable chief of the little state of Fumban in the Cameruns (whose dearest wish it was to be taken under British rule) had not only introduced an administrative system incomparably more advanced than those of his neighbours, but had even invented an alphabet, and reduced his language to writing.—See the interesting account by Capt. Stobart in 'Blackwood's,' March 1920, p. 380.

Such were the kingdoms of Uganda and Unyoro in the east, and of Dahomey, Ashanti, and Benin in the west. Even where this wholesale butchery was not a primary feature of the despotism, the social organisation was honeycombed by secret societies, whose ritual was a mystic secret, appeasing the deity by human blood, as in the ancient Yoruba nation under its semi-divine head, the Alafin.

But for the most part the progressive communities adopted, and owed their advance to the adoption of, an alien monotheistic religion, which brought with it a written language and a foreign culture. It is to the creed of Islam that this political and social influence has in the past alone been due. It has been the more potent as a creative and regenerating force, because it brought with it an admixture of Aryan or Hamitic blood, and the races which introduced it settled in the country and became identified with its inhabitants. They possessed greater powers of social organisation than the negro aborigines, and may therefore claim to be of a superior race-type.[1]

In West Africa the conquests of the Arabs and Berbers from the north-east introduced the creed of Islam in the belt bordering the southern edge of the Sahara early in the eighth century. The modern history of the advanced communities of Hausaland and Bornu in Nigeria "may be said to date from the period at which they accepted the Moslem religion, though the purer black races had established their domination over the inferior, and ruled by force of superior intelligence and cultivation long before that time."[2] They founded kingdoms which, in the zenith of their prosperity, rivalled the civilisation of Europe of that day. Their descendants, the Fulani, still form the dominant caste, and rule the Moslem States of Nigeria.

In East Africa, Arab Moslems from the Persian Gulf founded the dynasty of Zanzibar, and Bedouin Arabs became the rulers of the Nile Sudan; but though their creed has made its influence felt in Nyasaland and in the Tanganyika territory, and was at one time dominant in Uganda, they cannot

[1] "Neither in respect alone of colour nor of descent, nor even of high intellectual capacity, can science give us any warrant for speaking of one race as superior to another. . . . There is but one absolute test of superiority. It is only the race possessing in the highest degree the qualities contributing to social efficiency that can be recognised as having any claim to superiority."—Kidd, *loc. cit.*, p. 98.

[2] 'A Tropical Dependency,' Lady Lugard, p. 21.

claim to have founded any other native States in British East Africa.

Moslem rule, while enforcing the social regulations of the Koran, has generally incorporated whatever indigenous systems were worthy of survival. The system of government, of dress, and of social observance thus obtained a hold upon the people which the more alien habits and dress of Europe —ill-adapted to a tropical country—could not achieve. Islam looks for its language, literature, and culture to Arabic and the East. As a religion it does not evoke in the pure negro the ardent zeal which it excites in the races of alien or of mixed blood, and there is often little to differentiate the peasant or labourer who calls himself a Mahomedan from his pagan brother.

Islam as a militant creed which teaches contempt for those who are not its votaries, panders to the weakness of the African character—self-conceit and vanity. Centuries of lawless strife have made the African a worshipper of force, and he has been quick to adopt the creed of the conqueror, chiefly for the prestige it brought. Its very excesses, the capture of women as slaves and concubines, and the looting of villages, though hateful enough when he is himself the victim, form the beau ideal of his desires if he can be the aggressor. It is the law of might to which he is habituated.

And there is much else which appeals to the African and suits his conditions in the religion of Mahomet. It sanctions polygamy, which is natural to the tropics. It not merely approves the institution of domestic slavery, but has done much harm by countenancing the ruthless raiding for slaves. It has the attraction of an indigenous religion spread by the people themselves, or by men of like race with similar social standards, and not depending on the supervision of alien teachers. Its great strength lies in the fact that it combines a social code with simple religious forms, and is thus interwoven with the daily life of its followers. Originating in the tropics, it is essentially a code and a religion of the tropics, which has never made headway in the temperate zones, just as Christianity has been the religion of the temperate climates. Considering, however, the many centuries of unopposed opportunity which it had enjoyed, Islam has made singularly little progress in Africa, except among the Hamite and negroid tribes, and, generally speaking, has not been adopted by the negro races.[1]

Mr Bosworth-Smith shows that it is a religion incapable of the highest development,[2] but its limitations suit the limitations of the people. It has undeniably had a civilising effect, abolishing the gross forms of pagan superstition and barbarous practices, and adding to the dignity, self-respect, and self-control of its adherents.[3] Though its tenets among the ignorant peasantry are (as in India) far from orthodox, and much coloured by superstition, its general effect has been to encourage abstinence from intoxicants, a higher standard of life and decency, a better social organisation and tribal cohesion, with a well-defined code of justice.

Christianity, on the other hand, has not proved so powerful an influence for the creation of political and social organisations, though in recent years, combined with Western education, we have seen remarkable results in Uganda, and in a less degree among the Egbas and others in West Africa. Its more abstruse tenets, its stricter code of sexual morality, its exaltation of peace and humility, its recognition of brotherhood with the slave, the captive, and the criminal, do not altogether appeal to the temperament of the negro.

On the other hand, it has a most powerful auxiliary in its hymns and church music, which are infinitely attractive to him, as well as the frequent occasions it affords for a display of oratory. Christianity is, I think, sometimes apt to produce in its converts an attitude of intolerance, not intended by its teachers, towards native rulers,[4] native customs, and even to native dress, especially when wholesale conversions have overtaxed the supervision of the European mission staff. Its constructive efforts (combined with Western education) are to be found chiefly among the Europeanised natives, to whom I shall presently refer.

[1] Eliot, *loc. cit.*, p. 96. Sir F. Fuller, *loc. cit.*, p. 223. Even among the Nilotic negroes, most continuously exposed to its influence, Islam made little progress, and a Shilluk who became a Moslem was looked on as a disgrace to the tribe.—F.O. Handbook 98, p. 55.

[2] 'Mahomet and Mahomedanism.'

[3] Dr Blyden, who has been acclaimed as one of the most distinguished of native African writers, says of Islam in Africa: "It has been the most effective instrument in moulding the intellectual, social, and political character of the millions whom it has brought under its influence. . . . It is the most effective educational force in Negroland."—'West Africa before Europe,' pp. 39, 74.

[4] See Fuller, *loc. cit.*, p. 223, &c.

The advanced communities, then, whether their organisation was self-evolved by pagan races, or due to the advent of conquerors of alien blood, and the introduction of Islam, held sway over their less progressive neighbours, whom they raided and enslaved. They rapidly developed the commercial instinct, and the traders of the Hausa States, the Yorubas and others, carried the produce of one district, or the imported goods from the coast, to another, in organised caravans. They built great cities (but of no permanent material), and developed the industrial arts. They introduced a highly centralised form of government, systems of taxation, and courts of justice, and jealously guarded their own customs and social organisation from European interference. Agriculture, with the help of slave-labour, remained the staple industry, and the dyer continued to grow his own indigo, and the weaver his cotton.

I come now to the last group—the Europeanised Africans—who are chiefly to be found in West Africa. Since they form but an infinitesimal fraction of the thirty-eight million inhabitants of British tropical Africa—though south of the Zambesi they may be found in greater numbers—they would hardly seem to merit a class to themselves. But they occupy a position of importance out of proportion to their mere numbers. They sit on the Legislative Councils, and make their voices and opinions heard through the medium of their own press and in other ways. Whereas those progressive elements which assisted in developing the "advanced communities" penetrated Africa from the north-east across the desert,—for the Zanzibar Arabs from overseas added little to social progress,—European influence was the direct outcome of the conquest of the ocean, and its earliest origin dates from Vasco da Gama's circumnavigation of the continent in the fifteenth century. European connection with tropical Africa was at first sullied by the overseas slave-trade, and its educational and religious influence—which brought the Europeanised African into existence—can only be said to have become an effective force in the west in the middle of the nineteenth century, and some decades later in the east.

The Europeanised African differs not merely in mental outlook from the other groups, but also in physique. Doctors and dentists tell us that he has become less fertile, more susceptible to lung-trouble and to other diseases, and to defective dentition—disabilities which have probably arisen from in-breeding among a very limited class, and to the adoption of European dress, which writers in the native press say is enervating and inimical to the health of the African.[1]

Europeanised Africans represent no tribe or community, but form a class apart in the principal cities of the West Coast, where they reside in a varying minority among an illiterate population in the tribal stage of development, amid sordid surroundings for men of education and culture. They may belong to one or other of the neighbouring tribes and speak their language, or they may, as in Sierra Leone, be the descendants of liberated slaves, ignorant of any African language. Individuals complete their education in England and return as ministers of religion, barristers, doctors, and journalists. Some few are traders on their own account, but the large majority have a very incomplete education, and are content to fill subordinate posts as clerks in the service of Government, or of commercial firms. Some have shown a balanced judgment, and have been of assistance to the local governments as members of the Legislature and of Municipal Boards, but the native press is too often notable for its invective and racial animosity. The most popular professions are those of the law—which affords opportunity for the African's gift of oratory—and journalism.[2]

The educated African imitates European dress and customs closely, however ill adapted to his conditions of life, and may be heard to speak of going "home" to England. He has, as a rule, little in common with the indigenous tribes of Africa, and seldom leaves his native town except to travel

[1] The records in Sierra Leone "tend to show that the deaths considerably exceed the births," and the population of the colony is apparently maintained by immigrants from the protectorate.—F.O. Handbook 92, p. 8.

[2] Writing of the American negro, Mr Graham observes that "he has a passion for journalism in advance of his present development and capacity" ('Children of the Slaves,' p. 53). Each of the British colonies in West Africa boasts of several newspapers owned and edited by natives. The Governor of the Gold Coast has recently pointed out the injury to racial co-operation done by the local press. Its invective is much read by schoolboys, and Mr Carr (Acting Director of Education, Nigeria—a native) was of opinion that it does much "grievous harm." Dr Blyden remarks that at St Louis (capital of French Senegal), "where there is every facility for such a thing, they have not a single newspaper; and they are happier for it than their brethren in other parts of Africa, who rejoice in the advantages and 'freedom of the Press'" ('West Africa before Europe,' p. 90). The French law of 1881 regarding native newspapers has by a recent decree been made more stringent.

by sea or railway.[1] The Europeanised African is indeed separated from the rest of the people by a gulf which no racial affinity can bridge. He must be treated—and seems to desire to be treated—as though he were of a different race. Some even appear to resent being called negroes, the universal race-term in America. The Rev. R. Keable complains in 'East and West' that even native priests showed in the war a contempt for and aloofness from the natives in their spiritual charge unknown between white men of unequal social standing.

The "Montague-Chelmsford Report" describes the politically-minded Indian in terms which are singularly appropriate to the educated African. "He is a creation peculiarly our own, the product of an educational policy in the past, which aimed at satisfying the few who sought after English education, without sufficient thought of the consequences which might ensue from not taking care to extend instruction to the many." It was due to that policy (says the report) that the Indian adopted as a rule the non-practical professions of law, journalism, and teaching, which magnify the importance of words and phrases, and he has only recently been encouraged to create wealth by applying his knowledge to industrial enterprise. But the Indian progressive, however divergent from the mass of the people in habits of thought, yet speaks their language, shares their customs and religion, and knows their country. Though the percentage of Indians who speak English is infinitesimal compared with the total population, it is probably twenty times greater than the percentage of English-speaking Africans to the population of Africa, and includes a certain number who have administrative and municipal experience.

Perhaps it may be said that the number of Europeanised natives in West Africa is too small to justify any generalisations. Let us turn, therefore, to America, where for a couple of generations at least the African has had an opportunity of vindicating his status, and of proving his capacity for social progress. The negro population of the United States reaches some 12,000,000 souls, and though there is a considerable admixture of European blood, his progress there will afford some clue as to the capability of the race for intellectual development and social organisation. The 'Times'

[1] See the statement by Chief-Justice Sir E. Speed, quoted in Cmd. 468, p. 80.

correspondent draws a disheartening picture,[1] and American opinion seems to be equally pessimistic. Dr Stoddard,[2] like M. Beaulieu,[3] is emphatic that "black Africa is unable to stand alone," and quotes Meredith Townsend's observation that the negro race "has never evolved a civilisation, a literature, or a creed, or founded a stone city, or built a ship, or exercised the smallest influence over people not black." [4]

Such men as Booker Washington and Moton prove, however, that the negro race can at the least produce individuals of great force of character and high ideals. Dr Moton's recent book [5] combines high idealism with practical organising ability. Du Bois—albeit not of pure negro blood—is said to have the gift of leadership.[6] He touches the true source of the unhappiness and discontent of the Europeanised or Americanised negro, when he asserts that "in order to attain his place in the world the negro must be himself and not another." [7]

[1] "The intellectual negro," he writes, "seems to take rather kindly to socialism and organised agitation, and the further upwards they move in the social scheme the greater their discontent. . . . The fact remains that, after more than half a century of freedom and educational opportunity, they have not been able to rise to a plane above that of agitator, or to carve out for themselves a satisfactory position in the body politic."—'Times,' 16th Oct. 1919.

[2] 'The Rising Tide of Colour,' p. 102.

[3] "Bien plus nous croyons que l'autorité Europienne ne devra pas être temporaire dans la majeure partie de l'Afrique ; ce n'est pas une simple affaire d'éducation devant durer un ou deux siècles, c'est une organisation definitive. Le climat des regions equatorials et tropicales de l'Afrique ainsi de la race qui s'y trouve établie ne nous paraissent pas de nature à pouvoir rendre jamais compatible autant qu'on en peut juger la prospérité de ces contreés et leur absolue autonomie. Il serait à craindre que une fois detachés même dans deux ou trois siècles des Metropoles ces pays . . . revinssent apres deux ou trois generations à la barbarie primitive. Toutes les colonies ne sont pas destinés a s'émanciper."—Vol. i. pp. 291-2. See notes p. 198.

[4] 'Asia and Europe,' pp. 92, 356-358.

[5] 'Finding a Way Out.'

[6] 'The Children of the Slaves,' S. Graham, p. 261. See also article, "The Colour Problem," 'Edin. Review,' April 1921.

[7] 'The Souls of Black Folk,' Du Bois, p. 8. A series of interesting articles appeared in the Sierra Leone and Lagos native press in Feb. 1902. "The foreign and uncongenial life can only avail to display the oddities and eccentricities that naturally attach to abnormal or hybrid life," says the former ; while the Lagos writer laments that by adopting foreign education and a foreign mode of life Africans have become foreigners to their own people, with whom they can only converse through interpreters. There is no class, says the writer, which is less welcome to the lay Englishman than the "black white man" who has abandoned his racial integrity and is quick to learn European vices. Compare Locke's observation that to teach a child contrary to his natural bent is to produce affectation. "The negro," says Lebon, "will never be fit for institutions which are not in some way a direct outcome of the negro character." Dr Blyden expresses the same view : "Progress must be along the line of our own institutions. Intellectual development must be of his own powers—the present policy makes the African a caricature."—See 'W. Africa before Europe,' p. 107.

Dr Moton, head of the splendidly organised Tuskegee Institution, gave dignified expression to the same feeling when, after a prolonged tour in Europe, he wrote : "I landed on American shores with the feeling that whatever may be the disadvantages and inconveniences of my race in America, I would rather be a negro in the United States than anybody else in any other country in the world." [1]

This leads us to the consideration of the recent claims by the educated West African for a larger share in the government. I do not refer to the spectacle of Mr Garvey, "Provisional President of Africa, arrayed in a flowing robe of crimson slashed with green," claiming to found a single republic for the whole continent, and parading the streets of New York with six bands,[2] for such wild schemes can only fill the cultured and thoughtful African with regret and misgiving, and in the words of Dr Moton, lead "many honest and sincere white people to doubt the wisdom of educating the coloured man."

But movements such as the Pan-African Congress, which met at Paris under the presidency of M. Diagne—a native African, and Deputy for Senegal—during the Peace Conference, stand in a different category, and in so far as they give expression to the desire for a larger individual and collective responsibility and liberty—which is the natural outcome of British teaching—may be regarded as indications of progress. The principles to which the resolution of the Congress gave expression are in the main reasonable, and differ little from those which have guided Great Britain in her dealings with the tropical races,[3] but like the so-called "National

[1] *Loc. cit.*, p. 152. [2] 'Times,' 2nd Sept. 1920.

[3] The terms of the resolution were as follows :—

The Governments of the Allies and their associates should establish an international code of laws for the protection of natives. A permanent secretariat in the League of Nations should see to the application of these laws.

The coloured races of the world desire that henceforth the natives of Africa and peoples of African origin should be governed everywhere in accordance with the following principles :—

(1) *The Land.*—The soil and its natural resources shall be reserved and safeguarded for the natives, who shall have effective ownership of the lands they cultivate.

(2) *Capital.*—A system of concessions shall be so fashioned as to prevent the native from being exploited and the natural riches of the country from being drained. These concessions should be only temporary, and be under State supervision. Note should be taken of the growing needs of natives, and part of the profits should be used for the moral and material development of the native.

(3) *Labour.*—The abolition of slavery and corporal punishment of any nature.

Conference," which recently laid a petition before the King, the Congress could lay no claim to be considered as representative of Africa, which is, of course, too vast a country and with too diversified a population to be represented by any delegation from any particular region.

The latter body consisted of a group of native barristers and others, for the most part resident in the Gold Coast, whose claim to represent the advanced thought and progressive elements of that colony was indignantly repudiated by certain of its chiefs, while probably no one in Nigeria outside the coast towns had ever heard of their existence. The Governor (Sir H. Clifford) poured scathing ridicule on "the fantastic claim to a common nationality," or to represent either the advanced or the primitive peoples of Nigeria, and the leading representative of native opinion in Lagos "protested with all the emphasis at his command at the impudence of these people who style themselves representatives of Nigeria." In these circumstances it is not worth while to discuss their voluminous resolutions, but they were not couched in any spirit of disloyalty.[1]

In India the principle was enunciated that advancement in self-government must depend on the extent to which the educated class is in sympathy with, and capable of representing, the illiterate sections of the people. In this respect the claim of the African "intelligentsia" is, as we have seen, very weak, nor has the educated native, generally speaking, shown himself to be possessed of ability to rule either his own community or backward peoples of his own race, even under favourable conditions. "Can any one say that the Governments of Hayti, San Domingo, or even of Liberia are

The abolition of forced labour, except as a penal procedure for the punishment of crimes. The promulgation of official labour rules.

(4) *Education.*—Every coloured child shall be taught its mother tongue and the language of the trustee nation. Professional education shall be available.

(5) *Health.*—A service of medical assistance, composed of hospitals and doctors, shall be established by the State which shall be responsible for the welfare of the inhabitants.

(6) *The State.*—The coloured races of Africa shall be allowed gradually increased participation in the State, as their intellectual development improves, by virtue of the principle that governments exist for peoples and not peoples for governments.

[1] Mr Hayford, a member of the Delegation, quotes in his book, 'Gold Coast Native Institutions,' p. 312, the following appreciation of British rule: "We labour in vain to find one spot (upon the world-wide map of the British Empire) where the people possess in their own right such a rich and unhampered legacy of liberty, freedom, and enfranchisement as we should enjoy on the Gold Coast." See note on page 619.

successful," asks a native writer who does not fear to face the *facts*.[1]

However strong a sympathy we may feel for the aspirations of these African progressives, sane counsellors will advise them to recognise their present limitations. At no time in the world's history has there been so cordial a hand held out to Africa, such genuine admiration for the achievements of such men as Booker Washington and Moton, or a keener desire to assist the African in the path of progress, and in Mr Rhodes' words, to grant "equal rights to all civilised men irrespective of race." "I think," said the Secretary of State for the Colonies (Mr Churchill), when addressing the Dominion Premiers in June last (1921), "there is only one ideal that the British Empire can set before itself, and that is that there should be no barrier of race, colour, or creed which should prevent any man by merit from reaching any station if he is fitted for it."

Meantime there is abundant opportunity for the educated African, if he will avail himself of it, in the sphere of civic usefulness and the improvement of the conditions of the people in the cities in which he lives, and the community to which he belongs, and for whom he can claim to speak with knowledge. Let us learn from him how these opportunities can be enlarged, and he may rest assured that his opinions, and above all his visible efforts to realise the obligations of his own municipality, will be met with sympathy.[2] Booker Washington's "first and last word was co-operation"—the aspiration to serve others and not himself.

As a professional man the educated native can establish schools and obtain financial assistance under the educational code, or he can conduct hospitals and dispensaries. As a business man he can open hotels (which are much needed)

[1] Nigerian 'Pioneer,' 13th Sept. 1918. See Stoddart's account of Hayti, *loc. cit.*, pp. 141 and 100, &c. The speeches of the present and late Presidents of Liberia are excellent essays on the art of government by a foreign ruler, but the reports which reach us of disregard for native rights, insecurity of trade, and lack of educational facilities testify to an inability to put them into practice.

[2] The determined hostility of the civilised native community to the imposition of any rates strikes at the very basis of municipal independence. In Lagos a moderate water-rate to defray in part the cost of a pure and abundant water supply led to riots. In Sierra Leone the limitation of the hut-tax to the protectorate was adversely commented on by the Secretary of State. In the Gold Coast the Governor at one time had it in contemplation to abolish the small rates levied in certain coast towns, in view of the hostility of the people to them. This opposition has in all cases been led by an influential section of the educated classes.

or employ his knowledge and capital in scientific farming. In all the channels of civic responsibility he can establish his claim to municipal self-government. (See chapter xxix.)

The episode of the "National Conference Delegation" has served to give prominence to a principle of far-reaching importance, with which I shall deal more fully in the chapter on native rule—viz., whether the path to self-government alike among Oriental and African races may not better be sought by the education of their own rulers, and the gradual extension of their powers, than by the introduction of an alien system of rule by British-educated and politically-minded progressives. In a striking speech in the Gold Coast Legislature, Chief Ofori Atta, C.B.E., supported by the other three native members, maintained that the claim of a handful of educated lawyers and doctors to represent the people, instead of their chiefs, was a base attempt to denationalise the institutions of the country. In his cabled version of it to the Colonial Office, the Governor says that the delegates have brought discredit on education since "illiterates have now a just complaint that education leads to belittling and ignoring the native rulers." [1]

There is no colour bar in British Africa, and the educated native enjoys the fullest liberty. He is allowed the utmost licence in the newspapers he conducts, unless he oversteps the limits which render him liable for defamation or sedition. He engages in trade, in professional practice, and in recreations on equal terms with Europeans, and there are many highly-respected and influential native gentlemen who have availed themselves to the full of these facilities. Africans are appointed to such posts in the administration as they are qualified by education and character to fill.

In an article on "the colour problem" contributed to the 'Edinburgh Review' of April 1921, I summarised my conclusions in the following words, which the President of the United States recently quoted in a speech in the Southern States, as seeming to him to indicate "the true way out": [2]

[1] Telegram communicated to the Press by the Colonial Office at the request of the Governor. The assertions were later denied by other chiefs.

[2] Speech at Birmingham, Alabama, 26th October 1921. Individual dislikes, and aversion to social intercourse, which between persons of the same race would be ascribed to their real causes, are often indiscriminately attributed to colour prejudice. The desire to tread a separate path in matters social and racial is, as some coloured writers have assured us, as much desired by themselves as by whites.

"Here, then, is the true conception of the inter-relation of colour: complete uniformity in ideals, absolute equality in the paths of knowledge and culture, equal opportunity for those who strive, equal admiration for those who achieve; in matters social and racial a separate path, each pursuing his own inherited traditions, preserving his own race-purity and race-pride; equality in things spiritual, agreed divergence in the physical and material."

Addressing the Legislative Council in January 1921, the Governor of the Gold Coast said that he hoped to see 50 per cent of the present European staff in the technical departments replaced by natives, and announced the appointment of a committee to elaborate the organisation of a native Civil Service. In Nigeria a native African of exceptional ability has long held the second highest post in the Education Department in the south, and frequently acted as its head, and was appointed by me to the highest executive post under the Administrator of the colony. Four hold appointments as medical officers. In the Gold Coast the principal medical officer was at one time a native. That there are but few Africans in the higher branches of the Civil Service is in part due to the fact that few are well qualified by force of character and educational attainments, and in part to the fact that unofficial activities offer prospects of more lucrative employment to the really capable. Few adopt the profession of engineering, and it is obvious that difficulties are likely to arise if a young African engineer is placed in charge of British platelayers, artisans, and skilled foremen, but the Survey Department offers more scope. The subordinate clerical service is entirely manned by natives, as also the subordinate posts in the railway, engineering, medical, printing, survey, and other technical departments. In Nigeria it is roughly estimated that not less than 4500 posts in the clerical and 2500 in the technical departments are so held, with an aggregate of not less than £500,000 per annum in salaries.[1] Outside the Government service half the unofficial members of the Legislative Council of the colony and of the Town Council of Lagos are natives, and they are represented also in the Nigerian Council. Efforts have been made to enlist the active participation of African gentlemen on the advisory boards of the various townships, on school com-

[1] Cmd. 468 of 1920, p. 18.

mittees, and similar organisations, both in the colony and in the protectorate.

While, therefore, as we have seen, the educated native has not proved himself able to govern communities of which he is in no way representative, it is, on the other hand, most desirable that natives who have the necessary qualifications of character and education should be afforded every opportunity of participating in the government of the community to which they belong, whether as civil servants or as unofficial members of municipal boards and councils, even if at first their standards of attainment fall below those of the British staff, for it is only by the exercise of actual responsibility that efficiency can eventually be attained, and that a tradition of public service can be created. As Lord Milner, speaking at Oxford, observed: "We may even to some extent have to sacrifice efficiency of administration in order to promote contentment, though we cannot as honest trustees afford to sacrifice it too much." [1]

I am, however, reluctantly compelled to admit that, so far as my own experience goes, it is extremely difficult at present to find educated African youths who are by character and temperament suited to posts in which they may rise to positions of high administrative responsibility.[2]

It is a natural presumption that the illiterate tribes would have more confidence in one of their own race and colour, who could speak their language fluently, view life from their standpoint, and understand and sympathise with their prejudices as no European could. But I have been frequently assured by those who know them best that the illiterate native, even of the coast cities, is more ready to give his confidence to the white man than to the educated native.

With the object of creating a class qualified by character and educational attainments to fill responsible positions under Government, I have suggested the formation of a native Cadet Service, the members of which by prolonging their

[1] "We must be prepared to see Indian electorates hurt others—the helpless as well as themselves. It is the only way in which the spirit of trusteeship can be called into being and made to grow."—L. Curtis, quoted by Sir V. Chirol. 'Times,' 7th June 1918.

[2] My personal experience is limited to the colony of Lagos, where a considerable number of the leading native gentlemen are immigrants from the older colonies of Sierra Leone and the Gold Coast, in which, no doubt, a larger number are fitted for responsible positions.

studies during the earlier years of their service under special arrangements, and specialising in such subjects as would qualify them for the higher posts, would form a class from which the Government could with confidence select probationers for the Civil Service. I shall discuss this more fully in the chapter on education. The principle might perhaps be inaugurated by the formation at headquarters of a group of clerks specially recommended by heads of departments as qualified for positions of responsibility and control, and by affording them facilities for special study.

Some bitter criticisms have been made upon the educated African, and none perhaps more searching than that of his distinguished representative, the late Dr E. Blyden. A French writer draws the conclusion that a literary education on European lines has mischievous results, and that "Great Britain, though animated by a sense of duty and by a high ideal, is creating classes of natives who feel no gratitude to her, but, on the contrary, are bitterly hostile." [1] The educated native would indignantly repudiate this charge, for he loves to present loyal addresses to the Throne. But he sometimes fails to realise that loyalty does not begin and end by singing "God save the King," and is incompatible with racial antagonism, which treats with contempt the sympathetic efforts of those who, while recognising present limitations, seek his best welfare. The more honour is due to those Africans—such as Messrs Carr, Ajasa, and Sapara Williams in Nigeria, and many others in the Gold Coast and Sierra Leone—who with great moral courage have not feared to point the true way to their countrymen, and to expose and condemn false ideals.

When the Europeanised African has qualified in the school of municipal training, and proved his ability to control his own community and improve its conditions, he can claim, and rightly be accorded, increased representation on the legislative and other councils, and selection by elective vote. The area over which the Legislative Council exercises jurisdiction can be gradually extended to include the whole of the tribe to which the native councillors belong, whose customary law and language they understand, provided they do in fact represent the tribe and are not in conflict with the legitimate

[1] 'Lois Psychologiques de l'Evolution des Peuples,' Lebon. See 'Colonial Journal,' April 1914.

authority of the chiefs. But it would be unjust to place under their control the interior tribes, who themselves have a right to a measure of self-rule (see chap. x. and xi.)

But though the claim of the educated African to represent or to rule the people of the interior may be denied, though the foibles and the follies of some individuals may have brought discredit on his class, and chagrin to those who have a wider sympathy and culture, let us not forget the incalculable debt which Africa owes to her educated sons. Administration in West Africa would be impossible without the vast army of clerks and accountants who fill the departmental offices. Railway extension would have been equally impossible without the telegraphists, guards, signallers, storekeepers, and the rest of the trained assistants. In every branch of effort he bears his share, and both the Government and the merchant would find it difficult to exist without his services. He has, as I have said, a special claim to our sympathy, since he is the creation of the system of education we have introduced, and his aspirations are the natural outcome of the ideals we have taught him.

I will not discuss in this place the races of alien origin which have created so profound an influence in parts of British tropical Africa. Of the Fulani in particular I shall have something to say in the chapter on native administration.. But a little-known class in West Africa—the Syrians—merit a word in passing. It astonishes the newcomer to see a white man as pedlar or hawker in the streets of Lagos or Accra, but he soon learns that the Syrian has come to Africa to stay. He lives at first on the same plane as the illiterate African, but he does not inter-marry with him. He brings his wife, and rears his children in the tropics, and by rigid thrift he often rises to positions of considerable affluence. As a trader he is the counterpart in the West of the Indian in East Africa.

The recent riots in Sierra Leone, in which Syrians were attacked and their property destroyed, causes us misgivings as to the ability of the Europeanised African to deal justly by others when his material interests are involved—a misgiving which was enhanced by the inclusion among the "reforms" advocated by the "National Conference," of the expulsion of the Syrians, and their exclusion from West Africa, on the grounds that they were a menace to the good government of the land—a proposal stigmatised as "preposterous" by an unofficial councillor in Nigeria, where there has been no such movement. In French West Africa, however, "measures have been taken by the Government to control the entry of Syrian merchants into the territory and the conduct of their business with the natives," since they compete seriously with the French merchants.[1]

We are perhaps somewhat too apt to take it for granted that the introduction of civilisation must add to the happiness of the natives of Africa. The ascent of man to a higher plane of intelligence, self-control, and responsibility is a process not unattended by pain. We in England would not hesitate to prefer our present culture to the barbarism of our woad-painted ancestors, but who shall say that we are either happier or physically fitter than they?

Under the conditions of primitive communal life the law of might prevails. The community is at the mercy of its most combative members, and the older men are generally unable to control the headstrong young warriors who bring war upon the tribe. It is the weak who suffer. Women, after the first flush of youth, lead a life of perpetual toil and slavery. The aged and the sick succumb to the law of the survival of the fittest.

On the other hand, the enhancement of the value of life to the individual brings with it apprehension. From the ability to realise cause and effect spring many sources of fear unknown to primitive man. A more highly-developed brain and nervous system increases the sensibility to physical pain. Evolution and progress are a law of nature, and since the necessities of his existence compel civilised man to share the produce of the tropics, let us see to it that the process is accompanied by as much benefit and as little injury to the natives as may be. Let us admit that the "blessings of civilisation need not necessarily be limited to our civilisation, and of religion to our religion, without giving a thought to the value of other civilisations, older than and perhaps as admirable in practice as our own, and to other religions in which men have lived and died with comfort and hope for centuries before we ourselves emerged from the rudest barbarism."[2]

[1] Foreign Office Handbook, No. 100 of 1920, p. 14.
[2] 'Times,' 15th January 1907.

The practical man, however, recognises the futility of theoretical disputations as to whether or not civilisation is a benefit. Though the Allies in their reply to the German demand for the restitution of her colonies, state that a Mandatory Power will derive no benefit from the exercise of his trusteeship, it would be absurd to deny that the initial motive for the penetration of Africa by Western civilisation was (with the exception of the religious missions) the satisfaction of its material necessities, and not pure altruism. In the circumstances, as Sir Charles Lucas says, the best protection for the native against abuse of power by the white man is to place the white man under the control of a civilised Government.[1]

It is impossible to strike a balance of the immediate profit and loss to the native populations by the advent of civilisation. On the one hand, the freedom of inter-communication, which followed the cessation of inter-tribal war, has had the result of disseminating diseases previously confined to particular localities. It brought from the Congo the "Jigger," and the sleeping-sickness which decimated the population of Uganda. It has afforded to itinerant native traders access to primitive communities, which they did not previously dare to invade, and they have carried venereal diseases with them both in the east and in the west.[2]

On the other hand, medical science has mitigated the scourge of smallpox by vaccination, and is waging successful war against leprosy, ankylostomiasis, sleeping-sickness, yellow fever, and other endemic diseases. Civilisation has decreased the sum of human misery inflicted by man upon man by tribal war, barbarous practices, and slave-raiding. By promoting trade and increasing wealth it has raised the standard of life and comfort.

The white man was at first engaged in consolidating his own position, and making the tropics more healthy for Europeans engaged in their development. He has now accepted the principle that they must be made more healthy for the

[1] 'The British Empire,' Lucas, p. 207.

[2] A Nigerian resident remarks in one of his reports that Fulani herdsmen now penetrate unmolested into pagan areas, where before the era of British rule the cannibal tribes would have disposed of him "by the complete method of eating both him and his cattle."

native population.[1] If, then, we have to admit that the first impact of civilisation on barbarism—no less than on an Oriental social organisation—is bound at first to produce some untoward results, we may find encouragement and promise for the future in the undeniable alleviation of human suffering which it has also brought.

[1] Colonel Amery (Under-Secretary) in the debate on the Colonial Office vote, August 1919.

CHAPTER V.

SOME GENERAL PRINCIPLES OF ADMINISTRATION.

Nature and functions of the administration—Constitution of a Crown colony—Two principles of administration: (*a*) Decentralisation—Decentralisation and amalgamation—Reasons for amalgamation—The case of Nigeria—Decentralisation in departments—Method of amalgamation in Nigeria—The principles involved—(*b*) Continuity: of personnel—Of records—Of Governor's instructions and policy—Continuity in office of Governor—Scheme of continuous responsibility—Anticipated advantages—The former system—Objections by permanent officials—Object and limitations—The "Man on the Spot"—The scheme abandoned—Suggestions for promoting continuity and co-operation—Tenure of office of Governor.

The British Empire, as General Smuts has well said, has only one mission—for liberty and self-development on no standardised lines, so that all may feel that their interests and religion are safe under the British flag. Such liberty and self-development can be best secured to the native population by leaving them free to manage their own affairs through their own rulers, proportionately to their degree of advancement, under the guidance of the British staff, and subject to the laws and policy of the administration.

But apart from the administration of native affairs the local Government has to preserve law and order, to develop the trade and communications of the country, and to protect the interests of the merchants and others who are engaged in the development of its commercial and mineral resources. What, then, are the functions of the British staff, and how can the machinery of Government be most efficiently constituted for the discharge of its duties in those countries in Africa which fall under British control?

The staff must necessarily be limited in numbers, for if the best class of men are to be attracted to a service which often involves separation from family and a strain on health, they must be offered adequate salaries and inducements in the way of leave, housing, medical aid—or their equivalents in money—for their maintenance in health and comfort while serving abroad, and this forms a heavy charge on the revenues. Policy and economy alike demand restriction in numbers, but the best that England can supply.

Obviously a consideration of the machinery of British administration in the tropics involves a review of its relations to the home Government on the one hand, and of its local constitution and functions on the other. I will take the latter first.

The Government is constituted on the analogy of the British Government in England. The Governor represents the King, but combines the functions of the Prime Minister as head of the Executive. The Councils bear a certain resemblance to the Home Cabinet and Parliament, while the detailed work of the administration is carried out by a staff which may be roughly divided into the administrative, the judicial, and the departmental branches.

The administrative branch is concerned with the supervision of the native administration and the general direction of policy; with education, and the collection and control of direct taxes, which involve assessment and close relations with the native population; with legislation and the administration of justice in courts other than the Supreme Court; and with the direct government and welfare of the non-native section of the population.

The departmental staff is charged with duties in connection with transport, communications, and buildings (railways, marine, and public works); with the development of natural resources (mines, collieries, forestry, agriculture, and geology); with the auxiliary services of government (medical, secretarial, accounting, posts and telegraphs, surveys, &c.); and the collection of customs duties.

The task of the administrative branch is to foster that sympathy, mutual understanding, and co-operation between the Government and the people, without which, as Sir C. Ilbert has observed, no Government is really stable and efficient. Its aim is to promote progress in civilisation and justice, and to create conditions under which individual enterprise may most advantageously develop the natural resources of the country. The task of the departments, on the other hand, is to maintain the Government machine in a state of efficiency, and to afford direct assistance in material development. Their motto is efficiency and economy. The two branches work together, and their duties overlap and are interdependent in every sphere. The efficient discharge of those duties in combination constitutes the white man's title to control.

There are in my estimation two vital principles which characterise the growth of a wise administration—they are Decentralisation and Continuity. Though, as Lord Morley said of India, "perfectly efficient administration has an inevitable tendency to over-centralisation," it is a tendency to be combated. It has indeed been said that the whole art of administration consists in judicious and progressive delegation, and there is much truth in the dictum, provided that delegation of duties be accompanied by public responsibility. This is not applicable to the head of the Government alone or in particular, but to every single officer, from the Governor to the foreman of a gang of daily labourers. The man who is charged with the accomplishment of any task, and has the ability and discrimination to select the most capable of those who are subordinate to him, and to trust them with ever-increasing responsibility, up to the limits of their capacity, will be rewarded not only with confidence and loyalty, but he will get more work done, and better done, than the man who tries to keep too much in his own hands, and is slow to recognise merit, originality, and efficiency in others. His sphere of work becomes a training school, and he is able to recommend his best men for promotion to greater responsibility than he himself can confer. The Governor who delegates to his Lieut.-Governors, Residents, and heads of departments the widest powers compatible with his own direct responsibility to the Crown, will witness the most rapid progress.

But delegation to an individual who is not equal to the responsibility obviously means disaster, and it is therefore often advisable to entrust extended powers to the individual rather than to incorporate them as a part of the duties of his office. His successor, who must obviously have less experience, and may or may not be his equal in ability, will not then automatically enjoy the same latitude, until he has proved his capacity in the higher office.

Increased latitude to the individual is not, however, inconsistent with increased delegation of duties to the office, more especially in the administrative branch of the service, where posts must of necessity grow in importance as the country as a whole develops. It is a frequent ground of criticism that the Colonial Office has been somewhat backward in appreciating the value of this principle in these young and rapidly-growing dependencies.

The Governor, by delegating work to others, would seem to lighten his own task, but in point of fact the more he delegates the more he will find to do in co-ordinating the progress of the whole. Moreover, in order to have a right appreciation of the abilities, and of the personal character of each principal administrative officer and head of department, he must be in close personal touch with them, and make absolutely clear to them the essential features of his policy. He must be the directing brain, and leave the execution to others. The task he undertakes is no light one, and if he should be called on to create an administration *ab ovo*, or to lay down new lines of policy in an old one, the work may become more than the time at his command suffices for, and the personal touch with his officers may temporarily suffer from the insistent demands of his office, until he is able gradually to delegate to those in whom he has confidence.

In applying the principle of decentralisation it is very essential to maintain a strong central co-ordinating authority, in order to avoid centrifugal tendencies, and the multiplication of units without a sufficiently cohesive bond. I shall revert to this point when discussing the grouping of colonies.

There are in British tropical Africa several blocks of territory under separate administrations which are contiguous to each other, and the question arises whether it would be more advantageous that they should be placed under a single directing authority, with a single fiscal system, a common railway policy, and identical laws—more especially if one controls the coast area, and the other has no access to the seaboard. Such a process would, of course, be in no way opposed to decentralisation of the machinery of Government. Amalgamation (that is, unification) and federation are both natural processes of evolution, as we have seen in the United

States, in Canada, Australia, and South Africa, and more recently in Nigeria. The French have gone even further, and placed colonies widely separated from each other under a central authority. I will deal here only with the question of amalgamation. The federation or grouping of colonies raises a separate issue, which I shall discuss later.

Where one administration comprises the coast area, and collects the customs dues (which have hitherto formed the bulk of the revenue in most African dependencies), while another forms its hinterland, the latter must either establish an inland fiscal frontier, or share the duties collected by its neighbour. The former expedient adds to the cost of all imports—already enhanced by the inherent expense of long and costly transport services (involving a slower turnover of commercial capital),—and is obviously opposed to the progress of trade and development, apart from the heavy cost of the administration of an effective customs and preventive service. The latter course is rendered most difficult by the impossibility of arriving at a division of the customs revenue which will not be resented by both. Imported goods which have paid duty on the coast pass into the hands of native middlemen, and their ultimate destination, by a thousand byways of trade, may be in the hinterland; or the exportable produce for which they are bartered may originate in the interior territory. It is clearly impossible to discriminate with any accuracy in such circumstances between the value and volume of the trade properly belonging to each administration. The Liverpool Chamber of Commerce in July 1893 made strong representations in this sense to Lord Rosebery regarding Nigeria. The French Governor-General, M. Roume, referring to the fiscal reorganisation of the French West African colonies, observed that "it was not right to continue to allow the coast colonies alone to benefit by trade, a large proportion of which was destined for the interior," and Senegal had to make a subsidy to its hinterland.

A hinterland Government has not only to bear heavy transport charges from and to the coast on its imports and exports, but upon it falls the burden of frontier defence. In order to balance its budget it will probably have to depend on a grant from Parliament, paid by the British taxpayer, while the coast Government may have a surplus revenue. A grant-in-aid involves control by the Imperial Treasury—a department which knows nothing of local needs, and is solely concerned in reducing the charges—and the dual control of two departments of State is inimical to all progress.

With an increase of material prosperity, new and disturbing factors arise. An interior administration depends largely for its development on railways and improved waterways, for which capital is required—but loans are not permissible while as yet a country depends on an Imperial grant. Even if sufficient revenue for its needs were raised by taxation, payment of taxes must be largely made in kind, which can only be realised by conveying it to the coast. Some small part may be sold to merchants for cash, but they will not establish themselves, unless means of transport are available.

The organisation and control of railways, waterways, and telegraph lines traversing both territories must of necessity be in the hands of a central administration. It would obviously be inadvisable for one administration to treat the other as foreign territory, and to conclude railway and postal conventions with it in order to exercise separate control over its own section. Increased cost of administration, obstacles to trade, unnecessary accounting, and the certainty of friction must result. A comprehensive and far-sighted railway policy, to which the efforts of both would be consistently devoted, becomes impossible.[1]

When legislation pursues two different channels, differences in policy in regard to native administration, the courts of law, and other vital matters are bound to arise, and it is obviously inadvisable that contiguous communities should be under different systems of taxation, and different penal codes. The evil is accentuated by the fact that the frontiers between the two—often fixed at a time when their geography and ethnology were almost unknown, by lines of latitude and longitude instead of by distinctive natural features—must inevitably intersect tribal boundaries. It goes without

[1] The railway in East Africa does not actually traverse Uganda, and the difficulty is therefore not so acute, but it depends largely for its earnings on the carriage of merchandise to and from Uganda. Hitherto Kenya has appropriated its revenue. A railway Board has now been formed on which both countries are represented. The control of the Board (unless amalgamation of the two Governments is carried out) must presumably be exercised from Downing Street, —a retrograde step opposed to decentralisation, and tending towards that absentee control from London, which the Indian Railway Committee has so unanimously condemned.—See Cmd. 1512/1921.

saying that a single co-ordinated effort will achieve more for the permanent good of a country than the separate efforts of two administrators, not focussed on a common objective.

Such conditions were applicable to Nigeria, and are still probably applicable to Kenya and Uganda. They were fully described by me in a Memo. dated May 1905; but the amalgamation of Nigeria, though supported by the Governors of the coastal administrations, was not decided upon till 1912, when Mr Harcourt charged me with the task. To administer such enormous territories as East Africa or Nigeria as a single unit, decentralisation is more than ever necessary, but how it can best be effected is not an easy problem.

In the administrative branch the chain of responsibility from the most junior grade to the head of the Government —the District Officer, the Resident of a Province, the Lieut.-Governor—is easily forged, but the departments offer a more difficult problem. If on the one hand each department is under a single head, responsible to the Governor, the tendency is towards a highly-centralised Government, in which the Lieut.-Governors are deprived of initiative and financial control, and there is a danger lest their instructions to the local representative of the department may conflict with those of the departmental head. The Lieut.-Governor for all practical purposes ceases to frame his own budget. On the other hand, the duplication of departmental heads in each area under a Lieut.-Governor involves extra cost, and some loss of technical efficiency and co-ordination. There are, moreover, a number of departments whose functions are indivisible, and they must remain under the direct control of the central authority—such as the judicial, railway, military, &c.

The scheme of amalgamation adopted in Nigeria was designed to involve as little dislocation of existing conditions as possible, while providing for the introduction later of such further changes as were either foreseen, but not immediately necessary, or might be suggested by future experience. They would then be rather in the nature of natural evolution than of reversal. There are twenty-one provinces in Nigeria—exclusive of the Mandate territory in the Cameruns and of the colony proper—each with an average area of 16,000 square miles, and a population of 800,000. To invest each Resident of a province with large powers of autonomy, or at the least to create half a dozen Lieut.-Governorships, would not be a measure of decentralisation but the reverse, for the work arising from each of the separate units—as well as from all the departments—would be centralised in the hands of the Governor. The truest principle of decentralisation was to make the area placed under a Lieut.-Governor so large and important that the officer appointed to its charge could relieve the Governor of all the routine functions of administration, leaving him to direct the general policy, initiate legislation, and control those departments which must necessarily be centralised.

The old northern and southern divisions of Nigeria were retained intact (the colony being a separate entity), and placed under Lieut.-Governors, pending the unification of the laws, the judicial system, and the general policy. It was thought that when the fundamental divergencies in these should have been removed, it would be possible (should the experience gained point in that direction) to create a third Lieut.-Governorship, or to make other changes. The task of amalgamating and re-enacting the statute-books of the two administrations was one which would necessarily take some time.

The difficulty regarding the decentralisation of the departments to which I have alluded was dealt with in the following way. A central secretariat (which would naturally later become the principal secretariat of Nigeria) was set up, while Lieut.-Governors retained their own secretariats. The departments which I have described as necessarily indivisible remained under the Governor and the Central Secretary. The other large departments, such as the Medical and Public Works, were retained in each unit as fully organised entities, and their receipts and expenditure were included in the Lieut.-Governor's budget, but they were placed under the general supervision of an officer senior to both the departmental heads, who, without interfering with the Lieut.-Governor's control, preserved uniformity and technical efficiency, and acted as adviser to Government.[1] Minor departments, such as Police, Education, &c., whose spheres of action do not

[1] In proportion as the head of a department ceases to exercise executive functions, and acts as adviser to Government, he approaches to the position of a "Minister" in a self-governing colony, and the germ of a future development is introduced.

overlap, remained separate in each unit. Departmental promotion was in all cases to be determined by a common roster.

In fiscal matters the whole of Nigeria became a single entity. All revenue was paid into the common Treasury (a "central" department), and each Lieut.-Governor and the heads of the central departments framed and submitted his own estimates to the Governor, who personally examined them with him, and assigned such funds for new works or for departmental expansion as the requirements of the country as a whole permitted. I shall describe more fully the functions and powers of the Lieut.-Governor and other officers in the next chapter. It suffices to note here that the methods by which it was sought to secure effective decentralisation were (*a*) by the delegation of executive, financial, and administrative powers to Lieut.-Governors who would exercise responsibility and initiative, and not be merely Deputy-Governors with no executive powers of their own; [1] (*b*) the administration of native affairs, being regarded not merely as a department, but as the most important duty of the administration, the Resident of a Province was as far as possible relieved of all other administrative duties, in order that he might devote his undivided time and thought to this work; (*c*) the authority of its head over a department was unfettered, and subject only to the control of the Governor or Lieut.-Governor, as the case might be. This scheme of amalgamation was adopted in the particular circumstances then existing in Nigeria; and its general principles would of course require adaptation if applied elsewhere, and will require modification to the changing conditions of the development of Nigeria itself.[2]

To what extent the principles of decentralisation may be applied as between the Colonial Office and the local Government is a question I shall discuss in chapters viii. and ix.

The second of the two principles which I have described as vital in African administration is Continuity, and this, like Decentralisation, is applicable to every department and to every officer, however junior, but above all to those officers who represent the Government in its relations with the native population. The annually recurrent absence on leave, which

[1] Decentralisation is the key-note of the Sudan administration, where Governors of provinces have the widest powers.

[2] A full report was submitted to the Secretary of State, and published as Cd. 468 of 1920.

withdraws each officer in West Africa from his post for about a third of his time, the occasional invalidings and deaths, and the constant changes rendered unavoidable of late years by a depleted and inadequate staff, have made it extremely difficult to preserve in that part of Africa any continuity whatever. The African is slow to give his confidence. He is suspicious and reticent with a newcomer, eager to resuscitate old land disputes—perhaps of half a century's standing—in the hope that the new officer in his ignorance may reverse the decision of his predecessor. The time of an officer is wasted in picking up the tangled threads and informing himself of the conditions of his new post. By the time he has acquired the necessary knowledge, and has learnt the character of the people he has to deal with, and won their confidence, his leave becomes due, and if on his return he is posted elsewhere, not only is progress arrested but retrogression may result.

It is also essential that each officer should be at pains to keep full and accurate records of all important matters, especially of any conversation with native chiefs, in which any pledge or promise, implied or explicit, has been made. It is not enough that official correspondence should be filed —a summary of each subject should be made and decisions recorded and brought up to date, so that a newcomer may be able rapidly to put himself *au courant*. The higher the post occupied by an officer, the more important does the principle become.

It is especially important that the decisions of the Governor should be fully recorded in writing, and not merely by an initial of acquiescence or a verbal order. This involves heavy office work, but it is work which cannot be neglected if misunderstandings are to be avoided and continuity preserved. The very detailed instructions regarding the duties of each newly-created department which were issued when the administration of Northern Nigeria was first inaugurated, served a very useful purpose in maintaining continuity of policy, till superseded on amalgamation by briefer general orders.

In the sphere of administration there are obviously many subjects—education, taxation, slavery and labour, native courts, land tenure, &c.—in which uniformity and continuity of policy is impossible in so large a country, unless explicit instructions are issued for guidance. By a perusal of the periodical reports of Residents, the Governor could inform himself of the difficulties which presented themselves in the varying circumstances of each province, and think out the best way in which they could be met, and could note where misunderstandings or mistakes had been made. By these means a series of Memoranda were compiled, and constantly revised as new problems came to light, and as progress rendered the earlier instructions obsolete. They formed the reference book and authority of the Resident and his staff.

In a country so vast, which included communities in all stages of development, and differing from each other profoundly in their customs and traditions, it was the declared policy of Government that each should develop on its own lines; but this in no way lessens the need for uniformity in the broad principles of policy, or in their application where the conditions are similar. It was the aim of these Memoranda to preserve this continuity and uniformity of principle and policy. Newcomers, by studying them, could make themselves fully acquainted with the nature of the task before them, the problems to be dealt with, and the attitude of Government towards each of those problems. Senior officers were spared the labour and loss of time involved in frequent iteration, when noting any misunderstanding or ignorance in the reports of their subordinates, by simply inviting attention to the pertinent paragraph of the Memorandum. Subversive policies cannot gradually creep in, and any change must be deliberately inaugurated by the formal cancellation of the particular instructions in the Memoranda. Though the preparation of the Memoranda involves considerable labour, they result in an eventual saving in the time both of the Governor and of senior officers. They are the embodiment of the experience of the most capable officers, co-ordinated by the head of the Government, who has access to the reports and is familiar with circumstances of all. When any point of particular difficulty presents itself where opinions are in conflict, and the information insufficient to form a clear judgment on the principles involved, the Governor may perhaps cause a précis to be circulated before a final decision is reached. The little volume of 'Political Memoranda' has been of much use in Nigeria. It deals solely with the actual problems of practical administration.

The Statute Book, the Regulations and Orders made under

the laws, the General Orders, and the Governor's Memoranda on administrative subjects, contain between them in a readily accessible and compact form the whole structural policy of the Administration, and constitute the "Laws and Usages" of the country. Had such a quartette existed, revised decennially since the earliest origin of our Indian Empire and of our Crown colonies, they would have formed valuable material for the history of the Empire. In Africa we are laying foundations. The superstructure may vary in its details, some of which may perhaps be ill-designed, but the stability of the edifice is unaffected. You may pull down and re-erect cupolas, but you cannot alter the design of the foundations without first destroying all that has been erected upon them.

Important as it is that the British Staff, so long as they are efficient, should remain in the same posts without more interruption than is necessary for the preservation of health, and the prevention of ennui or "staleness," it is of still greater importance that continuity should be maintained in the case of an efficient Governor, who directs the policy of the whole country.[1] For in a rapidly-progressing country policy and legislation are developed from day to day, Regulations and Orders in Council for the carrying out of laws are matters of daily consideration; and in spite of every effort to decentralise and to delegate powers, the Governor has to deal daily with large numbers of Minute papers, each calling for a considered judgment on some problem of sufficient importance for reference to him.

It is above all important that he should be present towards the close of the year, when the estimates are framed in which the programme of material progress—railways, roads, buildings—and increases of staff, &c., are settled. These months, and the first quarter of the new year, are far more important from an administrative and business point of view than the remaining months, which form the rainy season in the tropics north of the Equator. The accounts are completed; annual

[1] The 'Times,' discussing the "Administrative problem in Equatorial Africa," in a well-informed article some years ago (1st Oct. 1901), pointed out that the entire absence of continuity in the administration of Uganda had produced results which were alike "deplorable and discreditable." The bewildering rapidity of the changes in Commissioners, each of whom experimented with the unfortunate country by introducing new and subversive policies, made it impossible to fix any responsibility.

reports from all departments begin to come in, and must be reviewed; and the yearly report to the Secretary of State, for which they form material, must be compiled. Communications are no longer impeded by washouts, or roads too soft from rain to carry vehicles, and the season permits of travel and inspection. In order always to be present at this season, a Governor in West Africa must take his leave either after eight or after about seventeen months in the country, and so make his absence coincide with the rainy season. By which arrangement will continuity be best preserved?

The seventeen months' tour of service involves a heavy strain. The Governor's absence on completing it would extend over a period of about 6½ months, including voyages, thus seriously encroaching on the working season. During so long a period many matters of first-class importance must be decided without awaiting his return, new legislation must be put through, and even questions of policy may be affected. By so long an absence continuity is seriously sacrificed. Another hand must guide the helm, or there must be a period of stagnation and delay. Important questions await his return, and leave him but little time to read up all that has transpired during his long absence, so that he finds himself wasting precious time in the hopeless endeavour to overtake arrears at a moment of exceptional pressure, or dealing with questions with which he is perforce imperfectly acquainted.

The eight months' period of residential service offers less disadvantage in these respects, and is already applicable to the judges in Nigeria. But even an absence of four months in each year (including voyages) is a distressing break in continuity, if the Governor during this period is wholly detached from his work. It was, however, found necessary by Lord Cromer—though the climate of Cairo or Alexandria is better than that of West Africa,—and I believe he attributed much of his success to his annual holiday. The Governor-General of the Sudan also takes an annual leave, bringing home with him during the rainy season many of his senior officers, and transacting much business for his Government during his time in England. During the absence of Lord Cromer, or Sir R. Wingate, the *locum tenens* could not initiate any new policy or legislation. This was the Foreign Office solution of the problem. The Niger Chartered Company had found it no less necessary for their highest officers (the Agent-General and Chief Justice) to come home yearly, though in their case the administration was directed from London.

After six years' experience in West Africa, during which an exceptionally robust constitution enabled me to adopt the sixteen to eighteen months' period of foreign service, and so to avoid absence at the essential period of the year, I realised very fully its disadvantages, and submitted to Mr Lyttelton, then Secretary of State for the Colonies, a proposal by which I hoped that this lack of continuity might be overcome, and at the same time a closer touch assured between the Governor and the Secretary of State and commercial interests in England. The proposal was seen by Mr Chamberlain, who had recently left the Colonial Office, and he was inclined to approve it. The principle was also approved by Lord Cromer and other statesmen.[1] Mr Lyttelton declared his intention of giving it a trial in Nigeria.

In brief, I suggested that "the Governor-General (of an amalgamated Nigeria) should spend six months of each year in Africa, and six in England, being on duty and not on leave while at home . . . whether in England or in Africa he would remain the sole working head of the administration." The scheme was not cordially accepted by the permanent officials, and did not at that time take effect; but when in 1912 I was invited by Mr (now Lord) Harcourt to undertake the amalgamation of the two Nigerias, he agreed to adopt it on the basis of seven months' residence abroad and five months' absence, including voyages—which I think is better than six and six. With rapid sea passages it might even be eight and four months.

The scheme was in operation for some years, and I doubt whether the task of amalgamation, with the added difficulties of the war, could have been satisfactorily carried through without it. Arrangements had been made so that the rôle of the permanent officials at the Colonial Office should in no way be interfered with by the presence of the Governor, while his residence in England for four months during the rains each year involved an absence from Nigeria no longer, though more frequent, than the normal period of leave. He was in

[1] Sir A. Hemming, who had served for thirty years in the Colonial Office, latterly as head of the West African Department, and subsequently as Governor of two Crown colonies, warmly supported it in a letter to the 'Times' (26th December 1905).

point of fact more closely in touch with his deputy than if he had been travelling in a distant part of Nigeria. His deputy in Africa was vested with full powers to deal with any emergency which might arise, and to carry on routine work.

It was hoped that the arrangement would have beneficial results in relieving the Governor for a period in each year, when he could best be spared, of the burden of routine work, and enable him to devote time to the study of larger problems,[1] and to maintain a close touch with commercial interests in England. For the latter reason it was welcomed by the merchants.[2] It was anticipated also that the Governor's presence in England—not on leave but on duty—might, if duly utilised, prove of value to the home authorities, and minimise despatch-writing.

Under the normal Colonial Office system, the Governor when on leave was rarely consulted, except on a matter of very exceptional importance, and was at liberty to leave England if he desired. No doubt it was the kindly intention that he should have complete rest. The Acting-Governor was vested with full powers, and for the time being entirely superseded the Governor, and was alone recognised by the Colonial Office. Since the Governor did not see the despatches sent to or received from his Government, he lost all touch, and on his return he had a heavy task to overtake arrears and possess himself of what had transpired in his absence. The Foreign Office, as Lord Lansdowne told the House of Lords, like the French Government, has a different tradition.

Experience did not lessen the hostility of the permanent officials to the scheme.[3] It was, they considered, contrary

[1] Compare Burke, addressing a member of the French National Assembly in 1791: "They who always labour can have no true judgment. You never give yourselves time to cool. You can never survey from its proper point of sight the work you have finished before you decree its final execution. You can never plan the future by the past. . . . These are among the effects of unremitted labour, when men exhaust their attention, burn out their candles, and are left in the dark."

[2] One of them had in fact advocated a very similar scheme—viz., that a Governor "should return home for six months after nine in Africa, and be responsible for his *locum tenens* and all his acts during the interval."

[3] An obviously well-informed article appeared in the 'Glasgow Herald' of 13th July 1912, before the scheme was brought into effect, stating that Mr Harcourt's decision "was strongly resented by the permanent officials . . . no other Crown Colony [they said] is carried on in this way, which means the practical supersession of the permanent Under-Secretaries."

to all precedent, and even to constitutional usage. This could not indeed be gainsaid, but the experiment could be, and was, legalised like other experiments in Empire Administration, by Letters Patent and Royal instructions. The apprehensions of the permanent officials were not unnatural, for the presence of the Governor at the Colonial Office seemed to threaten the anonymity of the Secretary of State, from which they derived the powers so absolutely essential to the working of the Colonial Office system. Regarding this system I shall have some remarks to make in chapter viii.; but in so far as this scheme is concerned, no interference with the functions of the permanent officials was ever contemplated, or alleged while it was in operation. The Governor, though working in close relation with the department, was not part of it, and had no claim to see the Office Minutes.

The primary object of the scheme, as I have explained, was to promote a true continuity of responsibility and control, in lieu of a continuity which was not real. That there is a tendency on the part of an Acting-Governor, vested with the fullest powers, to inaugurate policies of his own, had been the experience of more than one West African colony. It may not go so far as the reversal of legislation—which could be vetoed by the Secretary of State—and it may even be due to misunderstanding rather than to deliberate intention, but the result is equally deplorable.

The practicability of the principle of continuous responsibility of the Governor when absent from his post, and of his annual return to England, must, of course, depend largely on the distance of the colony and the time taken in sea voyages. It is adapted only to a group of colonies under a Governor-General—and the two Nigerias, in size, population, and wealth, might be said to represent such a group—and to colonies within a comparatively short sea voyage of England. A scheme which has been found feasible for West Africa, Egypt, and the Sudan would not be suitable for the Straits Settlements, Ceylon, or Mauritius, unless aviation introduces new possibilities in the future. The French system in West Africa—which I shall presently describe—is not dissimilar.

British public opinion is in favour of trusting the "Man on the Spot," who represents the King, and is held responsible by the nation. If trouble occurs through the action of his deputy, it is the Governor's policy which is blamed. He should therefore have the same control over his deputy when he is in London as he would have were he absent in some distant part of the protectorate, where for all practical administrative purposes he would be less in touch than when in London. But the scheme, as Mr Churchill wittily said, involves an enlarged definition of the "Spot," due to the rapid means of transport and communications which steam and telegraphy have introduced, in order to give effect to the essential principle—control by the man who is held responsible.

No project can, however, be successfully carried out to which one party is consistently opposed, and the scheme has been abandoned,—nor should I have devoted so much space to it were it not that its revival—possibly in some modified form—would certainly in my view be desirable, if the proposal to "group" colonies—which I shall deal with in chapter ix.—were adopted.

How, then, in the meantime can continuity of responsibility and co-operation best be preserved? It has been said that continuity is maintained by the permanency of the officials at the Colonial Office, whose rôle it is to oppose subversive policy by a new Governor based on insufficient experience, or the assumption of too wide powers by an Acting-Governor. This is, of course, an essential function of the Colonial Office under the present system—a function which, as we have seen, the Foreign Office had been accused of failing to perform in Uganda. The duty of acting as a drag on the wheels may indeed preserve continuity, but it is not necessarily a continuity of progress, and may even produce an attitude of mind tolerant of delays, and hostile to new lines of thought.

If it were made manifest to a Governor on leave that his presence and assistance is welcomed at the Colonial Office; if he saw all correspondence with the Acting-Governor, and were informed of all proposed changes; if the atmosphere of secrecy were exchanged for one of absolute frankness, not only by the seniors but by the juniors of the Office, and he were consulted in matters regarding his sphere of work, and invited to Conferences and Committees; if his period of leave were invariably to coincide with the rainy season—either annually with an absence of three to four months only, or (since conditions in West Africa now admit of longer residence) every alternate year, with a total absence not exceeding six months (say, from mid-March to mid-September); and finally, if the powers of the Acting-Governor were strictly curtailed, and the continuous responsibility of the Governor were officially recognised—much might be done not only to promote continuity, but also to forward the best interests of the country.

In the latter direction clear rules should be laid down and published. The initiation of legislation, the approval of important leases, and the appropriation of any considerable sums unprovided in the estimates, should be reserved to the Governor. His deputy should have no power to cancel or alter existing Regulations, General Orders, or Governor's instructions, or to issue any instructions contrary to these in letter or spirit, or incompatible with the general policy in regard to the native administration. He should not alter the boundaries of provinces, depose or appoint chiefs of the highest rank, alter the permanent distribution of the military forces, or give pledges to merchants or missionaries which involve important principles, without prior reference to the Governor.

The prosperity of a colony, and the welfare of its population, must obviously depend very largely on the character and energy of its Governor. It is therefore of the first importance that the best men should be selected for these posts, and that during their tenure of office the Secretary of State should have frequent opportunities of judging of their ability and sustained energy and enthusiasm.

The work and character of a Governor cannot be gauged by his popularity, or by the hearsay evidence of juniors, or of those whose pecuniary interests may have been affected by measures needed for the good of the country, for they are necessarily inadequately informed. Unpopularity arising from questions of public policy may indeed be a proof of strength of character and of a disinterested sense of duty.

It is manifest that when the right man is in the right place, it is to the benefit of the country that his tenure of office should be prolonged; but in order to avoid the retention of a man who has not come up to the expectations formed of him, or who, though thoroughly capable, is unsuited to the particular post, the period of Governorship should be limited as now to six years (though earlier transfers could, of course, be made), and the extension of this term should carry with it an increase of emoluments, so that the Governor may not suffer in pocket or status, and the extension may be regarded as a recognition of merit. There is a widespread feeling in the senior ranks of the service—the bitterness of which is probably not appreciated in Downing Street—that present methods provide no safeguard against inefficiency, and no guarantee for the selection of the best men.

A Governor is often a married man with a family. In the conditions hitherto prevailing in Africa, except in the eastern Highlands, he must be separated from the latter, even if his wife (probably no longer young) is able to accompany him. The best men, therefore, are apt to look for promotion to a colony which does not necessitate such separations. It is only within the last dozen years that Governors have remained for their full period of office in West Africa. Formerly they rarely remained for more than three years. Continuity again suffers, for Governors appointed from the eastern colonies (as so many have been in West Africa) have much to learn and unlearn before they become familiar with African conditions and African character—so essentially different from those of the East.

In the self-governing colonies limitation of tenure of office has special advantages. Continuity is maintained, not by the Governor-General, but by his ministers. Past controversies are buried with the advent of a new Governor, and the progress of democratic institutions in the Mother Country, and her relations towards the colony, are more accurately represented. The new Governor is, in fact, more up-to-date as the representative of the feelings and changes in Great Britain. In the tropical dependencies the case is otherwise. Personality counts for so much with native races that the departure of a man who has gained their confidence may set the clock back and delay progress—and the same may be said of material development. Given the right man, the longer he stays the better, provided he retains his energy and enthusiasm—as results have proved in Egypt and elsewhere. On the other hand, as decentralisation proceeds, the force of these arguments decreases. Continuity of method and policy is better assured, and the "new blood" which the Colonial Office constantly endeavours to infuse into the colonies has its advantages in bringing new ideas and new experience, and in preventing an administration from becoming limited in its channels of progress under the continued control of the same man.

Continuity may therefore suffer in three ways: first, by the short tenure of his post by a Governor; secondly, by his long absence on leave; and thirdly, by the indefinite powers given to his temporary deputy.

It may be said that as Faith, Hope, and Charity are to the Christian creed, so are Decentralisation, Co-operation, and Continuity to African Administration—and the greatest of these is Continuity.

CHAPTER VI.

THE MACHINERY OF ADMINISTRATION

The Legislative Council—Unofficial representation: (*a*) European unofficial members; (*b*) native unofficials; (*c*) representation of the masses—Method of enacting laws—The official vote—The Executive Council—Its duties, procedure, and composition—Value of Executive Council—Committees—The Nigerian Council—The Governor—The Governor's deputy—The Lieut.-Governor—The Resident—The Malayan and Nigerian systems—Conditions in Malaya—Contrast between the two—The District Officer—His training—Necessity for acquiring the language—Advantages of a *linguâ francâ*—Duties of the District Officer—Continuity at his post.

TURNING from general principles to the machinery of administration, the Governor and the Councils over which he presides first claim consideration. The powers and duties of the Governor and the constitution and functions of the Councils are laid down in the "Letters Patent" which constitute each colony, or the Royal "Orders in Council" which take their place in the case of a protectorate. These instruments are supplemented by "Royal Instructions," in which they are further elaborated.

The constitution of the Legislative Council varies greatly in different colonies and protectorates.[1] In some of the Crown colonies there is an unofficial majority, either nominated or partly elected by constituencies; but in the African dependencies the unofficial members are in a minority, and are nominated by the Crown except in the case of Kenya, which has eleven elected members. Colonial legislatures can only exercise jurisdiction in their own territories, unless special power is given to them to legislate for adjacent regions.[2] In

[1] See Taring's 'Law relating to the Colonies,' p. 61. Also Colonial Regulations, chap. i.—'Colonial Office List' (1921), p. 793.

[2] Taring, pp. 61 and 132.

Southern Nigeria, prior to amalgamation, the Legislative Council of the colony legislated for the protectorate,[1] but its functions are now limited to the colony proper, and the Governor legislates for the protectorate. Every protectorate Bill is placed before the Executive Council before the Governor's assent is given, a draft having been published in the official gazette for some time prior to enactment, unless the Bill is urgent, or there is other good reason for not doing so. This affords opportunity for the expression of public opinion in regard to it, a course which is the more necessary in West Africa, since the principals of most of the firms there retain the direction of their commercial affairs largely in their own hands in England, and their local representatives have, according to their statements, insufficient authority to voice their opinions.[2]

Unofficial membership of the Legislative Council is shared between the European and native communities. The "Montagu-Chelmsford Report" and the writings of Mr Lionel Curtis and Sir Valentine Chirol regarding the great experiment which is now being tried in India, have very clearly demonstrated the danger of enlarging the powers of criticism by increased unofficial representation—such as was accorded by the "Morley-Minto Reforms"—without the responsibility which men feel when they may be called upon to translate their theories into practice.[3] A community, therefore, which is ripe for responsible—or even for representative—Government should be able to provide individuals capable of holding high executive office.[4] I shall revert to this question in the chapter on native rule.

The petition of the "National Conference" from West Africa complained that nominated councillors were not representative of the people (though its leading signatories owed their position to nomination). It elicited from the

[1] These powers apparently grew out of the extra-colonial jurisdiction acquired by Governor Maclean in the Gold Coast hinterland. They were formally conferred on the Legislative Councils by a series of Orders in Council.

[2] See Cd. 6427 of 1912, question 99.

[3] 'Dyarchy,' by L. Curtis. Letters to the 'Times' by Sir V. Chirol, 7th June 1918, &c.

[4] "Representative government" is the term used for an unofficial majority in the Legislature, and is of course very different from "responsible government," viz., complete home rule. The danger of the premature grant of too advanced a form of government was shown in the case of Jamaica, where, after twenty years of friction and the refusal of the unofficial majority to vote supplies, the Constitution was remodelled.

Secretary of State (Lord Milner) his opinion that these dependencies are not yet fitted for the principle of election or of an unofficial majority.[1]

It may be accepted as a principle of British colonial policy that the interests of a large native population shall not be subjected to the will of a minority, whether of Europeans or of educated natives.[2] Thus in India the Governor General in Council legislated without reference to the Legislature for scheduled (*e.g.*, backward or primitive) districts and for native states.[3] In Natal, prior to the Union, the Governor had a commission as "Paramount Chief" for the control of extra-colonial natives, and the Legislative Council could not interfere with this jurisdiction, while at the Cape the High Commissioner governed the protectorates, and legislated for them, in a separate capacity from that in which he presided as "Governor" in the Cape Legislature. They remain under his control, and are not subject to the Union Government.

The weight which the British unofficials should carry is in West Africa impaired by the lack of authority to which I have referred. Though the local representatives of commerce are assured of a sympathetic hearing and a full investigation of any suggestions they may have to offer, the methods of Crown colony Government as applied in the African dependencies enable the principals of firms in England to carry their proposals direct to the Colonial Office, and thus to be somewhat indifferent to local representation.

There are already indications that the rapid progress of commerce in West Africa will bring with it a necessity for responsible heads of firms, who can speak with authority, to reside on the spot, and a fuller realisation of the duty and privilege of bearing their share in the councils of the countries in which their profits are made, so that as in the Eastern colonies local questions affecting trade will increasingly be decided locally without the delay and circumlocution involved by Colonial Office intervention. The claim of the British settlers in Kenya to representative or even responsible government may be justified in so far as control over their own

[1] The elective principle is about to be introduced into the Legislatures of Nigeria and the Gold Coast.

[2] Sir C. Dilke expressed the view that autocracy is preferable to a "veiled oligarchy" such as would exist if a small body of unofficial Europeans were invested with the power of taxing the natives.

[3] Ilbert, 'Government of India,' pp. 108, 121, and 214-15.

affairs is concerned, but to place some three million natives under the jurisdiction of a Legislative Council in which the unofficial vote predominated would, as I have said, be contrary to all British colonial precedent and tradition.

The Europeanised natives form a very important section of the community, and in proportion to their numbers have a substantial representation in the Legislature. They are necessarily drawn from the English-speaking section, and are not generally (as I have explained) representative of any but their own class. Owing, moreover, to the great distances and lack of means of rapid communication, the choice of native councillors is practically limited to the inhabitants of the capital city, whose commercial and other interests are not always identical even with those of their own class outside the colony.[1]

That the cry of "self-determination for small nations" should have awakened aspirations, while as yet no claim to a national status could be shown, is neither to be wondered at, nor indeed to be condemned. For these aspirations, though occasionally marred by ill-advised language in the native press, have, on the whole, been characterised by moderation, and conducted by constitutional methods.[2] Prosperity, combined with a wrong system of education and widespread illiteracy, has indeed, alike in Ireland, in Egypt, and in India, invariably given rise to unrest and sedition.[3]

The real problem is the representation of the bulk of the population, more especially the second of the two classes, which in chapter iv. I described as the "advanced communities." Some of these are literate in Arabic, or in their own language, but at present do not speak English, and are too far distant from the seat of Government (which in West Africa is unfortunately in all cases on the coast) to render attendance by responsible representatives a practical possibility.

The obvious remedies are the spread of education, and

[1] 'Times' correspondent in Nigeria, 24th May 1912.

[2] The only serious exception appears to be the "Ethiopian Church movement" fostered by American negroes, which was the probable cause of the Natal riots and led to bloodshed in Nyasaland in 1915.

[3] Never in the history of either Ireland or Egypt had a condition of such material prosperity been reached as immediately preceded the outbreak of disorder in both, while of India the 'Times' correspondent writes that "a standard of prosperity never previously approached coincides with a situation never comparably so menacing."—22nd December 1913.

especially the knowledge of English, the improvement of communications, and the delegation to such communities of the largest possible powers of control of their own affairs. But even so the desirability that the view of native rulers should be heard in Council on questions of legislation which affect them, and on other matters, cannot be denied. This could perhaps best be effected under present conditions by the appointment of an officer charged to ascertain and represent their views, and to act as their spokesman, both in the Executive and Legislative Councils—just as the Protector of Chinese in the Straits is charged with the interests of alien immigrants. His explanation to them of the Bills before Council, and the opportunity offered to them of expressing opinions, of asking questions, or of submitting motions through him, would be of great value in identifying them with the Government and in their political education.

Ordinances applicable to the colony are enacted by the Governor "with the advice and consent" of the Council. They are operative on receiving the Governor's assent, and are transmitted to the Secretary of State, and if not disallowed by His Majesty become part of the Statute Book. In Nigeria, in order to avoid duplication and tautology, Bills which refer—as the majority do, wholly or in part—to both colony and protectorate, are laid in full before the Legislative Council, and passed "so far as the provisions thereof relate to the colony," any clause which relates exclusively to the protectorate being outside the purview of the Council. If, as I have suggested in a previous chapter, the colony and protectorate were merged under a new title, the jurisdiction of the Legislative Council should remain restricted. It might perhaps be made co-extensive with that of the Supreme Court, where, as in Nigeria, that Court operates within "local limits." The Royal instructions direct that Bills relating to certain specified matters shall not be assented to, except in case of urgency, without prior instructions from His Majesty through the Secretary of State. Most ordinances contain a section empowering the Governor-in-Council to make any necessary Regulations for giving effect to the law, and the main heads under which such Regulations may be made are usually specified in the ordinance.

The influence on legislation which is exerted by the Council, and the extent to which Bills submitted to it are modified and improved before being finally passed, depends, of course, on the interest taken by members—especially by the unofficials—and the ability with which their views are presented. It is the desire of the Governments to appoint to the Legislative Council those members of the community who are most representative of its interests, and can best voice its opinions.

The procedure of the Legislative Council both as to motions and as to Bills is modelled on that of the Imperial Parliament. The Government majority is represented by the official members—viz., the holders of certain offices named in the "Letters Patent," who are expected to vote with the Government—while the unofficials represent the independent criticism of the Parliamentary "Opposition."

This principle was laid down in a circular, dated 17th August 1868, from the Duke of Buckingham and Chandos—at that time Secretary of State for the Colonies. Official members may, if necessary, be required to support the Crown —*e.g.*, to vote in favour of a Government Bill—but if an officer of the Crown has conscientious scruples, which the Governor is unable to remove, he may be excused from taking part in measures to which he objects on these grounds. He could not, however, continue to hold an office which carries with it a seat on the Council, if his conscience should not permit him to give to the Crown such support as may be necessary. In practice, therefore, an official member may in no case vote against Government.[1] If there is a unanimously hostile unofficial vote, a clause may (if the Governor so directs) be inserted suspending the operation of the ordinance until His Majesty's pleasure is known.

The Executive Council consists of the holders of the principal offices of the Government, who are named in the Royal instructions. They form an advisory body, before which the

[1] Lord Milner, speaking in the House of Lords on 12th May 1920, justified the official majority in the following terms: "The only justification for keeping an official majority in any colony is that we are convinced that we are better judges, for the time being, of the interests of the native population than they are themselves. Unless we thought that, we should not be justified in keeping our official majority. If that is the case, then I think that the argument that the unofficial vote was against you is not an argument which possesses any force. The responsibility rests with us. It is not as if we departed from the principle of trusteeship. On the contrary, on the principle of trusteeship, we keep the authority in the hands which we think for the time being most competent to use it, and we must not be fearful about making use of that reserve power." Lord Cromer expressed the same view.—'Literary and Political Essays,' p. 12.

Governor must lay all matters of importance, and in particular any Bill which he proposes to bring before the Legislative Council, or to enact for the protectorate, and any Regulation or Order which he proposes to make under any ordinance which requires that the Regulations, &c., shall be made by the Governor-in-Council.

In addition, various duties are laid upon the Council either by Royal instructions or by Statute, or by His Majesty's Colonial Regulations,[1] such as the final approval of all pensions, gratuities, and other expenditure not specifically provided in the estimates, the review of all capital sentences, the confirmation of sentences of deportation, and inquiry into cases of misconduct by any except very subordinate officers.

The Governor presides, and in case of divergence of opinion his decision prevails; but any member may record his dissent in the Minutes, which are periodically transmitted to the Secretary of State. Only such matters are discussed as are laid before the Council by the Governor; but a member who wishes to bring forward any question, and is not permitted by the Governor to do so, may in like manner record the fact with his reasons. The proceedings of the Council are confidential, and every member is bound by oath not to divulge the matters debated.

The Council may include unofficial members nominated by the Crown, if so provided by the Royal instructions. The advice of such members may on occasion be of great value to the Governor; but, on the other hand, a merchant may find his position embarrassing, should projects be discussed, or information acquired in his capacity as Councillor, which affect his personal interests, and are not known to his commercial competitors. An Executive Councillor, moreover, would usually be a member of the Legislative Council, and his position as an independent critic of any Bill is prejudiced if, as a member of the Executive Council—which is practically the Government—he has already committed himself before consulting public opinion. So far as Europeans are concerned, business men in the tropics have rarely time to devote to the

[1] These Regulations are merely directions given by the Crown to Governors of Crown colonies and protectorates for guidance. They do not constitute a contract between the Crown and its servants; on the contrary, they are alterable from time to time without the consent of Government servants.—Taring, p. 56.

details of executive government. The new constitution of Kenya provides for two unofficials on the Executive Council.

In Nigeria and other dependencies of great size the Governor (unless he delegates all powers to his deputy) must be able to summon a Council at more than one centre, if it be only for the transaction of statutory obligations. This need is met by the power vested in the Governor to summon officers as "Extraordinary Members."

The Executive Council is an institution of the utmost value. It affords the Governor an invaluable opportunity of inviting the criticism and suggestions of the ablest and most experienced of his staff, not individually but collectively, when the views of one are opposed or confirmed by another, weak points are detected and new aspects brought to light. Every dependency should be provided with an Executive Council. There was none in Northern Nigeria prior to its amalgamation with Southern Nigeria, and there is still none in Uganda.[1]

The Governor, of course, always has it in his power to appoint a committee to deal with any particular matter; and in formulating any large scheme, or in drafting any specially constructive ordinance, he would naturally have availed himself to the full of the advice of the officers who had special knowledge of the subject. But committees and departmental experts are alike liable to take too restricted a view.[2] When the results of their labours—expanded it may be by the Governor's own views and experience—are laid before the

[1] There are "Advisory Councils" in Zanzibar (see note, p. 34), the Sudan, and Northern Rhodesia. The latter, consisting of the Administrator and Secretary and five unofficial members elected by the European settlers, was created in 1918. The unofficials submit a list of questions, to which the Administrator replies, and resolutions are passed and recorded. In response to a petition from them for an increased share in the government, the Chartered Company has agreed that all details of revenue and expenditure, and all draft laws affecting Europeans (unless urgent and affecting Imperial policy), shall be laid before them, and their views submitted to the High Commissioner before the law is enacted. Lord Buxton's Committee recommends the creation of a Legislative Council.—Cmd. 1471/1921.

The Governor-General's Council in the Sudan was created in 1910, and consists of four *ex-officio* and two to four members nominated by him. The Budget and all laws must be passed in Council. There is no Legislative Council.—F.O. Handbook 98, p. 59.

[2] The East African 'Economic Commission' of 1919 (pp. 23, 24) suggests that decentralisation could be achieved by the creation of Advisory Boards, and in particular by an "Economic Development Board." The powers which it is suggested should be conferred on this Board go far beyond those of an Advisory Committee, and would almost certainly result in friction with the Legislative and Executive Councils.

Executive Council, it has in my experience constantly happened that suggestions of great value are made, and flaws detected, by the fresh minds brought to bear on the subject.

Government by committees is proverbially unsatisfactory, and may degenerate into a means of shirking responsibility or of limiting free discussion. Their chief value consists in sifting evidence and recording opinions, upon which a larger body, unbiassed as the representatives of particular interests, may form a considered judgment. Undue weight is apt to be attached to the recommendations of a committee of experts, whose conclusions are not infrequently the result of a compromise on points of very unequal importance.[1] The Executive Council forms an admirable body for full and free discussion, to which experts can, if desired, be summoned.

In a small colony in which the interests of the bulk of the population are focussed in the capital city, or in which the means of communication by railway are good, the Legislative Council may be a fairly representative body. Its unofficial members are influenced by a public opinion voiced in the Press, and made vocal wherever men meet and discuss affairs. Membership is a dignity which carries with it considerable responsibility.

Except perhaps in East Africa, where there is a large number of European settlers, these conditions are not usually found in an African dependency. Great distances intervene, necessitating many days' travel, and the Press is not an efficient organ of the best opinion—European and native. In Nigeria, for instance, there is a considerable European and educated native community, not only at Lagos, where the Council sits, but at Kano, Kaduna, Bukuru (Minesfield), Calabar, and Port Harcourt, none of which are less than three days' travel by sea or land from Lagos—equal in point of time to the distance between London and Gibraltar. Clearly no ordinary Council can succeed in focussing public opinion in such circumstances.

To afford in some degree a palliative for this difficulty, there has been established in Nigeria a Council which, like the General Council of French West Africa, meets yearly, usually on the last days of the year, and has a large membership, including representatives—British and native—from every important centre, and of all important interests—

[1] See Mr Bonar Law's opinions quoted on page 171.

banking, shipping, commerce, and mining (the Lagos and Calabar Chambers of Commerce, and the Chamber of Mines, each appoint a member). The official members include all Executive Councillors and Residents of Provinces, &c. The unofficial members comprise six Europeans and six natives, the latter including some of the leading chiefs from the most distant parts.[1] It is unfortunate that at present few of these can speak English, but this will be remedied in course of time, and the prospect of attending the Council will form an incentive to the rising generation to learn English.

The proceedings hitherto have consisted of an address by the Governor, in which he reviews the events of the year, gives the latest possible statistics of trade and finance, and explains questions of policy and legislation. This is followed by debates both on the address and on motions previously submitted by members to the president. Thus ample scope for criticism or suggestion is afforded in regard to legislation past and future—or in regard to development works (railways, harbours, &c.), or any other matter which members may desire to bring forward. The Council has no legislative powers.

The Nigerian Council is an attempt to bring together representatives from all parts of a vast country for purposes of discussion, at least once in the year, since distances and lack of means of communication render it impossible for them to assemble as frequently as is necessary in the case of a Legislative Council. As an experiment still in embryo, it may, I think, claim some success.[2]

West African merchants have raised the question of directors of firms coming to Nigeria to attend the Council as temporary extraordinary members, and the secretary of their association remarks that it is due to the proceedings of the Council that the merchants have been prompted to take a part in the dis-

[1] The honour of appointment is much coveted. The Sultan of Sokoto was eager to attend, though the journey involved 256 miles by road and over 700 by rail.

[2] The Member of the Liverpool Chamber of Commerce who was deputed to report for that body on the proceedings of the Council for 1916 writes: "After reading the report through, as I have done, several times, I have become much more firmly convinced that the Nigerian Council, so long as it is treated by the Governor of the colony as a deliberative and active body (as now), has in it the possibility of doing an immense amount of good service, and of developing the colony on sound business lines, and we merchants should appreciate . . . the idea of such a Council and its present formation and importance."

cussion of the problems of Nigeria, instead of merely criticising Government action, as they have usually done in the past.[1] In questions of capital expenditure and development an Economic Board (see p. 492) may also assist in creating and giving expression to public opinion.

Coming now to the official personnel of the administration;—the Governor is appointed by a Royal Commission, and his duties are defined in Royal instructions. "He is the single and supreme authority, responsible to and representative of His Majesty . . . entitled to the obedience, aid, and assistance of all military and civil officers."[2] He may grant pardons or remit penalties. He appoints, and subject to certain Regulations suspends and dismisses, public servants, assents or refuses assent to Bills passed by the Legislative Council, with the exception of Bills on certain matters reserved for the signification of His Majesty's pleasure. He issues warrants for the expenditure of money required for the public service. "The Governor is, of course, bound to obey the King's commands conveyed to him by the Secretary of State in his legislative as well as in his executive capacity, whether or not the course prescribed accord with his personal views and opinions."[3] A Secretary of State recently observed that "the authority and responsibility of the Governor is the basis on which Crown colony administration is founded, and it must not be weakened."

The apparent autocracy of the Governor is limited on the one hand by the control of the Secretary of State, who exercises a real autocracy, and whose sanction is required not merely in matters of importance, but in many which are absurdly trivial; and on the other hand, by the influence of the Councils.[4] A Governor normally holds office for six years. In West Africa he is, or was, expected, like all other Government servants, to take leave to England after twelve months' residence, involving an absence from his duties of upwards of five months (see pp. 105-110).

[1] The present Governor (Sir H. Clifford) has intimated that the Council will be abolished this year (1923) and the jurisdiction of the Legislative Council—now restricted to the Colony (p. 115)—will be restored over the whole of the southern provinces under the name of the "Council of Government."

[2] Colonial Regulations.

[3] Circular of 17th August 1868.

[4] It is interesting to note that in the island of Guam the American Governor exercises absolute powers, and lately issued a decree that since "the practice of whistling is an entirely unnecessary and irritating noise, no person shall whistle within the limits of the city," under penalty of $5 executive fine.—'Times,' 29th July 1920.

During his absence the officer who takes his place is vested with the full powers of Governor. He has the legal right to make or repeal laws or regulations, to inaugurate or abandon important works; and in matters of policy, especially as regards native affairs, he can give rulings and pledges to chiefs in the name of the Government. He occupies Government House, and is addressed as "His Excellency." He would not, however, in practice be allowed to reverse the policy of the Governor or to initiate radical changes.

The officer who acts as Governor is usually the Colonial Secretary, through whose hands all the Minutes and files have passed which relate to the various matters which have been submitted by the Governor. He is therefore familiar with the history and antecedents of each question which may arise, and has been in close touch with the Governor, and knows his views. These are undoubted advantages; but if we may assume that the guidance of the policy in regard to the native population, and discrimination in matters involving the interests of non-natives, constitute not only the most important of the functions of the Governor, but also the sphere in which the initiative rests primarily upon himself, and is not shared with the departmental officers of his Council to the same extent as his other duties, it seems clear that the officer who takes his place as Acting-Governor should be a man of administrative experience, rather than one with the training of a secretariat officer. To meet this difficulty the experiment has been tried of appointing as secretary the senior or most capable officer from the administrative branch, but this course has two disadvantages. In the first place, the administrative officer is without experience in the management of a large office, and out of touch with departmental requirements. In the second place, the staff of the secretariat (to which it is especially necessary to attract exceptionally good men) are afforded no prospect of attaining to the highest post in their department, and it consequently becomes unpopular.

It has been argued that a sacrifice of continuity is involved if a Lieut.-Governor acts for the Governor; but since it can be arranged that the same Lieut.-Governor should always act as deputy, continuity in the Governor's office would be maintained; and since the same Resident would usually act for the Lieut.-Governor (who as Deputy-Governor is himself present to ensure continuity), the argument does not seem to have much force. Moreover, since it is probable that the senior Resident would in due course succeed to the Lieut.-Governorship if he has proved his competence, a greater measure of permanent continuity would be secured.

In my judgment there should be at least one Lieut.-Governor in every African dependency, and he (or the senior if there is more than one) is the officer best qualified to act for the Governor. The normal duties of a Lieut.-Governor in Nigeria are (as we shall presently see) only less onerous and responsible than those of the Governor himself; and as a member of the Executive Council he is already familiar with most of the larger questions of material development, and in close touch with the Governor.

The appointment of the Colonial Secretary to act as Governor compels the Secretary of State, when selecting a new Governor, to choose between a man whose training has been chiefly in an office, and one who has wide experience in administrative work among the natives but has never been tested as an Acting-Governor. Possibly this may have prompted him to look outside the ranks of the Colonial Civil Service.

The Lieut.-Governor—who would, as I suggest, act on occasion as Deputy-Governor—would usually be selected from the ranks of the Provincial Administrative Staff, though, of course, exceptions would be made. He will bring to his new post a wide understanding of the people and their language, and as Resident of a Province will have had practical experience in the handling of men. A capable man will soon pick up the threads of his wider administrative duties, and his early course of training in the secretariat will have made him sufficiently familiar with its routine. His capability for the post will already have been put to practical test by acting for the Lieut.-Governor in his absence—and there are plenty of Residents from whom to choose if one proves unsuitable.

The secretariat-trained officer, on the other hand, has not that experience of actual administrative responsibility which is only acquired by the District Officer who has risen to be a Resident.[1] Nor does the proposal to combine the secretariat

[1] Lord Curzon, when Viceroy of India, set himself to meet the criticism that "the Government of India has been systematised and formalised to such a degree that the executive officers are the slaves of clerical routine, and the judicial ones

with the administrative branch as a single department appear to offer any better solution. Each requires specialised training, and the qualifications which make for excellence in the one are almost the reverse of those required in the other.[1] Moreover, since the number of administrative officers in a large protectorate may be twenty times that of the secretariat, the latter under such a system would suffer from constant change; and since it is a department of record on which the Governor depends for accuracy of reference and knowledge of precedent, this would be fatal to its utility. Some secretariat training is invaluable to a District Officer, and for this he can be temporarily attached as supernumerary.

These views will no doubt be opposed by the office men, who alone have the opportunity of writing Minutes on such subjects; but for my part I have no doubt as to which class will have the widest knowledge of and sympathy with the subject races, and the more practical experience of administrative problems. Neither have I any doubt from which class the more useful type of African Governor can be recruited.

A Lieut.-Governor in Nigeria is in supreme administrative charge of the group of provinces for which he is responsible. He prepares an annual budget, and submits it to the Governor, and when it is approved he controls the expenditure votes. Such of the Governor's powers, whether statutory or executive, as are delegated to him are precisely notified in the 'Gazette,' in order that there may be no misunderstanding either on his part or that of the public. They are as wide as possible, and, generally speaking, exclude only matters reserved by statute to the Governor-in-Council (which cannot be delegated), the initiation of legislation, the general direction of policy, and the approval of unbudgeted expenditure—in which the Governor himself has very limited powers.

The post of Lieut.-Governor was not a new one in West Africa, but hitherto the officer who held the appointment

of legal technicalities; that both alike have lost their old touch with the people; and that the only classes which benefit by this development are the office Babus, and the barristers and 'pleaders,' parasitic growths alien to the soil of India, but thriving on the system we have introduced . . . that the District Officers have lost their old touch with the people under the pressure of modern 'Secretariat' government."—'Times' (special correspondent), 13th November 1901.

[1] In the very interesting description of Lord Curzon's "New Province" in India, we are reminded that "a methodical and highly-trained administrative class in proportion to its scientific evolution becomes less and less adapted to pioneering in wild tracts."—Ibid.

had, so far as I am aware, no clearly defined powers or authority on which the public could rely. His functions and duties were shadowy, and depended on the latitude given by the Governor. When dealing with the subject of Decentralisation in the last chapter, I discussed the relations of the Lieut.-Governor with the Governor on the one hand, and the various departments on the other. His most important duty is to watch over and co-ordinate the political administration. "The question," wrote Lord Morley, "is whether the judgment of the Lieut.-Governor should be fortified and enlarged by two or more competent advisers, with an official and responsible share in his deliberations." Later, the Lieut.-Governor in India was provided with an Executive Council of three administrative heads—but no such step has as yet been taken in Africa.

Next to the Governor and Lieut.-Governor, the most important administrative officer in Nigeria is the Resident of a Province—the average area of which is 16,000 square miles, with an average population of 800,000. As the senior official, he is, generally speaking, responsible for the efficiency of the public service in his province, but his first duty is with the native administration, including the conduct of the provincial and native courts. The departmental services are controlled by their own heads, who assign to their subordinates their professional duties and responsibilities, and convey their orders to them direct.

The Resident is the backbone of the administration. He is Judge of the Provincial Court, of which his staff are commissioners. Through them he supervises and guides the native rulers—as I shall describe in chapter x. In the provinces with the most advanced native organisation he is counsellor and adviser, while among primitive tribes he must necessarily accept a larger measure of direct administration. His advice when given must be followed, and his authority is supported by the weight of the British Administration. His powers and duties are clearly and fully set out in the printed instructions which I have described in the last chapter. Alike for the information of the Governor—to enable him to maintain uniformity of policy—and to afford the Resident a means of setting out his difficulties and describing his progress, he submits a yearly report under specified headings (to which are appended a few statistical forms), dealing with the provincial and native courts, taxation and assessment, education, slavery, trade, general progress, and other matters of interest. These reports stimulate thought, and form valuable records. They afford to a Resident's successor a full account of all matters of interest, and enable him to preserve continuity.[1]

A Resident is relieved as far as possible of general administrative work (unconnected with the native administration) by the Lieut.-Governor, and by "Station Magistrates" appointed to the principal urban centres. The provinces in Nigeria are so large—Sokoto and Bornu are each larger than Ireland, and two others have a much denser population—that a Resident must rely largely upon his District Officers, and delegate many duties to them. He and they are the medium of all important dealings with the natives.

The Residential system of the Federated Malay States has been quoted as similar to that set up in Nigeria, but since both in its origin and development it differed essentially from it, it may be of interest to contrast the two.

When the Imperial Government replaced the Chartered Company in Northern Nigeria, and effective occupation had become necessary to establish British rights, the new Government found itself compelled to overcome the hostility of the Moslem Emirs, and to check their slave-raiding by force of arms. They were conquered, or submitted, and the country was divided into provinces, each of which was placed under the charge of a Resident, who was thus the representative of the Governor in a country in which the King's sovereignty had been asserted, and full responsibility for administration assumed.

In the early history of Malaya very different conditions existed. The British settlements were surrounded by wholly independent native states, with which the Imperial Government had no desire whatever to interfere, in spite of their requests for protection. In 1873 the chronic internecine war which existed among them, and their interference with the

[1] The report includes extracts from those of the Divisional Officers, so that the progress of each division may be separately related as part of the single unit of the province, under its various subject heads. Departmental statistics are eliminated, but a general summary of the work of departments in relation to their bearing on the provincial administration is given. The report deals with facts, events, and conclusions. Recommendations and discussions are excluded from it.

trade of the British colony, induced Lord Kimberley to suggest the possibility of appointing a British officer to reside in such of them as might consent to the arrangement—on the analogy of the Residents at the Courts of independent Rajas in India.

In the event a Resident was murdered, and a powerful military force exacted reprisals. The effect of this punishment, and the removal of obstructive chiefs, proved more effective than many years of futile advice. Though Residents were still instructed that they would be held answerable if they exceeded their rôle as advisers, they were now feared, and were able to engage a staff of Europeans, to raise a police force, and to collect the revenue. This was adequate for an effective administration, for the country was very rich. State Councils, on which the Resident and his assistant sat, were set up, and Courts of Law, with European magistrates.

Sir F. Swettenham, from whose book I am quoting,[1] speaking of one of the Residents, says: "No doubt he consulted the local chief in all matters of importance, but he received no help from that quarter, and simply pushed on alone, when he could not carry him with him." The British officers had, in fact, ceased to be "Residents" except in name, and were actually "administering the country in the name of the Sultan"—a rôle which, when it had first been proposed, was disapproved by the then Secretary of State. "Each Resident followed his own line in his own State without any particular reference to his neighbours," and resented any interference or suggestion from outside, until the differences, at first irritating, became unbearable, and led to Federation—with the approval of a Secretary of State of wider outlook (Mr Chamberlain). "The system," says Sir F. Swettenham, "was built up without much more than routine references to the Governor," who only knew what Residents chose to tell him—for Singapore was too distant for him to exercise any effective control. They submitted an annual report and a budget, which required the Governor's approval, and no vote could be exceeded without his sanction—a "very great and necessary safeguard," as Sir F. Swettenham observes.

From first to last the theoretical independence of the States was the governing factor in the system evolved in Malaya. The so-called "Resident" was in fact a Regent,

[1] 'British Malaya,' chapters viii. to xii.

practically uncontrolled by the Governor or by Whitehall, governing his "independent" State by direct personal rule, with or without the co-operation of the native ruler. He had no aggressive European neighbours on his frontiers, and in the last resort depended on his armed police and the military forces of the colony, and his abundant revenue made him self-supporting. This, as we shall see, is the very antithesis of the Nigerian system. Sir F. Swettenham describes how Downing Street disarmed the criticism of the non-progressive party at home by reiterating that the Resident must only give advice, and the onus of exceeding those orders was thrown on the men on the spot, as the only possible way of avoiding failure, and of carrying out the wishes of the Secretary of State.

Northern Nigeria up to the time of amalgamation was still dependent on a grant-in-aid, and in the early days it had no great source of wealth and no industrious Chinese to develop its resources, or to supply nine-tenths of the tax revenue. By the Secretary of State's instructions, it had to maintain a very large and costly military force, which absorbed all and more than all of its local revenue. To-day its native administrations are comparatively wealthy, but the railway which has created that wealth, and the whole machinery of Government—outside the native administrations themselves—was, and is, paid for from general revenue. The one "very great and necessary safeguard" imposed on the Residents of the Malay States—viz., that the votes in their approved budgets should not be altered or exceeded without the Governor's sanction (though the States they administered were independent, and solely self-supporting)—has, however, been ruled by the Colonial Office to be unnecessary in the case of the native administrations of Nigeria.

Dissimilar as the two systems were in origin and in method, the problems which confronted the Residents were practically identical, and have been solved with the same success in both cases. The conclusion emphasised by Sir F. Swettenham is "the advisability of letting people who live 8000 miles away manage their own domestic affairs without foreign interference."

Every province is divided into three or four divisions, each under a District Officer, who again has assistant district officers under him in charge of districts. The District

Officer comes of the class which has made and maintained the British Empire. That Britain has never lacked a superabundance of such men is in part due to national character, in part perhaps to our law of primogeniture, which compels the younger son to carve out his own career. His assets are usually a public school, and probably a university, education, neither of which have hitherto furnished him with an appreciable amount of positive knowledge especially adapted for his work. But they have produced an English gentleman with an almost passionate conception of fair play, of protection of the weak, and of "playing the game." They have taught him personal initiative and resource, and how to command and to obey. There is no danger of such men falling a prey to that subtle moral deterioration which the exercise of power over inferior races produces in men of a different type, and which finds expression in cruelty. The military officer turned civilian invariably becomes an ardent champion of his protégés, and no one shows greater aversion to militarist methods than he.[1] If occasionally some colonial officer suffers from "swollen-head" (as a member complained in the House), and exaggerates the importance of his office, may it not be charitably ascribed to that very devotion to his work, and realisation of its responsibility and magnitude which has made our Empire a success? No words of mine, after long experience, can do justice to the unselfish, conscientious work of these officers.

There is no career in which the aspirations of youth can take a finer form than in the service of the Empire, and

[1] "The administration so far as the masses are concerned is mainly carried on by the District Officers, . . . upon them the maintenance of law and order largely depends. They alone represent the British Raj in the minds of tens of millions who have not the faintest idea of what a Legislative Council means. The ultimate responsibility for the welfare of the native races rests not with the educated native, nor yet with the native rulers, but in the hands of the controlling power—*e.g.*, the District Officer, to whom the native ultimately appeals for justice. He is the exact opposite of the bureaucrat." So writes Lord Sydenham of India, and the words are equally true of Africa.—('Times,' 10th August 1917.) The code which must guide the administrator in the tropics is, as Mr Churchill has finely said, to be found in no book of regulations. It demands that in every circumstance, and under all conditions, he shall act in accordance with the traditions of an English gentleman, whose first quality it is to comprehend the point of view of the other side.—(Speech, June 1921.) Sir W. Geary, writing of West Africa, says that to each individual native there has come prosperity, and not merely acquiescence, but a joyous and friendly welcome of British rule. This he ascribes to the high character and judicious conduct of the officials of the Civil Service, which has admirably fulfilled its duty to the Crown and to Africa. —('West Africa,' 6th November 1920.)

there is none with less sordid ideals. To fit him for his duties, the candidate selected for an administrative post in the tropics must go through a special course of study in England. He attends the lectures prescribed, and must show that he has profited by them.[1] After he has arrived in Africa he must pass an examination in simple law, judicial procedure, and in the ordinances, regulations, and general orders of the local Government. If his duties lie in a Moslem State, he must know something of Koranic law, which controls alike the procedure of the courts and the social life of the people. He must study the native laws and customs, which react on Koranic law in Moslem districts, and replace it in pagan areas. Within a specified time he must pass a preliminary examination in one of the most widely-spoken native languages, to be followed by a more severe test later on. Failure to qualify in these tests may delay his promotion.

There is no need to emphasise how completely an officer who knows nothing of the native language is in the hands of his interpreter, who either from his imperfect knowledge of English, or by criminal intent, may wholly misrepresent what he was told to translate, or, on the other hand, may threaten an ignorant native that he will mislead the District Officer unless he is bribed. Incalculable harm has thus been done, and the interpreter becomes the real power. On the other hand, the officer who knows the language cannot fail to acquire a keener interest in and sympathy with the people. If the language used be some pagan dialect, and the officer can speak the more generally known language, it will be better for him to use it in speaking to his interpreter, for by so doing he ensures simplicity of diction, and the interpreter is more likely to understand his meaning than if he spoke in fluent English. If he uses English he should employ the simplest phrases, and make the interpreter repeat what he is about to translate; and later, if possible (if the matter is of importance), he should verify his accuracy by employing a second interpreter. The vital importance of this matter is my justification for this somewhat lengthy reference to it.

An officer is fortunate if there be a single language in his district, which has been reduced to writing with text-books and vocabularies. It is in the interest of the natives and

[1] See footnote, p. 138.

of good administration that the Government should use every endeavour to promote the use of a *linguâ francâ*—in Nigeria, Hausa; in East Africa, Swaheli. These are already generally understood even among primitive tribes, owing to their use by itinerant native traders; and they are simple languages, easily acquired by Europeans. When no such medium can be used, English—even though it be "pidgin English"—is already a means of communication, and will become more so as education increases.

The duties which a District Officer is called upon to perform are very varied. In an isolated station he may have to discharge the functions of all the departments—postal, customs, police, and engineer—in addition to his normal work. He is the medium of communication between the military or the departmental officer and the native chiefs in matters of labour and supplies, and is especially charged to see that labourers are fully paid and properly treated. To him alike the missionary, the trader, and the miner look for assistance and advice. The leper and the slave find in him a protector. As in India, he combines judicial with executive powers, and as Commissioner of the Provincial Court he deals with cases on the spot, within the limits of the judicial powers conferred upon him. These powers in Nigeria vary with the extent of his legal knowledge and proved judicial competence, irrespective of his rank. He is also charged with the constant supervision of the native courts (see chapters xxvii., xxviii.) He enforces the ordinances, issues licences, keeps up the prescribed records, and renders the prescribed returns. These are reduced to the minimum necessary, on the one hand, to afford his superior officers an insight into the way he is doing his work, and on the other, for the compilation of such administrative and statistical records as the Government may consider essential. "The work done by a political officer," said Sir H. Lawrence, "in his district surrounded by the people, is greatly superior to the work done in his office surrounded by untrustworthy officials." Recognising this great truth, it must be the aim of the Government to reduce office work in every possible way, and to leave the District Officer free to travel and work among the people.

His duties as assessing officer of the direct (income) tax effect much more than the mere collection of revenue. He is brought into close touch with the people, and gains an intimate knowledge of them, and of the personality and character of the chiefs and elders in every village. During his visit to each town he administers justice, inquires into and settles disputes, collects valuable statistics of population, agriculture, and industries. He uses every effort to detect oppression and extortion if it exists, and impresses on the village elders the allegiance they owe to their chiefs, and through them to the Government, the obligation to cease from lawless acts, and the right of every individual to appeal against injustice.

The primary object of travelling (accompanied when possible by the local chief or district headman) is that the District Officer may hear the complaints of the people at first hand. It is only by the advent of a British officer that scoundrels, misrepresenting the Government action, or extorting what they will from the natives in the name of Government, can be caught; for the villagers in their ignorance, supposing them to be genuine, dare not as a rule complain. It has been abundantly shown by experience that "unrest," resulting in murders and outrages, and eventually necessitating the use of force, inevitably takes place among primitive tribes when districts are not regularly and systematically visited. By frequent touring, abuses are redressed before they become formidable, the law-abiding people are encouraged to restrain the turbulent and lawless elements, and trust and confidence in Government is fostered. The results of the District Officer's careful and precise inquiries are contained in the 'Provincial Record Book' and in the map of the district, to which he is always adding the new information acquired on tour.

The District Officer who has achieved success in the assessment of his district will have done much to promote its progress and civilisation. The test of his work is the absence of crime and the efficiency of the chiefs and native courts. Nor must he neglect the development of its economic resources, the best method of improving them and enhancing their market value by proper preparation, and the cheapest methods of transport. For this purpose he should maintain touch with the traders, prospectors, and miners in his district. The measure of his efficiency depends largely on his interest in his work, and this is stimulated by the feeling of responsibility, which is the natural result of being trusted.

A District Officer's influence in his district naturally depends on the extent to which he has acquired the confidence of chiefs and people, mastered their language, and studied their local customs. It is therefore important that he should not be transferred to another sphere of work, where he has to begin afresh—least of all should contiguous colonies have a single roster of promotion as has been suggested. It may be valuable for the newly-joined officer to serve under different Residents, and in different districts, in order to enlarge his outlook, and enable him to learn from each ; nor is it possible to retain juniors permanently in the same district, or to gauge their qualifications and special aptitudes until they have had a varied opportunity. But as a District Officer gains seniority, and with it enlarged powers, it becomes increasingly important that he should remain in the district or province where he has acquired local knowledge and influence, for the African is naturally reserved and suspicious, and slow to give his confidence. It is, moreover, disheartening to the zealous District Officer to have to begin all over again in a new sphere. There are some who like change. They are not the best. When eventually he becomes the Resident of a Province he should never be changed without strong reasons. The war, and the inadequacy of the staff even prior to it, have no doubt militated greatly against the application of this principle.

CHAPTER VII.

THE BRITISH STAFF AND CONDITIONS OF LIFE IN THE TROPICS.

The classification of the staff—Selection by nomination—Selection by modified competition—Courses of study—Adequacy of staff—Cost of the staff in West Africa—Medical examination of candidates—Wives in the tropics—Housing in Northern Nigeria, 1898-1901—Causes of mortality—Improved conditions—Need of sanataria and recreation—Native huts as dwelling-houses—House-building in the tropics—Water-supply—Segregation—Food in the tropics—Medical and nursing staff—Private practice—Hints for health—Medical work among natives.

THE staff in the tropical dependencies may be divided into three classes—(*a*) the administrative and secretarial, corresponding to the Covenanted Service in India—to which may be added the judicial; (*b*) the Departmental, corresponding to the Indian Uncovenanted Service; and (*c*) the temporary staff, which consists either of officers seconded from the permanent staff of other parts of the Empire, or of men appointed on agreements with the Crown agents for specific periods, and non-pensionable, who, however, after completing a certain number of years' service, may be transferred to the pensionable staff. All military officers and some few civilians belong to the seconded class, while to the third category belong the large majority of foremen in the public works and railway employees.

The employment of seconded officers in the Postal, Public Works, Survey, and other departments has the advantage of bringing in up-to-date technical knowledge; but unless the department is entirely or mainly manned by such officers, their introduction in the senior posts disheartens the permanent staff by robbing them of opportunities for promotion.

The administrative staff of the Home, Indian, and Eastern Colonial services are recruited by open competitive examination. For the African tropics, candidates are selected by the patronage department of the Colonial Office (for the Sudan by the Governor-General). Selected officers must satisfy examiners that they have benefited by a course of lectures, which they are required to attend before taking up their appointments.[1] This preliminary training was suggested by me in September 1903, but proposals which were in advance of existing methods eighteen years ago demand reconsideration with the enormous increase of the Tropical Civil Service and its extension to the Mandated territories.

"The problem of maintaining order and creating civilisation in our African possessions," says Colonel Amery, "is at least as difficult as that of administering a settled country like India." The staff should, he considers, be recruited in the same way as the Indian Civil Service, and on terms of pay and pension equally attractive, and not by "the haphazard methods of personal nomination, which have survived from a bygone period." There is ample scope for the creation of an African Civil Service, capable of playing a part as distinguished as that which the Indian Civil Service has played in another field.[2]

While the Indian Civil Service seems likely to decrease both in numbers and in attractiveness, West Africa can no longer be regarded as a "death-trap," and the frequent leave to England is a great attraction to those who have children at school at home. Each group of colonies throughout the Empire has its own attractions and disadvantages. In one the climate is good, but long and bitter separations from children, and perhaps from wives, are unavoidable. Another offers better chances of promotion; in a third, the nature of the work is more attractive.

The results of an absolutely open competition have not, I believe, been considered to be an unqualified success in India; but competition, qualified by such conditions as

[1] Three courses, each of three months, held annually at the Imperial Institute, were inaugurated in 1908. Lectures were given in tropical hygiene, criminal law, procedure, and evidence, accountancy, and the cultivation, preparation, and uses of tropical products—vegetable and mineral. There was also a separate course in surveying, and facilities were afforded for learning Hausa, Arabic, &c. Officers of the police forces could be attached for six months to the Royal Irish Constabulary.

[2] 'Union and Strength,' p. 284.

would attract the right class from our public schools and universities, while excluding as far as possible the "bounder," the "prig," and the "book-worm," would secure the best that England can give, and would relieve the Colonial Office of much irksome work.

Sir F. Swettenham, recognising this necessity for tempering competition by selection, proposes that the candidates should be required to obtain a nomination by the Secretary of State before examination.[1] This would, however, perpetuate the burden on the patronage department, and the same result might perhaps be attained by a headmaster's certificate as to character and participation in field sports, &c., which, equally with the medical certificate, would be a necessary qualification for the open examination. The patronage department could still give nominations in exceptional cases. Alternatively the task of selection might be entrusted to a Standing Board—possibly a Standing Committee of the Council suggested in the next chapter. It would seem desirable that the subject should be thoroughly examined by an expert committee, with a view to fixing a uniform method of selection, and preliminary training of officers of the non-professional branch of the Civil Service.

The courses of study would in the main be common to all, but special classes would provide for special needs. They could be arranged at the universities, or by such agencies as the London School of Economics, the School of Oriental Languages, Kew, and the Imperial Institute. Since it is desirable that officers should not take up their appointments in the tropics until they are twenty-three years of age, there is ample time for taking a university degree. In the Indian Civil Service selection precedes the university course, and thus an opportunity is afforded for specialised study, which university candidates for the African tropics have missed.

Such a scheme as I suggest would ensure that the existence of these colonial appointments should be widely known in the public schools and universities. The conditions of service in each group of colonies (salaries, leave, pensions, &c.) could be studied by intending candidates. Ignorance of their existence has in the past restricted the list of well-qualified candidates, and inquiries add to the correspondence

[1] 'British Malaya,' p. 339.

entailed on the Colonial Office. The alternative methods are:—

(*a*) A list of special subjects, including those peculiar to any group of colonies, would be advertised. Young men desirous of entering the Tropical Civil Service would specialise in these at a university or elsewhere at their own expense. The Selection Board would be largely influenced by the diplomas obtained.

(*b*) Selection prior to special training, and the payment to the selected candidate of a salary while undergoing it.

Writing in 1903, I pointed out that the French had long had such a school. The course was three years, and the fees £4 per annum. Those who passed the examinations were granted diplomas which qualified them for the public service, and a list was sent to the ministers concerned. The Dutch system appears to be somewhat similar.[1]

It is of essential importance that the British staff, especially on the first inception of an administration, should be adequate for its very onerous duties. The lack of a sufficient staff in the first years of an administration, when the work is heaviest, means that wholly impossible demands are made on a few, at the cost of many lives and injured constitutions, that touch cannot be kept with the native chiefs, and the motives of Government explained, with the inevitable result of outbreaks due primarily to misconceptions and baseless reports. Of this there has been ample evidence, with needless loss of life, both in East and West Africa. Delays in filling appointments for which monetary provision has been made, and for which there was an abundant supply of applicants—as in the early days of Northern Nigeria—is especially deplorable, and has called forth protests from the Press.[2]

[1] Mr Alleyne Ireland states that "since 1864 no one is appointed to an administrative post in the Dutch East Indies who has not passed the grand examination for officials. . . . It covers only the history, geography, ethnology, laws, institutions, and customs of Netherlands India, and the Malay and Javanese languages"—the subjects required being exclusively local.—'Far Eastern Tropics,' p. 183.

[2] "This is a policy of unintelligent parsimony. The question which Ministers have consciously or unconsciously asked themselves is, 'What is the smallest sum with which we can keep things going?' What ought to be asked is, 'What sum is required to establish and maintain an efficient administration, and to put the country as speedily as possible into a position to meet its expenditure from its internal resources?' It is a form of economy which has repeatedly led to disasters which have cost hundreds of thousands to rectify."—'Times,' 1st October 1901.

When urging a more adequate staff for Northern Nigeria (in August 1905) I

On the other hand, it must, of course, be recognised that the staff of a tropical dependency must necessarily be small in comparison with its area and population. A liberal grant-in-aid—by way of loan if otherwise unobtainable—may at first be necessary to supplement the local revenue, which is inevitably very limited until its resources are developed. Large calls are made on that revenue, for the maintenance of troops and police to preserve order and to guard its frontiers. In the absence of railways and roads, the cost of transport for building materials and supplies is unduly heavy. Poor food and bad housing add to the effect of a trying climate, especially in West Africa, and necessitate frequent leave, with a consequential increase of staff to maintain the actual minimum for duty, and a disproportionately large medical staff is required.

Financial considerations therefore reinforce those of policy, and dictate the necessity of ruling through the native rulers themselves, while devoting the efforts of the British staff to making that rule at once effective and humane. This policy, however, takes time to inaugurate.

In West Africa, to supply the vacancies caused by the absence of officers on leave in England, one-third additional staff has hitherto normally been required. But if to this be added the deficiencies due to invalidings, extensions of leave for ill-health, and local absence from duty for the same cause, the proportion actually available for duty is, or certainly was, probably not more than half. In other words, the Revenue must provide for double the British staff required for the efficient conduct of the administration.[1] But it is not only or even primarily a question of cost, even though efficiency depends on meeting that cost. An even more serious aspect lies in the drain thus caused on the young manhood of the Empire.

wrote: "In 1902-3, three years after the inauguration of the administration, the Political department cost £30,545, and collected a revenue of £1250. In 1905-6 it cost £59,089, and collected £69,756, besides carrying out the whole of the administrative and judicial work. The cost was rather less than doubled, the receipts were multiplied by 56."

[1] The committee appointed to consider the desirability of revising the leave and pension rules for West Africa presented its report in March 1920. It is recommended that the normal residential period of service abroad should be from eighteen to twenty-four months, and it should be left to the discretion of the Governor to allow any officer to proceed on leave after twelve months—an extension of the former system in Northern Nigeria, which was afterwards abandoned. A curtailment of the period of leave in England is also recommended, with a grant of local leave, and officers are to be encouraged to take their wives.

Of late years this responsibility has been more fully recognised. Candidates for West African service must be twenty-three years of age, and have to undergo a medical examination before selection. If, as sometimes occurs, the local medical officers attribute the death of an officer to physical causes which ought to have ensured his rejection, the responsibility should be brought home to the officer who "passed" him. It never is. Such cases are not frequent in the Government service, but I am informed that they are comparatively common among the young employees of commercial firms.

In the debate on the Colonial Office Vote, the spokesman of the Colonial Office (Colonel Amery) said that it was the desire of the Secretary of State that married life should be the rule rather than the exception in the Crown colonies and Protectorates.[1] That is the desire of every Governor, but in the conditions of Africa it is difficult to realise. In some instances it would be impossible for a married man, accompanied by his wife, to discharge his duties efficiently, and such instances form no small part of the total—as in the case of District Officers, surveyors, and others, who are constantly travelling, often in districts where a man would hesitate to leave his wife alone in camp, while she would seriously hamper his work if she were by his side. But putting these aside, there remains the serious difficulty in regard to children—inherent in a career in the tropics. Those who are familiar with the conditions of life in India, which the writings of Mr Kipling and Mrs Steel have pictured to the British public, know that even there—where hill-stations with hotels and boarding-houses abound, and there is a large "Society"—the official tied by his work to the plains, and the "grass-widow" in the hills, present conditions of life not altogether attractive.

In the highlands of East Africa the case is, of course, different, and in other parts of tropical Africa we may hope that the reign of law and order on the one hand, and the creation of attractive sanataria in the uplands on the other, will in part at least provide a solution of the difficulty. The advent of heads of commercial firms will tend to facilitate conditions favourable to European family life.

The necessity of proper housing is now recognised, though

[1] Debate of 23rd August 1920.

the war interfered with this in the colonies no less than at home. When I recall the deplorable conditions which existed in 1898 and subsequent years, the measure of progress is striking. British officers in N. Nigeria then lived in temporary grass-huts—not rain-proof, and liable to be carried away by the violent tornadoes of the Niger Valley, and very inferior to the well-thatched mud-walled native house. A year or two later we considered ourselves fortunate when three officers, or five British N.C.O.'s, shared a wooden hut, with a galvanised iron roof, containing three rooms 12 ft. square. But it was long before all were thus accommodated, even at headquarters. The expenditure for the whole civil establishment, "including house-building, vessels, telegraph construction, railway survey, &c.," in the first complete financial year, 1900-1, is given in the official report as £96,407 only! And £35,593 was "saved" from the available funds, pitifully small as they were, "chiefly through the non-appointment of officials till late in the year, more especially the Director of Works, so that the urgent works—houses for staff, &c.—were not begun till towards the close of the year."[1] I recollect that at one time we desisted from retaining the flag at half-mast, which signalled another death, because its frequency had so depressing an effect.

I have served, with short intervals, for forty years in the tropics, mostly in places with the worst climatic reputation, and I think that the appalling death-rate in those early years in West Africa was due not so much to the climate as to the absence of the necessary housing, &c., and that the death-roll would have been hardly appreciably less had we lived in the Thames Valley all the year round in the same conditions of overwork, anxiety, housing, and food.

Looked at from the meanest point of view, it was false economy, for not only was efficiency sacrificed, but heavy expense was incurred by invalidings, and revenue was wasted by the inadequacy of the staff to collect it. It is, as I have already said, a cruel mistake to ask of the early pioneers—at a time of inevitable strain, anxiety, and heavy responsibility, with impaired vitality due to bad housing, unnutritious food, and latent malaria—that they should work incessantly by day and night with the harassing feeling of inability to overtake arrears of importance. Lack of adequate subordi-

[1] Annual Reports, No. 377 of 1901, p. 43.

nate staff, moreover, compels an officer to waste valuable time in trivialities and the maintenance of necessary records, and leaves him insufficient time to deal with essentials. He works on, as a British officer will, over-wrought and losing ground, till his health breaks down, and a new hand has to take his place, with a sacrifice of continuity and efficiency. That is the tale I heard too often in those days.

Much of this mortality and deficiency of staff might have been avoided by an Imperial loan charged against the revenues of the future, if the nation had appreciated the value of the country as Mr Chamberlain did. The Transvaal administration began with a loan of £30,000,000 ; Palestine and Mesopotamia have cost unknown millions—but the whole authorised civil expenditure of Northern Nigeria in the year of its inauguration was £86,000, with a further £50,000 for purchase of worn-out steamers and for buildings ! "If the British nation," I wrote in 1902, "is not prepared to bear the cost of an enterprise which promises good returns, and already shows substantial progress, it were better that it had never undertaken it." [1]

Experience thus acquired has taught the home authorities a better way. Great care is now taken to see to the physical fitness of officers selected, and of those returning to duty. But the chief cause to which the staff owe their improved conditions is the material prosperity of the colonies. The Secretary of State has no longer to persuade the Treasury, and can afford to approve of adequate housing, improved sanitation, and means of recreation, and even to contemplate the creation of a local sanatarium, since the colony, and not the Treasury, pays the cost.

A brief word as to what is needed. The diseases of tropical Africa are comparatively few—blackwater, malaria, dysentery, and anæmia are the principal ones. Lung diseases, enteritis, cholera are rare or unknown among Europeans. We have now in the African tropics a most efficient Medical Service, and, generally speaking, excellent hospitals, with an adequate nursing staff. To the skill of the doctors, and to the improvements they have effected in sanitation, &c., it is due that the returns of deaths and invalidings show such a wonderful decrease. It is time that the Governments in West Africa considered the feasibility of providing a sanatarium in

[1] 'The Making of Nigeria,' Capt. Orr, pp. 77 and 140.

the highlands, where men who are run down and need rest might recuperate. One of the minor worries of African life is the servant—especially the cook—difficulty. The sanatarium should therefore possess an hotel, where a man could stay at a reasonable cost. Various forms of recreation are essential.

It is indeed well worth the while of Government to encourage the formation of recreation clubs at every centre, by providing ground, and even by financial support at their inception. They should soon become self-supporting, under the management of local committees. Polo, tennis, golf, cricket, and even football have each their votaries, and Government might build a racquet (or squash-racquet) court at each large centre, as in India. A club-room, with a library, newspapers, and even a billiard-table, would add much to the amenities of life, and promote healthy intercourse between officials and non-officials.

So much has been written, and such admirable practical results have been obtained by the medical staff, in matters which come within the field of their endeavours, that notes which I had put together some years ago are now quite out of date. A few brief comments—the result of long tropical experience—may, however, be of some use, albeit from a layman. District Officers are not infrequently found to prefer a well-made native hut to a European-built house. It is cool and roomy, and if provided with properly-made doors and windows to exclude wind and rain, it is not unattractive. The preference should, I think, be discouraged. The thatch, though cool, becomes soaked with moisture in the rains, which is driven inwards, through decomposing matter, by the heat of the sun. The mud floor is unhealthy, and, like the roof, favours rats, scorpions, centipedes, white ants, and other unwelcome visitors. The darkness, especially in the apex of the conical roof, harbours mosquitoes. Nor is it an economical policy—apart from questions of health and comfort,—for the annual renewals, added to the compensation allowance, are more costly than the erection of permanent houses.

The style of house best suited to the tropics is a matter of much controversy and prolific experiment. My own view is that houses should, when possible, be built with an upper storey, which should contain the living, and especially the sleeping rooms, the ground-floor being used for dining-rooms, office, and stores. The practice common with commercial firms, of housing their employees in rooms built over produce-stores is, however, to be deprecated, for the effluvia cannot be conducive to health. The tendency to enlarge the verandah, close it in, and use it as the living and sleeping portion of the house, tends to make the interior rooms dark and uninviting. Its light roof is often insufficient protection from the sun. Floors should be covered with linoleum, which is easily washed, and prevents smells and draughts ascending through a boarded floor. The houses should be oriented, so that the sun passing over from end to end, as nearly as may be throughout the year, does not render the front and back verandahs alternately untenable. Windows should be low, and doors half-glazed.

The space between the ceiling and the apex of a sheet-iron roof in the tropics becomes filled with hot air during the day, and ventilators in the ceiling only increase the temperature of the room. Ventilation should be secured by open windows and doors, and by gauze-netting—or gratings in a masonry house—round the outer walls near the ceiling. Tiles are the best and coolest roofing material, and if locally made have been found to be not appreciably more costly than corrugated-iron sheeting, even though the framework of the roof must be strengthened to carry their weight. For wooden houses, corrugated iron or asbestos sheeting (uralite) laid on match-boarding is probably the best. Houses which have only a ground-floor should be raised above the surrounding level. If of wood, they should be built on masonry or iron pillars, 2 ft. from the ground. The eaves should descend to within 5 ft. 6 in. of the floor-level. Pitch-tar or siderothen paint is invaluable for preventing the access of white ants to any part of the wooden structure of a house.

The heat of a house in the tropics is caused, not so much by the direct rays of the sun, as by radiation from the ground. Some therefore prefer to break the back of the roof at the edge of the verandah, and extend it for a few feet, at a very gentle slope, supported by uprights outside the house. Of all vermin in the tropics, the most offensive and insanitary are bats. They will enter a building by incredibly small orifices, and establish themselves in the roof, or between the weather and match-boarding, and their odour is repulsive.

Particular care must therefore be taken to close every crevice, and protect every grating by wire-gauze.

The house should not be surrounded by so many trees as to exclude the breeze and light. Vegetation which harbours mosquitoes should not be allowed near to it. Compounds or gardens should not be too large, and the servants' quarters must be as distant as possible. Township by-laws will regulate the erection of private houses, so that they may conform to a reasonable standard for health and general amenity.

Mosquito-proof sleeping cubicles of copper-gauze are now much in vogue, but they have the disadvantage that mosquitoes which have gained access by the inevitable carelessness of servants are not as easily detected, or dislodged, as in an ordinary mosquito-net. They also exclude the air. Duplicate gauze windows and doors in an ordinary living-room are in my experience excellent. They can be closed in the evening, admit air, and exclude flies as well as mosquitoes, and temper too violent a breeze. Common-sense dictates that dark-coloured clothes which harbour mosquitoes should be kept folded up, and not hung on the walls, and that the mosquito-net should be carefully examined and well tucked in before going to sleep.

The purity of the water-supply—a matter of vital importance to health—is, of course, a question to which the medical staff devotes unremitting attention. There is no need, therefore, for me to dwell here on the desirability of a pipe-borne supply from an uncontaminated source; on the necessity of eliminating native villages from proximity to a stream which supplies the township; of keeping reservoirs stocked with fish, and drawing off the surface water (which contains most larvæ, &c.): of boiling drinking-water and using good filters; of protecting wells by a curb, and using a pump to draw the water; of preventing the sinking of wells near contaminated ground; of detaching pipes from rain-water tanks till the first showers have cleansed the roofs, and allowing feed-pipes to empty into a gauze bucket to prevent the ingress of lizards, &c.—for these are now well-established customs.[1]

[1] A writer in the 'Pioneer Mail' (3rd February 1905) advocates the sterilisation of water by chemicals in preference to filtration or boiling, since the latter are often neglected for lack of vessels or time, and are suitable for stations, but not for troops on the march. Permanganate of potash is not effective. Sulphate of copper has not been fully tested. He advocates the passing through the water of chlorine gas, "liquefied and stored in little cylinders like those used for carbonic

But it may be worth while to mention that in the early years in Northern Nigeria we practically eliminated dysentery from many centres by the use of portable condensers burning wood fuel. These were procured through the Crown agents, and are invaluable in isolated stations with a bad water-supply. They are simple, and can be managed by a native, and transported by two carriers.[1]

The question of the segregation of Europeans and natives is one which merits a word here. We have learnt that malarial germs—and at times those of yellow-fever also—are present in the blood of most natives, especially of native children, and their dark huts and insanitary surroundings foster mosquitoes, by which these diseases are conveyed. Doctors, therefore, urge that Europeans should not sleep in proximity to natives, in order to avoid infection.

We do not go to Africa for our health, and every other consideration must give way to the discharge of duties, which in some cases—such as the headmaster of a school, the keeper of a prison, missionaries, and others—must of necessity render the observance of this rule impossible. But where segregation is compatible with work and duty, commercial firms, no less than the Government, incur a moral responsibility not to expose their employees to infection which can be avoided.

With this object in view, new townships are divided into European and native reservations, separated by a non-residential area 440 yards in breadth, cleared of high grass and scrub. Europeans are not allowed to sleep in the native reservation, and natives, other than domestic servants and other necessary employees, may not reside in the European quarter.

The belt of clear ground which intervenes between the two quarters forms an effective fire-guard from bush-fires, and the conflagrations, so frequent in the dry zone, of the inflammable huts and enclosures of the natives,[2] which also harbour rats and other vermin. It may be used for recreation and parade grounds, railway and public works depart-

acid for soda-water, with a tube attached, liberating only one gramme at a time." The chlorine kills every species of germ in thirty minutes, and by adding sulphate of soda the taste is removed. A 5-lb. cylinder will sterilise 111,944 gallons at a cost of 1d. per 1000 gallons.

[1] Condensed water was discarded in the Philippines as lacking the natural salts. Artesian water was there obtainable.—Elliott, *loc. cit.*, p. 204.

[2] The serious fire which occurred in the Niger Company's premises at Burutu, with a loss of some half-million sterling, due, it is believed, to natives cooking over an open fire, is a case in point.

ment yards, cemeteries, &c., and even for buildings in which Europeans or natives do not sleep, provided that they do not form connecting links for the spread of fire, or resting-places for mosquitoes. They should for this reason never be allowed on the side on which the native reservation is located. In old townships these principles can only be introduced very gradually; and in order to avoid difficulties in the future, much care and foresight must be exercised when granting long leases in places which may eventually expand into a township. Europeans should never be permitted to reside in a native city, or close to but outside a township.

Such in brief is "the policy of segregation" [1] which Lord Milner considers to be desirable no less in the interests of social comfort and convenience than in those of health and sanitation.[2] It is obviously applicable only to large centres of population, and since Europeans and natives must necessarily be in close association during the day-time, it affords at best a very partial safeguard against insect-borne diseases, for which the only real cure is the extermination of the mosquito—or the rats which harbour the plague-flea—alike in the native as in the European quarter, and the isolation of persons suffering from insect-borne diseases.

The policy has given rise to bitter controversy, and the allegation by both British Indians and Africans that it is merely a manifestation of racial arrogance and prejudice.[3] This is, I think, in part due to a misapprehension, in part to an attempt to carry the policy to extremes. On the one hand the policy does not impose any restriction on one race which is not applicable to the other. A European is as strictly prohibited from living in the native reservation, as a native is from living in the European quarter.

[1] The members of the African section of the Manchester Chamber of Commerce declare that they are, "without exception, strongly in favour of the principle of the segregation of Europeans; but they stipulated (*a*) that the area proposed to be assigned to Europeans should be officially declared, and not subject to alteration, with a view to avoiding the erection of buildings which would become useless by a change of boundaries; and (*b*) that there should be no compulsion, and one or more Europeans should be allowed to sleep on the business premises as a guard against burglary."—Letter to Colonial Office, 6th May 1921. The latter proposal is open to the objection that it accords to Europeans an exemption denied to Africans.

[2] Debate of 14th July 1920.

[3] See the presidential address by Mr Jewanjee at the Indian Congress, Mombasa, 11th December 1920, and Indian and African press *passim*.

On the other hand, since this feeling exists, it should in my opinion be made abundantly clear that what is aimed at is a segregation of social standards, and not a segregation of races. The Indian or African gentleman who adopts the higher standard of civilisation and desires to partake in such immunity from infection as segregation may convey, should be as free and welcome to live in the civilised reservation as the European, provided, of course, that he does not bring with him a concourse of followers. The native peasant often shares his hut with his goat, or sheep, or fowls. He loves to drum and dance at night, which deprives the European of sleep. He is sceptical of mosquito theories. "God made the mosquito larvæ," said a Moslem deputation to me; "for God's sake let the larvæ live." For these people sanitary rules are necessary but hateful. They have no desire to abolish segregation.

In order that there may be no legitimate ground for alleging that public money is unduly spent on the "European" quarter, separate rates should be levied in each reservation, and spent wholly on the quarter from which they accrue, while any grant from public revenue to the township should be spent impartially on both.

Improvement in the quality of food in the tropics is a matter of great importance for health and efficiency. Meat (including fowls) is generally tough and tasteless, and, like tinned foods, is deficient in nutritive qualities, while vegetables and fruit (except bananas) are rarely procurable. "Mutton clubs" in India, by feeding the animals well—especially on grain—succeed in producing excellent meat, and the same system can be adopted in Africa, and extended to poultry, and the quality can be improved by crossing with imported stock. Vegetables can be raised in properly-tended gardens under municipal supervision, and sold to Europeans; but raw salads should be avoided in the tropics. Gardens in the dry zone depend on irrigation, which can be effected by raising well-water by windmills. The French have set us an example in the production of garden produce in Africa. "Cold storage" in West Africa, especially in the coast towns, now supplies imported joints, vegetables, and fruit, and is capable of extension to inland centres by railway. Above all, the need of training native cooks is a matter of such importance that it is well worth considering whether cookery classes could not be instituted as a special subject in Government schools. Mrs Ruxton and Mrs Tew have rendered a great service by their admirable books on simple tropical cookery.

Too much emphasis cannot, of course, be laid on the necessity of providing an adequate and well-qualified Medical staff, with specialised training in the splendid schools of Tropical Medicine which now exist in this country for research work. Well-equipped laboratories for local research work—like the Wellcome Institute attached to the Gordon College at Khartum, and the smaller institutions in Nigeria and elsewhere—are doing increasingly valuable work, and demand every encouragement from the local Governments.

It is to Mr Chamberlain's sympathetic foresight that we owe the creation of an adequate Medical Service in the tropics, the inauguration of Tropical Schools of Medicine, and, above all, the institution of hospital nurses. The Colonial Nursing Association, in which Mrs Chamberlain took a very prominent part, was formed in 1896 by private subscription, with the object of supplying trained nurses—a need which, I think, I was one of the first to advocate, for nursing sisters were unknown in Africa during my first eight or ten years' service there. The Gold Coast has recently appointed women doctors for the schools, to combat child diseases and mortality.

The utility of the Medical department can be greatly increased by providing motor-cars or cycles for the doctors, as we found in Nigeria during the war, when the bulk of our medical staff was lent for war work elsewhere. By thus covering long distances, even over the roughest of native roads, they are enabled to save many a life. The story of African development is full of deeds of self-devotion by doctors, who have travelled day and night under almost impossible conditions to save the life of a sick comrade in an isolated and distant post.

It is primarily due to medical research, and to the zeal of medical officers, that the wonderful decrease in mortality among Europeans in West Africa is to be ascribed, though better conditions of life, greater moderation in the use of alcohol, and other causes, have of course had their share in the result.[1] Further decrease will no doubt result from the

[1] Dr Sambon, Lecturer in the London School of Tropical Medicine, in an interesting paper contributed to the Press ('West Africa,' 3rd August 1918), states that 100 years ago the mortality of white troops in West Africa was 1500 per

improvement of sanitary conditions among the natives, and from the discovery of an effective treatment for the great scourges of blackwater fever and sleeping-sickness,—the case mortality of the former has already greatly decreased, and a cure for the latter appears to have been found in the German discovery known as "Bayers 205." The provision of dentists is a further departure of the greatest possible value.

I shall not here discuss at any length the debated question of private practice by medical officers in the Government service. Since there are but a few centres where an income can be made by this means, it is inevitable that there should be heart-burnings and friction in regard to the selection of officers for these posts. The salaries, pension, and promotion of Government medical officers should be sufficiently generous to attract good men, without such extraneous inducements; and if the acceptance of any fee, except as consultant, were disallowed, the field would be left open to private practitioners, and Government medical officers would have more time to devote to research, and to free hospital and dispensary work among the natives.

A few brief words to the newcomer to the tropics, before he has had time to acquire experience, or to benefit from the advice of the doctor, may be of use:—

Wear light flannel next to the skin, and use a cummerbund. Never be separated from your mosquito-net—a small one can be carried on the saddle,—and see that it is well tucked in at night, and that your feet or hands do not lie against it while asleep. Wear some head-covering when under an insufficient roof or in a verandah, and on no account go into the sun without a hat, even for a moment. When marching on foot, wear thick woollen socks and roomy boots. Bathe in warm water. Be moderate in eating and drinking; always eat something before going to work,[1] and eat frequently, but not largely at one time. Eat fresh food, even though unappetising, in preference to tinned food. Obtain all the vege-

mille! The average for the quinquennial period ending 1917 appears to have been 9·87 per mille for the Gold Coast, and 20·44 for Nigeria, in spite of war conditions. Dr Sambon looks forward to the time when the African tropics, like Panama, will be made colonisable by the conquest of parasitic diseases.

[1] Khatib Musa, who for forty years was Imam of the Mosque of Timbuktu, without a single day's illness, attributed his good health to the observance of three rules. "He never slept," he said, "exposed to the night air; he never missed anointing himself at night, and taking a hot bath in the morning; and he never went out without breakfast."—'Tropical Dependency,' p. 126.

tables and fruit you can, but eat sparingly of uncooked salads. Boil all drinking water and milk bought from the natives. Take five grains of quinine daily, preferably in liquid form—tabloids sometimes become so hard that they pass through the system without dissolving. If unavoidably exposed to mosquitoes, take an extra dose on alternate days for ten days. Personally, see to the cleanliness of all cooking utensils by frequent inspection. See that your clothes are not washed in water used for this purpose by natives.

Turning to the native population, we need not be disheartened because, as I have said, the first impact of civilisation has not brought with it all the alleviations and benefits which we had hoped. The discouraging reports of the Belgian Congo Commission,[1] and of the East African Commission,[2] Sir H. Belfield's assertion that the population of the Gold Coast is not increasing,[3] and Sir R. Coryndon's report to the same effect as regards Uganda,[4] will, rightly used, point the way in which our efforts should be directed in the future, no less in the sphere of administrative action than in that of technical research and medical treatment. In the one we shall learn to abstain from interference in the mode of life of the people, leaving them to work on their own land in their own way instead of as hirelings under conditions which do not suit them, or in places far distant from their natural climate and food. In the other, as Dr Sambon says, a very much larger staff is required to achieve adequate results. Vaccination should be more widely extended. Bad water, lack of drains, open cesspools, insanitary customs, such as burial in houses, overcrowding, and absence of sanitation in the cities, cause infant enteritis and dysentery, with an appalling

[1] Constituted under the Congo Charter. It reports a rapid and alarming depopulation, due partly to the spread of indigenous diseases, partly to the advent of hitherto unknown diseases, such as tuberculosis, typhoid, and meningitis, and partly to the increase of immorality and venereal disease. The Administration is making strenuous efforts to cope with these dangers, and has, *inter alia*, introduced a system of training native assistants in up-to-date methods of dealing with five or six special diseases, with periodical "refresher" courses.

[2] The report (p. 29) asserts that 50 % of the native population is relatively incapable of physical exertion, and the infant mortality is appalling.

[3] Cd. 6278, p. 12. The census returns of 1921, however, show an increase of about half a million in the decennial period. There was presumably a considerable under-estimate in 1911.

[4] In several districts statistics show that 33 % of the children are still-born, in others that the population is decreasing—due to venereal disease.—'United Empire,' June 1920, p. 396.

infant mortality. The efforts made through the native administrations by the establishment of dispensaries in the cities, the provision of sanitary gangs (prisoners and others) under expert supervision, of incinerators, and of improved latrines, above all, of venereal hospitals and leper settlements, need to be made on a more extended scale, and with a larger medical staff and trained subordinates who can speak the native languages.

On the other hand, in spite of inadequate resources in the earlier years, we can claim some successes. Loss of life by direct human agencies—tribal war, slave-raiding, witchcraft ordeals, and fetish practices—has been checked by administrative action, while an enthusiastic Medical Service has been established which affords treatment to the people. In Nigeria—which I quote in illustration, solely because I have more personal knowledge of that country than of others—vaccination, at first feared and disliked, is now, generally speaking, popular. The advanced "native administrations," which I shall presently describe, are showing increased appreciation of sanitation, and are establishing dispensaries supported by native funds. They have taken up the cause of the leper outcasts. When I left Nigeria the single asylum in Bornu had 534 lepers, and a venereal hospital had been established. In Sokoto, where leprosy is most rife, there has been a notable decrease, the cause of which is obscure, but probably due to better conditions of life—from 5 per mille in 1910 to 3·7 in 1916, and in the Gando division from 4·2 in 1911 to ·56 ; Illo, 3·14 to 1·14. A similar decrease in the number of blind is reported—from 6 and 7·6 per mille in two districts in 1911 to 1·2 and 1·9 respectively. The injection of chambuga-oil for leprosy appears to promise success, and a definite policy for leper settlements has received legislative sanction.

CHAPTER VIII.

THE HOME GOVERNMENT AND THE DEPENDENCIES.

The demand for reform—The constitution of the Colonial Office—The Secretary of State—The Parliamentary Under-Secretary—The permanent Under-Secretary and staff—The work of the Colonial Office—Results of congestion—Lord Elgin's reorganisation—Relations of the Colonial Office with the colonies—Grounds of dissatisfaction—Intervention by the Office—The Office view—Treasury control—The function of the Colonial Office—Results of the system—Ability of Colonial Office officials—Government by departments—Suggested palliatives—A second Under-Secretary—Sir C. Bruce's scheme—Alternative schemes—Direct responsibility of Under-Secretary—A Director of Protectorates—Committees and Councils—Standing Committees—Councils—The Indian Council—Contrast with the Colonial Secretary.

THERE has been for many years past a consistent complaint that the Colonial Office needs reform and adaptation to modern requirements. Several leading statesmen have foreshadowed changes,[1] and many of the principal newspapers and monthly journals have published articles with the object of demonstrating its deficiencies—its delays, its unnecessary interferences, and what not,—as exemplified in some particular matter or some particular colony ; but few have made any definite constructive proposals, viewing the subject as a whole.

I propose in this chapter to discuss the grounds of some

[1] Lord Selborne and Lord Emmott, both of them former Under-Secretaries at the Colonial Office, may be cited. The former says: "The Colonial Office, excellent as the work of that department has always been within my personal knowledge, has never been modelled to meet the conditions that are growing up in West Africa in the way that the India Office, for instance, was modelled to meet the conditions in India: and I suggest that we are on the eve . . . of political developments in connection with West Africa, as well as commercial developments."—Speech of 14th July 1917.

Lord Emmott says: "There must be, owing to this war, an enormous increase in the responsibilities and work of the Colonial Office, and with this there must be an increase of liberty so far as the colonies and protectorates which are governed by us are concerned."—Speech, July 1919.

of these complaints, and to offer, with much diffidence, some suggestions which may possibly form a basis for discussion and reform.

Through the Press and Reuter the public is made aware of what happens in the most distant colonies, and the Secretary of State is expected by Parliament to be conversant with their affairs almost from day to day. With their growing importance the office of Colonial Secretary has become one of the most important in the State, to be held by a Minister whose position in Parliament and in the Cabinet makes heavy demands on his time, wholly unconnected with the duties of his office. He comes to it generally ignorant of the problems of most, if not all, of the colonies, and holds office for only a brief period. Since Mr Chamberlain's time the average tenure has been only two and a half years.

The Parliamentary Under-Secretary is the representative of the Colonial Office in the House in which the Secretary of State does not sit. He defends the policy of his chief, and answers questions. He vacates his post on a change of Government, and may at any time do so on promotion. The average tenure of the post in the same period has been less than two years. He can call for any papers in the Office and minute upon them, and if so authorised by the Secretary of State, may deal finally in his name with the less important ones. He receives deputations, and acts as chairman of many committees. His energy is usually unbounded, and he forms a link between the department and the public. As most of the questions with which Parliament expects him to be familiar are new to him, his task is no light one; but the business of the Office goes on, whether he participates in it to a greater or a less degree.

The permanent staff of the Colonial Office consists of one Under-Secretary and four Assistant Under-Secretaries of State—one for the Dominions, one as "Accounting Officer," and two for the Crown colonies. The two latter are in charge of the five departments into which the Crown colonies are grouped, for office purposes. Each group is under the charge of a "principal clerk." [1] Papers on all subjects for sub-

[1] See Colonial Office List, pp. xv.-xviii. The latest issue shows the "Accounting Officer" and "Dominions" combined, and the fourth Assistant Under-Secretary as seconded from the India Office for Mesopotamia, Palestine, and Arab areas.

mission to the Secretary of State pass through the permanent Under-Secretary, who is his chief adviser, and acts in his name in any matters to which he is not personally able to attend. He deals with the diverse affairs of a couple of score of Dominions, colonies, protectorates, and Mandate territories; the representations of merchants, shipowners, and mine-owners; Imperial and other conferences and deputations; Parliamentary and Treasury questions; and a thousand other matters. He has, as one of them said to me, no time at all to *think*.

Since the Colonial Office was set up as a separate department in 1825—ninety-six years ago—the post of permanent Under-Secretary has only been held for an aggregate of eighteen years by promotion from the office itself, probably in order that its head may bring to his task a wider view than a lifelong training in the department would secure.

Almost the whole of British tropical Africa is the creation of the past three decades, for prior to 1890 it consisted chiefly of small enclaves on the West Coast. The work of the Colonial Office was, of course, greatly increased when, some fifteen years ago, it took over the control of the African Protectorates from the Foreign Office. From that time to the present day expansion has been extremely rapid, and of late the territory held under Mandate has been added, including Palestine and Mesopotamia.

The increase of work is, however, due not merely, or even primarily, to territorial expansion, but rather to the increasing diversity and complexity of the problems arising from the development of the material resources of these dependencies by railways (which have facilitated the exploitation of vegetable and mineral products, with the consequent influx of merchants and miners), the progress in medical and sanitary methods, the increase in British staff, and to a less degree the problems of native administration. The improvement in ocean and cable services has caused a more rapid turnover of business. Even a dozen years ago it was estimated that the correspondence had already increased four or five times in volume. The expansion of the department of the Crown agents, who transact the purely business requirements of the colonies, is typical. When I joined the Colonial Service they occupied a few rooms on the ground floor in Downing Street, but they now find it necessary to occupy a spacious block of buildings of their own.

It is clear that in these circumstances the Secretary of State must delegate some of his functions, or that all except the most important questions must be dealt with in his name by the permanent officials. It is equally clear that the work devolving upon the permanent Under-Secretary cannot be dealt with by a single man, however able and industrious, and that much must be left to the two assistants. These in turn are compelled to relegate much of their proper work to the clerks in charge of departments, who moreover are called upon to attend many committees, and devote much of their time to the endeavour to condense into minutes and précis for their seniors the contents of despatches on important questions which should be read in original. It is hardly surprising that the result gives rise to much dissatisfaction among the more zealous servants of the Crown in the colonies, the extent of which is probably unknown to the Secretary of State.[1]

In response to a Resolution adopted at the Imperial Conference in May 1907, Lord Elgin "reorganised" the Colonial Office. Under his scheme it was to consist of three departments, styled respectively "the Dominions," "the Crown Colony" (political and administrative), and "the General" Department; the latter included matters common to all the Crown colonies (currency, banking, posts and telegraphs, education, medical, pensions, &c.) The Crown Colony Department was divided into four geographical "Divisions," supplemented by four Standing Committees on patronage and promotion, railway and finance, concessions, and pensions. A single Under-Secretary remained as "the permanent head of the whole Office, and the principal adviser to the Secretary of State." Of the four Assistant Under-Secretaries, two were assigned to the Dominions, and one each to the other two departments.[2] This scheme was later modified in the way I have explained.

The object of this rearrangement was not to lighten the

[1] Sir Charles Bruce writes: "Seventy years ago, Sir H. Taylor, speaking with intimate knowledge from within, declared that the far greater proportion of the duties performed in the Office were performed under no effective responsibility. The whole history of the Office is a record of conflicts with the ablest, and even the most trusted of Governors."—'Broad Stone of Empire,' p. 182.

[2] Cd. 3795, 1907, p. 4.

burden on the Secretary of State and the permanent Under-Secretary by judicious delegation, but primarily to satisfy the Dominions, at whose instance it was undertaken, by assigning to them "a distinct division" of the Office, and facilitating the work of the Conferences. In point of fact, it would seem to have actually increased the congestion in the Crown colony branch, while the senior Assistant Under-Secretary for the Dominions had apparently little to do, and left England for a prolonged tour in them. The time is probably not distant when the Dominions branch at the Colonial Office will be transferred elsewhere.[1]

When Mr Chamberlain took office in 1895, "Downing Street" was not popular. The criticism was, no doubt, chiefly expressed by the self-governing colonies, for the Crown colonies were then even less vocal than now. When he left office a remarkable change had taken place; but it is impossible to talk with senior officials of the different colonies to-day without noting the recrudescence of the critical feeling. The cause of their dissatisfaction may be exaggerated, but it is none the less subversive of that cordial co-operation which should animate the two branches of a service engaged in a common task, for which both are spending themselves freely—not for reward, but for the sake of the work. I trust that in scrutinising the grounds for this dissatisfaction and in venturing to put forward some suggestions, I may be credited with the sole desire to promote the best interests of the Empire.

The dissatisfaction arises, I think, mainly from three alleged causes:—

(*a*) First, that the considered recommendations of the Governor and his expert advisers (which necessarily embody the best local opinion) are overruled in important matters by the senior Colonial Office officials, and in less important matters by juniors, whose decisions are recorded over the lithographed signature of the Secretary of State, against which there is no appeal.

(*b*) Secondly, that the Colonial Office shows an increasing

[1] The task of preparation for the Imperial Conferences is heavy, but the direct work with the Dominions concerns the Premier, the Foreign Office, the War Office, the Admiralty, the India Office, and the Board of Trade, equally with the Colonial Office—viz., treaties with foreign States, defence by sea and land, alien immigration, trade and Imperial preference, emigration, shipping rings, patents, and similar matters.

tendency to interfere in matters of detail in internal administration—an interference which is largely attributed to junior officials,—with consequent delay in those other matters which properly fall within its duties. This delay is prejudicial to the interests of the colonies, and complained of by both officials in the colonies and by business men.

(c) Thirdly that the Colonial Office lacks that element of actual administrative experience which would understand and sympathise with the difficulties of the man on the spot, and that the Secretary of State and his office are out of touch with the local administrations.

There seems to be no doubt that there exists at present a widespread feeling that there is a great deal of unnecessary interference from Whitehall in the sphere of actual administration—which under the Royal Letters Patent is the function of the Governor,—thereby increasing the work of the Colonial Office, while delaying and impeding the task of government in the colonies, and creating unnecessary friction—due, it is alleged, to "the deplorable system of government by junior clerks."

Sir A. Hemming, in a letter to the 'Times,'[1] claims to write with thirty years' experience in the Colonial Office, where he was head of the West African Department, and later as Governor of two Crown colonies. "A great portion of the work," he says, "has been entrusted to junior officials. These men have not and cannot have the experience and knowledge required for such duties, and it is naturally galling to high officials in the colonies to know that their suggestions are criticised by youths almost fresh from school or college, and their mature and well-weighed advice possibly rejected on the recommendation of these embryo statesmen. That the bulk of the work in the Colonial Office is done well and conscientiously I should be the last to deny; but the pressure on the seniors, and especially on the Under-Secretary of State, is too great, and the junior clerks consequently obtain a much larger portion of authority and control than their position properly justifies."[2]

[1] 'Times,' 26th December 1905.

[2] Sir Charles Bruce (who, after long colonial service, was Governor of the Windward Islands and of Mauritius) goes even further. The passage is too long to quote *in extenso.* He argues that the Secretary of State is not informed of all that is going on in his own office, and "must only know what it is good for him to know, . . . the tradition was upheld in the Colonial Office for many years,

The Office, it is said, intervenes in every detail of economic development and of administrative policy. It demands exhaustive reports—involving interminable despatch-writing—on matters often of trivial importance, and its sanction is necessary for unbudgeted expenditure, however petty. Sometimes, says Sir C. Bruce (and I can corroborate it from my own experience), a decision well adapted to the colony in which it was evolved is offered in substitution of carefully-considered proposals, as a solution of a problem where the conditions render it merely "grotesque." Consequential delay and apparent vacillation—perhaps for over a year—before a scheme is eventually carried out with little if any change, is placed by critics to the discredit of the local Government, and is heart-breaking to those on the spot.

That this criticism does not originate merely from the impatience of local officials and "prancing pro-Consuls" may be seen from the opinion expressed in the House of Lords by the late Lord Salisbury: "I do not think," he said, "that our government is of much advantage to the Englishmen who go into a new country. Almost everything that is done at home is apt to hinder them; and though we have officers unparalleled in the world, they come generally with their hands tied to their sides with red tape, and beside them sits the spirit of the Treasury, like care behind the horseman, which paralyses every effort, and casts a shadow on any enthusiasm they may feel. I do not think Governments aid our people much when they go into the possession of a new territory." [1]

The officer selected for the responsible post of Governor, especially when he has acquired long local experience, is

during which grave inconvenience to the public service was caused by circumstances known to every member of the Office except the Secretary of State. . . . The Office must decide to a large extent on what questions they may act without his direct authority under cover of his constitutional responsibility, . . . but the tradition is prolonged into a wider area of activity when the Office claims, as it does, a rigidly exclusive monopoly of access to the Minister either by documentary or personal communication." He explains, with emphasis, that he intends no reflection on the personal ability of the permanent officials, and quotes Sir F. Swettenham's panegyric on the admirable ability and efficiency of their work—the patient care with which each question is examined, and the anxiety to be just in every case,—a description in which I think all who have knowledge will concur. "What was deprecated was a system which placed in the hands of a group of officials, living in the artificial atmosphere of a public office in the centre of the Empire, absolute control over the destinies of communities" living far away.—'Broad Stone of Empire,' pp. 196-99.

[1] House of Lords debate of 14th February 1895.

justified in expecting to be trusted to decide (with the aid, if necessary, of his Legislative and Executive Councils and departmental advisers) such matters as the incremental pay of a foreman of works, the promotion of very junior officers, the engagement of a mechanic on some small increase of pay in special circumstances, the writing off of small sums of public money after full investigation by a committee and revision by the Council, the amount of baggage which an officer may carry free by local rail, or to take appropriate measures in similar questions of a purely administrative and local nature in Africa. Or at most it should suffice to call his attention to any apparent inconsistency, of which the Office may become aware—for it is, of course, well understood that such matters are dealt with by juniors. In some cases it is alleged that the Office has even undertaken the drafting of local ordinances, and drawn up departmental regulations, with the aid of subordinate colonial officers, for the Governor to enact. A case is quoted in which the clerk in charge of a department averred that a particular colony had for years been administered from his room and not by the local Governor.

In larger questions which do reach the Secretary of State, the Governor in Council may find his recommendations overruled, without opportunity of personal explanation. For the advice tendered to the Minister is "the office view," limited by tradition and precedent, and uninformed by personal experience. A strong Secretary of State like Mr Chamberlain (whose office nickname was "Our Master") will exercise an independent judgment so far as time permits of his studying the matter. A weaker, or an overpressed, or less industrious Minister may allow the office view to prevail, and be transmitted to the colony, justified and elaborated by its exponent, over the signature of the Secretary of State, whose decision must be loyally accepted.[1] By the fine tradition of British statesmanship, the mistakes of the permanent officials—if they make any—are accepted by the Secretary of State as his own, to be defended before Parliament with all the influence and ability at his command.

If a protectorate is dependent on a grant, Colonial Office

[1] "Every Secretary of State, however well-intentioned, energetic, and capable, is likely, sooner or later, to become the medium, conscious or unconscious, through which the permanent heads of the Office carry out their policy, . . . able and trusted, but necessarily academic advisers."—Bruce, *loc. cit.*, p. 200.

supervision is supplemented by Treasury control, which, says the 'Times,' "largely consists in interference in technical detail, refusing an extra draughtsman or a subordinate clerk, and generally hampering and exasperating the responsible administrator. It is this form of control in the past that has killed all sense of financial conscience in the public service." The Office then experiences something of the exasperation which its own methods are apt to produce in the local Government, when the responsible Administrator feels inclined to exclaim with Job, "No doubt but ye are the people, and all wisdom shall die with you, but I have understanding as well as you."

That the function of the Colonial Office is not creative or initiative—still less administrative—was a principle affirmed by Mr Chamberlain—a limitation ignored in the public pronouncements of several of his successors. Lord Onslow, his Under-Secretary (than whom the men on the spot have never had a more appreciative and generous supporter), stated that it was Mr Chamberlain's settled policy never to interfere with the decision of the policy of the Governor. All they asked for at the Colonial Office in return was that they should be kept fully informed of what the man on the spot intended to do, and what he advised the Government to do.[1] J. S. Mill thus formulates the principle in regard to India: "The Executive Government of India is, and must be, seated in India itself. The principal function of the Home Government is not to direct the details of administration, but to scrutinise and review the past acts of Indian Governments; to lay down principles and issue general instructions for their future guidance, and to give or refuse sanction to great political measures, which are referred home for approval." The Foreign Office apparently acts on this principle, for a recent

[1] 'African Society's Journal,' March 1907. The distinguishing characteristic of Mr Chamberlain as Colonial Secretary, which rendered possible the great development which took place during his eight years of office, and endeared him to those who served under him, was the trust he placed in his Governors and the latitude he allowed to those in whom he had confidence. The present Secretary of State (Mr Churchill), in his speech at the Corona Club in June 1921, alluded to Mr Chamberlain's success in inspiring co-operation and loyal comradeship, and himself struck the same note. "The Colonial service (he said) must be a self-reliant service, because its representative is constantly confronted with the problems on the spot, and must have the initiative and resolution and the conviction to decide upon the necessary action, and to take it when the decision has to be made. It would not be possible to govern the British Empire from Downing Street, and we do not try."

inquiry regarding the Sudan elicited the response that the Home Government is not concerned with the details of its administration since the country is self-supporting and manages its own affairs, the Home Government being only concerned with such important questions as may be referred to it.

The effect of unnecessary intervention in administrative affairs is to dishearten the higher ranks and to weaken their sense of responsibility, while engendering in the lower ranks a feeling that it is not to the Governor and his Council that they must look, but to an anonymous official at the Colonial Office. Delay and friction are inevitable. It does not suffice to say that these occasions of discontent are exaggerated, or even in some cases fanciful, so long as they exist. If the officials admitted their truth, they would no doubt regard such results as inherent in the discharge of their duties as "watch-dogs"—to quote a term recently used in a public speech by the Under-Secretary (Sir G. Fiddes). Watch-dogs are employed to guard against an enemy, not against a partner in a joint task.

I am anxious to emphasise the fact—as other critics have done—that it is the *system* that is criticised and not the individuals.[1] The individual officials have great experience, and uphold the traditions of a most honourable service. The seniors have grown grey in the study of Colonial affairs. They form an invaluable repository of knowledge and precedent. It would be a crucial mistake to undervalue the benefit of their moderating counsels, and of their influence in preserving continuity and checking hasty changes by a new and inexperienced Governor. That their lifelong training in the Office should leave its mark upon them is inevitable. The guardian of continuity may sometimes be slow to recognise progress and reform, and ignorance of the local conditions may lead to false analogies and misapplication of precedents. But all administrators alike have testified to the conscientious industry and ability and high sense of honour which the officials of the Colonial Office bring to their task, and their desire to do the thing that is just.

It has been said that "Government by Department is the worst of all forms of Government," and it is permissible, alike for the British public and the colonies, to ask whether in the interests of the Empire these high qualities are directed

[1] See footnote, p. 161.

into the best possible channels, and whether the officials should not bear a measure of public responsibility commensurate with the powers they exercise; and to demand that the duties laid on them should be limited to what a man weighted with responsibility can reasonably discharge with efficiency. The public at large knows but little of the administration of the colonies. Even an officer like myself, who has served for twenty years in the highest office abroad, knows so little of the internal organisation and methods of the Colonial Office, that suggestions must of necessity be made with diffidence and reluctance. Officials in harness may not speak, and those who have retired are glad to avoid controversy and seek rest and quiet.

The causes of friction to which I have referred can never be wholly removed. It is inevitable that dependent Governments should chafe at control, and perhaps equally inevitable that supervising departments should exhibit a tendency towards bureaucracy. It is common to every nation and to every department of State. We shall find the same tendencies even in local Governments, where the Executive officer resents Secretariat interference, and is sceptical whether the instructions he receives really emanate from the Governor. I suggest, however, that the objects in view may be facilitated in the following ways:—

1. By duplicating the post of Under-Secretary, and investing these officers with a measure of public responsibility.
2. Possibly by the creation of a Council, or Councils, to assist the Secretary of State in the discharge of his duties.
3. By allowing to Governors a wider discretion, especially in financial matters, with a minimum of interference with their direct responsibility to the Secretary of State.
4. By the delegation of some of the functions and responsibilities of the Secretary of State to Governors-General of groups of Colonies.

The volume of work at the Colonial Office has expanded like a bladder, but it has still to pass through a single narrow neck. It is suggested that there should be two permanent Under-Secretaries, as in the Treasury, mutually independent but acting in close co-operation, with independent access to the Secretary of State. The Office alone can judge how the duties could best be allocated between them. One might, perhaps, deal with the general work of the Office, and control its legal, financial, and other departments, and supervise the Mediterranean colonies with or without the Eastern groups; while the second would deal with the tropical dependencies, especially the large African groups, with or without those in the East and the West Indies. He would supply that closer touch demanded by the merchants interested, and would encourage enterprise, which, it is alleged, under present conditions has sometimes been driven to find other outlets; and he would maintain close personal touch with the Governors and senior colonial officials when in England.[1] This would ensure that all matters, other than mere routine, which were not dealt with by the Secretary of State himself, would at least pass under review of the most responsible officer. The first Under-Secretary would probably be selected from the ranks of the Colonial Office, the second from among the Governors, with actual administrative experience in one or more colonies, and his tenure of the appointment might be limited to the period for which a Governorship is usually held (five or six years), though renewable at the discretion of the Secretary of State if he proved especially suited to the post, in order that accumulated experience might be available. Under such a régime, Governors would feel that their difficulties were in the hands of a man who could appreciate them from his own experience. There would thus be two well-organised channels of communication with the Secretary of State, each under responsible and experienced officers, with time to deal adequately with the various questions, and to review the minutes of juniors.[2]

The appointment of a second Under-Secretary is preferable

[1] This suggestion was made by me to the Secretary of State in 1904. It was also made by Colonel Amery, writing in January 1908.—'Union and Strength,' p. 283, and the 'Times,' 29th April 1908. The transfer to the Colonial Office of Mesopotamia, Palestine, Aden, and "Arab areas," which has been announced since these pages were written, would suggest the provision of a third Under-Secretary for the Eastern and Far Eastern dependencies.

[2] The existing system is thus trenchantly described by an "outside observer" (of whose identity I am unaware) in the 'Times' of 28th August 1917: "The permanent Under-Secretary is frankly and undisguisedly head of the whole concern; his ability, his familiarity with precedents, his devotion to public interests, are all unquestioned. But his education has been purely literary, he has sat in the office since he left the university, . . . in a word, he is an official and not a practical man." The functions of the political head of a Government department, he argues, seem to resemble fairly closely those of the chairman of a company—"but in a Government department there is no general manager, no man that is trained in the actual practical conduct of business."

to the alternative of each assistant Under-Secretary dealing direct with the Secretary of State, for this would result in "water-tight compartments," tend to divergence and lack of co-ordination, and render the position of the Under-Secretary anomalous and indeed impossible.

Sir C. Bruce suggests a division into "two branches, one dealing with questions of politics and administration, the other with the development of the material resources of the colonies." The latter, he considers, lies "altogether outside the competence of the officials of the Colonial Office," and must be manned by men of the first scientific attainments. "Such an organisation," he adds, "would, of course, have to be carried out in detail, so as to put an end to the deplorable but apparently admitted system of government by junior clerks."[1] Those who have intimate inside knowledge can best decide whether such proposals are practicable from the Colonial Office standpoint; but if the administrative affairs of each colony are to be dealt with by one branch, and its material development in another, it can easily be imagined that there would be many occasions for overlapping, duplication, and friction. Moreover, the consequential amalgamation of the Colonial Office and the Crown agents would constitute a somewhat unwieldy machine, and the system proposed would probably result in a tendency to centralise administration in Colonial Office experts, and to usurp the duties and functions of the local Government. This is opposed to the spirit of the times, and imposes on the Colonial Office a rôle of direct administration which, as Mr Chamberlain said, is not its proper function.

Others have pointed out that the present organisation on a purely geographical basis postulates a competency in the officials of each section to criticise alike administration, finance, currency, railways, harbours, commercial questions, and every other problem of Government. The knowledge of each of these subjects displayed by officials is, they admit, surprisingly large, but it is purely critical and local. They suggest that an organisation according to subjects (though naturally subdivided geographically) on the lines of the War Office and Admiralty would produce "greater uniformity of policy, and a more helpful, active, and less purely critical attitude." They would amalgamate

[1] *Loc. cit.*, pp. 187-188.

the Crown Agent's Office with the Colonial Office, and the former would supply several of the branches. These might consist of administration, finance (including loans and currency), and public works and development branches, the heads sitting together as a Colonial Office Departmental Council.

But though the appointment of a second Under-Secretary would lighten the work of the present head of the Office, it would not relieve the Secretary of State. His constitutional responsibility at present necessitates the use of his signature on every despatch, however routine and trivial, and its lithographed reproduction is evidence of how farcical its use has become. Would it not be feasible to introduce a measure of decentralisation by allowing the two permanent Under-Secretaries to deal, over their own signatures, with correspondence which does not demand reference to the Secretary of State? For, as I said in chapter iv., decentralisation and delegation must be accompanied by public responsibility. The exercise of power without personal and public responsibility is the weakness of the present system. The anonymity conferred by the use of the lithographed signature, and even the time-honoured fiction of being "directed to say that the matter has received the consideration of the Secretary of State," would disappear. The responsibility for that large class of correspondence, which it is well understood that the Secretary of State has never seen, would then frankly rest on the Under-Secretary, while mere routine papers could be signed by an Assistant Under-Secretary, and addressed to the Chief Secretary of the colony. If in any rare instance the Governor considered that a matter dealt with by the Under-Secretary should be laid before the Secretary of State, he would be at liberty to ask that this should be done.

It may be argued that the Governor, as the King's representative, should take his instructions only from the King's Minister, and that the Under-Secretary is not his senior in rank and dignity. He would, however, be the delegate of the Minister (who is not himself a delegate but the representative of King and Parliament). In order to make this clear, and to avoid over-sensitive susceptibilities, the use of the first person might be avoided, and despatches (as in the Army) be signed "By Order." This proposal may appear to be of small moment, but I am convinced it would have a far-reaching effect.

When the Foreign Office controlled the greater part of British tropical Africa, the post of "Director of African Protectorates" was created. His duties included personal visits to Africa.[1] Were a second Under-Secretary appointed at the Colonial Office, it might be possible for him to make such occasional visits. It would, however, be necessary that his position *vis-à-vis* the Governor should be most clearly defined, in order to maintain that unchallenged responsibility of the King's representative abroad which, as we have seen, is "the basis of Crown colony Government." The object of his visit would be to study at first hand, with the friendly aid of the Governor, the local problems which could only be inadequately described in despatches, more especially in their relation to contiguous colonies and to the expressed views of the Secretary of State. He would explain what is being done in other colonies, and the opinion of the Secretary of State. He would not pose as one authorised to give orders or instructions, nor even as an adviser or critic, but as a learner. He would not advise or give pledges to either officials, unofficials, or native chiefs, or even interview them, except with the concurrence and generally in the presence of the Governor. Coming with the sole desire to acquire full information, with the object of making himself more efficient and his advice of greater value to the Secretary of State, his visits should prove very useful. If, on the other hand, he made any attempt "to go behind the Governor," to pose as a higher authority, or to collect *ex parte* evidence to support his own theories, he would probably find that the best informed were also the most loyal, and his information would be unreliable. I do not minimise the delicacy of such a task, and I recognise that its utility is open to question unless it is discharged with the utmost tact.

Mr Chamberlain even desired that the Secretary of State should himself visit the colonies, and did actually go to South Africa; while Mr Churchill, as Parliamentary Under-Secretary, visited East Africa. In practice, however, this is not generally feasible, and even were it possible, the information thus acquired is lost on a change of Government. The

[1] According to Mr Colquhoun, the French in 1908 were considering a scheme by which a council of experienced officials in Paris, aided by a body of inspectors (who were frequently to visit and report on the colonies), would be responsible for colonial affairs.—'Morning Post,' 18th April 1908. Sir F. Swettenham advocates this system.—'Malaya,' p. 340.

knowledge gained by a permanent Under-Secretary would be at the service of successive Secretaries of State.

The advocates of the system of Colonial Office reorganisation on War Office and Admiralty lines, which I have described in a previous paragraph, would carry their analogy further, and appoint an Inspector-General with a regular staff of subordinates, competent to inspect in each branch, and they express the view that such an organisation would strengthen the hands of a competent Governor. I think that there is little doubt but that the opposite would happen, and the Colonial Office would look to the Inspector-General rather than to the Governor, whose position would be almost untenable. It is essential to remember that the War Office and Admiralty are responsible for the direct administration of every detail of the Army and Navy. For the Colonial Office to assume such a rôle would be contrary to the traditions of the Empire, and I believe fatal to its prosperity.

My second suggestion referred to the creation of a Council. It is obviously desirable that the Secretary of State—and also the Under-Secretaries—should have the best independent advice on matters of policy, especially when they concern more than one colony. Such advice may be obtained by means of *ad hoc* committees—appointed with definite terms of reference to inquire into some particular matter, and to take evidence from all available sources—or by Standing Advisory Committees, or by a permanent Statutory Council.

The Standing Committee is usually concerned with a technical subject, such as medical and sanitary matters, surveys, &c., and consists of experts whose opinion must carry the greatest possible weight. Such committees, however, have serious drawbacks, and are not always satisfactory in operation, either to the Secretary of State or to the local Governments, of whose special and varying conditions they rarely have first-hand knowledge. They make large demands on the time of the permanent officials deputed to attend them as members or secretaries.

Once appointed, they are apt gradually to acquire powers not originally intended. A member of one of them remarked to me on the tendency shown to deal with matters of local and minor detail, thus usurping the functions and duties of the departmental heads, who may occupy seats on the Colonial Executive and Legislative Councils, and be in close touch with the Government policy. Subordinate officers are apt to look to the Committee rather than to their own departmental chief or Governor—especially if promotion depends on its recommendation. Lack of identity with the colony in which they are serving, and departmental indiscipline, are the results.

But perhaps an even more serious and inherent defect is that a committee of experts, without financial responsibility for the execution of their proposals, is almost bound by professional zeal to recommend counsels of perfection. "The tyranny of the expert" is the bugbear of the administrator, who has to balance the comparative urgency of many competing claims when framing his budget.

"Government by Committee" shares with "Government by Departments" the distinction of being dubbed the worst of all possible forms of Government, and it was probably to such Standing Committees that Mr Bonar Law referred in his speech in the House on 15th and 22nd April 1915, when he expressed, amid cheers, his disbelief in committees. "If you wish to get something done, do not set up a committee, but tell somebody to do it, and entrust him with it. . . . All business must be done by an autocrat more or less. It could never be effectively done in any other way."

A Council is a Statutory Standing Committee, and in some ways shares its defects. Its object is to place at the disposal of the Secretary of State the assistance of men of ripe experience, and sufficient leisure to study the problems presented to them. It may, like "the India Council," exercise important statutory functions, both in regard to legislation and finance, or it may be purely advisory.

The India Office is the only department of State to which we can turn for a working example of a Statutory Council, for the Boards of Trade, and of Agriculture, and the Local Government Board, in spite of their titles, possess no Boards. The Army Council and the Admiralty Board afford little or no analogy, for they are, as I have pointed out, the actual working heads of the Army and Navy, and they are not like the India Office, concerned with the administration of territories under their own local Governments overseas.

The "Council of India" is the descendant of the old East India Company's "Board of Control," and inherited some of its powers. It is the prototype of the Executive Council of the Governor of a colony. All orders emanated from the "Secretary of State in Council," thus establishing the principle of Executive control "in Council" as opposed to individual autocracy. "It was a consultative body without any power of initiative, and a very limited power of veto," but its consent was necessary in financial and some other matters.

Under Lord Morley its powers were greatly restricted, and what one Liberal statesman had begun, his successors, Lord Crewe and Mr Montagu, endeavoured to complete. By the Council of India Bill of 1914 (which was shelved by the war) the Secretary of State was empowered to transact business with the aid of individual members; and Lord Crewe's Committee (9th July 1919) recommended its abolition, and the substitution of a purely Advisory Council in its place, in order "to establish the individual responsibility of the Secretary of State to Parliament"—in other words, complete autocracy.

Thus the history of the India Council is that of a body vested originally with powers which curtailed those of the Secretary of State; of the efforts of the latter to free himself from these restraints, at first by ignoring and evading the Council, and finally by abolishing its powers altogether and retaining it only as an advisory body.[1]

The Secretary of State for the Colonies, on the other hand, exercises a practically unfettered control, alike over the legislation and the finances of the majority of the colonies. He can, if need be, instruct the Governor to pass a law with the aid of his official majority. He can disapprove any item in the annual budgets, which, though passed by the local legislatures, require his final approval.

The story of the India Council shows how strong is the modern tendency towards bureaucracy under the guise of "the undivided responsibility of the Secretary of State to Parliament"—at a time when the control of either Parliament or the Cabinet has dwindled to vanishing-point. It is idle, therefore, to discuss whether the Colonial Secretary's functions could be better discharged in the interests of the Empire, if he had to act as "Secretary of State in Council"

[1] See Ilbert, 'Government of India,' p. 112 *et seq.* Also the 'Times' of 29th June 1914 and of 10th July 1919, where the later history of the India Council is admirably summarised.

under the statutory restraints imposed on the Secretary for India for the last half-century. It would wholly depend on the individuality of the Secretary of State. A beneficent autocracy has much to commend it if the autocrat is sympathetic, industrious, and has time to devote to his duties. On the other hand, it may be doubted whether an Executive Council of this kind would lighten those duties. It would no doubt completely alter the position of the permanent Under-Secretary, who could no longer be "frankly and undisguisedly head of the whole concern."

CHAPTER IX.

THE HOME GOVERNMENT AND THE DEPENDENCIES.
(*Continued.*)

An African Council: Its functions; its constitution; its procedure—Wider latitude to Governors—Grouping of colonies—Position of Governor-General—Governor-General's Council—Advantages of federation—The French system—Summary of suggestions—Personal touch with the Secretary of State—With the Under-Secretary—Interchange of officers—Juniors—Seniors—Commercial intelligence—Cost of the Colonial Office—Crown colonies without means of expression.

If the principle of an Advisory Council were adopted at the Colonial Office, it would probably be recognised that the Secretary of State would require separate Councils to deal with groups of colonies with such widely dissimilar conditions as the Far Eastern, the Mediterranean, and the West Indian on the one hand—all of which are colonies with constitutions more or less advanced—and the group of African dependencies on the other hand. But whether there be a single council or two is immaterial, for their duties and functions would, I assume, be practically identical. It is sufficient to deal here with an African Council for tropical Africa lying between the Union in the south and Egypt in the north.[1]

The object of the Council would be to place at the disposal of the Secretary of State and the Under-Secretaries the experience, independent judgment, and local knowledge of men who had held office as Governor, and of others who had

[1] I suggested such a Council as long ago as 1893 (see 'Our East African Empire,' vol. ii. p. 658), and later in fuller detail to the Secretary of State. It has also been advocated by Sir A. Sharpe, Sir C. Bruce, and others. On the other hand, Mr Chamberlain, in 1901, dissented from its creation at that time, and preferred appointing a powerful commission to proceed to West Africa and report.—(Speech to Liverpool deputation. See Annual Report of Chamber for 1901.) The Liverpool merchants have consistently supported the proposal up to the present day.—See also 'Morning Post,' 18/7/1898.

special experience of its material problems, thus serving the same useful purpose as the India Council, without fettering the authority of the Secretary of State. As an official body it should not attempt "to make its voice heard, and to promote a continuous and well-informed interest in Africa," as suggested by the 'United Empire Journal,' for that is the sphere of an independent public body. Its advice would be confined to matters referred to it for report. These would embrace most of the really important questions, to the exclusion of those which are concerned with local administration, and lie outside the sphere of Colonial Office intervention. It might review and co-ordinate the policy underlying important legislation, and report on large schemes of development, changes in scales of emoluments affecting more than one colony, new methods of raising revenue which differ from those in contiguous colonies, and similar questions. It might, perhaps, with the consent of the President, discuss and make recommendations on matters laid before it by its unofficial members; and if so invited by the Secretary of State, it might submit suggestions for filling vacancies in the highest grades. It might even assist a local Government in the solution of a problem, by affording it information as to how a similar matter had been dealt with in another colony or in India. It might sift the accusations of philanthropic bodies, and hold the balance between them and the merchants and settlers.

The permanent Under-Secretary for the African dependencies (if that post were created) would preside, and the Assistant Under-Secretary would be a member. Two seats might be filled by Governors who had retired within the five preceding years, and in spite of the objection that officers if appointed while still in the service would be fettered in the expression of their opinions, I think that a seat might be given to an officer who had held office as Governor and had not yet retired. The knowledge he would acquire of the reasons which dictate the policy of the Secretary of State, the point of view of the merchants, and the way in which various problems of administration were being dealt with in different colonies, would be of great value to the colony (or group of colonies) he subsequently administered, while his local and up-to-date knowledge would be most useful to the Council. These three members would be appointed by the

Secretary of State, and would retain their seats for, say, five years, and be eligible for reappointment. If the system of grouping colonies, to which I shall presently refer, were adopted, the Governors-General should, I suggest, be *ex-officio* members of Council while in England, or at least attend its meetings.

In addition to the five official and salaried members there should, I suggest, be three unofficial members without salary. Representation on the permanent Council would no doubt be welcomed by the African sections of the London, Manchester, and Liverpool Chambers of Commerce, in lieu of the conferences held three or four times a year at the Colonial Office.[1] The object of these meetings was to afford information to the merchant, and not to frame recommendations to the Secretary of State.

All matters discussed by the Council would be regarded as confidential. The members would be brought into close working relations with the high officials of the Colonial Office, and benefit by their accumulated experience. A member of Parliament who had shown special interest in colonial affairs might on occasion be invited to attend meetings of the Council. A secretary would be provided to record proceedings, and the cost of the Council would be distributed between the several African dependencies.

Business, it is suggested, could be transacted partly by meetings and partly by written minutes. The former are useful when it is desired to hear the evidence of experts, or when the attendance of any Governor on leave is desired. When the problem is complex and controversial, involving reference to many documents, the best result will, however, probably be obtained by written minutes, after a short preliminary discussion. By this method the inherent defect of committees is to some extent avoided—viz., that the most fluent and argumentative members monopolise the discussion, and there is a difficulty in arriving at definite conclusions.

[1] Miss Kingsley, in an address to the Manchester Chamber of Commerce, in which she denounced the "Crown colony system" in very trenchant terms, advocated in its place an African Council composed entirely of the "trade-lords" who had pecuniary interests in West Africa, whether they had resided in the country or not. The German African Council appears to have consisted of twelve merchants. It seems unnecessary to discuss at length why it would be unwise for those members to predominate in the Council, whose advice, however disinterested, might be condemned by the ill-informed as biassed by personal interests, and who would have had no actual experience of administration.

Incidentally the time of the President (the permanent Under-Secretary), who has little to spare, would be saved.

A clearly-worded "reference" would be circulated to each member with the papers on the subject. He would briefly record his opinion, with the least possible delay, on the definite points raised, and the reasons on which it is based. If the opinions are divergent, a copy of them would be sent simultaneously to each member, who, with the opinions of his colleagues before him—which may modify his earlier view—would record his conclusion as though the final decision lay with himself. The members would be men who have had to deal with committee reports, and to base a decision on some degree of compromise, and on the particular weight which they attach to each recorded opinion. Sir A. Fraser told me that in his experience as Lieut.-Governor of Bengal this method had hardly ever failed to produce a unanimous conclusion. The Council minutes will form valuable records.

The Council would have no direct dealings with local Governments. Its object would be to bring together the heads of the service at home and representative men with administrative experience, with a view to mutual understanding and co-operation, and in order that their combined advice, together with that of representatives of commerce, might be at the disposal of the Secretary of State whenever he requires it, and he could use it or not in Parliament as he might desire. Such a Council would afford a means of retaining a lien on the services of men with a specialised knowledge, and the limit fixed for their appointment (though renewable) would enable the Secretary of State to dispense with their services, without appearing to undervalue them, when by reason of age, or of changes brought by time, they were no longer of the same value. Outstanding instances of specialists whose minds were stored with knowledge both accumulated and secret, and who knew more of particular and exceptionally complex situations than any other living authority, may be found in Sir John Kirk (East Africa and Zanzibar and African treaties, &c.), Lord Cromer (Egypt), and Sir John Jordan (China).

These suggestions are based on the assumption that the Council would be constituted on the model of the India Council (but without its very limited restrictive powers)—viz., that it would consist of men of weight and experience to assist the Secretary of State with their advice. I have, however, referred to the suggestion of a Council of a purely departmental type, consisting of the heads of different branches in the Colonial Office, on the War Office and Admiralty model. Such a Board would not be incompatible with the larger Advisory Council which I have discussed.

My third suggestion raises the question whether it is possible for the Secretary of State to entrust to a Governor a larger share of the responsibility which they divide between them for the administration of a British colony, without divesting himself of that ministerial responsibility which, as Sir W. Laurier, speaking of the Dominions, so emphatically insisted that it is necessary to maintain.[1] The Government of India Act claims to have set a precedent in this direction, by delegating large powers to the Viceroy and his Council which had hitherto been reserved to the India Office and the Secretary of State.

We have already seen that this principle was carried further by Mr Chamberlain than by any other Colonial Secretary, and it earned for him a devotion which no other has enjoyed in a like degree. Nor has any one been found to deny that it was justified in its results by the progress achieved during his tenure of office. Lord Milner has shown the same broad-minded statesmanship and desire to grant a larger measure of self-government. The stronger and more capable the ruler, whether he be the Secretary of State at home or the Governor abroad, the more ready he is to trust his subordinates, and to encourage their initiative, when he has satisfied himself that the trust will not be misplaced. "The tendency, however, to-day," says the 'Times,' "is to increase the numbers and the powers of the centralised bureaucracies, and to decrease the staffs and the independence of the local administrations."[2] Colonial Governors of acknowledged ability, such as Sir F. Swettenham and Sir Charles Eliot, when they had left the service and were free to speak, have urged the desirability of greater latitude to the local administrator.[3]

I have in a previous paragraph indicated how trivial are many of the matters on which a Governor is criticised, or regarding which his discretion is fettered. Nor does there

[1] Cd. 3795 of 1907, pp. 5 and 6. [2] 'Times,' 19th June 1920.
[3] 'East African Protectorate,' Sir C. Eliot, p. 204. 'Malaya,' Sir F. Swettenham, p. 340.

appear to be any discrimination between a Governor of long standing and experience administering an important colony, and one newly appointed to a minor post. Both alike are controlled by rigid regulations, some of which seem very inappropriate to the circumstances of a "first-class" colony.[1] I should weary my reader were I to go into details: it suffices to refer to the sanctions required for writing off petty losses —though investigated by committees and by the Governor and his Council—and for incurring petty expenditure, and the inconvenience caused by delay in approving the annual budget while Colonial Office clerks elaborate detailed criticisms of petty items.[2]

The principle of graduated responsibility would find appropriate expression if the colonies—or some of them—were formed into groups under Governors-General, and wider powers might, it is suggested, be conferred on the experienced and trusted officers, who would be selected for these responsible posts. The burden of the Secretary of State and his advisers would be proportionately reduced.[3]

I have in chapter v. discussed the advantage of *amalgamating* contiguous colonies, from the point of view of internal administration and economic development. The grouping or *federation* of colonies under a Governor-General (which was suggested by me to the Secretary of State in 1907) is an entirely different matter. For this purpose colonies need not have co-terminous frontiers, or forfeit their separate identity. The object is twofold: to promote some uniformity of policy among colonies with common economic conditions, and more or less identical problems of administration; and to relieve the pressure of work at home by decreasing the number of units, and increasing the powers and responsibilities of the high official selected to control each group. Some measure

[1] Sir F. Swettenham, *loc. cit.*

[2] The East African Economic Commission, 1919, is emphatic that there should be no Colonial Office interference except where Imperial interests are affected. They stigmatise Crown Colony government as "an autocracy disguised as constitutional government"—and hence indefensible. Their very sweeping proposals must of course be taken to refer to a colony such as Kenya, with a large and educated British unofficial population.

[3] Mr Churchill, speaking in Manchester so long ago as December 1906, expressed the view that "the day is not far distant when we shall be forced to embark upon a great scheme of amalgamating all our West African Colonies under a common organisation and control." He has more recently, as Secretary of State, expressed the view that the East African dependencies should as soon as possible be combined as an homologous unit.

of cohesion is advantageous, as, for example, the interchange of officials—in such varying degree as may be feasible, looking to diversity of native languages and conditions in the component colonies,—the training of native subordinates, a common penal code, a uniform coinage, and to such an extent as may be possible, uniformity in tariffs, mining laws, and other legislation affecting economic development. Some uniformity may also be possible in conditions of service and rates of pay for the Civil Service. Each unit would retain its own financial independence under its own Governor, though it may, as in the French system, be desirable that each should contribute, proportionately to its revenue, to a common fund for large works whose utility is shared by all. At present even contiguous colonies have no means of knowing what is being done by their neighbour.

It would be premature to enter here into a detailed forecast of the functions of the Governor-General, and the powers he might exercise without invading the ministerial responsibility of the Secretary of State, or unduly curtailing those of the Governors administering each unit. It would largely depend on the size of the groups, and is a matter which would require very careful consideration, and might well form a subject of reference to such a Council as I have suggested. Generally speaking, the more important legislation in each unit would be approved if not actually initiated—subject, of course, to disallowance by the Crown through the Secretary of State—by the Governor-General, with a view to preserving a measure of uniformity, and of identical policy, especially in such matters as native administration and railway construction.[1] The budgets of each would be scrutinised and approved by him, subject (if considered necessary) to the covering consent of the Secretary of State. The disposal of the common fund for public works shared by all, and the equalising of the incidence of the cost of military forces for frontier defence, would rest in his hands. The imposition of new taxation, and the inception of military operations, would be subject to his concurrence—advised in all matters by his Council. He alone would address the Secretary of State, but routine correspondence, as I have suggested,

[1] The High Commissioner of South Africa assents to all legislation in the Chartered Company's territories (Northern and Southern Rhodesia), and in the three widely separated Protectorates under his control,—Swazi, Basuto, and Bechuanaland.

would be conducted between the Governors and the Under-Secretary.

The "spot" over which he would exercise control would be so large, and its units might be so widely separated, that it would make little difference to any particular one whether he was within or beyond the ambit of his territorial jurisdiction, and his instructions to his Governors should operate wherever he may be. He would probably need no deputy to act in his absence from headquarters, for the officer administering each unit would have ample powers to take whatever immediate action might be required.[1]

Governors of units, with a few other high officials, would form a Council, as in the French colonies, meeting once a year for discussion, and at other times if summoned by the Governor-General. It has been suggested that the Council should consist of "Ministers" for industries, education, communications, &c. Though some of the high officials, such as the Judge of the Appeal Court, the commandant of troops, &c., would no doubt reside with the Governor-General at the capital of the principal colony, and be available as a subordinate Council if desired, the appointment of Ministers controlling the departments of the different colonies, and forming an Administrative Council, would probably be premature in the conditions of Africa, and would interfere with the functions of the Governors and the independence of the colonies, and tend rather to amalgamation than to federation. Sir H. Johnston suggests that each group should have its own agency in London to look after its own material requirements and commerce.[2] So far, however, as the principle of federation is concerned, there is no need to supersede the Crown agents.

Such a system of federation of contiguous dependencies could not, I think, fail to advance their material prosperity. It would also, as I have pointed out, enable the Secretary of State to delegate enlarged powers to the Governor-General, and by reducing the number of units for which the Colonial Office is responsible, would lighten his task. The proposal follows in principle the analogy of the existing Appeal Courts in

[1] A French writer (Mons. P. Millet) suggests that the British and French Governors-General should meet regularly and discuss problems of common interest—the use of ports, railways, and telegraphs, &c.—with a view to closer co-operation. This would tend to eliminate causes of friction and difficulties which are often due to exaggerated or false native reports.

[2] 'The African World,' 17th August 1918.

the East and West, and it is interesting to note that it received support from the Under-Secretary, when moving the second reading of the West India Appeal Court Bill on 30th July 1920.[1]

East and West Africa form two convenient groups, though if the Sudan and Northern Rhodesia be included, the East African group might, temporarily at least, be divided into two.[2] Southern Rhodesia belongs to the South African group, whether included in the Union or not.[3]

The French system in West Africa has been described, says the official White Book, by an American writer as the best and simplest in the world, and by French writers as a model of efficiency. It is claimed that in actual results it has transformed the French colonies from a costly incubus into prosperous and self-supporting possessions. It is therefore worth while to describe the system very briefly.[4]

[1] A single Appeal Court for East Africa, Uganda, and Nyasaland was set up by Order in Council of 15th February 1909. The "Full" Supreme Courts of Nigeria and the Gold Coast constitute a Court of Appeal for those colonies.

[2] The question of federating the various units in East Africa under a "Viceroy" has of late (July 1920) been brought into prominence by a motion by Lord Islington in the House of Lords, and in letters to the 'Times' from Sir T. Morison (July 21, 1920) and others, who dwell on the similarity of their problems, and the dissimilarity of the methods at present employed in their solution.

In round figures the whole of British West Africa would aggregate about 490,000 square miles, with a population of some 21,900,000. The whole of East Africa (including the Mandated Tanganyika Territory, the Sudan, and Northern Rhodesia) would cover about 2,140,000 square miles (twice the size of British India), with a population of 16,000,000. Were this divided into two, the southern group might include the Mandate territory, Nyasaland, and Northern Rhodesia, with an area of about 695,600 square miles, and a population of 6,000,000. The remaining units, with an area of about 1,444,200 square miles (including the great deserts of the Sudan), would have a population of 10,122,000. (See Table, p. 45.)

[3] Since these pages were written, an apparently authoritative announcement has appeared in the 'Times' (14th September 1921), that the Secretary of State (Mr Churchill) "is engaged in an important scheme for the reorganisation of the administration of the Crown colonies and protectorates, designed to give them among other things a greater amount of autonomy." The pronouncement has received no official confirmation, and cannot therefore be treated as accurately indicating Mr Churchill's intentions, but it is interesting to note the statement that "the main proposals are the grouping of the various colonies according to their geographical position under High Commissioners, to whose shoulders will be transferred some of the duties and responsibilities—especially in the way of public appointments and concerning financial problems—which now devolve on the Secretary of State." Each High Commissioner, it is said, will be assisted by a council, partly elected and partly nominated, and will have control of Imperial forces, naval and military, within his jurisdiction.

[4] See Foreign Office Handbook, No. 100 of 1920, and I.D.W.O. Memos. of October 1902 and October 1904. The trade of the French West African Colonies is stated to have increased from 66,200,000 francs in 1893 to 299,900,000 francs in 1913 (imports calculated on value in Africa, exports on value at destination). —'What every Frenchman ought to know of French Occidental Africa,' by G. Francois. See 'West Africa,' 9/8/19.

The French possessions in West Africa are placed under two Governors-General. One, with headquarters at Dakar, controls those which comprise "French West Africa"—viz., Senegal, Guinea, the Ivory Coast, Dahomey, Upper Senegal and Niger, Togo and Mauretania—an area of over 1,822,000 square miles and a population of nearly 12,000,000. The other, with headquarters at Brazzaville, controls "French Equatorial Africa"—viz., the Gabun, the Congo, Ubanghi-Shari, and Cameruns (late German).

Taking the former in illustration of the system, we find that as long ago as 1895 the necessity for co-ordination by a Governor-General was recognised; but it was not until the Anglo-French Convention of 1898, and the declaration of 1899 had enabled her to link up the various colonies, that M. Decrais in the latter year was able to procure the decree which gave effect to the new system. It was elaborated and completed by later decrees of 1st October 1902, and finally that of 18th October 1904. The powers of the home Government are in a large measure entrusted to the Governor-General, who exercises a more real control than can be exerted from France. Subject to the decrees and laws made by the President and Chamber, he exercises wide powers—often tantamount to legislation—by means of "*arrêtés.*" He appoints all but the most senior officials, and those of the Treasury—and these he recommends. All correspondence with the home Government must pass through him. It is his duty to survey French policy as a whole, and co-ordinate the activities of the different colonies. Himself relieved of all direct administrative functions, "he is absolute and responsible arbiter in all political and administrative matters." The Secretary-General, who was liable to encroach on his powers, was in 1909 replaced by departments of Finance and General Business, working solely through the Governor-General, with inspectors of the different departments in the various colonies. He has a Council consisting of the Lieut.-Governors, the principal officials, and the influential natives from each of the four important colonies—in all, from twenty to twenty-five members. It meets yearly, and votes the general and colonial budgets, and the Governor-General must consult it in matters of finance and taxation. The different units, separated by intervening British colonies, are under Lieut.-Governors, who can also issue *arrêtés* on local affairs, and have their own

Councils, which they must consult on financial matters. Each raises its own revenue, but all Customs dues and taxes on shipping are paid into a common fund at the disposal of the Governor-General and the financial experts appointed by the home Government,[1] from which assignments are made for railways and large public works.[2]

The adoption of some or all of the suggestions I have made would extend the principles of Decentralisation and Continuity from the circumference overseas to the centre at Whitehall. They would, it is hoped, lighten the task of the Secretary of State and the higher officials, and remove the chronic complaint that juniors usurp their powers, and would tend to the more rapid despatch of important business. It is of no use adding to the size of the bladder by increasing the junior staff while the neck remains too narrow to cope with the discharge. Merchants and others interested in material development would obtain in the Council—where every side of a question could obtain a hearing, and pertinent papers would be presented—a recognised *locus standi* for the expression of their views more appropriate and dignified than that they now enjoy.

The admission of administrative officers on the one hand, and of merchants on the other, to share in the counsels of Downing Street, would be in accord with the liberal tendencies of the time, and remove the complaint of bureaucratic rule and secrecy. Already there are signs that persistence in methods of exclusiveness may lead to a reaction under a Labour Ministry, which it should be the care of wise and prescient statesmanship to avert, by granting to the citizens of the Empire, whether at home or abroad, a reasonable voice in its development, and to the local Governments that larger latitude in the management of their own affairs which their growth and progress justifies.

The methods by which it is sought to give effect to these principles are mainly two. First, the delegation by the

[1] Decree, 12th December 1912.

[2] Mr Morel, who considers the French system incomparably superior to our own, points out that every French colony which is not directly represented in the French Chamber (as Senegal has been since 1834) is represented at the Colonial Office by a delegate elected by vote of the white inhabitants.—'Affairs of West Africa,' p. 24.

The system has lately been largely reorganised by the decree of 4th July 1920. For the General Council there has been substituted a Colonial Council of forty elected members.

Secretary of State of some of his powers and duties to new and responsible officers of the highest rank: at home by the creation of a second Under-Secretary, and the delegation to those high officials who now exercise power in his name, of a measure of public and executive responsibility; abroad, by the creation of Governors-General of groups of colonies with extended powers, who may relieve the Secretary of State of functions not essential to his ministerial responsibility, decrease the number of units, and promote continuity and a measure of uniformity of policy. Secondly, the utilisation in the service of the State of the knowledge and experience, on the one hand, of men who are no longer on the active list, and on the other, of representatives of commerce, in positions of public and responsible participation in the administration of the Empire.

Miss Martineau, when describing how in 1825 it had become necessary to have an additional Under-Secretary, remarks: "We are beginning to learn how absurd it is to expect the machinery of the Colonial Office to do the necessary work,"—the lesson has ever to be learnt afresh.[1]

One of the main objects in view—the promotion of closer touch between those responsible abroad and at home for the guidance and control of the dependencies—may be promoted in other ways, by far the most important of which is that the Secretary of State should be on terms of personal and unofficial intimacy with the Governors, of at any rate the more important colonies, when they are in England. They are not so numerous as to make it a matter of difficulty, and the advantage should be reciprocal. The Secretary of State would be enabled to form a personal estimate of the character and ability of his Governors, while they would enjoy the greatly valued opportunity of hearing from him any criticisms of their policy which may have reached his ears, and of verbally explaining their views and motives. There is a limit to government by despatches, and it is personal touch which stimulates the best efforts. That touch is lost if the Secretary of State is only a respected chief, accessible by rare interviews in his room at the Colonial Office.

Mr Chamberlain's success and popularity as Colonial Secretary no doubt owed much to the pains he took to know his Governors personally. Though I was one of the youngest

[1] 'Thirty Years' Peace,' vol. ii. p. 30.

of them, he spoke with such entire frankness and freedom from official reticence, as to make one feel how entirely he trusted one's discretion; and Mr Lyttelton adopted the same attitude. In his *official* relations the Governor, as I have suggested, should be given every possible facility for keeping in touch with the affairs of his Government, and be fully consulted in every important matter while in England, his deputy's powers being strictly limited.

But if it be desirable for the Secretary of State to be on terms of social intimacy with his Governors, it is equally desirable that the permanent Under-Secretary should personally know the senior colonial officials. It is he who makes recommendations for the filling of the highest posts, and personal knowledge is essential, for local popularity may be the worst of guides. Governors and high officials who know how irksome interruption is when pressed with work, hesitate to intrude in office hours, or to stay longer than the business demands, but the opportunities afforded by successive Under-Secretaries for meeting them on terms of social intercourse have been rare. The Colonial Service thus feels that an absence of personal knowledge among the permanent officials in Whitehall has been responsible for selections for promotion which in many cases have been considered to be marvellously ill-judged.

It has been suggested that it would be of great advantage, both to the Colonial Office and to the colonies, if officers were interchangeable between the two Services, or at least if officers from Whitehall served for some years abroad, and so gained personal knowledge of the colonies. There is already some misgiving that in the laudable desire "to know what people are saying in the colony," junior officials at home are led to discuss questions of policy with juniors on leave from the colonies, and be guided by their irresponsible and necessarily ill-informed views. The type of officer who lends himself to such discussions is often one who is full of theories of his own, and is rarely the best qualified to voice local opinion. It is disheartening to the responsible officers to discover that official opinions have thus been formed on a half-knowledge of the facts. It is to obviate such fortuitous and undesirable means of acquiring knowledge, that a closer touch between responsible officers at home and abroad is so much needed.

A brief visit to a colony is of little use, and even temporary service abroad of a junior Colonial Office clerk may do more harm than good if the officer on his return is posted to the section concerned with the colony he has visited. As a junior he will have had little opportunity for learning the reasons for any course of action adopted by the Governor and his Council, and may probably never even have heard of important matters outside his immediate sphere of work. On his return, the junior who has served temporarily in a colony is apt to be regarded as "the man who knows all about it," and it may be that his dicta may influence the views of his seniors, and be accepted in modification of those of the Governor and his Council. The only appointment in which an officer can become acquainted with the instructions of the Secretary of State, with the views of the Governor and his Council, and with the opinions expressed on matters of administrative policy by Lieut.-Governors and Residents, is as "Political Secretary" to the Governor (or "Secretary for Native Affairs")—a post which should not be held by too junior an officer.

Interchangeability between the services, as distinct from temporary service abroad, has, I believe, been adopted by the Foreign Office in all grades, and offers, I think, many advantages. Under such a system officers of the home service would serve for alternate periods at home and abroad, at all stages of their careers, interchanging with selected officers of the colonial service, as in the Navy and Army. The junior is no longer a specialist if his seniors have also served abroad. The exchange, for instance, of junior officers of the home service with colonial secretariat officers, for substantial periods of service, would afford to the former a considerable insight into the affairs of a colony, and to the latter a training in the excellent office methods of the home department. These conditions of service would, of course, have to be made clear to those who enter for the competitive Civil Service examinations. The old system in the Eastern colonies, which afforded a period of training at the Colonial Office to cadets before taking up their appointments, had much to recommend it.

The question of the interchangeability of officers in the highest posts is a more difficult matter. It presupposes, as Mr Wood reminds us,[1] not only interchangeable officers, but interchangeable duties, and the training of the services is essentially different and specialised.

[1] 'Report on Visit to West Indies,' Cmd. 1679, pp. 36-38.

"Evidence," says Lord Crewe's Committee on the relations of the India Office and the Indian Government, "has indicated the great value of bringing the superior officers of the Home and Indian Administrations into close touch with each other under daily working conditions, and it is presumed that the system of deputing these officers on special duty and with definite objects from one country to the other, will be continued and possibly expanded." But they "do not think it desirable or possible to arrange any formal system of interchange between members of the India Office and the Indian services."[1]

Before leaving the subject of Colonial Office organisation, a word may perhaps usefully be added on the subject of commercial intelligence. Mr Churchill, when Under-Secretary, said that while the business of the Office had doubled or trebled in the last twenty years, the most remarkable increase was in the commercial branch, which, however, had not been altogether successful, and it was desirable that the Colonial Office should get more in touch with business men.[2]

Each colony nominates a correspondent with the Commercial Intelligence Branch of the Board of Trade, and inquiries and samples can be transmitted to the Imperial Institute and to Kew. There are also the College of Science and Technology, and the Overseas Trade Department;[3] but sources of information are too confused—or diffused—whether for the colonies (which are somewhat out of touch with research and progress in other countries), or for business men who desire precise information, or direction as to where it can be obtained.

An African Council on which commerce was represented would no doubt go far to meet Mr Churchill's desires, but it should be reinforced by special facilities for obtaining information. The Imperial Institute is the natural Commercial Department of the Colonial Office. It does not require duplication, but the great possibilities of usefulness which it might afford seem to be hardly sufficiently utilised.

I suggest that the simple and inexpensive expedient of an expansion of the library and reference-room at the Colonial

[1] Report of 9th July 1918.

[2] Speech of 7th February 1907.

[3] See Board of Trade Memo. on 'Organisation of Commercial Intelligence.' Cd. 8715/1917.

Office, superintended (as now) by a thoroughly efficient librarian, whose services would be at the disposal of all inquirers, would serve a very useful purpose. Here the legislation of each colony on each special branch of material development would be collated for comparative study. Questions and answers and debates in Parliament on colonial subjects could be tabulated for reference, with all command papers and other Blue-books, and even useful and pertinent magazine articles.[1] Governors' despatches explaining the nature and object of new legislation affecting trade and industry, and the latest local regulations, Orders in Council and departmental reports, received mail by mail, and even Colonial Office White-books, might be made available for reference. Memoranda compiled in the colony, dealing with the soil, climate, and labour-supply, the charges and conditions under which land is available, transport by rail, river, and road, customs dues, local markets, openings in agriculture, forestry, or mining, should be supplied for the encouragement of new enterprise, with data as to the extent to which the Colonial Government would be able to afford special encouragement. These and all other pamphlets and monographs should be obtainable from the librarian without the formality and delay of application to the Office.

A small staff would be required, whose duty it would be to supply information needed by the colonies, and keep them posted in the legislation and progress in other tropical countries (including India) on economic subjects. A room might be set apart where merchants, mine-managers, and others could arrange meetings with Governors and colonial officials when in England, explain their wishes, and learn to what extent the finances would permit of their realisation. Much misunderstanding and ill-informed criticism would thus be avoided.[2]

Some of the suggestions I have made would involve additional expense, but there would seem to be no objection in principle were the colonies invited to bear a part of the cost

[1] Some years ago a very useful quarterly periodical, styled 'The Colonial Office Journal,' made its appearance, with Sir W. Mercer, one of the Crown Agents, as its editor. It was published with the approval of the Secretary of State, though he was not responsible for the opinions expressed in it. It is to be regretted that this excellent publication has ceased to appear.

[2] If for lack of space or other cause this suggestion were found to be impracticable, possibly an arrangement could be made with the Royal Colonial Institute on the same lines.

of the Colonial Office, as well as of an African Council, just as the Indian Government has hitherto borne the cost of the India Office. England, as we have seen, has treated her colonies with great generosity: at first by free grants in aid; later, by the use of Imperial credit. There seems no good reason why, when a colony has grown to prosperity, it should not pay for the large amount of administrative business undertaken on its behalf by the Colonial Office (in addition to contributing towards its defence, see p. 275), and so relieve the Imperial Exchequer at a time when it is burdened with such heavy liabilities incurred in the common interest.[1] Such contributions, in return for specific benefits received, appear to me much more dignified and legitimate than the profit of 50 per cent made by the Mint on silver coin supplied to West Africa prior to the creation of a local currency, in return for a hypothetical redemption risk.[2] It is said to have amounted to a very large sum per annum.

The Crown colonies and protectorates, like the Dominions, have in the last decades advanced greatly in wealth and importance. Many of them have a considerable population of British merchants and others, and the British public has invested large sums of money in their development. Under the progressive and liberal rule of Lord Milner, Malta, Kenya, and Ceylon have been granted wider powers of self-government, and Jamaica may perhaps shortly realise her ambitions in this direction. Mr (now Lord) Long, moreover, made a notable departure in asking for the opinions of the colonies on questions of economic policy and reconstruction after the war. But for the most part they remain as they were fifty years ago, without a voice which can be heard outside the walls of the Colonial Office. They lack touch with centres of progress in this country. Organisations have been formed in England to meet this need—the West India Committee, the China Association, &c.—but they can only proceed by way of deputation to the Secretary of State, by periodical banquets, and by press agitation. Philanthropic bodies interested in the tropics find powerful support—mission societies, anti-liquor, anti-opium, the Aborigines' Protection, &c.—but their sources of information are often very defective, and they can only proceed in the same fashion. It is becoming more

[1] See Sir F. Swettenham in the 'Empire and Century,' p. 889.
[2] See Mr Harcourt's speech to liquor deputation, August 1911.

and more an epoch of deputations, which waste much time, and usually give little satisfaction to those interested.

It may pertinently be asked whether the time has not come when the Crown colonies and protectorates may justly demand some representation on Imperial Conferences. They all have much the same administrative and economic conditions and problems. If an administrator of proved experience were nominated to represent them (preferably a member of the African Council if that body is formed), and if the nomination were publicly announced some time before the meeting of the Conference, and the colonies and home interests alike were encouraged to communicate with him as to any matter of sufficient general interest to be placed, with the Secretary of State's concurrence, on the agenda paper—a representation would be accorded which would do something to meet the present complaints of bureaucracy and lack of publicity in the conduct of the affairs of tropical dependencies. The party in the State which will realise the immense and growing importance of the tropics,[1] and the influence they will exert in the progress of this century, and the statesman who will take seriously in hand the problems of their administration and material development, will beyond doubt perform a great work for the Empire.

That abler men than myself have refrained from suggesting reforms can, I suppose, only be attributed to the fact that in criticising systems they must needs appear, however unintentionally, to criticise and offend the men who administer them.

[1] See 'The Empire and the Century,' 'The Tropics and the Empire,' by Lady Lugard, pp. 817-826.

PART II.

SPECIAL PROBLEMS.

CHAPTER X.

METHODS OF RULING NATIVE RACES.

The principle of co-operation—Divergent methods of self-government: (*a*) Representative government: The new system in India; (*b*) Complete independence the goal; (*c*) Dependent native rule—The Fulani of Nigeria—Recognition of the principle of rule through chiefs—Advanced communities in Nigeria—Relations with British staff—Revenues of native administrations—Courts and jurisdiction—The village unit—Essential features of the system—Application to non-Moslem States—Limitations to independence: (*a*) Armed forces; (*b*) Taxation; (*c*) Legislation; (*d*) Land; (*e*) Control of aliens—Disposal of revenue—Alien races as native rulers—Education of native rulers—Misuse of the system—System must vary with local traditions—Administrative procedure—Succession—Extra-territorial allegiance.

If continuity and decentralisation are, as I have said, the first and most important conditions in maintaining an effective administration, co-operation is the key-note of success in its application—continuous co-operation between every link in the chain, from the head of the administration to its most junior member,—co-operation between the Government and the commercial community, and, above all, between the provincial staff and the native rulers. Every individual adds his share not only to the accomplishment of the ideal, but to the ideal itself. Its principles are fashioned by his quota of experience, its results are achieved by his patient and loyal application of these principles, with as little interference as possible with native customs and modes of thought.

Principles do not change, but their mode of application may and should vary with the customs, the traditions, and the prejudices of each unit. The task of the administrative officer is to clothe his principles in the garb of evolution, not of revolution; to make it apparent alike to the educated native, the conservative Moslem, and the primitive pagan, each in his own degree, that the policy of the Government is not antagonistic but progressive—sympathetic to his aspirations and the guardian of his natural rights. The Governor looks to the administrative staff to keep in touch with native thought and feeling, and to report fully to himself, in order that he in turn may be able to support them and recognise their work.

When describing the machinery of Government in an African dependency in chapter vi., I spoke of the supervision and guidance exercised by the Lieut.-Governor, the Residents, and the District Officers over the native chiefs. In this chapter I propose to discuss how those functions should be exercised.

Lord Milner's declaration that the British policy is to rule subject races through their own chiefs is generally applauded, but the manner in which the principle should be translated into practice admits of wide differences of opinion and method. Obviously the extent to which native races are capable of controlling their own affairs must vary in proportion to their degree of development and progress in social organisation, but this is a question of adaptation and not of principle. Broadly speaking, the divergent opinions in regard to the application of the principle may be found to originate in three different conceptions.

The first is that the ideal of self-government can only be realised by the methods of evolution which have produced the democracies of Europe and America—viz., by representative institutions in which a comparatively small educated class shall be recognised as the natural spokesmen for the many. This method is naturally in favour with the educated African. Whether it is adapted to peoples accustomed by their own institutions to autocracy—albeit modified by a substantial expression of the popular will and circumscribed by custom—is naturally a matter on which opinions differ. The fundamental essential, however, in such a form of Government is that the educated few shall at least be representative of the feelings and desires of the many—well known to them, speaking their language, and versed in their customs and prejudices.

In present conditions in Africa the numerous separate tribes, speaking different languages, and in different stages of evolution, cannot produce representative men of education. Even were they available, the number of communities which could claim separate representation would make any central and really representative Council very unwieldy. The authority vested in the representatives would be antagonistic (as the Indian Progressives realise [1]) to that of the native rulers and their councils,—which are the product of the natural tendencies of tribal evolution,—and would run counter to the customs and institutions of the people.[2]

An attempt to adapt these principles of Western representative Government to tropical races is now being made in India. It is at present an Eastern rather than an African problem, but as a great experiment in the method of Government in tropical countries, the outcome of which "many other native races in other parts of the world are watching with strained attention," it demands at least a passing reference here.

Though the powers entrusted to the elected representatives of the people are at first restricted under the dyarchical system (which reserves certain subjects for the Central Authority), the principle of government by an educated minority, as opposed to government by native rulers, is fully accepted. It must be admitted that there is a considerable body of well-informed opinion in India and England—voiced here by the India Association, Lord Sydenham (who speaks with the authority of an ex-Governor of Bombay), and others—which expresses much misgiving as to the wisdom of placing all political power "in the hands of a disaffected minority unrepresentative of India," and regards it as "an attempt to govern India by the narrowest of oligarchies, whose interests often conflict with those of the millions." [3]

The experiment has so far shown much promise of success, but the real test is not merely whether the native councillors

[1] "The extremist Press," says Sir Valentine Chirol, "has already frequently denounced ruling princes and chiefs as intolerable obstacles to the democratic evolution of 'Swaraj'" (Home Rule).—'Times,' 10th February 1921.

[2] See the assertion of Chief Ofori to this effect quoted on p. 86. "We claim and we insist," say the spokesmen of the educated natives, while denouncing the present system, and advocating a new policy, "that such a policy can be adequately carried out only by giving an effective position in the legislatures to ourselves."

[3] 'Times,' 22nd December 1913. See also 'Spectator,' 5th February 1921.

show moderation and restraint as against extremists of their own class, but whether, when legislation has to be enacted which is unpopular with the illiterate masses and the martial races of India, there may be a reluctance to accept what will be called "Babu-made law," though it would have been accepted without demur as the order of "the Sirkar"—the British Raj.

It is, of course, now too late to adopt to any large extent the alternative of gradually transforming the greater part of British India into native States governed by their own hereditary dynasties, whose representatives in many cases still exist, and extending to them the principles which have so successfully guided our relations with the native States in India itself, and in Malaya in the past. It is one thing to excite an ignorant peasantry against an alien usurper, but quite another thing to challenge a native ruler.

Such a system does not exclude the educated native from participation in the government of the State to which he belongs, as a councillor to the native ruler, but it substitutes for direct British rule, not an elected oligarchy but a form of government more in accord with racial instincts and inherited traditions. It may be that while dyarchy and representative government may prove suitable to Bengal, and perhaps to some other provinces, the alternative system may be found to be best adapted to Mohamedan States, and to other of the warlike races of India, where representatives of the ancient dynasties still survive. Time alone will show. I shall recur to this subject in the next chapter.

The second conception is that every advanced community should be given the widest possible powers of self-government under its own ruler, and that these powers should be rapidly increased with the object of complete independence at the earliest possible date in the not distant future. Those who hold this view generally, I think, also consider that attempts to train primitive tribes in any form of self-government are futile, and the administration must be wholly conducted by British officials. This in the past has been the principle adopted in many dependencies. It recognised no alternative between a status of independence, like the Sultans of Malaya, or the native princes of India, and the direct rule of the district commissioner.

But the attempt to create such independent States in Africa has been full of anomalies. In the case of Egbaland, where the status had been formally recognised by treaty, the extent to which the Crown had jurisdiction was uncertain, yet, as we have seen, international conventions, including even that relating to the protection of wild animals, which was wholly opposed to native customary rights, were applied without the consent of the "Independent" State, and powers quite incompatible with independence were exercised by the Suzerain.[1] (See footnote, p. 35.)

The paramount chief might receive ceremonial visits from time to time from the Governor, and even perhaps be addressed as "Your Royal Highness," and vested with titular dignity and the tinsel insignia of office. His right to impose tolls on trade, and to exact whatever oppressive taxes he chose from his peasantry, was admitted, but his authority was subject to constant interference. The last-joined District Officer, or any other official, might issue orders, if not to him, at any rate to any of his subordinate chiefs, and the native ruler had no legal and recognised means of enforcing his commands. He was necessarily forbidden to raise armed forces—on which in the last resort the authority of the law must depend—and could not therefore maintain order.

The third conception is that of rule by native chiefs, unfettered in their control of their people as regards all those matters which are to them the most important attributes of rule, with scope for initiative and responsibility, but admittedly—so far as the visible horizon is concerned—subordinate to the control of the protecting Power in certain well-defined directions. It recognises, in the words of the Versailles Treaty, that the subject races of Africa are not yet able to stand alone, and that it would not conduce to the happiness of the vast bulk of the people—for whose welfare the controlling Power is trustee—that the attempt should be made.

The verdict of students of history and sociology of different

[1] That one of the stipulations of the Egba "Treaty of Commerce and Friendship" of 1893 should be the prohibition of human sacrifice, indicates that the community was hardly ripe for self-government.

nationalities, such as Dr Kidd,[1] Dr Stoddard,[2] M. Beaulieu,[3] Meredith Townsend [4] and others is, as I have shown (p. 82), unanimous that the era of complete independence is not as yet visible on the horizon of time. Practical administrators (among whom I may include my successor, Sir P. Girouard, in Northern Nigeria) have arrived at the same conclusion.

The danger of going too fast with native races is even more likely to lead to disappointment, if not to disaster, than the danger of not going fast enough. The pace can best be gauged by those who have intimate acquaintance alike with the strong points and the limitations of the native peoples and rulers with whom they have to deal.

The Fulani of Northern Nigeria are, as I have said, more capable of rule than the indigenous races, but in proportion as we consider them an alien race, we are denying self-government to the people over whom they rule, and supporting an alien caste—albeit closer and more akin to the native races than a European can be. Yet capable as they are, it requires the ceaseless vigilance of the British staff to maintain a high standard of administrative integrity, and to prevent oppression of the peasantry. We are dealing with the same generation, and in many cases with the identical rulers, who were responsible for the misrule and tyranny which we found in 1902. The subject races near the capital were then serfs, and the victims of constant extortion. Those dwelling at a distance were raided for slaves, and could not count their women, their cattle, or their crops their own. Punishments were most barbarous, and included impalement, mutilation,

[1] Dr Kidd writes: "There never has been, and never will be within any time with which we are practically concerned, such a thing as good government in the European sense of the tropics by the natives of these regions." He describes the collapse of prosperity in the West Indies and Guiana which followed the false conception that the British tropics, if given control of their own destinies, would develop into modern states—and points to the gloomy picture of Hayti, &c.—'Control of the Tropics,' pp. 37, 51, 73, &c.

[2] "Unless every lesson of history is to be disregarded, we must conclude that black Africa is unable to stand alone."—'The Rising Tide of Colour,' p. 102.

[3] "Les noirs d'Afrique sont au milieu de l'humanité des mineurs qui pour parvenir à un certain état de civilisation . . . ont besoin d'être dirigés, guidés, gouvernés pendant un bon nombre de dizaines d'années par les Européans. Il convient que chaque nation qui a la résponsibilité d'une Colonie Africaine puisse sur son territoire d'une absolue souverainité."—Beaulieu, *loc. cit.*, vol. i. pp. 361, 364. See note, p. 82.

[4] "None of the black races have shown within historic times the capacity to develop civilisation."—'Asia in Europe,' p. 92, quoted by the American writer, Sir Stoddard. He gives his reasons at great length for his conclusions.

and burying alive.[1] Many generations have passed since British rule was established among the more intellectual people of India—the inheritors of centuries of Eastern civilisation—yet only to-day are we tentatively seeking to confer on them a measure of self-government. "Festina lente" is a motto which the Colonial Office will do well to remember in its dealings with Africa.

That the principle of ruling through the native chiefs is adopted by several of the governments of British Tropical Africa can be seen from recent local pronouncements. The Governor of Sierra Leone, in his address to the Legislative Council last December (1920), remarks that "nine-tenths of the people enjoy autonomy under their own elected chiefs . . . European officers are the technical advisers, and helpers of the tribal authority." The Governor of the Gold Coast on a similar occasion observed: "The chiefs are keenly appreciative of our policy of indirect rule, and of the full powers they retain under their native institutions."[2] The powers retained by the Kabaka of Uganda and his Council are very wide indeed.[3]

[1] The dungeon at Kano is thus described: "A small doorway 2 ft. 6 in. by 18 in. gives access into it; the interior is divided by a thick mud wall (with a similar hole in it) into two compartments, each 17 ft. by 7 ft. and 11 ft. high. This wall was pierced with holes at its base, through which the legs of those sentenced to death were thrust up to the thigh, and they were left to be trodden on by the mass of other prisoners till they died of thirst and starvation. The place is entirely air-tight and unventilated, except for one small doorway or rather hole in the wall through which you creep. The total space inside is 2618 cub. ft., and at the time we took Kano 135 human beings were confined here each night, being let out during the day to cook their food, &c., in a small adjoining area. Recently as many as 200 have been interned at one time. As the superficial ground area was only 238 square feet, there was not, of course, even standing room. Victims were crushed to death every night—their corpses were hauled out each morning. The stench, I am told, inside the place when Col. Morland visited it was intolerable though it was empty, and when I myself went inside three weeks later the effluvium was unbearable for more than a few seconds. A putrid corpse even then lay near the doorway."—Northern Nigeria Annual Report, 1902, p. 29.

[2] Captain Armitage says of the northern territories: "The powers of the chiefs had largely lapsed, and it was the custom to put, one might almost say, the village idiot on the stool. Our policy has been to re-establish the powers of several big chiefs, and it has been a remarkable success."

[3] Before Uganda had been declared a British protectorate, and control assumed by the British Government, I wrote (in 1893): "The object to be aimed at in the administration of this country is to rule through its own executive government . . . the Resident should rule through and by the chiefs."—'The Rise of our East African Empire,' vol. i. pp. 649, 651.

Uganda proper is divided into *Sazas*, each of which has a *Lukiko*, which assembles weekly and deals with minor cases. They are inspected by the district officers, and report to the Central Lukiko at the capital. This consists of some

The system adopted in Nigeria is therefore only a particular method of the application of these principles—more especially as regards "advanced communities,"—and since I am familiar with it I will use it as illustrative of the methods which in my opinion should characterise the dealings of the controlling power with subject races.

The object in view is to make each "Emir" or paramount chief, assisted by his judicial Council, an effective ruler over his own people. He presides over a "Native Administration" organised throughout as a unit of local government. The area over which he exercises jurisdiction is divided into districts under the control of "Headmen," who collect the taxes in the name of the ruler, and pay them into the "Native Treasury," conducted by a native treasurer and staff under the supervision of the chief at his capital. Here, too, is the prison for native court prisoners, and probably the school, which I shall describe more fully in the chapter on education. Large cities are divided into wards for purposes of control and taxation.

The district headman, usually a territorial magnate with local connections, is the chief executive officer in the area under his charge. He controls the village headmen, and is responsible for the assessment of the tax, which he collects through their agency. He must reside in his district and not at the capital. He is not allowed to pose as a chief with a retinue of his own and duplicate officials, and is summoned from time to time to report to his chief. If, as is the case with some of the ancient Emirates, the community is a small one but independent of any other native rule, the chief may be his own district headman.

A province under a Resident may contain several separate "Native Administrations," whether they be Moslem Emirates or pagan communities. A "division" under a British District Officer may include one or more headmen's districts, or more than one small Emirate or independent [1] pagan tribe, but

forty Saza chiefs presided over by the Kabaka with his Katikiro and other ministers. The native administration has 20 per cent of the native tax—about £16,000. The system, says the Governor, "is an excellent example of the best results of indirect rule."—'United Empire,' June 1920, p. 395.

Sir H. Low and Sir F. Swettenham testify from their experience in Malaya that "the only way to deal with the people is through their recognised chiefs and headmen."

[1] By the term "independent" in this connection is meant "independent of other native control."

as a rule no Emirate is partly in one division and partly in another. The Resident acts as sympathetic adviser and counsellor to the native chief, being careful not to interfere so as to lower his prestige, or cause him to lose interest in his work. His advice on matters of general policy must be followed, but the native ruler issues his own instructions to his subordinate chiefs and district heads—not as the orders of the Resident but as his own,—and he is encouraged to work through them, instead of centralising everything in himself —a system which in the past had produced such great abuses. The British District Officers supervise and assist the native district headmen, through whom they convey any instructions to village heads, and make any arrangements necessary for carrying on the work of the Government departments, but all important orders emanate from the Emir, whose messenger usually accompanies and acts as mouthpiece of a District Officer.

The tax—which supersedes all former "tribute," irregular imposts, and forced labour—is, in a sense, the basis of the whole system, since it supplies the means to pay the Emir and all his officials. The district and village heads are effectively supervised and assisted in its assessment by the British staff. The native treasury retains the proportion assigned to it (in advanced communities a half), and pays the remainder into Colonial Revenue.

There are fifty such treasuries in the northern provinces of Nigeria, and every independent chief, however small, is encouraged to have his own. The appropriation by the native administration of market dues, slaughter-house fees, forest licences, &c., is authorised by ordinance, and the native administration receives also the fines and fees of native courts. From these funds are paid the salaries of the Emir and his council, the native court judges, the district and village heads, police, prison warders, and other employees. The surplus is devoted to the construction and maintenance of dispensaries, leper settlements, schools, roads, courthouses, and other buildings. Such works may be carried out wholly or in part by a Government department, if the native administration requires technical assistance, the cost being borne by the native treasury.

The native treasurer keeps all accounts of receipts and expenditure, and the Emir, with the assistance of the Resident, annually prepares a budget, which is formally approved by the Lieut.-Governor.

In these advanced communities the judges of the native courts—which I shall describe in a later chapter—administer native law and custom, and exercise their jurisdiction independently of the native executive, but under the supervision of the British staff, and subject to the general control of the Emir, whose "Judicial Council" consists of his principal officers of State, and is vested with executive as well as judicial powers. No punishment may be inflicted by a native authority, except through a regular tribunal. The ordinances of government are operative everywhere, but the native authority may make by-laws in modification of native custom—*e.g.*, on matters of sanitation, &c.,—and these, when approved by the Governor, are enforced by the native courts.

The authority of the Emir over his own people is absolute, and the profession of an alien creed does not absolve a native from the obligation to obey his lawful orders; but aliens—other than natives domiciled in the Emirate and accepting the jurisdiction of the native authority and courts—are under the direct control of the British staff. Townships are excluded from the native jurisdiction.

The village is the administrative unit. It is not always easy to define, since the security to life and property which has followed the British administration has caused an exodus from the cities and large villages, and the creation of innumerable hamlets, sometimes only of one or two huts, on the agricultural lands. The peasantry of the advanced communities, though ignorant, yet differs from that of the backward tribes in that they recognise the authority of the Emir, and are more ready to listen to the village head and the Council of Elders, on which the Nigerian system is based.[1]

Subject, therefore, to the limitations which I shall pres-

[1] "The development of self-government in India," says Lord Sydenham, "should begin with the *Panchayet*" (Village Council).—'Times,' 10th Aug. 1917. The Indian Commission of 1912 reported in favour of re-establishing the *Panchayet*, which previous reforms had tended to destroy, and this, too, was one of the planks of Gandhi's "Bardoli programme." In China the village head (*Tipao*) is all-powerful. Larger towns and cities are aggregates of the Tipao-governed units. The system has worked smoothly in spite of the chaos in the central and provincial Governments.—(C. Kadono at Washington Railway Conference, Feb. 1922.) In Egypt, however, the *Omdehs* of the villages were Government officials whose qualification was ownership of ten acres of land. The system inevitably led to great abuse and tyranny.—(Sir V. Chirol, 'Times,' 1/1/20.)

ently discuss, the native authority is thus *de facto* and *de jure* ruler over his own people. He appoints and dismisses his subordinate chiefs and officials. He exercises the power of allocation of lands, and with the aid of the native courts, of adjudication in land disputes and expropriation for offences against the community; these are the essential functions upon which, in the opinion of the West African Lands Committee, the prestige of the native authority depends. The lawful orders which he may give are carefully defined by ordinance, and in the last resort are enforced by Government.

Since native authority, especially if exercised by alien conquerors, is inevitably weakened by the first impact of civilised rule, it is made clear to the elements of disorder, who regard force as conferring the only right to demand obedience, that government, by the use of force if necessary, intends to support the native chief. To enable him to maintain order he employs a body of unarmed police, and if the occasion demands the display of superior force he looks to the Government—as, for instance, if a community combines to break the law or shield criminals from justice,—a rare event in the advanced communities.

The native ruler derives his power from the Suzerain, and is responsible that it is not misused. He is equally with British officers amenable to the law, but his authority does not depend on the caprice of an executive officer. To intrigue against him is an offence punishable, if necessary, in a Provincial Court. Thus both British and native courts are invoked to uphold his authority.

The essential feature of the system (as I wrote at the time of its inauguration) is that the native chiefs are constituted "as an integral part of the machinery of the administration. There are not two sets of rulers—British and native—working either separately or in co-operation, but a single Government in which the native chiefs have well-defined duties and an acknowledged status equally with British officials. Their duties should never conflict, and should overlap as little as possible. They should be complementary to each other, and the chief himself must understand that he has no right to place and power unless he renders his proper services to the State."

The ruling classes are no longer either demi-gods, or parasites preying on the community. They must work for the stipends and position they enjoy. They are the trusted delegates of the Governor, exercising in the Moslem States the well-understood powers of "Wakils" in conformity with their own Islamic system, and recognising the King's representative as their acknowledged Suzerain.

There is here no need of "Dyarchy," for the lines of development of the native administration run parallel to, and do not intersect, those of the Central Government. It is the consistent aim of the British staff to maintain and increase the prestige of the native ruler, to encourage his initiative, and to support his authority. That the chiefs are satisfied with the autonomy they enjoy in the matters which really interest and concern them, may be judged by their loyalty and the prosperity of their country.

Comparatively little difficulty, it may be said, would be experienced in the application of such a system to Moslem States, for even if their rulers had deteriorated, they still profess the standards of Islam, with its system of taxation, and they possess a literate class capable of discharging the duties I have described. No doubt the alien immigrants in the northern tropical belt afford better material for social organisation, both racially and through the influence of their creed, than the advanced communities of negro stock which owe nothing to Islam, such as the Baganda, the Ashantis, the Yorubas, the Benis, and others. But the self-evolved progress in social organisation of these latter communities is in itself evidence that they possessed exceptional intelligence, probably more widely diffused among the peasantry than would be found among those over whom an alien race had acquired domination. They too had evolved systems of taxation and of land tenure, and had learnt to delegate authority. The teaching of missions through many decades had in most cases produced a class who, if their energies were rightly directed to the service of their communities instead of seeking foreign outlets, would form a very valuable aid in the building up of a "Native Administration." That these communities are fully capable of adopting such a system has been proved in recent years in South Nigeria.

They have not produced so definite a code of law, or such advanced methods of dispensing justice, as the Koran has introduced, and they lack the indigenous educational advantages which the use of Arabic and the religious schools have conferred on the Moslem. On the other hand, many—especially the Baganda—have benefited greatly by the Christian schools, and a wider range of knowledge, including English. Some of their chiefs—notably Khama of Bechuana, and several of those in Uganda—have been remarkable men. Among many of these communities the chiefs exercise an influence different in its nature from that accorded to an alien ruler, and based on superstitious veneration.

The limitations to independence which are frankly inherent in this conception of native rule—not as temporary restraints to be removed as soon as may be, but as powers which rightly belong to the controlling Power as trustee for the welfare of the masses, and as being responsible for the defence of the country and the cost of its central administration—are such as do not involve interference with the authority of the chiefs or the social organisation of the people. They have been accepted by the Fulani Emirs as natural and proper to the controlling power, and their reservation in the hands of the Governor has never interfered with the loyalty of the ruling chiefs, or, so far as I am aware, been resented by them. The limitations are as follows :—

(1) Native rulers are not permitted to raise and control armed forces, or to grant permission to carry arms. To this in principle Great Britain stands pledged under the Brussels Act. The evils which result in Africa from an armed population were evident in Uganda before it fell under British control, and are very evident in Abyssinia to-day. No one with experience will deny the necessity of maintaining the strictest military discipline over armed forces or police in Africa if misuse of power is to be avoided, and they are not to become a menace and a terror to the native population and a danger in case of religious excitement—a discipline which an African ruler is incapable of appreciating or applying. For this reason native levies should never be employed in substitution for or in aid of troops.[1] (See p. 576.)

On the other hand, the Government armed police are never quartered in native towns, where their presence would interfere with the authority of the chiefs. Like the regular troops,

[1] This rule does not seem to have been enforced in Kenya. "Administrative chiefs, in order to assert and maintain their authority, have found it necessary to form bands of armed retainers, to whom they accord special privileges which are found to be oppressive."—Official Handbook 1216, p. 243.

they are employed as escorts and on duty in the townships. The native administration maintain a police, who wear a uniform but do not carry firearms.

(2) The sole right to impose taxation in any form is reserved to the Suzerain power. This fulfils the bilateral understanding that the peasantry—provided they pay the authorised tax (the adjustment of which to all classes of the population is a responsibility which rests with the Central Government) —should be free of all other exactions whatsoever (including unpaid labour), while a sufficient proportion of the tax is assigned to the native treasuries to meet the expenditure of the native administration. Special sanction by ordinance—or "rule" approved by the Governor—is therefore required to enable the native authority to levy any special dues, &c.

(3) The right to legislate is reserved. That this should remain in the hands of the Central Government—itself limited by the control of the Colonial Office, as I have described—cannot be questioned. The native authority, however, exercises very considerable power in this regard. A native ruler, and the native courts, are empowered to enforce native law and custom, provided it is not repugnant to humanity, or in opposition to any ordinance. This practically meets all needs, but the native authority may also make rules on any subject, provided they are approved by the Governor. (See chapter xxviii.)

(4) The right to appropriate land on equitable terms for public purposes and for commercial requirements is vested in the Governor. In the Northern Provinces of Nigeria (but not in the South) the right of disposing of native lands is reserved to the Governor by ordinance. In practice this does not interfere with the power of the native ruler (as the delegate of the Governor) to assign lands to the natives under his rule, in accordance with native law and custom, or restrict him or the native courts from adjudicating between natives regarding occupancy rights in land. No rents are levied on lands in occupation by indigenous natives. Leases to aliens are granted by the Central Government. (See chapters xiv. and xv.)

If the pressure of population in one community makes it necessary to assign to it a portion of the land belonging to a neighbour with a small and decreasing population, the Governor (to whom appeal may be made) would decide the matter. These reservations were set out in the formal letter of appointment given to each chief in Northern Nigeria.

(5) In order to maintain intact the control of the Central Government over all aliens, and to avoid friction and difficulties, it has been the recognised rule that the employees of the native administration should consist entirely of natives subject to the native authority. If aliens are required for any skilled work by the native administration, Government servants may be employed and their salaries reimbursed by the native treasury. For a like reason, whenever possible, all non-natives and natives not subject to the local native jurisdiction live in the "township," from which natives subject to the native administration are as far as possible excluded. This exclusive control of aliens by the Central Government partakes rather of the nature of "extra-territorial jurisdiction" than of dualism.

(6) Finally, in the interests of good government, the right of confirming or otherwise the choice of the people of the successor to a chiefship, and of deposing any ruler for misrule or other adequate cause, is reserved to the Governor.

The revenue of a native administration consists, as I have said, not of an arbitrary sum assigned to it by the Governor, but of a fixed proportion of the statutory tax collected by its agency, together with the fines and fees from native courts, market dues, and similar receipts assigned by the Governor. Thus, though the Suzerain power imposes the taxes (whether direct in the form of an income tax or indirect as customs dues, &c.), and the general *rate* of the former is fixed by the Governor, the actual assessment is in the hands of the native ruler and his representatives—the district and village heads—guided and assisted by the British staff. It therefore appears to the taxpayer as a tax imposed by his own native ruler, though he knows that the vigilant eye of the District Officer will see that no unauthorised exactions are made, and that any injustice will be remedied. Since the salaries of the ruler and the officials of the "Native Administration" are paid out of their own native treasury funds, they cannot be regarded by him as officials paid by Government.

The proportion assigned to the native administration in advanced communities is a half of the general income and cattle tax,—the proportion is less in pagan communities. On the inauguration of the tax in Nigeria the proceeds were quite insufficient to meet even the necessary salaries of chiefs; but with improved assessment, a more honest collection, and increased prosperity, the sum, without additional burden, has become so large that in the more wealthy Emirates there is a considerable surplus, when all the salaries of the very largely-increased establishments of native officials, police and prison staff, &c., have been paid.[1] From these funds native court-houses, treasuries, schools, and prisons for native court prisoners have been built, and the balance, invested in a reserve fund, totalled in 1919 £486,654, exclusive of the large sums voted by the Emirs towards the cost of the war. These reserve funds—originally created to meet any emergency, such as famine or cattle disease, when Northern Nigeria had no colonial reserve, and was dependent on a grant-in-aid—are now available for public works of benefit to the people.[2]

The revenues of the native administrations do not appear in the colonial budget of revenue and expenditure, and are independent of colonial treasury or audit control. The proper expenditure of these large sums—obtained by taxes imposed and enforced by the Suzerain Power—must obviously depend in part on the ability of each native ruler, and in part on the Resident who advises him. "Unfettered control" may in some cases mean that a Resident, and not the ruling chief, disposes of large revenues independent of the Lieut.-Governor; in other cases it may mean a tendency to multiply offices and pay high salaries, which either overburden the finances of other less wealthy treasuries, or cause discontent among its employees, and ultimately enhance the cost of labour throughout the country—a result which is inimical to production and progress, unless necessitated by economic causes. It is a tendency which a Resident, however much he has identified himself in the interests of the native administration, may not find it easy to resist, though he sets his face against nepotism and the reckless exercise of patronage and display—which are so apt to be regarded as the symbol of power by a native ruler.

Pending the growth of a fuller sense of public responsibility and of an enlightened public opinion, some check may

[1] The aggregate revenues at the disposal of the native administrations increased from £28,500 in 1906-1907 to £536,000 in 1919.

[2] A piped water-supply from a distant reservoir to Kano city was projected, but the undertaking was delayed by the war.

be afforded by the preparation of annual estimates of revenue and expenditure in a very simple form. These should require the approval of the Governor (or of the Lieut.-Governor), as the colonial estimates require that of the Secretary of State, and any subsequent alteration should require the like sanction. While refraining as far as possible from interference in detail, the Lieut.-Governor can, by suggestion and comparison, effect some co-ordination and uniformity where desirable, and can best discriminate between the scope which may be allowed to an individual, and the grant of extended powers of universal application.[1]

The habits of a people are not changed in a decade, and when powerful despots are deprived of the pastime of war and slave-raiding, and when even the weak begin to forget their former sufferings, to grow weary of a life without excitement, and to resent the petty restrictions which have replaced the cruelties of the old despotism, it must be the aim of Government to provide new interests and rivalries in civilised progress, in education, in material prosperity and trade, and even in sport.[2]

There were indeed many who, with the picture of Fulani misrule fresh in their memory, regarded this system when it was first inaugurated with much misgiving, and believed that though the hostility of the rulers to the British might be concealed, and their vices disguised, neither could be eradicated, and they would always remain hostile at heart. They thought that the Fulani as an alien race of conquerors, who had in turn been conquered, had not the same claims for consideration as those whom they had displaced, even though

[1] Some difference between the Colonial Office and local opinion arose in connection with these funds. The Secretary of State directed that they should only be used for works which the Government would not otherwise have undertaken, and refused contributions made to the cost of the war—limitations which seemed to hamper the utility of the projects undertaken, and to fetter the discretion and wound the susceptibilities of the chiefs and their councils. Opinions also differed as to the extent of the control over these large sums which should in the present stage of evolution be exercised by the Governor, and as to the desirability of some special accounting and audit staff, without unnecessary interference or time-wasting "red-tape." These, however, were not matters of vital importance. The principle at issue was that of dependent rule as opposed to independence, and perhaps the local opinion, in its insistence on the advisability of the former, was betrayed into too narrow a view in regard to financial control.

[2] As Professor Elliott-Smith has justly observed, a people becomes decadent, and population decreases, not so much from war or disease as from lack of interests in life.

they had become so identified with the people that they could no longer be called aliens.

But there can be no doubt that such races form an invaluable medium between the British staff and the native peasantry. Nor can the difficulty of finding any one capable of taking their place, or the danger they would constitute to the State if ousted from their positions, be ignored. Their traditions of rule, their monotheistic religion, and their intelligence enable them to appreciate more readily than the negro population the wider objects of British policy (see p. 220), while their close touch with the masses—with whom they live in daily intercourse—mark them out as destined to play an important part in the future, as they have done in the past, in the development of the tropics.

Both the Arabs in the east and the Fulani in the west are Mohamedans, and by supporting their rule we unavoidably encourage the spread of Islam, which from the purely administrative point of view has the disadvantage of being subject to waves of fanaticism, bounded by no political frontiers. In Nigeria it has been the rule that their power should not be re-established over tribes which had made good their independence, or imposed upon those who had successfully resisted domination.

On the other hand, the personal interests of the rulers must rapidly become identified with those of the controlling Power. The forces of disorder do not distinguish between them, and the rulers soon recognise that any upheaval against the British would equally make an end of them. Once this community of interest is established, the Central Government cannot be taken by surprise, for it is impossible that the native rulers should not be aware of any disaffection.[1]

This identification of the ruling class with the Government accentuates the corresponding obligation to check malpractices on their part. The task of educating them in the duties of a ruler becomes more than ever insistent; of inculcating a sense of responsibility; of convincing their intelligence of the advantages which accrue from the material prosperity of the peasantry, from free labour and initiative;

[1] Soon after the establishment of British rule in Northern Nigeria more than one "Mahdi" arose, and obtained a fanatical following, but in every case the Fulani Emir actively assisted in suppressing the disturbance. In the Sudan thirteen Mahdis arose between 1901 and 1916.—F.O. Handbook 98, p. 43. The Germans in East Africa, in order to check the spread of Islam, encouraged pig-breeding.—Cmd. 1428/1921, p. 30.

of the necessity of delegating powers to trusted subordinates; of the evils of favouritism and bribery; of the importance of education, especially for the ruling class, and for the filling of lucrative posts under Government; of the benefits of sanitation, vaccination, and isolation of infection in checking mortality; and finally, of impressing upon them how greatly they may benefit their country by personal interest in such matters, and by the application of labour-saving devices and of scientific methods in agriculture.

Unintentional misuse of the system of native administration must also be guarded against. It is not, for instance, the duty of a native administration to purchase supplies for native troops, or to enlist and pay labour for public works, though its agency within carefully defined limits may be useful in making known Government requirements, and seeing that markets are well supplied. Nor should it be directed to collect licences, fees, and rents due to Government, nor should its funds be used for any purpose not solely connected with and prompted by its own needs.

I have throughout these pages continually emphasised the necessity of recognising, as a cardinal principle of British policy in dealing with native races, that institutions and methods, in order to command success and promote the happiness and welfare of the people, must be deep-rooted in their traditions and prejudices. Obviously in no sphere of administration is this more essential than in that under discussion, and a slavish adherence to any particular type, however successful it may have proved elsewhere, may, if unadapted to the local environment, be as ill-suited and as foreign to its conceptions as direct British rule would be.

The type suited to a community which has long grown accustomed to the social organisation of the Moslem State may or may not be suitable to advanced pagan communities, which have evolved a social system of their own, such as the Yorubas, the Benis, the Egbas, or the Ashantis in the West, or the Waganda, the Wanyoro, the Watoro, and others in the East. The history, the traditions, the idiosyncracies, and the prejudices of each must be studied by the Resident and his staff, in order that the form adopted shall accord with natural evolution, and shall ensure the ready co-operation of the chiefs and people.[1]

Before passing to the discussion of methods applicable to

[1] See p. 82, footnote 7.

primitive tribes, it may be of interest to note briefly some of the details—as apart from general principles—adopted in Nigeria among the advanced communities.

Chiefs who are executive rulers are graded—those of the first three classes are installed by the Governor or Lieut.-Governor, and carry a staff of office surmounted for the first class by a silver, and for the others by a brass crown. Lower grades carry a baton, and are installed by the Resident, or by the Emir, if the chief is subordinate to him. These staves of office, which are greatly prized, symbolise to the peasantry the fact that the Emir derives his power from the Government, and will be supported in its exercise. The installation of an Emir is a ceremonial witnessed by a great concourse of his people, and dignified by a parade of troops. The native insignia of office, and a parchment scroll, setting out in the vernacular the conditions of his appointment, are presented to him. The alkali (native judge) administers the following oath on the Koran: "I swear in the name of God, well and truly to serve His Majesty King George V. and his representative the Governor of Nigeria, to obey the laws of Nigeria and the lawful commands of the Governor, and of the Lieut.-Governor, provided that they are not contrary to my religion, and if they are so contrary I will at once inform the Governor through the Resident. I will cherish in my heart no treachery or disloyalty, and I will rule my people with justice and without partiality. And as I carry out this oath so may God judge me." Pagan chiefs are sworn according to their own customs on a sword.

Native etiquette and ceremonial must be carefully studied and observed in order that unintentional offence may be avoided. Great importance is attached to them, and a like observance in accordance with native custom is demanded towards British officers. Chiefs are treated with respect and courtesy. Native races alike in India and Africa are quick to discriminate between natural dignity and assumed superiority. Vulgar familiarity is no more a passport to their friendship than an assumption of self-importance is to their respect.[1] The English gentleman needs no prompting in such

[1] "The Master said: The nobler sort of man is dignified but not proud; the inferior man proud but not dignified. The nobler sort of man is easy to serve yet difficult to please. In exacting service from others he takes account of aptitudes and limitations."—'The Sayings of Confucius,' L. Giles, p. 65.

a matter—his instinct is never wrong. Native titles of rank are adopted, and only native dress is worn, whether by chiefs or by schoolboys. Principal chiefs accused of serious crimes are tried by a British court, and are not imprisoned before trial, unless in very exceptional circumstances. Minor chiefs and native officials appointed by an Emir may be tried by his Judicial Council. If the offence does not involve deprivation of office, the offender may be fined without public trial, if he prefers it, in order to avoid humiliation and loss of influence.

Succession is governed by native law and custom, subject in the case of important chiefs to the approval of the Governor, in order that the most capable claimant may be chosen. It is important to ascertain the customary law and to follow it when possible, for the appointment of a chief who is not the recognised heir, or who is disliked by the people, may give rise to trouble, and in any case the new chief would have much difficulty in asserting his authority, and would fear to check abuses lest he should alienate his supporters. In Moslem countries the law is fairly clearly defined, being a useful combination of the hereditary principle, tempered by selection, and in many cases in Nigeria the ingenious device is maintained of having two rival dynasties, from each of which the successor is selected alternately.

In pagan communities the method varies; but there is no rigid rule, and a margin for selection is allowed. The formal approval of the Governor after a short period of probation is a useful precaution, so that if the designated chief proves himself unsuitable, the selection may be revised without difficulty. Minor chiefs are usually selected by popular vote, subject to the approval of the paramount chief. It is a rule in Nigeria that no slave may be appointed as a chief or district headman. If one is nominated he must first be publicly freed.

Small and isolated communities, living within the jurisdiction of a chief, but owing allegiance to the chief of their place of origin—a common source of trouble in Africa—should gradually be absorbed into the territorial jurisdiction. Aliens who have settled in a district for their own purposes would be subject to the local jurisdiction.

CHAPTER XI.

METHODS OF RULING NATIVE RACES—(*Continued*).

Arguments against the system in case of primitive tribes—Reasons for its adoption—Changed conditions in Africa—Decay of tribal authority—The task of the Suzerain power—Effect of direct taxation—Native opinion of the system—Selection of chiefs—Study of primitive institutions—Summary of objects—Results in Nigeria—Loyalty of the chiefs—Criticisms of the system of ruling through chiefs—Government responsibility for misrule—Inadequate supervision—Not applicable to Europeanised class—Interferes with departmental officers—Lessons from Indian policy—The policy in Egypt—French policy in Africa.

THERE are some who consider that however desirable it may be to rule through the native chiefs of advanced communities, such a policy is misplaced, if not impossible, among the backward tribes. Here, they would say, the Resident and his staff must necessarily be the direct rulers, since among the most primitive peoples there are no recognised chiefs capable of exercising rule. The imposition of a tax is in their view premature, since (they say) the natives derive no corresponding benefit, and learn to regard the District Officer merely as a tax-collector. Moreover, refusal to pay necessitates coercive expeditions—scarcely distinguishable from the raids of old times. To attempt to adapt such methods—however suitable to the Moslem communities—to the conditions of primitive tribes, would be to foist upon them a system foreign to their conceptions. In the criticisms I have read no *via media* is indicated between those who are accounted to rank as advanced communities, entitled before long to independence, and direct rule by the British staff.

Let us realise that the advanced communities form a very minute proportion of the population of British Tropical Africa. The vast majority are in the primitive or early tribal stages of development. To abandon the policy of ruling them through their own chiefs, and to substitute the direct rule of the British officer, is to forgo the high ideal of leading the backward races, by their own efforts, in their own way, to raise themselves to a higher plane of social organisation, and tends to perpetuate and stereotype existing conditions.

We must realise also two other important facts. First, that the British staff, exercising direct rule, cannot be otherwise than very small in comparison to the area and population of which they are in charge.[1] That rule cannot generally mean the benevolent autocracy of a particular District Officer, well versed in the language and customs of the people, but rule by a series of different white men, conveying their orders by police and couriers and alien native subordinates, and the quartering of police detachments in native villages. Experience has shown the difficulty in such conditions of detecting and checking cases of abuse of office, and of acquisition of land by alien and absentee native landlords. There is a marked tendency to litigation, and the entire decay of such tribal authority as may previously have existed.

The changed conditions of African life is the second important fact for consideration. The advent of Europeans cannot fail to have a disintegrating effect on tribal authority and institutions, and on the conditions of native life. This is due in part to the unavoidable restrictions imposed on the exercise of their power by the native chiefs. They may no longer inflict barbarous and inhuman punishments on the individual, or take reprisals by force of arms on aggressive neighbours or a disobedient section of the community. The concentration of force in the hands of the Suzerain Power, and the amenability of the chiefs to that Power for acts of oppression and misrule, are evidence to primitive folk that the power of the chiefs has gone. This decay of tribal authority has unfortunately too often been accentuated by the tendency of British officers to deal direct with petty chiefs,

[1] What a thoroughly efficient system of direct rule means, may be seen in the "new territories" of Hong-Kong. In the matter of land alone, 40,000 acres are divided into 350,000 separate lots, classified and described in 87 bulky volumes, which for working purposes are condensed into 9. 24,000 receipts for rent are issued yearly, the average value being 1s. The preparation of the annual rent-roll, and the collection of the rents, are tasks of some magnitude.—Hong-Kong Land Reports.

and to ignore, and allow their subordinates to ignore, the principal chief. It has been increased in many cases by the influx of alien natives, who, when it suited them, set at naught the native authority, and refused to pay the tribute which the chiefs were given no means of enforcing, or acquired lands which they held in defiance of native customary tenure.

But the main cause of the great change which is taking place in the social conditions of African life is to be found in the changed outlook of the African himself. There is, as a writer in 'New Europe' says, "something fantastically inconceivable about the policy of keeping the forces and ideas of the modern world out of Africa," and it is the negation of progress "to fasten down upon the African his own past. . . . Over most of tropical Africa the old order of tribal society is dead, dying, or doomed." He is apparently speaking of East Africa.[1] His views were strongly endorsed by the Governor, Sir P. Girouard—than whom few have shown a greater insight into problems of native administration. In his report on East Africa for 1909-10, Sir P. Girouard enumerates the various agencies which are "breaking down the tribal systems, denationalising the native, and emancipating him from the rule of his chief." "There are not lacking," he writes, "those who favour direct British rule; but if we allow the tribal authority to be ignored or broken, it will mean that we, who numerically form a small minority in the country, shall be obliged to deal with a rabble, with thousands of persons in a savage or semi-savage state, all acting on their own impulses, and making themselves a danger to society generally. There could only be one end to such a policy, and that would be eventual conflict with the rabble."[2]

From every side comes the same story. "For fifteen years," says Mr Wilson, writing of Nyasaland, "I have watched the tribal system breaking up—nothing could infuse new life into it." And with the rapid changes the native character has deteriorated. Stealing and burglary are rife, and the old village discipline and respect for chiefs has gone.[3]

[1] 'The African Mandates,' by Fulani bin Fulani. 'New Europe,' 7th and 14th July 1919. See also "Africanus" in the 'African Society's Journal,' January 1921, p. 98.

[2] Cd. 5467 of 1911, pp. 39 and 47. For a description of the system adopted, see Official Handbook 1216, p. 243.

[3] 'East and West,' January 1921.

In the West we find the mine manager with his wife and flower-garden established in a district which only a few years ago was the inaccessible fastness of a cannibal tribe. Ladies in mission schools teach nude savage children the elements of geography and arithmetic. The smattering of knowledge and caricature of the white man's ways acquired by these children react on their village, and upset tribal customs and authority. A few years ago one would find communities in which no individual had ever been twenty miles from his home. To-day the young men migrate in hundreds to offer their labour at the mines or elsewhere, and return with strange ideas. Some perhaps have even been overseas from West to East Africa during the war.

The produce of the village loom, or dye-pit, or smithy, is discounted by cheap imported goods, and the craftsman's calling is not what it was. Traders, white and black, circulate under the *pax Britannica* among tribes but recently addicted to head-hunting, and bring to them new and strange conceptions. The primitive African is called upon to cope with ideas a thousand years in advance of his mental and social equipment. "He cannot proceed leisurely along the road to progress. He must be hurried along it, or the free and independent savage will sink to the level of the helot and the slave."

Here, then, in my view, lies our present task in Africa. It becomes impossible to maintain the old order—the urgent need is for adaptation to the new—to build up a tribal authority with a recognised and legal standing, which may avert social chaos. It cannot be accomplished by superseding—by the direct rule of the white man—such ideas of discipline and organisation as exist, nor yet by "stereotyping customs and institutions among backward races which are not consistent with progress." [1]

The first step is to hasten the transition from the patriarchal to the tribal stage, and induce those who acknowledge no other authority than the head of the family to recognise a common chief. Where this stage has already been reached, the object is to group together small tribes, or sections of a tribe, so as to form a single administrative unit, whose chiefs severally, or in Council as a "Native Court" (see chapter xxviii.), may be constituted a "Native Authority," with

[1] Debate on Colonial Office vote, 26th April 1920.

defined powers over native aliens, through whom the district officer can work instead of through alien subordinates. His task is to strengthen the authority of the chiefs, and encourage them to show initiative; to learn their difficulties at first hand, and to assist them in adapting the new conditions to the old—maintaining and developing what is best, avoiding everything that has a tendency to denationalisation and servile imitation. He can guide and control several such units, and endeavour gradually to bring them to the standard of an advanced community. In brief, tribal cohesion, and the education of the tribal heads in the duties of rulers, are the watchwords of the policy in regard to these backward races. As the unit shows itself more and more capable of conducting its own affairs, the direct rule, which at first is temporarily unavoidable among the most backward of all, will decrease, and the community will acquire a legal status, which the European and the native agent of material development must recognise. "The old easy-going days, when the probity of the individual was sufficient title to rule, are gone. . . . Intelligent interest, imagination, comprehension of alien minds —these are the demands of to-day."

To this end the institution of the tax is the first beginning. It marks the recognition by the community of the Suzerainty of the protecting Power, and the corresponding obligation to refrain from lawless acts. Failure to impose it is regarded as a sign of weakness or of fear. The payment of "tribute" to a chief marks the transition from the patriarchal to the tribal stage. It forms no burden, and is only refused if a community deliberately desires to throw off all restraint and revert to lawlessness, in which case coercive measures become inevitable for the protection of the law-abiding. The most experienced Residents declare that it is not resented, and is a definite curb on the impulse to attack traders.

Throughout the whole of the British African tropics (except the Gold Coast) the sum levied on the pagan tribes is a substantial one, but in Northern Nigeria it has generally been nominal in amount,[1] and there at any rate it cannot be said to have been without a substantial equivalent, in the promotion of trade and prosperity, in the construction of roads,

[1] It was at first fixed at 3d. per annum per adult—or at most at 6d.—and later somewhat increased. In many protectorates it ranges up to 10s. or £1.

in the beginnings of education, and in the suppression of slave-raiding. "Since you have stopped slave-raiding," said a pagan chief to a Resident, "we are willing to do or give what you like."

The inauguration of a treasury, in like manner, though admittedly beyond the grasp of such peoples, is the embryo conception which will later develop with education, and they are quick to realise that the salaried chiefs and sub-chiefs are not merely paid officers of the Government, but receive a portion of the funds which they themselves collect from the people. They do not exist merely to collect an alien tax as the agents of Government, but are selected as men who will be trusted and followed by their people, and capable of expressing their opinions. Among the primitive communities it suffices that the share of the tax should be sufficient to meet their salaries only, so long as they are incapable of understanding or exercising any judgment regarding other expenditure. Without a tax there can be no treasury, and without a treasury no real eventual measure of self-rule. The imposition of a tax at a later stage of development would be resented as a breach of faith, and would generally lead to trouble.

It is not necessary that these embryo administrations should follow closely the model adopted for the Moslem communities, if any more natural line presents itself. Experience in the advanced pagan communities will suggest divergencies. For, as I have said, there is no desire to impose on the people any theoretically suitable form of government, but rather to evolve from their own institutions, based on their own habits of thought, prejudices, and customs, the form of rule best suited to them, and adapted to meet the new conditions.

Direct British rule among primitive tribes, unaccompanied by any tax, may perhaps, if a fully adequate staff is provided, be the least troublesome, and temporarily at any rate the most efficient—albeit the most costly—method. But it shirks the more difficult task of education, and when the time comes—as it inevitably will come—and the people demand a voice in the control of their own affairs, we shall find—as we find in India to-day—that we have destroyed the natural institutions of the country, that we have sapped the foundations of native rule, and have taught them only the duty of obedience. We can then only offer an alien system, evolved by Western nations to suit wholly different circumstances, moulded on European and not on native habits of thought.

The Moslem Emir of Yola and his Council showed, I think, a better appreciation of these principles than the critics I have quoted. The natural instinct of a Fulani, they said, when he has got over his fear of the pagans, is to treat them as slaves, and he would then either be murdered by them or convicted of oppression by Government. "If they think you are trying to make them Fulani or Moslems they resent it. I would not put a Fulani headman to live in their country, but he should constantly tour amongst them, and advise the pagan chief, and tell all the people that they may appeal to him, but he should not go behind his back." The Waziri added: "As the British govern us through ourselves, so we must govern the pagans through their own chiefs. If we think we can deal directly with the pagan peasantry, we are deceived. We should know nothing of what is going on, and we should do no good." This view was not dictated by a desire to please, for it was apparently opposed to the policy of the Resident at the time. How striking is this advance from the methods of the Fulani conquerors.

It is of the first importance that the chiefs should be elected by the community from among themselves, and be men of influence and strength of character, neither middlemen traders selected for their wealth nor Moslems. It is preferable also not to employ the latter as judges of the courts, or teachers in the schools, even though progress be slower. If the selection of an alien is inevitable he should not be allowed to retain any armed following. The District Officer must be tolerant of misrule due to inexperience in a chief who promises well, and avoid damaging his prestige and influence.

In order to develop a system suited to their needs, the District Officer must study their customs and social organisations; for without a knowledge of their institutions the result must be failure. These in some tribes take the form of a classification by age, the youths being circumcised in batches, each of which forms a class with special duties and standing.[1] Most tribes develop a number of societies

[1] The senior class among the Ibos of West Africa—who number several millions—form the "Akang" club, the juniors the "Ekpe" club. The clubs give entertainments, and arrange for batches of labourers when required, &c. Compare Sir C. Eliot's description of the age-classes of the Masai in East Africa, *loc. cit.*, p. 136, and Handbook 1216, p. 241.

with secret ritual, which will usually be found to have their origin in some sound principle, such as the maintenance of discipline among lawless sections or the promotion of tribal cohesion.

In some cases it is reported that a society which formerly existed for purposes of extortion, or even murder and human sacrifice, has, owing to the native court system, which allows of trial in open court, become innocuous. In other cases the power wielded by those who conduct the secret ritual may have caused the society to degenerate into a cruel Fetish cult, destroying its value as a social organisation. Or its prestige and influence may have been misused to cover the crimes or the greed of individuals, or a tribal "age-class" may have adopted a ritual, and formed a society inimical to the interest of the community. Careful investigation is necessary to distinguish between Fetish cults, which exist to terrorise the people by human sacrifice and witchcraft (such as the "Chuku Juju" of the Aros, or the alleged "Human Leopard Society" of Sierra Leone), and those which have their origin in social customs, and may afford a framework which, when divested of its harmful accretions, is capable of development and understood by the people—to which class very probably the "Ogboni" may belong.

These primitive tribes—as we shall see when discussing the courts—are capable, even in their present stage, of settling ordinary social disputes in a tribunal composed of chiefs—which, in default of rulers of sufficient individual importance and prestige, it is often necessary to endow with executive powers as the "Native Authority."

Turning now from the detailed discussion of the application of this system to advanced communities on the one hand, and to primitive tribes on the other, let us glance at its results and the criticisms it has evoked. I think that there are very hopeful possibilities for the future in the development of the "Native Administrations" of Nigeria. Already they bear a large share in the cost of the schools; they are showing an increasing interest in the establishment of dispensaries, in the sanitation of the great cities, and in leper settlements. Some, especially Sokoto, have taken a keen interest in afforestation and artesian well-boring. Kano, in view of its congested population, has developed a scheme of rough-and-ready delimitation of farm lands by native surveyors. Special classes for training youths in agriculture, forestry, veterinary work, and survey will provide young men (drawn from the provinces which need them) with some technical training for service under the native administrations.

The steady increase in the material prosperity of the peasantry of the Moslem Emirates is the frequent theme of the Residents' annual reports, and though this cannot be attributed solely—or even primarily—to the system of native administration, there can be no doubt that this system has had a large share in the result. The growing wealth of the people renders possible a steady increase in the tax, with a corresponding addition to the funds available for local development. That the system has been successful is proved by the contentment of the people and the loyalty of their chiefs. The Emirs and their councillors appreciate the liberality of the Government policy and the genuine sympathy of the Residents, and any breach of the peace has come to be looked on as an almost impossible occurrence. A perusal of the latest reports (1917-18) from his Residents cannot but fill the Lieut.-Governor of the northern provinces with satisfaction.[1]

The war, however, put the system to the crucial test. It was well known that Britain was fighting against Turkey, a Moslem State with whom the Senussi, whose emissaries from Tripoli find easy access to Nigeria, was in active alliance. A great rising took place in the vast regions under French rule bordering Nigeria to the north. Reports, fully credited

[1] I make a few extracts at random. Kano reports an increase of £32,000 in the revenue, and 1000 miles of unmetalled or partially metalled roads fit for light motors. Zaria, Nassarawa, Illorin, and other provinces state that the pagans, who for generations have lived on the hill-tops to escape the raids of the Fulani, and from their inaccessible eyries have been a menace to traders, are increasingly coming down to live peacefully in the plains in well-planned villages. In Zaria the revenue has quadrupled in four years; the facilities of the bank are used for surplus funds. The *Mallamai* take pride in their work, and now keep registers of births, deaths, and migrations. Sanitary reform includes the use of incinerators and refuse-bins. Sokoto reports a like progress in sanitation, and adds that the population has nearly trebled since the British advent in 1903, due largely to immigration over the frontier. Village heads report to the district head and to the native courts cases of cattle disease, breach of isolation rules, and any robberies in their vicinity. The prisons are admirably kept, the prisoners well cared for, and the discipline good. The officials of the native administration work cordially with those of the Government, both executive and judicial, and the "*Dogarai*" afford all assistance to the police. The credit of inaugurating and giving practical and successful effect to this method belongs wholly to the Residents and their staff—Messrs Temple, Goldsmith, Gowers, Arnett, Gall, Palmer, among others.

by the French themselves, reached the country that Agades —the desert capital—had fallen before a Moslem army well equipped with cannon. Hostile forces were said to be rapidly advancing towards Sokoto. The French asked our assistance. Half our own forces, and most of the officers well known to the natives, had already gone to East Africa. But not for a moment was there the slightest doubt of the loyalty of the Emirs. The garrison of Kano itself was withdrawn, and replaced by police. Sokoto and Katsena, the border States, were eager to raise native levies to assist.

Each year of the war the native treasuries offered £50,000 towards its cost. The last year they subscribed £11,000 to the Red Cross Fund—the Sultan of Sokoto preferring that he and his chiefs should subscribe from their private means for such a purpose rather than from the public treasury. Daily prayers in all the mosques were offered for the victory of the King's arms.

Dr Solf, when Minister for the Colonies in Berlin, visited Nigeria. He expressed to Mr Harcourt his appreciation of our methods, and wrote to me (for I was absent at the time) that he intended to adopt them in the German Cameruns.

The system described has, of course, like every other possible system, found its critics and opponents. The educated native very naturally dislikes it, for it places the native chief, who has no schoolroom education, and is probably ignorant even of the English language, in a position of authority over his people, and tends to make him independent of the educated native lawyer or adviser.

The criticism of Europeans is, so far as I am aware, chiefly confined to those who have not had personal experience of its working, or adequate opportunity to examine for themselves the truths of statements they have read in the native press. Bishop Tugwell, whose long and faithful service in West Africa has chiefly lain in the coast area and its immediate hinterland, writes: "'Indirect rule' is direct rule by indirect means. The Emir's position and salary are secure. His sway, backed by British authority, is rendered absolute, while his people become his serfs, or those of the British Government. Their life is thus robbed of all initiative or desire for progress—intellectual, social, moral, religious, or political." The Emir, he adds, who is appointed by the Government, is the instrument of the Resident, and "the name of Christ must not be proclaimed lest this blighting system should be overturned."

The statement is inaccurate, for there are very many cases on record in Nigeria, extending from the earliest beginnings of British rule in the north up to the present day, where not only the highest officials of the native administration have been deprived of their positions and subjected to the rigours of the law for misconduct, but even Emirs and principal chiefs have been deposed for misrule. As regards the peasantry, it is incontestable that they have never enjoyed such liberty and material prosperity as they now possess, such security of land tenure and immunity from oppression. The new Government schools are opening up avenues for intellectual and social progress. (See chap. xxii.) With the question of Christian propaganda in Moslem States I shall deal in a later chapter.

But Bishop Tugwell, unconsciously perhaps, gives imperfect expression to an aspect of the matter on which I have already touched. It was naturally a cause for anxiety and misgiving that the British Government, by supporting native rule, and the authority of the native courts, should accept some measure of responsibility for evils which its meagre staff of British officials was unable to control adequately, seeing that the one was exercised by men who had behind them a century's tradition of such tyranny and oppression as I have described, and the other had become corrupt and inflicted barbarous sentences. To overthrow an organisation, however faulty, which has the sanction of long usage, and is acquiesced in by the people, before any system could be created to take its place—before, indeed, we had any precise knowledge of Moslem methods or of native law and custom —would have been an act of folly which no sane administrator could attempt. The very necessity for avoiding precipitate action, and the knowledge that reform could only be effective, and enlist native co-operation, if it was gradual, made the responsibility all the more onerous. To infer that it was not realised, or was lightly regarded, is to do a great injustice to the administrative staff of the early Government of Northern Nigeria, who struggled to cope with a burden which taxed them beyond their strength. Some died, and some left with health impaired.

That the supervision exercised was insufficient, in spite

of their efforts, is a reasonable criticism, for the staff was quite inadequate. In the year 1903-4, in which the whole of the Moslem States first came under British control, Northern Nigeria provided in its budget for forty-four administrative officers.[1] Of these, as I have shown (p. 141), we can only assume that a half were actually at work. Thus in the fourth year after the administration was inaugurated there was only about one officer available for each 11,600 square miles and 400,000 head of population—and most of them very young and new to the work!

On amalgamation with Southern Nigeria in 1914 I had hoped that the finances would at last admit of an adequate provision of staff, and of decent houses for them to live in. But the Great War broke out, and the staff was again depleted below the uttermost safety limit, to allow every possible officer to join the fighting forces. The conditions have retarded progress in the pagan areas, and must be borne in mind by those who criticise the inadequacy of supervision in the past.

That the system is inapplicable to communities of Europeanised natives educated on Western lines is admitted. The method of their progress towards self-government lies, as I have said, along the same path as that of Europeans—increased participation in municipal affairs until they prove themselves fitted for the larger responsibilities of Government of their own communities, by a majority vote in the councils, by popular election, and by appointment to posts of responsibility in the Civil Service.

A local criticism is that the natives are taught to look to the District Officer only, that the latter is intolerant of any departmental officer exercising authority in his district, and that it is impossible for a departmental officer to feel a keen interest in his work, and achieve the best results, if he is practically dependent on a junior administrative officer, and can get nothing done without reference to him.

The reply is that orders to the local headman emanate, not from the District Officer, but from his own chief (to whom any wishes of Government in the matter are communicated by the Resident). The District Officer, who knows the headmen personally and speaks their language, is the natural and best means that the departmental officer can employ for

[1] 'Gazette' of 30th April 1903.

making his demands known, and obtaining the services of an agent from the chief to procure labour, &c. In technical details he gives his orders direct. In case of difficulty it is not to the District Officer but to his own chief that the headman appeals for instructions. The chief in turn only invokes the advice or intervention of the Resident if he needs it.

Our experience in India (to which I alluded in the last chapter) seems to me to afford a striking confirmation of the principles which underlie the policy I have advocated. "British India" (comprising nearly two-thirds of the country and over three-quarters of its population) has been subjected to direct British rule, which foreign critics have praised as a model of efficiency. But when the inevitable time arrived, and India demanded a measure of self-government, the bases on which it had rested for centuries are found to have been destroyed, and to-day the situation in British India is described as the most serious with which England has ever been confronted, for the policy of the past rated administrative efficiency more highly than education in self-government.

In the remaining part of India we have ruled indirectly through the native princes. The limitations to their independence were less onerous than those which are necessary in Africa,[1] for they were the inheritors of an ancient civilisation, and their relations with the Suzerain Power were established by treaty, and not by conquest. The conditions which obtain in their territories to-day are in marked contrast with the disorder around them. Their progress has been fostered by the tactful and devoted guidance of the British Residents at their courts.[2] Their loyalty has been so unquestioned that of late years they have been encouraged to maintain standing armies of their own, which have been freely placed at the service of Government, and we have ceded to them fortresses such as Gwalior, which we formerly maintained to overawe them. The institutions and enlightened rule of some of these States rival those of British India. Their peasantry are said to be happier and more satisfied under the rule of their own chiefs than under the system of direct rule.

[1] See Ilbert, *loc. cit.*, chap. ii. pp. 141-145, and chap. vii.

[2] It was not till 1909 that Lord Minto directed that Residents should no longer press reforms upon the native rulers. Their policy in future was to be one of non-interference in internal affairs. Direct British rule continued, however, to be exercised when the heir was a minor, and his education was the care of the Suzerain Power.

In Egypt European "advisers" were appointed to the various Ministries in Cairo, whose titular head was an Egyptian, and this system was extended to the provincial "Mudirates." Even under the watchful eye of Lord Cromer—tied as he was to headquarters at Cairo—the tendency for these "inspectors," as they were infelicitously called, to assume the rôle of *de facto* rulers, had already become marked. The mudirs, as Lord Milner observed [1] (writing in 1892), "did not so much mind taking orders themselves, if it was clearly understood that they alone were entitled to give orders to their subordinates. 'Tell us what you want done,' they say to their foreign monitors, 'and we will take care that your wishes are carried out, but do not attempt to see to their execution yourself.'" This is the whole difference between direct rule and rule through the native rulers. Until it has become a tradition, enshrined in precise written instructions (necessarily somewhat detailed), and maintained by constant personal touch between the head of the Government and his administrative officers, the tendency of the energetic, capable British officer to overstep his rôle as adviser will inevitably assert itself. "Instances, however, were not wanting (in Egypt) in which Englishmen have got on thoroughly well with provincial Governors, and come to be regarded by them as friends and helpmates, and not as spies and intruders." Lord Milner emphasises the absolute necessity of supervision and control over native officials. "The whole problem," he says, "is how to exercise this control, which is indispensable, without destroying the prestige of the permanent officials, which is equally indispensable." The problem could not have been better or more concisely stated.[2]

With the passing of Lord Cromer, the tendency to direct rule by the inspectors, appointed "to advise the Advisers," became more pronounced, and junior inspectors assumed the right to dictate to the mudirs, on whom in theory the responsibility rests.[3]

[1] 'England in Egypt,' p. 110-111. [2] Ibid., p. 334.

[3] See articles on "Egyptian Unrest," 'Times,' 9th September 1919, and 7th January 1920. The writer proposes that the British staff should become executive officers, responsible to their Egyptian official superiors—the mudirs—who are again controlled by the Egyptian Ministers with their British advisers. I have ventured to suggest that, however anxious both might be to fulfil their obligations with loyalty, nothing but disharmony and friction could result from such a system, and the best qualities of both would be nullified.—(Letter to 'Times,' 16th September 1919, with which Lord Milner expressed to me his general con-

Foreign nations have never, so far as I am aware, adopted a policy similar to that of Great Britain, in whose colonies, even where direct rule by British officers is maintained, the native chiefs retain their titular positions, and are allowed the exercise of restricted powers. In French West Africa chiefs are appointed as Government officials, but there is no organisation of former native kingdoms under their traditional rulers, as in Nigeria or Uganda. On the contrary, the sons of former native chiefs are deprived of all titles of sovereignty.

As native officials they are employed in matters of sanitation, the levying of taxes, road construction, engagement of labour, &c., and in subordinate posts under the Government. A portion of Senegal is governed directly and exclusively by white officials. Though the older conception of the assimilation of the native races appears to be giving place to one of trusteeship, the quondam native rulers remain mere subordinates of the Europeans, who conduct the native affairs.[1] The French system proceeds on the hypothesis that the colonies are an integral part of France, and its inhabitants Frenchmen, with consequent liability to conscription, &c. We learn, however, that the secret of General Lyautey's success in Morocco is that he introduced collaboration with the native chiefs, and the principle of dual administration between the protector and the protected, and by this means he everywhere conciliated the populations he subdued.[2]

The object of substituting for British rule, in which the chiefs are mere agents of the Government, a system of native rule under the guidance and control of the British staff, whether among advanced or backward communities, is primarily educative.[3] Among backward tribes the chiefs have

currence). The mudir should take his orders only from his official chief, the Egyptian Minister, and he alone should give orders to the village sheikhs. The British inspector tenders advice, and sees that abuses do not exist, and should be responsible only to his British chief—the adviser to the Minister. In the Sudan Egyptians and Sudanese are appointed as mamurs (police officers, and magistrates of districts), and their numbers are increasing. Foreign Office Handbook 98, p. 60.

[1] Foreign Office Handbook No. 100, 1920, pp. 6 and 10.

[2] 'La France au Maroc,' Berthe Georges Gaulis.

[3] Mr Gilmour, reviewing in the 'African Society's Journal' (April 1912) two books[1] in which this system of native rule was described, thus summarises: "Like a silver thread the proposition of the paramount importance of helping the African to become a better African, and not endeavouring to turn him into a caricature of a European, runs through both books, and is obviously regarded

[1] 'The Making of Northern Nigeria,' Captain Orr. 'Nigeria, its Peoples and Problems,' E. D. Morel.

to learn how to exert and maintain authority, and establish a chain of responsibility reaching down to the village head. Among the more advanced their interest is directed to education, forestry, sanitation, prevention of disease, and public works. In all alike the endeavour is to prevent denationalisation, to develop along indigenous lines, to inculcate the principle that the function of the ruler is to promote the welfare of his people and not to exploit them for his own pleasure, and to afford both to rulers and people the stimulus of progress and interest in life.

by both authors as the fundamental proposition of the Nigerian policy." "The policy of the administration," he says later, "is directed to developing the resources of the country, through the agency of the natives rather than by concessions to Europeans."

CHAPTER XII.

TAXATION.

Direct tax—The basis of native administration—Tax on Pagans accords with native custom—Tax in Moslem districts—Tax denotes progress—Delay in imposition inadvisable—On primitive people should be light—Taxation as an incentive to work—Is indirect taxation sufficient—The tax on advanced communities—Nature of the tax—Income and "profits"—Tax on average standard of production—Profits on trades other than agriculture—Rate of tax—Abuses of the old system: (*a*) Absentee landlords; (*b*) Tax-gatherers; (*c*) Disconnected areas of jurisdiction—Summary of reforms—Disposal of tax—Definition of village and town—Principles of assessment—Tax is not a land rent—Method of assessment: (*a*) Native officials; (*b*) The District Officer's task—Taxation of primitive communities—Payment in cash, kind, or labour—By whom payable—Drastic changes to be avoided—Personation—The hut-tax—Contrast with the tax proposed—Summary of results of direct taxation—Minor direct taxes—Licences and market dues.

APPENDIX.

The hut-tax in Africa—In Sierra Leone—Uganda—Nyasaland—East Africa—Northern Rhodesia—South Africa—Foreign Nations.

No system of rule can be effective—whether governmental or municipal—unless it enjoys some measure of financial independence; and, as I have said, the fundamental basis upon which the policy I have described in the last chapter rests, is the assignment to the native rulers of a definite revenue with which to pay the salaries of their officials, and to inaugurate schemes of development. This revenue must obviously be found by taxation, and in Nigeria (to which I again refer in illustration, because it is the dependency which I know best) it is derived from a direct tax—based on the principle of an income-tax—collected through the machinery of the native administration, in accordance with native law and custom, and under the close supervision of the British staff.

The native rulers and others who share it are not therefore salaried officials of Government, but derive their incomes as proper dues from their own people, in return for their work as rulers, or judges, or employees of the native administration. They, and even the more intelligent of the peasantry, can see that a substantial portion of the tax is spent by themselves in their own immediate interests, and can appreciate the necessity of devoting the remainder to the central Government. They thus have an interest in its collection in full, and there is no perennial complaint of an insufficient grant for the maintenance of the native administration, disproportioned to their particular claims.

Moreover, it is obvious that the native rulers must have some means of livelihood, and of maintaining their position. If there be no legal and recognised tax, the necessary income must be obtained by arbitrary levies on the peasantry, subject to no control by Government. In the Moslem States the tax is the corollary of the abolition of slavery.

It has been asserted that, with the exception of those communities which have accepted the Koranic system of taxation, the natives of Africa are unaccustomed to, and radically opposed to, direct taxation, and that it is therefore better to adopt indirect taxation, the incidence of which they do not understand.

The African is not peculiar in disliking taxes, but as soon as any degree of tribal cohesion is reached, the obligation to pay tribute to the head chief—generally in the form of slaves, concubines, food, and unpaid labour—is recognised. As the tribe advances in organisation, and its rulers become more powerful and luxurious—as in such pagan communities as the Baganda, the Yorubas, Benis, &c.—the demands become increasingly heavy. It is probable that the Moslem conquerors in Northern Nigeria merely superimposed the Koranic tithe upon the pre-existing scheme of taxation among the Habes. Mahomedan rule merely admitted of a more systematised method.

Only among the most primitive peoples, where the authority of a paramount chief has not yet emerged, do we find an entire absence of taxation, for there is no authority to demand or enforce it. Such communities regard the payment of tribute as the token of acknowledgment of a Suzerain, with the consequent obligation to refrain from murders and robberies. Provided that it is not collected by alien native tax-gatherers, and is not unduly onerous, they do not appear to resent its imposition; and, as I have said in the last chapter, refusal to pay is usually a formal and deliberate prelude to an outbreak of lawlessness.

A direct tax is not therefore contrary to native custom or prejudices among those who have reached the tribal stage,[1] and the dislike of it is not due to any objection to the principle, but to the imposition of a tax in addition to, instead of in substitution for, the tribute. The Yorubas, who at first resented it strongly, asked for its imposition when they understood the system, and the hostility of the Fulani was similarly converted to a whole-hearted co-operation.

The tax imposed by alien Moslem conquerors on those who adopted the Faith was the Koranic tithe, with a much more onerous levy on conquered pagans (which was doubled in case of rebellion), while unconquered tribes were regarded as slave preserves. With the growth of luxury the tendency is for the rich and powerful to evade it, while the peasantry, even though nominally Moslems, are subjected to increasing burdens. The rulers no longer lead in war, the *Jihad* degenerates into the slave-raid, and the tax is collected by deputy, while the chiefs live in luxury at the capital, surrounded by slaves, eunuchs, and concubines. The erstwhile leaders of the armies become fief-holders farming the taxes of large districts, or particular cities, and appointing their relatives and favourites as their deputies.[2]

The payment of direct taxes is in Africa, as elsewhere, an unwelcome concomitant of progress. It marks the recognition of the principle that each individual in proportion to his means has an obligation to the State, to which he owes security

[1] Sir W. Macgregor, who expressed this view, nevertheless recognised the obligation to pay the customary direct tribute to the chiefs, and himself undertook to reassess it among the Illeshas, when it had lapsed owing to the decay of tribal authority consequent on the advent of the British ('Gazette,' 16/1/04). The regular tribute among the Yorubas and Illeshas, paid by both men and women, is said to have varied from 5s. to 10s. It was supplemented by obligatory personal service, and there were special taxes, including death-duties.

[2] These were the characteristics of the decadence of Fulani domination in Northern Nigeria, which necessitated its overthrow by the British administration. The Sultan of Sokoto admitted that the fall of the Fulani dynasty was a just punishment for their misrule. All kinds of additional and irregular taxes—on special classes or on particular crops or possessions—had been introduced. The ancient kingdom of Bornu appears to have approached to something like an income-tax and death duties.

for life and property, and his increased wealth,—due to fair wages for his labour, improved transport, and a large competitive market for his produce.

By its means the upper classes can be paid salaries for public work; slavery, forced labour, and all other forms of exactions from the peasantry can be declared illegal without reducing the ruling classes to poverty. The freed slave, on his part, renders to the State a small and fixed proportion of the profits of his industry. The tax may thus in a sense be regarded as a means of promoting the recognition of individual responsibility, which is inseparable from liberty, but is destroyed by the system of slavery. It was by this means that in Nigeria we sought a solution of the difficulties attendant on the abolition of the legal status of slavery, and to support the ruling classes while protecting the peasantry.

It emancipates justice by freeing the salaried native judge from the temptation of bribes and unjust fines. It lightens the heavy burdens on trade, both by rendering possible the abolition of the tolls levied by native rulers, by decreasing the amount which must otherwise be raised by customs, and by promoting, as no other agency can, the introduction of coin currency. The task of assessment promotes an intimate touch between the British staff and the native officials who assist in it on the one hand, and the inhabitants of remote and almost inaccessible villages on the other hand, who but for this assessment might have remained unknown. The District Officer comes as the herald of a just and equitable tax to replace extortion.

Among unorganised communities, not previously subject to tax, where native rulers cannot be said to exist, the tax affords a means of creating and enforcing native authority, of curbing lawlessness, and assisting in tribal evolution, and hence it becomes a moral benefit, and is justified by the immunity from slave-raids which the people now enjoy.

Though the project of instituting a tax before the introduction of a coin currency should have afforded a means of converting it into revenue seemed at first impossible, I soon became convinced that postponement would be a weak and short-sighted policy, which would render the eventual necessity all the harder of attainment. For the time must come, as it has come to every community in the world, when some form of direct tax for revenue purposes must be imposed.

That necessity has been recognised (with, I believe, the sole exception of the Gold Coast) by every administration in British and foreign tropical Africa. If delayed, its imposition is certain to be resented, and to lead to trouble and bloodshed. If it is imposed at once it is recognised as part of the white man's rule, and accepted as such. The inauguration of British rule is the moment at which to lay the foundations, not merely in view of subsequent necessities for revenue, but in order to establish the principle of personal contribution to the State in proportion to wealth, to which I have referred.

But though the principle in my view should be asserted at the outset, it is of no less importance that the tax should in primitive communities be very light at first, since it is there intended to be educative rather than a source of revenue. If it is in principle an income tax (though in a primitive communal society it becomes a poll-tax) it will automatically be proportioned to the ability to pay. It will correspond in some degree with the expenditure incurred in the district. Now that new territories are falling under British control by the Mandate of the Powers, it is worth while to emphasise the necessity both for the early imposition of the tax, and for making it a light one.

There are those who advocate direct taxation primarily as a means of compelling the natives to work. This was the underlying principle of a clause in Mr Rhodes' "Glen Grey Act" (which, however, provided that the proceeds of the tax should be applied to their own benefit).[1] Mr Chamberlain ridiculed the idea that the South African method was akin to slavery. The native, he considered, should be made to work, because he had for so long forced his women to work in order that he might live in idleness. The substitution of labour for the payment of a tax, or the imposition of a heavier tax if the native cannot prove that he has worked for a specified time, are expedients which in the past have been adopted elsewhere.

If, as has been alleged regarding natives restricted to Reserves, the males of a community are found to be living in habitual idleness and drunkenness, special taxation may perhaps be justified in their own best interests; but in that case the native should be free to earn the money by working

[1] The clause remained a dead letter for eleven years, and was then formally repealed.—B. Williams' 'Life of Cecil Rhodes,' p. 212.

on his own land, or by offering his labour to whom he chooses. The object in view would be the education of the native, not the procuring of labour for Government or European employers, or the increase of revenue.[1] I shall recur to this subject in the chapter on labour.

Under normal conditions the African rarely needs compulsion to work, and this is not the object of the tax I have proposed, but in so far as the tax stimulates productive industry, and compels a man, as in England, to provide an extra margin wherewith to meet the obligation, or if it diminishes the large surplus of the grain crops, which among many pagan tribes is set aside for brewing liquor with which to indulge in frequent drunken orgies, its effect can only be good (pp. 603-4).

It was reported in Northern Nigeria that in districts where taxes had formerly been paid to the Fulani but had lapsed, considerable areas had gone out of cultivation, and the male population, deprived, as in South Africa, of its principal occupation of fighting, had taken to drinking and quarrelling. In Southern Nigeria the tribute to the chiefs had in many cases been discontinued on the advent of the British, and tribal authority had consequently been weakened. The High Commissioner of Uganda expressed the view that the direct tax "will prove to be the making of the country, not only because of the revenue it brings, but because of the habits of work it inculcates, which are rapidly altering one of the natural characteristics of the people."

It may be asked whether, so far as revenue is concerned, a sufficient sum could not be raised both for Government requirements and to support the native administration, by indirect taxation? The only substantial source of revenue from indirect taxation accrues from customs duties. It is not possible that such duties should provide a revenue adequate for the needs of the Government, and none at all could be spared for native administration. In Nigeria the customs duties were estimated in 1919 to provide less than a third (29½ per cent) of the total revenue (including the sums retained by the native administrations), in spite of the fact

[1] See chapter xix. Lord Milner in the Transvaal, and Sir G. Lagden in Basutoland, both agreed that the primary object of the tax should not be to compel labour. Lord Milner's later pronouncements as Secretary of State, both in a despatch published as a White-book and in the debate in the House of Lords, are quoted in the chapter referred to.

that they had been recently increased by a third, by special export duties which were not intended to be permanent.[1] In East Africa—taking a mean between the years 1913-14 (pre-war) and 1917-18—the customs provided only 13½ per cent of the revenue [2]—in the Sudan only 12 per cent.[3]

The trade of the tropics consists of the export of raw materials in exchange for manufactured goods, and customs duties offer the simplest and cheapest form of taxation, but they have their limits. Though a necessary adjunct, they retard the development of trade, and fall very unequally on the population. Provinces distant from the sea and the railway consume the minimum of customable goods, and hence pay but little indirect tax, though they are the most costly to administer by reason of the heavy transport charges. Other forms of indirect taxation, of which fines and fees of court are probably the most considerable, are not easily expandable.

Where direct taxes already exist, the object in view is to consolidate them into a single annual payment, based on native law and custom and the indigenous institutions of the country, while ensuring that the sum demanded is just and reasonable, and that the method of collection is such as will distribute the burden equitably in proportion to the wealth of the individual, and finally to see that it is clearly understood by chiefs and people alike that any demand in excess of this authorised tax is illegal. The chiefs must be warned that any attempt to make a larger demand—even indirectly as compulsory labour, or the exaction of supplies or food without payment—will lay them open to a charge of extortion, and the peasantry are informed that in such a case they can appeal from the village to the district head, or in the last resort, to the Emir and the British staff.

In the Moslem States of Northern Nigeria the immediate task was to consolidate the multiplicity of taxes into a single "general" tax, payable on a single demand after the harvest, and whenever possible in currency instead of in kind. The

[1] Prior to the abolition of the import of "trade spirits," an abnormal revenue was raised by the duties imposed on these imports, which in 1913 amounted to about two-thirds (64 per cent) of the total customs receipts (£1,138,000 out of £1,760,400). The duty was about 250 per cent *ad valorem*. Customs were 51 per cent of revenue.

[2] 'East African Economic Commission's Report,' p. 7.

[3] Handbook 98, p. 158.

task of the District Officer was to assist the district and village headmen to assess it, year by year improving the graduation in proportion to wealth. It rests with the head of the Government to see that as far as possible some measure of uniformity, and of equality of incidence, is introduced in the different provinces.[1] Among primitive communities, where no recognised tribute exists, the communal basis of society compels a capitation tax, but this is susceptible of gradual modification as rights in individual property emerge with the growth of tribal organisation, and of individual enterprise in trade.

The tax most suitable for Africa is, in my judgment, an income or property tax—in other words, a contribution to the needs of the State by each individual according to his means, whether he be an agriculturist or a craftsman, a trader or a collector of sylvan produce, a nomad herdsman or a dweller in cities, a chief or a peasant, or, on the other hand, whether he be a Moslem, a Christian, or a pagan.

It should not be levied on a man's hut or cultivated land, to neither of which has the State any right, and any claims on which he will cordially resent, but on the income or profits of each individual, regardless of the source from which he derives it. This is the basis of Mohamedan taxation according to the Koranic law, and is therefore in strict accord with native law and custom in Moslem States. It is not an "economic land rent."

The vast bulk of the population of Africa are agriculturists, and it has been argued that if a community consumed all

[1] The first tentative effort in Northern Nigeria, before the country was fully brought under administrative control, was "to secure to the revenue a certain proportion of the taxes on land and produce levied by the native chiefs, and did not in any way touch the nature of those taxes or restrict the power of the chiefs as to the extent to which they might tyrannise over or extort from the peasantry." In due course, when adequate information had been collected, this was followed by an enactment, the object of which was "to lay down limits to the taxation by native chiefs, to define and legalise the various taxes, and to place them under the supervision of the administration, and at the same time to assign an adequate portion of the revenue so collected to the Government."—Governor's Despatch of 26th April 1905. Even if the Government were to take no share of the proceeds, the task of assessment and the supervision of the payment of the tribute is a duty which cannot be avoided, so long as the system of ruling through the chiefs is maintained. For "if Government enforces their demands, it must see to it that they are reasonable and not extortionate; otherwise, not only would Government be the instrument of misrule, but revolt would take place in every province"; for already, owing to the extortion of the past, the peasantry were declining to pay any dues whatever.—Governor's Despatch of 23rd August 1905.

its corn and stock in feeding itself, there being no profits, no tax could be levied, and the result would be that the industrious who produce a surplus would be penalised, and the idle, who only produce enough for their own wants, would escape taxation. Moreover, it would be exceedingly difficult to determine what proportion of produce and stock should be properly assigned to the actual needs of the cultivator.

The argument has special force in a country like Africa, where primitive man has few wants, and lacks incentives to accumulate wealth, where even among the advanced communities the bulk of the peasantry would seem to have few inducements to increase that margin of profit which among civilised nations becomes a necessity. A minimum of labour —largely done by his women-kind—is required to build his hut, to weave his cloth from his own cotton, and to furnish his needs in food. But the African, as soon as he has ceased to be nomadic, and has settled down on the land,[1] is not immune from the natural human desire to make profits.[2] As soon as he has emerged from primeval savagery—often indeed before he has done so—he becomes a keen trader, eager in the pursuit of gain. Even the least progressive are anxious to set aside some margin for the purchase of articles outside their bare necessities,—whether it be gaudy cloths and beads for ornament, or potent spirits, or to grow a surplus of corn with which to brew the beer that they love.

In order, however, to meet the case of the idle and the least progressive, I enacted in the "Native Revenue Proclamation" of Northern Nigeria (March 1906) that "the principle on which the estimate or valuation of lands shall be made, shall be the amount of produce or profit which can be annually obtained from, and the number of live-stock that can be annually raised and supported on such land, by a person cultivating and using the same, in the manner and up to the average standard of cultivation and use prevailing in the

[1] The nomadic pastorals have, of all the peoples of Africa, the least use for the amenities of civilisation and the least desire to trade. They are generally content to go naked or clad in skins, and look to their cattle for all their requirements.

[2] See Adam Smith on profits, *loc. cit.*, Bk. II., chap. iii. "The desire of bettering our condition . . . comes with us from the womb, and never leaves us till we go into the grave"; it is a "universal, continual, and uninterrupted effort" (pp. 19 and 27). Compare Malthus, "That master-spring of industry, —the desire of improving our condition," p. 468, &c.

neighbourhood." This clause introduces the important principle that the tax is not an income tax pure and simple, but a tax on the potential profits—viz., profits realisable by the expenditure of ordinary and normal industry and effort. It is described by the "Northern Nigeria Lands Committee" as embodying "the principles of a regular revenue assessment," which, however, owing to lack of staff and other reasons, had not in 1907 been applied in their entirety.[1]

To assess the tax due on the potential yield of a given acreage of land under cultivation, which has no special facilities of transport, or proximity to a good market, or exceptional water supply, &c., is not an insuperably difficult task. The normal yield of such land would be known, and would have a recognised value, varying slightly from year to year, and easily estimated by the village headman. This forms the basis so far as the agriculturist is concerned. It remains to ascertain how much cultivable land and stock is held by each farmer, and whether its value is augmented by special conditions. The cultivator must therefore exert himself to cultivate his land to at least the normal standard, so as to produce sufficient to pay his tax in addition to his own consumption. Agricultural "profits" therefore means the usufruct or yield of the land if cultivated to a normal standard, inclusive of the consumption of the owner.

If the term "profits" be applied to sources of income other than land, it means the gross revenue derived. Property from which revenue is derivable, though none be actually realised, is of course assessable to tax as in England—*e.g.*, a house inhabited by its owner. In the rough-and-ready system which in the early years replaces the lack of any system at all under a native despotism, the tax paid by the normal agriculturist forms the datum of assessment, and the peasant who lives on the same general standard, whether he be a craftsman or a fisherman, &c., would pay the same tax. It is assessed by the village headman and his council of elders, who are the only competent judges of the comparative wealth of individuals. This may to some extent be gauged by the number of a man's wives, his live-stock, and the style of his hut. Nomad cattle-owners can pay a fixed sum per head of stock.

The rate of the tax is fixed by the Governor, and in Northern

[1] Cd. 5102 of 1910, p. xv.

Nigeria it is nominally the Koranic tithe (under the name of *Haraji*)—viz., a tenth of the gross annual income; but there are probably few who pay so much, and the poorer classes may be rated at 4 per cent to 8 per cent only. In the case of the small farmer it is estimated that this 10 per cent of gross profits is the equivalent of 25 per cent net profits (a ratio, I believe, accepted in Burma). It may be more convenient to take the *net income* as the basis in the case of those who, like traders, live on the profits of capital, or in localities where the cost of living is unduly high, but it is difficult to define the term. In primitive Africa, necessary living expenses, other than food, are negligible.

In Northern Nigeria the highest average for a district is given at about 5s. to 6s. (probably equal to 9d. per cultivated acre) per annum, and in some pagan districts it does not exceed 6d. Remissions are freely made in case of local failure of crops, and there are some few exemptions, such as the salaries of native officials of Government and of the native administration, ex-soldiers who have won decorations, and the blind and infirm. This compares favourably with most other tropical dependencies, where the tax is fixed at 10s. or £1, and it is undoubtedly a great relief to the peasantry.[1] Yet the amount realised (including receipts from native courts, &c.) has increased in fifteen years from £20,861 in 1904-5 to about a million sterling in 1919.

It is desirable to take note of the principal defects in the native system that we may avoid them in the new system.[2]

Apart from the multiplicity of taxes and their undue severity, absentee landlordism was a fruitful source of evil. Alike in Uganda[3] and in Northern Nigeria it was customary for a territorial chief to reside principally at the capital, leaving his district to be misgoverned by a deputy, or through agents and tax-gatherers, whose chief aim it was to squeeze all they could out of the people, both on their own account, and in order to earn favour with their chief and retain their

[1] 'Colonial Office Annual Reports,' 476 of 1905, p. 21. Lord Cromer writes that, "in countries such as Egypt and the Sudan, low taxation should be the keystone of the arch." Works, however desirable, should be postponed "rather than that the principle of maintaining taxes at a low figure should be in any degree infringed."

[2] Compare the abuses described by Lord Cromer, 'Modern Egypt,' vol. i. p. 169.

[3] It was in Uganda obligatory for a chief to reside for three months at the capital (Felkin, 'Notes on Waganda,' p. 46). The "Sazas" when absent now appoint a deputy to represent them in the lukiko (council) at headquarters.

posts. The territorial chief held his lands at the will of the paramount chief. He was afraid to be absent from the capital lest reports—true or false—to his disadvantage should reach the ear of the ruler, or some other favourite should replace him. The ruler on his part feared to let these powerful provincial chiefs out of his sight, lest they should grow independent and defy his authority. Both employed tax-gatherers, who seem to have generally collected their demands through local headmen.[1]

These tax-collectors became a veritable curse to the country, and were the most hated feature of the system. They not only collected, but assessed the demand. Their arbitrary powers, and the fact that they alone had the ear of the chief, enabled them to practise what extortion they pleased. Naturally they made as much as they could, both for their employers and for themselves. They acted as spies, informers, procurers, and accredited agents, and were universally detested by the people.

The lands thus arbitrarily assigned to the rapacious rule of the Emir's nominees were frequently not homologous. A district which happened to be available, owing to the death or removal of its feudal chief, would be granted to a favourite, irrespective of whether it lay near his territory or not. Moreover, in the confusion of war it might happen that a party of fugitives settled down on a spot far removed from the rest of the community, but continued to recognise the ties of clan and affinity, to pay allegiance to their own tribal chief, and to ignore the authority of the local district head.

Thus a chief might exercise jurisdiction over, and claim taxes from a number of detached areas, situated like islands in another chief's territory, accentuating the evils of absenteeism, and inviting a conflict of authority. It is clearly necessary that such extra-territorial allegiance should be gradually abolished, while all new migrants acknowledge the local authority as a condition of settlement.

The urgent reforms which would seem to be of universal application in Africa, wherever a system of indigenous taxation exists, may be summarised briefly, nor are the principles

[1] In Southern Nigeria (Yoruba-land) there was a tendency for the "Balés" of the great cities (some of which had a population of over 100,000) to settle down and create a court of their own.

they cover less applicable if taxation is being introduced into a district *de novo* :—

(*a*) The abolition of a multiplicity of taxes, and their consolidation into a single tax, due at a fixed time, and limited to a known amount, and the abolition of the system of farming out taxes.

(*b*) The selection of competent men (whether the former territorial chief or another), and their appointment as salaried district headmen, directly responsible to the native ruler, and residing in the districts assigned to their charge.

(*c*) The collection of the tax *from the individual* (in cash if possible) by the village headman and his advisers, supervised by the district head and the British staff; *from the village* by the district head; with the abolition of the tax-gatherer, and a right of appeal to the head chief and to the British staff.

(*d*) The recognition of the undivided authority of the native ruler and his delegates, and the payment to them of the taxes, of which the ruler retains the portion assigned to him, and transfers the remainder—in cash if possible—to the Government. ***The tax must be in substitution of tribute and all other demands*** from the peasantry, and not a white man's tax imposed in addition to them.

The district headman can and should have a house at the capital, where he can attend to receive the instructions of the native ruler and answer for his stewardship. But the former fief-holders who prefer to reside permanently at the capital would cease to be recognised as part of the native administration, and would receive no salaries unless selected for an official post under the native ruler. Some would become traders, others farmers of their own lands. Unauthorised demands on the peasantry must be treated as criminal offences. Accredited messengers of the chief or native court should carry symbols of office to prevent personation by scoundrels.

The tax, as we have seen, is collected in the name of the native ruler, who in the advanced communities usually retains a half for the native administration and pays half to the Government. In primitive communities, where there are no highly paid officials, and the whole machinery of a native administration is in embryo, a quarter of the total may suffice, while in districts where it has not yet been possible to create any such machinery, 5 per cent or 10 per cent may be enough for the remuneration of the village headmen.

The principle of participation in the proceeds of the tax, however small the percentage assigned to primitive communities may be, should be introduced simultaneously with the tax to promote co-operation. The proportion to be credited to the native administration is fixed by the Governor, and may not be altered without his sanction. Of the moiety retained by an advanced native administration, from 5 per cent to 10 per cent is paid to the village headmen. This payment may take the form either of a percentage of the amount actually collected by him—which ensures his interest in the collection—or, when his integrity has been fully established, of a fixed salary. The amount would vary in proportion to the work he is called upon to do. In small farm villages his duties may hardly encroach at all on his ordinary occupation of farming, and the prestige of the position, with a small bonus, will suffice. But in large villages, which include a number of craftsmen and traders, the duties of the village head may become very onerous, and may probably occupy his whole time. In such cases he would generally be put on a fixed salary.

The district headman, who will probably require at least one scribe and several messengers to assist him, must receive a liberal salary, to enable him to maintain his position without resorting to illicit practices. The ruling chief, and the principal officers who form his council and transact the business of the treasury, &c., must also be liberally paid.[1] Probably 50 per cent of the native share of the tax in an advanced community may be devoted to these purposes, the remainder being available for the pay of the police, the maintenance of the prison, the salaries of the native staff in the schools, and other administrative expenditure, leaving a considerable surplus for public works, such as court-houses, treasury buildings, roads, &c. The inclination to spend an undue amount on the capital city must be avoided. A forward step in decentralisation and delegation of responsibility would be taken by the ruling chief assigning a portion of this surplus to each of his district headmen, to be spent in development work for the general benefit of the taxpayers.

[1] In North Nigeria the principal Emirs receive £4800 per annum.

The French have, I believe, recognised this principle in some districts.[1]

On the first inauguration of the tax in Northern Nigeria, the native ruler and all officials were paid in percentages, but as on the one hand experience was gained as to the salaries requisite, and as on the other hand the revenue increased, fixed salaries were, as I have said, substituted in all cases except the small village head. The receipts from the native courts fully balance the expenditure on the salaries of the judges, &c. The undesirable parasites—favourite slaves and eunuchs—who, under a native despotism, are invariably to be found surrounding the native ruler and exercising a baleful influence, soon disappear when their maintenance becomes a charge on the chief's personal income, but he is relieved of the cost of police and other officials charged with public duties. Unfettered financial independence has a tendency to multiply superfluous court officials and parasites.

I referred in the last chapter to the recognition of the village as the unit of administration, and to the difficulty of defining it, since with security to life and property the tendency of the peasantry is no longer to congregate in walled towns, but to build their huts on the land they till. In an advanced civilisation like that of England, the State has a personal account with each individual citizen, but in tropical Africa (as in India) the village must be the unit of taxation. For this purpose scattered groups of tenements, which cannot even be dignified with the name of "hamlets," must be considered as forming part of the town or village from which they emanated, and to which in association they belong.

On the other hand, the tendency to group a number of contiguous villages under a single head must in my opinion be avoided, for it strikes at the root of the principle of the village unit. That principle is that a measure of responsibility in the assessment for taxation (as in other matters)

[1] Monsieur Roberdean, Governor of the Ivory Coast, when introducing the direct tax, is reported to have said that the necessity for its imposition "makes it equally necessary that the authority of the chiefs should be more extended and efficient. For it is the chief who should assess the tax, should distribute it fairly, and should be charged with applying the necessary proportion to the interests of the village taxed." It was to supersede all direct tributes, and was to be divided as to one-third to the chief, one-third to public works in the village, and one-third for the local administration.

should be conferred on the chief of each distinct village, assisted by councillors selected by the villagers themselves. Its practical efficiency depends on the recognised headman having some personal knowledge of the standing and wealth of every member of the community, and a personal influence over them, and being able to collect the tax himself without employing tax-gatherers, while he in turn is under the influence of their opinion.

When the size of the community and the diversity of its occupations begin to render this impossible, the village may be said to have become a town or city. For purposes of taxation (and of general administration) a town is divided into wards, each under a ward head, who occupies a status similar to that of a village head. They are responsible to the district head either directly or through a headman of the town.

The tax is based on the principles which characterise the evolution of taxation in all countries—viz., the right of the ruler, on behalf of the community, to a share of the usufruct of the land. This was the basis of the Hebraic as of the Islamic system. It was the ancient custom in India, and still obtains in some of the smaller States. The British system in India, though theoretically founded upon it, revolutionised its fundamental principles, by taking immense trouble to ascertain the *average* yield of each field, and its money value, and then demanding from the cultivator the Government share in cash. Thus in a bad year the ryot was often driven to the money-lender, and he lost also by the conversion into cash.

This ancient method of dividing the produce of the land between the overlord and the cultivators has survived in France under the *métayage* system, but the share was the due of the landlord and not of the State. In the Moslem States of Nigeria the greater part of the land was now held rent-free by peasant proprietors paying their tax to the State. (See chapter on land.)

The difficulty in giving practical effect to the principle lies in the necessary inadequacy of the British supervising staff, and in the ignorance of the native subordinates, their fear of assuming responsibility, and their liability to succumb to temptation and to adopt irregular practices. An ideal assessment cannot be effected without a trained and costly staff, but it is well to keep the ideal in view. Assessment on an average yield need not, however, necessarily produce unfair results, provided that the unit of area is not too large, that the Government is ready to make remissions in exceptional cases, and above all that the *average price* (as distinct from the *average yield*) of produce is not fixed. For if a failure of crops is fairly universal over a wide area, the diminished output will probably fetch a higher than the average price, and as the tax is paid in cash and not in kind, the peasant should not suffer.

We have seen how a rough-and-ready assessment of the amount due from each cultivator may be arrived at by the district and village headmen, as a percentage of the potential yield of his land—viz., a tax on his profits or wealth. To call this (as the Northern Nigeria Lands Committee do) a "land rent" is, from the point of view of the native occupier, the same thing as asserting that the land belongs to the Governor, who is to him the embodiment of the abstract idea of "the State." If he can only obtain the right to use it by payment of a rent, he considers that the land has been taken from him, and it is for this reason that the people of Southern Nigeria and the Gold Coast have evinced such a dread of the application of the Northern Nigerian system to their lands. I shall deal with this subject in chapter xiv.

Moreover, if the tax is treated as a land-rent and proportioned to the area occupied, each cultivator naturally endeavours to reduce his acreage, especially if he has a risky crop, which may fail and leave him nothing with which to pay his rent.[1] The taxpayer is only liable for the authorised percentage of the harvest which his land should yield in any particular year if properly cultivated, whether that yield be large, or whether, in consequence of drought, or locusts, &c., it be small. A rough survey by natives to assist in the calculation of area under cultivation, total yield, and individual holdings, is very useful. (See p. 301.)

The District Officer, aided by the native district and village headmen, assesses in a rough-and-ready manner the amount

[1] This was illustrated in Sokoto, where a fixed rental resulted in 3641 rice farms (about half the total area of that crop) going out of cultivation, with a corresponding decrease in the tax collected. Sir H. Fowler (Secretary of State), in the Indian Budget debate of 1906, asserted that "the land-tax in India cannot be called taxation in any shape or form. It resembles (he said) the relation of landlord and tenant . . . (since) the land in India has for centuries belonged to the Crown." The land-rent was 1s. 8d. in the £, other taxes 1s. 10d. per head per annum.

which each village has to pay, by taking a census of the population and live-stock, and noting the amount of cultivated land, the proximity of markets, water-supply, &c., and the number of craftsmen and traders it contains. The profit on village cattle (as on those owned by nomads) is for convenience calculated at an average rate per head (1s. 6d.). Craftsmen (blacksmiths, tanners, weavers, dyers, &c.) may be assessed by a comparison of their standard of living with that of the agriculturists, or grouped in classes according to their visible profits.[1] Fees for special services or privileges are, of course, additional to the tax, such as market dues (spent on the control and improvement of the market).

This assessment is obviously not an easy task, but when once the tax of a normal village, enjoying ordinary facilities as to markets, &c., has with much pains and discussion been arrived at, additions and deductions can be made with sufficient accuracy for other villages in the district. To the ordinary value of the usual crops must be added that of special irrigation crops, and of live-stock, together with the profits of the non-agricultural population, including traders. The total is then divided among the adult population in proportion to their wealth by the village headman. If an individual earns a separate income—as, for instance, by working as a casual labourer during the season when his farm does not demand his attention—he would be liable for the percentage of his profits in the place where they are earned, and no account of them would be taken in the village assessment.

The district headman collects the tax from the various villages, and takes it to the ruling chief, unless (as in a small community) he is himself the chief. The list of villages with their assessments is carefully checked by the chief and his council each year just before the harvest, when the crop can be estimated with fair accuracy, in order that any small additions due to increase of population and wealth, or decreases due to migration and other causes, or alterations due to seasonal variation may be effected. As time permits the District Officer would check these revisions on the spot. The modifications, and the reasons for them, are explained to the villages by the village head, who is thus trained and encouraged to accept responsibility. The final assessment is, of

[1] In Bornu they were grouped in four classes—paying respectively 3s., 2s., 1s., and 6d. per annum.

course, subject to remission by the Governor for any exceptional cause.[1]

The District Officer on his part compiles a statistical register, showing the number of men, women, and children, of live-stock and huts, with notes on the area under cultivation, the special conditions affecting each village, and the method by which he arrived at the amount of assessment. The report, illustrated by a map, contains such historical and ethnological information as he has been able to collect, with notes as to the incidence of former taxation, the existence of any communities which own a separate allegiance, the prospects of introducing new cultures, and any other matter of interest. In Northern Nigeria these assessment reports are admirably compiled, and have been found of quite extraordinary interest.

The task is obviously a laborious one, though full of in-

[1] The apportionment of the tax by the village head is adopted in India (as indeed it must be in any tropical dependency). The magistrate, says a writer in the 'Asiatic Quarterly,' appoints the *Panchayet* (Council of Five), under the Act of 1856, to apportion the tax, and this is done either "(*a*) by actual valuation of property, which is rare, or (*b*) by their general knowledge of the circumstances of each individual, a system which works much better."

The method followed at Sokoto is thus described by the Resident: "First there is a discussion with the district headman regarding taxation prospects generally, condition of crops and trade; whether an increase of last year's tax is justifiable, and what changes are desirable (whether increase or decrease) for particular villages. Then the village headmen are called in, each in turn; the district headman makes his recommendation, the village headman is invited to express an opinion, and the tax is then decided. The Political Officer records the tax in the Tribute Register, and writes the name of the village, the amount of its tax, with initials and date, on a slip of paper. He hands this slip to a native scribe, who writes the name and the amount of tax in the vernacular, while at the same time a second scribe enters the name and amount in the vernacular on a list. When the district is complete the vernacular list with its total is handed to the district headman together with the separate slips which he will distribute to the village headmen. The village head has this documentary record of the amount due, to show to the village elders when they assemble with him to distribute the tax among the people and draw up the annual list of taxpayers. Many villages will be paying the same as the previous year, but probably 75 per cent are changed, generally by a slight increase.

"Not every district is summoned to Sokoto every year. In most years the European staff admits of some districts being revised on the spot—viz., at the headquarters of the district. This has the advantage that in cases of doubt as to the capacity of the village, an inspection and census can be taken. The object of this annual revision is to adjust inequalities caused by inter-village migration, between the five or six years that elapse between one assessment by a District Officer and the next. . . . The Sarkin Musulmi (*e.g.*, Sultan of Sokoto) has ordered all district heads to prepare a census annually, on which their tax revision will be based. . . . There is no doubt that the periodical visits of the headmen to Sokoto has done much to strengthen the Sarkin Musulmi's control."—Resident Arnett, 11th October 1916.

terest. The result is called an "approved assessment." Until it can be undertaken, the tax imposed must necessarily be a mere guess, based on information derived from the district head and the former tax-gatherers, which in all cases has been found to be unreliable, and very much less than the proper amount. These assessments have been in progress for many years in Northern Nigeria, and though interfered with by the depletion of the staff during the war they are approaching completion.

The education of the district and village headmen in the duties of assessment and apportionment of the tax is a very important part of a District Officer's work, but he must be content to find that the results of his efforts will only be very gradually apparent, and be satisfied with uniformity in principles.[1] He is responsible to the Resident, as the district head is to the native ruler. He hears appeals in consultation with the district head, and a final appeal to the Resident is provided by law. Defaulters are dealt with by the provincial or native court.

Collection by natives is apt to give rise to fears of malpractices, but the replacement of the tax-gatherer by responsible native officials, the prior notification of the amount due, the check exercised by the native ruler and his council, as well as by the British staff, and the right of appeal to both —all these are efficient checks. It is, moreover, most desirable, on the one hand, to train the native administration, and on the other hand, that the peasantry should regard the British officer not as a tax-gatherer, but as a friend to whom they can appeal against injustice; and he has an opportunity of judging of the capacity and the integrity of native headmen.

Among primitive tribes the work of the assessing officer is simplified, for in the communal stage the tax falls equally upon all, and is in fact a levy on the common stock. From that stage of evolution onwards through the tribal organisa-

[1] In some of the provinces of Northern Nigeria, however, the amount at which each individual has been assessed is entered by the village head in a register, and receipts are given on application. Copies of this register are kept up to date in the Waziri's office at the capital. Such a result would have been considered a counsel of perfection a few years ago. The individual account is, however, superfluous, except in the case of wealthy traders. Papers of different colours, showing the amount due and receipts for payment, are useful as being easily distinguishable by illiterates.

tion to the "advanced community," the bulk of the people have—though in a constantly decreasing ratio—an identical standard of living, and of "wealth." The tax therefore develops *pari passu* with the progress of the community from a poll or capitation tax to a graduated income tax.

Until efficient district heads have been trained, the District Officer will have to collect the tax himself from the family or village heads. The important point is to ensure that the rate is widely known, otherwise the village head, if a strong man, may practise extortion, and if a weak man will fail to exact it from those who refuse to pay, and will seize an excess amount from those who are unable to resist. Experience in Northern Nigeria shows that independent pagans are not unwilling to pay, provided they can do so direct to Government and not through an overlord or tax-gatherer.[1] Police should never be employed in the collection of the tax.

When discussing native administration I remarked that among such folk the institution of a treasury seems to be a farce, for they are incapable of understanding it, but (as in the case of the primitive native courts) I think that much value attaches to these early beginnings, for they are steps towards the fulfilment of the aim of the Government, to push each community a step further up the ladder of progress, by the realisation of the conception of individual and civic responsibility.

Though the collection of so small a tax from primitive tribes may seem to-day to give more trouble than it is worth, its chief value does not lie in the revenue collected. The most useful result—as the French and Belgians have also found—is the close contact between officials and natives which assessment and collection necessitates, and the consequent mutual understanding and confidence which invariably results. Moreover, those who pay the tax are quick to resent the immunity of others.

The tax should be collected simultaneously in all provinces immediately after the harvest. Quick collection minimises opportunities for misappropriation, and obviates the necessity

[1] Yola and Bauchi are two provinces with a large population of independent pagan tribes. The Resident of the former writes (September 1919): "I do not think the tax is resented even by the wilder tribes—refusal to pay is generally rather a revolt against all constituted authority than objection to paying the tax itself." The latter reports that "the tax is brought promptly even by the most backward tribes, and there is no trouble."

of large working balances in the native treasury. The single demand is popular. The cattle tax should be collected during the rains, when the flocks and herds have all returned from the marsh-lands to their own districts.

To avoid the trouble of transporting bulky produce, the native quickly appreciates the advantage of securing sufficient cash to pay his tax, thus promoting the adoption of currency, which facilitates trade.[1] If payment in cash is not possible, the produce most easily saleable would be accepted, and its sale if possible witnessed by the payers; but as Khama pointed out, European traders should be urged to pay cash for the produce they buy, in order that the native may get cash to pay his tax.[2] (See p. 490.)

I have said that the amount of the tax on primitive tribes should be very small—the equivalent of a few days' labour. In Uganda a month's labour is, or was, I believe, exacted in lieu of the tax—a system I deprecate as being liable to be misunderstood for forced labour. It is, I think, desirable to avoid the acceptance even of labour's equivalent—*e.g.*, wood fuel for steamers, &c.,—it is better to pay for such things in cash, and receive the cash back as tax, that there may be no possible mistake as to forced labour. Such a course, moreover, lessens the chance of the whole tax falling on the poorer classes, while the traders and well-to-do escape. Since women are at least equally with men the producers of wealth, all adults pay the tax, but women usually pay one-third less than men.

All persons in Northern Nigeria who are subject to the native jurisdiction pay the tax through the machinery of the native administration. Native traders and others not subject to the native jurisdiction, but "residing or being" in a province to which the ordinance applies, pay to the British staff, deducting any municipal rate to which they may be

[1] In Uganda, where distance from a seaport renders the realisation of produce paid in kind equally difficult as in Northern Nigeria, the administration was fortunately able to form a "local produce scheme," by which the natives were encouraged to cultivate or collect saleable produce and bring it to the Government stations, where it was handed over to merchants for cash. The feasibility of such a scheme depends of course on merchants being available at a sufficient number of stations throughout the country.

[2] "The white men who trade with us object to pay money. They like to give us the goods they sell in exchange for such things as we have a desire to dispose of. In order that we may find money for paying our taxes . . . the white traders must pay money for what they buy."—Letter of 11th November 1895, Blue-Book.

liable in a township. Natives not resident in the area to which the ordinance applies remain liable in respect of any property or income derived from that area.

The lack of precision in the original scheme of taxation in Nigeria, which the Colonial Office was disposed to criticise, is not in my view a defect. For the object is to evolve reform by organisation and adjustment, without dislocation of customs and traditions to which the people are accustomed, so that these conservative forces may be auxiliary and not antagonistic to the improved methods—in a word, the development of indigenous institutions rather than the sudden introduction of alien methods, however excellent. "There has been no great shock and no convulsion, only into the veins of a decadent civilisation new blood has been introduced which has brought with it the promise of a new era of life." [1]

The most serious obstacle experienced in Nigeria when the tax was inaugurated was the difficulty of suppressing personation. A credulous and illiterate people, long accustomed to oppression, were easily victimised by any scoundrel who, producing an old envelope picked up in a deserted camp, or even a piece of newspaper, as his credentials, would declare himself to be the authorised emissary of the Government, and demand what he chose. If the villagers demurred he would threaten their extermination by Government, or bring lying accusations of disaffection. Patient investigation, the gradual education of the peasantry, and very deterrent sentences on the culprits when caught, can alone deal with this offence, which causes the Government to be misrepresented and hated.

In most parts of Africa direct taxation has taken the form of a hut tax. The hut was, of course, intended as the symbol of population, and there was no intention of claiming property in it, or of charging a rent for it. But the method was unfortunate, for as Miss Kingsley justly observed, the African assumes that "the thing you pay any one a fee for is a thing which is not your own," [2] and that Government has confiscated his hut.

Apart from the defects in form and operation of the tax on a native hut which experience has brought to light, this tax differs from the one proposed in this chapter, in that it

[1] 'A Tropical Dependency,' p. 500.
[2] Letter to 'Spectator,' 19th March 1898.

appears to be superimposed upon any system of taxation by the chiefs, which in Uganda at any rate must, I presume, be tolerably substantial. It thus becomes a purely white man's tax. The method I have advocated has this essential difference, that the tax is imposed in the name of the paramount chief, is shared with the native administration, and is substituted for all existing forms of taxation.

The general results which may be anticipated to accrue from a system of direct taxation shared with the native administration may be thus summarised :—

(*a*) In the case of advanced communities a substantial revenue should be secured to the native chiefs and officials, to replace the loss of slave-raiding and slave-trading, the levies on traders which crushed trade, the extortions from the peasantry, and the fines and bribes which perverted justice. As individuals they would have adequate salaries, which they *earn* by discharging responsible duties for the administration, and as rulers they would have revenue for the progress of the country.[1]

(*b*) A considerable and increasing revenue can be secured to Government, due to better organisation and collection of the tax, and its universality; while coin currency with its immense influence for trade and progress is promoted.

(*c*) The peasantry is emancipated in the true sense of the word to an even greater extent than would be the case by the abolition of domestic slavery. The tax they pay should be very moderate, and they are freed from arbitrary exactions. Industry and personal initiative are encouraged instead of being the mark for spoliation.

(*d*) The absentee ruler or landlord is replaced by the district headman, who has responsible executive duties, delegated by the ruling chief, instead of being an idle placeholder. Decentralisation of powers relieves the ruler of work he could not properly perform, limits opportunities for maladministration by him, increases the Resident's effective

[1] The revenue of the native administrations in the northern provinces of Nigeria amounted in 1918 to £492,663. The salaries of all grades, including native courts, police, and prisons, amounted to £304,996, being about 9½d. per head of population, and leaving about £188,000 for other expenditure (public works, education, &c.) In 1919 the total collected was over £950,000, of which the native administration share was £536,000. In the Kano Emirate, with a population of 2¾ millions, the returns have increased by 300 per cent in ten years and by 46 per cent in the last four years, but the tax is still under 1s. 6d. per head of population (2s. per adult).

supervision, and facilitates the delegation of powers by Government, with confidence that they will not be abused, and so enables the Government to rule through the chiefs.

(*e*) The former territorial chiefs, who invariably deteriorate by the exercise of unchecked licence, have either to accept responsible duties as district heads or officers of State, or have to take to trade or agriculture, and lead a life dignified by personal exertion.

(*f*) The multiplication of titular office-holders and others, including the tax-gatherers, who live on the industry of the peasantry, and the tendency of the rulers to grant such offices to relatives or favourite slaves, will be checked, and only such officials will be appointed as have substantial duties to perform, and as have been selected for their ability.

Among primitive communities the introduction of the tax, simultaneously with the assumption of control, lays the foundation for future expansion for revenue purposes, whereby the burdens on trade, which are unequal in their incidence, may be reduced. If imposed at once it is more likely to be received without friction. It has the effect of curbing lawlessness, of accelerating progress to a higher plane, and of stimulating industry. The amount in the early stages should be small, and should increase with the evolution of the community, and the benefits it receives.

A brief note as to the form and amount of the direct tax in various British and foreign dependencies in Africa is appended.

The most common direct taxes which it is the object of the income tax to supersede, partake either of the nature of class taxation, or are levies on trade in one form or another.

Caravan tolls are immemorial in Africa—existing in Abyssinia to-day to a degree which almost stifles trade.[1] As peace and security of property are introduced, evasion is increasingly easy. The employment of police offers great temptation for bribery direct and indirect. The examination of bales of goods is a grievance, and the frequent demands for payment as the caravan proceeds from centre to centre is greatly disliked. The collection of the taxes involves very heavy work on the district staff, and evasion adds to the list of punishable offences. Nevertheless, from long usage these tolls were not unpopular in Northern Nigeria, and had the strong

[1] See footnote, p. 46.

support of the native rulers, even after they ceased themselves to benefit by them. Canoe licences are a necessary adjunct of this tax, for a trader who conveys his goods by water would otherwise obtain an undue advantage over the merchant who travels by land.

Northern Nigeria was compelled by lack of revenue for essential needs to adopt these taxes, until the success of the direct income tax was proved. In 1906, however, all produce for export overseas, and goods imported by those who held trading licences, were exempted, so that the tax fell solely on the internal native trade—chiefly soda from Lake Chad to the great cities—which had paid no customs duties.

As a temporary expedient these tolls were not wholly without merit, for they fell on the class best able to pay, which otherwise practically escaped taxation. They acted to some extent as a deterrent to the abandonment of agriculture in favour of petty trade—a tendency especially noticeable when slavery was abolished, and the roads made safe. The collection, moreover, enabled the infant administration to gain a knowledge of the internal trade of the country, which it would otherwise have taken many years to acquire. Trading and shopkeepers' licences fall into the same category, and hamper trade and development. These also have long ago been abandoned in Nigeria.

Vehicle licences—especially on private motor-cars—are justified as a contribution to the maintenance of the roads they use. If used only in a city or township, the licence fees form a useful addition to municipal revenue. Market dues, if in excess of the sums required for the supervision and improvement of rural markets, are a restraint on trade and objectionable, but a township is justified in deriving a moderate revenue from them for municipal purposes.

Licences for the most part are not imposed with the object of raising revenue, but in order to give effect to some special restriction—*e.g.*, those for shooting game or bearing firearms —or to recoup some special expenditure.

APPENDIX TO CHAPTER XII.

THE HUT TAX IN AFRICA.

A house-rate is a form of levy well adapted for raising municipal funds in a city, where modern amenities require a special outlay. The native householder sees that it is paid equally by Europeans, and can appreciate the necessity for providing funds for water-supply, street-lighting, good roads, and sanitation. Mr Chamberlain himself took exception to the fact that the hut tax in Sierra Leone had not been made applicable to the Colony and its capital city Freetown, where much of its proceeds would be spent. The rate was 5s. per hut. The very serious rising in Sierra Leone in 1897, though it was popularly known as the "Hut-tax Rebellion," was probably only partially caused by that tax, and had its deeper origin in the efforts of the local Government to check misrule by the inland chiefs, and in the malpractices of its own police.

In Uganda a hut tax of 4s. (or alternatively of one month's labour) was said to have had ill effects in rendering the natives unwilling to occupy separate huts, and decreasing marriages. The *lukiko* (native council) then suggested a tax of 2s. 8d. on those who did not occupy huts. The result, said the High Commissioner, was "to lessen the distinction between the married man and bachelor, to promote morality, induce the bachelor element to settle down, and to encourage married life." The labour equivalent of the tax seems to have been very high. The German substitute would have been eight days' labour instead of a month. *Vide inf.*

In Nyasaland the Ordinance of 1901[1] imposed a tax of 12s. on the owner or occupier of each hut in a "proclaimed district" (viz., 95 per cent of the population) and of 6s. elsewhere, with a rebate of half the amount if the occupier could prove that he had worked for a European for wages for a month. This would seem to partake of the nature of a subsidy payable from revenue to European employers of labour, while the distinction between "proclaimed" and other districts seems to penalise the natives of the settled districts, for presumably the un-proclaimed districts were those in which the tax could not easily be collected, unless the native made himself liable by seeking work from Europeans.

These anomalies have been removed by the recent Ordinance,[2] which imposes a tax of 6s. per hut, with an additional 6s. for every wife after the first, and an alternative poll-tax for any native not liable to hut tax. The penalties are severe. Default for six months involves liability to a fine of 2s. or a month's imprisonment, further default for two months involves a fine of 4s. or three months' imprisonment, and forfeiture of his hut. The tax remains recoverable as a judgment debt.

[1] 'Gazette' of 31st December 1901.

[2] No. 4 of 31st March 1921.

Taxation in Kenya takes the form of a poll-tax, and the signatories of the Economic Report express the view that the African could not conceivably be assessed to income tax.[1] The tax was raised to 16s., a rate which was found to be excessive in a country where the wage-rate was only from 6s. to 8s. per mensem, and it was reduced to 12s. It is stated that by far the larger part of the revenue thus raised is spent on the requirements of the British settlers.

In Northern Rhodesia the tax may not exceed £1, and is fixed at present at 10s., with an additional 10s. for each wife after the first. Half the revenue is derived from this source.[2]

The South African Native Affairs Commission recorded their opinion—

(1) That it is necessary to impose direct taxation upon the natives.

(2) That it can best be imposed by means of a hut tax or poll-tax.

(3) That the tax should not be less than £1 per annum, payable by every male adult native, with an additional £1 for every wife after the first.

(4) That farm servants in *bona fide* and continuous employment and natives domiciled within an urban area who pay local taxes should be exempt.

In addition, the Commission favoured the extension of the principle of local taxation for beneficial purposes on the lines of the Glen Grey Act.[3]

Dr Unwin reported in 1911 on the system of taxation in force in German Togoland. Every male over sixteen years ef age must pay 6s. or twelve days' labour at his option. Treasury officials preferred the former, district officers the latter. Headmen of villages were called upon to declare the number of adult males and to bring them up annually. The numbers were checked by the district officer. The headman was given a German field-cap as a mark of office. In the Cameruns the tax was, I believe, 3s. per adult male, with 2s. additional for each wife after the first.

Mr Migeod writes: "In French territory the poll-tax varies from 5 francs in some districts to 12.50 francs in others. . . . The Belgians have a graded tax, variable to meet the earning capacity of the native. In the big towns near the coast it is as much as 25 francs. A man who has four children by the same wife is exempt—with the dual object of stimulating monogamy and child-bearing. All wives after the first have to be paid for. The tax in both French and Belgian Congo is collected by the European officer."[4] In India the tax is stated to average 3s. 6d. a head.[5]

[1] Economic Commission's Report, 1919, p. 25.

[2] 'Gazette' of 25th February 1921; Ordinance 2 of 1921. In Southern Rhodesia there is a poll-tax of £1.

[3] In Basutoland the poll-tax is £1, with an additional £1 for each wife up to £3. In Bechuanaland a hut tax of £1, plus 3s. for a native fund for education is levied.—Annual Report 1057 for 1919-20.

[4] 'West Africa,' 25th June 1921.

[5] 'Times,' 19th December 1913.

CHAPTER XIII.

TAXATION (*continued*) AND METHODS OF RAISING REVENUE.

Taxation of corporate bodies—Trading—Mining—Banking—Taxation of individual non-natives—Taxation and representation—Import and export duties—The case for export duties—Duty on salt—Adjustment of duties to area of consumption or origin of articles—Rebates to compensate for transport — Differential export duties — The economic effects of the war—The Paris economic resolutions—Committee on oil-producing seeds and nuts—Committee on commercial and industrial policy—The action taken and its justification —The case of cotton—Proposals of the E.R.D.C.—Alternative proposals—Contribution for defence—Imperial preference—Retaliation by foreign Powers.

In the two chief forms of European enterprise and investment in the tropics—trading and mining—we find that local governments have imposed two principal forms of indirect taxation—viz., customs duties for the one, and royalties for the other. The operation of these two methods of taxation differs considerably. In the first case the merchant adds the amount of the import duty to the retail selling price, and thus transfers the tax to the consumer. In like manner the amount of any export duty is deducted from the price paid for the produce, and is thus passed on to the producer. In neither case is it paid by the merchant, whose profits are neither increased nor diminished by such duties, provided the industry can bear them—viz., that the consumer will continue to buy the merchants' goods, when the duty, plus the reasonable margin of profit on capital invested, has been added to prime cost, inclusive of transport, and provided that the producer will continue to sell for the price offered, including marketing and all other charges.

The merchants' profit therefore depends primarily on the degree of competition to which he is subjected by other merchants, while the amount of the customs duty which the local government can impose is limited to the amount which the consumer of imports, or the producer of exports, can pay. In other words, customs duties are an indirect tax on the native consumer or producer, and not on the importing or exporting merchant. Competition will secure to the native the maximum price which rival traders can possibly pay for produce, and customs duties act directly in diminution of this price or profit to the native, so long as the market is free. If a monopoly is introduced, or a trading combine or ring is formed to control the market, and interfere with these natural laws, then the duties will operate in diminution of the profits of the monopoly or combine.

This is also true of the rents and premia paid to the Government, or to a private owner, for the land occupied by a merchant in the pursuit of his business. They are not added directly to the selling—or deducted from the purchasing—price, like import or export duties, but if there is unrestricted competition they decrease the price which the competitors are able to offer for the produce, and increase *pro rata* the price asked for imported goods. The produce exported by the merchant, whether animal or vegetable, is annually renewed by the processes of nature and the toil of man, and is in that sense inexhaustible, and its value in the home markets depends on the demand and supply of the world.

The case of the miner stands on a different basis. The minerals he exports are not perennially renewed by Nature, and when exported are permanently lost to the country. There is no local competition (except in the labour market), for whatever quantity he may win from his particular mine does not appreciably affect the value of his neighbour's output. He is subject only to the fluctuations of the world's prices—equally with the merchant. His local efforts are confined to the endeavour to reduce the cost of winning the minerals, and by so doing he does not decrease the exportable output of his neighbour, but merely increases his own individual profit. The rents, licences, and royalties he pays to Government are in direct diminution of those profits, and cannot be passed over to the native, except in the form of a reduction of wages, and this is not feasible to him, since the wage-rate is fixed by the competition of all industries alike, and by the profits of private production. Profits in the mining industry are regulated, therefore, by cost of production, and the world's prices for the product. Royalties must be proportioned to "what the industry will bear," and should therefore be fixed on a sliding scale—increasing or decreasing with the world's prices.

It thus appears that whereas the mining companies (whose exports decrease the capital assets of the country) contribute directly to the local revenue, trading companies (though increasing by their operations the productive output) do not contribute directly, for whatever customs duties are levied on the goods they import or export are transferred to the consumer or producer as the case may be, and thus become a form of indirect taxation, which chiefly falls on the natives, who are the principal producers and consumers.

The profits of both industries are taxed (whether before or after distribution to the shareholders) in the country where the company is registered, and it would seem reasonable that companies should register not only in the country where the profits on the use of capital are distributed, but also in the country in which the profits are made, and that a certain proportion of those profits should accrue to the country in which they are earned. With the phenomenal increase in the material prosperity of the British African tropics, and the formation of innumerable companies, British and foreign, many of which in normal circumstances earn large profits, the question of the contribution which commercial and mining companies formed by Europeans should rightly make towards the administration, and development by railways, &c., of the countries in which their profits accrue, becomes one of increasing importance and urgency. It has already received some attention in Uganda, Northern Rhodesia, the Congo State, Jamaica, Trinidad, and the Straits Settlements.

Turning now from Joint Stock Companies, and the taxation of profits on the use of capital, to the individual non-native in Africa, we find that they consist—with the exception of missionaries and the settlers in the East African Highlands—almost entirely of Government officials and the employees of companies. Their incomes may consist of a fixed salary, with or without a share of profits or a prospective pension, or contingent easements, such as free housing, medical attendance, full-pay leave, &c., which we will include in the term "income." The incomes earned by the senior employees of companies, whether engaged in trade, mining, or banking, are believed to be considerable, but whether small or large they are free from any form of local income tax in Africa. "Why," it has been asked, "are the natives subjected to an income tax from which Europeans are exempt?"

As in the case of companies not registered in the colony, so also in the case of individual non-resident traders and others who derive profits from their business in the colony, it is manifestly desirable that they should contribute a fair share of those profits to the revenues of the local government which bears the cost of the administration, and assures to them security of life and property, and renders it possible for them to earn their profits.

It is probable that the imposition of an income tax on the profits of business carried on in the colony would have but little effect on the salaries of agents employed in Africa; for presuming that the existing salaries are the minimum sufficient to attract men of the type required, it may be assumed that if the salaries were diminished by the imposition of an income tax, they would (unless unduly inflated by post-war increases) be augmented by the employers to the previous tax-free standard.[1]

[1] Since these pages were written the "Report of the Inter-Departmental Committee on Income Tax in the Colonies not possessing Responsible Government" has been issued (Cmd. 1788 of December 1922). The Committee arrives at the conclusion that "the most appropriate scheme for the colonies generally is one which imposes tax upon income which either has its origin in the colony, or while having its origin outside the colony, is received in the colony"—viz., the taxation of income that comes within the colonial jurisdiction. The most important item of income, it declares, is undoubtedly profits from business. The tax should be levied on the "chargeable income" of the year preceding that of assessment—viz., on the aggregate income of any person after deducting the expenditure incurred in acquiring it, together with various other deductions. The method of assessment, and the deductions admissible from this "chargeable income," are fully discussed. It is recommended that companies registered in a colony should be entitled to deduct from the dividends payable to their shareholders the amount of the tax paid, and that they should furnish each shareholder with a certificate of the amount in order that he may obtain the relief allowed by the Finance Act, 1920—viz., up to half the amount of the United Kingdom tax. Since the profits of companies not registered in the colony cannot be taxed at the source, such companies would be taxed at a flat rate.

All individual non-natives would be liable to the income tax (including officials), and since "it is clearly desirable that non-residents who derive income from a colony should contribute their fair share to the expenses of the Administration which renders it possible to earn that income," the taxing authority—when the amount of profits derived from his trade by a non-resident cannot be actually ascertained—would fix (as in the United Kingdom) such fair and reasonable percentage as the facts may justify.

A model Ordinance—which appears to be excellently drawn—is attached to the Report, embodying these principles for enactment in the several colonies.

Government officials should, as in the United Kingdom, be equally liable to income tax, and if in some cases it were necessary in consequence to augment salaries, the local revenue would still benefit by the relief afforded to colonial taxpayers by the Finance Act, 1920. Missionaries and others engaged in educational work might well be exempted.

In East Africa there is a poll-tax on every non-native of £1 (R. 15) per head per annum, and an Estate Duty Ordinance was passed in 1918. Allowance is made in the case of small incomes.[1] The Economic Report observes: "The Europeans consist of civil servants, tradesmen, professional men, and settlers. To subject the first to direct taxation is obviously economically unsound. A tax on the so-called profits of the settler would yield little or no return, if assessed on any basis which would not endanger positions as yet not firmly established. The only section of the community from whom income tax could be collected comparatively cheaply and easily appears to be the European merchants and professional men, who form too small a proportion of the community to justify the imposition of a general income tax, with the attendant disabilities. . . . A score or two of Indian firms in the towns are probably the only Asiatic sources from which any appreciable amount of income tax could be collected by ordinary methods."[2]

It has from time to time been argued that the bulk of the revenue is derived from customs dues paid by merchants, who should therefore have a more effective voice in the government of the country. We have seen, however (pp. 235-6), that customs duties provide not more than from 12 per cent to 30 per cent in the countries named, and that they are paid by the producer or consumer and not by the merchant, as they themselves freely admit. On the other hand, it is a recognised principle that the Government should be conducted by men trained to the work, who have no personal interests to serve, and whose conduct of affairs offers a target before which no shield of self-interest is interposed to prevent the critic from discharging his shaft. The merchant who embarks his capital in, and devotes his time and thought to, overseas trade does so naturally and rightly for the sake of

[1] 'General Information *re* East Africa,' Overseas Trade Department, 1919, and 'Handbook of Kenya Colony,' I.D. 1216 of 1920.

[2] *Loc. cit.*, p. 25.

profit, and does not wish to be bothered with administrative problems. But in my experience, while seeking for profit, he has shown a laudable desire that it should be shared with the native producer.

The educated native on his part contributes, in Nigeria at any rate, a very small proportion indeed of the revenue. At present he pays no income tax, and even the institution of a small rate to pay a part of the cost of the water-supply for his own city was resented in Lagos. The highest claim to guide the State is based on service to the State, and those who claim to participate in its control must bear their full share of the burdens and the work of citizens.

Customs duties in most colonies provide the bulk of the revenue derived from indirect taxation. The tradition of the Colonial Office — based, no doubt, on their accepted superiority in civilised countries — has been in favour of import as against export duties, while the Foreign Office, when in control of African protectorates, maintained that "at the Berlin Conference the Powers had deliberately pronounced against import duties, and in favour of export duties." Such duties were approved as regards the Congo State to meet expenditure on the suppression of the slave trade, and were enforced in the territories under the control of the Foreign Office in both East and West Africa, in spite of the arguments of the Liverpool merchants in 1893.[1] The merchants preferred import duties on the grounds that "whilst on the one hand the customs houses and staff required to deal with imports may entail more expense than those required in dealing with exports, it may be pointed out that in the case of exports the duty has to be paid before the produce is shipped for the home markets, compelling an outlay of capital restrictive of the bulk of trade."

British Chambers of Commerce have always opposed export duties, arguing that since the amount of the duty must be deducted from the price offered by the purchaser of produce, the native suffers, and that if the duty were removed his purchasing power would be stimulated (thus increasing the demand for imported goods). "To tax exports in an undeveloped country," says the Manchester Chamber, "is held

[1] The Sudan Government continues to levy an export duty of 1 per cent *ad valorem* on produce exported; but the import duty is 8 per cent on ordinary goods.—Handbook 98, p. 155. The Seychelles, Somaliland, and Bechuana all impose an export duty.

to be wrong in principle, and calculated actually to retard development."[1] They prefer, in case of necessity, increased import duties, and the imposition of duties on articles which enter duty free, and an increased duty on salt.

It is argued, on the other hand, that the native pays the duty equally whether it is levied on exports or imports. If the duties on the latter are increased to a point which would compensate the revenue for the abolition of export duties, the cost of imported goods becomes prohibitive, and as recent experience has shown, the native refuses to buy. For, as I have pointed out, his wants are not at present absolutely essential necessities, and if Manchester textiles rise above a reasonable price he turns to his own looms, not merely depriving Manchester of her market, but absorbing the raw cotton which she needs. The native producer may perhaps be tempted to sell his produce for cash if the price is improved by the abolition of export duties, but he will probably hoard the cash rather than buy imported goods whose price is enhanced by exorbitant duties. The hoarding of cash after the war from this cause contributed to the stringency of current coin, and inflicted considerable injury on trade.

The comparative expediency of import and export duties in an industrial country has, of course, no bearing whatever on their expediency in a country which has no exportable manufactures, and where the consumer and the producer are the same person, who pays the duty whether levied on imports or exports. The Economic Commission in East Africa shares the view that the duty should fall on the consumer, but in that country the European settlers form a large section of the producers. Even in a country like West Africa, which exports raw materials only, the weight of opinion is strongly

[1] Letter to Colonial Office of 6th May 1921.

The International Chamber of Commerce lately (1st July 1921) endorsed this view. "Considering," says the resolution, "that every tax on export of raw materials must necessarily increase the cost of production, and thereby hinder economic restoration," their abolition is recommended. If necessarily retained provisionally for revenue purposes "they should be adopted without any discrimination whatever as regards countries." See also Mr J. H. Batty's reply to question 1239 by the Edible Nuts Committee.—Cd. 8247 of 1916.

Major Wood, Under-Secretary, asserted in the debate on the Colonial Office vote (7th July 1922), that for export duties to be effective, the country which imposes them should have a practical monopoly of the commodity on which the duty is levied, and that it should be a non-substitutable requisite for manufacture.

Export duties if imposed should be proportioned to the home market price, on the *ad valorem* principle, and not a fixed sum per ton.

opposed to export duties. This view is reinforced by the psychology of the African, who will continue to produce so long as he gets a good price,[1] and though he may hoard his receipts for a time, will eventually buy what he requires regardless of its price. The increased cost of imported goods must, it is argued, increase the volume of exports with which to pay for them. The import tariff should aim at placing on the free list all articles of food, and, as far as possible, building materials and the like, and the gradual substitution of specific duties for an *ad valorem* list.

The advocates of export duties in Africa have, however, some cogent arguments to support their case. Raw materials and foodstuffs are easily recognisable, and there is no need for the duty to discriminate as to value arising from quality, since the equal tax has the effect of penalising inferior qualities, and thus promoting a higher standard.

Imports, on the other hand, are very varied, and textiles in particular may differ by every shade of gradation and price. The notable and practically universal integrity of the British merchant, and the shame and loss of standing which a conviction for fraudulent declaration would involve, are insufficient grounds to justify a system under which officers, charged by law with the duty of exercising a close supervision, are necessarily unable to give full effect to it. For goods could not justifiably be subjected to a specially rigorous examination on mere suspicion, involving loss to the importer. Bales of goods for the African market have often to be packed at considerable cost in waterproof material, and in hooped and sizeable loads for transport to the interior, and if opened can with difficulty be repacked. Goods for export, on the other hand, can be dealt with solely by weight —the allowance for receptacles being uniform. Under a system of export duties it is easy to grant exemption or reduced duties on any particular product, the culture of which it is desired to encourage—*e.g.*, cotton, or newly-introduced products. These critics do not, of course, suggest the entire abolition of import duties, but in the peculiar circumstances of African trade, they maintain that the prejudice against export duties is without adequate foundation.

[1] Mr Churchill pointed out that the cotton export tax was followed by a very large increase in production, and that the Gold Coast tax on cocoa had not prevented a steady increase in the quantity shipped.

There is one article of native food which is largely imported, and often—as I think wrongly—heavily taxed, viz., salt. The tax in Nigeria is £1 per ton—a rate which appears to be much less than the tax imposed in India.[1] In my view the taxation of this article, of prime necessity to the native population, is to be deprecated.

Commandant Binger, the French explorer, states that the lack of salt was one of the causes which promoted the internal slave trade in the region of the Upper Niger. For the salt came from the north, and in the absence of portable produce the vendors took slaves in payment. "When Europe [he says] can import salt at a reasonable price in the Niger bend, she will have rendered a true service to the native."[2]

It is obvious that when imposing import—and more especially export—duties, the question of the regions in which such imports are chiefly consumed, or in which such exports originate, is a matter of importance in regard to the incidence of taxation. Thus the import duty on "trade spirits" in West Africa fell entirely on those coastal regions in which their sale was not prohibited. By their recent prohibition those regions in Southern Nigeria pay about a million sterling less in indirect taxes. An export duty on palm kernels, and on cacao, falls on the inhabitants of the moist equatorial regions, from which alone these products are exported (which are, in fact, the same areas as those in which spirits are consumed); while a ground-nut duty falls chiefly on the people of the drier uplands. If, therefore, it is desired to impose a larger share of indirect taxation on those who do not pay a direct tax, or to relieve those whose produce has to bear enhanced transport charges, a careful adjustment of customs duties can be made to redress the balance in some small degree. Excessive import duties will, however, result in diminution of the stimulus to production—temporarily, at any rate—since the wants of the African are rarely necessities, and he can leave them ungratified.

[1] The salt tax in India is 1s. 8d. per maund—viz., 45s. 6d. per ton. Prior to 1903 it had been double that amount, and in the 'seventies had stood as high as £8, 10s. approximately. By recent legislation it has been restored to the higher level (91s.). The duty in Nigeria is 40s. per ton. Since the daily wage in India is much lower than in West Africa, the burden on the Indian taxpayer was correspondingly greater. The price of imported salt at Kano (Nigeria), with 700 miles of rail freight, fell from 30s. per cwt. in 1908 to 11s. in 1913.

[2] For the various sources of supply of local salt see Binger, 'Du Niger au Golfe de Guinée,' vol. i. p. 375.

The keen competition between merchants, and the comparatively heavy and bulky nature of African produce relative to its value, impose, of course, a heavy handicap on the merchant who essays to develop regions in the interior, especially if they are remote from railways and navigable waters, in comparison with the trader who buys the same produce in easily accessible regions. In order to encourage the development of these remoter regions, it may be worth while to consider a system of customs rebates on a sliding scale, calculated in proportion to the distance from the coast, and from rail or river, supported by certificates of origin. If in the most remote district the revenue derived no benefit by way of customs duties on imported goods, or on produce for export, the trader on the one hand would still have to meet his heavy transport charges, while the administration would benefit by the increase of trade and wealth, and the extension of the coin currency, which would facilitate the payment of the direct tax.

But whatever may be the comparative advantages and disadvantages of import and export duties as a normal means of raising revenue, there is, of course, no question that—unless precluded by treaty—either is capable of being used as a powerful agency to restrict imports from, or exports to, foreign countries in favour of home or Empire markets. Moreover, if a country produces an article which is in great demand, and the supply of which is limited and regional, the advocates of export duties point out that revenue may undoubtedly be obtained at the expense of the foreign consumer by a preferential export duty.

After the war a preferential export duty was introduced in the West African dependencies, admittedly in order to secure for the Empire a monopoly of palm kernels. It has been the subject of much controversy in both Houses of Parliament,[1] and in the Press; and, since its imposition affects fundamental principles, the matter merits careful consideration.

The war profoundly changed the economic conditions of the world. Some of the economic results affecting the relations of British African tropics to the United Kingdom may perhaps be briefly summarised as follows :—

(*a*) Great Britain now realised that it had been the de-

[1] 'Debates' of 17th December 1919 and 13th May 1920, &c.

liberate policy of Germany—taking advantage of the "open door"—to monopolise the supply from the British dependencies of certain raw materials which were essential to some of our principal industries, and for the manufacture of munitions in time of war. Great Britain and her Allies determined in future to safeguard these supplies.

(*b*) The financial strain resulting from the war gave rise to various proposals for rehabilitating the finances of the United Kingdom, opposed to the accepted principles which had hitherto guided the policy or practice of England towards her tropical dependencies. Those put forward by the Empire Resources Development Committee were very influentially supported.

(*c*) The realisation of the importance of drawing together all parts of the Empire, and making it self-supporting, strengthened the hands of those who had long advocated "Imperial Preference," and it became the accepted policy in regard to the Crown colonies.

As regards the first of these three heads, representatives of the Allies met in Paris in June 1916, and passed a series of resolutions,[1] which were accepted by Mr Asquith's Government, in so far as they related to the transitional period after the war.[2] By Resolution B. iii., "the Allies declared themselves agreed to conserve for the allied countries before all others their material resources during the whole period of reconstruction." The Government thereupon appointed an extremely strong Committee, under Lord Balfour of Burleigh (which included the chairmen of a number of departmental committees previously appointed by the Board of Trade), "to consider the commercial and industrial policy to be adopted after the war, with special reference to the conclusions reached at the Paris Conference."

In the previous year—1915—the Colonial Secretary (Mr Bonar Law) had appointed a Committee to study the trade in palm kernels and other oil-producing nuts and seeds, and "to make recommendations for the promotion in the United Kingdom of the industries dependent thereon."[3] The Committee reported in May 1916. Germany, they said, had before the war monopolised three-fourths of the export of kernels, and on the assumption that with her mills undamaged

[1] Cd. 8271 of 1916.

[2] Cd. 9035 of 1918, paragraph 3.

[3] Cd. 8247 of 1916.

she would after the war be ready to offer extravagant prices to regain her monopoly, it was necessary, in order to induce British crushers to erect mills at heavy outlay, to offer them a guarantee for a limited period (five years), until their mills were established, so that they should be able to obtain kernels at reasonable prices. The Committee recommended legislation in the colonies, on the lines eventually adopted. A precisely similar recommendation was, as we shall see, made by the Textiles Committee (set up by the Board of Trade) in regard to Indian jute.[1]

Lord Balfour's Committee reported in December 1916 that "effect cannot be given to these (Paris) Resolutions unless export restrictions are placed during the transitory period on a certain number of important articles, . . . and any measures taken for the purpose should aim at assuring to the British Empire and the Allies priority for their requirements, and at preventing the present enemy countries from gaining by the use of such materials an initial advantage in the competition to recover markets which will follow the war."[2] They refer to the proposals made in regard to palm kernels, and suggest that India should be asked to devise measures with a similar object in view, and add: "We do not overlook the fact that objection may be taken to the restricted policy which we recommend, on the ground that the burden may fall unduly upon the individual producer, whose price may be lowered by the restriction of his market. In our opinion it is particularly important to avoid even the appearance of any such penalisation, especially in cases in which the interests of native subjects of the Empire are concerned. We think, however, that if the policy is limited, as we have recommended, to materials of which the greater part of the supply can be absorbed by the United Kingdom and the Allies, it will be possible, in consultation with the various Governments concerned, to devise satisfactory safeguards to meet the danger."[3]

Ordinances to give effect to this policy and restrict the export of palm kernels to Empire markets were accordingly introduced by order of the Secretary of State in the Legislatures of the West African colonies. The unofficial members

[1] Cd. 9070-73 of 1918.

[2] Cd. 9034 of 1918, paragraph 4.

[3] Ibid., paragraphs 21 and 22. In debate on 10th May 1922 Lord Buxton quoted Mr Bonar Law's assurance that the duty would be withdrawn if it proved detrimental to the interests of the natives.

of the Gold Coast voted unanimously against it, though palm-kernels are a negligible export from that colony. In Nigeria, where they are a staple of trade, the matter was debated both in the Nigerian Council and in the Legislative Council of the colony. There was no dissentient opinion, and the leading native speaker cordially endorsed the proposals.

The justification of these measures lay in the fact that they were designed to meet special conditions arising out of the war, and were of a temporary nature. They were based on the recommendations of two very representative Committees, with the object of giving effect to a policy which had received international sanction, and to transfer to the United Kingdom an industry essential to defence in a future war.[1]

This, if properly explained to the people of West Africa, would not be resented, since the United Kingdom was able to take the whole of the output, and the unrestricted market for the manufactured article, and keen competition between merchants assured fair prices to the producer. If, however, the position of the British mill-owners is already assured, it devolves upon them voluntarily to forgo the benefit of an implied assurance, as I have ventured to suggest.[2]

But whatever may be the merits of the controversy which has raged so fiercely in Parliament and the Press, it has one aspect in which all who are interested in the Empire can only rejoice. It has shown that our professed concern for the rights of the natives, and our obligations as trustee on their

[1] In a striking passage that ardent free-trader, Adam Smith, after setting out an overwhelming case against the restrictive principles embodied in the "Act of Navigation," says that, "since defence is of far greater importance than opulence," that Act "was perhaps the wisest of all the commercial regulations of England."—'Wealth of Nations,' vol. ii. p. 195.

[2] 'Times,' 31st December 1919. While some maintain that the duty has enabled the crushers in England to control the kernel market, knowing that importers could not ship their kernels abroad, others hold that the tax was justified and had more than served its purpose. Germany, they argue, with her mills intact, with special facilities for supplying the markets of Austria, Russia, and Eastern Europe generally, by rail without breaking bulk, desired again to invade West Africa and capture the kernel trade. She had, however, been prevented by the duty, and had therefore substituted copra, principally from the Dutch East Indies, thus relieving the palm-kernel market of a serious competitor, and extending the demand for kernels. The natives, they maintain, have not suffered, since prices had been maintained by competition, as was evident from a comparison between the prices ruling for kernels and for copra, which for all practical purposes supplies the same needs. The subject is fully discussed in the Report on Trade and Taxation in West Africa, Cmd. 1600, 1922, pp. 59-64.

A similar duty under home instructions had for some time been imposed on tin. Compare also the Malayan duty, imposed to prevent a foreign monopoly.—'Malaya,' p. 333.

behalf, are neither camouflage nor "unctuous righteousness," but that it is a tradition held deep in the hearts of the British people, for any infringement of which, however temporary and exceptional, an explanation and justification is at once demanded.

The vindication of the principle that a trustee Power is not justified in arbitrarily restricting the markets of its ward leads us to the consideration of the case of cotton. The increasing absorption by the United States of her own cotton for her own industries, and the consequently decreasing quantity available for export, has compelled this country to adopt a programme for the growing of cotton within the Empire, on the assumption that the cotton so grown will be available for the looms of Lancashire. In so far as the cotton is the product of British-owned plantations (as in the Sudan, Gezirah, and Nyasaland), no question can of course arise; but where (as in Nigeria and other protectorates) it is a native crop, is the market to be restricted to Great Britain? That colonial revenues have been spent in improving the quality, &c., gives the British market no claim to a monopoly, for such revenues belong to the colony, and are rightly spent in developing its resources. But if funds belonging to the taxpayers of England, or if private capital has been spent in promoting the industry in a British colony, is Germany or Japan to have the right to underbid the British merchant and buy the crop?

In 1916 the Board of Trade appointed a Committee to report (*inter alia*) regarding the textile industry, and its report was issued in 1918.[1] Following the general lines of Lord Balfour of Burleigh's Committee, it recommended that the Empire's resources in raw material should be safeguarded, and utilised for the requirements of the Empire, and for purposes of negotiation with other countries, and that an export duty (*e.g.*, on jute) should be imposed in India, with a total rebate for the United Kingdom. But the Cotton Committee, appointed by the Government of India in September 1917, affirmed that the interests of the cultivator must be paramount—a stipulation to which the Empire Cotton Growing Committee "heartily agreed."[2] Thus any restriction of the market in the interests of the United Kingdom is

[1] Cd. 9370 of 1918.

[2] Cmd. 523 of 1920, p. 42. See also the debate in the House of Lords of 12th July 1920. This latter "Committee" has now been constituted under Royal

ruled out, and if the growth of cotton is increased in India, the surplus may go to the country which offers the best price instead of to England, whose manufacturers and taxpayers have spent money in its development. Or to put it in another way, it might seem equally beneficial to promote cotton-growing in China as in the Empire.

The figures given by the Board of Trade[1] show that for the quinquennial period 1912-13 to 1916-17, only 7 per cent of the Indian crop was received by Great Britain, while 55 per cent went to Japan. In the last year (with the elimination of Germany and other countries) the proportion was 9·7 per cent to the United Kingdom, and nearly 70 per cent[2] to Japan. Though the bulk of the crop is stated to be at present of too short a staple for the needs of Lancashire, this is only a temporary condition, and our efforts to increase the length of staple will presently begin to show results. Japan, moreover, will also require a longer staple as the standard of her manufactures improves.

The Empire Cotton Growing Committee has, of course, carefully considered this matter. Its view is that the grant of public money is principally for the benefit of those parts of the Empire in which cotton is grown,[3] and where it would not be grown unless it was to the advantage of the country growing it. They hold to the great principle that "any specific control of the destination of the crop is impracticable and undesirable"—but they think it certain that an indefinite preference will be indirectly secured for spinners in the British Empire; and finally, it is beyond question that in case of war it is of the first importance that supplies of cotton should be available in the Empire itself, so that we should not have to depend solely on other countries, however friendly they may be. Thus the general principle is affirmed that any restriction forcibly imposed upon the markets of the pro-

Charter as a permanent "Corporation" for the promotion of cotton-growing in the Empire, with an Imperial grant of about a million sterling accruing from certain war profits in Egypt.

[1] 'Board of Trade Journal,' 2nd May 1918. See also Cmd. 51 of 1919, p. 322.

[2] See also Indian Progress Report for 1917-1918, published in 1919, where the percentage is given as 71 per cent (p. 101).

[3] This view will not, I think, find general acceptance. Parliament agreed to this additional burden on the British taxpayer, not as a subsidy to India, Nigeria, or Uganda, but in the interests of the great Lancashire industry. Such assistance may, however, be placed to the Imperial credit in the commercial bargains which Lord Balfour of Burleigh's Committee suggested as a form of Imperial preference, the colony recognising the prior claim of the United Kingdom to the crop as an act of reciprocity. [See pp. 277-278.]

ducing country for the benefit of the Controlling Power is contrary to the theory of trusteeship.[1]

I come now to the second of the headings, under which I summarised some of the economic effects, resulting from the war, on the relations of the African dependencies to the United Kingdom—viz., the proposals for rehabilitating the Imperial finances by schemes such as those put forward by the "Empire Resources Development Committee."

I have, I think, conclusively shown in an article in 'The Nineteenth Century'[2] that such of these proposals as relate to the African dependencies, and aim "at promoting the development for profit under State auspices, and participation of selected resources," cannot be adopted except at the sacrifice of fundamental principles. These particular proposals have not been pressed of late, and it will therefore suffice to refer my reader to the article alluded to, in which they are examined in detail. They appear to contemplate a complete or partial monopoly by the controlling Power, by which the natives would be compelled to sell their produce to its agents, so that the profits may be acquired not by the individual merchant, or even by the local Government for the benefit of the country, but in liquidation of the British war-debt, under a system which must necessarily involve the fixing of prices for labour and produce, and the restriction of markets. The patriotic proposers had not, I venture to think, fully realised the implications of their scheme, which in essential principles appears to resemble the former régime of the Congo State, on the abandonment of which the British Government insisted before it accorded its recognition of the reversion of the State to Belgium.[3] The market is at present well supplied with capital.[4]

[1] The 'Times' (18th December 1919) gave publicity to an unpublished letter from the British to the French Government, dated 28th May 1918, which stated that, after the needs of this country had been met, "the resources in raw materials of the British Empire will be at the disposal of France and other Allies. Only after the Allies have obtained what they require for their economic development will the resources of our Empire be offered to neutral Powers, and lastly to the countries with which we are now at war." This would seem to be a formal and precise pledge of a very sweeping nature, unrestricted in time, or as to the nature of the raw materials, or the consent of the colonies concerned, and would seem to assume the right of the British Government to deal as it may think fit with the produce of the tropical dependencies.

[2] "The Crown Colonies and the British War-debt," August 1920.

[3] Prof. Keith, 'African Society Journal,' July 1918, p. 256, citing State Paper 107, p. 352.

[4] The chairman of the Association of West African Merchants wrote to the

But if such schemes as these must be ruled out as inadmissible, are we to accept the conclusion that the peoples of the tropical dependencies are to bear no share in the financial burden of the war, which was fought no less for their liberties than for our own? National liberty in these days depends largely on national wealth, for only the wealthiest nations can afford to maintain the great armies and navies and air services on which the defence of those liberties depends. It is therefore to the self-interest of the subject races that Great Britain should remain wealthy enough to support the burden. But the war has left her with a colossal debt, and a scale of taxation which cripples enterprise.

From these financial burdens the tropical dependencies are to a large extent exempt. To some of them the war and the period succeeding it even brought added prosperity, and notwithstanding any temporary set-back, the demand for their foodstuffs and raw materials is assured, and promises a prosperous future. They helped to win the war; are they incapable of some voluntary self-sacrifice in order to help "to win the peace"? State monopolies, fixed prices for produce and labour, confiscation of lands, compulsory service—none of these things should we ask of them. But is it too much to ask of the native producer that he should voluntarily give a preference to British requirements for a definitely limited period, and acquiesce in the limitation of his market, provided that the whole of his output is absorbed at remunerative prices, and that the particular product is one of essential importance to British industry? In the case of cotton, for instance, he would not thereby be contributing to "capitalistic profits," for the Empire Cotton Corporation is pledged to make no profits, and the British consumers have imposed upon themselves a tax of 6d. per bale to provide funds for its activities. Competition by merchants on the spot will assure fair prices.

Voluntary acquiescence, if genuine—that is to say, if it can be obtained by a widespread knowledge of the facts—is

Press (10th November 1916) that "British merchants have been and are prepared to find all the capital required for its (Nigeria's) development, and have at present invested there probably two million more than before the war." Much capital has been invested since that date, and in addition we have Lever Bros., Jurgens & Co., and other large capitalists outside the Liverpool group. Moreover, the credit of West African dependencies is good enough to enable them to raise whatever loans they may need.

the better way. But the trustee Power is also entitled to consider, if need be, what definite obligations are being incurred by its ward for which an adequate return is due. I do not refer to financial assistance in the early years, nor am I oblivious to the indirect advantages which accrue to a trustee, however freely "equal opportunity" is accorded to the commerce of all nations.

But can it be said that there is any violation of fundamental principles if a colony, when it has reached a stage of prosperity, should be asked to make some contribution to the Navy on which it is dependent for its defence from its surplus revenue—viz., from the balance remaining when ordinary administrative expenditure has been met—which is a measure of its prosperity, and is normally devoted to development? The principle has long been in application in our Eastern colonies, where a military contribution is levied—not with their consent, and not for the purpose of maintaining troops for the preservation of law and order in the colonies themselves. The Empire is based on the relations of the family, and not on those of the syndicate. The African, who shares with us its benefits, must learn that it is his duty and his privilege to share its burdens. This ideal should be more adequately explained to him.

On the other hand, it has been alleged, both in East[1] and West Africa, that the local forces maintained by the African dependencies are in excess of the needs of the colonies for local defence and police purposes. Many of these dependencies —Nigeria, the Gold Coast, Kenya, Uganda, and Nyasaland —had frontiers coterminous with German colonies, and the events of the war have shown that so long at least as that aggressive Power remained a menace to the world, the colonial forces were necessarily maintained at a high strength. Whether they can now be reduced is a matter for consideration.

I come to my last heading—Imperial Preference. This stands on a different footing, for it has no necessary relation to war legislation or post-bellum economic conditions, and is in principle wholly voluntary. The case for the imposition of a tariff was put by Colonel Amery—than whom no one is

[1] Mr Wallis, late Chief Secretary of Uganda, asserts that the King's African Rifles are not required by Kenya or Uganda, and should be disbanded or paid for by the War Office.—'Times,' 23rd August 1921.

better qualified to state it,—writing from East Africa so long ago as January 1908 :—

"What inducement is there," he asks, "for the British taxpayer to undertake all this increased expenditure—or, at least, increased financial responsibility? . . . Under the fiscal system at present prevailing both in England and in the territories under Colonial Office control, there is no guarantee whatever that the market, when developed, will be a market for English rather than for foreign goods, or that the raw materials will go to British factories rather than to the factories of our rivals. Why should not British industry have that guarantee in return for the expenditure and risk incurred by the British taxpayer? Why should not the producer in these new territories give that guarantee in return for the establishment of the settled conditions which make this industry possible?" Colonel Amery even goes so far as to say that "No one can suggest that a preference in favour of British imports into East Africa, or—what is more desirable—a differential export tax on raw materials exported from East Africa to foreign countries, is likely to inflict hardship upon either native or settler, or to retard the development of the country."[1]

It is worth while to examine these proposals carefully, for they appear at first sight to enshroud the principles of the palm-kernel export duty under the comforting title of Imperial preference. A preferential export duty may, as we have seen, inflict considerable loss on the producers, by depriving them of the high prices which foreign nations are willing to pay for their raw materials. The controlling Power would benefit, as in the old plantation system, by a monopoly. Nor does the export tax even benefit the local revenue, for in effect it is rarely levied. It is intentionally made prohibitive, so as to ensure the monopoly. Such a differential export duty, if forced on a reluctant colony for the benefit of home trade, is, as Lord Emmot says, the absolute negation of the voluntary principle.[2] The question of voluntary assistance to the Mother Country by African dependencies—even though it may involve sacrifice—is a separate issue, with which I have already dealt.

But Colonel Amery does not contemplate compulsion. He

[1] 'Union and Strength,' L. S. Amery, pp. 290, 291.
[2] House of Lords debate of 17th May 1920.

assumes the export tax to be self-imposed voluntarily, with the object of inducing the British Exchequer to incur further expenditure in the development of the country, and to guarantee to the British taxpayer the benefit of the money so expended. In my view, private capital, attracted by the prospects of the country, or raised by way of loans on the security of the revenues—if need be with the assistance of an Imperial guarantee—is preferable to grants from the Exchequer.

African products do not suffer appreciably from foreign competition. Already they have a duty-free market in the United Kingdom, and the object in view is not to exclude foreign competition, but to attract to England produce which otherwise would find a more remunerative market abroad.

What, then, has the controlling power to offer in return, so that it may properly come under the designation of a reciprocal preference? There are duties (for revenue purposes) on tea, sugar, coffee, cocoa, and tobacco, and these could be remitted, as proposed by Lord Balfour of Burleigh's Committee, "as a first measure of colonial preference,"[1] but they do not touch the bulk of the exports from tropical Africa, which are imported duty-free into the United Kingdom. To give a preference to these, it would be necessary to impose duties on all such articles imported from foreign countries, and to remit them for Empire-grown produce. If the principle of equal opportunity be applied absolutely without reservation, what advantage, asks Colonel Amery, does the controlling power gain to compensate for the burden it sustains? I shall deal with this question in my last chapter.

Colonel Amery's alternative, which he regards with less favour, is a preference on British imported goods. Since the local revenue (which in some dependencies is largely derived from customs) could not afford a reduction in existing customs duties (for the loss would have to be made good by some equivalent tax), the preference would no doubt take the form of additional duties on goods of foreign origin. Leaving out of account the question of commercial and other treaties (viz., the Berlin and Brussels Acts and the Conventions of

[1] Cd. 9035, p. 48, paragraph 237. The East African "Economic Commission," while expressing readiness to give a preference to the United Kingdom, apparently asks in return for a subsidy to shipping lines for special freights for certain products for a limited time. *Loc. cit.*, p. 26.

June 1898 and of September 1919), and that of retaliation by foreign Powers—both very important considerations—how would such action affect the purely Imperial preference point of view?

It would be a genuine preference, and it would probably not be opposed by the dependencies, for the bulk of their imports are already from the United Kingdom, and would remain unaffected. The colonial consumer would suffer in some degree, no doubt, by the loss of cheap foreign goods, but there is much to be said for such a preference if the Mother Country can offer some equivalent. There may be some articles in which the Empire output is insufficient to supply the home market and foreign competition makes itself felt. In such a case duties could be imposed, and in the words of Lord Balfour's Committee, "preferential treatment should be accorded in respect of any customs duties now or hereafter to be imposed in the United Kingdom."[1] The Committee suggests also "the expediency of considering measures of Imperial preference other than the imposition of differential customs duties—as, for example, Government contracts to purchase for a term of years, at guaranteed minimum prices, part or the whole of the output of materials of great industrial importance . . . or financial assistance from the home Government towards the development of Imperial resources."[2]

Following these pronouncements, a notice appeared in the 'Board of Trade Journal' announcing that reduced rates as specified therein would be charged on certain goods "consigned from, grown, produced, or manufactured in the British Empire."[3]

It is, of course, more than probable that if Great Britain restricted the produce of her colonies to her own markets, she would provoke foreign countries to a policy of retaliation. It was pointed out in the palm-kernels debate that the United States and Belgium (Congo) were bound by treaties to exact no preferential duties against Great Britain, on the grounds that they have free access to her colonial markets. France has deprived herself of the weapon of retaliation by her own exclusive policy, and in the letter quoted by Lord Mayo in

[1] Cd. 9035 of 1918, paragraph 254.

[2] Ibid., paragraph 239. For the application of this principle to Empire-grown cotton, see p. 272.

[3] 'Board of Trade Journal,' 9th September 1920.

that debate, the French Government formally notified to our Foreign Office her intention to retain for her own sole use the raw materials of her colonies.[1]

Thus the fear of jeopardising our commercial relations with foreign Powers, no less than the extreme reluctance we should feel in forgoing the proud boast that Britain alone holds her colonies open to all the world, would add to the regret with which we should adopt such a policy otherwise than as a temporary measure arising out of the war, affecting one group of colonies, and one or two products only. Exclusive tariffs are dangerous weapons, apt to injure the hand which uses them, opposed to the traditions of British trade, and contrary to the agreement of the Economic Conference, which pledged the Allies "to adopt measures for facilitating their mutual trade relations."

Let us hope that the nations whose destinies the war has shown to be closely interdependent may learn that reciprocity is a better word than restriction, and carry its operation even beyond the sphere of tariffs. Nigeria, for instance, has assisted France by allowing French goods to pass over her railways to Zinder. Mutual reciprocity would guarantee like facilities over any railway which France may build thence to the Mediterranean.

[1] "After the war," says a French writer, "France must as far as possible live on the products of her colonial lands . . . by reserving for French commerce her colonial market, so that neither enemy, nor neutral, nor ally shall profit unduly from the colonies of France."

CHAPTER XIV.

LAND TENURE AND TRANSFER.

The natural evolution of conceptions of land tenure—The problem in West Africa—Committees on West African lands—West African land tenure: (*a*) Tribal and family; (*b*) Individual ownership; (*c*) Absence of tenure—Summary *re* land tenure—Rights of conquest—Recognition of private rights—Necessity for declaration of policy—View of the Committee—Nationalisation—The economic doctrine—Criticism and fears—Actual practice in Northern Nigeria—Summary of criticism of Northern Nigeria land law—Encouragement of small holdings—Large estates—Transfers between natives—Acquisition of land by Government and aliens in conquered countries—Shifting cultivation—Curtailment or increase of tribal or village lands—Summary of Government and native rights in controlled lands—Freehold and communal tenure.

I PROPOSE in this and the following chapter to discuss the question of land in the British African tropics, only in so far as it presents itself as an administrative problem. Speaking generally, it may, I think, be said that conceptions as to the tenure of land are subject to a steady evolution, side by side with the evolution of social progress, from the most primitive stages to the organisation of the modern State. In the earliest stage the land and its produce is shared by the community as a whole; later the produce is the property of the family or individuals by whose toil it is won, and the control of the land becomes vested in the head of the family. When the tribal stage is reached, the control passes to the chief, who allots unoccupied lands at will, but is not justified in dispossessing any family or person who is using the land. Later still, especially when the pressure of population has given to the land an exchange value, the conception of proprietary rights in it emerges, and sale, mortgage, and lease of the land, apart from its user, is recognised.[1]

Conquest vests the control of the land in the conqueror, who in savage warfare also disposes of the lives and chattels of the conquered, but he usually finds it necessary to conform largely to the existing law and custom. In civilised countries conquest does not justify confiscation of private rights in land.

These processes of natural evolution, leading up to individual ownership, may, I believe, be traced in every civilisation known to history. Ahab, 900 years B.C., was unable to dispossess Naboth of the private ownership of his vineyard without violation of accepted principles; China for centuries has recognised individual property in land, as did Babylon 5000 years ago,[2] and as the nations of Europe do to-day.[3]

In Africa every stage of this process of evolution may be encountered. The problem with which a Government has

[1] There are, says Professor Berriedale Keith ('African Society's Journal,' April 1912), two opposing theories as to the evolution of the ownership of land. Some, following Sir H. Maine, hold that the land is first owned by the tribe, then by the village community, and finally by the individual. Others maintain that the individual was the original owner, and that ownership by the community or tribe, so far as it is real and not a matter of territorial sovereignty, is a later conception.

I venture to think that neither theory is exclusive. When a swarming horde of invaders enters an inhabited country the earlier possessors are ousted. Each unit seizes the land it requires, and eventually village boundaries are recognised. If the invaders had already attained to a tribal organisation, vacant lands are at the disposal of the tribal head; if not, they remain indeterminate, until that stage is reached. They are at the disposal of the territorial chief, not as owner, but in his capacity as sovereign of the tribe. On the other hand, where possession has been acquired by the occupation of uninhabited and unclaimed lands—a condition which applies to areas left derelict by pestilence, slave-raids, or famine—or by gradual encroachment on grazing lands, which the tribe in possession is no longer able to defend, individual settlement and ownership probably preceded that of the family or tribe. These academic theories are, however, immaterial to the indisputable fact that, whatever the origins of land tenure, the inevitable tendency has been towards the recognition of individual proprietary rights in land *pari passu* with social evolution.

M. Delafosse—a translation of whose admirable memorandum on land tenure in French West Africa may be found in the 'African Society's Journal,' 1910, pp. 259-273—asserts that this difference in the original method of acquisition affects the existing tenure of land. "Depending," he says, "upon whether the conquest or original occupation was the work of a single chief or of a community acting without any one directing force, so will ownership of land be found to be vested either in the chief or in the community." In the former case, he says, the chief has the rights of proprietor, and "real owner," and can alienate at will—in the latter he has no such rights, and acts only as trustee.

[2] 'Ownership, Tenure, and Taxation of Land,' Whittaker, p. 40.

[3] "Nobody is at liberty to attack several property and to say at the same time that he values civilisation. The history of the two cannot be disentangled."—Maine, 'Village Communities,' p. 230.

to deal consists, on the one hand, in adjusting land questions between natives, which otherwise would lead to quarrels and bloodshed—questions often complicated by the disintegration of tribal authority and native custom, due to extraneous influences. On the other hand, the Government must control generally the acquisition of land by non-natives.

As regards the second of these two tasks, it is manifest that there exists a fundamental difference between those countries in which there is a dense native population, and Europeans and others enter for a more or less temporary residence, and those in which the climate attracts European settlers, and the sparsity of the native population admits of the settlement of non-natives—European and Asiatic. The group of West African colonies and protectorates are typical of the former, and since their population and the volume of their trade with the outside world is much greater than that of all the remainder [1] put together, I propose to deal with them at some length.

In 1908 Lord Crewe, then Secretary of State for the Colonies, appointed a committee to investigate the subject of land tenure in Northern Nigeria, and to advise as to the system which should be adopted by Government.[2] In 1912 Mr (now Lord) Harcourt (Lord Crewe's successor) appointed another committee under the same chairman, with similar instructions as regards the remaining dependencies in West Africa. They were to report "whether any, and if so what, amendment of the laws is required, either on the lines of the Northern Nigeria Lands Proclamation or otherwise." War broke out before they had completed their report, which was never made public.[3] Earlier in 1912 Mr Harcourt had already sent the late Sir Henry Belfield to make inquiries

[1] The population of British West Africa is estimated at 21,823,000, and its trade is valued at £49,820,000. The aggregate population of the whole of the remaining British dependencies in tropical Africa (excluding Mauritius, the Seychelles, St Helena, and Ascension) is put at 16,149,600, and the value of their trade at £26,759,000 (see Table, p. 45).

[2] Cd. 5102 and 5108 of 1910. The committee sat for two months and examined eight witnesses, two of whom were members of the committee, two were Englishmen connected with commerce, and the remainder were officials. They also had at their disposal memoranda on the subject issued by the Governor and his predecessor to Residents in Nigeria.

[3] The second committee was appointed in June 1912 and finally dissolved in 1915. They examined a very great number of witnesses, including natives, and a great mass of correspondence was laid before them, in addition to the voluminous evidence taken in West Africa, and Sir H. Belfield's report.

into the system of administration of land in the Gold Coast, and his report was published in July of that year.[1]

An immense mass of evidence was taken on commission in Africa for the "West African Lands Committee." That from Nigeria passed through my hands, and from it and Sir H. Belfield's report on the Gold Coast it is possible to arrive at some broad conclusions as to the conceptions regarding the ownership and transfer of lands held by the people of West Africa, the more so that the system of land tenure is known to be very similar in all these dependencies.

It may be assumed that Africa was densely populated long before the tribes which now hold sway settled on their respective lands.[2] Title to land accrued to the latest conquerors, and where land had become derelict as a result of extermination, slave-raids, migration, or pestilence, the individual who first reclaimed it claimed ownership of it for himself and his descendants. The title to such land was vested in the head of the family, and further areas reclaimed by its members were added to the family lands. Intervening unoccupied areas were later included. The tribal chief allotted the conquered lands to families, and the disposal of any vacant lands not included in those claimed by any family was vested in him. In some tribes the family remained the important unit, as in the Gold Coast and Yorubaland, in others it became merged in the tribe. In the former case there would be two classes of unoccupied land—family and tribal.[3] Primeval forests, unoccupied by man for centuries, the natural barriers between warring tribes, became gradually included

[1] Cd. 6278 of 1912. The report is dated 18th June 1912, and is accompanied by notes of evidence, addresses, &c., by fifty-seven persons. His instructions are not quoted, but in an address to the chiefs and others Mr Belfield stated that "the principal object of my mission is to make inquiry into the system of administration of land in the Gold Coast Colony" (p. 4).

[2] Many, especially of the native witnesses, appear to ignore this fact, and speak as if the earliest founders of the existing tribes came, like the sons of Noah, into a wholly uninhabited land, and pegged out claims which developed by a symmetrical process from the original founder, through the family and the tribe, to the kingship—though nothing, I imagine, is more certain than that the populations of this continent have been subject to constant displacement by more powerful neighbours. The Yoruba and other native legends (like the Hebrew myths) are apt to attribute the foundation of the tribe to a single semi-divine ancestor, who settled in a waste land and gradually populated it. These witnesses testify that the idea of unoccupied and unappropriated land is contrary to all native conceptions, but fail to see that this strong assertion is incompatible with the thesis on which they found the claims of existing tribes.

[3] Belfield's Report, paragraphs 19-26 and 48. See note 1, next page.

in one or the other class, and were recognised as the inalienable property of the neighbouring community.

Starting from these hypotheses, the evidence appears to show that the following general principles—with local variations—became consolidated. The tribal land at the disposal of the chief might be allotted either to families which had outgrown their family lands, or to strangers who desired to settle among the tribe, provided that they paid the customary tribute and dues. Family lands are at the disposal of the head of the family, and every member of the family has a right to a share in the land—a right which is not forfeited even by prolonged absence. The holder and his descendants have undisturbed possession in perpetuity, and all rights of ownership, except that they cannot alienate the land so as to deprive the chief of his ultimate control over it. The occupier's title is held by virtue of his membership of the family, and perpetuates in the name of its head.

The produce of the land is the property of the occupier, and he may own trees planted by himself, either on unoccupied land or on land occupied by another. He may sell or pawn the crops on his land, or trees owned by him, but not the land itself. He may be ousted from his holding for offences against the community, including failure to pay customary tribute; and upon the general acknowledgment of their right to allocate land, and to enforce punishment in respect of it, depends the prestige of the chiefs. Hence the system of ruling through the chiefs depends on the recognition by Government of these powers. A chief acts as trustee for the tribe in regard to land. "He is joint owner with his people, and he cannot exercise any proprietary rights without the co-operation of his people," said the deputation on the Gold Coast Forest Bill.[1] Consequent on these assumptions, it is maintained that "every acre of land is the property of some tribe, family, or individual," including forest and swamp.[2]

[1] Native deputation to Secretary of State, July 1912. Monsieur Delafosse notes that among the northern tribes, as contrasted with "the tribes of the forest zone," control of the land is more often exercised by an individual chief, there is usually less tribal land, and absolute alienation of land to a stranger is less difficult than among the forest tribes. *Loc. cit.*

[2] Belfield, paragraph 22. See Maine, *loc. cit.*, p. 121. "The so-called waste lands (in India) are part of the domain of the various communities which the villagers theoretically are only waiting opportunity to bring under cultivation." Some witnesses before the Committee made the same assertion as regards Northern Nigeria, but in my opinion it is unquestionable that in that country there are

It is clear from this description that African land tenure is not "communal" in the sense of tenure in common.[1] Its fundamental characteristic seems rather to be an individual tenure of land derived from the common stock at the disposal of the tribe or family.[2] Such a tenure would tend to develop very rapidly into individual ownership, and evidence that this was the case was given by several witnesses—and much more is available.

Side by side with these primitive conceptions of land tenure, we find a growing recognition of the conception of individual ownership. This is due in part to the natural evolution to which I have referred, and in part to the introduction of European conceptions of land tenure. The spread of these European ideas may be attributed in the first place to ignorance of the native system. We find the Supreme Courts issuing writs of execution for the seizure of land from a judgment debtor, though by native customary law—of which the court was bound to take cognisance—he had no individual property in it. This was much aggravated by the tendency to charge the Supreme Court with the duty of deciding all land cases to the exclusion of the executive officers.

large tracts of land which have become derelict and ownerless as the result of the slave-raids of the past. They are known as "Jagin Allah" (God's jungle), and villages of ex-slaves have been formed on such areas without protest or any opposing claim. Even the evidence from Southern Nigeria did not appear to be very consistent on this point, for more than one witness referred to vacant lands, and one Lagos witness spoke of "No-man's land," which he said was called "Tedo." When, however, the right to collect sylvan produce on vacant lands is regularly exercised they cannot properly be regarded as waste lands.

[1] Mr Gower's evidence. Cmd. 5103, 1910, p. 94. Questions 866, 867.

[2] Professor Keith, in the very interesting article already quoted, doubts whether there was "any conception of the community as a whole as a land-owner." It is impossible, he remarks, to say from the evidence before the Northern Nigerian Lands Committee "that there is any clear recognition of a legal entity, namely the tribe or village, as owning the land . . . the Hausa customs as to the inheritance and division of property on death are quite contrary to any such conception."

The power of expropriation by the head of the tribe is, he argues, a political control, which does not necessarily connote tribal ownership, nor does the moral control exercised by the family head denote family ownership. He appears to consider that the land is individually owned by the head of the family, and is divided among the members at his death. "None of the evidence adduced shows that the property ascribed to the tribe or community amounts to more than the fact that the village has recognised boundaries," within which the land required by any member is assigned to him by the head. Compare Baden-Powell: "It seems to me quite clear that a sense of individual 'property' in land may arise coincidently with a sense of a certain right in others to have a share of the produce."—'Indian Village Communities,' p. 131.

Secondly, the English conception of land tenure was carried far and wide throughout the country, by the desire of every European trader or miner to obtain a freehold right to the land occupied by his residence. And thirdly, especially in the large coast towns, by the influence of the Europeanised native lawyers. To these may perhaps be added in some districts the influence of Mohamedans. In the larger cities of the coast the conception of individual ownership in land, with the right to sell, mortgage, and bequeath it, has thus become fully recognised, while in the interior the idea has become more and more prevalent.[1]

On the other hand, the conception has no doubt also arisen from natural processes, where the density of the population in and around the native cities gave to the land an economic value for residence or for its produce.[2] Even among some very primitive tribes the principle of private ownership seems to be recognised, for there is evidence of land having been sold or rent charged for its use, even where pressure of population was not the cause.[3]

The conception of individual ownership is promoted by the cultivation of permanent crops which take long to mature, such as cocoa, rubber, &c.[4] It is remarkable with what tenacity the native mind holds to the idea of private ownership, or at least of the absolute right to tenure in perpetuity. It was difficult in Lagos to dispose of Crown land to natives on any terminable lease, however favourable its terms.

There are considerable areas in Africa under the domination of nomadic tribes—such as the Masai of British East

[1] Mr Dennett states that to alienate land by sale, formerly held to be a crime among the Egbas, is now becoming a custom. A deputation of natives urged on the Alaké the view that land is not inalienable, but the private property of the occupier.—'African Society's Journal,' and 'Morning Post,' 14th March 1910.

[2] There is evidence in the Blue-book (5103) that this stage had been reached in various parts of Northern Nigeria—especially in and around the cities of Sokoto, Kano, and Zaria.

[3] Mr Cardinal tells us that in the Northern Territories of the Gold Coast the "Tindana"—the priest of the earth-god—and not the secular chief, owns and disposes of the land. The person who first reclaimed a piece of land "becomes the owner for all time. . . . It is private property, much as we know it in our own country," and he derives his title from "the caretaker or agent of the earth-god—the Tindana."—'The Natives of the Northern Territories of the Gold Coast.'

[4] Speaking of the spread of the cocoa industry in Ashanti, Sir H. Belfield writes: "The necessity for creating a form of land tenure in the nature of individual ownership is therefore becoming apparent. . . . The people will have to admit into their system of land tenure an exclusive right to land, which has only been recognised up to the present time in the case of concessions to Europeans."—Report, para. 51.

Africa—who have established grazing rights for their cattle, but otherwise claim no rights of user in the land. The desire of the agricultural tribes for land is replaced among these nomadic pastorals by the desire for ownership of cattle. In other regions—such as Bornu in Nigeria—the poverty of the soil, and the migratory habits of the people, lead to the frequent transfer of villages from one site to another, and consequently to a similar absence of any rigid system of land tenure. Elsewhere we find wandering tribes of pastorals traversing the lands occupied by the settled tribes, who accord to them rights of grazing for their cattle—as the Fulani and Shuwas in Nigeria. Some of these tribes do possess a small amount of cultivated land—witness the Ol-moruo of the Masai. These are usually cultivated by a helot race of serfs, who have no rights in the usufruct.

It is not easy to focus into a paragraph a general conception of African land tenure. The general principles would seem to be that the assignment of land to the individual is entrusted to tribal or family authorities, in whom is vested the control of common grazing lands and forests; that every individual has a right to a share of the use of the land, and holds it in perpetuity, subject to the performance of tribal obligations, but may not alienate it; that these principles are held more tenaciously by the forest tribes than by those farther north, where, in some cases, it is the representative of the earth-god who assigns the land, in others an individual chief, while pastoral nomads are indifferent to questions of land ownership and value grazing rights only. The forest tribes jealously maintain that all unoccupied land belongs to some community or other, while the northern tribes are less insistent on such claims. All alike recognise the right of the conqueror to dispose of the land. The inevitable tendency to individual ownership is meanwhile constantly asserting itself, with the evolution of the tribe, and is fostered by pressure of population, by foreign example, and by the replacement of annual by permanent crops.

We have seen that in the struggle for existence among the aboriginal inhabitants of the African continent, the land—upon the possession of which survival depended—fell to the conqueror. The earlier Committee, dealing with Northern Nigeria, based its conclusions on the assumption that the whole of the protectorate was either conquered by British arms, or had submitted to a threat of force, and that African peoples—whether Moslem or pagan—recognised that all land is at the disposal of the conqueror. They accordingly assert that "the whole of the land, whether occupied or unoccupied, is subject to the control of the Government, and that no title to the occupation, use, or enjoyment of any land is valid without the consent of the Government." [1] A word of comment on this general assumption, which as they say forms the basis of the report, is desirable.

It has been laid down as "a principle from which no civilised Government would think of departing, that in countries acquired by conquest or cession, private property, whether of individuals or communities, existing at the time of the cession or conquest, is respected." In that portion therefore—even though the people admitted our right to deal with their lands and their lives as we should see fit—we are, as a civilised nation, precluded from assuming such "dominion and control" over the land as would interfere with the communal or private rights of the conquered people.[2] Moreover, a large part of Northern Nigeria had never been conquered by the Fulani, and was unconquered until it submitted to the British.

In the other portion the British conquered the dominant race, which was Moslem, and as such recognised the Maliki law of Islam.[3] But these conquerors, as the Committee re-

[1] Cd. 5102, paragraphs 20, 32, and 72.

[2] See also judgment of Privy Council in the Oluwa land case, July 1921.

[3] A very interesting document, called the *Ta'limu' Radthi* (land law) of the Sokoto Empire, by Mallam Abdulahi, brother of Dan Fodio, whose Jihad led to the Fulani conquest, has recently been discovered. It probably describes what, in the view of the writer, the land tenure should be under Moslem rule, rather than what it ultimately became, owing to the influence of existing customs. Land assigned by the Imam (he says) is private property, and can be given away or bequeathed, but the Imam cannot assign ownership of cultivated land captured in war, or ceded by treaty, even though held by unbelievers. Such lands are *Wakf* or public lands, and only the user of them can be granted. He can assign ownership of deserted lands, but lands still in cultivation by the ancient inhabitants "belong to them and to no one else."

The Maliki law lays down that all conquered lands under cultivation become *Wakf*, and cannot be sold or inherited. They are assigned to Moslems or converted owners. Neither the ruler nor the occupier has the power to dispose of the land itself. Rents are paid to public revenue. Land not under cultivation, including cities, may be assigned by the ruler to whom he pleases. A part may be set aside as "public lands" for the public good, if there is a clear need of them, if their area is small, and if they are absolutely waste.—Ruxton's 'Maliki Law,' pp. 78, 79, and 254.

In the Mohamedan Protectorate of Zanzibar, lands are either *Wakf* or freehold. Most of the latter are mortgaged to Indian traders, and the Arab owners are

cords,[1] are believed to have adopted to a large extent the pre-existing system of native law, including that of land tenure, which we may assume was based on the general principles I have described as being common to this part of Africa. Thus the rents receivable under Koranic law from *Wakf* (cultivated) lands were not demanded, being contrary to native custom, and a tribute tax based on the usufruct was substituted. The occupiers—who professed Islam—were confirmed in their holdings.

There is one other principle in dealing with conquered lands to which there can be no dissent. It is that, whatever may be the intention of the conqueror in regard to the land, it must be declared as soon as possible after the conquest is completed.[2] The Government of Northern Nigeria recognised this obligation.[3] Each Emir on appointment or reinstatement, received a letter which was publicly read, stating clearly that whatever rights in the land had belonged to the Fulani would now inure to the Government—rights which may be said to follow as a matter of course on the right to depose or appoint chiefs. No attempt at that time was made to define those rights, for we had not the necessary information, and it requires careful study to discriminate between the rights claimed by native conquerors over the inhabitants, as distinguished from rights over land. This was followed as soon as possible by an Ordinance, under which the Government claimed the right to dispose of unoccupied lands, and lands which were the property of conquered or deposed rulers, which were called "public lands." For these the Government became trustee. The immediate control of occupied lands was not interfered with, and remained in the hands of the native rulers, and no rent was demanded from the owners or occupiers.

The Government at the same time claimed *ownership* of certain lands, which had been acquired in perpetuity for specified public purposes (administrative sites, &c.), including lands leased to non-natives. Acquisition by Government had been effected by voluntary cession, any occupier being free to take up land elsewhere (of which there was abund-

in a dependent position.—Report for 1914, Cd. 7622, 1915. The Government claims ownership of all waste lands.—Government Notice, 'Gazette,' 15th June 1907.

[1] Cd. 5102, paragraphs 3 and 4.

[2] Belfield's Report, paragraph 47.

[3] Cd. 5102, paragraph 17.

ance), but for the most part the sites occupied were on waste lands. It was recognised that compensation in the form of alternative land should be made. These were called "Crown lands," and included certain lands transferred by the Chartered Company. The assumption of the right to dispose of waste land and unoccupied lands was not in conflict with the theory that all land has an owner, since, as I have shown, there were derelict lands in Northern Nigeria.

It would perhaps have hardly been worth while to devote so much space to the rights (and the limitations to them) resulting from conquest, and the course adopted in Nigeria, were it not that the question may again come into view in regard to the Mandated territories acquired by conquest from Germany.[1] On the two hypotheses—viz., that they were dealing with conquered lands, and that the control and disposal of such lands passes to the conqueror—the Committee recorded its conclusion that "the fundamental basis on which the law should rest are (1) that the whole of the land is subject to Government, and (2) that that control must be exercised as far as possible in accordance with native customs."[2] The adoption of these principles, they add, "seems to exclude the English conception of private ownership of land, or of any fixity of annual payment on account of the occupation of land." The Committee would impose a "special contribution on the occupiers of land, which would rather be in the nature of a rent than a tax on agricultural profits," and this rent should increase automatically in order to secure to the Government the expanding values of land due to the increase of wealth.[3] "It would, in fact, be the economic rent."[4]

[1] The Germans declared all vacant lands to be Crown lands, and a European could only acquire title to any land from the Crown.

[2] Cd. 5102, paragraphs 16, 20, 32. [3] Ibid., paragraphs 45, 46.

[4] Ibid., paragraph 45. What Sir T. Morison calls the "economic doctrine" is, I understand, "the claim of the State to the unearned increase in the rent of land, or a great part of that increase," due to improvements made by the State or by the community, as apart from those made by the occupier. "Since land is the free gift of nature . . . the economic doctrine would seem to require that all lands should become the property of the State."—(Morison, 'Industrial Organization of an Indian Village,' p. 19.) See also Whittaker, 'Ownership, Tenure, and Taxation of Land,' p. xxi.

Sir P. Girouard (my successor, and at that time Governor of Northern Nigeria) declared himself whole-heartedly in accord with the principles laid down by the Committee, which he construed as a declaration of the nationalisation of the land (Cd. 5102, p. xxvii.). In printed instructions to his staff he subsequently explained that land is "nationalised" when the economic rent

The Committee suggest that if it is impracticable to charge this rent by legislative methods, it should be imposed "administratively"—a course which the Attorney-General reported as contrary to the native revenue ordinance.[1] The Committee, however, admits that "an economic rent has not yet emerged, and forms no part of the indigenous system of taxation."[2] Its imposition would therefore be contrary to native customary law, and would thus violate one of the "fundamental bases." It had never been introduced by the Moslem conquerors, and, as we have seen, when an attempt was made to apportion the general tax in relation to the land in occupation, the result was that about half the valuable rice land in Sokoto went out of cultivation. The existing tax on the produce of land is in accordance with native law, but to exact a rental is to create "the new and strange idea of property in the land itself"—which the Committee condemns,—for the native not unnaturally considers that the person who claims the right to receive rentals is the owner of the land, and *Government becomes the owner and not the trustee.* Colour was lent to this view by the opinion of the Committee that any distinction between "Crown lands," in which the Government claimed *ownership* by purchase, &c., and the rest of the land over which it claimed control, was "unnecessary and may be misleading," and "superfluous."[3]

The Ordinance, which was drafted in England in accord-

is paid to the State, and not to an individual. "Proprietary rights will be created whenever an individual pays for the use of land to another individual, and not to the State." "There is therefore a necessity of separating the agriculturist and his land-revenue from taxes on all other walks in life." "Where economic rent has emerged it should be *added* to the amount assessed as an income tax." Lord Elgin defined the share of Government "in the unearned increment in the value of land" as being "that portion of its value which is due to the growth around it of an organised economic and political system."—Cd. 4117/1908, p. 30. These extracts appear to embody the theory of "Economic Rent."

The school of political economists who hold the view that the State alone should have any rights in land, appear to be ready to admit the indefeasible title conferred by conquest and spoliation, while denying the rights acquired by user, improvement and reclamation, or by purchase as the result of success in other forms of industry.

[1] Report, Cd. 5102, paragraphs 28, 29.

[2] Ibid., paragraph 46. Sir P. Girouard observes that "to attempt to assess an economic rent for lands that have not yet acquired a market value is impossible. This course would not be practicable in the case of natives, and would be opposed to their native law and custom in the Mohamedan States at any rate." "The native system is based on profits made out of the land."—Ibid., p. xxix. and 48.

[3] Ibid., paragraphs 23 and 27.

ance with the Committee's recommendations, evoked some criticism. The people of Southern Nigeria and the Gold Coast, as I said in the last chapter, were much perturbed at the inference in the terms of reference of the second Committee lest it should be applied to them, and they organised deputations to England to protest. It is worth while, therefore, to recapitulate briefly the grounds of this criticism and apprehension.

The law enacted that no title to occupation should be valid without the Governor's consent, and he was precluded from granting a right of occupancy except on rental, revisable septennially. This gave rise to the criticism that to turn an occupier who under native law holds his land rent-free in perpetuity "into a rent-paying, short-term lessee on a precarious tenure is bluntly confiscation," and both inexpedient and unjust.[1] Since, however, it was obviously impossible to issue certificates to millions of native occupiers, with no adequate staff or survey, the Colonial Office explained that native holders might continue to be dealt with by their rulers, acting in theory as delegates of the Governor. In the result, therefore, no certificates (without which rent is not chargeable) were issued, and the law remained a dead letter so far as native occupiers are concerned. They were unaware that it had declared their titles to be invalid, unless granted under a certificate by the Governor.

The native apprehension in the coast colonies was centred on the question of ownership. They could not understand how the lands could be described as "native lands," of which the Governor was trustee, if no occupier had a valid title without his consent, or that of his delegate, for a limited time, on a rental. Ownership they considered was transferred to Government by such an assertion. The Crown could no doubt claim ownership by right of conquest—as appears from the judgment of the Judicial Committee of the Privy Council in the Rhodesian Lands case (see pp. 343-4)—in respect of territory actually conquered, but since the preamble of the Ordinance appeared to repudiate this claim, and recited that its object was to assure to the natives their customary rights in the land, and since the terms of reference suggested similar legislation in the south, the people there feared lest the Government should claim the same powers in respect of their lands.

[1] Sir W. Geary, 'African Society Journal,' April 1913, p. 245.

The Ordinance has been amended in some respects, and in practice at any rate no interference with native occupation or title, or the right of the chiefs to dispose of the land to persons under their rule, and no attempt to impose a rent, has been made. An occupier if expropriated (unless for fault) is compensated. On the other hand, the original claim of Government to dispose of waste lands has been maintained, and the alienation of land by the chiefs to non-natives has been prevented. This right I imagine would not be disputed by the advocates of native rights. The native of the Gold Coast or Southern Nigeria would however assert, first, that his land was not conquered territory, and secondly, that there were no waste lands. The Aborigines' Protection Society contends that "where lands are *beneficially occupied* by natives they should not be dispossessed." [1] "We want," says Colonel Wedgwood, "an independent people on their own land, whether held individually or communally." [2] Up to the time when I left Northern Nigeria in 1906, the question of land tenure was not so pressing as other urgent matters, and I had myself been inclined to favour a land-rent, but I speedily changed my opinion, on grounds both of equity and expediency, when on my return to Nigeria in 1912 I made a closer study of the subject.

The object in view—namely, that the system of taxation shall be such that "the Government revenues will partake automatically in any increase in the general wealth" [3]—is equally ensured by the income tax described in the last chapter, in a manner, as it appears to me, the most effective possible, without violating one of the most fundamental of native prejudices. For the native pays in proportion to his wealth, whether it arises from the expanding values of land or otherwise. The cardinal principles of native law are not infringed, for the occupiers' tenure is a holding in perpetuity, subject to the payment of a portion of the usufruct, but not of rent for the land itself. The validity of his right is not dependent on the issue of a licence to occupy. On the other hand, the right of the ruler to revoke it for good cause, or to appropriate it if need be in exchange for land elsewhere, is not questioned.

[1] Sir S. Olivier, May 1920.
[2] Debate on Colonial Office vote, August 1919.
[3] Report, *loc. cit.*, paragraph 45.

It is inevitable that the examination of the land law of Northern Nigeria, which has been claimed by some as a model ordinance, should be somewhat technical and detailed. I make no apology, therefore, for a brief summary of the points of criticism. The Committee assumed that the whole of the lands of Northern Nigeria were conquered lands, and apparently ignoring rights which conquest does not annul, enacted that no title (including those of existing occupiers) was valid without the consent of the Governor, whose consent was to be granted in the form of a "certificate of occupation," which imposed a rent, revisable septennially. This naturally gave rise to fears in Southern Nigeria that the Government claimed *ownership* of all lands. Subsequent alteration of the law and practice has maintained the right of native occupiers to the lands they occupy, and the right of native rulers to assign lands to natives in their jurisdiction, without any certificate of occupation. Compensation for eviction by Government (save for "good cause") is given, and not merely for unexhausted improvements. No land-rent is demanded, as being contrary to native custom.

As land acquires an economic value, there is no doubt a natural tendency towards its accumulation in the hands of the wealthier classes, with the consequent creation of a landless peasantry. It has been the beneficent policy of British Governments in India and other dependencies to counteract this tendency to the best of their power, and to encourage the class of peasant proprietors. In conquered countries, where Government has claimed the control of the land, it would seem that that control cannot be better justified, or exerted with greater benefit to the people, than by imposing such restrictions on the transfer of lands as may preserve an ignorant peasantry from the consequences of its own improvidence. Mr Rhodes shared this view, and was an ardent believer in the efficacy of individual small holdings as an aid to self-respect. I shall discuss his scheme in the next chapter.

The restriction on alienation matters little, I think, to the African cultivator, provided he enjoys fixity of tenure in perpetuity. This indeed is "ownership" in the native sense of the term. I believe that there is nothing which can so effectively tend to eradicate the servile habit of mind in a people who have for generations been accustomed to regard themselves as slaves or serfs, as the sense of responsibility of the free occupier of the land. Emancipation of the body is a lesser benefit than emancipation of the spirit. It is not enough to set a man free from his legal status as a slave unless he learns his responsibilities as a citizen. That has been our aim in Nigeria.[1]

The labourer who works on land which is not his own, whether as the serf, or even as the paid servant of an estate owner, or as a unit in a communal estate, has little interest in its improvement during, and none beyond his own lifetime. And so we find in Africa, "the oldest of the continents," no permanent irrigation works, such as those which terrace every hillside in Afghanistan, India, and China.[2] The African plants few trees, and is careless of the productivity of the soil. Individual proprietorship is no doubt inimical to the supply of wage labour for large estates, but it makes for individual progress, thrift, and character. It is the strongest inducement to good farming, and politically an asset to the Government, to which the peasant owes the security of his holding. The French verdict is the same. "The system of individual ownership is incontestably the one which is most favourable to production." [3]

A policy of encouraging small peasant proprietors is not inconsistent with the recognition of the value of a limited number of larger estates employing paid labour. These, if held by local natives, as is still the case in the Sokoto and Yola provinces of Nigeria, add to the prestige and influence of the ruling classes, and promote their desire for peaceful progress, since they have "a stake in the country," and they bring these classes into closer touch with the peasantry. Paid labour is, however, difficult to procure as long as there is abundant land for the asking. (See chapter on labour.)

Plantations of limited area, owned by Europeans, are useful as object-lessons in improved methods. On the other

[1] A Senior Resident writes: "At the present time (1917) the whole Hausa country is covered with holdings ranging from one to four acres, cultivated by one man and his children and servants or slaves. That man may be an Emir, a Hausa, or a Fulani." Very many others bear similar witness to the result of British policy. "The country is covered with small holders—there are no estates now."

[2] In West Africa water is led on to small plots where intensive cultivation is practised, but there is no extensive system. In East Africa irrigation is practised to a small extent. See note 2, p. 518.

[3] Colonial Budget Report, 1910, No. 375, p. 91.

hand, the native land speculator, who is a trader or money-lender, and acquires an estate of which he is an absentee landlord, is often the worst type of profiteer, whose aim it is "to make rapid profits by sweating native labour, and by grievous exploitation of the soil."[1] A due proportion between wage-labour and small proprietors is probably the most desirable in the interests of the peasantry. (See page 419.)

The first and most important step to preserve the peasant proprietor is the prohibition of the sale or transfer of land, without the consent of the Governor, to any person, European or other, who is not subject to the local native jurisdiction. The sale of permanent improvements appurtenant to the land, and involving a transfer of the user—which is for practical purposes indistinguishable from a transfer of the land itself—would have the same effect in converting the free peasant proprietor into a wage-earner on the estate of another. Wherever possible, it should, I think, be the duty of Government to withhold from the native chiefs the power of allowing such sales to persons not subject to their jurisdiction, and to enact that mortgages and sales of permanent improvements to such persons should have no legal recognition, unless approved by the Governor. The recovery of advances on crops would be limited to the result of the harvest, and no claim to the trees or to the land would be recognised. Recovery of debt should, moreover, be restricted, so as to leave sufficient for the bare necessities of life and seed for the coming year. I shall presently discuss the question further in cases where Government cannot exert these restrictions.

In brief, while peasant occupation is the best as a general rule, the ownership, even in regions where white settlement is not possible, of estates of limited area by Europeans for the cultivation of new or improved products is most valuable, but estates owned by absentee native landlords engaged in trade or usury is inimical to the interests and productivity of the country.

Transfers of land between natives subject to the local native jurisdiction can best be controlled by the native authority, which is the natural guardian of native custom, under the watchful scrutiny of the Resident. In Northern

[1] Report by the late Mr Farquharson, Nigerian Agricultural Department. He desired to see every alien native landlord compelled, like the small crofter in Scotland, to apply a certain minimum of tillage and manure to his holding.

Nigeria the regulations are that there is no restriction on sale, transfer, or bequest to a blood relation. The consent of the district headman is necessary for transfer to a non-related native of the same district, and the additional approval of the Resident is required for transfer to a native non-resident in the district. An appeal is allowed, and transfers must be registered by the native court. In order to add to the security of the peasant holder, all transfers should be so registered; and as native administrations become more efficient, and a rough survey by native officials becomes possible, the head chief should be encouraged to keep a Domesday Book with a record of all holdings.

The right of the State to acquire land for necessary public purposes—*e.g.*, administrative sites, railways, &c.—is recognised by all Governments. In conquered countries where Government controls the land—viz., acts as trustee for its use—it seems reasonable that this power should include the acquisition and disposal of all land over which the Government considers it necessary in the interests of the people that it should exercise direct control—namely, over all lands occupied by persons not subject to the jurisdiction of the native rulers. The Government would assume the responsibility of deciding whether, and to what extent, an application for land by an alien, engaged in the development of the country or in mission work, was reasonable and justified in the public interest. In any important decision of this nature the Secretary of State exercises a controlling decision.

The land required might, for instance, have been used for generations by a family for low-grade cultivation or as grazing land, and have become valuable because of its proximity to a railway station built at the cost of public funds. Its appropriation by Government, with a view to securing a good rental from a non-native—to be applied in diminution of taxation or for development works—is undoubtedly in the general interest of the natives. In the case cited the native occupier would, under the Northern Nigeria Lands Committee's proposals, receive no compensation, since there were no improvements; but it seems equitable that he should be compensated for disturbance, and provided with equivalent land elsewhere.

Thus in regions where the Government exercises control over the land, it would become the landlord of all aliens, and the conception of landlord and tenant would not be prematurely introduced into the native system of land tenure. Moreover, where land is rapidly increasing in value, and it is considered advisable to institute periodical revisions of rent, these can best be fixed by Government, and should accrue to the State, to whose action the increasing value is generally due.

The maximum acreage for the various types of lease—residential, agricultural, grazing, &c.—are laid down by ordinance or regulation, and will be discussed in the next chapter. No freehold grants are made. Leases to Europeans inside a native city are to be deprecated, and the grant of large blocks of land to "concessionaires," unless uninhabited, is altogether opposed to the principle of trusteeship. The peasantry on their part, by the advent of the railway and the traders who follow it (and require sites), obtain prices hitherto undreamt of for their produce, and they can buy European goods at cheap rates.[1] They derive a direct advantage, while the Government, by leasing sites to traders, puts the land to its most remunerative use, and adds to the funds which make further railway extension possible.

Before passing to the consideration of the conditions applying to land in countries in which the Government does not claim the rights of conquest, a few remarks regarding the native method of using the land will, I think, not be out of place. The general characteristics of the low-lying equatorial zone (though there are curious exceptions) are heavy rainfall, luxuriant vegetation (including belts of forest), a soil enriched by decayed vegetable matter, and a climate unsuited to live-stock. North of this zone the rainfall is often very meagre, the soil light and devoid of humus. Annual fires sweep over the prairie grass in the dry season, and cattle and other live-stock are plentiful.

Where the density of the population had limited the land available for each cultivator, the agriculturist in the dry zone has learnt that it can be rendered more productive by manure from his live-stock; but even with this resource he must leave a certain portion fallow, in order that the exhausted soil may recover. In the equatorial zone the cultivator finds that the soil, at first most productive, rapidly deteriorates,

[1] When the railway reached Kano (in Nigeria) ground nuts were sold at £3, 10s. a ton. They later fetched £40 to £45.

and he too has recourse to the expedient of leaving it fallow for varying periods. But lying close to hand are areas of virgin soil covered with forest. This he reclaims by ring-barking the trees—which remain like gaunt skeletons—and clearing and burning the undergrowth on the spot. Thus each year the valuable evergreen forest disappears, never to reappear, and is replaced by secondary deciduous forest, and if the process is repeated the forest is eventually replaced by grass, liable to frequent fires. Forests serve as a reservoir which feeds the head-waters of streams, and with their destruction the torrential rains carry away the surface soil, and deposit sand and debris on the plains, thus rendering them unfit for cultivation, while the rivers cease to be navigable. The rainfall decreases.[1]

Mr Thompson, Director of Forests in Nigeria, and a very high authority, estimates that by this process—known as "shifting cultivation"—the acreage of land taken up for cultivation is from five to nine times in excess of the requirements of the cultivator under a less wasteful system. Shifting cultivation, he says, is not tolerated in any but the wildest and most uncivilised parts of the world, and even there it is restricted. In India it is not recognised as a right. The checks on the increase of population under savage conditions—war, pestilence, and famine—are alone responsible for preserving such forests as remain in large areas of tropical Africa.

The essential necessity of conserving the forest wealth of the country compels the introduction of better methods, but these are not learnt in a day. Where Government controls the land, it may be argued that the imposition of rentals would operate to restrict the wasteful use of land. But restriction can be equally well secured and forests protected by the agency of the native rulers, and by the operation of the tax levied on the produce of the land if cultivated to an average standard, without incurring the additional opposition which land rentals would cause. The problem as it affects uncontrolled lands belongs to a later paragraph.

The question of the assignment to the village of its proper proportion of uncultivated land—for grazing, fuel, &c.—is one which in many localities requires constant supervision,

[1] See Mr Thompson's report on Forest questions in the Gold Coast, Cd. 4993, 1908, and pp. 526-9 *infra*.

owing to the migratory habits of the people, and the rapid increase or decrease in the population of the villages. This is a matter for adjustment by the ruling chief, subject to the supervision of the executive staff. The larger question of the augmentation of the area held by a tribe, or by an advanced community, whose increasing population has caused acute land hunger, while perhaps a neighbouring tribe has so decreased in numbers that its lands are in excess of its needs, is one for the Government to deal with. Several such cases have occurred in my own experience. If the facts are established a transfer of land must be made, but in my opinion, in no case—whether the country is conquered territory or not—should a rental be demanded from the community which receives the additional land. In days not distant it would have seized the land, and would probably have exterminated its owners as well. The peaceful adjustment of such economic claims, when proved to be well founded, is the function of the suzerain Government.

The conclusions which it seems reasonable to deduce from these considerations may be briefly summarised. When a European Power succeeds to the domination hitherto wielded by a native conquering race, the control of the land, in so far as it was exercised by the latter, passes, if publicly claimed, to the new suzerain, and should be exercised in accordance with native law and custom. If the dominion was not vested in a conquering race, the controlling Power should interfere still less with customary law. Private and communal rights must be respected.

In practice, therefore, the Government should not intervene between the native rulers and the people under their jurisdiction as to the disposal of lands or the tenure upon which they are held, except to advise, and to maintain justice. Land rents should not be charged to natives, since Government is the trustee for and not the owner of the land, and rentals are opposed to native law. But the Government should prohibit the transfer of lands to aliens, and reserve to itself the right to grant leases to them, and to appropriate the rentals to public revenue, paying full compensation. The Government may also develop, for the public good, lands which are not in beneficial occupation, and not likely to be required for such purpose. Lands which are beneficially occupied may be appropriated for any public purpose, or for lease to aliens, if justified for the encouragement of trade or mining, and in the interests of the public revenue. Such alienated land should be strictly limited in extent, and subject to provisos (which will be described in the next chapter) to ensure its proper use and development. In such cases the original occupier must be fully compensated. Any such expropriation should be effected through the native administration, and under the immediate authority of the native ruler.

The exercise by the native authority of his control of the land should be supervised and guided, equally with his other executive acts, by the British staff, and there should be an appeal to the Resident. The guidance of the British staff should be directed towards the encouragement of small holdings, and their preservation against absorption in large estates, or alienation for debt; to the utilisation of the land to the best advantage by permanent improvements; and to the curtailing of shifting cultivation. It is their duty to see that the revocation of any holder's right of occupation is justified by native law, and they report to the Governor whether any application for land by a non-native can be granted without injury to the rights of the natives.

When the pressure of population in any district has resulted in enhancing the value of land, it is expedient that holdings should be roughly surveyed by natives trained, paid, and controlled by the native administration, and records kept by it.

These principles appear to me to be in accord with the system of ruling through the native chiefs on the one hand, and with those general bases of taxation which are not repugnant to native custom on the other hand. A system of land rentals, leases, and licences to native occupiers, and of the expropriation of holders without compensation except for their own improvements, appears to me not only incompatible with the principle of ruling through the chiefs, and the system of taxation recognised by the people, but also to violate the cardinal tenets of native customary law.

It seems preferable that the natural evolution of land tenure should not be arbitrarily interfered with, either on the one hand by introducing foreign principles and theories not understood by the people, or, on the other hand, by stereotyping by legislation primitive systems which are in a transitional state. Each advance should be duly sanctioned by native law and custom, and prompted by the necessities of changing circumstances. Such a policy of patient progress is best adapted to the country. Tribal tenure at one end of the scale has its defects, in that it provides no check on the wasteful use of land, by allowing large areas to lie fallow, while valuable forests are destroyed in the search for virgin soil, and in that it checks individual enterprise and industry. Unrestricted freehold tenure at the opposite extreme has its failing, in that there is no check on the mortgage or sale of his land by the peasant holder who is likely to become a tenant or serf on the lands he once owned. The owner of freehold land, moreover, obtains without any effort on his part, any increase in the value of the land due to the expenditure of public funds, or the industry of the community. It is reasonable and just that the community as a whole—viz., the State—should participate in these increased values by periodical revision of rentals, or preferably by a graduated income tax.

CHAPTER XV.

LAND TENURE AND TRANSFER—(*Continued*).

Countries in which rights of conquest have not been claimed—Ignorance of native law—Conditions in the Gold Coast—Definition of areas under English law—The law applicable to remaining lands—Transfers of land to non-natives — The executive, not the judiciary, should deal with land cases—Duties of Government as trustee—Disposal of rents of tribal lands — Government as landlord of aliens in unconquered countries — Need for fixity of tenure — Land held by "strangers"—Modification of native law—Grants relating to the produce of the land—Forest licences and leases—Communal plantations—Leases of Crown lands to natives—Differences in meaning of terms—The problem in Eastern Africa—Acquisition of land by, and status of British Indians—The Indian case—Obligations to native races—The case of the British settler—Suggestions—Native reserves —Divergent views as to policy—The interpenetration policy—Management of reserves—The Glen Grey Act—Mr Rhodes' views—Land tenure in East Africa—Conditions for settlers in Kenya—Uganda — Nyasaland — Summary of conditions in East Africa—Population in relation to land areas—Conclusions.

THERE remains to discuss the attitude of Government towards the land in those territories where rights of conquest cannot be claimed, or where the claim, though valid, was not set up, and no declaration of policy was made. The latter seems to have been the case after the conquests of Ashanti [1] and Benin [2]—the only two cases in British West Africa (apart from Northern Nigeria) in which native dynasties were overthrown—

[1] "In Ashanti . . . had the lands of the country been proclaimed at the time of conquest to be the property of the Crown, they would unquestionably have so vested. . . . The claim to ownership was waived, and cannot now be asserted." —Belfield Report, paragraph 47. The Chief Commissioner is empowered to take any lands required by Government, but only on payment of compensation for improvements and disturbance. In the "Northern Territories" of the Gold Coast the control of all lands by Government appears to be as absolute as in Northern Nigeria.—(Cardinal, *loc. cit.*)

[2] In Benin, consequent on the massacre of 1896, the Oba was deported and Government assumed direct control. A few Crown leases were then issued, thus showing that the Government of the day had adopted the view that Benin lands

and the same may be said as regards the various military expeditions, such as that arising from the " hut-tax rebellion " in Sierra Leone, the Jebu, and the Aro expeditions in Southern Nigeria, and the many minor operations brought about by murders and outrages, which the Government was compelled to suppress by force of arms. In these, and in other cases in which tribes submitted to a threat of force, no definite claim to control the land was asserted. If, apart from conquest, there are any districts in which a Government has by usage, sufferance, or otherwise established a claim to control the land, or special privileges in regard to the acquisition of land, its claim should be publicly notified.

The absence of any definite and consistent policy in regard to land in these dependencies seems to have arisen from the failure to investigate the system of native tenure. The legislatures, though desirous of giving due weight to native custom, were not apparently familiar with it, and we find that the various Ordinances relating to land are couched in terms often quite inapplicable to native tenure, and the leases and other instruments are often drawn on an English model. The Chief Justices of the Supreme Courts have in many judgments where particular issues of importance had to be decided, shown much knowledge of the principles of native land law—of which they were bound to take cognisance—but as I have described in speaking of individual tenure, the issues have become confused by the permeation of English conceptions of land tenure among the natives themselves, so that it was often difficult to decide to what degree these conceptions had influenced the grantors, and further difficulty arose from the terms of the law which the judges had to administer.

Thus during Mr Chamberlain's tenure of office, when the first attempts to deal comprehensively with this question of land tenure in the Crown colonies appear to have been made, the Government of the Gold Coast introduced (in

(except of course those held in private ownership) had by right of conquest become Crown lands. The restoration of the Oba in 1916 was made conditional on the recognition of Government control over the land. In 1917 an agreement was substituted, under which the Oba was left free to deal with the land occupied by Benis, while rentals received for land leased to aliens and "strangers" might, at the discretion of the Governor, be shared between the protectorate and the native treasuries. Only one area, already leased as Crown land, was retained as such.

1897) a Bill based on individual ownership. It "aimed at encouraging the native to settle permanently on cultivated land by assuring to him the right of proprietorship therein, if occupation is continuous. . . . He may by occupation secure a good title against any chief or any one else . . . though forfeiture results from abandonment; . . . a permanent, hereditable, transferable right of proprietorship which the Supreme Court will enforce."[1] The Bill was opposed on the ground that it vested in the Crown powers over the land which belonged to communities or individuals, and it was not pressed. The alienation for ninety-nine years of tribal lands, by chiefs and families, to Europeans for money payments, which had grown to be a scandal,[2] continued to be recognised by the courts.

The object of the Gold Coast Ordinance as finally passed in 1900 was to induce the vendors to bring the transaction before the Court, that it might see that it was fair, and that the rights of the natives to cultivation, &c., were protected. It left the chiefs free to make their own bargains with the purchasers, though the Court had power to modify the terms. I do not propose to discuss this much-debated measure, which was the subject of an exhaustive inquiry by Sir H. Belfield. But it raises many important issues which are pertinent to the subject under discussion. Sale of tribal lands had also taken place in the Lagos hinterland, though not to the same extent.

To the native mind, uninfluenced by foreign ideas, land is an unsaleable thing. "We have power to dispose of the land; we cannot sell the land; no chief can sell the land," said a Lagos chief in evidence before the Supreme Court.[3] If an alien requires land, whether he be a native stranger who desires to cultivate, or a European who desires to trade or mine, the question to the native mind would be, whether or not the stranger's presence is desirable and to the benefit of the community. If it is, he is given land rent-free. He

[1] Cd. 5103, p. 23.

[2] Belfield Report, paragraph 35. It has been freely stated that the chiefs had alienated an area in excess of the total area of the Colony—the inference being that the whole was alienated, and many concessions overlapped. Sir H. Belfield states that the total alienated was 899 sq. miles out of 24,300. There were some 3000 sq. miles additional "under notice," but in the great majority of cases no further action was contemplated (paragraphs 39-40).

[3] Cd. 5103, p. 32.

may or may not give a part of his profits or produce in return for the favour conferred upon him. If he does, it has no connection with the land, and is not in proportion to its area. Similarly if the Government takes land for a recognised public purpose, no payment would be demanded, but any person dispossessed would obtain land elsewhere through the chiefs.

In all these dependencies, however, English law is largely if not exclusively applied in the big coast cities, and to a varying degree beyond them. No doubt European concessionaires, holding land devised to them in deeds drawn by native barristers in English legal terms, understand that they hold title under English law. Moslems and other native aliens probably have their own ideas as to the tenure of their holdings. And it seems clear that the grantors themselves have only the vaguest conceptions as to the conditions of the grants. Obviously the courts—bound by Ordinance to take cognisance of native law and custom—have in these circumstances a very difficult task in determining land cases.

The first and most urgent step would seem, therefore, to be the determination by Ordinance of the area in which English land law applies. This might be limited in the first instance to the urban and suburban districts on the coast, and fixed by the legislative councils of the respective colonies, to be extended if need be by resolution of the council. Within that area all land titles would, of course, be registered.

Outside these districts it would seem to be desirable to enforce registration (within a prescribed period) of all holdings not already registered, in which individual ownership is claimed, whether by aliens or by natives. The remainder of the land should be declared to be subject to native tribal tenure and (except to Government for public purposes) alienable only in accordance with the principles of native law—*e.g.*, the freehold could not be granted. If at any time it were desired to extend the application of English law to any transfer of land in such areas, the consent of the Governor would be required, in order to ensure that the grantor fully understood the transaction. The conditions applicable to individual ownership might be laid down by Ordinance in simple language—viz., that the land can be sold or taken in execution, &c.—with a correspondingly simple form of lease. A similar form for tribal land alienated on leasehold might be added.[1]

[1] See the forms suggested by Sir H. Belfield, Report, paragraph 103.

This procedure would not arrest natural evolution, or perpetuate by legislation a system which is in course of development, but it would ensure that native tenure could only be modified to accord with changing circumstances, after due consideration, and with the assent of the Government. It would in no way interfere with the right of native owners (subject to the conditions I am about to suggest) to dispose of their lands, and to make their own bargains, and if so desired, to include special terms in the lease.[1] It would ensure to the grantee the clean title he desires, and a clear understanding of the law to which it is subject. It would, I presume, considerably simplify the work of the courts.

Although in territories where no claim to the control of the land has been set up, Government thus explicitly recognises the right of the native owners to dispose of their lands as they like; no interference with native rights or customs can be alleged if Government asserts its unquestioned jurisdiction over non-natives, and directs that they must obtain its consent before acquiring land from a native, and its final approval of the lease. It would seem desirable, in the interests alike of the grantors and of the grantees, that this rule should be enforced, and that registration should be obligatory within a prescribed period. A notification to this effect was issued by the Gold Coast Government on 10th October 1895, and appeared in the 'London Gazette' and five leading London papers.[2] It has also been the law in Lagos since 1908, and in Southern Nigeria since 1900. At the present time in Nigeria an alien may be called upon by the court to prove that he is in legal occupation, and may be evicted and fined if he fails to do so. Nor may he occupy land with the consent of the native owner without acquiring it.

The Governor, before giving his consent, would see that the lease was not in any way manifestly opposed to native interests, and he could insert a clause making the possession of the land dependent on its efficient development.

If a native cultivator sells or mortgages his permanent

[1] The term "concession" is one of evil association. All grants should be in the form of leases not exceeding ninety-nine years.

[2] It read as follows: "No document hereafter made, purporting to grant or convey any rights over or interest in land, forests, or minerals, or monopoly in economic products, save and except the right to occupy building land for the erection of a native house, will be recognised in any way by the Government, unless it shall bear the signature of the Governor, &c."

improvements—*e.g.*, a plantation of cocoa-trees—to an alien (which for practical purposes involves the transfer of the land), the transaction should, as I have said, require the assent of the Governor equally with a sale of the land, and a definite period for the duration of the transaction should be fixed. As a further safeguard against the alienation of tribal land by rights of user originating in a sale or mortgage of permanent crops, the right of the native ruler to demand a ground rent should be recognised.

By such means the Government, through the District Officer, could assist the native chiefs in their dealings with Europeans. He would see that there was no overlapping of leases, that the terms proposed were understood, and that the bargain was equitable to the native owners. On the other hand, the Government would be able to transfer to the executive the onus of protecting the rights of the people against any improper transactions by the chiefs or others in regard to land.

This task is by the Gold Coast Concessions Ordinance thrown upon the judiciary. Sir H. Belfield writes in this connection: "It is undesirable that the work should be entrusted to the judges, because they do not possess any first-hand knowledge of the land with which they are dealing, and because their decisions are not open to revision except in contested cases. I believe the work can be performed more efficiently, more expeditiously, and more economically if entrusted to executive officers." [1]

Disputes regarding land boundaries, not only of lands sold or leased, but the ever-recurring inter-tribal quarrels regarding land, can be dealt with more effectively by inquiry on the spot by the District Officer than by the courts, and costly litigation avoided. Boundaries once decided should be recorded by the native courts. The intervention of the Supreme Court in land cases is indeed a matter of very serious importance in the southern provinces of Nigeria and in the Gold Coast, for which successive Governors and Chief Justices have failed to find an effective remedy. Sir H. Belfield describes at great length the remedial procedure he advocates.

[1] See Report, paragraphs 67 and 68; also 84-106, &c. Application should, in the first instance, be made to the District Officer, who makes all inquiries and advises the natives in their interest. When the lease has received the Governor's approval, conditional occupation may be allowed, pending survey. In order to avoid any conflict as to title, the proposed grant should be notified in the 'Gazette.' Registration may then be accepted as a guarantee of title.

If recourse to the courts is necessary the case should be dealt with by the Provincial Court, in which legal practitioners are not heard, and the prevailing evil of lawyers' touts to foment land cases is thereby to some extent diminished. In such cases the right of appeal to the Supreme Court (where the debt, damage, or default exceeds £50) should be abolished. The judgment is reviewed by the Chief Justice in a non-judicial capacity as an automatic appeal, and he can, if desirable, order a transfer to or a rehearing by the Supreme Court. (See pages 544-45.)

The importance of excluding native lawyers in these cases cannot be over-estimated, for judges of the Supreme Court of long experience have stated that by the action of these native lawyers ignorant chiefs are involved in costly and needless litigation, and often plunged into debt.[1]

It is the first duty of a Government to watch over the interests of the governed, and if there is one section of these which claims a special share of consideration and thought, it is the one which, by reason of poverty and of ignorance, is least able to take care of itself. It follows that a civilised Power in Africa, while fully recognising the rights of the native chiefs to dispose of tribal lands on behalf of their people, cannot escape responsibility for seeing that those powers are rightly exercised. To do otherwise is the negation of the functions of a Suzerain. Claims to the individual ownership of land must be scrutinised in the interest of the communities; alienation must not deprive the people of sufficient land for their needs, and their rights of cultivation, grazing, &c., must be safeguarded; the consideration received from aliens for the use of land must be adequate, and the money received must be paid to and expended on behalf of the owners—the community. Have the several Governments in West Africa discharged their obligations fully in this latter respect?

By universal consent the land belongs to the people, for whom the chiefs act as trustees or agents, and it is the

[1] Of this there is abundant evidence. As to the Gold Coast, see Belfield's Report, paragraph 33, &c. So great have been the evils of this land litigation that a high official expressed a doubt whether its economic results were not as bad as the former inter-tribal wars. As to Nigeria, see Cmd. 468, 1920, appendix iii.

Sir E. Speed, Chief Justice, pointed out that these land cases very rarely referred to individual rights or disputes, but were generally concerned with tribal boundaries long ago settled by the district officer.

function of Government to see that that trust or agency is carried out honestly. Sir H. Belfield informs us that the custom in the Gold Coast is that the consideration money is divided into three parts, of which the chief, the elders, and the chieftainship fund each take one. This practice, he writes, "is at variance with the traditional conditions which underlie the authority vested in the headman. They are supposed to exercise their authority for the common benefit of the tribe as a body, but they actually spend this money for purposes from which the ordinary members of the community can derive no advantage, therefore the tribe finds itself despoiled of a substantial area of its land for a period which leaves it dispossessed for two or three generations, and receives no sort of compensation for the diminution of its property."[1]

He recommends that a quarter of the money should be retained in a fund for the general benefit of the people, but it is impossible to deny that the proceeds of the sale of communal lands belongs entirely to the community, and should be spent in their behalf, and I so instructed the district staff in Southern Nigeria.

I was at that time engaged in setting up in the districts most affected—Yoruba, Egba, and Benin—native treasuries such as I have described in chapter x. Rentals for communal land are properly paid into such treasuries, which constitute the common fund of the community. Since it is from them that the chiefs, under the system of "native administration," receive their salaries, and the expenses and dignities of the chieftainship are defrayed, they have an interest in the augmentation of the funds. Where native treasuries are not established, a communal fund can still be created, and it would be the duty of the district staff to see that it was not misspent, and to hold the chiefs accountable. Sir H. Belfield's statement is a very serious indictment both against the native chiefs—though the whole tenor of his report shows that he did not lack sympathy with them—and against the control and supervision exercised by the Government on behalf of the lesser people.

I have expressed the view that in territories where the control of the land is vested in the Government, it is in the public interest that Government should become the landlord

[1] Report, paragraph 35.

of all aliens, since, *inter alia*, it can by periodical revision of rentals, or by appropriate taxation, secure for the public revenue the expanding value of land, which arises directly or indirectly from the expenditure of the taxpayers' money. These values may be shared by the taxpayer by means of an income tax on Europeans and others.[1]

It is worth a moment's consideration how far this general principle is possible of application in territories—other, of course, than those districts declared to be under English land law—where Government does not claim the disposal of the land.

Before constructing a railway in such territories a colonial Government acquires the land "for a public purpose," including a sufficient area on either side of the track, on terms which are equitable to both parties. The method of doing so is usually laid down by law. Or it may be that in anticipation of the benefits which will accrue to their trade, the native communities are willing to cede the land in perpetuity, in order to induce the Government to construct the line. In such cases, and also in the case of building plots in a projected township, where Government has acquired the land in anticipation, the object in view is attained.

But when the land is not required for a public purpose, but by a non-native for commercial or other purposes, it may be a matter for consideration whether Government should acquire the land from the native owners, and lease it to the non-native applicant, in order to carry out the principle which I have advocated of Government being the landlord of all aliens.[2] It might be argued that the native owner would not in that case obtain so good a bargain. To obviate this the terms might be fixed by a Land Court on which natives would sit as assessors. The acquisition, however, of land nominally for a public purpose, and its subsequent disposal on lease to non-natives, is clearly irregular, and unjust to the native owners, unless the phrase "acquisition for a public purpose" has been specifically defined to include acquisition for sublease to non-natives.

In the southern districts of the West African dependencies the introduction of cocoa and other permanent crops, which

[1] See Model Ordinance, Section 5 (*c*), Cmd. 1788 of 1922.

[2] This was formerly the system in Uganda, but is now abandoned.—Annual Report 1918-19, No. 1054, p. 10.

take several years to come to maturity, has accentuated the desirability of affording to the cultivator some guarantee of his right to continued occupation. I have quoted Sir H. Belfield's view that native land tenure will require some modification. Moreover, the density of the population (in Southern Nigeria though not in the Gold Coast), and the long immunity of the people from slave-raids, together with the prevalence of shifting cultivation, has resulted in there being no superabundance of land in considerable regions.

Interference with native customary law, which may be relied on to adapt itself to changing circumstances, is much to be deprecated; but if intervention is found to be necessary in the interests of the people, the first step might usefully be to abrogate the rule that the claim of a member of the family to land does not lapse, however prolonged his absence.[1] This means that an individual who left his village in boyhood may return after many decades—perhaps as a wealthy lawyer—and claim land. If the undeveloped land at the disposal of the family is exhausted some peasant must be ousted, a course which militates against fixity of tenure, without which it is hopeless to expect any permanent improvement of the land. Abandonment for two years, except for the recuperation of the soil, should, I suggest, involve forfeiture of the claim to land.

The cultivator who has the greatest need of protection is the "stranger" who, owing to deficiency of land in his own district, has been driven to seek it elsewhere, and has been allowed to settle in another community where land is abundant. Such "strangers" may be welcomed by a tribe whose numbers are decreasing, as adding to its strength. But so jealously guarded is the ownership of land in the west equatorial belt that the stranger may probably only be admitted on condition that he shall plant no trees (cocoa, &c.), the ownership of which would give him a claim to the land beyond the term of his own life.[2]

[1] Evidence from Nigeria was to the effect that an educated native who had spent the greater part of his life in Lagos could, if he desired, return to his village and claim land as of right.

[2] The Resident of a province in Southern Nigeria remarks that "there have been several instances where the owners of the land, so soon as they see the valuable crops maturing, have made attempts to regain possession of the land, including the cocoa; and many farmers, who in the ordinary course would probably be allowed to occupy land in perpetuity, hesitate to embark on cocoa-planting for want of sufficient security against their landlords."

This is so manifestly disadvantageous to the progress and permanent good of the country, that I essayed to modify native customary law by securing the adhesion of all the native authorities (after full discussion with them) to a native court rule, which aimed at securing continuous occupation to "strangers" under specified conditions, while placing a check on the irregular acquisition of tribal lands by undesirable strangers. These immigrants are of three types—(*a*) those who intend to identify themselves with the tribe, and by intermarriage become merged into it in the second generation (these require no special protection); (*b*) those who settle on the land, but remain aliens to the tribe; and (*c*) land speculators, who are generally absentee landlords, and may perhaps have acquired title to land from a chief who had no right under native law to grant it, but did not understand the effect of the deed—probably drawn by a native lawyer—conferring individual ownership.

In some cases the stranger may have sold his title to another native, or may have assigned its use to a European (thus evading the law), or may assert his independence of the local native authority. Or he may have acquired the land purely as a speculation on its expanding value, and prove an obstacle to development. In this case it is the native authority, and not the stranger, who requires protection—and, indeed, in some cases the community has been disintegrated by the acquisition of land by such "strangers."[1]

The new rule recites that by native law no stranger can acquire an interest in tribal land except by consent of the native authority, nor can he permanently deprive the community of the use of the land. It then lays down that the grant must be approved by the native court, and recorded by it in writing, with the signature of the parties. The Resident's approval is also required, and he will see that the

[1] Mr R. E. Dennett—a high authority—bears witness to the disintegration of tribal authority caused by "the creation of a class of irresponsible landowners who pay no tribute."—'African Society's Journal,' and 'Morning Post,' 14/3/1910.

Natives of the colony of Sierra Leone residing in the protectorate, where the land is regarded as belonging entirely and unreservedly to the natives, pay to the local chief a rent of £1 for the right to occupy, or £1, 10s. if adjacent to an improved road. Land leased for permanent buildings must be transferred by deed and attested by the District Commissioner. A lease of agricultural land of under 50 acres must be approved by him. If over 50 acres and under 5000 the Governor's approval is required, and if over 5000 that of the Secretary of State. A chief cannot be compelled to alienate land, nor may he do so for his own benefit.—Sierra Leone Report, 1908, p. 51; Cd. 4448 of 1909.

record is properly made, and that it assures to the stranger the right to plant permanent crops, or erect buildings, and to receive compensation if dispossessed otherwise than for misconduct or breach of the conditions. Rents (if demanded) must be paid to the communal fund. The grant would usually be for an indefinite time (except in a native city), and the occupier may assign his rights to another with the consent of the grantor and court.

On the other hand, every stranger already in occupation of communal land must attend, if summoned, and satisfy the court as to his right of occupation, and its conditions. Failure to attend may, with the consent of the Resident, involve forfeiture. The court, if satisfied, makes the necessary record. Any member of the community may appeal to the court if the chief has exceeded his powers. Conditions of occupation may include any special reservations.

If a native stranger desires to acquire the full rights of individual ownership, he should only be able to do so by the same process as a non-native. Native court registration may perhaps be usefully extended to native occupiers of land under permanent plantations, who are not "strangers." In territories where the land is under Government control, strangers who desire to settle in a native city or elsewhere must obtain permission from the native authority, and unreservedly accept its jurisdiction. They are treated as regards taxation, &c., in all respects as local natives, otherwise they must reside in the native reservation of a township, or acquire land under the same conditions as apply to non-natives.

As a general rule it is undesirable that leases or licences should be granted to non-natives for the collection of sylvan produce which the natives are capable of exploiting themselves—such as palm-fruit, wild rubber, gum-copal, &c.; but where the exploitation involves the use of capital, and of appliances beyond the resources of the natives (as in the case of heavy timber for export), licences to non-natives are fully justified. Exceptions may also be made of small areas held in conjunction with experimental plantations, or to encourage the introduction of machinery for producing a better or a partially-manufactured product, or for saving labour. Such exceptions would be justified by their economic and educative value.

In a former paragraph I alluded to the important rôle

which the evergreen forest of the equatorial zone plays in the climate and the conservation of rainfall, apart from the great value of its products. These forests are rapidly being destroyed by shifting cultivation, and hardly less damage is done by indiscriminate felling for mining purposes. Until education in forestry and agriculture has made much greater progress, it is manifestly the duty of Government, as trustee for posterity against the reckless destruction by the present generation, to safeguard what remains of these forests, while not disputing the claims of native ownership.

"The keystone of all forestry conservation," says Mr Thompson, "is reservation, by which a sustained and increasing yield of produce can be assured."[1] It is therefore essential that reserves should be created and kept inviolate from depredation. Licences to fell timber in them may only be granted with the consent of the Governor. They are limited as to time and area, and as to the classes and girth of trees which may be felled, and they impose conditions as to replanting. The revenue goes in part to the native owners, and in part to the public funds.[2] Natives in adjoining villages may take timber and other produce for their own needs, but not for sale. Outside the reserves "protected trees" may only be felled for sale by licences, issued for short periods.

In Southern Nigeria an ordinance to give effect to these principles has long been in force, but in the Lagos hinterland its acceptance was formerly made contingent on the assent of the native councils, and it was practically inoperative. It has lately been revised and re-enacted for all Nigeria. In the Gold Coast a similar measure was opposed in 1910, and though passed with amendments later on, was not brought into operation. As in the case of the Concessions Bill, deputations visited England to protest against its interference with native rights. In Nigeria steps have been taken to associate the native authorities with the Government in the control of the forest reserves, with excellent results.

[1] Cd. 4993, p. 197.

[2] The Government, it will be noted, shares the proceeds arising from the sale of forest produce with the native owners. This share, whether small or large, passes into general revenue and is expended for the benefit of the country. Its appropriation therefore differs essentially from the former "domain privée" of the Congo State, where the profits went into the private pocket of the concessionaire.

We have seen that land held in communal tenure is cultivated by the family or individual, but that its products as a rule belong solely to the cultivators. The attempt to form communal plantations of rubber under Government auspices has not been a marked success in the southern provinces of Nigeria. In a loosely-organised community they must be tended by forced labour, for no individual has any interest in them, and their general supervision, tapping, &c., falls on the Forestry or Agricultural Departments. Even in a more highly-organised native administration, when the labour is performed by paid employees, it would seem to be more advantageous to promote individual initiative and ownership in the crop. Communal fuel plantations in timberless districts for the benefit of large cities are, however, very desirable, and they require little or no care once they are established.

In the southern provinces of Nigeria, Crown lands are leased to natives either for an indefinite or for a specified term, and for any specific purpose. The leases are only terminable by voluntary surrender, breach of covenant, or if the land is required for a public purpose. In the latter case full compensation is, of course, given, and in the two former the value of all unexhausted improvements would usually be paid. Such leases would be under English law, or under the rules applying to individual ownership, according as they were in or beyond the area declared subject to English law, but they can only be transferred to natives, and with Government consent.

Before leaving this branch of my subject, it will be useful to point out that the difference of meaning attached to words or phrases, familiar to us in their English sense, when applied to African conceptions may be a fruitful source of misunderstanding, and of apparently contradictory assertions by experts; for, as M. Delafosse observes, "there are certain ideas in native law which correspond to nothing analogous in our own laws." The term "ownership," for instance, as applied to land, is relative even in England, and is qualified by the right of Parliament to expropriate the owner if his land is essential for railway construction, &c. In Africa it is still more qualified, and the owner of land possesses it subject to certain well-understood limitations and obligations towards the community to which he belongs. Thus, on the one hand, when it is asserted that "all rights in land are vested in the chief," or that he is the ultimate "owner," the assertion is accurate only if the term is used in its native sense, for his "ownership" is subject to most important limitations. It is equally true, on the other hand, that the peasant proprietor of a farm does not "own" it in the full sense of the English term, and if he sells it to a non-native he does so with the well-understood limitations and obligations imposed by native law. To assert that property in land is unknown in West Africa is, in my view, as inaccurate as the assertion that "individual ownership" in the English sense is recognised because the land may be sold, or bequeathed, and descends from father to son. African individual ownership is none the less real because it is qualified by concurrent rights and obligations, in the north more especially to the chief, and in the south by still further restrictions and obligations to the family.

From a perusal of this chapter it will, I think, be evident that the same discrimination must be exercised in referring to such terms as "waste lands," "sale," &c.

Considerations of space, and the lack of personal experience in the evolution of the land question in East Africa, combine to place a limitation on the remarks which I have to make on the problems that present themselves in this group of dependencies. Much of what has been said regarding African conceptions of land tenure, and the rights exercised by Governments, will apply, equally with West Africa, to those areas which lie at low altitudes, but in the regions which have been found possible for European settlement an entirely separate problem arises, to which the proximity of India, and the immigration of its people, adds complexity.

These conditions are peculiar to a comparatively small portion of the colony of Kenya, and to small areas in the Shiré highlands of Nyasaland, which lie at altitudes from 4000 ft. to over 9000 ft. above sea-level. On these highlands the experiment of establishing British settlements is in progress. They cannot, however, be regarded as true colonies, for the reasons given in Chapter II. (see pp. 41-42). Kenya and Nyasaland have also attracted a considerable influx of British Indians, and the result has been to reproduce—especially in the former colony—the racial and economic rivalries and troubles which were witnessed in South Africa, but in an even more acute form.

The case as between the British settlers and the Indians may be broadly stated as follows: The settlers claim that the highlands were discovered and opened up by British explorers and pioneers, and that it is due to their enterprise and capital alone that the economic progress of the colony is due. The claim of the Indians to be the earlier arrivals is discounted by the fact that they were confined to the Zanzibar coast as traders and money-lenders, where they played a not very creditable part as slave-owners and usurers. Indian regiments took part in the campaign in German East Africa during the war, but the settlers accuse the local Indian residents of pusilanimity in the defence of the country.[1] It cannot, however, be denied that in the early days the police and military forces both in East Africa and Nyasaland were recruited from India, and that Indians have manned the railways and workshops and filled the subordinate clerical posts.

The Indians, on their part, claim as British subjects the right to acquire land without any restriction anywhere in the colony, and, in fact, " to stand on a footing of unquestioned equality with other settlers of whatever nationality," with no segregation, and with a common franchise and electoral roll on a reasonable property basis, plus an educational test without racial discrimination.[2] The question was discussed by the recent Imperial Conference (1921), and on this point alone its report was not unanimous. The resolution passed " reaffirmed that of the Imperial War Conference of 1918, that each community of the British Commonwealth should enjoy complete control of the composition of its population, by means of restriction on immigration from any of the other communities," but it added the following rider : " The Conference recognises that there is an incongruity between the position of India as an equal member of the British Empire, and the existence of disabilities upon British Indians lawfully domiciled in some other parts of the Empire. The Conference accordingly is of the opinion that in the interests of the solidarity of the British Commonwealth it is desirable that the rights of such Indians to citizenship should be recognised." The representatives of South Africa could not accept this resolution, and the matter was relegated for direct negotiation between India and South Africa.

[1] The charges—including that of treachery—are made in a Memo. signed by Lord Delamere and Mr C. K. Archer. They are denied in an article giving "the Kenya Indian's Case" in the 'Times,' which throws doubt on the fairness of the trials, and asserts that some whose innocence has since been proved only owed their lives to the intervention of Sir R. Hamilton, ex-Chief Justice, and Colonel Northey.

[2] Lord Chelmsford's despatch of 21st October 1920, later endorsed by the Government of India, and supported by the Secretary of State for India.

The resolution—to which the Colonial Secretary subscribed —refers only to Indians "lawfully domiciled in other parts of the Empire," and affirms the right of "each community of the British Commonwealth"—presumably including Kenya, which enjoys an advanced form of Crown Colony Government —to exclude new immigrants. All the Dominions, except South Africa, having already excluded Indians, were thus able to subscribe to it.

To the Indian claim the settlers are vehemently opposed. They maintain that if it were granted, the Indians, who are already more than double their number,[1] would eventually have political control of the country,[2] in spite of any present disavowal of such intention on their part. They demand that the franchise shall be on a communal basis, and that Indian immigration shall be restricted. They defend segregation on the grounds of the lack of sanitation in the Indian quarters, which they say are almost invariably the foci of each successive outbreak of plague,[3] and they formulate charges of moral depravity debasing to the Africans. These charges (including incitement to crime) are indignantly repudiated by the Indians, and, in fairness to them, demand a full investigation.[4]

The Indian delegation, on its part, expressly disavows any desire to acquire political control. They are willing to forgo any claim to the higher colonial appointments, or to equal representation on the Legislative Council, provided that the official majority is an effective instrument so as to leave

[1] By the last census (1921) the Indians are returned at 22,822 and the British at 9651, including officials. The adult male British settlers, however, probably do not number more than between 2000 and 3000, the adult male Indians being probably eight times as many.

[2] Their view was supported by Lord Sydenham and two other members of the Joint Select Committee on Indian affairs. To grant an equal status to Indians, they say, would convert a British colony into "an Indian independency," and lead, in due course, to the absorption by them of the whole Government of the Colony—an ambition already definitely avowed by their spokesmen ('Times,' 1st August 1921). This, Sir Valentine Chirol retorts, means that "the measure of the rights enjoyed by subjects of the Crown is to be determined by the colour of their skin, and the civilisation for which the British Empire stands is not an ethical but a purely racial civilisation" ('Times,' 5th August 1921).

[3] See 'Admiralty Handbook,' p. 326. Sir R. Coryndon, when Governor of Uganda, stated that the better-class Indians own 40 per cent of the cotton-ginning business and are of a good moral standard, but the great majority are petty traders who have few moral scruples. They are demoralising to the Baganda.—'United Empire,' June 1920.

[4] Report of 'East African Economic Commission' of 1917, p. 21. The charge is repeated in another document on the authority of Dr Burkitt, senior unofficial medical officer.

the control of native affairs entirely in the hands of the colonial officials.[1] This, if the future can be so pledged, would dispose of the most serious of the settlers' anxieties.

Finally, the settlers claim that they were invited by the British Government to come to Kenya, on the express promise of Lord Elgin and successive Secretaries of State that the highlands would be reserved to them.[2] In this matter also the Indian delegation is willing to meet their view, and not to press their claim at present, while not abandoning their rights. They, too, may well claim that they were encouraged to come to Kenya, but it is pertinent to note that Mr Churchill, when speaking of Indian settlement, referred (as I did myself thirty years ago) to Indian colonists, and not to temporary residents and shopkeepers.[3]

Such are the salient points in the controversy between the claims of the British settlers and the Indians, which are now (June 1923) the subject of investigation by the departments of State concerned. Both sides are very much in earnest. The settlers have let it be known that they are prepared to go to almost any extreme in case of an adverse decision, while the

[1] "Indians in Kenya," says the spokesman of the official delegation, "have again and again authoritatively declared that they have no desire whatever to take any part in the direct administration of native affairs. . . . In the allocation of posts for the higher Colonial Civil Service, Indians have not in the past been appointed in Africa. The Kenya Indian deputation, speaking on behalf of their community, have no wish to disturb that arrangement, and are ready to give a guarantee in writing to that effect. . . . There is no ambition whatever in Indian minds to make either Kenya or any part of Africa an Indian Colony" (C. F. Andrews, 'Times,' 8th May 1923). In a later letter (5th June) he declares that the relegation of the control of native affairs, and of the legislative power to the Imperial Government, is "the key to the whole Indian position." The moderate Indians suggested a "fixed number of representatives of each community—eleven Europeans and five Indians" ('Times,' 27th January). "They authorise me to state that they have no desire now or in the future to control the Administration, and are willing to give any pledge or agree to any safeguards which will meet the fears of the Europeans" ('Times' correspondent, 3rd February).

[2] Lord Elgin announced that, while imposing no legal restrictions, grants of land in the uplands should not be made to Indians, while grants in the lowlands should be restricted to agriculturists (Cd. 4117 of 1908, pp. 27 and 33). Mr Churchill, as Colonial Secretary, confirmed this undertaking. Mr Shastri challenges the assertion that any pledge was given that the European settlers should have the exclusive occupation of the highlands in perpetuity ('Times,' 2nd June 1923). Active propaganda were originally instituted to attract settlers from the United Kingdom and South Africa, and more recently the Soldier Settlement Scheme was widely advertised.

[3] "The Government welcomed their entry into the country," said Mr Churchill on his return from his visit to East Africa as Under-Secretary. It was hoped by the Colonial Office "that Equatorial Africa might offer a compensating field for the colonising enterprise of our fellow-subjects in India" to ease the Transvaal difficulty.

Indians declare that any departure from the resolution of the Imperial Conference can only result in breaking the Imperial connection between India and Great Britain.[1]

With the ventilation of these opposing claims in the Press, it may, I think, be confidently assumed that British public opinion has very definitely come to the conclusion that our responsibility as trustee for the 2,500,000 African inhabitants of the colony demands that their interests should be paramount. The Indian delegation, as we have seen, agrees to this, but it asserts that, "in spite of the official majority, the Legislative Council and the Governor himself have again and again been dictated to by the European settlers, and have given way on such vital matters as forced labour ordinances, hut and poll taxes," &c.[2]

The first step towards the solution of this very serious problem must necessarily lie in a frank admission and reversal of the errors in policy which have created it. Among these I venture to think the following may be included :—

1. The premature transformation of Kenya from a Protectorate to a Crown Colony (which confers on wild border tribes not yet fully brought under administrative control the status of British subjects), merely, it would appear, in order to comply with the wording of the Colonial Stocks Act (which could have been altered) when raising a loan.

2. The grant to the European settlers of seats on the Executive Council, and of elected representatives of constituencies in the Legislative Council, ostensibly as instalments towards self-government, whereas they meant in point of fact increased control over the native population.

3. The failure of both the Colonial Office and the local Government to formulate a definite native policy, and to use the official majority effectively to carry it out.

4. Lack of co-operation between the Colonial and the India Office, with a view to informing and obtaining the co-operation of the Government of India before enunciating decisions.

The solution of the problem would seem to lie in defining the area to be appropriated to British settlement, and granting to the settlers within that area representative government

[1] Andrews, *loc. cit.*

[2] Mr Shastri ('Times,' 6th June 1923). It is stated that the bulk of the revenue raised from the natives has been expended in the interests of the white settlers.

leading up eventually to that complete self-government which a virile and progressive British colony may rightly claim. Outside the limits of the Settlement no land would be alienated other than such limited sites for commercial depots as the Governor might consider to be in the interests of the economic development and trade of the native territories, without racial discrimination. The jurisdiction of the Legislative Council should, I suggest, be confined to the Settlement, which alone should have the status of a colony, while the Governor, assisted by an Advisory Council, would legislate, as in South Africa and in other Protectorates, for the native territories. Such an advisory body might form the nucleus of a council for a future federated East Africa.

The control of railways, harbours, and customs and such other matters as equally affect not only the British Settlement and the native territories of Kenya, but also Uganda, would be largely entrusted to separate Boards, and the Legislative Council would (as hitherto in Nigeria) only deal with them in so far as the area to which its jurisdiction is confined is concerned. The Governor's assent would be required to such legislation, and he would legislate separately and simultaneously for the native territories. Large towns in the Settlement in which there is a considerable Indian population would be organised as municipalities, and since it is essential to the settlers to retain the services of the shopkeepers, who constitute the Indian section, there need be no fear that they would not be liberally dealt with. The same argument applies to such native communities as might unavoidably be included within the limits of the Settlement. Compensation or equivalent land could be given to any who might desire to leave.

The fact that the British self-governing Settlement would—like the Transvaal before the Union—have no seaboard would of course create difficulties,[1] but it is clear that no solution free from difficulty is now possible. It is in the nature of compromise between the competing claims of the immigrant races, while ensuring the fulfilment of our responsibility to native peoples. It would be opposed by those settlers—if there are any such—whose real aim is not to secure self-government, but the control of the native population, with all the evils inseparable from the rule of such an oligarchy. (See page 116.)

[1] The British Government some years ago made a definite offer, I believe, to the Jewish community to establish a self-governing colony in the Kenya highlands.

It would be equally distasteful to the Indians, who, it is understood, do not desire a similar settlement of their own—for they are not colonists and settlers—and profess to regard such a proposal as an exaggerated form of segregation.

It may be therefore that H.M.'s Government will find the line of least resistance in retaining the existing or a nominated Legislative Council for the whole colony, and either depriving it of jurisdiction in regard to native affairs, or endeavouring to ensure that the official majority is effective and properly utilised. The difficulty, however, of deciding what are purely "native affairs," or of ensuring that an influence which has hitherto proved itself so powerful shall in future be under official control are so great, that I am convinced that such a solution will only give rise to continued friction (especially if the Africans are educated to demand representative institutions), and that the Indian community will, after practical experience, find itself driven to ask for the solution I have proposed.

These suggestions to a large extent dispose of the controversies which centre round the questions of franchise, immigration, and segregation. To the Advisory Council the Governor would, at his discretion, invite the attendance of Europeans and Indians when questions affecting their interests were under discussion. A separate Lieut.-Governor would represent the Governor—and through him the Crown—in the British Settlement, and assist him in his relations with the settlers. If political control is effectively exercised by the official majority, the franchise becomes unimportant. British immigration would be limited on the one hand by the available land in the settlement, and on the other, equally with Indian immigration, by the economic needs of the native territories as determined by the Governor. Throughout the group of territories which form part of the Empire in East Africa, whose interests and policies are largely identical, the way would lie open for the federation which I have advocated in Chapter IX. (pp. 179-182).

The second problem peculiar to those limited regions in the tropics in which European settlement is possible, is that of "native reserves." On the high plateau lands the native population is not dense, the most populous tribes being the Wa-Kikuyu and the Wakamba, in the provinces of Kenya and Ukamba, who are agriculturists, and the Masai, and other pastorals in the Naivasha province, who are nomads. The areas inhabited by the settled tribes are reserved for their occupation, but do not appear to have been accurately delimited, and are not "reserves" in the usual acceptation of the term. "The Masai alone," says Sir P. Girouard, "have had their reserves assigned to them by treaty."[1] Formerly this tribe roamed with its herds over a great expanse of country, but it was greatly reduced in numbers by the outbreak of rinderpest, which destroyed the cattle in 1800. With the advent of European settlers the segregation of the Masai into reserves appeared to be a necessity, the more so on account of their lawless and predatory habits and disregard of human life.

The policy of native reserves had long been accepted in South Africa, where Europeans form 21·93 per cent of the population.[2] Its adoption in East Africa, where the natives outnumber the Europeans by about 246 to 1,[3] was based on the assumption that the European settlers would rapidly multiply and take up the vacant lands; for as Sir C. Eliot, the first Commissioner, wrote, "the interior of the Protectorate is a white man's country, and it is mere hypocrisy not to admit that white interests must be paramount, and the main object of our policy and legislation should be to found a white colony."[4] Provided that the area assigned to the natives was fully adequate for their needs, and for future expansion, and that proper steps were taken for their material and moral welfare, few will be found to dispute the advisability or justice of the formation of reserves for the nomad Masai in the circumstances.

Sir C. Eliot, however, dissents from this view. "As a general principle," he writes, "I am opposed to the creation in this protectorate of native reserves, meaning by that name not plots of land kept here and there to meet the needs of natives, but territories in which natives are segregated and left to themselves; . . . reserves by isolating natives tend to perpetuate bad customs, and to retard civilisation and missionary work." Where, however, it is not possible for natives to be restricted, "they should be allowed to immigrate to lands reserved for their use"—a qualification which deprives

[1] 'Annual Report, 1909-10,' Cd. 5467 of 1911, p. 38.
[2] Census of 1921, 'Statesman's Year-book,' 1923, p. 233.
[3] Ibid., p. 200. The native population of three highland provinces of Naivasha, Kenya, and Ukamba is given as 1,268,000 and the Europeans as 4571 in 1917-18.—'Admiralty Handbook,' Appendix "A.," p. 581.
[4] 'East African Protectorate,' pp. 105 and 310.

his objection of much of its point. Reserves may, he thinks, "sometimes be advisable in dealing with very strong native races, or where it is desired to prevent the destruction of a vanishing race, but they tend to isolate a tribe and prevent their fusion with other stocks, and so forming the hybrids to which virility and improvement are due."

Sir P. Girouard when Governor expressed a similar view. The creation of reserves, he writes, "amounts to the dedication of lands for the perpetuation of barbarism. It would appear to me desirable to place all native reserves in the hands of trustees, who might conceivably be drawn from the judiciary or mission bodies," since they would protect the natives and favour Government proposals for their benefit.[1] But Government is itself the trustee, and should be competent to take its own measures for the good of the natives.

Sir C. Eliot's alternative to the system of reserves is that "native villages should remain on the estates of Europeans in order to supply workmen, the villages and a sufficient amount of land round them being the property of the natives, and excluded from the area of the European's property."

The Economic Commission strongly supported this "interpenetration policy," as being more favourable to the natural development of the country, which they frankly place in the foreground, since "every one, including the civil servant, is concentrated on producing wealth," and secondly, as more conducive to the welfare and progress of the natives. The policy of reserves is, they say, more suited to South Africa as an industrial country than to an agricultural country like East Africa.

By strictly limiting the extent of the reserves to areas already in beneficial use by the natives, and allowing no margin for increase of population, they propose to force the surplus to settle in villages interspersed among the European settlers, and to encourage them to become "labour tenants on European farms." The areas in which the natives are concentrated are to be distributed as widely as possible throughout the reserves, with tracts between them for white settlements. The labour available for European scientific production will thus be largely increased. "Exploitation," they consider, is not possible where no economic pressure exists, and the demand for labour exceeds the supply. They are opposed to small holdings. "The natives (they say)

[1] 'Annual Report, 1909-10,' Cd. 5467 of 1911, p. 38.

can only stagnate under a system of peasant proprietorship." They condemn the existing reserves, which are "practically identical" with the game reserves, and (they infer) are without medical and veterinary facilities, or adequate education. They consider them strongholds of savagery, ignorance, and superstition. The chiefs, they say, are not tribal chiefs, but the nominees of Government, without authority and engaged in enriching themselves.

But these are not the conditions which ought to exist in a native reserve, and if they do exist in East Africa there can be no question of their continuance. With adequate medical supervision the population will increase, for the Africans are a prolific race; and though the ratio of natives to whites may decrease, the time must eventually come when the original, and numerically greater, population will learn to resent the status of labour tenants to Europeans.

The results of "interpenetration" would, it is only too probable, reproduce some of the worst features of the old slave plantations—immorality and irresponsibility. The policy is one which can hardly be said to be compatible with the principles which this country has advocated, through its statesmen, at Brussels and at Paris, as those which should guide our action towards subject races. And looking to the future, I am convinced that it would be fraught with danger and disaster. This criticism of "the interpenetration policy" does not, of course, mean that employees who of their own free-will prefer the conditions of permanent wage-earning labourers on an alien estate should not live with their families upon it, cultivating their own allotments in their spare time, or as herdsmen in charge of stock on a European ranch. This is a different proposition to that of breaking up tribal organisations and distributing the people among European estates, and suppressing reserves with the same object.

Mr Rhodes' opinions on this subject were embodied in the Glen-Grey Act,[1] which was a carefully-considered scheme for the organisation of a model reserve. It provided for the division of land—not already hypothecated—into locations, each of which would be subdivided into allotments of about four morgen (eight and a half acres), with sufficient commonages for general use. Each location is controlled by a Board of three resident landholders, and a certain number of the

[1] Act No. 25 of 1904, enacted 15th August 1904.

members of these Boards are appointed to a District Council, presided over by the Resident Magistrate. The Council is empowered to raise and expend rates, and generally to manage the location. A land rental of 15s. must be paid by each holder, with an additional 3s. for each morgen over four. Default involves distraint and eventual cancellation of title. The allotment passes by primogeniture to male descendants. It thus creates a system of freehold hereditable holdings in a reserve, controlled by native Boards and Councils, supervised by a European officer.

The motives which prompted this legislation are explained in the numerous works on Mr Rhodes' life and policy.[1] His conception was, I think, a finer one than those I have discussed. He firmly held to the view that social progress and development among the natives could best be promoted by individual holdings in land. "I find," he said, when moving the second reading of the Bill, "that there are certain locations for natives where, without any right or title to the land, they are herded together. . . . I hold that natives should be apart from the white men and not mixed up with them. . . . We will put them on the land, we will let them manage their own affairs."[2] In conversation he frequently asserted his belief that individual possession of land was the key to the social elevation of the natives, and created self-respect. He considered segregation necessary to preserve them from liquor and European vices, and desired that they should enjoy self-government in their own locations, but should not interfere in colonial politics which did not interest them. He believed in taxation as a means of compelling natives to work. The four principles of the Glen-Grey Act are described as, "Work, segregation in the reserves, individual property in land, and local self-government."

The adequacy of the area assigned for reserves, so as to allow for increase of population, is a difficult matter, especially when it is complicated by the possession of large and rapidly

[1] See especially the 'Life' by Basil Williams.

[2] 'Cecil Rhodes,' by Vindex, pp. 361-390. Nine years later (1913) a select committee of the Cape Assembly reported the result as having been most beneficial to the natives. "Individual land tenure and self-government have done much." Mr Williams tells us that in thirteen years the rates reached the sum of £46,750, half of which was devoted to education, in which great progress was made, and £12,700 to roads. New reserves were added, the natives were eager to take up plots, and in three years numbered 6576. With the prohibition of all liquor, and the increase of education, the inclination to work increased.

increasing flocks and herds, for which extensive grazing is required. It must necessarily be controlled by the Secretary of State. In Rhodesia the Commission appointed by Mr Harcourt reserved "twenty-four acres for each man, woman, and child for exclusive and permanent native occupation." [1] The area cannot be decreased without the consent of the Secretary of State.

The East African settlement does not appear to have been so generous, judging from the evidence of the Colonial Secretary (Mr Hollis) and the medical officer, Nairobi.[2]

With regard to land tenure generally in East Africa a very interesting paper was presented to Parliament in 1912,[3] from which we learn, on the authority of the different Governors, what are the principles which have been accepted, and the conditions regarding land in each of the African dependencies. Within the ten-mile coast strip in East Africa—now the Kenya Protectorate—individual tenure is recognised, but a native must substantiate his claim to the land he occupies before he can obtain a certificate of title from Government. No restriction is placed on alienation. In Kenya Colony Government claims the right to dispose of all land, but the settled tribes have not been disturbed where they are in actual occupation of land. "Native chiefs," says the report, "are tenants under Government of the areas occupied by their people." These areas, as we have seen, are called native reserves, but only the pastoral Masai have been confined in properly delimited reserves assigned by treaty.[4] The land in the reserves "is supposed to be held in communal tenure,

[1] Letter from the Secretary of the Chartered Company to the 'Times,' 3rd July 1920, and Cmd. 507 of 1920. The cattle are stated to have increased from 55,155 to 652,776 in eighteen years. The chairman states, moreover, that there is no legal restriction against natives purchasing land outside the reserves, and they do in fact do so for very large sums of money.—Report, 28th October 1920.

[2] Mr Hollis states that all the most fertile land in the Rift Valley and Leikipia grazing grounds was taken from the Masai and sold to white settlers, "solely in the interests of the settlers."—Cd. 5584, 1911. The medical officer of Nairobi on the Government Commission of 1912-13 states that "the inadequacy of the reserves in Fort Hall and Nyeri districts for future development is patent."

[3] Command Paper 68 of 1912-13.

[4] In 1913 the Masai tribe brought an action against the Attorney-General, *e.g.*, the Colonial Government, for breach of pledges in regard to their reserves. The Judge of the High Court ruled that the acts of the defendants were acts of State, not cognisable by a Municipal Court. "If a wrong has been done, it is a wrong for which no Municipal Court can afford a remedy." The matter was allowed to drop, with this very inconclusive judgment.—Cd. 6939 of 1913.

and is alienable." Vacant lands were disposed of by Government, and very large blocks were sold to syndicates or individuals. It is estimated that nearly 5¼ million acres (8132 sq. miles) were disposed of in this way—much of it as freehold.[1]

The conditions on which settlers may obtain land in East Africa have been the subject of much controversy and many changes. In 1906 Lord Elgin raised the question of speculation in land, and laid down the principles of periodical revision and a graduated land-tax.[2] The present position seems to be that leases for agricultural land are for 999 years, the rent for the first 33 being 10 cts. an acre, for the second 33 at 1 per cent, for the third at 2 per cent, and for every subsequent period of 33 years at 3 per cent of the unimproved value. Preliminary occupation licences and the land-tax (to prevent accumulation of land by any one person) have been dropped. Not less than certain specified minima must be spent on improvements—classified as "permanent" and "temporary." An important clause empowers the Governor to veto an assignment of land when the assignee is of a different race to the assignor.

In Uganda proper, by the terms of the 1900 treaty, "natives own large areas as freehold, they can dispose of it as they like among themselves, but no individual can hold more than thirty square miles as private property without the consent of the Governor." The return shows that under the

[1] The East African Syndicate obtained 320,000 acres (500 square miles) on a nominal rental with option to purchase (under conditions) as freehold. Three other blocks of 100 square miles each are referred to in the return, which states that the total area held from the Crown on terminable leases was estimated (in 1911) at 4,550,065 acres, "with an additional 654,765 acres of freehold." East Africa was under the Foreign Office at the time these large concessions were granted. Correspondence relating to them was published in two Blue-books.—Cmd. 2099 and 2100 of 1904. See also Cmd. 2163, and Sir Charles Eliot's book, 'The East African Protectorate,' p. 309.

[2] The earlier conditions of unrestricted freehold were embodied in Ordinance 21 of 1902 ('Gazette,' 31st July). When the control of the protectorate passed to the Colonial Office, Lord Elgin insisted on the dangers of accumulations of enormous areas of land in the hands of individuals through the operation of free transfer, instancing Australia. He proposed a graduated land-tax, and a maximum limit for holdings, together with periodical revision of rentals, in order that Government should obtain its share of the unearned increment in the value of the land.—Despatch, 19th March 1908. Cd. 4117 of 1908, p. 30. These proposals met with much local opposition, but Mr Harcourt supported his predecessor's policy (Despatch, 3rd February 1911). The area of grants was limited according to the quality of the land, with a corresponding scale of rentals. Leases were to be for ninety-nine years only, and revisable at the thirty-third and sixty-sixth year (5 per cent of the unimproved value, with fixed maxima).

Baganda, Busoga, Bunyoro, Toro, and Ankole agreements 6,156,570 acres were assigned as freehold to the chiefs, 72,477 as freehold to missions, and 12,650 acres to other non-natives, while 99,143 were under lease. The remaining 54 million odd acres were apparently at the disposal of Government, no chief or other person being recognised as having "either a freehold or leasehold interest in them." There is no allusion to the nature of the pre-existing native tenure.[1]

"No chief or tribe is now considered as being the owner of any land in Nyasaland," says the Governor. Prior to British rule, "many chiefs had sold large tracts of country to private individuals without conditions. Many of these were confirmed later, subject, *inter alia*, to the condition "that existing villages be not disturbed. The balance of land, originally owned by chiefs and tribes, was handed over to the Crown by tribes before and after the protectorate was proclaimed." 6000 square miles are shown as alienated, all but 63 square miles being freehold. The remaining land is classed as "held by the Crown."[2] Leased land may not be assigned or sub-

[1] Sir H. Johnston's large work on Uganda deals very briefly indeed with the land question. The agreement (of 1900), he says, "transferred a little less than half of Uganda as the private property of the king, princes, princesses, and chiefs, and a large number (some 2000) of native land-owners," viz., all that they occupied, cultivated, or used for grazing, and "they were pledged to a proper treatment of their native tenants." The remainder, including the forests, "was handed over to the British Government to be dealt with on the same lines as Crown lands in a Crown colony. . . . Any landless native of Uganda can acquire cultivable land from the Administration at an almost nominal rental." Agreements were made with Ankole, Toro, &c., on similar lines.—'Uganda Protectorate,' vol. i. p. 250. Mr (now Sir F.) Jackson writes that "the land occupied by the natives belongs to them, and only unoccupied land belongs to the Government." The onus of proof that the land is not waste (and therefore Crown land) lies on the claimant.—Handbook 98, p. 128.

[2] A full description of his original settlement is given by Sir H. Johnston in his book on Nyasaland. Villages were as a rule excluded from the alienated lands, and "the natives were informed that the sale of the surrounding land did not include the alienation of their houses and plantations. . . . The tenure of the land was in reality tribal—viz., theoretically the chief had no right to alienate the land, . . . one of the results therefore was to completely free . . . the natives by restoring to them the inalienable occupancy of their villages and plantations." Finally, treaties were concluded with all the chiefs of the protectorate "securing Crown control over the remainder of the land, which the natives were henceforth unable to alienate without the sanction of the Commissioner. In some cases (says Sir H. Johnston) large sums were spent in buying up waste lands, where complete control over its disposal was desired. A percentage of the selling price or rental was paid to the native chief when portions of the Crown lands are let or sold."—'British Central Africa,' pp. 112, 113. The Official Handbook No. 95 states that the "British Central African Company" owns 350,000 acres, the "African Lakes Company" and the "Blantyre and East African Company," 150,000 each (p. 69).

let without the Governor's written permission, and no rent or service may be exacted from any native on the land.

From this brief summary it appears that throughout these three protectorates the Government has assumed to a greater or less degree not merely the right to control, but the actual ownership of the greater part of the land. In the available records—the Blue-books of the time and the works of Sir C. Eliot and Sir H. Johnston, their earliest administrators and historians—we do not find any record of investigations as to the native systems of land tenure. English terms are used, and English conceptions of land tenure seem to have guided the principles of the settlements or agreements. In Uganda, "kings, princes, princesses" and others are granted freehold lands, and the rest of the people are referred to as their "tenants." The Government is regarded as the owner of the land not included in these freeholds, which apparently embraced the land actually occupied at the time. The demands made by any increase of population since that date (1900) are to be satisfied by Government, whose rent-paying tenants these "landless natives" were to become.

In Nyasaland the settlement appears to have assured to the natives the possession at least of their actual villages and plantations, though it is stated that no chief or tribe now owns any land. Settlers in some cases obtained their land at prices as low as ½d. an acre (27s. a square mile).

The density of the population has, of course, an intimate relation to the importance of the land to the natives, the amount available for expropriation to aliens, and the labour supply. A glance at the table on page 45 reveals the astonishing paucity of the population of British tropical Africa, even though it be considerably greater than that of the French possessions. The density per square mile (14·4) is in striking contrast to that of British India (225 in 1921) or of Hong-Kong (1600 in 1921).[1] These figures bear eloquent testimony to the sufferings of the people of Africa in the past, and to the possibilities of the future, when, with the aid of peace and prosperity on the one hand and of medical science on the other, the vacant places fill up under British control.

Calculations of average density over vast areas are, how-

[1] The Statesman's Year-book, 1923,' gives the population of the colony (exclusive of leased territory) as 512,460, area 35 sq. miles—viz., a density per sq. mile of 14,641 !

ever, apt to give a wrong impression, for the people are very unequally distributed. Northern Nigeria, for instance, with an average density of about 40, includes areas where the density reaches 350 to the square mile, with corresponding depopulated lands with perhaps not more than one or two to the square mile. The Sudan, with its million odd square miles, has an average density of three only, but stretches of desert have no population at all.[1]

The table is interesting. The average density of the group of West African dependencies appears to be six times that of the eastern. The Gold Coast, which has been most clamant of its land rights, shows a density of less than twenty. In all except in the few very densely populated districts, it may be said that there is ample room for the legitimate needs of alien enterprise and development.

In those regions, whether in the east or west, where European settlement is not possible, the demand for land by non-natives is so limited, the area available is so large, and, except in limited districts, the native population is so small, that, whether the Government in theory owns the land or not, it is not likely in practice that the native cultivator will find any difficulty in obtaining all the land he needs.

It would, however, seem desirable that the claim of the natives of the soil to sufficient rent-free lands for their needs should be explicitly recognised, and there should be no question of "landless natives becoming Government tenants." For the rest, since by treaty, consent, or established usage the Governments in Eastern Africa have for a long period exercised a control of the land at least equivalent to that conferred by conquest, the extent and the limitations of that control might well be embodied in the local legislation as a guide to the British staff. The claim of the State should be that of trustee and not that of owner, and in other respects the legislation would, I hope, embody the principles which I have discussed as relating to conquered countries, which it will have been noted diverge in some important respects from the proposals of the Lands Committee regarding Northern Nigeria.

[1] The Halfa Province (112,300 square miles) has only 1 person to 3 square miles; Dongola (124,300 square miles) only 1, and Berber and Red Sea (125,800) only 1½ per square mile, while the Shilluk country is said to be the most densely populated in Africa.—Handbook 98, pp. 1 and 20.

CHAPTER XVI.

LAND TENURE AND TRANSFER—(*Continued*).

General conditions of land grants—Building leases—Agricultural leases—Mining leases—Grazing leases—Revision of rentals of all leases—Premium — Rents — Auction — Improvements — Surrender — Interdependence of lease conditions—Compensation—Object of lease conditions—Views of Liverpool merchants—Acquisition of land—Mission lands—Registration—Southern Rhodesia—Other British tropics—India—Burmah — West Indies — Malaya—Fiji—Hong-Kong—Non-British tropics—French—Portuguese—The Congo—Java—Philippines—China.

MINERALS.

Ownership of minerals—Justification of Government ownership—Alienation of mineral rights by Suzerain—Conditions of native ownership—Varying conditions of mining laws—The function of Government—Prospecting licences—Mining leases—Government monopoly in coal—Oil-fields.

I PROPOSE now to offer a few comments on the conditions on which land may reasonably be granted by Governments to non-natives, in the hope that they may perhaps prove useful or suggestive to administrators, though probably the general reader may feel disposed to "skip" the next few paragraphs. My comments refer to the tropics proper, and are not, generally speaking, applicable to homesteads and farms held under conditions of English law in East Africa.

It has for many years past been an accepted principle in British Crown dependencies that land granted to non-natives must be held on terminable leases and not as freehold—whether the grant is by the Crown or by a native,—but occupation rights to a native may be for an indefinite term. Land grants are exclusive of mineral rights. The conditions of general application—such as those relating to security of title, payment of rent, rights of way, survey, &c.

—are usually contained in ordinances and regulations, and are implied in the document of title, which contains any additional covenants. The Crown usually reserves the right to lay telegraphs or pipes across the land if necessary, on payment of compensation, and waterside leases usually reserve a strip of land as a public right of way along the water's edge. Native rights are safeguarded, and payment must be made for all unexhausted improvements assessed by Government. It is usual also to require that the lessee shall effect certain specified improvements within a stated time. These may be either in fulfilment of the purpose for which the lease is granted—*e.g.*, to erect buildings of a certain value under a building lease, &c.—or they may effect permanent improvements on the land, such as raising its level or reclaiming swamp, or filling in pits, &c. Improvements of the former class are the property of the lessee, but those of the latter class are in the nature of a contract between the lessor and the lessee, whereby the latter undertakes to do certain work which otherwise must be done by the lessor. The cost is repaid by an equivalent remission of premium or rental, and they belong therefore to the lessor.

The term of leases of residential sites in the European quarter of a township must be sufficient to encourage a lessee to spend capital in permanent buildings, &c.—say for ninety-nine years. If the land is only used for warehouses, or for temporary houses outside a township, the term would probably be less. The length of the lease is usually stated in the auction notice. The covenant requires that buildings of a specified value shall be erected within a specified time. To prevent overcrowding, the number of persons who may reside on a native plot may be restricted.

The area of European residential sites in a township is usually not less than one or more than two acres, and in a native location, quarter to half an acre (which may not be subdivided), exclusive of separate garden allotments. Outside a township they may extend to five acres or more. Leases of wharves, railway sidings, &c., are subject to special terms and conditions.

Agricultural leases in Nigeria are limited to 1200 acres, and a separate building lease is required for permanent European residences, but labourers' huts, store-sheds, &c., are allowed. Natives resident on the land do not become tenants, and no rent may be charged to them. The term of an agricultural lease may be from forty-five to sixty years, or longer if costly machinery is installed—oil-mills, saw-mills, &c. The lessee should bring at least one-eighth of the area under cultivation each year. The same lessee should not hold two coterminous leases so as to evade the limit of size. "Dummying" must, of course, be guarded against in all leases. Such leases are intended for rubber, cocoa, and similar plantations in regions not suited to European settlement. Allotments for gardens around a township are usually granted on short-term leases to natives at very low rentals. Forest licences convey no rights whatever in the land.

With regard to mining leases—I am only concerned here with surface rights. When the mines are underground these are unimportant, and consist merely of the area required for the erection of machinery, disposal of tailings, and residential areas for Europeans and labourers. Where, however, the workings are alluvial or open-cast, surface rights are, of course, all-important. Leases and "mining rights" may in Nigeria be for 800 and 76 acres respectively. Surface rights can be claimed over any area certified by the Inspector of Mines to be actually required for mining purposes. For permanent residences, recreation grounds, trading stores, or plantations, a separate lease is required. If the grant of surface rights would deprive the natives of sufficient cultivable land for their support, the mining lease might be refused.

As to grazing leases—in a populated country where pastoral tribes own millions of cattle and flocks, grazing land for stock and ostrich farming is, of course, only available where lack of water or fodder-grass prevent its use by the natives. It follows that a trustee in control of the land for the benefit of the natives can grant no extensive grazing rights in such countries to non-natives, except in regions at present useless for the purpose. There are great areas in Nigeria where these conditions apply—lack of water and of forage; there are still greater areas in the Sudan and the Kalahari and Rhodesia.

The pioneer should have security for a good return on the capital he has risked, by an option after the first twenty years to renew for a further period of, say, fifty years, over all land which he has rendered useful. A grazing lease should not exclude native settlements on the land, which, with proper safeguards regarding cattle disease and the use of water, would be advantageous to the lessee. The natives would not, of course, be his tenants, but free occupiers. Exclusive grazing rights would be confined to fenced areas on leased land, and it would be the duty of the District Officer to see that, if the lessee were allowed to graze stock outside his leased area, no preference whatever was obtained over native herds, and the non-native cattle-owner would pay a cattle tax or licence. The land must, of course, be used for the purpose for which it is granted—including the raising of fodder and corn for cattle or ostriches.

The Colonial Office has of late years insisted that leases of all kinds by Government to non-natives should be subject to revision of rental periodically. In East Africa, as we have seen, leases are revised at the thirty-third and sixty-sixth years.[1] In Northern Nigeria the ordinance, as recommended by the Committee, enacted septennial revision,—the term was later extended (for building leases only) to twenty years.

Revision is based on the exchange value of the land exclusive of improvements by the lessee. For leases of sixty years and upwards revision at one-third and two-thirds of the term seems reasonable—shorter leases at half-time with exemption for those of ten years or less. The period should, however, vary according to situation, being shorter in a rapidly-growing township, newly served by a railway, and longer in back districts where the land is unlikely to appreciate rapidly in value. If land held under an agricultural lease has become valuable for building purposes, the lessee, if required to surrender any portion, should be entitled to full compensation both for improvements and disturbance, with an equivalent extension in another direction. Leases of Crown lands to natives not subject to income tax should be equally liable to revision, but land leased for purely mining purposes should be exempt. An appeal to the courts or to arbitration against the revised rent should always be allowed.

This system has naturally been opposed by lessees as involving State interference, and introducing an element of uncertainty as to future rents which would render it difficult to borrow money on mortgage. Its advocates, on the other hand, maintain the right of the colonial revenue to participate directly in the increasing value of land (due in great part to the expenditure of public money), and they argue

[1] Also in Uganda. See Annual Report, 1918-19, No. 1654.

that the revision system enables the Government to encourage pioneer effort by very low initial rentals.[1] The alternative, as I have said (p. 293), seems to lie in an income tax by which the State receives its share of the expanding profits made from the land, or the graduated land-tax on Europeans, proposed by Lord Elgin and Mr Harcourt.[2] It cannot, however, be denied that revision at such short intervals as seven years is harassing and deterrent to private enterprise.

Premium may be regarded as a capitalisation of a portion of the rent due up to the date of the first revision, and is a reimbursement to the public revenues of the day of the expenditure incurred in providing necessary access to sites and other amenities.[3] It also forms a convenient basis for bidding at auction. As a rough-and-ready hypothesis, the premium should not exceed the annual rental, multiplied by half the period up to the first revision. In some colonies the premium charged is fixed at four to ten times the rental, apparently without regard to these considerations. If the amenities provided (roads, drains, water-supply, &c.) are defrayed from municipal funds, the municipality and not the general revenue would receive the premium. The rent fixed at revision is the original annual value without premium, plus any increased value of the land apart from the lessee's improvements.

Rents depend on the exchange value of land, and in a country where as yet land has little or no exchange value, and there is more than enough for all demands, it can only be arbitrarily fixed in relation to the amenities of the site, and the profits to be made by occupying it. Auction in such a case is of little value in determining it, for except in a restricted township there is probably no person other than the

[1] A critic of this system writes: "X, Y, and Z take up plots at a certain rent and proceed to improve their holdings. After a time W wants a plot. The amount of trade that the enterprise of X, Y, Z has drawn to or developed in the place has enhanced the value of the land, and at an auction W is content to pay such enhanced rate. Now if X, Y, or Z's first revision falls due, W's value can form the basis for the increase. If that does not mean that X, Y, and Z are being charged on their own improvements, what does it mean?" The system is not the fancy of any local Administrator, but has been laid down, for East and West Africa alike, by His Majesty's Government. The officer employed in dealing with such questions must necessarily be an expert, and it is for him to judge to what extent enhanced rentals are due to the expenditure of the State and the community in general, and to what extent they are due to the individual enterprise of the lessee.

[2] Despatch of 29/2/1911 in 'East African Gazette' of 1/3/1911.

[3] See Table, "Present Value of Lease," Whitaker, p. 399.

applicant who is interested in acquiring the land. Even in a new township, the boundaries of which can be extended without difficulty, there can only be competition based on the comparison between two particular lots, unless fewer lots are put up for auction than there are known to be applicants.

It is, however, manifest that where the profits of occupation have increased a thousandfold by the advent of a railway built out of a local revenue, that revenue (*e.g.*, the local tax payer) is entitled to a fair share of the profits, especially if those profits are made by persons with a foreign domicile, and only partially expended in the country. For the revenue (whether obtained by an income tax, or by revision of rentals) is spent for the benefit of the country and its taxpayers. Comparison with rental values in England, where tenants have heavy rates and taxes to pay, is of course misleading.

The principle to be adopted seems, therefore, to be that the rent and premium should bear some relation to the estimated profits of occupation within the first revision period, in comparison with the direct taxes levied on the native population. In an old colony the price at which land has changed hands by private sale, and the price obtained for similar lots at auction, afford data on which the upset price and rental can be fixed with accuracy. As between lots in a particular locality, the extent of frontage on the sea, or on a navigable river, or on a railway or road, will of course afford data for *comparative* valuation. Rentals for land owned by the Government must be distinguished from a land-tax. In agricultural leases the rent should be low for the first six years, until the trees come into bearing. In Penang the rent is quadrupled after the sixth year.

Surface rentals for land leased for open-cast or alluvial mineral workings should, when the minerals belong to the State, be merely nominal, and they are only imposed at all because, when the land is in private ownership, such rentals belong to the owner, and must be distinguished from the mineral lease.

Penal rents may be imposed by ordinance for failure to carry out covenanted improvements or obligations within the specified time. Reduced or even pepper-corn rents may be charged if the land is required for a purpose conducive to the public welfare, such as sites for schools and hospitals, or for religious purposes or public recreation.

The system of auction is the best method of securing strict impartiality in the disposal of land. The auction may be held either on the land or at any other place convenient to bidders. A bid may be made by letter, and announced at the auction. The public notice (in consecutive gazettes and otherwise) should give the fullest particulars, with ample time for inspection of plans and inquiry, and bidding should be on the upset price (premium), and not on the rental. In default of competition, the lot goes to the original applicant on the terms previously agreed.

The amount which an applicant declares himself willing to expend on improvements, and their permanency, is an important factor in deciding the terms of a lease. They are defined as "anything or any quality permanently attached to the land, directly resulting from the expenditure of capital and labour," and include buildings, fixed machinery, plantations of long-lived crops or trees, fencing, wells, roads, clearing for agriculture, irrigation or reclamation works, and even betterment of the soil which is not the result of ordinary cultivation. Improvements of which the cost has been deducted from the premium or rental belong of course to the lessor, but all other improvements remain the absolute property of the lessee. They only revert to Government (in the case of Crown lands) if the occupier vacates his lease at his own wish, or if his title has been revoked for good cause—*e.g.*, breach of covenant, &c.—or finally, in the case of the expiration of a terminable lease. The object of requiring "improvements" as a condition of the covenant is in order to prevent speculators buying up land, and leaving it undeveloped till an opportunity of selling at a profit should occur.

Surrender of a lease, though permissible, is usually subject to a statutory fine to prevent applications for land which the applicant has no intention of keeping. It may, of course, be reduced or remitted. The land must be left in good condition, and no permanent fixtures attached to the soil may be removed.

It is obvious that the length of a lease, the rent, premium, revision period, and value of improvements to be effected, are all interdependent, and must be considered in their mutual relations when advertising the conditions upon which a piece of land shall be put to auction. The applicant has to state, on the form of application, the value of the improvements he is prepared to effect, and the length of the lease would largely depend on the amount of this capital expenditure, whether in the form of permanent buildings on a building site, or of extensive plantations and machinery on an agricultural site, or of water-supply, irrigation, and importation of stock on a grazing lease. No definite scale can be laid down, for the situation of the site has an important bearing on the question. Whether the land is let on a "long-term" or a "short-term" lease depends, therefore, chiefly on the value of "improvements."

Compensation for unexhausted improvements, the property of the lessee, must be paid in full if the land is taken by Government for any purpose, but not if the lessee surrenders for either of the three reasons named. It would, however, be open to Government to refund to him any part of the value of his improvements which might seem just. If the land with its unexhausted improvements is re-leased, the value of these should be kept distinct from the ground rent, and added to the premium. The Government manifestly cannot be expected to pay for the whole of the unexhausted improvements, whenever an occupier may choose to surrender on revision of rental, however just the revision might be, and even if it were below the proper rental value. An unlimited liability would thus be imposed on the Government, which, if there were valuable buildings or plantations on the land, might amount to a large sum, while Government could be saddled at the caprice of the holder with an estate which it did not require, and of which it might be unable to dispose. Compensation is, of course, due for any damage caused by public works on leased land, and if more than 4 per cent of an agricultural lease is taken, compensation should also be given for the land itself. Full compensation must of course be paid to natives for any crops or dwellings, and also for disturbance if the land is leased to a non-native or acquired by Government.

Some of these principles, as might be expected, are by no means concurred in by those who have embarked their capital in the development of purely tropical lands in Africa. The Englishman is accustomed to freehold and to long leases on fixed rentals, and such conditions best suit his interests. It is the object of British policy to promote those interests by every legitimate means, while safeguarding the revenue of the future, and the interests alike of posterity and of the native populations. Its task is to distribute the burden of the contribution to public revenue equally between all. The object of the methods proposed is in brief to ensure that the native shall hold his land rent-free in perpetuity, paying a tax assessed yearly on its usufruct, while the non-native, who occupies lands whose value is rapidly increasing, has a terminable lease, with rent periodically revised.

The Liverpool Chamber of Commerce communicated their views to the West African Lands Committee in a series of resolutions.[1] They consider that if, as Sir H. Belfield states, the population is sparse and not increasing, it would be a mistake inimical to development to recognise the inalienable right of natives to the whole of the available land; "that where the lessee can prove an expenditure of, say, £500 per acre upon buildings or other permanent works, he shall be entitled to purchase the freehold of the land on specified terms," which the Chamber suggests should be ten years' rental; that on the expiry of a lease, failing renewal on acceptable terms, the lessee be compensated for all improvements, the amount being settled if necessary by arbitration; that the rent of an agricultural lease should be commutable "for a period not exceeding twenty years by paying a lump sum under discount at 5 per cent per annum"; that mining leases should include such superficial rights as would enable the lessee to sublet sites for dwellings for employees, and those who cater for them; that agricultural leases should not be limited to ninety-nine years; that no export duties on the produce of European estates (or otherwise) should be imposed; that the transfer of individual rights in land should be facilitated, and no distinction made between foreign or native individual owners; and finally, that neglect to utilise a mining or agricultural lease for two years should render it liable to forfeiture.

In a later Memorandum the merchants recognised the claim of Government to the unearned increment on land, and did not criticise the system of rent revision "if imposed in an equitable manner, and upon a settled basis." They ask for "trading and residential" leases of not less than ninety-nine years, with revision at twenty-one years—existing leases being converted if desired; that at the last revision the lessee should

[1] Published in the report of the Chamber of Commerce.

have an option of renewal to be exercised within five years of the expiry of a lease; that auction should be abolished, and that palm-oil plantation leases should be not less than ten square miles! Remaining stipulations are practically as already discussed.

When land (other than that in a township) at the disposal of Government is demanded on lease for any purpose, it devolves on the District Staff to make the fullest inquiries as to whether the grant will interfere with native rights of cultivation, grazing, or forestry, and how such rights can best be equitably adjusted—whether by the grant of equivalent land elsewhere, and by compensation for crops and disturbance or otherwise, or whether the grant should be curtailed or abandoned, and in the case of surface rights for mining, the minimum which is necessary. The District Officer informs the applicant of his intended recommendations as to the lease conditions. These data are carefully considered by Government before the lease is granted. To avoid delay and inconvenience, it is desirable that Government should permit occupation prior to survey and the completion of the lease, when the terms have been satisfactorily settled. Short-term leases—for five years or less—renewable from year to year, without compensation for improvements, may be granted when desirable—*e.g.*, for land which will later be required for a public purpose, or where the lessee does not wish to commit himself to a long lease. In the case of native-owned lands, the District Officer ascertains whether the proposed lease is by a tribal authority or by an individual, and in the latter case whether he has a title to the land, and he reports whether the proposed terms are in his opinion equitable to the owner.

Missions in Uganda occupy a specially privileged position, and 72,477 acres were assigned to them as freehold in the 1900 treaty. An alien mission is, of course, "non-native," and as such would be bound to obtain the Governor's sanction for the acquisition of land—though if the land is at the disposal of Government the grant might be made rent-free or on special terms. Like any other application, it would be investigated by the District Officer, and in particular he would ascertain whether the people were desirous of the establishment of a mission among them or hostile to it.

It may sometimes happen that a party of converts, with or without the consent of their chief, may erect a church and other buildings, with a residence for any missionary who comes to visit them, towards the cost of which they may or may not have received help from mission funds. The mission body disclaims any rights in the land or buildings (though they may have an indirect interest in them), and the transfer is not therefore cognisable as a transfer to a non-native. It is advisable that the Government, in the interests of peace and good order, should be cognisant of such matters, and this would be impressed upon both the missions and the people.

All transactions regarding land which are in writing should be registered within a prescribed time, and if not registered should be void, and not admissible in evidence. Boundary settlements made by District Officers, and approved by the Governor, should be endorsed by the chiefs and registered. A record should also be kept in the provincial office. An entry in the register, properly authenticated, should be a guarantee of title against the world, and to effect this verbal transactions must be held to be invalid by the courts, unless reduced to writing and registered. Individual owners in districts not declared to be under English land law (p. 306) should recite the grounds of their claim to title. Mortgages on land, and on permanent crops, should be included in the definition of "transactions in land."

The position in regard to land in Southern Rhodesia (though outside the tropics) is particularly worth noting, since it has been the subject of an important judgment of the Privy Council. The Chairman of the Chartered Company explained that there were four claims:[1] (1) The white settlers claimed that the Chartered Company held the land only as administering it for their benefit. (2) It was claimed on behalf of the natives that the land was theirs. (3) The Colonial Office claimed the land as belonging to the Crown. (4) The Chartered Company claimed the land as their property. The Privy Council found that the Company, acting on behalf of the Crown, conquered the country, and the Crown thus became possessed of the land by right of conquest; that it had not by any formal act transferred its rights to the Company, which rightly disposed of the land as its agent, but the Crown

[1] See report of 22nd meeting, August 1918, and note on page 24. The judgment did not apply to Northern Rhodesia, and since no claim there could be based on right of conquest, Lord Buxton's Committee recommended a new reference.—Cmd. 1471/1921

was liable for all necessary administrative expenditure, less the receipts from the land. The Privy Council did not apparently consider that the natives had any private or communal rights which the Crown, though conqueror, was bound to respect—other than the assignment to them of adequate reserves.

It may be of interest to add a few comments regarding the systems adopted in some other British colonies and dependencies outside Africa.

In India the Government claims a portion of the unearned increment when the enhanced value of the land is due to State expenditure. Sir T. Morison writes: "It is useless to discuss nationalisation of land, since the Indian Government has definitely repudiated such a conception of its rights in land. . . . The British Government has everywhere conferred or recognised a private right in land, . . . and in large areas has expressly declared the rights of landlord and village owners, . . . the economic doctrine has never been applied to the ownership of land in India." He adds in a later passage: "The general conclusion is that the Indian system of land tenure is something intermediate between complete nationalisation of land and absolute private property in land. To the extent of a half the State is able to appropriate that increased increment which is due to the development of the country." [1]

Individual ownership is safeguarded by legislation designed to prevent the transfer of land from the peasant proprietor to the money-lender—a process which at one time was rapidly taking place.

In Upper Burmah, after the British annexation, nothing was said in the regulations about defining the nature and extent of rights in land, but a "record of rights" was instituted, in which the facts as they came to light were simply stated, with all changes in ownership, &c. Practically every one, though not legally defined as "occupant" or "owner," had the enjoyment of his land on showing his possession and right thereto, provided the land was not State or Royal land. Royal lands were separately and carefully defined. About three years later a rough-and-ready assessment was made.[2]

[1] *Loc. cit.*, pp. 21, 22, and 39. See also Baden-Powell, 'Land Systems of British India,' and 'Village Communities of India'; also N. B. Baillie, 'The Land-tax of India.'

[2] Sir E. P. Girouard in Cd. 5103 of 1910, p. 47.

In the West Indies the policy of small holdings has been pursued. A Royal Commission in 1897 recommended the purchase (compulsory, if necessary) of areas held by large proprietors, with a view to their conversion into small holdings of about five acres each, and this proposal was adopted.

In Malaya practically all the land was the property of the Government, and it took some time, says Sir F. Swettenham, to convince the Malays of the desirability of obtaining a clear title in return for a low rental. Leases were issued for 999 years or in perpetuity. When Federation of the States was accomplished a uniform land code was adopted. Prior to this the land laws had differed widely.[1]

In Fiji, by the deed of cession, all land not at the time already alienated to foreigners, or actually being used, or probably required for use of the natives, was vested in the Crown, but in practice the Crown's rights were ignored, and the proceeds of sales were credited to the natives, so that the Crown is now without land.

In Hong-Kong the land vested in the Crown, and up to 1848 building sites, were leased without premium on seventy-five year terms—other leases were for twenty-one years. 999 year leases, with premium, were granted till 1885, when the older term was again adopted, and in 1898 these were made renewable for a second seventy-five years, with revision of rentals. In the New Territories all titles held under Chinese law were recognised, and in a total area of 40,000 acres over 20,000 certificates were issued, in addition to the mortgages registered. As on the island, all land vested in the Crown, if not held by individual title. Compensation for resumption of cultivated land is put at thirty-three times the annual rent.

Space does not admit of a lengthy examination of the way in which " the land question " has been handled by other nations in tropical Africa and elsewhere. We have seen that M. Delafosse agrees with our own authorities in regard to the principles which underlie the native system of land tenure in West Africa, but that the French nevertheless believe that individual ownership is incontestably the most favourable to production. This view is enforced throughout his volumes by the great French writer on Colonial Economics, Mons. P. Leroy Beaulieu.

[1] 'Malaya,' p. 236. See also Straits Annual Report, 1910, Cd. 5389.

As regards Portuguese possessions, a Lisbon decree some years ago was designed to promote free native holdings on vacant lands. No rent is charged for five years, and after twenty years a freehold is granted. Two-thirds must be cultivated, and the title is inalienable. Holders are exempt from forced labour of any kind, and from service in the police or military forces. Lisbon decrees are, however, not always operative in the colonies.[1]

The former system in the Congo State apparently not only denied any rights in land to the natives, but in the *domains privées*, which are said to have included nine-tenths of the area, they were forbidden to collect ivory and rubber except for sale to the Government. Purchasers of such produce were accounted to be receivers of stolen goods. This system has happily been replaced by a juster and more liberal régime. Individual ownership by natives is encouraged, and the right of Europeans to land they have reclaimed is recognised.

Mr Ireland tells us that all land in Java, other than the comparatively small area sold outright to Europeans and Chinese in the early days, is the property of the State, but free play is allowed for the operation of native customs, with the result that all agricultural land (with the exceptions noted) is held in hereditary leasehold tenure by individuals, or in communal holdings. The assessment of the land-tax follows the methods adopted in British India. Natives may sell their tenure rights to one another, but the sale to a European or to a foreign Asiatic is absolutely prohibited. This has been completely successful (he says) in protecting the native from the loss of his vested interest in the land, but it is generally felt that the Government has gone too far in its desire to protect the native, and has thereby retarded the development of the land.[2]

In the Philippines the United States, by the treaty with Spain, had become possessed of the public lands. With the exception of those reserved for military or Government purposes, these were placed under the control of the local Government, to be administered for the benefit of the people. "The sale of public lands was so carefully hedged about with restrictions that the development of the country has been retarded.

[1] Described by Mr J. H. Harris in 'The African Mail,' 9th August 1912.
[2] 'The Far Eastern Tropics,' Alleyne Ireland, p. 182.

In order to develop a class of small landowners, the sales of public lands were limited to 40 acres to one person, and 2500 acres to a Corporation." 406,730 acres were held by the Friars, and leased on three-year terms, generally renewed. The Government acquired these lands.[1]

In China the original right to all land vests in the State, and titles may be acquired by individuals, by reclaiming waste land (by permit), and on payment of the tax. Waste is not subject to tax, and cannot be owned by an individual. When reclaimed it is assessed for tax according to quality. All titles are entered in the *Tsik* ('Domesday Book') and *Tsak* (rent-roll). The last assessment was in 1771. There can be no title without payment of tax, and a penalty is imposed for using land which is not registered.

If in this chapter I have, on the one hand, appeared to go into unnecessary detail, and, on the other hand, to enunciate well-understood principles as though they were something new, my apology is that though the conditions of land tenure and transfer do not differ very materially in different parts of Africa, there has, as we have seen, been but little uniformity of principle in the treatment of the question, and it may be useful alike for the young administrator, and for the applicant for land, to have before them a brief summary of the principles on which, as I have ventured to suggest, the acquisition of land, rents, compensation, premia, &c., should be based.

MINERALS.

The Parliamentary Paper already quoted purported to render a return showing the ownership of minerals in the Crown colonies and protectorates.[2] From this it appears that the ownership of all minerals is unreservedly vested in the Crown in East Africa, Uganda,[3] Nigeria (in the south since 1916), Malaya, Trinidad and Tobago (since 1902), and British Honduras. The statement is not very clear as regards the remaining colonies, but apparently ownership of minerals is

[1] 'The Philippines,' Elliott, vol. ii. p. 68.

[2] Parliamentary Paper 68 of March 1912.

[3] The Governor, in a public paper, states that "the holders of land in the kingdom of Uganda have the right to minerals found on their estates, subject to the payment of a royalty (10 per cent). Elsewhere in the protectorate minerals belong to Government." See also Sir R. Coryndon in 'United Empire,' June 1920, p. 300.

claimed by Government in all controlled lands (which in Nyasaland and British Guiana are practically synonymous with the whole country), and all rights in minerals are reserved in leases of Crown lands.

The ownership of all minerals is claimed by France in her African colonies, and by the United States in the Philippines.[1] "The formal claim of the State to . . . all unworked minerals may be readily conceded by both international and municipal law," writes Professor Keith.[2] The reservation of the right of the natives to work any minerals which are necessary for their own industries or requirements—*e.g.*, iron, salt, &c.—is eminently just, and should always be conceded.[3]

In countries which are not highly industrialised, the bulk of the minerals are worked for export, and not for local manufacture, and the royalty imposed by Government is in fact an export duty, which the Government has an unquestioned right to levy for revenue purposes. The claim of ownership therefore means in effect that the right to grant licences for the working of minerals, not required by the natives for their own use, is vested in the Government, and that the owner of the surface rights in the land may not impose any additional royalties *in situ*.

The claim of Government to unworked minerals does not deprive the natives of any customary rights or profits. Their discovery is generally due to the technical knowledge of alien prospectors, and the possibility of their exploitation usually depends on the scientific methods, and the use of the machinery imported by Europeans. In those countries, therefore, in which the Government exercises the right to dispose of vacant lands and of mineral rights to aliens, it secures two important sources of revenue, to defray the cost of administration and development, without encroaching on the customary rights or requirements of the people. The revenue thus realised is expended wholly on the country to the benefit of its inhabitants, and diminishes *pro tanto* the amount it is necessary to raise by taxation for this purpose.

On the other hand, the Government is better able to take measures—impossible to a native grantor—to exclude those

[1] 'The Philippines,' Elliott, vol. ii. p. 69.

[2] 'Journal of African Society,' July 1918.

[3] In Nigeria tin had been worked in small quantities for ornaments or barter, and the small group of villages engaged in this industry were compensated.

concession-hunters who desire to obtain a title merely for manipulation in the money market, and to ensure that the interests of the *bona fide* miner are, as far as possible, identical with those of the country in which his profits are made. These objects can best be effected, *inter alia*, by requiring a guarantee that the grantee, or his assignee, has adequate capital for his enterprise, and by insisting on an annual minimum of development work, so that mineral resources may not be locked up for speculative reasons.

Government control should also result in the elimination of much litigation, due to overlapping or to badly-drafted concessions. The licensee is relieved of the initial purchase price of his concession, and his working capital is thus increased. He can therefore afford to pay a somewhat larger share of his profits by way of rents and royalties—a system more advantageous alike to the industry and to the country, which thus retains a direct interest in mineral development. The position of the grantee is more secure when he has to deal with Government alone, and enterprise is thus attracted, while Government is less hampered in securing adequate development and the best conditions for labourers.

Minerals, as I have already remarked, are a part of the capital wealth of a country, not perennially renewed like its vegetable products, and their development should afford a means for creating other assets of permanent utility, such as railways, harbours, irrigation works, &c., which shall continue to benefit the country when the minerals are exhausted.

Viewed from this standpoint, it seems a short-sighted, even if it is a justifiable policy, for the Suzerain Power to barter these assets, as was done in the case of the transfer of the Niger Chartered Company's territory to the Crown.[1] The Company, which claimed to have secured mineral rights by treaty from native chiefs, was entirely justified in making the best bargain it could for its shareholders, and no one will

[1] Parliamentary Papers, C. 9372 of 1899, 39 of August 1900, and 304 of February 1901. Within a defined area embracing the greater part of Northern Nigeria, whether covered by the Company's treaties or not, the Government undertook to impose such royalty on all minerals exported from a British port, or passing through a British Customs House, as may be compatible with the development of the industry, and to institute no specific taxation on the mining industry as such, which would prevent its imposition. The Company and its assigns were to receive half the royalty for ninety-nine years. As the price of its land and mining rights in the remainder of its territory a sum of £150,000 was paid.

be found to grudge to these patriotic pioneers the fullest recompense for their efforts. But one wonders how many of them have benefited from the prosperity of the mining industry in Nigeria. Shares have changed hands, but the onus on the industry, and on the revenues of Nigeria—upon which falls the whole cost of the Mines Department, survey, collection of royalties and rents, &c.—remains. It is to be regretted that a money payment, as in the case of the commercial lands, was not made, even if it had remained a charge on the revenues of the country.[1]

Where native ownership of minerals worked for export is recognised, the monies received for the concession, rents, &c., are, like the rents of tribal lands, the property of the community, and should be expended for the common benefit—viz., paid into the native administration treasury or communal fund, and not used (as it appears that they often are) as the private perquisite of the chiefs. If the land has changed from tribal to individual tenure, the ownership of minerals requires elucidation. They should, I think, be vested in the Government on behalf of the whole community.

The terms upon which prospecting rights and mining leases may be granted must obviously vary according to the mineral sought, and the form in which it occurs. The task of the administrator of a colony when drafting legislation on this complicated subject has been lightened by the recent publication of the mining laws of the different parts of the Empire in a compendious form. The conditions, for instance, which affect the winning of gold when found in quartz rock lying perhaps at considerable depths below the surface, and those affecting alluvial or placer deposits, must differ essentially, and the mining law must deal fully and separately with each class. I do not propose to do more than make a few general notes on this subject here.

The function of the Government is, on the one hand, to facilitate in every possible way the enterprise of the prospector and miner, and, on the other hand, to protect the native occupier of the land from injury resulting from mining operations, and to ensure fair treatment and reasonable comfort for the native labourer.

The exploitation of the mineral resources of a country

[1] The annual payment to the Niger Company amounted to some £70,000 in 1917, and is steadily increasing.

can best be promoted in the first instance by a comprehensive geological survey, such as is now being undertaken by most of the Governments of the Crown colonies. When minerals have been found, the first demand of the industry is for a clear and understandable mining law and regulations, and expert Departments of Mines and Surveys, which shall deal rapidly with claims, and surveys of leases, &c. Means of access by railway, to facilitate the import of machinery and supplies, and where necessary, the export of ore, is essential to development. All these things take some time to provide, especially if the revenues of the country are small, and delays are apt to give rise to acrid criticism, however anxious the Government may be to assist.

On the other hand, it devolves upon the Government to protect the interests of the natives, more especially in alluvial or open-cast workings, where surface rights, including the acquisition of land, and interference with water-courses and the supply of water for the agricultural and domestic needs of the natives, are involved. Nor can the duty of protecting the country from deforestation be neglected. There is a natural tendency to denude the country of timber for pit-props and fuel, which, while affording only a temporary advantage to the industry, inflicts a permanent injury on the country, as may be seen in the mining districts of South Africa.

General prospecting licences are usually granted for a year at a time, for a small fee, and unrestricted in area. They should, in my opinion, convey no important rights, such as cutting of timber, damming of streams, &c., and are more in the nature of a registration fee than a payment for special privileges. Exclusive prospecting licences, on the other hand, convey definite rights, for which a corresponding payment can be demanded. No other person may prospect the area simultaneously, and the prospector has the right to acquire one or more mining leases in the area included in his exclusive licence. He may cut timber, and use water under conditions, and on compensation to natives for injury. These licences should be very limited in area and in time, in order to avoid locking up the country to the exclusion of other enterprise. An exclusive prospecting licence should not be transferable without permission, and this should be clearly endorsed upon it to prevent its being used for purposes of speculation.

Mining leases for alluvial and open-cast workings should not exceed one square mile.[1] The term might be fifty years, and the rent need not be high, for the industry is taxed by royalties. Premia are unnecessary. Royalties on metals, whose price is constantly varying, can best be fixed by a sliding scale, framed on the value in the London market. In the facilities granted for prospecting and mining there should, of course, be no discrimination between natives and non-natives. Minerals such as gold and tin, which by erosion have been detached from their matrix and carried down by streams—falling by their weight to the stream-bed—are naturally sought for in streams, and in the beds of former streams. The winning of these minerals in such circumstances must involve interference with water-courses, and necessitates the use of water for washing the soil containing the ore. Special care is therefore needed to safeguard the native rights in the water-supply and in the disposal of tailings. To facilitate the exploitation of ground not rich in ore, and to assist the operations of the miner with small capital, "mining rights" as opposed to "mining leases" are granted in Nigeria. These are tenable for a year—renewable from year to year—and convey certain privileges as regards wood and water.

There is no temptation to Colonial Governments to interfere with private enterprise by creating monopolies in the working of minerals other than coal and oil. A temporary monopoly in the working of a coalfield may not only be justified but highly expedient, in order to prove the extent and quality of the seams, and to enable the Government to form a reliable estimate of the cost of winning, and the value of the coal at pit's mouth or delivered at the coast, with a view to determining what royalty the industry can bear, and what would be a fair price to fix for supplies needed by Government.

It will, moreover, be more than probable that a railway must be built to the coalfield, and since (for reasons I shall discuss in the chapter on Transport) it is advisable that all railways should be built and operated by the Colonial Government, it becomes essential that the Government should have the best possible independent technical advice as to the

[1] Sir F. Fuller mentions that the Ashanti Gold Fields Syndicate were granted mineral and other rights over 100 square miles.—*Loc. cit.*, p. 227.

value of the field before committing itself to the cost of railway construction. The scheme of development of a coal-field is a highly technical matter, depending on geological and other conditions, and in order to avoid wasteful methods it is necessary that Government should be in full possession of all data regarding the deposits before leasing the whole or any portion to a company, so that the conditions of development may be carefully prescribed.[1]

Initial investigation would cost a considerable sum of money, and delay must be incurred before the railway facilities can be created. A private company would demand very liberal terms to induce it to accept these risks and delays, and the lease would therefore necessarily be of a highly speculative nature. In these circumstances it cannot, I think, be disputed that an enterprise so vital to the future of the country, and involving railway and probably harbour construction, should be initiated by the Government. When the industry has been proved, the Government can, if it desires, reserve a portion of the field for its own railway and steamship requirements, and lease the remainder to private companies. Its expert staff on the spot will then be able to carry out the periodical inspection necessary to see that the lease conditions of development are being fulfilled.

Boring for oil offers no obstacle to private enterprise, since the oil if found can be piped without railway connection. If the geological investigations conducted by Government have afforded indications, correspondingly favourable terms can be demanded from the lessee. The lien on the supply for the needs of the Imperial Navy, to which I have elsewhere referred, is justified by the dependence of the colony on the Navy for its defence.

[1] This is the policy which has been followed in regard to the Enugu coalfield in Nigeria. Germany, by a decree of 4th December 1901, reserved any coal found on north-west of Nyasa as a Government monopoly.

CHAPTER XVII.

SLAVERY IN BRITISH AFRICA.

The origin of slavery—Effects of slavery—Growth of opinion adverse to slavery—The position in East Africa—The nature of Central African slave-trade—Realisation by Europe of the real facts—Effect of the scramble for Africa—The Brussels Act—Suppression by force—Slavery as an administrative problem—Tribal slavery, or alien masters—Predial and domestic slaves—Moslem slave-law—Evils of slavery and extenuations—Internal slavery in Africa—Slavery in protected Moslem States—Compensation and alternatives—Meaning of the abolition of the "legal status"—Results of abolition of legal status—Its application at Zanzibar.

Of all African problems there is none more engrossing than that of slavery, and as to assist in its solution has been the consistent object of my efforts since I first entered tropical Africa in 1888, I will ask indulgence if in discussing it I digress somewhat beyond the strict limits of present-day administrative problems.

Though the institution of slavery appears to be as old as the records of the human race,[1] and exists to-day in China [2] and in Moslem countries, it is from Africa alone that large sections of the population have, in at all recent times, been

[1] For an exhaustive historical review of the subject, reference may be made to Dr Ingram's learned article in the 'Encyclopædia Britannica,' 9th edition, vol. xxii. pp. 129-144. It may be noted that "slave-holding and its ally polygamy" have exhibited a tendency to flourish in the tropics rather than in the temperate zones. In the latter, the transition to serfs or villeins—*adscripti glebæ*—and from serfdom to a free peasantry has generally been a normal process not unduly prolonged. Adam Smith points out that the transition from the serf to the freeman is encouraged by the sovereign, who grows fearful of the power of his feudal retainers and their armies of serfs.—Book iii. chap. 2.

[2] Slavery in China assumes a mild form. Sale of the freeborn is illegal though common. Girls are bought, often as infants, and become household drudges until marriage, when they are free. Slaves are recruited chiefly by the sale of themselves or their children by a starving peasantry in time of famine or inundation. See Dyer Ball, 'Things Chinese,' pp. 623-628.

deported for use as slaves overseas.[1] The institution, though fundamentally opposed to the principles of Christian ethics, was not specifically condemned by St Paul, who even directed the rendition of a fugitive slave,[2] probably because in his day it had become so integral a part of the social system that to have condemned it would have conflicted with his teaching of obedience to constituted authority; but the influence of the Church has been opposed to it from the earliest times.

The incorporation in the tribe of the captives of war as slaves is indeed regarded by Dr Ingram as a "universal and inevitable accompaniment" of the stage of human evolution when sedentary habits replaced nomadic tendencies; and since it taught the necessity for continuous labour, he characterises it—as did Zebehr Pasha—as "a necessary step in social progress," superseding the earlier law of massacre and cannibalism.[3]

But however inevitable in the earliest stages of development the institution of slavery may be, its moral results are undeniably disastrous. To the slave-owners the exercise of despotic power, without external check, in all the relations of daily life is demoralising. Self-control is weakened, susceptibility to flattery, harshness or even cruelty, as well as immorality, are encouraged, and indolence, with a contempt for industry, becomes natural.

To the slave the effect is hardly less demoralising. He is deprived of the dignity of manhood. He is without responsibility and without incentive to work other than the fear of punishment. His status approximates to that of his master's cattle.[4]

[1] Calculations of the number of human beings killed or enslaved are purely guesswork. Pruen ('The Arab and African,' p. 224) estimates that fully 100,000 reached the East Coast yearly, and Livingstone and others considered that at least 10 are killed or left to starve for each one who arrives. This gives 1,000,000 per annum for the East Coast alone—a figure which may presumably be at least doubled for the rest of Africa. This has been going on for centuries!

[2] Philemon 10 and 16.

[3] So also Congreve, commenting on the passage of 'Aristotle' quoted in the next paragraph, "the human rival is the food of his conqueror. The first step out of this state of things is taken when the prisoners are not sacrificed and eaten, but kept and made useful."

[4] See Ingram, *loc. cit.* Also Clarke, 'Lavigerie and Slavery,' p. 246. The slave laws of various countries have a striking similarity to each other. The Moslem law varies little from that of the Hebrews described in Deuteronomy, or of Rome, or that of the Anglo-Saxons.—(See Green's 'History of the English People,' Colonial Press Edition, p. 18, and Buckland, 'The Roman Law of

"Certain peoples," says Aristotle, "are naturally free, others are naturally slaves. For these latter slavery is both just and expedient," and the same view has been held by able and influential men of our own day. To the African, they argue, owing to his lack of prevision and self-control, such a state of dependence is not altogether distasteful, and philanthropic effort can best be directed towards regulating the conditions of slavery as a recognised institution.[1] But they overlook two vital facts—first, that the history of slavery in all countries shows that the system cannot be maintained without constant recruitment, involving all the horrors of slave-raids, or of kidnapping and purchase, with depopulation of the country, decrease in its productivity, and stagnation in its development;[2] and secondly, that by perpetuating the institution of slavery the African is denied the opportunity of rising to a higher plane of individual and corporate responsibility and progress in social life.

The intellectual and moral progress of Europe and America had, at the beginning of the last century, led their people to condemn the overseas export of slaves from Africa,[3] which had been inaugurated by Portugal in 1442, but it was not till the middle of the nineteenth century that the majority of the nations abolished the system of employing slave labour.[4]

Slavery.') The slave may not give evidence in court. His master is responsible for his crimes. Wrongs to him are regarded as wrongs to his master, who has absolute power over him. These laws were modified by the "*jus naturale*" in Rome, and by the growth of a more liberal practice in other countries, as the predial slave passed to the status of a serf, and the domestic slave became included in the family.

[1] The notorious German, Dr Karl Peters, is reported to have proposed that a "fair arrangement" would be that the natives should be hired out by the State to work for eleven hours a day from the age of twenty to thirty-five years. The African, he contends, does not understand freedom, and "such a system would form a convenient half-way house between slavery and the European system of free labour—the result of centuries." Herr Zimmermann's policy differs only in degree (*loc. cit.*, pp. 39-45). English apologists for slavery, needless to say, do not advocate such methods.

[2] The writings of all African explorers are full of evidence of the ruthless destruction of life and the human misery caused by slave-raids, and of the appalling cruelties of the march to the coast. A résumé of the evidence may be found in Rev. R. Clarke's book, 'Cardinal Lavigerie and Slavery in Africa,' pp. 254-287. For an account of the appalling devastation in the Sudan, where the population was reduced from 8½ millions to under 2 millions in a few years, see Foreign Office Handbook 98, p. 26, and the authorities there quoted.

[3] Denmark led the way, 1802; England followed, 1806; America in 1808; the Dutch in 1814; Spain in 1820. The movement which led to these decisions had been growing both in England and America for 100 years previously.

[4] England emancipated her West Indian and other slaves in 1833; France in 1848; Portugal in 1858 decreed emancipation without compensation in 20 years. America, Brazil, and Cuba alone remained.

This was not effected in America till after the Civil War, while serfdom in Russia was abolished the year before.

There was naturally no sympathy with the movement for the abolition of slavery in Moslem countries like Turkey, Arabia, and Zanzibar, where the institution was an integral part of the social system, sanctioned alike by religion and by the civil law.

Though the export of slaves from Africa to America had been prohibited, the traffic was so lucrative, so long as slave labour continued to be employed, that it lingered on as a smuggling trade from the West Coast till late in the 'sixties. Great Britain took steps to suppress it, and for this purpose formed settlements and forts at the Gold Coast, and in 1861 acquired Lagos. With the cessation of the traffic she proposed in 1868 to abandon them. From the Mediterranean ports (especially Benghazi), and from those on the East Coast, however, an active export was carried on to supply the requirements of Turkey, Arabia, and Persia, and also Madagascar.[1]

In the 'seventies Zanzibar was a powerful independent State, claiming an undefined sovereignty over the mainland of Eastern Africa as far as the Great Lakes. The Sultan and the ruling class were Arabs from Muscat in the Persian Gulf. The British Consul-General was Sir John Kirk, companion of Livingstone, and a man of very exceptional ability, who had acquired great influence over the Sultan. As early as 1873 he had succeeded in inducing him to make a treaty declaring the export of slaves from the mainland illegal, and in 1876 an edict was issued prohibiting their arrival at the coast from the interior. The edicts, however, remained a dead letter.

For over half a century Great Britain had maintained a squadron in East African waters for the suppression of this trade. After the Sultan's edicts, H.M.S. *London*, especially equipped with a mosquito fleet, seized many dhows, which were condemned in the Consular Court. She was withdrawn in 1883, and two Vice-Consuls were appointed on the coast and one on Lake Nyasa. The latter, as I have said (p. 29), was without jurisdiction, and when he was seized by a slave-trading chief, stripped, and imprisoned, nothing was

[1] There can, I fear, be little doubt that, unknown of course to Lisbon, the Portuguese in Africa, at least as late as 1888, continued to transport slaves rom one of their possessions to another (nominally as deportees for some trivial offence) in order to recruit their local levies.—See 'Rise of East African Empire,' vol. i. p. 13.

done. These operations had been costly both in lives and money,[1] and the result was wholly inadequate. Of the thousands of slaves arriving at the coast, the Uganda railway survey report estimates that only about 120 per annum were rescued. The squadron, though a check on the sea-borne traffic, was of course unable to touch the trade on the mainland, or even to control the transport of slaves thence to the islands, which continued to be abundantly supplied with slaves.[2]

The withdrawal of H.M.S. *London* was marked by a considerable increase in the slave-trade, though British naval vessels continued to capture dhows. In 1885 the Berlin Act was signed, Turkey being a signatory Power. It stipulated that each of the Powers "binds itself to use all the means at its disposal to put an end to the slave-trade, and to punish those engaged in it." But the export by Arab dhows continued; and even when in 1889 a joint blockade of the coast was instituted by Great Britain and Germany, ostensibly to deprive the slave-traders of arms, but practically in order to withhold from the Arabs—with whom the Germans were at war—weapons with which to defend themselves, it was estimated that not 5 per cent of the slaves exported were rescued. These measures were moreover of little value to the slaves themselves, for it was impossible to repatriate them.

The trade was carried on by the Arab, Swaheli,[3] and Beluchi subjects of the Zanzibar Sultan. Many of these men had made very large profits by trading in ivory and slaves. With these they purchased weapons and armed their "Ruga-ruga"—at first as elephant-hunters. Taking part in some tribal quarrel, and increasing their armed bands, they and their allies soon became the dominant power, and could raid the

[1] The cost was estimated by a writer in the 'Times' at £200,000 per annum (29th August 1893). Consul O'Neill, formerly an officer of the *London*, considered that not less than 5 millions had been spent in the last 50 years.—'The Mozambique and Nyassa Slave Trade,' p. 9. Mr Waller stated that between 1880 and 1890 our crews had suffered 282 casualties, besides invalidings.—'Ivory Apes and Peacocks,' p. 44.

[2] Africa, No. 6 of 1893, p. 1. These facts and figures are given at greater length in my book, 'The Rise of our East African Empire,' vol. i. chapters vii. and viii. The statements there made were either prompted or viséd by Sir John Kirk, the highest authority on the subject, who for 20 years was Consul-General at Zanzibar, and later British plenipotentiary at the Brussels Conference.

[3] Literally "coast men," some of them the offspring of Arabs and female slaves, others slaves from the interior who had become domiciled at the coast.

entire district for slaves. Many tribes had also become slave-raiders on behalf of the Arabs, and sold their captives to them.

Many following in the path opened by Stanley and Cameron, like Tippoo Tib on the Congo, became powerful despots, practically independent of Zanzibar. Their dhows sailed on all the Great Lakes. By the year 1888 they had grown to be the greatest militant power in the interior of the Continent. Already they had almost turned the shadowy claims of Zanzibar into an actual Moslem Empire, no longer controlled by the Sultan, whose influence had been weakened by the advent of the British and Germans at the coast. Throughout Central Africa they poisoned the minds of the natives by saying that Europeans were cannibals, &c. There is some evidence that they had formed a league. The loss of the Nile Sudan by the Mahdist rising had dealt a heavy blow to European prestige. On Nyasa alone, one of their most important raiding centres and routes, the slavers were opposed by a band of Scottish traders. They now threw off the pretence of friendship, and attacked the little garrison at Karongas, which held the gate.[1]

But England had at last realised the futility of the attempt to suppress the slave traffic by chasing dhows at sea, and that if the evil which the Powers at Berlin had pledged themselves to check was to be suppressed, it must be dealt with at its source. While Emin on the Albert Lake, and the garrison at Karongas on Nyasa, were doing what they could with inadequate resources on the spot, Cardinal Lavigerie began his crusade in Europe. He preached a "Holy War" against Moslem domination in Africa and the slave-trade—a "Continental blockade," with a line of "anti-slavery stations supported by gunboats on the Great Lakes, and a central force of 500 European crusaders."[2] Others, like Victor Hugo, advocated European settlements; others again thought that the redemption of Africa must be by Africans, and looked to the return from America of a great body of emancipated negroes to liberate the country of their birth.[3]

[1] The story is told in my book, 'The Rise of our East African Empire,' vol. i. chapters iii., iv., and v.

[2] 'Lavigerie and the Slave Trade,' pp. 327, 343, &c.

[3] I prepared a scheme myself in much detail, supported by estimates framed with the advice of experts. Its basis was a well-armed and equipped native force, located on the plateau between Lakes Nyasa and Tanganyika, with armed transport steamers—not gunboats—on both lakes, capable of transport-

It was at this critical moment that the realisation by the industrial nations of Europe of the vast commercial resources of Africa led to the competition for territorial sovereignty between Great Britain, Germany, and France to which I have already referred—a movement, no doubt, accelerated and strengthened by the powerful support of those who advocated the suppression of the slave-trade by force in the interior, and the defence of mission and trading stations. Events marched quickly. In 1889 Great Britain and Germany took over the Sultan's territories on the mainland, and the latter declared war against the Arabs. In 1890 Uganda made a treaty with the British Chartered Company, and the Mohamedan party there was finally defeated. A British mission was sent to Nyasa, and shortly afterwards a protectorate was declared. The Congo State declared war on Tippoo Tib; France annexed Madagascar—a great receiving depot for slaves from the mainland—and began her long campaign against the Mohamedans of North Africa.

The days of the oversea slave-trade were numbered. The power of the great resident slavers in the interior was broken, but for the moment the organised Moslem despotisms on the Nile and in West Africa were too powerful to be affected by these measures, and they continued to raid and depopulate the countries over which they ruled.

Already, in 1889, sixteen of the principal nations of the world had assembled at Brussels, and agreed to take common action for the suppression of the slave-trade. They declared "in the name of Almighty God" their "firm intention of putting an end to the crimes and devastations engendered by the traffic in African slaves." The Act was signed on 2nd July 1890, but was not finally ratified till April 1892.[1]

Its framers could not foresee the astonishing rapidity with which the effective occupation of tropical Africa was to proceed; and though the opening words declared that "the most effective means for counteracting the slave-trade in the

ing a striking force with its supplies, &c., to any point where a slave-caravan was heard of. I hoped eventually to control a line from the north of Tanganyika to the mouth of the Zambesi—1100 miles—of which all but 200 was waterway, and so occupy the line which Livingstone had said would cut the slave-trade in half. Mr Rhodes agreed to finance the project, but other events interfered.—See "Two Ends of a Slave-Stick," by Rev. H. Waller, in 'Contemporary Review,' April 1889.

[1] C. 6048 of 1890.

interior are progressive organisation of the administrative, judicial, religious, and military services " of the Powers concerned, they proceeded to indicate, as a means to this end, the establishment of strongly-occupied stations, fortified posts on navigable waterways, expeditions and flying columns for repressive action, the use of cruisers on the great lakes, and stations of refuge, in addition to maritime suppression. More appropriate in the event were the recommendations to adopt administrative methods—such as the construction of roads, railways, and telegraphs, the use of steamers on navigable waters, and the encouragement of commerce and missions.

But the most essential and operative clauses of the Act (Arts. 8 & 14) were those binding the signatories to prevent the import into Africa, except under strong guarantees, of all firearms and ammunition, other than flint-lock guns and trade powder, between lat. 20 N. and 22 S. Great Britain had been one of the principal importers of arms to Africa, but since the ratification of the Act she has been foremost in her efforts to observe its obligations. Articles 62 to 70 referred to countries which are the destination of slaves, and contained special undertakings by the Sultans of Turkey and Zanzibar and the Shah of Persia, who were signatories.

This Act was the *Magna Charta* of the African slave, and Sir John Kirk's share, as our plenipotentiary, in its production was a fitting consummation to his life-work. With the ratification of the Brussels Act a new era dawned. Africa had passed, or was passing, under the control of different European nations, and though occupation had not yet become fully effective, the obligations of those who claimed territorial sovereignty were now clearly acknowledged.

It was not till the Mahdi was conquered by Kitchener in 1898 that effective control could be exercised in the Sudan. In Nigeria, where the Moslem Emirs annually employed large armies in raiding for slaves and had depopulated great regions,[1] the Imperial Government assumed control in 1900, and in spite of the pressure of the South African and the Ashanti wars, the power of the Fulani was broken in 1902 and 1903, and slave-raiding put an end to. A system founded on the tyrannical and bestial misuse of force had been crushed by force—the only method which could be understood by the

[1] Northern Nigeria Annual Report, Colonial Office Series 409 of 1902. See also Barth's 'Travels in Central Africa,' vol. iii. pp. 225, 233-236, *et passim*.

people. Omelettes cannot be made without breaking eggs. There were those, no doubt, who said that slave-raiding could only be suppressed by the construction of railways and the introduction of currency—neither of which was possible in a country openly hostile, which admitted the ingress of no Europeans. Such methods would have required one or two decades to accomplish. From a distance they advocated patience. Why hurry, though villages were burning and the remnant of the people was being wiped out?

The atrocities of the slave-trade and the decision to abolish it were the immediate expression of a conflict between two rival ideals, supported by two great world forces—that of militant Islam [1] on the one hand, with its disregard for life and its selfish appropriation by the powerful of all that was desirable; and that, on the other hand, of the nations assembled at Brussels in 1889—as they assembled at Paris three decades later—to declare their Mandate, "in the name of God Almighty," as trustees for "protecting effectively the aboriginal populations of Africa, and ensuring to that vast continent the benefits of peace and civilisation." Not all perhaps of those who have given their lives to the task recognised the greatness of the issue. Material as well as moral forces were at work—and it is well that the conflict came when it did.

With this brief historical and descriptive introduction, I pass to the discussion of slavery from the standpoint more proper to the object of this volume—viz., as an administrative problem. In the first place, it will be useful to consider what slavery is, and what are the conditions which distinguish the lot of a slave from a freeman. We may, I think, assume that there are three factors which affect the lot of a slave most nearly: (*a*) whether he is of the same race as his master; (*b*) the nature of the law (if any) affecting his status; and (*c*) what facilities it gives him for advancement or redemption.

Slaves captured in tribal war, or sold by one tribe to another

[1] It fell to my personal lot to fight *militant* Islam in the Sudan, on Nyasa, in Uganda and in Nigeria, but the repatriation of the Moslem Waganda by me, and my subsequent relations with the Moslem rulers in the latter country, will, I think, show that it was against it as an aggressive force, and not as a creed, that I found myself on so many occasions opposed to it in arms. My action gave rise to charges of militarism in Press and Parliament, and Mr Woolf (whose book is otherwise devoid of humour) describes me as possessed by a homicidal mania.—'Empire and Commerce,' p. 273.

for crime or debt, though they may not speak the language of their captors, are generally closely allied to them in race, and in the same stage of social development. Apart from the possibilities of fetish sacrifice, of reservation for a cannibal feast, or of being killed at their master's death to accompany him to another world—all of which may, I trust, be accounted to be horrors of the past—the life of such a slave would not differ greatly from that of his captor, except that he would have to work harder. He would become the lowest grade in the social scale, while the condition of women captives would generally be identical with those of the tribe. Probably in course of time the male slave would also become identified with the tribe.[1] In some cases the institution of slavery may have been copied from alien slave-dealers. Slaves, on the other hand, whose owners were either Arabs or Fulani, would be subject to either harsh or liberal treatment, according to the temperament or whim of their master, like the Gibeonites in the Hebrew State, or the Helots of Greece. Last of all came those who were shipped overseas, or sent to a country and a mode of life as different from their own as Egypt or Morocco.

The predial slave, employed to till his owner's fields, has, as we have seen, a tendency to become a serf attached to the land, and eventually a free peasant, like the Bakopi in Uganda,[2] rendering a portion of his produce to his landlord. But until he gains this higher status he may be punished with severity, or sold, or his family may be taken from him and sold. Nothing he possesses during life can be called his own, and at death any substance he may have been allowed to acquire passes to his owner. To what extent these harsh rights may be enforced depends on the law and custom to which his master is subject.

The lot of the domestic slave differs with sex. The male, unless he be a favourite, has a harder time than the predial slave, his work is more arduous, his family life more pre-

[1] The conditions vary according to tribal usages. Dr Laws writes of Nyasaland: "Domestic slavery, as far as I know, exists among all the tribes, and varies in severity from a nominal connection to the power of life and death exercised by the master." Among the Waganda, on the other hand, the predial slaves are practically serfs, with few disabilities.—See 'Our East African Empire,' vol. i. p. 171, Wilson's 'Uganda and Sudan,' vol. i. p. 186, and Monson's Report, Cd. 1631 of 1903, p. 2.

[2] Felkin, *loc. cit.*, pp. 46 and 50.

carious, and he has less of the responsibility of a human being. Slaves are, however, often so attached to their masters that they do not desire their freedom. The question of female slavery is inextricably mixed up with that of concubinage—on which I shall have something to say later. At the worst, by transfer or loan, a female slave may become a prostitute by order. At the best she is mother of her master's child, and freed.

The Koran inculcates kindness to slaves, and the liberation of a slave is an act of piety. Though the native courts are empowered in a British protectorate to administer Mohamedan law, it is superseded by any ordinances enacted by the Government. In West Africa the Malaki law and the local custom are extraordinarily liberal—probably more so than the Mohamedan law of East Africa. The sale of a house-born slave, except for gross misconduct, is regarded as an unjustifiable act, and so is the separation by sale of a slave family. Slaves may attain to high rank and power. Ill-treatment of a slave is strongly condemned, and if a slave can prove it, he would be liberated by the court. Slaves may even be allowed to give evidence in court. A woman who has borne a living child to her master is freed. While Arab owners claimed that since a slave has no existence as a man, his liberator stands *in loco parentis*, and can claim the rights of a father, the Malaki law recognised no rights whatever over the slave once freed.[1]

Slavery as an institution is, as I have said, essentially bad, demoralising to the master, and debasing to the slave, whom (except in rare instances) it robs of ambition, initiative, and responsibility. It is economically bad, for the freeman does more work than the slave, who, moreover, is indifferent

[1] Slaves were given every facility for ransoming themselves under a system known as "Murgu."—*Vide infra*, p. 383. Household slaves were generally treated as members of the family, often with affection. Predial slaves were not transferred with the land, and except for arbitrary demands, when their master needed money, were practically independent. The master supplied seed and implements, and claimed a percentage of the produce. Manumission was decreed if a slave were ill-treated, and if a slave wished to educate himself, a grant might be made from the charity fund. The Resident of Sokoto (Mr Arnett) writes: "In discussing slavery matters with the Sokoto chiefs, one is always conscious of their extremely enlightened and surprisingly liberal views. They are as ready as any European to deplore the inhumanity and moral and material ravages caused by slavery."—See also Sir A. Hardinge's Report on slavery in East Africa, Cd. 8683 of 1897, and Consul Monson, Cd. 1631 of 1903. He strongly defends the liberal character of the slave-law in East Africa.

to the productivity of the soil and careless of posterity. Barth noted, as we do to-day, the more thorough agricultural methods of the independent tribes compared with the land under slave cultivation. Domestic slavery creates a demand for new slaves to replace losses, and hence encourages the slave-trade. It is the most serious charge against Islam in Africa that it has encouraged and given religious sanction to slavery.

On the other hand, in an early stage of civilisation, *provided that it is not recognised by law*, so that the slave, if ill-treated, can leave his master, the temporary continuance of domestic slavery has certain advantages as a form of labour-contract between a more advanced and a very primitive people, where the conception of labour as a saleable commodity (but without the sale of the labourer himself) has not yet arisen, and currency with which to pay wages is unknown, or exists only in a very primitive form. The master must look after his slave in sickness and old age. He clothes, feeds, and protects him. If the public opinion of the community is sound and enlightened, the slave is assured of good treatment, and even the dead hand of inertia may be lifted by giving him the aspiration of redemption. In tribal slavery, however, where the owner is in the same stage of evolution as the slave, these obligations would not be recognised.

The point of view of an intelligent African regarding slavery was well expressed by Zebehr Pasha in conversation: "Slavery you say is bad. I agree that it is bad, but slave-labour is to the interior of Africa what steam-power is to your country. In your great factories where steam is used, is all well with the employees? Is there not much misery and suffering? You admit there is. Well, if the angel of God came and saw the unhappiness of your factories and said: 'This must not continue—abolish steam,' would you think it a wise decree? Would you not think it wiser to find means of alleviating the suffering? And so it is with slavery. You cannot say abolish slavery all at once because in some cases it has caused much suffering."

"The slavery question" naturally divides itself into two distinct though closely-related branches—the acquisition of and dealing in slaves, and the status of slavery as a social institution.

Prior to 1888 it was not, I think, fully realised in England that the acquisition of slaves for overseas export formed only one phase of the evil. The internal demand was also very great. Morocco, Tunis, Tripoli and Egypt, the Zanzibar territories on the mainland and islands, and the Moslem States of Nigeria and French West Africa—all these required enormous numbers of slaves. Still less perhaps was it realised that slavery is an indigenous institution in Africa. The native despotisms of Mtesa in Uganda, of Benin, Ashanti, and Dahomey made great demands for slaves, a large number of whom were sacrificed.

Even among the primitive tribes slavery was rampant. Sir J. Marshall gives a graphic account of his expedition to the tribes of the Lower Niger to endeavour to put a stop to the wholesale slave sacrifices there. "There is," he writes, "a terrible form of slavery prevalent throughout the whole of the Dark Continent which is not under European control. This is the slavery which every tribe is ready and anxious to practise upon other tribes. The very people who are constantly captured and carried off by the more powerful Arab tribes, are themselves everywhere addicted to the practice of doing the same thing to any neighbour they can conquer." [1] The same state of things prevails in Central and Eastern Africa.[2] Prisoners of war were enslaved if not killed. It was formerly asserted in Nyasaland that you could not send three men on a mission, or two would combine to enslave the third.

At the present day, however, sacrifice of slaves to fetish deities is, I hope, rare, and is dealt with whenever detected as ordinary crime. Inter-tribal war, and the capturing of slaves as prisoners, is practically a thing of the past. There remains an illicit traffic, chiefly in children, which twenty years of vigilance has failed to exterminate in Nigeria, and a certain amount of surreptitious kidnapping and slave-dealing, which will no doubt continue until education, combined with severe deterrent sentences, finally stamps it out.

The declaration of a protectorate over Zanzibar, and the inclusion of the Mohamedan regions of Nigeria and the Sudan under British administration, lead us to the consideration of the question as to how the institution of slavery should be dealt with in a Moslem country under the protection of a

[1] 'Lavigerie and Slavery,' p. 284 and pp. 316-327.
[2] Ibid., p. 342.

European Power, where the institution is not only recognised by the civil law, which we have adopted as the fundamental law, but also by the religion with which we have pledged ourselves not to interfere. In Zanzibar, for instance, the valuable clove plantations depended entirely upon slave labour.

However justly the vested rights of the slave-owner might be dealt with, it is clear that sudden emancipation would dislocate the whole social fabric. Men wholly unaccustomed to any sense of responsibility and self-provision would be thrown on the streets to fend for themselves. Slave concubines would become prostitutes. Masters, albeit with money in their pockets, would be ruined; industry would be at a standstill; and plantations would be wrecked before the new order could adjust itself.

An effort was made by England when she emancipated the slaves in the West Indies to bridge over this period of social upheaval by an apprentice system, which Mr Sturge,[1] M. Beaulieu and others, have conclusively shown to have been a disastrous failure. It was practically a temporary legalisation of slavery. In that case the owners had acquired their slaves under a system recognised by our Government, the validity of their claims was admitted by Lord Grey, and £20,000,000 was paid to them in compensation. But in Zanzibar the case was different. In view of the Sultan's edicts of 1873 and 1876, and the admitted fact that slaves do not multiply,[2] and rarely live more than eleven years on the coast, it was undeniable that in 1890 the large majority had been illegally acquired. Owners could urge no just claim for compensation in such a case—nor yet in Nigeria for slaves captured amid all the horrors of raiding expeditions. It would be monstrous, said Lord Grey, to reward those who trade in slaves.

What then should be our attitude towards masters and slaves respectively? Sudden emancipation had not proved a success, either in the West Indies or when adopted by the Chartered Company in the case of certain batches of slaves in East Africa,[3] whether viewed from the standpoint of the Government, which had to pay heavy compensation; the

[1] 'Compensation to Slave-Owners,' p. 13.
[2] Clarke, 'Lavigerie and Slavery,' p. 250. Ingram, *loc. cit.*
[3] Cd. 1631 of 1903, p. 4.

owner, who could obtain no labour for his estates; the community, which was disorganised; or the slave himself, who was demoralised.

Sir John Kirk, as ever, was ready with a solution. The East India Company had, he pointed out, eradicated slavery in British India without injustice, dislocation, or compensation, by enacting in 1843 the abolition of its legal status, and slavery had died a natural death.[1] Alternatively, as Portugal did in 1858, emancipation without compensation could be decreed at a date sufficiently distant to give the owners time to prepare for the change. Preferably the two methods should be combined by enacting, simultaneously with the abolition of the legal status, that all children born and all persons brought into the country subsequent to that date are free. This was the course adopted in Northern Nigeria. That the question is a social and not a religious one was shown by the action of the Sultan of Zanzibar—a strict Mohamedan—who of his own initiative decreed the abolition of slavery in the northern ports of his dominions, and again by the acquiescence of the Nigerian Emirs.

By abolishing slavery as a status known to the law, *permissive freedom* is granted to the slave. He becomes endowed with full civic rights. He can sue for ill-treatment, and cannot be seized if he leaves his master and asserts his freedom. The institution of domestic slavery is not thereby abolished, as would be the case under a decree of general emancipation. A master is not compelled to dismiss his slaves, and so long as the two work harmoniously together the law does not interfere. But the slave has the power of asserting his freedom at any time, and his master is actionable if he resorts to force to recover him.

The proposal, of course, only applies to Moslem countries, which possess a regular code of law—which we have accepted unless opposed to local ordinances or the dictates of humanity.[2]

[1] The decree of 1843 did not (as Lord Salisbury pointed out) affect the Native States in India. The universal abolition of the legal status in Northern Nigera was possible because the Moslem emirates were (as I emphasised in chapter x., p. 196 *et seq.*) constituted as dependent and not as independent States, though enjoying a large measure of self-rule. It is not in harmony with British traditions that British courts should recognise slavery, as they must do unless the institution has been expressly repudiated as a status known to the law.

[2] Since the acceptance of Koranic law is thus limited in a British protectorate, the abolition of the legal status is not an arbitrary interference with the *lex loci* as argued by the apologists of slavery.

In non-Moslem countries the institution of slavery has no legal status, and should be absolutely and entirely abolished in all its forms, and no claim or argument based on the existence of slavery in such countries should be recognised, either judicially or executively ; nor can Moslems outside the limits of the districts in which Moslem law is recognised have any claim to be dealt with otherwise than under the *lex loci*.

We have seen that sudden emancipation—compulsory alike on owner and slave—although it might be strictly justifiable, on the grounds that the slaves had been acquired in violation of treaties, or in opposition to the teaching of the Koran (which condemns slave-raiding, though admitting the right to enslave infidel captives of war), would be inexpedient and disastrous in its results. It would moreover create a bitter feeling of injustice, especially when the slaves had been inherited or bought for cash. The abolition of the legal status is, on the contrary, intended to be gradual and progressive in its operation—thc initiative lying with the slave and not with the law.

The owners, realising that slaves who assert their freedom cannot be recaptured or replaced, are compelled to treat them with kindness—a result which was at once apparent no less in East Africa (as Consul Monson relates) than in West Africa. Slave-dealing is simultaneously prohibited, and any attempt to sell would be rare, for the slave would not consent. A free labour market is encouraged. The secret acquisition of raw slaves, except small children, is not worth the risk, for they cannot be recovered if they desert. The continued existence of slavery under such conditions can only be temporary (for all children are born free), and domestic slavery ceases to be an incentive to the slave-trade.

It is to be regretted that this step was not at once taken when Zanzibar was declared a British protectorate, seeing that our Government had for years urged it upon the Sultan.[1] The edict of August 1890—issued under British auspices in spite of the Sultan's decrees of 1876 and 1889—even implied recognition of the rights of owners. Pressure was brougnt to bear upon the Government in the important debates of 1894 and 1895, when Mr Chamberlain, with Mr Pease (now Lord Gainford) and others, fought the battle of the slave,

[1] See Sir J. Kirk's despatch to Lord Granville of 11th November 1884, quoted by Mr Pease in the debate of June 1894.—Hansard, p. 239.

and I, with Sir John Kirk as my referee, was privileged to supply him with some of the facts and figures he needed.

It was not, however, till 6th April 1897 that the Sultan, at the instance of the British Government, at last issued a decree abolishing the legal status. At that time there were still about 100,000 slaves in the islands. The decree was subjected to severe criticism in the debate of 11th February 1898, on the ground that it extended to the islands only and not to the mainland, that concubines were exempted from participation in its provisions, and that it prescribed such elaborate procedure that not more than twenty or thirty slaves had been able to obtain their freedom in six months.[1]

That the Government was right in its endeavour to prevent a wholesale assertion of freedom, and so precipitate the evils I have described, no sensible man will deny, but the method adopted by the Foreign Office was open to criticism. "The abolition of the legal status," said Mr (now Marquis) Curzon, "means that every slave is at liberty to go to a court, constituted for the purpose, and claim his freedom." If the status is no longer recognised by the law, how can a person be held in a state of slavery, with the cognisance and approval of Government, until a court has adjudicated on his case? To make it a necessary antecedent to the recognition of freedom, that a slave should appear before a court and show adequate means of subsistence, is, in fact, a recognition of the slave-status by the court, which, if it refuses liberation, illegally relegates the applicant to continuance in slavery.[2]

An American after reading this chapter remarked to me that had the system here advocated of gradual and permissive freedom been adopted in the southern States of America, it is conceivable that the Civil War might have been averted.

[1] An excellent summary of the action taken in regard to slavery in the Sultan's dominions may be found in the Admiralty Handbook on Kenya, pp. 501-503 and 577-580.

[2] The debate afforded an excellent illustration of the peculiarly British methods of ignoring opportunities of consulting men of experience which our great Departments of State adopt. When challenged as to the reason why concubines were excluded from the decree, the Under-Secretary cited the recommendations of a young man who had been sent out by the Anti-Slavery Society to report on their behalf, instead of referring to the man whose verdict would have been accepted without question, who had been twenty years Consul at Zanzibar, was British plenipotentiary at Brussels, and was an experienced man of affairs.

CHAPTER XVIII.

SLAVERY IN BRITISH AFRICA (*Continued*).

The legal status and native courts—The change must be gradual—"House-rule"—Method of checking undue haste—Justification of methods—Results in Nigeria—Women and slavery—Purchase of wife or concubine—Employment of ex-slaves by Europeans—By natives in Government service—Enlistment of slaves—Self-redemption and ransom — Slave-dealing — Pawning — Disposal of freed slaves: (*a*) adults; (*b*) children—Inheritance in slaves—Special cases—Women-husbands—"Igba" in Benin—Slave-chiefs—The task of the past and of the future.

UNTIL the Government policy has become well understood, and acquiesced in by the Moslem rulers and judges, all slave cases should be heard in a British court. Later the native courts may be trusted to deal with them,—under the close supervision of the British staff until they have proved themselves thoroughly reliable. Native courts in Moslem districts administer Mohamedan law (which recognises slavery), and so long as the institution is not illegal they must continually be dealing with civil suits in which the existence of the status cannot be wholly ignored, and in particular it is desirable that they should issue certificates of freedom to ransomed slaves, since these have a special value in a Moslem community when issued by the acknowledged exponents of the Koran. How is this difficulty to be met?

In the first place, though native courts administer native law only, that law is superseded by any ordinances by Government. Native courts are bound, therefore, to recognise in their judicial decisions that slave-dealing is an offence, and that slavery has no legal existence. They cannot assist in detaining a slave or in enforcing the return of a runaway, nor can they discriminate in a judgment or sentence by reason of the fact that the defendant or accused is or was a slave, or because the fault or damage was committed by or upon a slave. But in civil suits they can use their powers of arbitration and conciliation with a due appreciation of all the facts, including the fact that one party has of his own free will accepted the relation of unpaid servant to another person, in return for food, lodging, &c. In order, however, that there may be no doubt as to the legality of the ransom paper, a special authorising clause is inserted in the Nigerian ordinance.

But if every slave can leave his master at will, what, it may be asked, is to prevent a sudden exodus, which would fill the cities with vagrants, criminals, and prostitutes, and pauperise the ruling classes, whom it is our desire to support and strengthen? If slaves were encouraged to assert their freedom wholesale, there would only be a difference in degree between this method and that of sudden and enforced emancipation, and those owners who, prior to the British rule, had under Moslem law legally acquired their slaves by inheritance or purchase, would be justly entitled to compensation for the loss of their property.

For the sake, therefore, alike of justice to the owners and in the interest of the slaves themselves, the Government (as Zebehr urged) must do all in its power to make the change as gradual as possible, and to give time for its constructive policy to mature. This was the dilemma which, as we have seen, embarrassed the Government of Zanzibar.

In Southern Nigeria, though not under Moslem law, the Government, faced with the same difficulty, enforced by ordinance the authority of the head of the "house" over all its members, who were chiefly recruited by slaves, and thus under the name of "house-rule" it practically legalised slavery. Government police actually arrested without warrant and restored fugitive slaves to their masters, nor was any person, European or native, allowed to employ a "member" without the consent of the head of the house.[1] These

[1] The ordinance was passed at a time when the local Government was almost powerless to enforce its authority on the tribes, armed as they were with Snider rifles. It was repealed shortly after the amalgamation. In his address to the Nigerian Council in December 1920 (delivered since these pages were written), my successor, Sir H. Clifford, speaks with regret of the "abolition of house-rule, since nothing was contrived to take its place." House-rule was never abolished, though the ordinance, which gave to its worst features the support of the law and of Government police, was by order of the Secretary of State (with my entire concurrence) repealed. A scheme which I had suggested, with

"houses" were a unique institution on the West Coast, and were primarily large native trading concerns. The house-rule system is more likely, I think, to have owed its origin to the powerful slave-trading chiefs, who in former days acted as purveyors of slaves for the overseas traffic, than to the patriarchal authority of the father of the family or tribe, as asserted by Mr Morel.[1] With the cessation of the slave-trade the houses for some years exercised a monopoly of the general trade with the interior. It is not, however, necessary to resort to either of the courses adopted in Zanzibar and in Southern Nigeria, which in effect are a denial of the pledges of Government.

We have seen that slaves are of two classes—household and predial. The household slave, born or long resident in his master's house, would rarely desire to assert his freedom unless he were a loafer and bad character, or his master had ill-treated or threatened to sell him, or unless he had been recently acquired. He would have become too dependent on his master, and unaccustomed to exercise initiative and free-will. He would have nowhere to go and no resources, while he sees around him the poverty of the vagrants in the great cities. He is generally apathetic, tolerant of control by nature, and prefers even to endure much ill-treatment rather than make a change, the consequences of which he cannot foresee. Moreover, master and slave are often much attached to each other, and the slave knows that in case of sickness, &c., his wife and children will be cared for. Even if recently captured in a raid, he knows that his home is destroyed, or if kidnapped, that his family will already have been broken up.

With the abolition of the legal status and the prohibition of slave-dealing, he no longer fears to be sold away from the connections he has formed, and he is fairly contented.[2] Africans of the lower classes, moreover, love to attach themselves

the hearty support of those who knew the country best, to strengthen the legitimate functions of the "houses" was not approved by Mr Harcourt. For a fuller description of the ordinance, see Cmd. 468/1920, § 23.

[1] 'Nigeria,' Morel, pp. 62, 63.

[2] In the days of unchecked slavery, slaves did desert in considerable numbers, especially from the Arab plantations on the mainland of East Africa, and founded stockaded villages such as Fuladoyo, in spite of the reprisals taken by the Arabs on tribes which harboured them.—'Rise of East African Empire,' vol. i. p. 231. In Nigeria, the capture of fugitive slaves was a lucrative trade for villages on the main routes.

to a "big man." Ex-slaves will do so—not necessarily to their late master. The master, aware that his slave can leave him at will, and cannot be reclaimed by force, or replaced by purchase, is compelled to treat him with kindness. All these are reasons which operate to make the household slave chary of asserting his independence; many of them apply to the predial slave also.[1] Those, however, who have been brought into contact with the system of free labour learn to value freedom to earn wages, with which to buy what they like, for slavery and free labour cannot long exist side by side.

If the slave asserts his freedom, it is generally in the form of an appeal for other employment. The executive officer inquires into his case, and if there is good cause, such as ill-treatment, he gives him a liberation paper, and finds him some Government employment on wages, and would encourage any individuals who show initiative and a real love of freedom to engage themselves as free labourers. In such a case native opinion is fairly satisfied. If, however, there is a wholesale movement of domestic slaves to leave their masters, he would refuse employment, or asylum in a Government township, to those who had no good cause. In the last resort, if a fugitive slave is claimed by his owner, and the officer is aware that his decision is being awaited by large numbers of others, and may be the signal for a wholesale rising or exodus, it would even be expedient to avoid the issue by conniving at the escape of the fugitive, or to place the town under special rules for the public safety. These were serious contingencies at one time in Nigeria, but have long ceased to exist.

It is, however, the predial slaves who are generally the first to assert their freedom, by declining to work or to bring the produce of their fields to their master. They desire to be free of all restraints, taxes, and obligations either to a master or to the State. Here again inquiry will establish whether or not the assertion is justified. If not, the slaves can be told

[1] In Sokoto, in former times, owners of refractory or idle slaves were accustomed to transfer them temporarily or by sale to the Zabermawa settlers, who were notoriously hard and merciless, making the slaves work in chains in the fields, with a bare subsistence and no family life, and brutal punishments. These Zabermawa now own very few slaves, and their large farms went out of cultivation at the British occupation of Nigeria, and have since been taken up by others.—Report of 1918.

that so long as they live in a house, and work on land which does not belong to them, the native court can and will enforce an adequate return in labour; at the same time an offer of payment for definite work would be made, and this would probably soon develop into ordinary paid labour and a contract enforceable in court.

But very possibly the reply of the slaves may be that they desire to take up new land, and build themselves huts. If it is imperative at the moment to exert a temporary check, the Government may decline to grant the land, except to those who have made out a good case. They are, however, at liberty to assert their freedom and offer themselves as labourers for wages, and the masters would be urged to accept all who so offered. "A large number of slaves at Sokoto have acquired a practical freedom, because their masters have encouraged them to earn their own living and become independent. The slave has his own house and family and occupation, and is entirely free except for occasional calls for such work as repairing the master's house; occasional presents of 6d. or 1s. may be given, more as a mark of goodwill than a quittance of real obligation." [1] The case of women is complicated by questions of marriage, concubinage, dowries, and divorce, and merits a separate paragraph.

Such measures may seem to constitute an arbitrary interference with natural laws of progress, and even to place the executive in a spirit of antagonism towards the full operation of the law. But they are conceived in a spirit of equity to the owner, and for the real benefit of the slave. They are suited only to a brief period of transition, which can be hastened by judicious explanations to master and slave alike. They will not arrest or defeat the operation of the law, but only make it more gradual. A sympathetic executive intends that every slave in the country shall have full knowledge in due course that he can assert his freedom if he desires, and will be supported in his action by Government. The object in view is to restrain an ignorant class from rushing into precipitate action, and to allow time for employers and labourers to grow accustomed to freed paid labour, and for Government to assist in facilitating that result.

An adequate currency for the payment of wages is essential

[1] Extract from report of June 1918, by Mr Arnett, Resident of Sokoto (Nigeria).

to the creation of a free paid-labour market, for if an employer is compelled to pay in kind, by instalments as they become available, and at arbitrary valuations, the employee is unable to save wages with which to purchase what he may desire, and, in fact, the conditions approximate to the slavery system. If a slave is in debt to his master, the fact raises no bar to his assertion of freedom. The creditor has the same remedy in the courts as in the case of a freeman.

Civilised countries in the twentieth century have their labour difficulties—though in a different form,—of which a writer pertinently remarks: "If we are to legislate to any purpose, we must not be content with denouncing them as anachronisms, or as contrary to Christian principles. They may be both, but they exist. It is not a question of what we would like to do, but of what we can do to abate an evil without causing more mischief than we can cure." It is surely very striking that words written of the situation in England to-day should be so literally applicable to the difficulties I have been discussing.

In spite of the difficulty created by the widespread belief that the advent of British rule meant that the whole slave population would be free to leave their work and do what they chose, the methods adopted have succeeded in Nigeria, where, owing to the tact and sympathetic counsel of the district staff, it has hardly ever been necessary to exert these restraints. The transitional stage has been negotiated without any social upheaval, without payment of compensation, and without any resulting bitterness on the part of owners. The records show 21,980 liberated by the native courts in the Sokoto Province alone, and a total of over 55,000 so liberated in the northern provinces to the end of 1917, a period of some fourteen years. The slaves on their part, influenced by custom and by public opinion, are willing and anxious to pay the ransom money. Many villages of ex-slaves have been formed. To-day, generally speaking, it may be said that in the Moslem States in Nigeria there are no slaves who are not well aware that they can assert their freedom if they choose; that the masters recognise these facts, and are ready to acquiesce in the methods of liberation approved by native law and custom, and accepted without any coercion whatever by the slave, and that the native courts administer the law freely, impartially, and liberally.

" Slavery in its strict sense is already dead," says Mr Gowers (now Lieut.-Governor of Northern Provinces of Nigeria); " the so-called slaves who still remain are rather servants than slaves."

These are methods adapted to a Moslem protectorate, and their success depends on their sympathetic application. They are, of course, unnecessary in a Crown colony, since slavery is illegal, though I am told there are slaves in the Gold Coast. Nor should they be necessary in any non-Moslem protectorate or district, for in these, as I have said, slavery should be absolutely abolished.[1]

The rights claimed over the person of a woman by reason of her status as a slave are complicated by the rights claimed over her as a wife or concubine, based it may be on payment of the " dowry." The sale of a girl, often of immature age, for the purpose of forcible concubinage with a man whom she may fear and loathe is one of the worst aspects of slavery, while the purchase of slave concubines by the powerful and wealthy classes to gratify their own desires, deprives the class from which these girls are drawn of their proper complement as wives. I am, however, concerned in this chapter to view the question rather from the point of view of " slavery " than from that of morality.

Concubinage is a recognised relationship under Moslem law, and applies only to female slaves who have sexual relations with their masters, since a man cannot marry his own female slave,[2] and concubinage with a free woman is illegal, and constitutes the sin of " *Zinat* " (adultery). A slave concubine who has borne a living child to her master is, however, practically freed during his life, and invariably liberated at his death.

Dowry is, properly speaking, given to a wife only. If a concubine has received presents from her master, they should be regarded as having been liquidated by his sexual relations with her, and if she asserts her freedom (as she has a perfect right to do when the legal status is abolished), he can neither claim their return, nor any rights over her on the grounds that she is in his debt, nor can he retain her children as being his slaves.

[1] The Slavery Ordinance 1916 decreed the emancipation of all persons "heretofore or hereafter born in or brought into " Southern Nigeria.

[2] 'Malaki Law,' Ruxton, chapter iii., section 3, sub-section 9.

If a slave woman is married to a man—whether slave or free—and wishes to leave him and marry another man (who is willing to ransom her), the matter must be decided solely by the marriage laws. She can obtain a divorce on repayment of the dowry—for Moslem law holds that it is futile to attempt to detain a woman who has made up her mind to go—and she can assert her freedom without ransom; but it is more usual for the intending husband to ransom her, and obtain a certificate of freedom from the native court. The ransom money is indeed often an equitable return from a household slave for the maintenance she has received in her master's house.

It must be made clear to persons who ransom a woman, and if necessary to native courts also, that since ransom money is not dowry, if a ransomed wife or concubine leaves her ransomer he cannot claim the ransom money from her, or from her new husband, or the return of presents given to her parents or others. He can only claim the dowry money given to her. Nor is a court justified in refusing to allow the new husband to retain the woman unless he repays the ransom money. On the other hand, the payment of ransom gives the ransomer no rights in the woman, and if he treats her as a slave, he is liable for slave-dealing. She was freed when ransomed, whether as a wife or concubine.[1] Native opinion in Nigeria strongly upheld this view. It was pointed out by a native judge that, although the ransomer apparently suffered hardship if the woman left him, it was generally his own fault, because, though he had nominally ransomed the woman, he had treated her as a slave, and so caused her to leave him; that if he could claim the ransom money back it became, in fact, purchase money and not ransom; and, finally, that if no man could marry such a woman without repaying her ransom as well as dowry, no one would be willing to do so, and she would remain unmarried and probably become a prostitute.

I have said that concubinage with a free woman is unlawful, and the effect therefore of the abolition of domestic slavery is to abolish the system of concubinage among Mos-

[1] So jealous are the Mohamedan judges of the enforcement of the spirit of the law, that I am informed that at Sokoto they hesitated to recognise ransom by an intending husband lest the girl should consider herself his slave.

lems,[1] a result which is only deferred by the enactment that all children born after a certain date are free. There is no doubt that this result is one which is exceeding obnoxious to the slave-owning classes.[2] Already in Nigeria it has given rise to an evasion of the law. A rich man promises to give a native court liberation certificate to a slave-girl whom he desires as a concubine, but instead of declaring her free before the native judge, he states that he ransoms her and "places her in his house"—a phrase which is understood to mean that while she remains there (as his concubine) she is still a slave —and hence the Koranic law is not violated—but the moment she leaves him she is free. The result is a curious anomaly. He cannot restrain her, for she has been freed. She can leave her ransomer at will and marry whom she likes. She is even more free than the wife, for she need get no divorce, and has no dowry to repay. Cases have occurred of girls inducing rich men to ransom them as concubines, in order that they may immediately leave them and marry some one else.

The immediate effect of these conditions in a Moslem district is to restrict large harems, for the master has to pay ransom money for each concubine, and his possession of her is precarious. The master is also compelled to treat his concubine well, for fear of losing both her and the money he paid for her ransom.

It is customary for the suitor to pay not only the dowry— which must be applied to the use of the bride—but also to give presents to her parents. It is obviously difficult to distinguish between the sale of a girl by her parents, and their acceptance of large presents for their consent to her marriage or concubinage. But since a child is not the slave of its

[1] The Moslem judge of Bida (Nigeria) ruled that "all concubinage proceeds from sale, and any one who procures a concubine, and pays a monetary consideration in respect of her, in fact buys her, whether she was previously free or a slave."

[2] I have even been informed that the majority of owners would now view with indifference the abolition of slavery, were it not for "the concubine question." It is easy to be contemptuous of prejudices we do not share, and to say that the four wives allowed to a Mohamedan by his creed should suffice, but to the Arab or the Fulani the matter wears another aspect. It is often, I believe, the fact that wives of their own race are sterile, and they desire concubines of the more virile African races to rear their children, nor is it unnatural that they should hesitate to adopt by marriage into their own social class, slave-women of a lower social grade. These prejudices, however, will have to give way.

parents, it follows that if they hand over a daughter to be the concubine of a Moslem—*e.g.*, his slave—both the parents and the man who acquires her are guilty of enslaving if she is free-born (as all under twenty are now in Nigeria), or of the transfer of a slave if she is slave-born.

If a master accepts a sum of money as a " present " for allowing his slave-girl to marry, and does not liberate the woman before a native court, he would be liable to prosecution for the sale or transfer of a slave.

Among non-Moslem communities—whether professing Christians or pagans—it is perhaps even more difficult to distinguish between the payment of dowry and the purchase of a female slave. If the principle that the dowry is given to a bride and to no one else, and that no one except the real parents may receive any present (and then only of limited amount) is observed, a step would have been taken towards putting down this detestable traffic; but so engrained and so universal is the conception of wife purchase, that I fear it will be long before the progress of education will effect the emancipation of women. Were the repayment of the dowry by the man with whom a wife had eloped to be done away with, the only check to promiscuous intercourse would be removed among tribes whose standard of morality is very low.

Slavery, as I have said, should be totally abolished in every non-Moslem country, but if for some sufficient reason this is not possible, it should at least be abolished in the case of women. In Moslem countries the abolition of the legal status, as I have shown, practically destroys concubinage. For the rest, if a woman slave desires to remain with her master, and marries a fellow-slave, she may well be allowed freedom of choice as to her husband.

The employment—of course for wages—by Europeans, or on public works, of slaves liberated by Government, is a matter in which great care should be exercised, for any seeming inconsistency is jealously noted, and it is said that Government, while depriving the owners of their rights in their slaves, connives at their acquisition by its employees or other Europeans. It should therefore be a rule that a freed slave child should be paid a small wage, even though its maintenance may be more than sufficient recompense for the small services it is called on to perform.

To avoid the suspicion of any ulterior motive by Government in its slavery policy, it should also be the rule that no slave liberated by a British court or by executive order should be given to a native in Government employ, either as wife or servant, except with express sanction.

In East Africa in former times, probably the majority of the "porters" who composed a Government or private caravan into the interior, were slaves who paid the greater part of their earnings to their masters on their return. This, it was alleged, was a direct encouragement of the slave-trade, since it enabled the owners to make large profits, with which they could buy more slaves. Access to the interior could at that time only be gained by employing human transport, and as long as Zanzibar was independent, few porters could be obtained who were not slaves. I arranged with the owners a scheme of self-redemption, but it was unfortunately not pushed with energy after I had left.[1]

Circumstances have changed, and since slave-dealing is now a criminal offence, the acquisition of new slaves is impossible under a vigilant administration, and the employment of slave-labour can no longer increase the number of slaves. The rule should, however, be made that no slave may be employed, either on Government work or by any non-native, unless under a contract for ransom—viz., that the slave on payment of a specified sum from his earnings shall receive a liberation certificate from the native court. In that case a deduction could be made from his wages, but the slave would himself pay over the ransom money to the native court. Of course if the legal status had been abolished, such an arrangement would be entirely at his own option, since he would, if he desired, be able to assert his freedom without any payment. If in the beginnings of British rule in a Moslem State there was no free labour for urgent Government work, and none could be imported, it might be necessary to accept

[1] 'Rise of East African Empire,' vol. i. p. 231. An interesting case recently arose at Sokoto which is illustrative of the native point of view in such cases. The native administration maintains a number of "Dogarai" (unarmed police), many of whom were formerly slaves of the Sultan and chiefs. An owner demanded some slight service from one of these, who had been his slave. The Sultan and Council condemned his claim, on the ground that the man had previously been employed by the chief in duties similar to those he now performed, and not for private gain. They considered it, they said, an honour that their slaves had been selected for these public duties. They were therefore all officially freed.

men who still were slaves, but their wages would be paid to themselves, and no claim of their owners would be recognised.

It would be desirable that no person in Government employ should be allowed to keep a slave, but in Moslem States it would be invidious to place high-class Mohamedan "political agents," &c., under disabilities from which others of their own standing were exempt; and since every slave can assert his freedom at will or claim the right of self-redemption, the rule is unnecessary.

In the case of soldiers and constables, however, the prohibition has for many years been enforced in Nigeria, for these men are apt to attach to themselves wives, or small boys or girls, and it is impossible to prove whether they have been acquired by purchase or other illicit means, or have voluntarily attached themselves to them, with the prospect of good food and little work. If an ex-slave, the wife or servant must be in possession of a native court liberation certificate, and the commanding officer insists on some small money wage being paid as a public acknowledgment that the servant is free, or lest the relation of master and slave should grow up between them. Those authorised are entered on the company register, their numbers are strictly limited, and every care is taken to see that they are not disposed of, especially when the soldier or constable goes on furlough or after his discharge. If he desires to ransom a woman in order to marry her, he may receive an advance for the purpose under the rules applying to ransoms. No person, whether a Government employee or not, should be allowed to keep any slave in a colony or in a township. All persons in the permanent service of Government must, of course, be free.

In furtherance of the policy of discouraging too rapid an exodus of slaves from their masters, it was formerly the rule in Nigeria that fugitive slaves should not be enlisted as soldiers or police, and a recruit before being enlisted had to agree to ransom himself, if he were later proved to be a slave. If, however, a slave succeeded in enlisting, under no circumstances would he be ordered to take off his uniform on the grounds that he was claimed as a slave. These rules are now relaxed, but any recruit who acknowledges himself to be a slave is encouraged to obtain a native court certificate by self-redemption.

With the abolition of the legal status a slave can assert his freedom without payment, but so strong are the traditions of slavery that native opinion does not readily admit that liberation by a British Government removes the stigma of slavery. A slave so liberated is a "white man's freedman," but remains *de jure* of the slave caste in public opinion, and, indeed, in his own; for the slave habituated to slavery has learnt to regard himself as the property of another, and if he has embraced Islam he feels that he is not really freed by the "unbeliever's" act. If he be a household slave he may also feel a filial duty towards his master, and his conscience is not satisfied until he has liquidated the debt. Ransom is indeed only justifiable in the case of slaves born or bred in slavery.

If, however, a slave receives a certificate of freedom from the judge of the native court—the exponent of the Koranic law—he is *de jure* free, and it is a crime to re-enslave him. These native court certificates are therefore greatly valued, and I have known cases of men freed by the administration who have voluntarily paid their redemption money to obtain them. In one case an ex-sergeant-major asked that the ransom should not be made unduly low, as his old master had treated him well.

Self-redemption and ransom, though entirely voluntary on the part of the slave, are worthy of encouragement by Government. It is creditable to the slave, and adds to his self-respect, and in many cases it is equitable to the master, who may have acquired his slave by what were at the time perfectly legal means. Redemption may be effected either by the system of *Kitabah*—viz., ransom by instalments—or by that of *Kita'ah*—viz., immediate payment.[1] The native

[1] The Koran, surah xxiv., paragraph 33, enjoins on every master the duty of agreeing to his slave's request to ransom himself, and of giving him every facility for acquiring the means to do so. The first system is known as "Murgu" in Nigeria, and under its provisions a slave would be allowed to retain his land with complete freedom while earning his ransom money, or he might work in his own time (one or two days a week being given to him) for wages, or he might pay a fee as earnest of his intentions, and be free for a year to earn the money, or he might be allowed to pay for his board and lodging, and liquidate the ransom by instalments in his own time. Whichever method he selects, he should be able to redeem himself within the year. The second method—viz., the payment of a lump sum down, known as *Kita'ah* (*pansa* in Hausaland)—would be resorted to by men who wished to redeem a woman for marriage, or by ex-slaves freed by Government who desired to get the native court certificate.—See Ruxton's 'Maliki Law,' chapter li.

courts, acting on the liberal instructions of the Koran, may usually be trusted to fix the amount of the ransom money with fairness and liberality,[1] but care must be taken to see that liberation is unequivocal and not a "ransom for concubinage," and that persons born after the date of the edict are not regarded as slaves for ransom. Certificates are also given when a slave is set free by a native court because of ill-treatment, or when voluntarily freed by his owner.

The slave-trade and open dealing in slaves in British Africa is now happily a thing of the past. Illicit dealing takes the form of kidnapping, or purchase by trading caravans, especially of children, who are often sold by their parents in time of famine, and being taught the language of their purchasers are passed off as part of his family, and told how to reply to any questions. Strict vigilance and heavy punishments upon offenders (including villages which are aware of the circumstances and fail to report them) are the only remedy.[2] Adults driven by starvation may also attach themselves to a trading party, or undesirable persons may be sold by a tribe. In former times it is said that porters, left sick in a village by a passing caravan, were also generally sold as slaves. The purchase of children for adoption or religious education is slave-dealing, even if the child is immediately liberated, and encourages the traffic by creating a demand.

The holding of persons in pawn for debt—which, unless voluntary, is forbidden by Moslem law—often results in the pawn becoming a lifelong slave, without a slave's privileges. If the contract is voluntary and limited in time, there is little to object to, but if unlimited in time the pawn's labour should be set against the debt, and the pawn should be free to abandon the contract and defend his case in court if he prefers. The onus of proof of the debt must, of course, be on the creditor. The seizure of a pawn by or for a creditor, including the pawning of children for debt, is by the Nigerian code classed as slave-dealing. The pawn is released, and the

[1] Recently it was found at Sokoto that many of the Government mail-carriers had been the slaves of chiefs. The Resident was inclined to call on them to ransom themselves, but the chiefs said that the services they had been accustomed to render to their masters were so light that they did not deserve ransom.

[2] In Nigeria, Hausa traders and Nupe fishermen carry on this traffic among primitive pagan tribes. The worst offenders are said to be the nomad Fulani herdsmen, who fill the children with terror of Europeans so that they fly or conceal themselves on the approach of an officer.

period of his detention is counted in liquidation of the debt. The plea of adoption of a child-pawn cannot be considered as valid as between creditor and debtor, and indeed adoption without ulterior motive is rare.[1]

The disposal of slaves when freed after recent capture often presents difficulties. Those freed at sea on the East Coast were at first sent to Bombay or to Mauritius, later they were generally handed over with a small capitation grant to missions (£5 by the British, 25s. by the Germans). It is rarely possible—though most desirable—to restore a freed slave to his home. A few years ago he would almost certainly have been re-enslaved (unless protected) *en route.* Children are unable to say where their home is, and there is always the danger that children who have been sold by their parents, or adults sold by their tribe, would again be sold if returned.

Men after being given a liberation paper and registered can usually be left to follow their own inclinations, and work can be found for them if they desire it. Women can be employed in or about a hospital, or as servants to a European lady, or they may be allowed to engage in trade or other useful occupation in the native quarter of a township. Failing any other method, a freed slave woman may be entrusted to the care of a reliable village headman till she marries, if there is no freed slave village or home to which she can be sent. In any case it is practically certain she will find a husband in a very short time, and he should pay her the usual dowry money due to a freed woman. It is necessary to exercise great care that he does not sell or transfer her as a slave.

Unmarried females are always children. In Nigeria there is a Native Children's Ordinance designed for the protection of juvenile ex-slaves. A child is entrusted to the custody of such guardian as may be named in the mandate, who is bound to care for and educate it properly, and may not transfer it. The mandate is for a limited period, which may be extended, and the children are periodically inspected by a Government official.

The "guardian" may be a Government establishment,

[1] Only in the present year (1920) has the system of debt-slavery been finally eradicated in the unfederated Malay States under British protection. There the debt was treated as hereditary. Children were taken in pledge for parents, and no reduction in the debt was made for the labour of the debtor.—Cmd. 470, 1920.

such as a freed slave home or village, or a department to which a boy is apprenticed, or it may be a mission, or a private person. The child may not leave its guardian—who is vested with parental authority—till, if a girl, she reaches the age of eighteen. Boys over twelve should be apprenticed, or may take service on wages. On attaining the age of fifteen they would be given freedom papers, and allowed to go where they please, unless bound as apprentices. A full periodical report is, of course, demanded from any institution or mission which obtains a grant from Government for receiving freed slaves.

The disadvantage of transferring freed slaves to missions is that liberation should not be open to the charge by bigoted Moslems that Government frees slaves only in order to convert them forcibly to Christianity.[1] I prefer myself a freed slave home for children, and "liberty village" for adults, both under Government auspices, for such freed slaves as cannot readily be absorbed into the village population.[2]

Adoption by individuals is, as I have said, open to a similar accusation—viz., that Government robs owners of their slaves in order to bestow them on its nominees. The willingness of the ordinary native to take a girl child gives colour to the assertion that he hopes to make a profit out of her. If adoption must be resorted to, the selection of guardians should be exercised impartially as between responsible Mahomedans and Christians.

A slave desirous of remaining in his master's house passes at his owner's death to his heir, but if he is taken out of the family, or by a distant relative (except with his own consent),

[1] We can hardly be surprised that the forcible detention of a "freed" woman, and her recapture by force if she "escapes" from a mission, should be confusing to the mind of the late owner.

[2] At the instance of Mr W. E. Forster a home was established in Cairo in 1884, and Lord Cromer in 1900 reported that it was still necessary and desirable. It had the advantage (impossible in Nigeria) of the continuous superintendence for twenty-four years of an Arabic-speaking lady—Mrs Crewe. Probably over 1000 women passed through the home.—('Anti-Slavery Reporter,' May 1900.)

A freed slave home was established in Northern Nigeria at Government Headquarters, but it was found almost impossible to control the women, the majority of whom preferred to leave the home and lead an immoral life. It was devoted, therefore, almost exclusively to children, of whom more were rescued—generally in an emaciated and starving condition—than could be accommodated. The home was under a trained nurse, and was visited daily by a doctor. It received a grant from Government and from the Rebecca Hussey and Giles trusts. After I left Northern Nigeria it was broken up, and the children transferred to the Sudan United Mission with a capitation grant. A second home, and also a "liberty village," were established in Bornu to meet the large influx of slaves from the German Cameruns.

a charge of "transferring" could be preferred. The family of a slave should not be broken up for purpose of division among heirs, nor is joint ownership permissible, for some single individual must be held accountable for good treatment. If an owner dies intestate, the slaves are freed.

The custom of elderly women procuring young girls, whom they call "wives," and with whom they go through a marriage ceremony, appears to be prevalent among tribes with widely different origins and customs. The purchase money is misnamed "dowry," and the woman-husband becomes absolute owner of the girls. The same thing is sometimes done for an identical purpose by very old and decrepit men. In some few cases it may be that the purchaser wishes to assure herself of a "wife" who will tend her in her old age, but the more usual reason is in order to claim fees for adultery, and to gain possession of the children of such intercourse, who by native custom are the property of the "husband" who has paid the dowry. In such cases, no doubt, the woman, who is in fact the keeper of a brothel, would be prosecuted on a criminal charge, and awarded no compensation for the loss of her "wives" and their dowries.[1] Or it may be that the girls are "married" by women traders, who pay a higher dowry than the young men can afford, in order to provide themselves with labour to transport their goods, since the men of the tribe refuse such work.[2]

"It was the custom in Benin (writes the Resident) when a father and daughter, husband and wife, or brother and sister quarrelled, if the man chose to say 'Igba' to the woman, she became at once 'devoted' to the Oba (king), and had to become one of his wives. Since April 1918 all these devotees have been released by the Oba, and the use of the word 'Igba' has been prohibited."

In Nigeria, as in other Moslem countries, favourite slaves often became very wealthy, even owning slaves of their own, and held appointments as chiefs of villages or districts. In Bornu, where these slave-rulers had in many cases been distinguished for generations, and were often held in higher account than freemen, the system has died hard. It arose from the fact that during an era of constant revolt by the provincial chiefs, the *Shehu* (Sultan) could only trust his own slaves—and provincial chiefs were in like case.

[1] One such woman was found to have nineteen wives.
[2] "Dan Gizo" in 'West Africa' of 15th May 1920.

Since all the property amassed by a slave-chief reverted to his overlord at his death, the system was lucrative to a despot. It was thoroughly bad in its results, for the slave-ruler, having no rights himself, could not be expected to regard those of others, and he oppressed the peasantry.

It has been the good fortune of this generation to witness not only the practical extinction of the overseas slave-trade, but also of slave-raiding and open slave-trading; there remains only the illicit dealing in slaves.[1]

The first step is to deal with slave-raiding as murder, and with the enslaving of a free man as a felony, and thus to cut off the supply of new slaves. The second is to regard any " transaction in slaves " as a serious offence, and to give the slave the right to assert his freedom if he desires to do so, and thus to destroy the value of property in slaves. The third, and perhaps the most difficult task, is to eradicate the servile habit of mind, bred by long traditions of slavery, to inculcate the right to be free, and to educate the native to a sense of personal responsibility, initiative, and aspiration, in order that he may learn the dignity of free labour and appreciate his duty as a citizen and to posterity.

This is being done everywhere in British Africa, partly by example, for the people see that the British officer makes no caste difference between slave and free, and promotes for merit alone; partly by the teaching of missions and the spread of education; partly by the creation of small land-holders with a title in perpetuity to their holdings, and, above all, by the creation of a free-labour market, with which I shall deal in the next chapter.

The only country in Africa in which slave-raids and the slave-trade are still openly practised is Abyssinia, and the nations of Europe must presently consider how they can reconcile this state of things with their solemn declarations to put an end to it in Africa. The very intelligent and progres-

[1] There is much still to be done before this curse of Africa is eradicated. In Nigeria as late as 1918 we hear of slave-dealing in Onitsha, of kidnapping of children in Bassa, of coast-traders buying slaves from the Aros at Owerri, of slave-dealing between the pagan Mamas and Bauchi, and of the Shuwa Arabs buying slaves from the Cameruns. These offences are dealt with under the Criminal Code.

In the Sudan the Abyssinians and lower Nile tribes still actively engage in the slave-trade, which, says the official Handbook (No. 98, pp. 27 and 44), would revive to-morrow if the British hold on the Sudan and French control in Wadai were relaxed.

sive Regent, Ras Tafari—whose personal friendship I value—recognises and deplores this blot on his country's reputation, and would gladly do his best to suppress it were he afforded the means of doing so.[1]

[1] In 1919 a British official mission traversed Abyssinia under Majors Athill, R.F.A., and Darley, and an account of the journey was given by Major Athill in a paper read before the Geographical Society ('Journal,' November 1920). Major Darley, whom his colleague described as one of the best type of British pioneers, gives a very startling account of the devastation which had been wrought in Southern Abyssinia by slave-raiding. For days or weeks, he says, the expedition traversed areas which he had formerly known as thickly peopled with prosperous villages. It was now entirely depopulated. He ascribes this deplorable state of things to the uncontrolled rapacity of provincial chiefs, who, especially when leaving the province, would seize all the people they could round up, and carry them off to be sold as slaves for their own profit. He describes such a scene of which he was an eye-witness in 1911.

The apologists, on the other hand, maintain that these descriptions refer to a period subsequent to the death of Menelik, when the Central Authority was very weak, and unable to control the provinces. They assert that recent raids are the work of bands of robbers, which the Central Government under Ras Tafari has done its best to restrain, though handicapped by lack of effective weapons, due to the embargo on the import of arms. Tafari himself has pointed out that Abyssinian slavery is based on the Mosaic Law, which does not forbid domestic slavery, and that the advent of Mohamedans into Abyssinia is alone responsible for existing abuses.

Finally, in a message recently communicated to the 'Times' (19th June 1923) by its correspondent at Adis Abeba, Tafari declares that he is willing to place full information at the disposal of the League of Nations in its enquiries regarding slavery in Africa, and to co-operate with it in any measures for the suppression of the trade. "Meanwhile they were acting energetically themselves. Heavy punishment was inflicted on persons caught slave-running. A new edict was about to be promulgated making slave-running a crime liable to capital punishment," and the chief of the province through which most of the slaves were conveyed to the borders of French Somaliland had been warned that he would be degraded unless he took adequate steps to stop it.

When we consider how secluded from European thought and sentiment Abyssinia is, and how confusing must be the whispers in the ear of the Regent—naturally, and not without reason, prone to suspicion—by the rival Powers, each accusing the other of interested motives, we shall perhaps be more willing to assist, and less ready to condemn. The problem is how to strengthen the hands of the Regent so as to enable him to curb the excesses of his provincial chiefs, with adequate safeguards against the misuse of his power.

CHAPTER XIX.

LABOUR IN TROPICAL AFRICA.

Free labour and slavery—Policy of H.M.'s Government—Decisions *re* East Africa—Criticisms and charges—Local opinion—Difficulty of applying the Government policy—Inadequacy of the solution proposed—Contrast East and West Africa—Inevitable conclusions *re* East Africa—West African products and conditions—The cocoa industry—The African as a worker—The African as a wage-earner—Quality of the work—The wage-rate—Method of payment of wages—Conditions of free labour—Labour regulations—Unpaid labour.

WE have seen that where a native conquering race holds an aboriginal people in control, a system of slavery and forced labour becomes practically inevitable by reason of mutual mistrust and the absence of such social organisation as renders possible a written contract, and payment for services in a recognised medium of exchange.

That system, though demoralising both to master and slave, and opposed to progress both moral and material, was by no means wholly one-sided when humanely enforced in accordance with the teaching of the Koran. It laid heavy obligations on the master, who is now quick to recognise that the free labourer can claim his day's wage and no more; and if he breaks his contract and does not do his work, the courts, which would have given the master no assistance in such a dispute with his slave, will help him, and that he is no longer responsible for the faults of his employee, or compelled to support him and his family in sickness and old age.[1]

Our task is to discuss how free labour can best be pro-

[1] Consul Monson writes of the institution of slavery in East Africa as "so repugnant in principle to English ideas, so little injurious in practice to its supposed victims." The owners "had been forced to treat their slaves liberally in order to retain them."—Cmd. 1631 of 1903.

vided in a country in which industry has hitherto been largely conducted by slave labour, and where most of the necessities and many of the incentives to work for wages which exist in civilised countries are lacking. In England the peasant must buy his daily food. Men and women may not go about quite nude. They are not physically inured to extremes of heat and cold, and need fires and fuel. We have, in fact, all acquired the habit of using many things which by long custom have become necessities of life. On the other hand, though I have warmly advocated the principle of small individual holdings, it is not a reasonable thesis (as some writers seem to infer) that every predial slave should become a peasant proprietor, for no country in the world can do without casual paid labour.

In a despatch to the Governor of East Africa, Lord Milner laid down the "traditional policy" of the British Government on the subject of native labour, "in order that there may be no room for doubt in the matter."[1] Such a pronouncement is particularly opportune at a moment when the claims and demands which arise out of the dual responsibilities of the Controlling Powers in the tropics—viz., as trustees to civilisation for the adequate development of their resources, and as trustees for the welfare of the native races—may seem in some cases to be mutually antagonistic, and have given rise to controversy. It is especially important in East Africa and Tanganyika, where our declared reason for ousting Germany was because of her misrule.[2] The "traditional policy," he says, "is absolutely opposed to compulsory labour for private employment. . . . It is a point of fundamental importance . . . that there is no question of force or compulsion, but only of encouragement and advice through the native chiefs and headmen."

The particular policy of His Majesty's Government to-day in regard to the difficulties which have arisen in East Africa "aims at the advancement and wellbeing of the native races

[1] Cmd. 873 of 1920.

[2] The Official Handbook quotes the German writer Hassert: "Colonisation consists in the utilisation of the soil, its products, and its men, for the economic profit of the colonising nation"; and Fischer: "Colonising Africa is making the negro work."—No. 113, p. 40. The Governor's report states that the Germans had reduced the natives to abject submission as permanent serfs, and they were rarely fully paid for their work. Unless they were able to prove their complaints they were flogged for making them.—Cmd. 1428 of 1921, p. 35.

in the protectorate, no less than the meeting of the settlers' requirements." It may be summarised as follows :—

(*a*) "Natives may be required to perform certain paid labour for Government . . . (viz.) works of a public nature, subject to the express proviso that no native shall be required to perform such work for more than sixty days in any one year, and that any native who is fully employed in any other occupation, or has been so employed during the preceding twelve months for a period of three months shall be exempted from such labour." Works of a public nature are defined in the ordinance as work on Government transport, or on roads and railways, "and other work of a public nature, whether of a like kind to the foregoing or not." The three months includes, of course, any work on his own account.[1]

(*b*) That natives in their own interests should seek outside employment when not engaged in work in their own reserves, and it is desirable that the young able-bodied men should become wage-earners, and should not remain idle in the reserves for a large part of the year.

(*c*) That "the Protectorate Government would be failing in its duty if it did not use all lawful and reasonable means to encourage the supply of labour for the settlers" engaged in the production of raw material much needed by the Empire.

(*d*) That for this purpose the principle of working through the native chiefs is right, but they must be closely watched by Government officials. On the one hand, any attempt to abuse their authority must be promptly checked, and on the other hand, "any unwillingness to act on instructions must be taken note of and recorded."

(*e*) That native labour shall not be procured by Government for a particular employer, and "the native is free to choose where and for whom he will work."

(*f*) That women and children may be employed, but "must return to their houses at night, and that only when the husband is employed, and living in the plantation should his family be permitted to remain there at night." It is inferred that their labour will be light—chiefly coffee-picking, and for half a day only.

[1] This was made clear by Lord Milner in reply to a question in the House of Lords on 27th October 1920, and affirmed by the Under-Secretary in the Commons. Mr Harris states that the settlers resent this interpretation of the ordinance.—('Manchester Guardian,' 3rd August 1921.)

(*g*) Finally, there is no objection to recruiting from an adjoining British administration (whether under Mandate or not), provided there is a surplus of labour over and above that required in the territory itself. Recruits may bring their wives with them.

It is permissible to examine these most important pronouncements by the light of personal experience and the criticism of the public Press. The "traditional policy" applies to the whole of tropical Africa and to other Crown colonies and Protectorates, but not to the Dominions, which frame their own policy. The detailed decisions apply *imprimis* to the conditions of East Africa.

The conditions resemble, with one exception, those of South Africa, and Lord Milner was able to say that he spoke from personal experience. They resemble South Africa in that Europeans are settlers depending on native labour, and not true colonists like Canadians and Australians,[1] while the natives are to a greater or less extent relegated to reserves. They differ in that the population of South Africa is less nomadic and pastoral, and has been in contact with Europeans for a longer time. The fact that the settlers came on the direct invitation of Government—first in 1905 and again after the war—obviously saddles the Government with a very special responsibility for making good the inducements which it held out.

The immediate cause of the Government pronouncement was the issue of a "Memo. of policy," and a circular by the local Government, on the subject of native labour, which called forth a very trenchant manifesto by the Bishops of Mombasa and Uganda. They asserted that though there was "technically no compulsion, practically compulsion could hardly take a stronger form." The Memo. was also severely criticised in a Memorial by the Aborigines' Protection Society, by the Conference of Mission Societies, and by the Press.[2] The

[1] As Mr Grogan picturesquely phrases it, "the European is not merely the individual producer as he is in Canada or Australia—he is the yeast that leavens the inert dough of Africa's peoples."—'Times,' 9th February 1920.

[2] See 'The New Statesman,' 21st February, 27th March, 10th April, &c. Sir S. Olivier, one of the signatories of the A.P.S. Memorial, asserts in the 'Contemporary Review' (August 1920), that "the permanent principles of our policy in dealing with native peoples are being whittled away," and the rights of the natives are to an increasing extent being recognised as subsidiary to the interests of white men. In a note on an article on "Labour in Nyasaland" ('East and West,' January 1921), the editor writes of East African conditions: "While

subject gave rise to a debate in the House of Lords on 14th July 1920, in which Lords Islington, Bryce, Emmott, and the Primate passed severe strictures on the policy.

It is of special importance to note that the Sub-Committee of the Labour Party, appointed to report on the administration of the dependencies, repeats and even exaggerates the charges brought against the East African Administration in this connection, for that Party assumes that sooner or later it will become the executive power in the British State, charged with the control of African policy. The author of the Memo. prepared by this Sub-Committee, while advocating in the main the principles for which I have contended in these chapters, accuses the Governments of Kenya and Nyasaland of "aiming at the evolution of a race of servile labourers in European employ divorced from their lands. The conditions (he says) in these countries in some respects reproduce, and even exaggerate, the evils of slavery"—bad food, disease, bad sanitation, severe punishments including flogging, lack of supervision by Government, desertion punished as a criminal offence resulting in lack of labour for the production of food, sedition, and grave danger of insurrection. Such is the picture which the Labour Party is invited to believe forms a true presentment of British rule in East Africa.[1]

The bishops recognise that the white settlers "all depend for their very existence as farmers on native labour," and they go so far as to recommend that compulsion should be definitely legalised, and directed primarily to State work under certain safeguards.[2] No doubt strong pressure has been brought to bear on the local Government by the settlers, whose views are recorded in the report of the Commission of 1917-19, to which I have referred, and at greater length in that of the earlier Commission appointed in 1912 to examine this question.[3] They were, in brief, that the native reserves should be restricted to the present needs only of the natives, that individual tenure should be substituted for communal,

nominally the law compels no one to engage in any but public service, it has the intention and the effect of imposing wage-earning on all, partly because the wages for Government departments are fixed so low as to be no attraction (about 3d. a day), and partly because in practice only wage-earners for private employers are exempted from the legal obligation to work for wages."

[1] See also 'Empire and Commerce' by L. Woolf, which is "a report for a Committee of the Labour Research Department," and is published by it. Part III., chapter 2, &c.

[2] Cmd. 873 of 1920, p. 8.

[3] Report of August 1913.

that "squatting" on European estates should be encouraged, and that labour camps under official supervision should be formed.[1]

These recommendations have not, however, as we have seen, been accepted by Government, and we have Lord Milner's assurance that the policy he defined is being carried out by the local officials. It will, however, be exceedingly difficult, if not impossible, to ascertain in the case of each individual native whether he has worked on his own land for three months, and the attempt to do so must open the door to all kinds of abuses by native subordinates. Among the agricultural tribes, I should doubt whether there are any individuals who do not devote at least that time to their crops. The pastoral tribes tend their cattle—which is presumably "occupation," and falls entirely on the males. Agricultural labour would be as irksome to them as penal servitude.

Then again there is the vital question—at what time of the year is the compulsory labour to be called for? If at the season when the native crops demand attention, the hardship may be great, and result in a reduction of the native food supply. If, as stated, it is to be demanded by Government from the more distant tribes, leaving the remainder for private labour, is the time taken in coming from and returning to these remote districts to be counted in the sixty days to be paid for? If so, there will be little margin for work. We are told, moreover, that the great variations in climate, and the different diet of tribes, causes much sickness and mortality when labour is transferred from its natural environment.[2] Age-limits for labourers are difficult to determine; medical examination for fitness is impracticable in areas so great, with a small medical staff overwhelmed with work, and the supervision of the District Officer is, we are told, negligible for the same reason.

[1] See 'Handbook' 1216, p. 466. The policy of closing the reserves to European penetration, which they say "has lately taken shape in the publicly-made official statement of the Chief Native Commissioner, that 'he did not see why a native should turn out to work for a European if he wanted to develop his own lands,' should (they consider) be reversed in the interests of the development of the country."—Report of 1919, p. 19.

[2] The Wakamba and Wa-Kikuyu tribes are practically the only sources for labour actually on the Highlands, for the climate is too cold even for the Wa-Kavirondo from the sub-tropical Lake region (who, however, are largely employed), and these tribes suffer equally if transported to the tropical coast regions, where a mortality of 145 per mille was recorded.—'Handbook,' pp. 324-467.

It is manifest, therefore, that there are serious difficulties in applying the policy laid down; but setting these aside, does that policy provide any permanent solution of the problem? The present labour supply, we are told, amounts to about 100,000,[1] which would seem to be a fairly large proportion of the adult males, allowing for an adequate contingent to cultivate their own crops. But this number is said to be wholly insufficient, even for the present small number of settlers and for Government requirements. But if the public works which the country so greatly needs were taken in hand, the Government demand alone would absorb the whole or the greater part of the available supply. If, at the same time, the number of settlers were multiplied (as is expected) tenfold, what solution does the present policy offer for the difficulties of the not-distant future?

An essential feature of that policy, as stated by Lord Milner, is "the advancement of the wellbeing of the natives." As they are educated in improved agricultural methods, and as they learn to grow exportable produce and find that they can realise good prices, and as their live-stock increases under peaceful conditions, the available supply of wage-earners is likely to decrease. Since it is opposed to the traditional policy of the Empire that the native population should be converted into labour-tenants of Europeans, it is imperative that the real facts should be faced without delay, if still further difficulties—or indeed disaster—is to be avoided in the future.

I shall presently explain how labour difficulties have been dealt with in West Africa; but such methods are only very partially applicable in East Africa, where there is no vast reservoir to draw upon, and differences in climate make it more difficult to transfer labour from one part of the country to another. Rates of pay are low in East Africa (from 8s. to £1 for the best men per mensem),[2] but higher rates will not permanently increase the supply. Something may perhaps be done in the way of better housing, better and more liberal food, and more sympathetic treatment by both recruiters and employers, and improved medical attendance.[3] But the truth

[1] Cmd. 7622 of 1915, and 'Times,' 11th August 1921.

[2] Handbook 1216, pp. 465 and 469. The shortage of labour began to be felt in 1907, and became acute in 1912.

[3] Ibid., p. 466. In the Sudan there is a "Labour Bureau" which appears to have been a success.—(Handbook 98, p. 95.) Pilgrims from Nigeria passing through or settled in the Sudan supply a considerable part of the labour demand.

of the matter is that the policy proposed is incompatible with the conditions as they exist.

In West Africa, where European settlement is out of the question, it is recognised that the native must be the producer of all agricultural exports. The Departments of Agriculture, Forestry, &c., endeavour to improve the quantity and quality of his output. Wage labour is chiefly required for public works—roads, railways, and harbours, &c.—and for mining operations. It is to some extent possible to allow the labour gangs to look after their fields at the crucial season without abandoning such works.

In the Highlands, and to a lesser extent in the sub-tropical zone of the Lakes—and even in the Lowlands of East Africa—the European desires to be the producer of agricultural exports. There is no large labour reserve, and the European requires his labourers for his crops at the very time when the native desires to tend his own fields. The requirements of the settlers, to put it bluntly, are incompatible with the interests and advancement of the agricultural tribes, nor could they be otherwise than impatient of native development as a rival in the growing of coffee, flax, and sisal.[1]

In justice alike to the old settlers and to the new-comers (who, it is said, have been tempted to enter the country by the specious prospects held out by emigration pamphlets and the like), and in justice to the natives, British immigrants should be fully warned of the deficiency of native labour, and discouraged from coming to the country unless they are prepared to dispense with it.[2] This was not done in the case

[1] The Official Handbook on Tanganyika observes that "all the tribes are capable of maintaining themselves without working for wages, and object to doing so. Hence the establishment of great estates demanding large supplies of labour must, if continued, lead to perpetual discord and trouble."—No. 113, p. 40.

[2] Mr Grogan, a Member of Council and of the Economic Commission, suggested some years ago ('Times,' 5th April 1903) that grants of land snould be offered to attract such settlers. The Germans, as we have seen (p. 391, note), had no scruples as to compelling the natives to work, and they had a particularly good labour supply in Unyamwezi, but they were soon faced with the same difficulty as Kenya. The recently-issued report by the Governor of Tanganyika (Cmd. 1428 of 1921) states that the German system resulted in "an over-crowded and discontented native community on the one hand, and large and valuable properties handicapped for lack of sufficient labour on the other" (p. 70). They were forced to the decision to alienate no more land to settlers, in view of the labour difficulties (p. 35).

Mr Duff, Resident of the British Cameruns province—a good German scholar—reported, after a long study of the German archives, that in 1912 the Government had decided to change its policy radically in view of the success of British

of the soldier settlers who were invited to the country after the war, and the Mombasa correspondent of the 'Times' describes the result. "Kenya," he says, "has not yet disclosed the *modus operandi* by which a small farmer can make a home and a living . . . the outlook is dismal in the extreme . . . the soldier settlement is dying."[1] It would in any case be a dangerous experiment, for men ignorant of the climate may imagine that they can do physical work, which the altitude forbids.

Since, then, the labour supply of the country is insufficient for the needs of the white settlers; since it is doubtful whether the small proprietor can dispense with native labour, and quite certain that the existing large estate owners cannot do so; and since it is the declared policy of His Majesty's Government "to meet the requirements of the settlers," for whose advent they are responsible, there is only one conceivable solution remaining—viz., imported contract labour, which, after all, differs only in degree from the recruitment of labourers from remote tribes to serve under conditions of climate, food, and language wholly alien to them.

The cost would no doubt be greater than that of the existing local labour, and the settler will be anxious to reduce the number of labourers asked for by employing labour-saving devices and improved methods of transport, by closer supervision and increased efficiency of the employees, by concentrating on crops which require scientific culture, and yield the highest returns. The native will then be left to grow the cheaper and more easily-cultivated products, and to build up a trade which will add to the prosperity and revenues of the country. I shall presently discuss the subject of imported contract labour more fully.

The critics who write for the Labour Party contrast the "amazingly successful" economic progress in West Africa with that of East Africa, and ascribe it primarily to a difference in policy. Whole-hearted advocate as I am of the principle of "free native labour on native-owned land," no impartial man can regard the comparison otherwise than as

methods. It abandoned its hopes of any considerable German colonisation, and determined to encourage native-owned plantations of cocoa, rubber, and oil-palms, as against German estates and hired labour, with an elaborate scheme of inspectors, and the distribution of vast numbers of plants from Government nurseries.

[1] 'Times,' 11th November 1920.

grossly misleading, and I digress for a moment to make this clear.

Figures are quoted which hold up to derision the output of East Africa (except Uganda) compared with West Africa. In the latter, it is said, the exports vary from 10s. to £5 per head of the population, and that in East Africa they are less than 2s. (See, however, table, p. 45.) But what comparison can be made between the exports of a densely populated agricultural country and one whose much sparser population consists largely of nomad pastorals ? [1] Between a country where the uncultivated oil-palm alone produces exports to the value of about six million sterling, and one in which every agricultural export—coffee, sisal, flax, cotton, &c.—has been introduced in quite recent years by the enterprise of the European settlers ? [2] The natural wealth of the west has enabled those countries to build railways, and so increase their output by geometrical progression.

The cocoa industry on the Gold Coast is the favourite instance of what free labour, employed for its own sole profit, can do, and it is a truly wonderful record. In 1891 the output was 80 lb., value £4 ; in 1919 it had reached 176,151 tons, value £8,278,500 ; and now that little colony, with a population of only 2,000,000, produces more than half the cocoa consumed in the world.[3] But while giving hearty praise to the initiative of the Gold Coast native, and to the methods which produced such results, it is misleading to cite them as evidence of astonishing industry, due to a policy however excellent, when they are due primarily to an exceptionally favourable soil, climate, and rainfall.

The Governor of the Gold Coast (Sir H. Clifford) remarked that " cocoa is notoriously one of the least exacting forms of permanent cultivation known to mankind." The natives would probably not have undertaken it otherwise, " or any

[1] Consul Monson (*loc. cit.*) says that three of the chief tribes of East Africa—the Masai, the Somalis, and the Gallas—are utterly unsuited for labour both by character and tradition. This is perhaps too sweeping a statement, for the Gallas are the serfs of the Abyssinians, and in that country have shown themselves industrious labourers, while the French railway from Jibuti to Addis-Ababa was built chiefly by Somali labour.

[2] The Economic Commission asserts that the native of East Africa, without European supervision, has no surplus products for external exchange, whereas 7000 whites have created over £6,000,000 of overseas trade in thirteen years (Report, p. 3).

[3] Annual Report, Cmd. 1103.9 of 1921, pp. 35-36, and 'Colonial Office List,' p. 212.

task of the sort that made a more severe demand on their physical energies." It is admitted that even that small amount of exertion has not been given to it, and a danger of fungoid and other disease on the "indolent and slovenly farms" is the result. The quality, too, is very inferior for lack of proper care and trouble in its preparation. The rush for large profits in cocoa has replaced the more laborious palm-oil industry, and the haste to get rich without toil has resulted in a serious shortage of food, and the destruction of irreplaceable forest lands in the search for virgin soil. The cocoa-farmers, we read, have become indolent, and the work is left to the women. Boys despise labour, and have a horror of manual work. Maize and other native food has now to be imported.[1] Another result has been to enhance the cost of labour to such a degree that there is great difficulty in carrying out public works and private undertakings.[2] These conditions are increasingly evident in the Lagos hinterland also.

We must not, however, forget that cocoa is the first permanent crop introduced into West Africa for native cultivation. It is to the native a novel experiment, and if he has failed as yet to realise that greater energy and improved methods are necessary, and that failure with a permanent crop means more than a seasonal disaster, we must not be in haste to blame him.

It has long been the fashion to speak of the African as

[1] Dr Unwin, late Forest Settlement Officer in Nigeria, a very competent observer, writes of the Gold Coast plantations: "Disease is already rampant, and thousands of the plantations remain unweeded and uncleared, a prey to further disease of all kinds. This is chiefly due to lack of labour and of appreciation of the necessity of keeping a plantation clean. . . . However, it is an easy crop to grow, and up to now it has been possible for the people to leave the trees alone till they bear, and then pull off the cocoa-pods at leisure. . . . We have now thousands and millions of acres of magnificent forests devastated each year in order to plant cocoa. . . . In about a decade the climate will be too dry for the growth of the cocoa-tree, and disease will, at the same time, have practically prohibited its growth . . . already there is a food shortage." He goes on to argue that as trustees for the African in economic affairs, we have no right to allow him "to go on blindly to face the rigours of ruthless natural laws," and the impending disaster to a crop which appeared to him a gold-mine. Sir D. Prain, Director of Kew, says: "The dangers which now threaten cocoa in the Gold Coast bid fair in the near future to extinguish what is now a profitable industry." Great emphasis is laid on the necessity for grading, and a graduated price for quality.—Handbook 93, p. 33. See Mr Farquharson's statement, p. 507 *inf.*

[2] The Governor (General Guggisberg), speaking at Liverpool in September 1920, stated that labourers earned 10s. to 15s. a day for carrying cocoa on their heads. "Naturally they would do that in preference to mining or agricultural work at 1s. to 2s."

naturally lazy, leaving work to his women, and contented to lie in the sun and eat and drink. It would seem, however (as I observed in the chapter describing the characteristics of the people), that there are few races which are more naturally industrious. The fertility of the soil, his few wants, the physical capacity of his women for manual work, are all prompting causes for idleness, yet except when relegated to reserves, or when his status as a slave deprived him of all incentive, he is usually industrious. Even as a slave his natural aptitude for work often makes him a willing and good worker. As a wage-earner he has not the plodding application of the Chinaman, and "he makes no pretence of taking pride in planting cotton or tobacco for some one else," says Mr Wilson; but this writer emphatically denies that the native in Nyasaland is idle and leaves most of the work to his women, and he "cannot think why Europeans persist in assuming that a native lives in degrading idleness unless working for a European."[1]

The free pagan tribes in West Africa often cultivate more than it seems possible to consume. There is no question of merely "scratching the surface," and the deep trenches in the Yoruba yam-fields show how thoroughly his work is done. Though in most districts the pressure of population, which compels hard and continuous work to provide the necessities of life, is absent, you may see him in the very early morning, and even in the heat of the tropical day, hoeing his fields—sometimes so engrossed that he will hardly pause to look at a passing European with his long train of carriers—and though his needs and desires are so small he willingly engages for wages.

It is the tradition of Africa that the men tend the cattle and fight, while the women work in the fields; but throughout the greater part of the continent the men share the field-work with the women, and in many districts do by far the larger part of it. The cattle-owning tribes had to be ready at any moment to fight for their herds, and thus it was the task of the men to tend them. The use of oxen in agriculture would thus free the women, and leave cultivation more largely in the hands of the men. The labour expended in collecting and preparing for export some £4,000,000 worth of palm produce in the Southern Provinces of Nigeria, and of £1,500,000

1 "The Labour Problem in Nyasaland."—'East and West,' January 1921.

worth of ground-nuts from the Northern Provinces, must be prodigious.[1]

We are told that the African, though a hard worker in his own fields, "does not like or understand the European capitalist system of wage-earning." In point of fact, this seems to be quite untrue. It would indeed be natural to expect in a country like Nigeria, where in the north there are large areas of fertile vacant lands which the peasant can now occupy secure from eviction or arbitrary exactions, and where in the south sylvan products which command high prices are provided without cultivation by the bounty of nature, that the very security for life and property, and the individual freedom enjoyed under British rule, would result in the peasantry taking up land for themselves, or engaging in trade, and would militate against the supply of free casual labour for wages. This, however, has only been the case to a limited extent.

The Government has been able to count on a fairly adequate supply of labour, and some 20,000 seek employment on the mines, in addition to other unofficial requirements. During the time I was in Nigeria there was never any shortage of free voluntary labour for the arduous work of quarrying coal underground, even in night shifts, and in a temperature which makes the work most exhausting, in spite of the fact that the colliery was opened in a district of primitive and turbulent pagans, where no previous demand for labour had existed.

It would seem that in proportion to the population the supply of wage-earners in East Africa, Uganda, and Nyasaland is very considerable. The conception of free wage-labour is not indeed entirely new, for wages have long been paid to carriers of goods. Time payment is recognised in West Africa, and Krumen engage for twelve months as ships' labourers and stevedores at the various ports. Native land-owners can engage labour at low rates in Nigeria. At Yola hired labour is reported as common, and slave-owners say that they would not mind if all their male slaves now asserted

[1] 'Les Colonies et Marine' estimates that the export of only 20,000 tons of palm-oil from French West Africa employs 600,000 carriers for transport alone —viz., 12,000,000 days' work—or 40,000 men a year.—'West Africa,' 30th October 1920.

their freedom. At Sokoto chiefs declared that they had found by experience that hired labour was cheaper than feeding and clothing slaves who had little work to do for a great part of the year. In one somewhat backward district even the system of piece-work was found to exist, the ground being marked out into plots of ten cowries (1d.) worth of work. In Zanzibar, long before the legal status was abolished, many Arabs declared that they preferred free labour, and later Consul Cave succeeded in introducing signed labour contracts.[1]

The native is tempted to earn wages by his desire to purchase the attractive goods offered for his choice, and though it is true that he can equally obtain money by selling produce grown or collected by himself, he is glad when his fields do not require all his energies to earn extra money to satisfy his new wants. There is also a large class who are not disposed to settle down to agriculture—perhaps because the pressure of population in their own particular district has left no fertile land available, and they do not care to go elsewhere; more often, probably, because once having been induced to leave his home, the labourer has become impatient of tribal life, and "often prefers being a wage-earner to a capitalist, and following a free life to the discipline and restraint of his elders"—as Sir E. P. Girouard says, speaking of East Africa,[2] and Mr Wilson as regards Nyasaland.[3] The African has also a love of being associated with the ruling class, whether European or Native. The conditions of paid labour are, moreover, not unattractive,—good and prompt payment, which admits of the purchase of little luxuries in the way of food; the absence of any need for taking thought; and freedom from anxiety as to rainfall, locusts, and the other cares which beset the small farmer. If he refuses work,

[1] The Arab, however, has been unable to accommodate himself to the changed conditions of labour since the abolition of the legal status of slavery in 1897. Most of the clove estates are now mortgaged to Indians, and the population is not increasing.—(Monson's Report, Cd. 1631 of 1903.) The negro appears to deteriorate as a worker in the West Indies. A correspondent of the 'Spectator' (31st August 1901), writing of Trinidad, quotes an ex-Governor as saying that the negro population looks on agricultural labour as degrading, and Dr Cumins in his report on Indian emigration says that since emancipation the negroes do less and less work. The Royal Commission of 1897 reports that they are disinclined to continuous labour.

[2] Report 1909-1910. Cd. 5467 of 1911, p. 47.

[3] 'East and West,' *loc. cit.*

it is generally because he knows that his would-be employer is unfamiliar with his language and customs, or because he can make more money in another way, or because he dare not leave his crops.

As to the quality of the work done by the wage-earner, Captain Orr says, I think very truly: "The whole question of industry and idleness depends almost on incentive. When the African native is given an incentive to work, he will work in a way that is sometimes almost astounding. . . . Give him an interest in his task, encourage his initiative by making him think for himself, thrust responsibility upon him, demand results, and not the mere mechanical performance of labour, and he will be found surprisingly industrious."[1]

His output of work depends very largely on the popularity and tact of the European overseer and on the class of work to be done. No white man could carry so heavy a load or for so long a distance as he does without over-fatigue, and at heavy earth-work with his own implements he can show good results. At skilled trades he is an apt pupil—a subject I shall deal with at greater length in the chapter on education. In West Africa natives trained as apprentices man the workshops and the printing offices, and make efficient turners, fitters, smiths, and ship-carpenters, and even engineers of launches. In East Africa the Waganda, the Somals, and others are said to have mechanical aptitude.

It is an economic disadvantage to any country if the wage-rate for unskilled labour is unduly high, for it arrests development. It is particularly unfortunate when free labour is struggling to assert itself against slave labour, for it is deterrent to employers. If, however, labour is really "free," the wage-rate must be determined by natural laws, and not by any arbitrary standard. Employers have, of course, a perfect right to settle among themselves what is the highest wage the industry can afford to offer—as the mine managers did in Nigeria—and the lower the rate the better, so long as it will attract voluntary labour.

Since, however, the wants of the African peasant are few and are not necessities, and since he can generally obtain sufficient cash to purchase them and pay his small tax (where a tax is levied) by the sale of a little produce, there is, as I have said, but little incentive to earn wages, and it may

[1] 'The Making of Nigeria,' by Captain Orr, p. 216.

often happen that as soon as the small sum he requires has been obtained he will cease to work.[1] The higher the wages in such a case the less the work, as the Indian industrial report says is the case with the Indian coolie.[2] Whether the wage is unduly high or not depends, of course, solely on its purchasing power. A daily wage of 9d. may be considered to be high in those districts where it would probably be more than four times the cost of a labourer's daily food, but in other districts it might be barely sufficient.[3] When the rate has become standardised it is difficult to reduce it, except by the introduction of alien labour.

The first and most important of all conditions to attract free labour is that the wage should be paid in full, without deductions, into the hand of each man, and not through a headman, contractor, or chief, who may find some means of appropriating a part of it. It should be paid in cash—which incidentally stimulates currency—and not in a note divisible among several men, and above all, not in the form of an order on a store. The latter form of payment is apt to lead to abuses, and discourages free labour. Inexperienced young agents, eager to show profits, may be tempted to palm off unsaleable stock. The recipient who requires cash either to purchase articles offered for cash, or to pay his tax, sells the goods he has received for what they will fetch in the market, very possibly not more than half the wages due to him, and the result is that you may often purchase imported goods in the native market much below their price in the adjoining European store.

Wages should be paid at short intervals—at least weekly,—and I think that an employer will find that it is to his eventual

[1] The principal determining factor in the wage-rate must (subject to modifying causes) obviously be whether a man can make more money by wage-earning or by growing and selling produce, or by trading himself.

[2] Cmd. 51/1919, p. 151.

[3] The usual pre-war wage for unskilled labour paid by Government and Europeans in Nigeria was 9d. per diem in the interior, but native employers could generally obtain workmen at a lower rate. In East Africa, the rate is stated to be as low as 3d. per day for an eleven- or twelve-hour day, and in Uganda and Nyasaland it appears to have been about the same—in Northern Rhodesia, 1½d.—'Gazette,' 14/8/20. In the Sudan it is 9d. or 10d., but reached 9s. 4d. in some places in 1919.—Handbook 98, p. 95. In the Union of South Africa the rate was about 1s. 10d. per day, but inclusive of food, housing, and other contingencies, it was some 63 per cent higher (Cd. 873 of 1920, p. 24; 'East and West,' *loc. cit.*; 'Times,' 12th July 1912, &c.). It is curious to note that in all countries the daily wage of unskilled labour is approximately the same as the local value of a fowl.

advantage to pay such small fines as may be authorised by regulations into a fund, to be employed in any way he thinks fit for the good of the labourers rather than credit them to himself. It has a marked effect in establishing confidence.

The next most important consideration to the labourer is the establishment of a native market close to his camp, where he can readily buy his food, salt, tobacco, and anything else he requires. Precautions would be taken that the prices asked are reasonable, and no intoxicating liquor would be allowed. In stores close by he should be able to purchase for cash imported goods at low prices. Something may be done towards improving his standard of comfort by exhibiting for sale useful articles, such as enamel-ware utensils, blankets, &c.

It is the custom in Nigeria to pay a labourer "subsistence money"—generally half wages—for the period necessary for him to return to his home or place of engagement, together with any steamer or railway fare, and also "detention money" if he is kept unemployed. It is essential, if an employer wishes to retain a hold on his labourers, that they should be released punctually at the date on which their contract expires, or when they desire to go to look after their crops. The village sees that its members who had gone to work for wages have not been forcibly detained, as they had feared, and the cloth, &c., which they have purchased with their earnings is a great attraction to others to come forward for work.

It is all-important that the man who actually handles the labourers should possess those instincts of fair-play and tolerance which we like to think are eminently British, and that he should have the knack of getting on well with his men. For the man they like, Africans will do double the work they will for another. Jones may be quite as just and kind as Brown, but Brown "has a way with him" of exciting a laugh and of good-natured chaff which is irresistible to an African. A free labourer can, of course, choose for whom he will work, and Brown will have the pick of those who offer. Decent hutments must be provided rent-free, and groups of men from different tribes should be housed apart. They should be encouraged to bring their women to cook for them. The gift of a blanket—instead of treating it as an advance—may be found to be an economy in the long-run.

Elaborate regulations under a "master and servant," or

similar ordinance in all our Crown colonies and protectorates, now amply safeguard the welfare of the native labourer, and provide for many of the points I have mentioned. They also prescribe places, methods, and conditions of recruiting, maximum periods for which men may be engaged, conditions of repatriation, maximum distances for which a carrier may be called on to carry a standard load, conditions as to medical attendance and sanitation, inspection of labour camps, and especially the punishments (from which flogging is wholly excluded) which may legally be inflicted by an employer. They provide the machinery for entering into labour contracts, as security against desertions, but good employers are found to prefer casual labour. These ordinances must necessarily vary according to the circumstances of each protectorate, and though some years ago some of them left much to be desired, they may now, I think, be said to be generally fair and just both to the employer and the employee.

It is, I think, important in such regulations to keep in view the following points, *inter alia* :—

(*a*) That breaches of contract by a labourer should be prosecuted as civil actions by the employer, and no contract should be enforceable against a labourer under the sanctions of the criminal law.

(*b*) It should be the recognised duty of the District Officer when inspecting labour camps to satisfy himself on behalf of illiterate natives that the conditions of contracts are being observed, and to take appropriate action in case of any breach by employers.

(*c*) A clear distinction should be drawn between labour recruited on the spot and that engaged by an agent at a distance. In the latter case, though engaged within the protectorate, the conditions may for all practical purposes assimilate to those of labour imported from overseas, since the labourer cannot desert if detained overtime or ill-treated, and cannot speak the local language.

(*d*) The authenticated certificate of the person who actually pays the labourers, that he has paid the full wage in cash to each man, as set down against his name, should be substituted for the receipt, made in the form of a mark against his name, by an illiterate labourer who is ignorant whether he is acknowledging the payment of £5 or 5d.

(*e*) Finally, it is above all desirable that regulations which must inevitably become inoperative, because impracticable, and will remain a dead letter, should be avoided. They are unfair to the native, to the honest employer, and especially to the District Officer who is charged with the duty of enforcing them.

A Memorial of the Aborigines' Protection Society to the Secretary of State describes the safeguards which the Society considers as essential to schemes of Government "corvée." The application of this term—corvée (*travail obligé et gratuit*) —to the conditions of compulsory free labour is misleading and mischievous. All labour employed in British East Africa or elsewhere, whether by Government or by private persons, is fully paid, and this is made clear in Lord Milner's despatch. The concessionaire system, formerly sanctioned in the Belgian and French Congo, depended for its existence on forced labour. It failed, we are told, under the French, because of their dislike to the use of such methods. It has since been abolished by the Belgians.

The exponents of the Labour Party's policy approve, I understand, the use of compulsory unpaid labour "for purely tribal purposes in tribal areas." Tribal forced labour is, however, even less justifiable than a Government corvée for public works would be. To urge the sanction of native law and custom is absurd, for that customary law would sanction slavery, and many other things contrary to humanity. If labour is employed at all under such conditions, it should only be by special rule, promulgated, with the approval of the Governor, by the native authority, for purposes of road repair and sanitation. But I would prefer to see the total prohibition of all forms of unpaid labour, with the exception to which I shall refer in a moment. It is in my view by no means the least advantage in the system of "native treasuries," described in chapter x., that it enables the native administration to pay for the labour it needs for repairing city walls and gates, for new road construction, for sanitation and buildings, and that it deprives the salaried chiefs of any excuse for employing unpaid labour to build their houses. A native administration has, moreover, at its disposal for public purposes the use of its own prison labour. The peasant who pays his tax has a right to be relieved from all such arbitrary obligations.

The one and only form of unpaid labour demanded by the

Government in Nigeria is the "cleaning of the roads." Each village is called upon to clear the road which passes by it of weeds and grass, to patch ruts, and clean the side-drains. It is to its own interest to do so. This does not include the repair of metalled roads or the construction of new roads—tasks which devolve upon the public works department, or the native administration funds, with paid labour. If villages are so far apart as to make the task onerous a subsidy is given. It is occasionally reported that a community is anxious to make a road in order to facilitate its own trade, and will supply all labour if Government will lay out the trace. It is not always safe to accept such representations at their face value, for it may be that they emanate only from chiefs and wealthy traders, and that the peasantry are forced to make the road (very possibly on the pretence that it is the order of Government) greatly against their will—even the native courts assisting by fining recalcitrants. It is probable that the serious disturbance which took place in Egbaland (South Nigeria) in 1917 was largely due to this cause.

CHAPTER XX.

LABOUR IN TROPICAL AFRICA (*Continued*).

Compulsion by Government when justified—How enforced: (*a*) pressure on chiefs; (*b*) by legislative authority—Taxation for labour—Recruitment from contiguous territory—Alien immigration and labour—Contracts for repatriation—Compulsion for self-advancement—Wage-earning and peasant ownership—Necessity of European ownership in certain cases—Co-partnership and profit-sharing—Exceptional justification of pressure on chiefs—Native contractors—Substitutes for labour—Conclusions.

If the safety of the State is imperilled, it is universally admitted that the government of a free and civilised people is justified in resorting to compulsion by means of obligatory military service for the young and able-bodied males, and to taxation limited only by the needs of the State on the rest of its citizens. This is, of course, the extreme case. The Secretary of State for the Colonies, speaking for the British Government, in a State paper has, as we have seen, laid down the principle, "in order that there may be no room for doubt in the matter," that the Government of an African dependency is justified in resorting to compulsion for paid labour required for works of a public nature, subject to express provisos. This dictum was not contested in the debate in the House of Lords,[1] and has been supported by various high authorities.[2]

[1] 14th July 1920. Lord Bryce admitting the necessity, pointed out that since such works are conducted in public any abuse would be known and rectified. The Primate concurred.

[2] The Aborigines' Protection Society quotes Lord Cromer: "We reluctantly admit the necessity of compulsory labour in certain cases, and we do not stigmatise as slavery such labour, when under all possible safeguards against the occurrence of abuses, it is employed for indispensable and recognised purposes of public utility. On the other hand, we regard the system when employed for private profit as wholly unjustifiable, and as synonymous with slavery." "Forced labour," writes Sir S. Olivier; "under the authority of tribal chiefs, is a permissible institution for the execution of public services, as in the

In what circumstances and by what methods, then, is it justifiable for a Government to resort to compulsion in the employment of paid labour? The reasons given in the blue-book for compulsion in East Africa do not appear to be limited to Government necessity, but include also the desirability of training of natives to work, so that they shall not "live in idleness and vice." The payment of tax by labour in lieu of cash, as in Uganda, is a different matter, and, as I have said (p. 251), it is preferable that the labour should be paid in full and the amount of the tax subsequently refunded, so as to make the distinction perfectly clear.

The educative results of compulsory labour depend on the conditions under which it is employed, and are not a primary reason for resorting to compulsion for public works, for it is, of course, possible to compel natives to work for their own or their community's benefit instead of for the white man's wages. In East Africa sixty days' compulsory labour is enforced by ordinance, and since this will not be demanded if a native works on his own fields or in other occupations, the object is manifestly purely educative. It is improbable, as I have pointed out, that it will result in procuring any appreciable supply of labour for Government—apart from the great difficulty of enforcing the law without injustice,—and therefore the problem of an adequate contingent of labour for railway construction, &c., is left practically untouched.

Compulsion is only justified where labour cannot otherwise be procured for public works of an essential and urgent nature. It is preferable that it should be avoided if possible for ordinary and continuing works, since it militates against the evolution of voluntary contract by rendering Government employment unpopular. Primitive tribes are suspicious, and fear employment by the white man. In such a case the wages paid, and the good treatment received, should have the effect of removing these fears and suspicions, so that compulsion may no longer be necessary, and free voluntary labour take its place.

The question of the measure of compulsion which is admissible or advisable in order to induce the African to work, solely for his own moral and material benefit and advance-

old brig-bote and burg-bote of our own ancestors" ('Contemporary Review,' January 1919). But the precedents of early Anglo-Saxon times are hardly applicable to the rule of a modern State in Africa.

ment, is one which belongs rather to the subject of education than to that of labour. An informative article in the 'Colonial Journal'[1] cites Belgian and French criticism of British methods of free labour. The Dutch in Java, we are told, compel the natives to work, "with the result of extraordinary prosperity, and the natives have flourished." The population has increased from four to twenty millions in 120 years, and is stated to be more industrious, trustworthy, and intelligent than the same races under British rule. The Germans in Samoa compelled the natives to plant and maintain a certain number of cocoanut palms per man: the population has quadrupled, the area of cultivation has increased, and the natives, it is said, so appreciate the system that defaulters are reported.

The results in British neighbouring dependencies are quoted in contrast. In Malaya and in Sarawak the Chinese are displacing the Malays and Dyaks. Indians are dispossessing the aboriginals in Fiji, and Sir Everard im Thurn writes that "either the Fijians themselves must in some way be persuaded to do a fair share of work, or more and more coloured labour must be brought in from outside."

The question at issue is whether a trustee Power has fulfilled all its obligations towards an indolent and apathetic ward by assuring to it complete security of life and property and the opportunity of a literary education, and then allowing it to commit racial suicide. We have upset the old order, and in many regions have weakened tribal authority. Our rule is not popular, for new generations forget the old hardships which their fathers suffered, and from which they have been relieved. They care less for our impartial justice than we like to think they do. It is at least arguable that they are not yet fitted for the full measure of individual liberty which it has taken us centuries to evolve for ourselves.

Such are the arguments of those who uphold compulsion, not as an unavoidable and disagreeable necessity, in order to carry on the work of administration and development, but as being in itself a justifiable means to an end—"the advancement of the natives themselves."[2] In those rare instances

[1] "Problems of Empire," April 1914—citing the 'Bulletin de la Société Belge d'Etudes Coloniales,' December 1913, and Lebon, 'Lois psychologiques d'évolution des peuples.'

[2] This view was supported by the East African bishops. The commission appointed "for the protection of the natives of the Congo" (which consisted

where the African is apathetic or indolent, such means may be of educative value, provided that the native is made to work on his own behalf and not for an alien master; but I think that there are other methods more essential, which I shall discuss in the chapter on education.

Among more advanced communities, familiar with the conception of wage-labour and contract, the "educative" argument recedes farther into the background. In Nigeria private employers—*e.g.*, mine managers and others—knowing that their labour supply depends wholly on the inducements they can offer, have succeeded in attracting a fair labour supply, and there is no reason why a Government should not do the same, though the supply may not at first be obtainable so quickly, in such large numbers, or at so low a rate of pay, as when compulsion is resorted to.

When in cases of exceptional emergency it is necessary to resort to compulsion, how should it be enforced? In primitive communities an executive order—though an undesirable method—may suffice; but under an organised native administration, even though the demand be only in a grave and temporary emergency, such a method is still more undesirable. The Criminal Code of Nigeria, as Mr Gowers, the Lieut.-Governor, points out, makes it a felony, punishable by five years' imprisonment, for any one to threaten with injury to himself, his reputation, or property, any person, or those in whom he is interested, or to induce him or them to believe that he will become an object of displeasure to the Government, or to a Government official, if he does so with the intent to compel the person to do any act which he is lawfully entitled to abstain from doing. But is not a native chief who is told to provide labour for Government ordered to commit this felony?

The employment of chiefs and headmen for this purpose can only weaken the native authority, for it exposes them to the very probable contingency of a refusal on the part of some individual, and unless he is coerced by illegal means, their authority is defied. In any case, a chief would be called on to do precisely that kind of arbitrary act which the District

largely of Roman Catholic priests) reported in 1912 that "it is necessary to impose labour on the blacks in order to secure the modification of their mentality, and to bring them to realise their duty as civilised people do."—'Diocesan Magazine, West Equatorial Africa,' July 1912, p. 13.

Officer has been constantly telling him the Government will no longer tolerate. Consider, moreover, the actual working of the order. The headman is directed to produce a specified number of men. Those able to afford it offer bribes to be let off, others refuse or disappear. In one case a village head, being a butcher, ordered all the butchers to go, so as to enjoy a monopoly himself. The most law-abiding are penalised. At best the incidence is purely arbitrary, and almost certainly attended by abuses difficult to detect or suppress. If the chief fails, he is accounted to have insufficient influence and authority for his position.[1]

The recommendation of the bishops in East Africa that compulsory labour should be legalised, " preferably for Government purposes," was, it is understood, made with the object of regularising the action of the District Officer and the native headmen, and providing them with the authority to enforce their demands. It is without question essential that, for whatever purpose compulsion may be resorted to, it should have the sanction of a law clearly defining the extent and conditions of the service required.

It is, however, in my opinion, preferable that special legislation should be enacted in each case where the necessity may arise, or, at least, that the Governor should be empowered to declare by Order in Council or proclamation that the necessity has arisen, and to specify the proportion of the adult able-bodied male population of a named district who are called upon through their chiefs to come forward, and for what period they will be required, and for what length of time the special emergency will continue.

If direct taxation is in force the District Officer will have an approximate census of every village, and can arrange the numbers to be called up for each relief gang. The formalities

[1] The evidence of Mr Hollis, C.M.G. (Colonial Secretary), before the East African Commission of 1912-13, is quoted: "Whenever an agent wants labour he goes to the chiefs and bribes them, with the result that a number of men are brought to the District Commissioners and registered,—one could not call this voluntary labour." Lord Milner, though emphatic that no form of compulsion for private employment is admissible, and that only "judicious advice" may be tendered, adds that "any unwillingness on the part of chiefs to act on the instructions conveyed through responsible Government officers would naturally be taken note of and recorded." "Instructions" are a very different thing from "judicious advice," which, whether given by the District Officer or by missionaries, does not so far appear to have produced the desired effect.

Mr Churchill has lately ruled that officials shall take no part at all in recruiting labour for private employment.—Cmd. 1509, 1921.

of this procedure will vest it in the eyes of both educated and uneducated natives with the character of emergency legislation. The close supervision of the British staff will minimise abuses, and the responsibility rests, where it ought to rest, on the Head of the administration.

In countries where the population is not inadequate for the supply of reasonable demands—in which category Uganda and Nyasaland may perhaps be included [1]—any unwillingness of the people to come forward may be diminished by the more equitable incidence of the demand which would thus be ensured, and by greater inducements in the welfare and treatment of the labourers, more especially by being allowed to return to their villages at seed-time and harvest.

We have seen that the Glen-Grey Act imposed a tax upon natives who could not prove that they had worked beyond the borders of the district for three months. This was an Act of the Cape Legislature for which the Imperial Government was not responsible. The clause was never operative, and the South African Commission of 1903-5 recorded its view that "any measure of compulsion is to be deprecated, not only as unjust, but as economically unsound." A similar undesirable system has recently been abandoned in Nyasaland. If the payment of the ordinary tax must be made in currency, natives will work for wages in order to earn the small sum required, and as a result will often become regular wage-earners.

The Aborigines' Protection Society lays stress on the undesirability of recruiting labour from a Mandated territory for service beyond it. Lord Milner has no objection to such a course, provided there is a surplus of labour available. If both are under the same controlling Power, the desirability or otherwise would seem rather to depend on distance—a matter equally important if the labour is recruited within the protectorate—a point on which I have already laid emphasis.

If labourers are conveyed long distances by steamer or

[1] In the latest Uganda report we read : "Voluntary enlistment of labour is the recognised policy, and is expected to furnish the quota required, always presuming that terms and conditions of employment are reasonably inviting. The current wages for unskilled labour averages between 2d. and 4d. per diem." This wage, contrasted with the money to be made by growing cotton (for which the Governor says 4s. a lb. was paid in Manchester), seems hardly sufficiently inviting.—Cmd. 508 (37), 1920.

The Governor (Sir R. Coryndon) says that "the available supply of labour is much more than adequate if it would come forward."—'United Empire,' June 1920, p. 298.

rail, it may be that neither the climate nor the food are suitable, and the conditions approximate to those of indentured rather than of free local labour.[1] If the employer fails to repatriate the men at the agreed time, they have no remedy. For this reason it seems desirable that when men are engaged for service at a destination over 100 miles from the place of engagement, they should be registered before a magistrate, a copy of the contract being deposited with the District Officer at the place of engagement, and a duplicate sent to the officer of the district in which they are to serve. The duty then devolves upon the former of seeing that the labourers understand the terms of the contract, and where they are going; and on the latter of seeing that the contract is fulfilled and the labourers are properly treated, and repatriated on its expiry. If engaged for over a month, it is desirable that they should take their wives with them. In most, if not in all, colonies recruiting agents must be licensed.

I have in the last chapter shown that since the British settler is unable to perform the manual work on his estate in East Africa, there is no really permanent solution to the labour difficulty which will meet the demands of the future, other than the importation of contract labour under Government supervision and control, supplemented by labour-saving devices.

Alien labour may either be of the class which intends to remain in the country permanently as colonists—being either free immigrants or labourers who have completed their period of indenture—or it may consist of labourers who are prohibited from settlement, or who do not desire to remain. To the colonist class belong the Indian immigrants who have settled in British Guiana, the West Indies,[2] and Fiji, and also to a large extent the Chinese in Malaya. To the non-colonist

[1] The export of labourers from Nyasaland to the South African mines some years ago, where they died in large numbers, seems to have been a lamentable failure. It is now discouraged by the Government, even though entirely voluntary. Consul Monson declared that nothing short of force would induce natives of East Africa to go.—Cmd. 1631 of 1903, p. 8. A similar export from Senegal to the French Congo was stopped by the French Government.

[2] In Trinidad half the population consists of naturalised immigrants, and that of the West Indies generally consists of the descendants of imported African slaves. Sumatra, Borneo, Mauritius, Java and Madagascar, offer parallel cases. It has been maintained that white men in North Queensland can be inured to labour in the sugar plantations under tropical conditions, but no one has so far had the temerity to maintain this view as regards Africa, except in the Highlands.

class belong the Tamils in Malaya, the Indian labour in Ceylon (where half a million indentured coolies serve their time and return to India of their own wish), the Chinese imported into South Africa, and the Kanakas in Australia, for whom repatriation was a condition of service.

It is, of course, desirable that the profits arising from the development of the resources of a country should as far as possible accrue to its own people. But it is manifest that when the population is too scanty, or too apathetic to develop those resources, or to supply sufficient unskilled labour for their development under alien supervision, there is no injustice if the people of countries where land is insufficient for the needs of a congested population are called in to help to develop it. If, indeed, the adequate development of the resources of the tropics be regarded as a trust, fertile lands capable of producing raw materials and food greatly needed by mankind cannot be allowed to lie unproductive. It may therefore be contended that if British capital, energy, and expert knowledge are available to develop waste lands in Africa, but lack sufficient manual labour, there is sufficient justification for importing alien labour.

The importation of labourers, however, a considerable portion of whom intend to remain as colonists, presupposes a policy of Asiatic colonisation, and I have already (in chapter xv.) discussed the many serious difficulties inherent in such a policy in our African dependencies. It would, moreover, only afford a very temporary relief to the labour difficulty, which would become as acute as ever as soon as the land assigned for Asiatic colonisation was filled up, and fresh immigrants could no longer be encouraged.[1]

If therefore Indian immigration, whatever its merits or demerits from other points of view, offers no solution to the labour problem, there remains only the possibility of importing labourers—like the Chinese in South Africa—who are under an obligation to leave the country on the expiry of their contract. This form of labour contract has been condemned by a large section of British opinion, as the debates in Mr Lyttelton's time testify. The allegation that it was equivalent to slavery must, I think, be regarded as insincere or ill-informed, looking to the safeguards employed, the high rate of wages, and the fact that it was a voluntary and a strictly

[1] This, Sir H. May informs me, is the present experience in Fiji.

limited contract. But the fact that such labourers were unaccompanied by their wives—with the inevitable result of trouble—was a serious objection.

It is obvious that the future necessities of Government development and of private enterprise will demand a large supply of native labour in Kenya, and if that supply is not locally available without retarding the progress of the natives of the soil as producers on their own lands, or limiting the area available for their future expansion by the introduction of an alien peasantry, it becomes necessary to consider the alternative of imported contract labour. Let us glance, then, at the conditions under which labourers on limited contracts, which provide for repatriation on their expiration, are employed in Malaya and elsewhere.

The labourers are generally " assisted," for they lack money for the sea-voyage and maintenance, and would land as destitutes wholly at the mercy of the employer. It is therefore in their own interests that Government insists that they should either embark under contract, or form a contract as soon as they arrive.

There is no need to describe here in elaborate detail the rules made in British tropical dependencies for the protection and care of alien labour. They may be studied in the ordinances of Hong-Kong, the Straits Settlements, British Borneo, and British Guiana by any one interested. It suffices to say that both in the country (if British) from which the labourers come and that to which they go, a " protector " who knows their language and understands them is appointed to look after their welfare, and scrutinise the contracts in the interest of the immigrant. Stringent rules are enforced as regards the duration of contract, recovery of advances, facility for repatriation, working hours, and method of payment. The labourer is medically examined, and care is taken that he has medical aid and hospital treatment, and food at reasonable prices. Housing, water-supply, and sanitation are regulated. He may not be separated from his family (if he has one), or employed in prescribed unhealthy districts, and must be repatriated at his employer's expense if unfit to remain. He is assured of a right of complaint and of redress.

Contract labour under such conditions has been a boon to the Indians and Chinese who have been employed in Ceylon, Fiji, Malaya, and other British colonies. Its use should be limited to countries in which the population is at present insufficient for the essential needs of the country. Where there exists an adequate native population, it is a confession of failure that we should have to resort to imported contract labour, whether it be Chinese labour in the Transvaal, or Indians in Natal. The education of local labour should progressively reduce the demand.

When discussing land questions, I maintained that the cultivation of exportable products by natives on their own holdings is unquestionably preferable to a system of European-owned plantations worked by paid labour, provided that the enterprise does not require large capital or technical skill and management, and that the crop is an indigenous or naturalised one. The native holder occupies a higher status, and working in his own sole interests and at his own time, will produce more than if working for another, as we have seen in the palm produce, cocoa, and ground-nut industries.[1]

On the other hand, it must be admitted that, though the cost of European supervision is heavy, it is compensated by improvement in the quality of the output, and by more continuous returns due to better care of the soil ; but European ownership on a large scale has in all cases resulted in the demand for alien or for compulsory labour, by which alone large foreign-owned estates can be kept going. I am not, however, disposed to regard the system of wage-earning with the aversion of those who consider that " capitalism " and " landlordism " are anathema. The agricultural wage-earner is free from the anxieties inseparable from an industry dependent on climatic variations, the fluctuations of markets, the outbreak of plant disease or insect pests, and the lack of necessary funds at a critical moment.

In the case of the mining industry the technical skill and appliances of foreign experts, and their continued supervision, is of course essential to the development of a minefield. But even in this case free native labour can be encouraged by the system of " calabashing " or " tributing " in the tin-mining industry, by which a labourer is paid for the clean ore he extracts by washing, and can seek the field where he will obtain the highest remuneration for his labour. Mining industries, moreover, often yield high returns, so that they

[1] Beaulieu lends the weight of his high authority to this view, and is emphatic that Africa should be developed by free African labour.—Vol. ii. p. 116.

are able to release a considerable portion of the labourers to attend to their crops at the critical seasons.

Nor is foreign skill less essential for the introduction of new vegetable products, or the improvement and adaptation of existing ones—*e.g.*, flax, or the curing of tobacco for export,—until the natives have learnt to cultivate and prepare them for the foreign market. Such industries, mineral and agricultural, are the means of adding to the wealth and prosperity of the country, and though they create—for a time at least—a large demand for wage-labour, the natives so employed are being educated in new and better methods of applying their labour, which they can later—as in the cocoa industry—undertake on their own account. The attempt to establish plantations on a basis of communal labour is, as I have said, an experiment of doubtful value. This subject is one which touches so many native interests that I have already had occasion to refer to it in the chapter on land, and shall again recur to it in speaking of economic development.

Experiments aimed at identifying the interest of the native labourer with that of the European employer, and of the native producer with that of the alien merchant, are as yet unfortunately rare. The system of cotton-growing adopted in the Sudan is an excellent example, for here the Government, private capital, and the labourer all share in the profits.[1] (See p. 525.) The problem of applying any system of mutual participation in results naturally offers greater difficulties in Africa than in countries where labour is highly organised and less exposed to interference by unnecessary middlemen (p. 480).

I have in a previous paragraph strongly deprecated the application of pressure on native chiefs as a recognised administrative method of obtaining labour, whether for Government or for private enterprise. Where the urgency of the public service leaves no possible alternative to compulsion, I suggested that a legalised *ad hoc* conscription, properly supervised by the district staff, through the chiefs, is preferable to informal and illegal " pressure."

In the earliest inauguration of an administration, however, before the machinery is fully organised, the experiment may be

[1] The Germans instituted a system in the Lindi district (East Africa) by which the planter prepared the ground by machinery, supervised the manuring, sowed the crop, and bought it at a fixed price from the natives.—Handbook 113, p. 69.

justified, if the reluctance of the natives to work is due to fear of the white man, and terror of the treatment to be expected from him, assuming that tribal authority is strong enough to enforce obedience, and that in consequence this method is the least likely to give rise to disturbance and trouble.

In such circumstances in Nigeria, in order to construct the Baro-Kano main trunk railway, and again when the Eastern Railway was undertaken in a district but little under administrative control, orders were sent to each chief to supply a given quota of men. The advantage that a railway would be to their trade was in the latter case pointed out to them, and this was not without its effect, and added a personal interest in the results of their labour. The district officers in the first case themselves supervised the labour from their districts; in the second case, where the work was more concentrated, a senior district officer was told off, whose sole duty it was to look after the interests of the labourers, to settle their differences, and to see that they were housed and fed, and were regularly and fully paid. They were in charge of an engineer who had gained a well-deserved reputation for handling natives with success. The result was that on discharge at the time appointed, they returned to their homes with cloth and goods bought from their wages, and presently came flocking back to engage of their own freewill.

The coal-mine at Udi was another example. Here, as I have already described, a particularly truculent tribe, during the time I was in Nigeria, supplied an entirely voluntary and adequate contingent for work underground of an unusually strenuous kind, in a suffocating temperature, from the first initiation of the work in 1914. 145,400 tons were placed on the railway in 1918. It was even possible to reduce the wage-rate considerably, and to introduce piecework. Both on the railway and in the coal-mine it was found that the labourer readily grasped the idea of piecework, and appreciated the option of leaving as soon as he had completed his task, or of earning double money by doing double work.[1]

[1] The educative value may be gauged from the following extract: "Recently the re-lining and heightening of the main drift, including the blasting out of 2 ft. of stone from the floor, and re-timbering, was successfully done chiefly in night shifts, under the sole supervision of a native foreman engaged in 1915. A section of the mine has also been placed under a native."—Report 468/1920, p. 53. Some of the mining companies are replacing their European foremen by Africans.

The primitive native does not discriminate between employment by one white man or another, unless and until he has found cause to do so. Since Government employment had become popular, he was equally ready to engage for work with any white man. The mining companies now employ about 19,000, many of whom travel considerable distances to seek work. It was the same in Nyasaland when I was there in 1888. The Scottish planters treated their labour well, and got as much and more than they needed at 2s. 6d. to 5s. per mensem. The employment of agents and touts recruiting labour on their own account among primitive tribes is to be deprecated.

It is obviously desirable to employ native contractors to carry out a specific task, as in more advanced countries, in order to minimise the need of personal supervision of unskilled work by officials. A contractor, however, pays his own labourers, and experience has shown that native chiefs who have undertaken contracts for Government have not only in some cases failed to pay their labourers, or paid them a wholly inadequate sum, but were apt to keep them for many days unpaid before the material for their work was supplied. The rule in Nigeria therefore is that whenever work for Government, or for a native administration, is given to a native contractor, he must engage to pay his labourers at an agreed rate for every day they are detained (whether at work or not), and do so weekly in the presence of a European if the contract is for Government, or of a responsible officer of the native administration when works are executed for or through the agency of a native administration, unless the British officer is fully satisfied as to the integrity of the contractor, or knows that his labourers are so independent that they would not remain unless they received their full and regular pay. Care is taken that each labourer is paid a full day's wage, and that no peculation or misappropriation of the money takes place, whether it is paid by Government or from a native treasury, and the principle of piecework is encouraged.

Lord Milner instanced Government transport as one of the tasks for which compulsory labour was authorised—viz., for porters to carry the effects of officials, so as to enable them to travel on duty,—which is a vital necessity. It is, however, economically unsound, especially in a country where labour is scarce, to employ men merely as beasts of burden, nor is it done in any other country in the world. Since it requires one hundred men to convey a ton of produce for three days' march only, the enormous numbers withdrawn from productive labour for the conveyance of the hundreds of thousands of tons annually shipped from these colonies may be conjectured. It therefore becomes the first duty of a Government to provide a better means of transport, and it seems indefensible that forced labour should be used for such a purpose, except where any other form of transport is impossible. I shall refer at greater length to this subject in the chapter on transport, and when discussing economic development I shall have occasion to discuss the desirability of economising human labour by the use of domestic animals in agriculture, and of machinery for the preparation of produce for the market.

The subject of the education of labour will be more appropriately dealt with in the chapters on education; but I may note here that the opportunity afforded for teaching a trade to long-sentence prisoners should not be overlooked, and it is desirable that special pains should be taken in the education of all forms of prison labour.[1]

The facts which have thus been briefly reviewed will, I think, lead us to the following conclusions. While the compulsory enlistment of fully-paid labour by Government for the essential needs of the country is justified, it should, when resorted to on any large scale, be legalised by special emergency legislation, and every effort should be made to render it as attractive as possible, with a view to encouraging timid and suspicious savages to return voluntarily. Where an adequate population exists, any form of compulsion should be only a very temporary phase.

Where, however, the population is inadequate to supply the necessary contingent of labourers for the construction of railways and other essential works without constantly resorting to compulsion, not merely of a surplus of un-

[1] In Nigeria the Director of Prisons, in his last report (1919), contrasts the present-day results with his earlier experience. "Reports (he says) for idleness against prisoners employed on industrial labour are almost non-existent, and during this period only two men who have been taught a trade in the prison have been known to return." In Hong-Kong great care was taken to train all long-sentence prisoners to a trade, and on discharge they were eagerly sought after at high wages.

employed, but interfering with the ordinary industry of the native population, the only solution appears to be imported contract labour, which, in certain circumstances, may also be tolerated for private enterprise.

If imported labour is resorted to, it should be employed under the strictest Government control and supervision. When possible, indentured labourers should be encouraged to become colonists, the period of indenture forming a kind of apprenticeship to enable them to realise the conditions of the country, and to accumulate a little capital to assist them in making a beginning on their own account. Where this is not possible or advisable, and the imported labour must be repatriated, it can only be justified for private enterprise where immense areas of vacant lands suitable for European settlement and development exist,—where it has been conclusively proved that the local labour supply, in spite of all inducements by good treatment, is insufficient, and that the temporary transfer of voluntary African labour from more distant parts of the country is not feasible, by reason of sickness and mortality due to change of climate and food. Except where conditions such as these exist, the development of the resources of the country should be carried on by the native himself, working as a voluntary wage-earner, or preferably on his own land as a free producer.

CHAPTER XXI.

EDUCATION.

Objects and ideals of education—Effect of European influence and education—The example of India—The system in British colonies—In West Africa—Mission responsibility—The need of co-operation—Principles adopted in Nigeria—Formation of character—Residential schools—The British staff—School monitors—Field sports—Grant dependent on tone of school—Moral instruction—Religious instruction—Contrast of Africa with India and China—The machinery of education—Unassisted schools—Assisted schools—Grant code must be attractive—Suggestions for a grant code.

If a life happy and progressive so far as the individual is concerned, useful, sympathetic, and stimulating in its relations with the community, may be said to constitute a worthy ideal, the object which education in Africa must have in view must be to fit the ordinary individual to fill a useful part in his environment, with happiness to himself, and to ensure that the exceptional individual shall use his abilities for the advancement of the community and not to its detriment, or to the subversion of constituted authority.

Its results should be manifest in the adaptation of the people to the existing conditions of life, and in enabling them to effect some betterment and progress in those conditions. It should train a generation able to achieve ideals of its own, without a slavish imitation of Europeans, capable and willing to assume its own definite sphere of public and civic work, and to shape its own future. The education afforded to that section of the population who intend to lead the lives which their forefathers led should enlarge their outlook, increase their efficiency and standard of comfort, and bring them into closer sympathy with the Government, instead of making them unsuited to and ill-contented with their mode of life. It should produce a new generation of native chiefs of higher integrity, a truer sense of justice, and appreciation of responsibility for the welfare of the community. As regards that smaller section who desire to take part in public or municipal duties, or to enter the service of Government or of commercial firms, education should make them efficient, loyal, reliable and contented—a race of self-respecting native gentlemen. Finally, the policy should popularise education, should extend it to the ignorant masses instead of confining it to the few, and should increase the output of youths well qualified to meet the demand, whether clerical, professional, or industrial.[1]

The diffusion of education throughout the country, and especially the education of the sons of native rulers, is particularly desirable in order to avoid the present danger of a separate educated class (in West Africa chiefly confined to the coast cities) in rivalry with the accepted rulers of the people.

The impact of European civilisation on tropical races has indeed a tendency to undermine that respect for authority which is the basis of social order. The authority of the head, whether of the tribe, the village, or the family, is decreased, and parental discipline is weakened—tendencies which, as Lord Macdonnell observed, are probably inseparable from that emancipation of thought which results from our educational system and needs the control of scholastic discipline.[2] These tendencies are no doubt largely due to the fact that each generation is advancing intellectually beyond its predecessor, so that "the younger men view with increasing impatience the habits, traditions, and ideas of their elders."[3] From this standpoint we may even regard this restlessness as a measure of progress.[4]

These tendencies became very marked in India towards the close of the nineteenth century. The failure of the system of Indian education is graphically described by Sir V. Chirol,[5] and appears now to be very generally admitted.

[1] The opposite ideal is that ascribed to Germany, as shown by her own publicists. "Her object was mainly to teach a sufficient number of natives trades and handicrafts in which they could be of use to European employers." Handbook 113, p. 38.

[2] Selected Records of Indian Government, 265, p. 11.

[3] Sir A. Croft, ibid., p. 142.

[4] 'The British Empire,' Sir C. Lucas, p. 220.

[5] 'Unrest in India,' chapters xvii. to xxi.

"A purely literary type of education was the only one generally provided by Government," says the Industrial Report of 1919, and the intellectual classes eagerly grasped at the prospect of Government, professional, and clerical employment, with the result that a disproportionate number of persons with a purely literary education were created, and industrial development was arrested.[1]

Prosperity would seem to be a contributory cause—as in Egypt and Ireland,—for, as the special correspondent of the 'Times,' writing in 1913,[2] observes: "The people of India have never been so well off, never so wisely cared for, never so secure as they are to-day." Yet the undermining of all authority is rapidly proceeding. Parents complain of the intractability of their boys. The local press preaches sedition, and racial strife is stirred up by misrepresentation and false reports. If "the influence of education for good depends on the qualities of character it is able to evoke," it must be judged to have failed. Its aim, it is alleged, has been to train the intellect, and to gauge the product of the schools by the ability to pass tests in prescribed fields of knowledge, to the neglect of moral discipline and standards of duty. Positive knowledge as tested by competitive examinations has constituted the key to success.

As long ago as December 1887 the Government of India drew the attention of the local Governments to "the growth of tendencies unfavourable to discipline in the rising generation," and various suggestions were made to counteract this tendency. They included the establishment of hostels and boarding-houses, the appointment of British headmasters and of school monitors, the recognition of field sports as a part of the school training, the adoption of disciplinary punishments which should fall more directly on the offender than fines, and of prizes for good conduct, together with moral instruction based on the fundamental principles of natural religion, and having a direct bearing on personal conduct. The suggestions were favourably received, and the replies of the local Governors and of educational experts were published in the Blue-book from which I have quoted, under the title, 'Discipline and Moral Training in the Schools and Colleges of India' (255 pages). It is a volume so full of ripe

1 Cmd. 51 of 1919, pp. 65 and 93.
2 'Times,' 19th-22nd December 1913.

experience and suggestion that the Colonial Office would do well to place it in the hands of the Director of Education in every colony.

On 18th June of the following year a resolution was passed which recognised the necessity for abandoning the purely literary scope of education, and it was followed in 1889 by a still wider recognition of the defects of the system. The results were, however, small, though they led the way to Lord Curzon's Educational Conference, and the very important resolution of March 1904.

The system which had proved so disastrous in India had its counterpart in the Crown colonies and dependencies, and its results were similar.[1] The lessons of India were ignored. I have already quoted the opinion of a French writer that a literary education on European lines has mischievous results, and only produces hostility and ingratitude. The results achieved by Holland, and to a lesser degree by Germany, in their Eastern colonies are contrasted to our disadvantage. In South Africa General Smuts has recently described the existing system as "wholly unsuited to native needs, and positively pernicious, leading the native to a dead wall, over which he is unable to rise, and becomes a ready prey to the agitator."[2]

The results in West Africa were described by the Secretary of State (Mr Harcourt) in 1916 as "very unsatisfactory," a verdict endorsed by Dr Blyden and by many other leading Africans, including the (native) Acting Director of Education in Nigeria (Mr Carr).[3] The output of the schools is described as unreliable, lacking in integrity, self-control, and discipline, and without respect for authority of any kind. The vanity of the young men produced by the schools had (said the senior native councillor in Lagos) become intolerable, and

[1] Mr (now Sir James) Currie, formerly Director of Education in the Sudan and Principal of Gordon College, strongly condemns the Crown colony system of education. "Wellnigh all critics (he writes in 1905) of systems of education among backward races, if agreed on nothing else, seem to be sceptical of the results hitherto attained. . . . Their indictment seems to be that the educated product in the tropics has proved himself out of touch with his proper social environment, and as a member of society, fruitless on the economic side."

[2] Speech on second reading Native Affairs Bill, 26th May 1920.

[3] "There is hardly a sign of the growth of mental power or of self-control. They are, generally speaking, not intelligent and not reliable." Sir W. MacGregor, when Governor of Lagos, referred to the class of "Mission-educated young men who live in the villages interfering with the native councils, and acting as correspondents for the mendacious native press."

something, he urged, must be done to rescue the rising generation from these evils. It is only to be expected that the result of the present system should be to create a prejudice against education, since, as a Sierra Leone chief remarked, "it teaches youths to despise their elders," while others ascribed the increased cost of food to the unwillingness of youths from school to work on the land.[1] Provincial reports speak of the contempt for manual work shown by boys from schools.

Education has brought to such men only discontent, suspicion of others, and bitterness, which masquerades as racial patriotism, and the vindication of rights unjustly withheld. As citizens they are unfitted to hold posts of trust and responsibility where integrity and loyalty are essential, or to become leaders of their own community in the path of progress. They have lost touch, as I said in chapter iv., with their own people. Fortunately there are many and brilliant exceptions.

Since education has in the past been largely in the hands of the Missions, to whom moral training would naturally be of the first importance, how are these results to be explained? Was there no means by which the disruptive forces of education could be minimised in a country like Africa, where the problem is comparatively simple? The lack of discipline among Mission converts has indeed occasionally led to political disturbances, both in Nigeria and in Ashanti.[2]

The fault has, I think, lain primarily on the Governments, for the grant on which the aided schools depend has been based on a purely intellectual test. Great as are the results achieved by the Missions in Africa—and they are great indeed in Uganda,[3] Nyasaland, and West Africa—they too must

[1] That a serious prejudice against education may be created by the usurpation of the prerogatives of the native rulers by "intelligentsia" who call themselves the "natural leaders of the people" was recently shown by the speech of the Gold Coast chief Ofori, and by the press comments and the speeches of leading natives of Nigeria, in regard to the claims of the members of the "National Conference," who presented a petition to the King in 1920. The Governor of the Gold Coast laid emphasis on this aspect of the matter. See p. 86.

[2] Prior to 1905, when the cost of the Bonny school first appeared in the estimates, education in Southern Nigeria was left entirely in the hands of the Missions. Government non-denominational schools were first established in Ashanti in 1911, because the Christian converts had refused service to the chiefs.—'A Vanished Dynasty,' Sir F. Fuller, p. 223.

[3] In Uganda education is still entirely in the hands of the Missions, and there are no Government schools. The number of pupils is 79,000. A grant of £2100 is made from revenue. [Annual Report, Cmd. 508, 1920.] The Governor says that good discipline is maintained in many of the schools.—'United Empire,' June 1920, p. 299.

bear their share of the blame in having set too slight a value on discipline, and concentrated too much on the acquisition of such knowledge as would enable their pupils to do creditably in the Government examinations, and the training of a specialised class for evangelical work.[1]

If these ill-results are to be avoided in the future, it is essential not merely that the local Missions should act in co-operation with the secular authority, but that the experienced and able men who control the policy of the great societies should take counsel with colonial administrators in England. It is also no less vital that the local Governments should exercise some control over all unaided schools.

I cannot too strongly emphasise this need for co-operation between all those who are interested in the education of the native races. No adequate results will be achieved if Government and Missions work in separate compartments, nor can the Government discharge its obligations—as it has attempted to do in some cases in the past—by the mere payment of a grant from revenue, based on examination results. Co-operation can only become effective by the creation of Boards of Education, and local committees, upon which not only managers of schools (both assisted and unassisted) should be fully represented, but also influential members of the community (European and native), and intelligent chiefs. There are very many subjects upon which the most experienced and the most sincere may hold different views, which can only be adjusted to some measure of uniformity by discussion and compromise, and concentration of effort on clearly defined lines. This co-operation must not be limited to those actually engaged in educational work, but must extend to the administrative staff and the native chiefs, on whose help and goodwill the education officer must largely depend for his prestige and standing in the native estimation, for the removal of prejudices, and for the popularity of his work.[2]

[1] Mr Rhodes expressed the view that Mission education only produced "Kaffir parsons and editors." There are of course notable exceptions to the general charge of indiscipline (largely due to the insufficiency of the Mission staff). Two stand out in my personal experience—that of Dr Laws on Lake Nyasa, and that of Archdeacon (now Bishop) Melville-Jones at Oyo in Nigeria. Kid-glove discipline is no more suited to the African than to the English boy.

[2] In Nigeria a Central Board under each Lieut.-Governor considers all proposals and suggestions, and makes its recommendations to the Government, while each provincial (Government) school has an Advisory Committee, on which natives are largely represented.

In the endeavour to give effect to the ideals which I have described as the primary objects of education, and to profit by the experience of the past, an ordinance and regulations were drawn up in 1915 in Nigeria, but did not obtain Colonial Office approval for a year. They were enacted in 1916, and they sought to embody the following principles :—

(*a*) That the primary object of all schools should be the formation of character and habits of discipline, rather than the mere acquisition of a certain amount of book-learning or technical skill, and that the grant-in-aid should be in part based on success in this direction.

(*b*) That the teaching should be adapted to the needs of the pupils, whether they are intending to qualify for clerical or other like service, or desire to become mechanics or artisans, or, on the other hand, have no wish to leave their village and the pursuits their fathers had followed.

(*c*) That the proportion of teachers to pupils should be adequate, that they should be properly qualified and their status improved. Adequate grants must be given to assisted schools (from which Government and commercial clerks are largely drawn) to enable them to pay adequate salaries to their staff.

(*d*) That educational agencies, whether controlled by Government or by Missions, should co-operate with a common object, and as far as possible by similar methods of discipline and instruction.

(*e*) That continuation and evening classes for advanced and for specialised study, and institutions and classes for the training of teachers, should receive special encouragement.

(*f*) That the value of religion, irrespective of creed or sect, and the sanction and incentive it affords, should be recognised and utilised as an agent for this purpose, together with secular moral instruction.

(*g*) That Government should exercise some measure of control over all schools, even though not assisted by grants, and endeavour to bring them into line with the general policy.

To which I may add :—

(*h*) That the schools should, as far as possible, be conducted in accordance with native customs in matters of dress and etiquette, in order that the pupils may not become denationalised or consider themselves a class apart.

I have placed the formation of character in the foreground of African education, for if this be recognised as a primary function of education in communities whose standards have been moulded by centuries of Christian ethics, whose youth even in its most squalid surroundings is subjected, however unconsciously, to the influence of those standards, whether in the board school or the picture palace, how much more necessary is it in Africa, where, as a rule, such influences are absent? Among the primitive tribes ethical standards must be created—among few are they a vital and potent force. If, for instance, in his village home the African boy perceives that self-indulgence and lack of self-control excite no reprobation; that thrift, ambition, and initiative are conceptions as foreign to his associates as an alien tongue, for which his language has no appropriate terms; if justice, fair-play, truthfulness, and mutual obligation have no influence in guiding the actions of those around him,—then these conceptions must be created and built up. I do not for a moment mean to infer that there is a complete lack of such qualities among Africans who have not been brought into contact with the higher standards, for I profoundly believe that these conceptions are all innate in humanity, and are exhibited in a greater or less degree, even in the primitive savage, but they are generally undeveloped, and are not enforced by the public opinion of the community, and lack the sanction of local custom.

If, then, it is admitted that it is inevitable that education should produce a ferment of new and progressive ideas, subversive of the old order, the function of a sound system must be to guide these tendencies so that they may conduce to the betterment of the body politic and not to its disintegration. If, further, it be granted that this result can only be obtained by placing the formation of character and habits of discipline above the training of the intellect as the primary object of education for Africans, it remains to discuss how this can best be effected.

The agencies which are indicated as most effective for this purpose are: (1) residential schools; (2) a more adequate British staff; (3) the delegation of responsibility for discipline to school monitors; (4) encouragement of field sports; (5) the classification of the order of merit of schools, and the grant to aided schools to be partly dependent on tone and discipline; (6) religious and moral instruction to be recognised. I will make a few comments on each of these heads.

Character is formed "by the public opinion of the schoolboy world in which a boy moves"—by example and influence rather than by precept. The first object, then, must be to see that the pupils are brought continuously under the right influences. This can best be effected by the boarding-school, in which a boy lives wholly in the atmosphere of the school, and is removed from the subversive influences of his normal environment.[1] It is here that he learns to be less self-centred, and to take pride in the corporate body of which he is a member—the school, the "house," or the sports "team,"—and to understand the meaning of "playing the game," of loyalty, and of co-operation in a common ambition and a united effort. It becomes therefore essential to give the fullest and most careful consideration to the principles which should guide us in the constitution and the conduct of such schools.[2]

The boarding-school must not be too near to a native town. It should approximate to the model of an English public school in its internal organisation—in regard to school-houses, dormitories, class and living rooms, playgrounds, and the rules respecting school boundaries, roll-calls, "exeats," meals, and hygiene.

The vital and essential importance of a British head-master for each primary school, and at least two British masters per 100 pupils in a secondary school—exclusive of

[1] The importance of boarding-schools, or of hostels and boarding-houses attached to schools, is strongly emphasised in the Indian Blue-book (see p. 5, &c.). It was again insisted on at the Educational Conference of 1904—(Chirol, *loc. cit.*, p. 231). It was laid down as one of the essential principles at the foundation of the Hong-Kong University, that all students must reside in the University quarters or in approved hostels.—"Appeal" of June 1910.

The same principle was recognised by the Gordon College at Khartum, where there are 231 boarders. It was, as I have said, emphasised in the policy of Nigeria, and I am glad to note that the Governor of the Gold Coast has recently (January 1921) spoken in the same sense. Moral training, he observed, is impossible in day-schools, and his Government therefore proposes to increase the number of boarding-schools, and to encourage Mission hostels. The native press has begun to adopt the same point of view—(Nigerian 'Pioneer,' December 1920). The disastrous results of the opposite policy are graphically described in chapter xviii. of Sir V. Chirol's book.

[2] Mr Maugham, in his 'Republic of Liberia,' speaks of a system of native education which has existed from time immemorial. Both girls and boys, he says, are taken away from their families for a period of about three years, to undergo a course of instruction in tribal usages and duties under strict discipline —showing that the boarding-school is in no way opposed to native ideas.

those absent on leave—cannot in my judgment be too strongly emphasised. It is they who, by the stimulus of living example, will set the standard of the school. It is their influence which will form the character and ideals of the boys, and introduce the English public school code of honour. "Considering," says Sir V. Chirol, "how immeasurably more difficult is the task of training the youth of an entirely alien race according to Western standards, and how vital that task is for the future of British rule, the conditions should be such as to attract not average men, but the very best men that we can produce."[1] The status and salaries of the British educational staff should be equal to those of the administrative branch. Upon the influence exerted by these men will depend the co-operation and loyalty, or the estrangement, of the rising generation of educated Africans, upon whom will devolve in an increasing degree the conduct of municipal affairs, and a responsible share in the work of Government. No consideration of cost should be allowed to weigh against an issue fraught with such momentous possibilities.[2] It is, of course, a part of the system that the teaching staff—British and native—should also be resident in the school or hostels, and in constant touch with the boys.

The character and influence of the native teaching staff is a matter second only in importance to that of the British masters. Much weight is attached by the Government of India to the system of "monitors," and Mr Jacob's letter is quoted with approval: "It is the delegation of this disciplinary power to the prefects that emphatically marks the trust reposed in them, and brings them to look upon the reputation and prosperity of the school as partly committed to their keeping. If you withhold this power, and require the prefects not to preserve discipline, but merely to report breaches of it to the masters, you reduce the prefects to the position of mere tale-bearers. Self-government becomes

[1] *Loc. cit.*, p. 227. See also p. 215, where he describes the result of a deficiency of British staff: "From the point of view of mere instruction the results have been highly unsatisfactory. From the point of view of moral training and discipline, and the formation of character, they have been disastrous."

[2] "The character of the head of the school, with respect to the healthy influence he is likely to exercise over the boys, and his power of moulding their character, is the most essential qualification for the post."—Sir A. Macdonnell, Indian Report, p. 14.

government by espionage, and with a decided tendency to develop nothing but ignoble traits of character in those who are allowed to play no higher part in it than that of menials."[1] Every Englishman who has been at a public school will, I think, heartily endorse these views.

For the purposes of field sports, so wisely recommended by the Indian resolution, it is, of course, essential that playgrounds and gymnasia should be provided. In Nigeria we have found that polo was a specially good game for the sons of chiefs and others who could afford it, while for other boys cricket, football, and "athletics" bring the staff and pupils into close touch, and have the best effect in training character.

Finally, in order to show the importance attached to the training of character, I suggest that up to 30 per cent of the marks awarded to qualify a school for the Government grant should be allotted for tone, discipline, manners, and character, so far as they can be judged by outside indications—dress, demeanour, &c.[2]

Government schools, though not applicants for the grant, should be inspected by the same staff, and their comparative merit and place among the schools of the colony (Government or other) should be determined by the same tests.

Though character can best be moulded by example and personal contact, something can also be done in the class-room by what for lack of a better name is called "moral instruction." This consists in placing before children in an attractive way, by illustration and anecdotal biography, the social and other incentives to gentlemanly conduct, and the success which rewards honesty, self-control, and industry. Truthfulness, courage, fair-play, respect for authority, good manners, &c., are treated from the secular point of view of their value in social intercourse, and their results in attaining success in life, leaving the higher sanctions to be dealt with in the class of religious instruction. In the higher standards moral instruction might include "civics"—the duties and privileges of citizenship, the true meaning of patriotism, &c. These principles would also be enforced by the stories and dialogues selected for "school readers" and text-books. Very

[1] Indian Report, p. 5.

[2] This principle is not new. Lord Macdonnell quotes a circular issued by the Council of Education in the United Kingdom, in which a reduction in the grant is ordered if discipline and a high moral tone are not maintained. Parliamentary Paper C 1964 of 1878.

much must depend on the ability of the teacher to point the moral in an interesting and vivid way, and to avoid being too didactic.[1]

Just as the evangelist looks on education as a means for the spread of the gospel, so the educationalist regards religion as a powerful auxiliary in the formation of character. Experience in India, China, and Africa seems to demonstrate that purely secular education (including moral instruction), divorced from religious sanctions, produces among races not habituated to the ethics of a monotheistic religion a class which lacks reverence and respect, whether for parents, social superiors, employers, or Government. To inculcate this discipline, and to overcome the natural proclivities of the African boy, requires every influence which can be brought to bear, and there is no doubt that no influence can be stronger with youth—perhaps especially in Africa—than that of religion.

It is however necessary, in order that religious instruction may rank in the estimation of the pupils as of at least equal importance with the rest of the school syllabus, that it should be regarded as an "examination subject," to which they must pay the same attention as to their other lessons. In Moslem schools the instruction would be imparted by a selected Mohamedan teacher, and in all other schools the Christian religion would be taught. The late Sir V. Buxton declared himself in agreement with the suggestion that a common non-denominational syllabus should be drawn up—at least for elementary schools—for teaching religion and moral training, so as to admit of Government inspection and examination.[2] Others maintain that non-sectarian teaching must necessarily be devoid of all vitality.

[1] See the exhaustive and most interesting report on this subject by Sir A. Croft in the Indian Blue-book cited, pp. 140-157. He fears lest the inclusion of "morals" in the school time-table may be inadvisable.

The "Moral Education League" has published a number of text-books and essays on this subject, and the "Duty and Discipline Movement," founded by Lord Meath, has issued a great number of useful papers. Mr Harward, late Inspector of Schools, Nigeria, has compiled a series of readers, suited to each school standard, and a volume in three parts suitable for senior, junior, and preparatory pupils (Nelson & Co.). See also a small book, 'Formation of Character,' by J. B. Watson.

[2] The late Chief Rabbi would, I am sure, forgive me for quoting a conversation in which he hazarded the conjecture that if the Primate, the Cardinal, and himself could meet to determine upon a system of religious education which could be universally taught in the schools of England, each being empowered to erase anything to which he took essential objection with the words "I bar," and without discussion, he was confident that they would find no obstacle to success.

In the Government schools of the Sudan "every boy is taught his own religion." In Nigeria the same rule is applied, and a time is set apart each day for religious teaching; but any pupil may—if his parents so desire, as in the case of a Mohamedan attending a Christian school or *vice versa*—be excused attendance and set some other task. Assisted schools are, of course, entirely free to teach their own beliefs, whether Protestant or Roman Catholic, in whatever form seems right to them. The religious class in a Government school would probably be taken by a missionary in the district.

In India the teaching of religion is surrounded with special difficulties, and it has not been found feasible to introduce it in Government schools; but "the Governor-General in Council would be sincerely glad if the number of aided schools and colleges in which religious instruction is prominently recognised were largely increased."[1] Even the teaching of the doctrines of natural religion, from which the moral duties flow as necessary deductions, is impracticable to Hindus, for "these conceptions are essentially violated in theory as in practice in every one of the idolatrous religions of India."[2]

This was a problem for which a solution had to be sought when we founded the University of Hong-Kong, for the Chinese, though singularly tolerant, could not be expected to acquiesce in the compulsory teaching of Christianity, or the Christian supporters of the university in the teaching of ancestral worship.[3]

Fortunately in Africa we are not faced with the terrible dilemma, "To what theory of life, to what ultimate basis of conduct, can we appeal in addressing members of a society whose religions, and therefore whose ethical principles, have been fatally undermined by Western education?"[4] Islam carries with it its own religious sanctions, while the Animism and Fetish of the pagan represents no system of ethics, and no principles of conduct. Christianity by replacing the terror of the supernatural supplies incentives, constructive as well as emotional, which may prove a basis for social organisation, creating and not destroying "the instincts of order, obedience, and reverence—the cement of the fabric of society."

[1] Indian Blue-book, p. 15. [2] Ibid., p. 150.

[3] The problem was dealt with in a paper read by me at the Imperial Education Conference of 1911 on "Character-training in Non-Christian Universities."—Cmd. 5666 of 1911.

[4] Indian Blue-book, p. 146.

Turning from these general considerations, let us briefly review the existing machinery of education in our tropical dependencies.

Schools for the education of youth in the Crown colonies and protectorates are either conducted directly by Government, or by some other agency which may be "assisted" by Government financially, or may be "unassisted." Adults and youths are also educated by means of an apprenticeship system, and by "continuation classes." The educational agencies — other than Government — which exist in Africa are chiefly Mission societies, but there are also private venture schools conducted for profit by individuals or bodies.

This last class includes in a Moslem country the schools in which boys are taught to memorise passages of the Koran, and to read and write in the Arabic character, of which there are estimated to be some 25,000 in Nigeria, with perhaps a quarter of a million pupils. Apart from these Mohamedan institutions, unassisted schools may either be conducted by Missions which do not desire to accept the conditions attached to Government assistance, or have failed to satisfy those conditions, or they may be private venture schools conducted by natives.

Speaking on behalf of the English Education Bill, Mr Fisher, Minister of Education, said that he feared that many private venture schools were frauds on the public. The new Bill would enable the Board of Education to call for particulars as to the quality of the education afforded. The London County Council went further (January 1918), and urged upon the Board of Education the necessity of the registration and inspection of all such schools.

If such criticism is justified in England, where the force of public opinion is strong, and where parents are themselves educated, or at least literate, it applies with much greater force in Africa. Among many primitive tribes the possession of a school is looked upon as conferring prestige and dignity upon a village. Half-educated youths, and others who are quite incompetent to teach, set up so-called "schools" for profit, and are treated with deference by the ignorant parents, who are wholly indifferent to the nature of the teaching given. Such establishments are a danger to the country. The local chiefs find it difficult to control them, and they are reported to be lacking in discipline and in loyalty to any constituted authority whatever.[1]

In order to qualify for a Government grant, a school must conform to the conditions prescribed by the "grant-code" or other regulations. Since in tropical Africa practically all assisted schools are conducted by Missions, with whom education is considered secondary and ancillary to evangelisation, the popularity of the code will depend very largely upon the encouragement to, or the seeming restrictions it may impose upon, religious teaching. In Nigeria, prior to the ordinance of 1916, many excellent Mission schools preferred to forgo the grant. This can only be regarded as a misfortune, for it is in assisted schools only that Government can prescribe, and enforce by trained inspectors, considered schemes for the improvement of education, and can promote uniformity of method.

It is therefore of great importance that the conditions of the code or regulations should be made attractive to the Missions. This may be done: (*a*) by inviting the co-operation

[1] The Nigerian Education Ordinance of 1916 anticipated to some extent the provisions of the English Education Act, 1918, by obliging the manager of every unaided school to submit an annual return showing the subjects taught, and the qualifications of the staff, &c., but the Colonial Office would not agree to any further control or inspection. Not till 1919 was an ordinance enacted empowering the Director of Education, or the Resident of a Province, to inspect a school which in their opinion ought to be closed, and enabling the Governor, on the report of a commission of inquiry, to close such a school for certain specified offences or defaults.

The hesitation of the Colonial Office contrasts unfavourably with the action of the High Commissioner in South Africa, for in Northern Rhodesia no school may be opened without Government consent, and all are subject to inspection. Any school may be closed by the Administrator if he is satisfied after due inquiry that the general conduct of the teacher or pupils, or the manner in which the school is carried on, is detrimental to good order and government, or if the natives on reasonable grounds desire it. Every teacher must be properly qualified, and married, and may be removed if he interferes with the tribal control of a chief, or with officials.—Ordinance No. 3 in 'Gazette' No. 5 of 1918.

The efforts of Government in Nigeria to bring these schools under control were the subject of an outcry by the native press of Lagos—with the honourable exception of the paper owned by Hon. K. Ajasa,—and they appealed to the Secretary of State against this form of "moral slavery"!

The absence of Government control over educational institutions is one of the four defects to which Sir V. Chirol attributes the failure of education in India. —*Loc. cit.*, p. 248. The Sudan Government goes so far as to make a small grant to "Kuttabs" which agree to inspection, but they are for the most part under teachers trained at Gordon College.

The policy of the Colonial Office appears to have changed, for it has recently been announced that all unaided schools in the Straits and Federated Malay States shall be registered with their teachers and subjected to Regulations.—'Times,' 6th October 1921.

of the managers of their schools in the general scheme of education, and giving them an opportunity of expressing their views as members of educational boards, &c.; (*b*) by recognising religious teaching as part of the school course, or at least by removing what may be considered by them to be gratuitous difficulties in the way of teaching religion; (*c*) by making the financial assistance sufficiently substantial, and unhampered by conditions which are considered obnoxious, or which tend to destroy the individuality of the school and its development upon its own lines.

The policy laid down by the Government of India resolution No. 199 of 1888 appears to me to formulate the principle which should guide Crown colony administration—viz., that the Government should encourage private enterprise in education as in all other matters; that it should pioneer the way, and maintain schools in which the system of instruction and discipline shall afford a standard for the emulation of aided or private institutions, and that it should assist their efforts by reasonable subventions.[1]

When I left Nigeria an experiment was in progress on the following lines: Grants are no longer awarded on the basis of an annual and necessarily hurried examination in certain set subjects, but on frequent inspections and examinations extending throughout the school year. Thirty per cent of the marks which determine the amount of the grant are awarded for the tone of the school, discipline, organisation, and moral instruction; 20 per cent for the adequacy and efficiency of the teaching staff by whom those results are achieved; 40 per cent on the result of periodical examinations and general progress, and 10 per cent for buildings, equipment, and sanitation.

Since it is far easier to train the characters of pupils who are boarders than of day scholars (while the former are very much more expensive to the school), the grant for a boarder in an assisted school is double that for a day scholar. The boarding-schools must be well found, with good dormitories and a recreation-room and grounds. The different grades of masters and teachers are defined in regard to their qualifications, and the minimum requirements of staff in proportion to pupils are laid down. There are special grants for training institutes for teachers.

[1] Indian Blue-book, p. 3.

There are no obligatory subjects, but no school (other than a rural school) is eligible for a grant unless its pupils show satisfactory results in English and in arithmetic. The list of school subjects is strictly limited, for a curriculum which is overloaded and too advanced means the neglect of English and other essential subjects. A clear distinction is drawn between those that remain as part of the school syllabus, and " special subjects " which are taught (to selected boys in the secondary schools in substitution for a subject in which they have qualified, or in a more advanced standard) largely by means of " continuation " and vacation classes. Eighty-one new schools came on the grant list the year after this code was introduced (an increase of 94 per cent), showing that it had the cordial approbation of the Missions.

The system necessarily leaves large powers in the hands of the inspector, for instead of the fixed criterion afforded by an annual set examination, the progress of the school is gauged by repeated visits and informal examinations. The inspector's reports are, however, subject to careful scrutiny and verification by the Director of Education, and the school managers are represented on the Board of Education, so that any complaint may be fully investigated. But it is obvious that in such a system the very best and most experienced men must be selected as inspectors. The appointment of men who have only a training as Board School inspectors in England, or who are without enthusiasm for their work, will go far to wreck the best-devised system of education in a tropical dependency.

CHAPTER XXII.

EDUCATION (*Continued*).

The three types of education required—Literary training—The demand—Provincial Government schools—Village schools—Central industrial schools—Clerical apprentices—Technical training—The African as a worker—Technical institutes—Technical courses—Details of educational methods—Subjects of tuition—Adequacy of teaching staff—Moslem education in Arabic—The language difficulty—Higher education—Continuation and special classes—The education of girls—The cost of education—Compulsory education—The essential conclusions.

ASSUMING, then, that the Government takes the lead in the task of education, let us consider the nature of the problem which it has to solve, so far as class-room instruction is concerned. There may be said to be three objects which educational agencies have in view—viz., (*a*) the literary training required for posts in which a good knowledge of English and accounting is necessary ; (*b*) the technical training of mechanics and artisans employed with power-driven plant and other technical work ; and (*c*) the teaching of crafts and agriculture and the very elementary schooling suitable to village life.

We sometimes hear the opinion that it would be better if the African confined himself to agriculture and artisan work, and left literary education alone.[1] We read that in India the output of the schools and universities is in excess of the demand, and creates an unemployable class which becomes a prey to the agitator. In tropical Africa, on the contrary, there is an unlimited demand, not only for subordinates but for doctors and for the Civil Staff, if men with

[1] Dr Moton, Head of Tuskegee College, tells us that Booker Washington himself was often accused of being opposed to higher negro education, but his real view was that education for the negro must be thorough, and suited to his reasonably immediate needs. He desired to raise the masses by an industrial and economic education widely diffused.—'Finding a Way Out,' p. 215.

the proper qualifications both of education and of character were available.

The progress made in the development of Africa would have been impossible were it not for the enormous number of Africans who fill posts in which a knowledge of English, of reading, writing, and arithmetic, and, to a lesser degree, of book-keeping and accountancy, is required. Those who are employed in the technical departments, such as surveyors, telegraphists, printers, and skilled men in the workshops, require the same initial training.[1] With the extension of railways and the expansion of Government departments and of private enterprise, the demand for such men has become very large indeed.

The result in West Africa is that boys who have only half completed their education are tempted to leave school, and are able to obtain posts which demand much higher qualifications than they possess, so that two or three may be necessary to do the work, with ill success, which one efficient man should perform. Thus the standard of efficiency is lowered, and wages, as compared with the cost of living and the value of the work done, increase beyond the scale paid in England and elsewhere for similar work. The wages paid to clerks react on the technical departments,[2] and it becomes increasingly difficult to secure an adequate number of apprentices with elementary schooling, or of teachers for the schools. The latter deficiency tends further to restrict the supply at its source. So difficult has the situation become in Nigeria that the Acting Director of Education—himself a native African of great distinction—urged the necessity of importing clerical subordinates in large numbers from the East.

It is clear that in dependencies so situated the Government cannot rely on the output of the Mission schools only—much as the British African tropics are indebted to them in the past,—and the creation of an adequate number of Government primary and secondary schools is a matter which must not be left (as it has too often been) until the deficiency has already caused grave injury to the country. Schools are

[1] See page 87 as to the numbers required in Nigeria as clerks, accountants, dispensers, dressers, sanitary and other inspectors, station-masters, railway guards, &c., &c. Probably at least another 1000 are required by banking, commercial, and mining firms.

[2] The cost of African skilled labour, measured by results, is estimated by the Director of Works, Nigeria, to be double the cost in England.

required at every provincial and at many divisional headquarters. Whenever it is possible, the boys should be boarders, for the reasons already given, and the school should not be nearer than one or two miles from a native city. An age limit should be fixed for each class or standard.

The medium of instruction, except in the lower standards, should be English, and as many scholarships as possible should be provided. In the northern provinces of Nigeria the cost of buildings and native staff is borne by the native administrations (42 per cent in 1913), that of the British staff and inspectorate by general revenue. Each school would, of course, have its "normal class" for the training of teachers, and its continuation classes. Uniformity in the "standards" of the various schools is of importance, so that the degree of proficiency of any boy, who is certified as having passed a certain standard, may be known to his prospective employer.[1]

The chief function of Government primary and secondary schools among primitive communities is to train the more promising boys from the village schools as teachers for those schools, as clerks for the local native courts, and as interpreters. For these the higher standards are not required.

The village schools must depend on these primary and secondary Government schools for their supply of teachers; and since the teaching in the village schools is chiefly industrial, each of the "literary" schools should have a class in which native crafts and industries (especially agriculture) are taught, so that boys who desire to become teachers in village schools may be properly qualified.

Village schools should, in my opinion, be adapted to the requirements of the peasantry, who do not seek either a literary education to qualify them as clerks, &c., or a technical training for power-driven workshops. Their object is to improve the village craftsmen and agriculturists, to raise the standard of life, comfort, and intelligence in the village community, and to teach habits of discipline, industry, and truthfulness. At these schools trades should be taught

[1] There are six such primary schools in the Sudan, where English is taught, but no industrial training is given. Each year about thirty boys are selected from the elementary vernacular schools and sent to them, and about 15 per cent go on to the Upper School at Gordon College. The entrance age is about eleven, and the course is for four years. The schools are intended for the sons of Government employees and better-class natives, who, after a further training at Gordon College, will be qualified to fill junior posts under Government.

(carpentry, blacksmithing, agriculture, &c.), together with some rudimentary schooling in elementary hygiene, colloquial English, and such moral and religious instruction, whether Christian or Mohamedan, as may help to free the peasant from the cruel domination of superstitious and inhuman practices. To this may usefully be added simple explanations of British aims—the advantages of railways, roads, currency, and free labour, the reasons for taxation, &c. In the higher classes some small knowledge of "the 3 R's" may be included, which shall render the pupil—and through him the village—less liable to be the victim of misrepresentation and fraud.

These schools would not be intended to qualify a boy for Government employment, or to develop into literary schools. They would be affiliated to the nearest Government primary or secondary school. In non-Moslem districts Mohamedan teachers would not be employed, and in practice no doubt these schools would be largely in the hands of the Missions.[1] They would be conducted by a carefully-selected native teacher, and would not be boarding-schools. The medium of instruction would be the vernacular—in the higher classes English or a local *lingua franca*—such as Arabic, Swaheli, or Hausa. The boys would at first spend about half their time in elementary education, and later practically the whole time in learning some craft. The instruction imparted would be very simple, and given from the most practical standpoint,[2] special attention being devoted to the introduction of better appliances, in order to improve the quality and increase the quantity of the output.[3]

[1] The late Sir Victor Buxton emphasised "the growing consensus that industrial training should be given a more prominent place in the Mission schools."—('African Journal,' April 1918.) It is in these rural schools that these objects can best be carried out.

[2] The elementary vernacular village schools (kuttabs) in the Sudan number about 74 with 7000 pupils. They are under native teachers. Reading, writing, drill, simple arithmetic, and elementary religion are taught, but no industrial crafts.

In the village schools of Sierra Leone boys are taught to write their own language in the Roman character, and instruction is given in elementary arithmetic and the rudiments of English, but the chief subject of instruction is agriculture. "We find by actual experience that a Mendi boy can be taught to read and write his own language, and to work out simple calculations in less than a year." The Governor complains of the rivalry between denominational schools, of which there may be "three, four, or seven in a single small village, with results fatal to teaching, to discipline, and to the proper payment of teachers."—(Speech to Legislative Council, December 1920.)

[3] The native loom is only capable of weaving a strip of cloth a few inches wide, and can only be worked out of doors in the dry season (owing to its

The instruction given at each school should be especially adapted to the occupations most suited to, or traditional in, the village. In some weaving, in others smelting, dyeing, or tanning may be time-honoured crafts. Similarly in regard to agriculture, the care of those crops which are chiefly cultivated in the district would receive special attention—cotton in one, cocoa in another, and so on.

The Indian Industrial Report—published since these instructions were issued in Nigeria—recommends practically identical methods in regard to the "cottage industries" of India, which, it is suggested, may be assisted by peripatetic instructors, teaching improved processes, and introducing new patterns and designs and labour-saving devices. The report emphasises the difference in training needed for these cottage industries, and the class-room study and apprenticeship necessary to produce skilled mechanics.[1]

The teaching of the village school may be carried to a higher stage in the agricultural classes (*vide inf.*) on the one hand, or in a Central Industrial School on the other. In the latter native arts and crafts would be taught by skilled native craftsmen, under the supervision of a British foreman. The object would be to preserve all that is best in native design and art, while introducing better methods, appliances, and tools. Carpentry and wood-carving, metal-work and engraving on brass and copper, blacksmith's work, smelting and casting, leather-work and tanning, weaving and embroidery on cloth and leather, and other native industries, would be taught. To these might be added such new crafts as are suitable for cottage industry, such as brickmaking and the construction of country carts and wheels. There would be no class-room instruction—though pupils would be encouraged to attend the evening classes at the provincial school,—and

length), but with the aid of an imported loom a native weaver was able without expert guidance to make a piece of cloth of full breadth.—(Ibid.)

As to the value of native crafts in Nigeria, Captain (now Major-General) Mance, R.E., asserts that "European manufacturers cannot put on the market cotton stuffs approaching the quality and the wearing power of the Kano cloth at the same prices as it is charged for by the natives." He even anticipates that these durable hand-woven cloths of excellent design will compete with imported textiles throughout West Africa, "and might even make an inroad on the English summer market," since they are already being used by Europeans "for strong tropical suits, riding breeches, and ladies' dresses." This may be exaggerated praise, but indicates the excellence of native cloth.

[1] Cmd. 51, 1919, pp. 97-99 and 162-167.

no attempt to train boys for wage-earning employment.[1]

It is very desirable that provincial schools—and essential that all village schools—should possess a good school garden, in which boys can acquire a knowledge of the various plants under cultivation, and of the use of garden tools and agricultural implements.

Before passing to technical education, I have a very tentative suggestion to offer, to which I have already referred in chapter iv. Parents deplore the tendency of young men to embark prematurely on an independent career, which in such circumstances can offer little prospect of success, and exposes them to temptation, and to the cost of maintaining a separate establishment beyond their means. In order to check this tendency and to maintain parental discipline, it may perhaps be feasible to institute a scheme of clerical apprentices somewhat on the following lines. Youths between the ages of seventeen and twenty, recommended not merely for intellectual ability but for sterling character, would be selected from among the seniors at the best schools for employment on progressive salaries during four or five years. They would reside during this apprenticeship with their parents, and be attached to the Secretariat or Treasury, but in order to acquire proficiency and fluency in English and thorough qualifications for their duties, they would continue to attend school for certain hours. They might be called "student clerks" or "cadets," and if they pass the required tests at the end of their term, they would have received a much better and more prolonged education than the ordinary clerk. They would be bound to enter the Government service, if wanted, for a period of, say, five years, and would be eligible for accelerated promotion. Eventually the cadets might become a *corps d'élite*, and aspire to high posts.

We have dealt with two of the great classes for whom educational facilities are required—viz., the literary (clerical)

[1] Such a school has been established at Kano (Nigeria) with excellent results. Its cost (exclusive of the British superintendent) is provided by the native administrations, and pupils are sent to it from all the Moslem provinces, which make proportionate subscriptions from their native treasuries. A separate school is required for Christians and pagans. Pending the completion of the Technical Institute, it has recently engaged in the making of "furniture, office fittings, drills and tools, boots, and book-binding," but this is a departure from its original and proper purpose.

class, and the rural (industrial) class. The third group consists of the artisans and mechanics employed in Government and commercial workshops—by the railway, marine, public works, and printing departments,—most of whom are engaged in handling power-driven machinery. For these a primary education is a necessary preliminary, but the "manual training," which has found favour both in Government and in Mission schools, is of little or no use. The workshop staff reports that not only is a training in box- and chair-making useless for a boy who desires to become a trained mechanic, but that he must unlearn much of what he has learnt, and begin all over again. Much valuable time is also lost in giving such teaching to boys whose intention it is to become clerks, and have no need of it.

The Indian Industrial Report (as I have already said) endorses this view, and emphasises the necessity of discriminating between the industrial training needed for cottage industries and the class-room study, and the apprenticeship necessary to produce skilled mechanics.[1]

As soon as the youth has passed the required standard he should become an apprentice in the department which he desires to adopt. It is of the utmost importance that every technical department should train a large number of apprentices. Their training must be conducted by a special instructor, and not left (as used to be the case) to the chance assistance of men engaged in work themselves. In other words, each technical department should have a technical class attached to it for the training of apprentices. The instructor would also hold classes for special instruction in theory and drawing, &c., for those who show special aptitude —not in night-schools, when they are too tired to learn, but during working hours,—and they could improve their general education by attending continuation classes at the provincial school. The aim should be to put the apprentices on the

[1] The Indian report to which I have referred is a mine of research and practical suggestion on this subject. The Commissioners find in India the same necessity as I have found in Africa for taking measures to improve the social status of the artisan, and to counteract the tendency to prefer a clerical education. They corroborate the view that the necessary theoretical instruction of apprentices cannot be given in night-schools when the youths are too tired to assimilate knowledge; they endorse the necessity for special instructors for apprentices in the workshops; they dwell on the need for training a class of native foremen; and they recommend the provision of hostels, &c., as I have done for Africa.—Pp. 100-108.

same level as the clerical branch, in pay, housing, opportunities for recreation, and general status, so as to attract to it an equally good class. During his five years' indenture an apprentice is, of course, paid a progressive wage.[1]

The aptitude of the African as a skilled worker is abundantly in evidence in the railway, printing, and other workshops. In West Africa, as an "engineer correspondent" testifies, he has replaced Europeans in many departments of skilled work, and he does not require an undue amount of European supervision. Even in such highly technical work as acetylene welding and cutting, in pattern-making from dimensioned drawings, and in the use of the lathe and of modern machine tools, he bears witness to his efficiency.[2]

If the African does not yet aspire to the position of foreman, it is because he has hitherto lacked sufficient general education, and has not entered the shops at a sufficiently early age. When boys of sixteen or seventeen, having passed the fifth or sixth standard so that they can make accurate calculations and correctly interpret plans and drawings, can acquire in the shops from a special instructor some knowledge of the theoretical side of the work and the reasons for the various processes, there is no reason why they should not become efficient managers and shop-foremen. The weak point of the qualified African engineer who holds a technical degree is that his ability to memorise enables him to fill his head with formulæ of which he does not appreciate the full meaning. He must also acquire the ability to control men, and a greater sense of responsibility in his work.

In the Sudan the Gordon College provides an extra departmental institute for technical training. A similar institution is in course of erection in the northern provinces of Nigeria, a considerable part of the funds having been provided by a bequest of the late Sir Alfred Jones. Such an institute supplements, but cannot supersede, the value of the training acquired by apprentices in workshops, but it has a special value in Nigeria, since it provides an opportunity of training

[1] The rates of pay in Nigeria for 1st-grade apprentices (viz., those who have passed standard V.) commence at £12 and rise to £36, and for heavy machinery from £18 to £42. An apprentice is on probation for three months, and is pledged to remain in Government employ for five years if wanted. It was proposed to fix the number under training at 760—an annual output of 150.

[2] 'West Africa,' 4th September 1920. We have seen (p. 421) that in Nigeria Africans are now employed as foremen in the mines.

Mohamedan youths who do not readily mix with the artisans from the coast.

It has also an additional value in providing a means of showing that the skilled workman occupies no inferior status to that of the clerk, and of promoting healthy rivalry in sports between the two classes. By these various means the tropical African dependencies should be able to produce competent native foremen of works instead of being dependent on British artisans, who are very costly, and of whom the supply is strictly limited.

Apart from the departments to which I have referred as using power-driven machinery—railway, marine, public works, and printing—there are others which afford technical training —*e.g.*, agriculture, survey, forestry, veterinary, telegraphs, and medical—to youths who desire to specialise in any of these subjects with a view to entering the service of Government, or of a private employer, or of a native administration.

Such training in its earlier stages can be given in special classes while the boy is still at school, and later by apprenticeship to the department concerned. Trained agriculturists are wanted as instructors, and overseers in the department, and for the charge of model plots and botanical gardens, &c. Education in forestry, like agriculture, is both theoretical and practical. For instruction in agriculture model plantations, and for veterinary work a small stock farm, are essential. It is very desirable that pupils—whether trained for the Government service or for service under a native administration—should be selected from various parts of the country.

Surveyors are required to replace Europeans in making simple surveys of leases of land, &c., and in the medical department there is great need of trained sanitary inspectors, dispensers, dressers, and female nurses.

My object in this chapter is rather to discuss the general scope and object of education in Africa than to deal with the subject from the detailed and educationalist standpoint. I have preferred therefore to speak of "provincial" and "village" schools rather than of "secondary," "primary," "elementary," "infant," or "trade" schools, for I am concerned here only with the general purpose which they are intended to serve. The provincial school, when first instituted, would not aspire beyond the primary standards; later it would become a secondary school. The village school combines the last three.

Nor is it possible within the scope of a single chapter in a volume such as this, to discuss in detail the subjects which should find a place in the school curriculum, the degree of scholastic attainment which should constitute each "standard" and class, or those which should be demanded in a "qualified" teacher, the age-limits of pupils, or the methods of inspection, &c. The way in which each of these problems has been handled in the various Crown colonies and protectorates may be studied in the admirable series of "special reports on educational subjects" issued by the Board of Education, which are probably too little known in our African dependencies. They are now somewhat out of date, since they bring their review only up to the end of 1902.[1] I will content myself here with one or two comments only.

It is, I suggest, a mistake to include in the syllabus of an ordinary primary or secondary school such subjects as Greek and Latin. Their place as classics should be taken by English. French and German would be taught as "special subjects" if there were sufficient students to form a class. Exception would no doubt be made by any special secondary school for youths who intend to take up the professions of law, medicine, &c., and to attend an English university.

The first essential—apart from character training—is to have a good knowledge of English, and "the 3 R's," whether a boy intends to adopt a "literary" (clerical) or a technical career, or whether as the son of a ruling chief he desires to be able to take his place some day on a Government Council, and represent there the needs and aspirations of his people. For the latter a course in practical "economics" and commerce would be of greater value than a knowledge of the foreign languages named.

The usual subjects of a school curriculum should, I venture to think, be treated somewhat differently for African than for English boys. It is, for instance, more useful that a student of geography should acquire a general knowledge of the British Empire, and of Africa in particular, with some elementary knowledge of physical geography, than that he should

[1] See Volumes V., XII., XIII., and XIV., Cmd. 417, 2377, 2378, and 2379. The Sudan is not included, and I have therefore given some notes of the system adopted there.

be familiar with the names of the English counties. The history of Africa is more appropriate than a knowledge of Hengist and Horsa, and a cursory acquaintance with the evolution of democracy under Cromwell may do more harm than good, by inducing " the boy patriot to deplore the woes, and discuss the regeneration of his country, instead of attending to his lessons," and encouraging him to believe that he can accomplish in a decade what England has taken some centuries to achieve. History, said Sir H. Hadow, in his presidential address to the Teachers' Guild in January 1921, " ought to be taught from the point of view of showing what England has been in the past, what England has done for liberty and civilisation, for invention, for industry, and for the spiritual, moral, and material welfare of mankind."

A " general knowledge " class may be more useful in developing the faculties of original thought, and in affording an opportunity of explaining the economic causes of present-day " unrest," than time spent on conic sections or the later books of Euclid.

I have already referred to the vital necessity of an adequate and properly qualified staff, and to the importance of resident British masters, and a highly-trained British inspectorate. The latter should be composed of men with a knowledge of the science of teaching, and suited temperamentally for work which needs much tact and patience. They should visit each school once a quarter, and remain a few days—or more, if required—in order to assist the staff by their advice, and in order to form a thorough opinion of the value of the teaching and the tone of the school. Each school should in addition be visited once in the year by a senior inspector.

The native staff, no less than the British, must be selected from the best men available, for it is on their example no less than on their teaching that success depends. The cry is everywhere the difficulty of procuring teachers—even at Gordon College, with its reservoir in Egypt.[1] To secure the

[1] The great difficulty in the "emirates" of Northern Nigeria was to provide teachers professing the Moslem faith, and no others would have been tolerated or have exercised any influence. Progress was necessarily slow till youths could be first taught themselves, and then trained to teach, but in a little over a dozen years (by the end of 1919) the enthusiastic efforts of the British staff had succeeded in establishing twenty-one schools. Ten years after the institution of British rule only twenty teachers had been trained. The original class consisted of pupils varying from six to sixty years of age, and was primarily industrial. By indefatigable patience and tact on the part of the administrative and education

right type of teachers in countries where the acquisition of wealth by trading offers great attractions, adequate salaries must be offered, and revenue cannot be laid out to better purpose, whether in Government schools or by increased grants to assisted schools. It is impossible, as the Governor of Sierra Leone observed, to expect men who are underpaid and overworked to continue in the same routine all their lives, and the quality of their teaching must suffer. The number of pupils under a single teacher should never exceed forty. The village schools, as I have said, must look to the provincial schools for their supply of teachers, and it is essential that every school should have its "normal class," in addition to a central training institute for teachers, with liberal free scholarships. The staff should be changed as little as possible, in order that the masters may acquire the confidence and an intimate personal knowledge of the pupils, and that British officers may become fluent in the local dialects.

The treatment of the problem of education must necessarily differ widely in Moslem and non-Moslem countries. In the former there already exists a literate class, held in respect by the illiterate peasantry. The goal of their ambition is to read the Koran, and to study the laws and traditions of Islam. No Mohamedan considers that he can claim to be properly educated unless he is able to do this. His outlook is towards the literature of the East—not of the West. In countries where Arabic is not the spoken vernacular (as it is in the Sudan), secular education, and the reading of their own language in the Roman character, does not offer to this class the same attractions as it does to non-Moslem natives. Arabic, says Blyden, is learnt for religion and for entrance to heaven, English for the things of this world.

There is, however, no reason why the two aims should conflict. In Nigeria the Government schools in the Moslem provinces have an Arabic class, in which, like "the classical

officers, the schools have now become so popular that it is difficult to meet the demand, though the cost is largely borne by the native administrations, who thus regard them as "their own schools." The keenness of the pupils is evidenced by the average attendance, in Zaria 87·75 out of 88, and others but little less.

The Ngala Agricultural Institute in Sierra Leone aspires to provide teachers for all the village schools. The pupils are fed, housed, and taught free of cost for a two-years' course.—(Governor's Speech, 19th July 1919.)

side " in our public schools at home, the study of an ancient language and literature can be fostered, without hindrance to the more utilitarian subjects required for the production of a class who can take their share of the appointments—clerical or technical—which Government has to offer in the departments of the public service. Moslems should recognise the disadvantages of allowing these posts to be held by aliens of a different creed, while a certain number of the Arabic scholars will be required to fill posts under the native administrations and as judges of the native courts. In the Sudan the *Kadis* (native judges) are trained at Gordon College.

This system has so far had excellent results in Nigeria, and the fact that the Government has viewed Arabic education not merely with tolerance but with active encouragement, has gone far to enlist the cordial co-operation of the Moslem rulers in the scheme of Government schools, of which —fearing they would undermine their religion—they were at first very suspicious.[1]

The diversity of languages in Africa surrounds the problem of education with special difficulties. Where a widely-spoken language easily acquired by Europeans exists—such as Hausa in the west and Swaheli in the east—it would appear desirable to promote its use as a *lingua franca*, for natives easily acquire an African tongue. Elsewhere English must form the medium of instruction, and of intercommunication between tribes, as it has already to some extent done in West Africa, and to a more remarkable extent among the Chinese, where it has become the " business " (pidgin) language. No greater benefit can be conferred on the African, whether as a means of enabling him to make known his desires, or for purposes of trade, or as affording an access to a great literature, than the teaching of English as a universal medium.

Missions, on the other hand, being concerned with evangelisation only, have no desire to promote intercommunication for trade and other purposes, and are generally content

[1] In Sokoto the Sultan, who is recognised as the Head of Islam in the western Sudan, visits the British school weekly, and the Wazeri spends several hours there on most days, and the same in varying degrees obtains in most other emirates.

Contrary to expectation, it has now been found that in some of the schools—notably in Sokoto and Bornu, the religious headquarters in East and West—English is becoming more popular than Arabic, but the latter will always serve a useful purpose for the sons of Emirs, and for the training of native judges.

to study a local dialect, and translate the Scriptures and text-books into it. I concur with Lord Kimberley's dictum, that though instruction in English must of necessity at first be given through the medium of the vernacular, Government encouragement should not be exerted to stimulate or preserve these native tongues.

Lord Kitchener's great institution in the Sudan, the Gordon College, stands as a model—short of a university [1]—for a central institution for education both literary and technical, and most other African dependencies have one or more special schools for higher education—notably Furrah Bay College, Sierra Leone, affiliated to Durham University.

Such schools are attended by sons of educated and well-to-do parents, who can afford heavy fees, or by promising youths who have won scholarships. Their aim is to enable boys who go to England for degrees in law, medicine, or theology to complete most of their education locally, and so to curtail their period of absence, and also to qualify youths to fill high posts in the Civil Service.

It is essential that such schools should be residential if boys are to imbibe the traditions that give to English public schoolboys that discipline and training which have fitted them for the work of the Empire. The schools must have junior classes, and not merely receive from other schools boys who have already formed habits which should have been moulded under the influence of the school; and they should, of course, have normal classes for the training of teachers.

If the institutions for higher education are at present but few in British tropical Africa, we must not forget that the problem hitherto has been to keep abreast of the demands of Government and commerce, and to supply the requirements of the teaching staff. The educated African demands a university for West Africa, and nothing could be more desirable than that African youths, who wish to qualify for the

[1] The Omdurman training college for teachers in the elementary schools was in 1916 absorbed in the Gordon College, Khartum, which in addition has an upper school divided into four sections, to train pupils for the several vocations of engineers, kadis (magistrates), teachers, and general service under Government or business houses, in the proportion of 1, 1, 5, 4½. It affords the only facility for higher education in the Sudan. In addition, it has a primary and a technical school. There are 231 boarders, and great attention is paid to field sports.

professions, should be able to take their degrees locally. But its advocates, and the native press which points to the present expense required for "a four or seven years' stay in England" for professional qualification, do not offer any suggestion as to how the endowment fund—without which, of course, the founding of a university is impossible—can be raised. This absence of initiative and self-help among those who are foremost in demanding advanced institutions militates against the fruition of their desires. They cannot fail to realise that the financial support which the local Government can legitimately give, from revenues raised by general taxation, to a project which benefits a comparatively small section, must necessarily be limited by the imperative demands for popular education. It is, moreover, more than doubtful whether there are at present a sufficient number of candidates to make a university a practical possibility.[1]

That these difficulties may be met, and that the idea may materialise in the not distant future, must be the wish of all who deplore the consequences of sending African boys to England to complete their studies—not seldom with the result that they become denationalised, and lose touch with their own people.

Secondary, and even primary, schools must always be supplemented by "continuation" and special classes. The object of these is to provide opportunity for boys to learn some special subject not included in the syllabus, or to carry their studies beyond the school standards in subjects taught in the schools; and finally, to enable young men, who are no longer pupils at any school, to receive instruction which they could not otherwise obtain. These special classes thus relieve the syllabus of a number of subjects for which there is no time in school hours, or for which the number of applicants for tuition is small. They can be encouraged by special grants, and any qualified person, official or unofficial, can be

[1] It was generally agreed that before the idea of founding a university in Hong-Kong could be considered to be a practical proposal, an endowment of at least $1,000,000 must be raised in addition to the cost of buildings (about $300,000) already promised. The money was subscribed chiefly by the Chinese themselves. Before founding the Khartum College as a memorial to Gordon (not so ambitious a proposal as a university), Lord Kitchener asked for a fund of £200,000. The African progressives, who lightly say that "the time has come to found a West African university on lines of African nationality," do not indicate a single donation from the wealthy members of their community towards its realisation.

employed as a fee'd lecturer. They include, of course, technical demonstrations, for which purpose Government laboratories, workshops, and apparatus can be used. The award of diplomas to students who pass a test examination will add to their popularity.

A movement has lately been set on foot by an African lady to collect funds for the establishment in the Gold Coast colony of a training institute for girls—who, she considers, are fully fifty years behind their brothers in educational development. The intention is to teach all branches of domestic science and child-welfare, and to train girls in dressmaking, millinery, market-gardening, poultry-farming, and typewriting. To these midwifery and nursing might be added, with a view to decreasing the present heavy infant mortality in Africa.

In a Christian monogamous community there are many girls who require to earn their own living, but throughout the greater part of Africa a girl is married at a very early age, and "domestic science" and child-welfare must be learnt in her school-days. The movement is one to which all well-wishers of Africa will desire success in the limited number of places where its need is felt.

I am not qualified to discuss female education from any detailed or particular point of view. What I have written regarding the principles of education in Africa applies equally to girls as to boys—viz., that the primary object should be to fit the individual to fill a useful part in her environment, with happiness to herself. The immense value to the educated youth of Africa, of having wives who can share their thoughts and sympathise in and understand their work, is only less important than the influence which the mother should exert in forming the character of her children. Improvement in the standard of private life is fully as important as in that of public life.

The Governments of our Crown colonies and dependencies have, I think, been too ready to leave the burden of education to be borne by the Missions. In most of the African dependencies the proportion of revenue devoted to this all-important object might well be doubled or even trebled. Regarding our task from either of the two standpoints which I have emphasised in this volume—viz., our duty to the natives, and our responsibility to civilisation—the obligation is insistent. It is from the natives that the bulk of the revenue is ultimately derived, and it is our duty to train them so that they may take that share in municipal and governmental work for which they prove themselves to be qualified; that they may fill the posts, both clerical and technical, for which good salaries are offered; that they may learn to adopt scientific methods in business and agriculture, so as to make the best of their opportunities, their labour, and the resources of their country, and hold their own in the world's competition.

The merchant, the miner, and the trader need the help of educated natives, whether as clerks and accountants or as artisans, to assist in the development of the country—a development in which Africans are themselves taking an increasingly prominent part. It is useless to build railways if you have no clerks, accountants, telegraphists, or signal-men, and no artisans for the workshops—and the same may be said of every other department. The employment of natives of the country by Government and commercial firms not only benefits the country by keeping the money in it, but saves the passage-money of aliens, and promotes continuity, which is sacrificed by employing Europeans, who have constantly to go on leave. Alike, therefore, from motives of moral obligation or material progress, there can be no way in which the revenue can be better applied than in promoting education.[1]

Though little material reduction in the cost of education can be expected from school fees, it is, I think, important that they should be imposed, however nominal in amount.[2]

[1] The cost of education in Nigeria (including grants to aided schools) was only about 1·5 per cent of ordinary revenue in 1913. This would have been largely increased but for the financial stringency due to the war. It is, however, exclusive of the large sums spent by the native administrations, and of the cost of training apprentices. The cost in Sierra Leone in 1919 is stated to have been 3·5 per cent of "available revenue." Education was started in this colony as far back as 1737.—(Governor's Speech.) In the Gold Coast the cost was 2 per cent in 1917 and 2·9 in 1918. In East Africa the amount spent on *native* education appears to be altogether negligible. It is stated by Mr Woolf to have been £1835 out of £666,000 in 1909-10—viz., ·3 per cent.—*Loc. cit.*, p. 344. In Uganda lump-sum grants are made to Missions (without qualification tests) aggregating in 1918-19 £2100 out of a revenue of £351,835—viz., ·6 per cent.—(Report, Cmd. 508 (37) of 1920.) See note, p. 429. Similar grants are made in Nyasaland of £1000—viz., ·5 per cent of revenue in 1918-19.—Cmd. 508 (24) of 1920. There is evidence of a greatly-increased interest in education in all the West African colonies.

[2] In the Sudan the village schools are supported by an educational rate, usually on crops, land, or date-palms, imposed by the Governor of the Province

The African is not singular in regarding as of little value what costs him nothing. The primitive savage is indeed apt to think that he should rather be paid for allowing his children to attend school, since he loses their household labour.

The time has not yet come for compulsory education in Africa, if for no other reasons than the paucity of qualified teachers, and the enormous cost. When, however, a boy receives his education free of cost, it would seem desirable that he should be compelled to remain and complete the school course. In most of the African dependencies there is an eager demand, both on the part of the parents and children —a demand which may be expected to continue unless the results of education are such as to create a prejudice against it. But although universal education is as yet a distant ideal, it should, I think, be a primary object of British policy to disseminate education throughout the country, with a view to breaking down the distinction between the educated and Europeanised class in the capital cities, and the bulk of the population in the interior. Each provincial capital to begin with should become a centre from which educational progress may radiate.

So important in my view are the main considerations in regard to education, which it has been the purpose of this and the preceding chapter to present to my readers, that I will venture briefly to recapitulate them, lest they should be obscured by the minor matters of detail referred to. I have emphasised the fact that not only as trustees for their advancement are we pledged to afford to the races of the tropics the best education we can give to fit them for an increasing share in governmental and municipal duties, but that the irresistible material progress of the country demands an ever-increasing supply of Africans with both a literary and a technical education—a demand which we ourselves have created, and one which may be the greatest and most potent factor for good if rightly used; for evil, and ultimate disaster, if the basis of our structure be founded on wrong principles. Moreover, great as are the claims of the minority, from whose ranks the demands of Government and commerce are supplied, they must not obscure those of the great majority who are

and approved by the Governor-General. Non-ratepayers are charged 2s. per month. The fees at Government primary schools are £4, 2s. per annum; at Gordon College £7, 10s., and for boarders £20 per annum.

content to live the life their fathers have lived in their villages.

The coloured races of the world are awakening to self-consciousness under Western influences. In Africa tribal rule is disintegrating. On the form which the new aspirations take will depend the future relations of these peoples with the white races of the world. Are the foundations being truly laid? Is the education provided by our schools such as to guide those aspirations into the channels best adapted for the evolution of individual character and racial progress? This is the great problem upon which incalculable results may—nay, must—depend.

My aim has been to urge that these results may best be achieved by placing the formation of character before the training of the intellect, and to make some few suggestions as to how this may be done—by boarding-schools; by an adequate British staff; by so framing the grant code and regulations as to enlist the co-operation of the Mission Societies, and extend the control of Government over all educational agencies; and finally, by the encouragement of moral and religious instruction. And by this I do not mean any particular system of philosophy or of creeds. "I speak of the controlling force and guiding principle which ministers through creeds and systems of philosophy to spiritual needs—the force which inspires a man to a sense of duty, to unswerving integrity and loyalty, whether in the public or the private relations of life. It is additional to and greater than the secular and utilitarian education of the class-room. It is founded generally on religious sanctions, and finds its highest expression in the noblest of creeds. It is an essential part of the environment and atmosphere of any institution fit to train and educate a nation."[1]

[1] Speech at the opening of the Hong-Kong University, 11th March 1912.

CHAPTER XXIII.

TRANSPORT.

Cheap transport a necessity—Necessity for railways—Selection of routes—Pioneer lines—Methods of construction: (*a*) contractors; (*b*) "the departmental system"; (*c*) by the Local Government; (*d*) by private enterprise—Application of railway revenues—Location of central workshops—Standardisation—Narrow-gauge development lines—Tramways—Mechanical transport—Animal transport—Roads and carts.

In Africa, even more than in most other countries—owing to the great distance of its interior regions from the seaboard, and to the comparatively low value of raw materials in proportion to their bulk and weight,—cheap transport is a vital necessity for the development of trade and commerce.

For uncounted centuries the African has been his own beast of burden, and a simple calculation shows that the cost of land transport by such means, with a wage-rate of 9d. a day, is about 3s. per ton mile.[1] This is somewhat reduced by the use of pack-animals in those districts where they can be employed—as in the far interior in the west,—but they cannot traverse belts infested by the tsetse fly, or survive in the coast regions, and were unknown in Uganda and Nyasaland.

It follows that produce worth £30 a ton at the port of shipment will have cost its full value to transport over a distance of less than 200 miles, leaving nothing for original cost of production and profit to the producer. The distance therefore over which produce can be conveyed by human transport

[1] A man carrying 65 lbs. for a distance of 12 miles per diem for six days in the week would at 9d. a day cost 2s. 6d. per ton mile. To this must be added subsistence money on the return journey, and a margin for sickness and supervision, so that 2s. 6d. a ton mile is less than the actual cost for long distances. The rate per ton mile for long distances may be put at four times the daily wage of the labourer. For bulky loads the cost is much more.

in competition with that of regions, in Africa or elsewhere, situated nearer to the coast, or to a navigable waterway or railway, is extremely limited.

Moreover, the native producer in such circumstances has great difficulty in disposing of his exportable produce, and has therefore no money wherewith to buy imported goods. He can only pay his tax in kind, which the Government, for like reasons, is unable to realise. With meagre imports (and therefore no customs dues) and with no direct tax, the revenue from territory so situated must be so small that it can devote no funds to development works. The vicious circle is completed by the excessive cost of the machinery of administration—not in money alone but in human life,—for the cost of conveying food supplies and building material is so great that officials are neither housed nor fed as the climate demands to maintain health. These facts are now recognised as the axioms of African administration. If they had been accepted earlier, very many lives might have been saved, and also much of the taxpayer's money,—spent in grants-in-aid which were no remedy.

It is, however, now recognised that the construction of arterial railways and the development of waterways, though involving subsidies or loans upon which the country may not for some time be able to pay interest, is the truest economy, and the postponement of such works involves unjustifiable waste.[1] For the development of the African continent is impossible without railways, and has awaited their advent. They have generally proved remunerative,[2] in spite of the fact that their route has been determined by administrative policy rather than from motives of profit. A railway reduces administrative expenses in the transport of stores, and in

[1] It is interesting to recall the fact that while Lord Selborne was telling an audience at Reading in December 1898 that the delay in starting the Uganda railway was responsible for the Fashoda crisis, Monsieur Leroy Beaulieu pointed out in the *Debats* that France's delay in constructing the trans-Saharan line had cost them the Fashoda rebuff. Had this line been built, he argued, France could have seized Sokoto and Kano by sending 60,000 men from Algeria, and could have held Northern Nigeria as a hostage.

Just as the precipitate haste of the Powers to acquire territorial sovereignty in Africa compelled us effectively to occupy districts which might otherwise have been developed by a more gradual process, so the activity of our rivals in railway construction has compelled us to push forward in the same direction, unless we were prepared to lose the markets we had secured.

[2] There is no need to urge these facts in the present day, as there was in 1892, when I advocated the building of the Uganda railway. Of that line, which so many stigmatised at the time as a waste of public money, Mr Lloyd George,

the time of officials in reaching their work; it saves the lives and health of officers; it reduces the number and cost of the troops required for policing the country by increasing their mobility; it renders direct taxation possible by affording a market for produce, and increasing the wealth of the people; it opens up new markets for British trade; it has killed the slave-trade; it renders labour now engaged in transport available for productive work; and by proper methods of construction it forms the most valuable of educational agencies for a free labour supply. It has been calculated that one railway train of average capacity and engine-power will do the work of 13,000 carriers at one-twentieth the cost.

Arterial lines of communication are, moreover, a necessary precursor of roads, for, as we shall presently see, neither mechanical nor animal-draught transport—for which they are constructed—can be of any great service for the development of interior regions, except as feeders to a railway or navigable waterway.

A railway should, of course, when possible, have some definite objective, as the Uganda railway had in the Victoria Lake, to the shores of which (extending for 800 or 1000 miles) the produce of the surrounding countries can be brought, and hence transported by water to the railway port. Or the objective may be a mineralised area like the tin-fields, or the coal deposits of Nigeria or Gwelo, or the copper mines of Katanga. Or the railway may connect some great centre like Khartum or Kano with the sea, or link two navigable sections of a river with each other, as the Matadi line on the

speaking in the House of Commons on 25th June 1912, said: "In 1902-3 Uganda exported nothing. In 1907-8 it exported 17,000 cwt. of cotton. In 1910-11, 83,000 cwt., and this year it is expected that 105,000 cwt. will be exported. In 1902 there were three or four trains in each direction. Now there are fifty or sixty in the course of the week, and the traffic is bursting all bounds." Nearly half the revenue of East Africa is derived from the earnings of the railway.—Economic Report, *loc. cit.*, p. 7.

The Uganda railway is not, however, called upon to pay interest on the capital sum expended by the Imperial Government on its construction. The latest report of the Nigerian railways shows that in 1920 they continued to meet all interest and sinking fund charges on the loans raised for construction, in spite of the heavy expenditure incurred in bridging the Niger, and the fact that the line traverses about 300 miles of almost unpopulated country, which is not, therefore, remunerative to the railway finances. It has, of course, entirely superseded the trans-Saharan trade by camels from Tripoli.

Lord Morley in his Indian budget speech (21st July 1906) stated that the railways had doubled their revenue in five years.

Congo, the Keyes-Bamako on the Upper Niger, or the Sudan railway on the Nile.[1]

But failing such definite objectives as these, which formed the first inducements to railway construction in Africa, any railway built reasonably cheaply through a populous country is bound to be remunerative, and, as East Africa has proved, it may be equally successful, in rare instances, in inducing settlers to develop a sparsely-populated region with a good climate. The main object is to tap trade-routes and connect populous cities. But before the trace is pegged out it is of essential importance (*a*) that the general railway policy and arterial system should be well thought out, so that each link may fit into the system, and (*b*) that a thorough survey should be made so that the best possible route may be selected.[2]

Sir Guildford Molesworth has observed that capital cost is too frequently increased by adherence to "the traditional excellence of railway construction." In constructing a pioneer line in Africa, the one and only object should be to get the track through somehow, and begin to earn receipts. Construction must begin from every point to which it is possible to transport material cheaply, or where earthworks can be undertaken in anticipation. Any work of magnitude, such as the crossing of a great river, must be postponed, and a substitute, such as a train-ferry, must be used, or bulk broken.[3]

[1] The Cape to Cairo railway can only be justified in so far as each section has a definite objective, which offers reasonable prospects of being remunerative. Railways in Africa must lead by the shortest route to the seaport, and not along its length. The estimates both as to distance, time, and cost of construction given in the 'Times' of 11th February 1899 were so fallacious as to lead the sceptical to conjecture that the real object was to tap cheap labour supplies for South African mines.

[2] I do not here discuss the probable railway development of the future in West Africa, but it will not be amiss to bear the following facts in mind. Nigeria is by far the largest and most densely-populated of our West African dependencies. The present terminus of the line is at Kano, a great collecting centre for the hides, skins, and produce of the nomad cattle tribes to north and east. Kano is 712 miles from the port of Lagos, and thence 4000 by sea to England. Bornu, bordering Lake Chad, is another possible centre of cotton development, and of hides. If linked up with the Kano line, its distance from the sea would not be less than 1000 miles. From these places to the Mediterranean in a direct line is about 1200 miles (to Tripoli). France talks of a railway to Agadir and thence to Timbuktu and Chad (connecting eventually with a Camerun line). Italy talks of reviving the Tripoli-Chad trade. In time of war, if not in peace, the desert route by railway would supersede that to the Guinea coast.

[3] The Ganges bridge was not constructed for thirty years after the railway crossed the river. The Brahmaputra bridge has not yet been built. The

Terminal reclamations and accommodation, if they interfere with progress, must wait. All above-rail works which are not absolutely essential—and even ballasting unless the material is on the spot—should be deferred. The telegraph and the block system must do the work of railway signals. Triangles can replace turn-tables ; platforms, waiting-rooms, and other buildings eventually necessary to a railway can be postponed. It must suffice if the train can travel by day only and at twelve miles an hour ; all the improvements can come later, when the railway is already beginning to earn and to reduce administrative charges. In permanent-way material (weight of rail and number of steel sleepers), however, and in the quality and adequate supply of rolling-stock, economy must not predominate. These were the principles on which Sir Percy Girouard built the Nile railway, and Sir J. Eaglesome the Baro-Kano line in Nigeria, and the results amply justified them.

Railways in Africa have either been built by contract, or under what is known as "the departmental system,"[1] or (as in Nigeria and the Sudan) by the local Government. The nature of the contract may be (1) by "lump-sum," or (2) by "schedule of rates," or (3) by percentage on work ("time and line"). For the first a detailed survey and specifications are necessary, and the Government must maintain a costly checking staff to measure up quantities, and to see that the work done and the quality of the materials used are in accordance with the specifications. Such a contract is impracticable in a little explored country, the geology of which is unknown, since the contractor's margin to cover risks and unknown factors must necessarily be prohibitive.

The "schedule of rates" contract, under which a rate is agreed for each class of work, with a fixed commission for contractor's profits, is more feasible, but it does not fully meet the demand—which is the chief argument in favour of contracts—that the total liability and the length of time required for construction should be known and guaranteed under penalty before the work is commenced. Nor does such a contract share the advantages which are claimed for the

Uganda railway instead of traversing Busoga stopped short at the lake, and made its connection by 160 miles of waterway. Though the Niger bridge was perhaps constructed prematurely, and before adequate investigation had been made, the river was crossed for some time by a train-ferry.

[1] For the official description of these systems see Cd. 2325 of 1904.

system of construction by Government, in such matters as recruiting and control of labour, assistance by every Government department, &c. (*vide inf.*). The penalty clauses of a contract are in practice rarely if ever enforced.

A modification of this method of contract (which has lately been adopted for the Guas' Ngishu Railway in East Africa) appears to minimise as far as possible the demerits of construction by contract. An estimate is arrived at with a stipulated commission for the contractors' profits. The contractor receives a progressive percentage on any savings he may effect on the estimate, and bears 10 per cent of any excess. The system, however, tends to over-estimating, for the contractor naturally desires to fix as high a datum-line as possible. The Government, moreover, has to maintain an expensive checking staff. Generally speaking, the more fully a country is developed, the more possible it becomes to construct railways by contract.

The terms demanded by contractors for construction and operation of a line have in some cases included a Government guarantee of a minimum profit for a term of years and the alienation of rights in land and minerals, which have *pro rata* mortgaged the future of the country, or have interfered with native rights.[1] Such concessions are greatly to be deprecated, and if granted a right of expropriation by Government on reasonable terms should be carefully preserved.

Under the "departmental system" consulting engineers are appointed by the Crown agents. They carry out the preliminary survey, and appoint a resident engineer, who controls the work on their behalf. He and his staff are nominally under the local Government, but he corresponds direct with the consulting engineers, whom he naturally regards as his real employers. The consulting engineers are bound by no contract, either as to cost or time. They usually submit

[1] The contractors for the abortive Suakim-Berber railway in 1885 employed English navvies on exorbitant rates of pay, in the fierce heat of the desert. Those who, like myself, were there can vividly recall the sequel of drunkenness, insubordination, and mutiny which followed. The constructors of the Bechuana railway were, I believe, given every alternate mile of land (including mineral rights), a Government subsidy of £20,000, and a lien of 12½ per cent on net profits.—'Times,' 11th February 1899.

The French decree of 1901, which conceded the construction of the Dahomey railway to Monsieur Borelli, allowed an annual subsidy of £80 per kilometre for 8 years, and special tariffs, with tracts of land aggregating 1150 square miles, including mineral rights. These terms evoked a protest from French, British, and German merchants, on the grounds that it made the colony the property of a commercial syndicate.

a preliminary estimate, safeguarded by many reservations as to contingencies which they cannot foresee or control. There is no incentive to keep the estimate low,[1] and every reason to avoid the odium of exceeding it, but in my experience it has always been exceeded. Their profits are subject to no risk. Materials are ordered through the Crown agents, who receive a percentage on the cost of all supplies. The local Government has to pay the bill with the very minimum of control over expenditure which it is possible to conceive.

The high standing and unimpeachable integrity of the consulting engineers and of the Crown agents are its only protection. Against errors and needless expenditure by the resident engineer, or enhancement of the labour-rate to the permanent detriment of the colony, it has none, for it is practically impossible for the local Government to change the resident engineer, even though satisfied as to his incompetency or unsuitability. Such a system must needs be expensive, and must needs cause friction. In my own experience its results have not been happy, while the strictures passed by Colonel Waghorn—an Indian expert who inspected the Lagos railway—formed a condemnation of the system. The rate of progress was stated by Mr Churchill to be twenty-five miles a year for the Sierra Leone railway, and thirty-one for the Lagos line, which, however, was said to have "many defects owing to hasty construction!"[2]

[1] In Nigeria an estimate for a light line, 3 ft. 6 in. gauge, was reduced by consulting engineers from £7000 to £3000 per mile, when a policy of independent construction was advocated. The cheaper estimate of course involved the elimination of most of the above-rail works, and presupposed cheap contracts for sea and river freight, but these possibilities did not come to light until the estimates were challenged by the alternative method of construction.

[2] Sir F. Swettenham gives a graphic description of the "established system" for the construction of railways in Crown colonies. "The system is that the consulting engineers to the Crown agents (and no dependency is allowed to choose its own consulting engineers) undertake the whole job." They survey the line, appoint as many engineers as they like, on salaries fixed by themselves, decide the weight of the rails, the type of the bridges and rolling-stock, and purchase the whole of the materials, and the colony pays the bill. "Neither the colony's chief engineer, nor its governor, nor its executive or legislative council have any real responsibility for the work, even though it takes twice as long to construct as the time originally estimated, and costs twice as much. . . . The work is executed thousands of miles away from the people who are responsible for it, who very probably have no personal knowledge of . . . climate and rainfall, labour conditions, local prices, and local materials." The engineer in charge has probably to buy his experience at the cost of the colony. "No one is responsible. The Secretary of State only insists on the system . . . the Crown agents have clearly nothing to do with it, the whole business only gives them trouble. The consulting engineers cannot be held responsible" if local conditions and prices are not what they expected. "Worst of all, the consulting engineers

The home Government under this system assumes through the Crown agents a direct control, and is responsible for the proper and economical expenditure of the funds, whether as trustee to the British taxpayer for an Imperial subsidy or to the local taxpayer for colonial funds. Every line so constructed should therefore be inspected by an independent authority—preferably from India—and his report made public. The present tendency, I am told, is to employ consulting-engineer-contractors, who deal direct with the manufacturers, and are responsible for both design and execution.

There remains the system of construction by the local Government. To ensure success the engineer-in-charge must be a man of high reputation. He and his staff—temporarily increased for the purpose—are the direct employees of the local Government, and stand or fall by the results of their work. The Government selects its consulting engineers, to whom it refers for advice regarding any large bridge, &c. For the port terminus it can employ separate consultants, as experts in harbour works, wharves, and terminal facilities. If there is a competent man in the colony, consulting engineers are no more required for ordinary railway construction than for buildings or roads, but for such special constructions as harbour works, moles, &c., in which a mistake cannot be subsequently rectified, consulting engineers are essential. Their employment ensures continuity of responsibility when the colonial staff has disappeared. The whole resources of Government are invoked for the work. Administrative officers engage and look after the interests of the labourers. Government steamers assist in transporting material. Troops (and also convicts) may help in the construction. When once the system has been started the first object should be to maintain a regular construction staff.

The Northern Nigeria railway, built by Sir P. Girouard and Sir J. Eaglesome under this system (which I had strongly recommended), was considered to be the cheapest, most

disappear as such, and are replaced by construction engineers, who pass the work of their own man, or of the contractors they employ." He thus concludes: "Therefore whatever the kind of work put in, the Government has to accept it; whatever the bill, the Government has to pay it; however the time of construction is exceeded, the public must bear it patiently; because this is the established system under which railways are made in Crown colonies. It might almost be added that unless a man believe in the system faithfully he cannot be saved." —'Malaya,' pp. 281-283.

rapid, and in every way the most satisfactory line hitherto constructed in tropical Africa.[1] If the local Government cannot undertake the work, it should at least have control over all local expenditure on labour, &c., and the railway staff should be responsible to it.

The earliest Indian railways were constructed and operated by private companies, with a guarantee of about 5 per cent and a share of profits in excess of 5 per cent. Experience has shown this method to be unsatisfactory, and the private companies are now nearly all expropriated. The general opinion, said Lord Morley, is that for India a system of construction by Government and working by private enterprise is the best, and this system was adopted in respect of 52 per cent of the mileage of Indian railways.[2] The great aggregate profits made by Indian railways, in spite of the fact that many were constructed for famine relief, or for strategic purposes, and not expected to be remunerative, affords a strong argument in favour of State ownership in such countries.[3]

I strongly share Mr Chamberlain's opinion that railways in our African dependencies must be owned and maintained by the Government. It alone should be responsible for the acquisition of the land, the provision of labour for construction, the training of skilled labour in the workshops, and the control of subordinates—too apt to take advantage of an ignorant people—when the line is in running order. The administration, moreover, is itself too dependent on the railway to admit of its being in other hands. The local revenue, and not the foreign investor, should benefit from the profits

[1] The railway built later to the coal-mines in Nigeria under the same system has been an equal success. The first experiment (preceding the Baro-Kano railway) consisted of a light 2 ft. 6 in. line, 22 miles long. Sanction was obtained in the spring. The rails were rolled in England in June, and the first train reached its destination by Christmas. The cost was £1480 per mile, which had been declared to be impossible. The railways in the Malay States, constructed in the same way, were equally successful.—'Malaya,' p. 281.

[2] The system of management by companies domiciled in England was unanimously condemned by the Committee of Inquiry appointed by the Indian Government in October 1920.—Cmd. 1512 of 1921. Half the members recommend management by the State, the other half prefer management by companies domiciled in India.

[3] The Committee, whose expert authority must carry great weight, do not question the principle of State ownership, but they point out that the estimate of profits is vitiated by the failure to write off depreciation of wasting assets, such as bridges, rails, and rolling-stock, so that their original cost should have been refunded from revenue by the time their useful life has expired. This absence of "commercial accounting methods, in a commercial undertaking" extends, I think, in some of the African dependencies to marine vessels and plant.

realised, or it may be desirable in the interests of the country to forgo or to decrease the profits from a railway. An exception may occasionally be made in the case of a short branch to develop a particular mine or industry if the right of expropriation on payment of capital cost and interest be reserved.

It should, in my view, be a recognised principle that railways must not be regarded as directly revenue-earning.[1] After paying their running expenses and depreciation, interest on capital cost, and a small contribution to a sinking fund for the extinction of the debt, any net profits should be devoted to the improvement of the line (including workshops and rolling-stock), and to reduction in freight rates. As an indirect agency in increasing trade, they are the greatest of revenue-earners.

There is perhaps a tendency in Africa to place the central workshops at or near the coast terminus. Modern experience is averse to this. The North-Western Railway of India has its shops at Lahore, not at Karachi. The Bengal-Nagpur and East Indian Railway workshops are at Jabalpore, not at Calcutta, and the same holds for all English railways. Workshops near the coast are in a more vulnerable position in case of war, and if seriously damaged might paralyse the whole line. But in Africa there is an additional reason for this principle, since the coast climate is enervating and usually malarial, and the seaport offers greater temptations to the European and African staff alike. The workshops afford unrivalled schools for the training of native apprentices, and it is a short-sighted policy to expose them to avoidable influences for evil, even were it shown that there was some material advantage in such a location.

The cost, both of construction and maintenance of railways in the tropics, could be very appreciably decreased by a system of standardising the requirements in equipment and rolling-stock, including bridging and wharfing material, constructional iron-work for buildings, signalling and electrical installations, pumping plant, &c. The system of indents,

[1] Most of the African dependencies adopt this vicious principle, and so retard development. East Africa derived 48 to 49 per cent of its revenue from railway profits (Economic Report, p. 7), a system lately abandoned, and the Sudan about 35 per cent.—(Handbook 98, p. 158). The Indian Committee insists that railways should have "a separate budget, and be responsible for earning and expending their own revenue." See note, p. 99.

according to the particular views and designs of each engineer, involves unnecessary drawing-office work, inspection, and cost in manufacture, as well as delay in execution. Standard types should be fixed by a committee of men with actual African experience, assisted by one or more experts, who would bring new inventions to their notice. "There was," says the Indian Industries Report, "a totally unnecessary diversity in orders for the same class of articles, instead of standard types, only to be deviated from where there are express reasons for doing so."[1] British engineering trade in China has suffered greatly in the competition with the United States from the lack of cheap standardised types.

Opinions differ as to the advisability of constructing narrow-gauge railways (2 ft. or 2 ft. 6 in. gauge) as feeder lines. If it is intended eventually to replace such a line by one on the standard gauge, the initial saving is chiefly limited to permanent way material and rolling-stock, for the cost of survey and alignment is no less, and bridges and culverts must be built wide enough and strong enough to carry the eventual standard-gauge line. Freights in proportion to train mileage are reduced, and the maintenance staff is not appreciably less. Above all, the complication of gauges prevents interchanges of rolling-stock, and involves breaking of bulk. It necessitates separate workshops, while there is a temptation to use heavier engines than the rails will bear. If, on the other hand, there is no expectation of a development of traffic sufficient for a standard-gauge line later on, the cost would, of course, be somewhat reduced, but would rarely be justified.

I am inclined to the conclusion that a line of less than the standard gauge should only be built when for financial reasons it is impossible to build a standard-gauge line; when there is a reasonable expectation that it will eventually be replaced by a standard-gauge, and the narrow-gauge rails can be taken up and used elsewhere; when the length is sufficient to compensate in some degree for the duplication of gauges, and to make the saving in construction cost appreciable—say, 100 miles; and when there is every reason to believe that, while production will be increased, the traffic will not exceed the capacity of the narrow-gauge line for a considerable period—say, fifteen years—as in the case of areas

[1] Cmd. 51 of 1919, p. 126.

newly taken up by settlers, where bulk freights cannot be expected until experimental plantations have been tested and come into bearing. Or again, in the case of an unproved mineral field, or where the best route to be followed by a permanent line is in the circumstances difficult to determine. There is, I think, an almost unanimous opinion against shorter and more temporary feeder lines on a narrow gauge. If in any circumstances they are constructed they should be worked on the principle of a tramway—without stations or station staffs, &c.—rather than on that of a railway.

These remarks do not, of course, apply to any form of light line on which the haulage is not done by locomotives. Light Decauville 2 ft. lines, and mono-rails (where the haul is not against the gradient), may be laid for any temporary purpose with great advantage, and taken up again when the purpose is achieved, the trucks being propelled by hand, or by animal traction.[1] The "loco-tractor" or "road-rail" system, in which the waggons and the guiding wheels of the locomotive run on narrow-gauge rails, but the driving-wheels of the locomotive, bearing most of its weight, run on a pair of narrow macadam tracks laid beside the rails, may prove to be the best and most economical form which such a method of transport can assume, since it claims to be independent of bridges, culverts, and gradients. The Under-Secretary stated to the House that extensive trials were being conducted in Uganda, the result of which has not yet been made public.

Generally speaking, it may be said that the initial cost of railways is high, while their running and maintenance expenses are low compared with road transport, so that if there is a prospect of sufficient volume of traffic developing within a reasonable time over which the initial costs can be distributed, a railway is the most economical form of transport. Its running expenses are reduced proportionally to a greater degree than in the case of road traffic by the development of passenger traffic. The freight rates can at first be fixed high, and yet offer considerable reductions on the form of transport which it supersedes. A railway develops the trade of a district more rapidly than any other method, and

[1] Such short temporary lines, laid alongside a road for animal traction, may prove to be the cheapest method of conveying cotton or other produce from a producing centre to a central market or the railway, where there are no severe gradients, and no bridging is required.

thus indirectly increases the revenue derived from customs duties, &c. On the other hand, while the whole cost of construction and maintenance of roads falls on the Government, it derives no revenue from private traffic except such licences on vehicles as it may impose, and these act in restraint of development, and are unlikely to produce any substantial sum.

The use of mechanical road transport has made great progress in Africa of late years, but it has serious limitations. Calculations of cost are apt to lose sight of the heavy expenditure incurred in construction and maintenance of the metalled roads necessary for any continuous and heavy traffic of this nature. Light vans may indeed run for a few months of the dry season on unmetalled roads, but continuous traffic, even of light vehicles, soon churns the surface into deep dust or sand.

If a full load can be secured both ways the cost of running may be as low as 1s. per ton mile when the return journey can be accomplished in a single day; but for greater distances, when liquid fuel must be stored in advance depots, and garages and repair shops provided, the cost rapidly equals that of human or animal transport, and the gain is only in the saving of time. Moreover, in order to keep the costs anywhere in the neighbourhood of 1s. per ton mile, native drivers must be employed, and since they are not competent to execute any but the lightest running repairs, the vehicles must return each night to headquarters, and can therefore cover no more than an outward journey of about twenty-five miles.

To avoid the heavy cost of metalling and maintaining roads, "roller-track" vehicles, which, being without wheels, create instead of destroying the roadway, offer attractions. The system has been made familiar by pictures of "tanks" during the war. The revolving sleepers present so large a surface and so distribute the weight that the pressure on the ground is reduced to a minimum, and loose sand or swamps present no difficulties. There are several types. One of them, the "Ped-rail," is fitted with an ingenious "ankle-joint," which enables it to turn in a narrow radius, and by minimising the road resistance, the draw-bar pull is so reduced that a couple of men can push or pull a ton load on the level without difficulty. It is claimed that tractors of 100 B.H.P. drawing trailers with a load of twenty tons can be worked very economically, while smaller vehicles of one or two tons can be drawn over any kind of ground by draught animals. To discuss the subject of mechanical road transport in any adequate way would demand more space than I can afford. It is dealt with more fully in my report on Nigeria.[1]

It is the immemorial custom of Africa for man (with a load on his head), equally with the wild game, to follow in single file a narrow path, twisting now to the right and now to the left, as some obstacle, long since passed away, may have dictated. The invaders from the north introduced the camel, the horse, the ox, and the ass, to share as pack animals in the burden of transport, and where they are in use the immemorial path has become widened, but no effort is ever made to remove obstacles or snags.

The utility of these animals is limited to the dry zone in the west, but they should be available throughout the greater part of East Africa. Mechanical road transport must take their place in those regions in which they do not thrive, or where the tsetse-fly exists. Human carriers may have to be used occasionally on military expeditions, or in close, precipitous, roadless districts; but, as I said in the chapter on labour, Government should set the example of abandoning this archaic and wasteful form of transport.[2]

Oxen are specially valuable, since most of the tribes understand their management. They are, of course, much more useful as draught than as pack animals.[3] The draught ox

[1] Cd. 468 of 1920, appendix vii. The "Yubo" also appears to be a useful type. Though the Ped-rail train, and the small vehicles for animal traction, appear useful for their respective purposes, they do not meet the need of a mechanically-propelled vehicle capable of carrying a load of 2 to 4 tons.

The question of the best and most economical substitutes for petrol for internal combustion engines for road transport has lately received much attention. The Colonial Economic Development Committee speaks favourably of "Natalite"—which consists of denatured alcohol mixed with a proportion of ether,—and also of "producer gas." The latter appears to have great possibilities, and experiments are being made with it in both East and West Africa. It is claimed that petrol-driven engines can be converted for its use, and that the saving is equivalent to the use of petrol at 3d. a gallon. It is, however, at present in the early experimental stage, and is not spoken of so hopefully by others. See note, p. 513, *re* "power-alcohol."

[2] Unknown to the employer, hardship may be caused by the impressment of men who are unused to the work but unable to bribe a village chief. Prompt payment should be made when their task is done, and villagers employed as carriers should not be taken against their will more than a day's march. On the other hand, care is necessary to see that they do not rob villages *en route* in the name of the white man—an offence at one time common. The French found that main routes were often deserted for this reason.

[3] A native chief in Nigeria aptly described the plough and the cart as "the white man's slaves."

is the most valuable animal in ordinary country, the camel in loose sand, and the mule in steep country intersected by ravines. But the use of the wheel has remained unknown in Africa, even among the Hamitic negroids in the northern tropical belt, and is only now being slowly introduced. Where the use of animals is possible the first lesson for the African is to learn to employ the country-cart of India and China (which can be repaired in any village, and requires no metalled roads), and to abandon a method of transport suited only to the precipitous gradients of the Himalayas.

The African does not excel in the care of animals. He will kill them by overwork, and sore-back them by atrocious pack-saddles. He fails to realise such elementary facts as that an animal in hard work needs a grain ration, or that oxen (which will not graze at night) must be given adequate time to feed by day.

There are those who have condemned roadmaking in Africa because roads do not assist the human carrier. But roads are intended to abolish human transport, to facilitate the use of country carts where draught animals are possible, and of mechanical transport where they are not, and so to act as feeders to a railway.

Where traffic is heavy and a road is likely to develop into a metalled track and even into a tramway or narrow-gauge line, it is worth the time and cost of a good surveyor to lay it out, so that unnecessary gradients may be avoided, and it may be serviceable all the year round. A detour of twenty times the vertical height may be taken as generally permissible to ease an ascent, with ruling gradients of 1 in 20 for distances over 100 yards, and 1 in 10 for short ramps. A common error is to make the road too broad, and so to deprive it of shade. A 24-ft. track—12 ft. of metal if required—is ample. Rest-houses and native camps must be provided at suitable distances where water is obtainable.

It is a matter of the first importance to interest the native administrations in road-construction, and to train native road-makers who should be capable of directing the work under occasional supervision, leaving the bridging to be done by the public works department. Ballast, where necessary, can be collected and broken by villagers, and placed in readiness along the roadside, being paid for by the cubic yard.

As with the pioneer railway, so with the road—" le mieux

est l'ennemi du bien." It is better to run a rough road from point to point along the surveyed alignment, with stumps and snags cleared, and improve it later by bridging and draining, than to complete a few hundred yards of first-class metalled road for the same cost and time, which effects no definite purpose, and arouses no emulation in the native administration.

Roads, as I have said, being ancillary to railways, should be constructed as feeders, and not parallel to them, so as to compete for freights. With regard to carts, it is useful to remember that the greater the diameter of the wheel the more easily will it surmount loose sand, and that a narrow tyre offers less resistance than a broad one—a lesson I learnt by practical experience when crossing the Kalahari desert.

CHAPTER XXIV.

TRADE.

Nature of trade in Africa—The fixing of price—Monopoly and combination—The middleman—The native trader—The native merchant—British *v.* native merchants—The Indian trader—Government and trade—Government and private enterprise—Concessions—Concessions for oil-mills—The principles involved—Produce inspection—Cash trade *v.* barter—Currency—A trade department—An Economic Board—French Chambers of Commerce—Trade commissioners and home agencies—The Crown agents—Criticisms of the system.

THE object of trade may, I presume, be defined as the exchange of the commodities of one country for those of another, with mutual benefit to each, while the function of a Government is to facilitate the operation, so far as may be in its power, and to see that the benefit is reciprocal. Trade in the African tropics assumes at present its most simple form—the exchange of raw produce for manufactured goods. In most countries of the world the producer, in order to obtain a livelihood, is compelled to go on producing as long as there is the barest margin of profit. In Africa, however, as a general rule, owing in part to the sparsity of its population, in part to the fact that the native has few needs, and in part to favourable conditions of climate and soil, the producer is not under any compulsion to produce for sale or exchange, while he can at the same time produce more cheaply than in most other countries.

Since the wants of the African are few, it would seem at first sight natural that any considerable rise in the price of imported goods would result in a decrease of production. Enhancement of the price of the goods he desires may indeed result in a temporary inclination to hoard his money, which in itself is not altogether undesirable, since it adds to his capital reserves, but the African is more influenced by the price obtainable for his produce than by the price he has to pay for his purchases.

If the price obtainable for his produce is a liberal one, even though relatively less than the increased price of imports, he will continue to produce, and the increased price of imported goods does not affect the quality of the produce offered for sale; while a decreased price for produce, though reducing its quantity, will operate to improve its quality, for the demand being less, the better quality is more likely to find a purchaser.

It has been argued that the profits derived by the native producer, when competition is unfettered, are in some cases unduly large, and would be more properly distributed among the agencies which have made such profits possible, as for instance, when the price paid for ground-nuts at Kano rose from £2 or £3 a ton to £50. Provided, however, that increased prices do not have the effect of checking production—a result which may happen among primitive tribes when the vendor of produce only requires a limited sum, and ceases to sell as soon as he has acquired it,—the rule operates in Africa, as in other countries, that the greater the price the merchant can afford to pay, and the larger the profit made by the native vendors, the greater is the prosperity of the country, and the greater its wealth. The wealthier the native producer becomes, the more he spends on the purchase of imported goods, which in turn adds to the profit and wealth of the merchant. The wealth of its native population tends to the rapid development of the country. Even the increased wealth of the foreign merchant, whose capital is embarked in the country, tends to the same result. Nor must we overlook the fact that even the peasant producer does not wholly escape from the increased cost of living, which is a concomitant of development, or that he shares his profits with the middleman. The absurdly low prices paid for produce a few years ago may conceivably have been relatively almost as beneficial to the peasant producer under the conditions then prevailing as the higher prices of a later period under changed conditions. The price which the agriculturist can obtain for produce grown for home consumption must always control the price at which he is willing to produce for export.

Since, as Adam Smith says, it is the object of the merchant

in every age, and of every nationality, to buy in the cheapest market and to sell in the dearest, the object of a trade combine or trust is to oust competition, and so to cheapen commodities—viz., to reduce prices to the producer. Unless, however, monopoly is supported by State aid, it is difficult to establish, for the monopolist must be continually buying out the independent trader, or underselling him, which means increasing the purchase price, even up to the point when no profit remains.

I have already in chapter xiii. discussed one aspect of the question of monopoly, and there is no need to restate the arguments here. Experience has shown that whether the monopoly is national, as established by the old navigation laws, or State-aided like those of the chartered companies, or created by private firms, they have alike proved inimical to the expansion of trade. The tendency in modern no less than in ancient times has nevertheless been towards co-operative societies, "combines," and "trusts," by means of which the powerful group has sought to exclude the smaller merchant, and to enhance profits at the expense of either the producer or the consumer. The State, as the guardian of the public, has usually sought to oppose these monopolies, and to encourage competition. On the other hand, a "combine" by reducing the "overhead expenses" of several different managements may be able to sell more cheaply, and any tendency to "cut prices" or form a monopoly is checked by the competition of the native trader.[1]

"I will give the native producer a fair price," says the monopolist, "sufficient to encourage production (which excessive profits retard). The extra profits I make shall be carried to reserves, which will enable me to take risks, and incur losses in opening up new markets." By such arguments, no doubt, the Niger Chartered Company would have defended its action in amalgamating the competing European trading interests on the Niger, and establishing a virtual

[1] Lord Balfour's Committee argues that "every encouragement should be given by [Government] to the formation of combinations of manufacturers, and others concerned, to secure supplies of materials."—Cd. 9035, p. 37. Compare Herr Dernburg, German Colonial Minister: "The production of raw materials is more and more being included in the operations of great foreign industrial enterprises, syndicates, and trusts, which tend to eliminate the middleman and to concentrate in their own hands every process of particular industries from the field or mine to the finished product."—'Times,' 14th January 1907.

trade monopoly which enabled it to secure Nigeria for the Empire.[1] Similar arguments would no doubt be used by modern combinations in West African trade. The temptation to reduce the purchase price when it depends solely on the will of the purchaser is great; but in practice, as I have said, it is doubtful whether a monopoly can be maintained, unless State-aided, or unless it controls shipping, especially when the profits to be made are large. The form of monopoly which is of all the most intolerable and injurious is one in which the State participates, as under the former Congo régime, or the proposals of the Empire Resources Development Committee, which I have already discussed.

If, on the other hand, as a result of unrestricted competition, the native producer seems for a time to make unreasonably large profits, his standard of living will rise, and the imports which he requires will increase. So far as the home consumer is concerned, the price of African produce is regulated not by the price paid in Africa, but by the world's supplies and prices, which the output of any particular region in Africa is rarely large enough to modify appreciably.

The native producer, we have seen, gains by a competitive market, but the profit does not all go to him, for much of it is absorbed by the middleman. In the case of Nigerian ground-nuts it was affirmed that he received three-fifths of the price, and the producer only two-fifths.[2] In so far as he is a mere unproductive exploiter of the labour of the peasant, the middleman is without justification, and can only be an ephemeral incubus until the producer learns, with the assistance of Government, to do without him. When, however, as he generally does, the middleman performs a useful function as a small trader, opening new fields for trade, he is

[1] Amalgamation of interests in the circumstances of the Royal Niger Company was also necessary for purposes of mutual defence, and to overcome foreign State-aided competition.

[2] The Kano Resident reported that a large number of middlemen arrive at that centre of the ground-nut trade at the season when the crop is ready for the market. They picket the roads, and induce or compel the producer to accept the price they offer, and return south when the season is over. The Government had to take action in the interests of the producer, and the Emir forbade the sale of produce outside the authorised market.

The same phenomenon presents itself in India. "The export trade from country districts (says the Industrial Report, p. 9) generally suffers from the existence of an undue number of middlemen, who intercept a large share of the profits."

entitled to his gains. As communications improve he is driven farther afield to open up new markets. The merchant is glad to employ him to distribute his goods, and to bring exportable produce in return. Here again a "cut-throat competition" may prove a deterrent to legitimate trade. In West Africa, especially among the German merchants, the desire to secure the services of middlemen took the form of affording unjustifiable credits to them, with the object of creating monopolies.[1]

If the export trade suffers from a superabundance of middlemen who intercept profits, the remedies would seem to be that British merchants should get in closer touch with, and as far as possible buy direct from, the producer, and that the producer should be encouraged to adopt a better system of marketing by co-operative selling.

The African, as I have known him, is a keen and expert trader. I speak more particularly of Nigeria, and of the Hausa and Yoruba races—each numbering several millions—and of the coast population, educated or illiterate. The native traders bring produce to the export merchant and distribute his goods either by head-carriage or by caravans of donkeys and pack-oxen in the north, and by canoes on the waterways in the south,—imported textiles and hardware for hides, palm-produce, seed-cotton, and other exportable goods. Or they exchange the products of one region for those of another—salt, kola-nuts, natron, live-stock, and skins—for the cloths and leather goods of Kano and other cities.[2] Throughout the length and breadth of the land, weekly or bi-weekly markets, often held by night, are attended by thousands of vendors, who obtain much of their supplies from the itinerant trader.

The rôle of the latter is entirely useful, and if in the past he has sometimes been convicted of extortion, personation, and spreading false reports, of combining slave-dealing with

[1] A prominent West African merchant remarked to me that the abuse of the system of giving credit to native middlemen was the curse of South Nigeria. He had been present in court when a case was heard in which a native with a borrowed canoe and labour, who on his own showing had never possessed £5, was found to be owing four different firms a sum of about £700 for goods supplied without any guarantee whatever. I was told that the outstanding credit at a single port was fully £200,000.—See Cmd. 468/1920, p. 41. As regards the Gold Coast, see Handbook 93, p. 34.

[2] The trade of Kano for many centuries consisted of manufactured articles—cottons, shoes, leather, &c.—chiefly in exchange for salt, slaves, and kolas.

his legitimate trade, and of spreading venereal disease, these are matters susceptible of improvement with the progress of the times, and already to a large extent obsolete.

The native traders on the coast, on the other hand, are engaged to a greater or less degree as principals in the import and export trade. The most wealthy employ middlemen, who penetrate through the network of creeks and rivers in canoes, exchanging their goods for palm-oil, palm-kernels, and other produce.

As an exporter the native merchant trades at an advantage over his European rival, for he has had no excess profits duty and no income-tax to pay. During the war he was loud in his protests if the European shipping companies did not accord him ample cargo space. He does not, as a rule, care for the risk of opening up new markets, and is content to compete in those opened by his rivals. Many native merchants have in these conditions amassed, I am told, considerable fortunes.

As the native trader learns the advantage of association, and as individuals acquire the command of increased capital, they will become more serious competitors with the British trader, who, however, in spite of his home taxes, has always been able to hold his own by better business methods and a larger command of capital. It was, I believe, only during the abnormal conditions created by the war that the native export merchant became a serious rival and made large profits, with a resulting tendency to combination among the foreign merchants, so that they might command their own shipping. It would probably be advantageous that every trading company should be compelled to register in the country in which it operates.

I claim no knowledge of the conditions of trade in the eastern group of our African dependencies, but I conceive that these remarks also apply, generally speaking, to the Indian trader and merchant. As a petty trader the Indian shares the praise and the dispraise of the Hausa and Yoruba. He opens up new markets, but his methods are not above criticism.[1] As a merchant his standard of living, his assiduity, and his frugality enable him to a greater degree than the native trader in the west to reduce his establishment charges to a minimum, and undersell the European. By remitting

[1] See note, p. 321.

money out of the country, he minimises the benefit of trade to the district of origin.

Not only is the wealth and prosperity of a country dependent upon its trade, but it is obvious that it can only pay for its administration and for its development works by its exports and the results of its industry. It is manifest therefore that it is of the first importance that a Government should do everything in its power to promote and encourage commerce. Some of the principal ways in which this can be effected are the following :—

(*a*) By promoting scientific research a Government may prove the suitability of the climate and soil for introduced products, improve the quality of existing ones, and check animal and plant diseases.

(*b*) While refraining from competition with private enterprise, a Government can pioneer the way and prove the possibility of remunerative undertakings. It can, for instance, run a service of lorries or a line of river steamers for the transport of produce, until private enterprise is ready to undertake it.

(*c*) It can, as I have said, afford some protection to the producer and the small trader from the coercion of the combine on the one hand, or a fraudulent middleman on the other.

(*d*) It can assist commerce and industry by educating clerks, accountants, mechanics, and others required in the transaction of business.

(*e*) It can avoid all taxation in restraint of trade, and take every care that the necessary taxes fall as lightly as possible on it.

(*f*) It can provide facilities for transport and communication by railways, improved waterways, and roads, by shipping, and by an effective postal and telegraphic service.

(*g*) It can improve the quality of produce by inspection and rejection of inferior qualities at the port of shipment, and by stringent laws against fraudulent adulteration.

(*h*) It can provide and maintain an adequate coin currency, and promote its use in many ways.

That a Government should not be a competitor against private enterprise is admitted, and is, in fact, one of the chief objections to chartered company government. It has, however, been suggested that a Government may with advantage *participate* in such enterprise, and so secure a share of the profits for the public revenue, provided that by so doing it enjoys no preference or advantage which competitors do not share.

The principle appears to me both unsound and dangerous. If the undertaking is one beyond the scope of private enterprise, or one in which it is so impossible to forecast the conditions and profits that a private firm would not engage in it unless offered very substantial inducements by Government,—as in proving a coalfield, which can only be opened up by the construction of a railway and port,—it is better for the Government to take the initiative on its sole responsibility. If, as in a case of oil-boring within my experience, a company asks for financial assistance, the Government is not justified in accepting a speculative risk which financiers will not incur. If, again, the venture is one in which private enterprise is already engaged, such as the schemes foreshadowed by the Resources Development Committee, participation by Government must inevitably create conditions unfair to competition. Even the investment of surplus funds in well-established local concerns may give rise to suspicions of preference, however unjustified. It is in every way more desirable that such funds should be invested in new development works undertaken by Government itself, such as railways and harbours. The inherent objection to the participation of the State in speculative enterprise is that the Government cannot become bankrupt, and hence if its action proves ill-advised the taxpayer must redeem the position.[1] Competition in, or participation in, enterprises for profit is, of course, a very different matter from encouragement of nascent industries by Government (see p. 499).

When speaking of monopolies I referred to the grant of

[1] The East African Economic Commission elaborates in some detail a project for a "development bank" under Government control—half its directors being officials. The capital, which must in that case be chiefly or entirely found by Government (though it is stated that "Government itself is unable to execute urgent reforms of certain economic utility for want of funds"), would be applied to financing promising schemes "on the security of their potential value," and the bank would float companies, in which it would take shares, and appoint officials and others as directors.—*Loc. cit.*, p. 28.

The Congress of the International Chamber of Commerce, sitting in London, passed a resolution on 1st July 1921, declaring "that Government control of or participation in industry and commerce discourages individual initiative, and renders trade conditions uncertain and artificial, and that it should be discouraged."

"concessions"—a term susceptible of various meanings. Under the regime of King Leopold in the Congo, the State, it is said, claimed all "vacant lands," and compelled the natives to collect the produce under a system of "labour taxes," whether directly for the State or for the concessionaires, to whom vast blocks of land were leased. In four-fifths of the country, remarked a German newspaper, all ivory and rubber belong to the State, and a European who buys them is looked on as a receiver of stolen goods. Under the wise and liberal rule of King Albert this system has been abolished. The French adopted a similar regime in their Congo territories.

This system has not been tolerated in British tropical Africa, though we read of concessions to collect rubber in areas of two square miles in Uganda, and enormous blocks of uninhabited land have been granted to concessionaires in East Africa. Concessions on the Gold Coast have been based on a system the very antithesis of that on the Congo—viz., on a recognition of the right of native chiefs to dispose of lands, minerals, and even of the sole privilege of collecting sylvan produce, ostensibly in the name of the tribe. The subject, in so far as the Gold Coast is concerned, is exhaustively dealt with in Sir H. Belfield's report, to which I have already referred at some length.[1] Viewed solely from the economic standpoint, the one system, if carried to the same lengths as the other, would be equally effective in creating monopolies detrimental to sound development. The term "concession" is unknown in Nigeria.

Applications have been made for a concession of a very different kind—viz., for the sole right to erect oil-mills in a given area. Their object is to obtain the fruit of the oil-palm while fresh and free from the fatty acids which cause rancidity, and rob it of 50 per cent of its most valuable contents, rendering it fit only for making soap instead of margarine. The monopoly is asked for in order to protect the mill-owner from the risk of a rival mill benefiting by the development effected at his expense. The proposal has attractive features. It suggests a vision of the forest of wild palms reduced to an ordered plantation, the improved varieties of trees properly spaced and tended, so that the maximum yield per acre should be obtained, and the fruit collected by

[1] Cmd. 6278 of 1912. *Vide supra*, pp. 305-309.

means of light tramways intersecting the plantation.[1] Such improvements would, however, involve very heavy initial outlay and annual expenditure, which it is very unlikely that any concessionaire would undertake unless he had proprietary rights in the land itself. As a practical proposition, moreover, it would be difficult for the mill-owner to secure the guarantees he desires. He could only do so by separate agreements with the owners of the land—whether tribal or individual—that they would not allow the erection of a rival mill within the agreed area for a term of years, and enforce a like stipulation on any land alienated by them. Others have demanded, not protection against a rival mill, but that the natives shall be prohibited from selling to any one other than the concessionaire, and compelled to bring in the fruit while fresh—a type of concession inconsistent with British policy.

The opponents of concessions fear lest the acquisition of any form of exclusive rights should lead to the gradual acquisition of the land itself, so that the natives should eventually be reduced to the status of paid labourers. To prevent anything of the kind must be the first duty of those who are charged with the protection of native rights. On the other hand, the introduction of capital and organising ability, by increasing output and improving quality, is a benefit not only to the country, but to mankind. Intelligent appreciation of the world's progress and needs compels us to recognise with Lord Leverhulme [2] that vast areas of exceptionally fertile land cannot for all time remain as unreclaimed jungle, and large quantities of a commodity of great value as food be allowed to rot ungathered, at the caprice of primitive races who lack the incentive to make the most of nature's gifts. In one district, says Mr Farquharson, the natives when shown how to make biscuit rubber cut down their para trees because it was too much trouble. The native grows kola-trees, he says, because they require even less labour than cocoa, and the jungle fire he kindles to prepare the land for his shifting cultivation destroys oil-palms and the humus of the soil.

The education of the natives in scientific agriculture and improved products can be promoted (as I said in chapter xiv.) by the lease to Europeans of small agricultural estates, even

[1] See Mr Smart's evidence, Edible Nuts Committee.—Cmd. 8247 of 1916, pp. 111-125.

[2] Paper at Royal Colonial Institute, 7th April 1919.

in a country where European settlement is not possible, for they are invaluable as models for the native cultivator to emulate, and as an ocular demonstration of what scientific culture can produce. On this subject I shall have more to say in the next chapter. Large " concessions " are not necessary for this purpose. He is no true friend to the African who would deprive him of the incentive which an object-lesson can alone bring home to his intelligence. The problem is to avoid the evils of the concessionaire,[1] while ensuring the proper and adequate development of natural resources, and the example of the European-owned plantation will assist in its solution.

But it is of even greater importance in those countries where the native must be the producer, to ensure that the produce he grows for export is shipped in the best possible condition. The quality of cocoa is greatly enhanced by proper grading, drying, and uniform fermentation; palm-oil should not contain more than 10 per cent of fatty acids, and should be extracted from the fresh fruit and not kept till it is rancid; palm-kernels should show at least 48 per cent of oil;[2] oil should be brought to market "soft," and not "hard," by the expenditure of a little extra trouble; rubber should be marketed as "biscuit" and not "lump"; hides can be better flayed, more uniformly stretched, and denuded of superfluous offals, which add to their weight and bulk; cotton from distant villages can be reduced to a third of its bulk and weight by hand-ginning and crude presses, and its quality improved by careful sorting; gums need to be graded—one might go on indefinitely to show how the quality and value of raw produce can be increased by proper preparation.

It goes without saying that it is of the first importance to the trade of a country that its exports should bear a high reputation for quality, and command a high price in the world's markets. If the reputation for a particular article

[1] A concessionaire's rights under British law are at best precarious, as was shown in the case of Messrs Cook *v.* Sigcau, when Pondoland was transferred to the Crown. It was admitted that the concessionaire had given good value, but on appeal the Privy Council upheld the cancellation, mainly on the ground that "the concessions created no legal obligation, because their execution depended solely upon the will of the paramount chief, and there existed no possible means of enforcing them."

[2] Letter of Mr Robert Miller to the West African press, 22nd October 1919, from which most of these percentages are taken.

from a particular country be bad, it is difficult for an individual producer, or a discriminating merchant, to obtain full value for the exceptional quality of his exports, and progressive deterioration is likely to result.

Stringent laws, strenuously enforced, against fraudulent adulteration must be supplemented by fixing a standard of purity for exports in collaboration with the merchants, and by prohibiting shipment of produce which does not comply with the tests. The Government of Nigeria held the view that the Government inspection should take place prior to shipment only—viz., after purchase,—and that it was the function of the merchant to discriminate as to quality by giving a better price for a good article. The Governments of India and of Natal arrived at the same conclusion.[1] The view which has been advanced, that the merchant is in theory concerned only with the exchange of commodities, and not with their quality, would in practice be not unlikely to result in difficulty in disposing of stocks, and the eventual loss of his market.

Some merchants, on the other hand, have desired the appointment of Government inspectors in the native markets prior to purchase. Such a system obviously affords opportunities for peculation and extortion on the part of the subordinate native officials employed on the work, which it is exceedingly difficult to detect and check. Nor does it appear justifiable to make it an offence to offer inferior produce for

[1] A Committee on this subject appointed by the Government of India reported that the most effective method for securing a good standard was by combination among buyers. The issue of certificates of purity would involve a large staff of inspectors, to which the Committee was "emphatically opposed." "Control at the port of export, and refusal to allow the export of produce below a minimum standard of purity, fixed in consultation with the trade," was, they considered, the best system. It should be carried out by the Customs Department, and a small charge made. While it is the duty of the Government to protect the cultivator, "the Government of India has (they declare) time and again decided that it is not for them to take any steps in the matter, and the remedy lies with the trade."—('Indian Trade Journal,' 19th April 1918.) These views are endorsed by the Indian Industrial Commission.—(Cmd. 51 of 1919, p. 143.)

In Natal the quality of maize for export had fallen to a very low standard, when the Government found it necessary to intervene by grading and marking, and the rejection of all below a fixed standard. The inspection was carried out at the port, any other method being found impossible, and an enormous improvement resulted. The French on the Ivory Coast instituted an "office guinéen" for the inspection of rubber at the port of shipment, rejecting all that was not up to standard. Rejections, at first 25 per cent to 30 per cent, soon fell to 3 per cent. Shippers held buyers responsible for the loss.

sale, provided that there is no fraudulent intent. The Government, moreover, cannot accept responsibility for the results of inspection conducted in a distant market without any check on subsequent deterioration or adulteration.

The increase in West Africa in the number of small native exporters who have no business reputation to lose, and whose profits are not greatly affected by the colony's standing in the produce market, increases the urgency of the need for Government intervention. The first necessity is for merchants to employ expert buyers and middlemen.[1] They reply that it is very difficult in the conditions of West Africa to get expert buyers, for their British staff is constantly changing. It should, however, be no more difficult for merchants to find expert and honest native buyers than for Government to find the qualified inspectors who would be necessary if produce were inspected before shipment. Two of the most experienced witnesses before the Edible Nuts Committee condemned the system of produce inspection by Government prior to purchase, while others supported it.[2] Government through its Agricultural Department can assist in educating the producer. Export duties—since they are levied equally on inferior as on valuable produce—exert an influence in the right direction.

A difficulty no doubt arises in regard to inspection prior to shipment at small ports, and complaints may arise as to delays caused by inspection at large ports, where the volume of exports is great. The latter could perhaps be met by granting exemption to a shipper whose consignments had been found for a specified period to be invariably well above the standard, provided that he satisfied the Government that

[1] The late Mr Farquharson, of the Nigerian Agricultural Department, observed that the employment of low-paid buyers, with ready reckoners and a flat rate, instead of skilled, highly-paid men with special knowledge of produce, had led to deterioration. Rubbish, he remarked, should not be allowed to occupy cargo-space when shipping is scarce.

[2] Captain (now Major-General) Gray, with very long local experience, stated that when buying kernels he could tell the percentage of shell and dust within 1 per cent or 2 per cent, and "any man who deals in the business should be able to do the same." Inspection, he insisted, "is a matter for the merchants themselves to arrange." Mr Trigge, of the Niger Company, with long experience of the home markets, was equally emphatic.—Report of Edible Nuts Committee, Cmd. 8247 of 1916, questions 1409 and 1681-82. For the evidence of merchants —for and against—see questions 819, 1409, 1679, 1887, 2593, 4909, 5493. (Also 818, 5443, and 5492 *re* the practice in Dahomey.)

his uninspected shipments had realised the standard prices at their destination.

The Uganda Produce Protection Ordinances, 1913 and 1918, empower the Governor to make rules for licensing buyers, dealers, and growers of produce. I am not aware how this ordinance has worked in practice, but as a general principle I think that the less Government interferes in trade, and the fewer the number of licences, the better.

A feature of African trade which merits a passing reference is the tendency to direct barter, under the mistaken notion that a double profit is thus secured, since the vendor of produce must buy where he sells.[1] It is a short-sighted policy opposed to the true principles of trade. The inexperienced agent may think that he is doing a smart stroke of business in foisting unsaleable stock upon the ignorant native, and that by refusing to pay cash he prevents his purchasing in a rival store, or he makes the mistake of offering goods ostensibly one-third more in value than the cash price, instead of inviting purchase by variety and cheapness. The result is to discourage trade, as those have found who have adopted a more liberal and far-sighted policy. The concensus of reports is to the effect that trade has increased greatly wherever cash has been introduced.[2] It may even be considered justifiable, by a "Truck Act," to give the vendor of produce the right to claim payment in cash, at a rate equal to that of the goods offered, and the right to purchase for cash goods offered for public sale.

Nor must the trader in distant regions lose sight of the fact that his interests are largely identical with those of the administration, and it is to his advantage to assist the Government, as far as he is able, by promoting the circulation of currency. Since a portion of the output of the country must

[1] Mr Neville, of the Bank of British West Africa, who claims personal knowledge of West Africa since 1874, writes that "British merchants as a body, prior to the establishment of regular banking, showed a decided disinclination for cash dealings, believing the barter system to be more profitable, and it was left to the Germans at Lagos in particular to import British silver, freight and insurance being paid by the British Mint. This cash advantage, in conjunction with a large supply of Hamburg gin, gave them a practical monopoly of the produce trade." —'African Societies' Journal,' June 1917.

[2] In Nigeria it is reported that a peasant bringing goods for sale, and requiring cash to pay his tax, or to buy some special article, has in some districts been paid in goods he does not want. These he sells in the local market for what they will fetch, and imported goods may thus often be bought more cheaply in the native market than in the neighbouring store.

go to pay for its administration and development works, and be collected in the form of a tax (whether at the coast as customs dues, or in the interior as a direct tax), it is for him to assist in converting it into a form in which it can be readily collected for revenue, and transmitted in payment of indebtedness at home. The Government on its part is able to afford him substantial assistance in return by cashing his bills or *vice versa* in distant trading posts.

It is unnecessary to observe that the introduction of a coin currency is an immense aid to trade. Primitive currencies such as cowries, brass rods or rings, "manillas," &c., being heavy and bulky, increase in value the farther they have to be carried into the interior, so that there is no stable rate of exchange.[1] Cowries can soon be eliminated by prohibiting their import—for they rapidly break and disappear,—but to forbid their use so long as they exist would be unjust to owners. They remain in use in India to this day, but are reported to have entirely disappeared in the trade centres of Zaria and Kano in Nigeria.

It is important that the lowest values should be represented —tenths of a penny are a convenient unit,—for prices rise if the unit is large. The Currency Board, under the chairmanship of Sir G. Fiddes, introduced a local coinage into West Africa—though in the interests of a universal Empire currency one could wish it had been possible to retain the British coins, while securing the mint profit to the colony.[2] East Africa is unfortunate in sharing the fluctuations of the Indian rupee. Notes are not adapted for use by a primitive people, and destroy confidence. Being constantly exposed to the weather, they are soon reduced to pulp, and they are often torn in half to be shared between two persons.

The subject of trade departments or boards in the colonies, and of home agencies for the dissemination of commercial intelligence, is one which demands attention. The African dependencies, owing to their great size, have special need

[1] In the early days in Nigeria it was necessary to stabilise the value of the cowrie by forming Government reserves at different centres. Difficulty was experienced for some time, for a soldier could not understand why his shilling was only worth 1200 cowries at one station and 2000 in another, though its purchasing value in food might be greater in the first than in the second.

[2] The Board was established in 1913, and in four years (deducting British coins repatriated) shipped silver coin to the face value of over four million sterling. The assets of the Board on 30th June 1917 stood at £1,867,000, an average of £497,000 per annum.—Cd. 8883 of 1917.

of a department to co-ordinate the mass of information on commercial subjects derived from various sources, internal and external; to supply information both to the local Government and to the Board of Trade and the Overseas Trade Department; to conduct correspondence with the Imperial Institute and Kew regarding the commercial value of potential products; to reply to inquiries, and to examine applications in regard to new enterprises. For this purpose a special department or a commercial branch of the secretariat is required.

It would be the business of the officer in charge of such a department to compile information "as an expert for experts, as bases for an active policy, and not merely to explain changes years after they have occurred." He should be familiar with the publications, the pertinent legislation, and the development of other tropical dependencies, and have an expert knowledge of and touch with the home and foreign markets, and be competent to report on the prospects, and the needs as regards transport, &c., of any district (or any special product) which appears to offer opportunities for development.

The issue of a trade journal or supplement to the 'Gazette,' with useful extracts from local and other reports, and the prompt publication of an annual trade report, could not fail to be of value to merchants, and to promote the trade of the colony. The latter should include information as to railway, river, and ocean freight rates, postal and telegraphic services and charges, and terms of leases of lands and minerals, as well as a review of each line of commerce and industry.

An Economic Board, such as exists in the Sudan, might usefully be instituted in all the African dependencies, especially if it included unofficial members, and so assisted in bringing together officials and producers. It would assemble from time to time, to consider any important proposals regarding trade and development, and advise the Government. It could meet at various places in the country, so as to hear local opinion and study the economic needs on the spot. The report of the East African Economic Commission, to which I have frequently referred as an authoritative statement of the views of the European community in that colony, devotes much space to recommendations in this connection, but the wide executive and financial powers which the Commissioners would confer on the Economic Board would seem —in spite of their disclaimer—to invite conflict with the Government and Legislative Council.[1] Such powers would certainly be unadapted to West Africa.

The French, it is said, refer all questions relating to trade and commerce to the local Chamber of Commerce, and their action has been held up as a model for British imitation. So far as my experience goes, however, British Governments have been only too anxious to avail themselves of the expert advice of the local Chamber; but owing to the fact (on which I have elsewhere commented) that the principals of firms are not themselves resident in British Africa, and decline to allow their representatives to speak with authority, the reply to any reference from Government is often colourless, and any matter of importance is referred home by the Chamber.

A French Chamber of Commerce differs, moreover, very essentially from a British Chamber. It is formed, not by the merchants themselves, but by the Government under an Order of the Council of Administration, which prescribes the number of French, foreign ("European and suchlike"), and native members, with elaborate definitions of the electorate and the conditions of the annual election. The Chamber recently created at Lome is constituted under thirty-seven articles. Even "corresponding members" (without a vote) must be qualified under the commercial code, and their election is subject to the approval of the Commissaire de la République. It receives a subsidy from Government in the form of an addition to the licence fees and customs dues, and it partakes of the nature of a municipal body in that it can, with the approval of the Commissaire, incur debts, and collect taxes or rates for the erection of buildings, &c.

I venture to think that the British system of dividing these duties and powers between a Municipal Council and a Chamber wholly and entirely appointed by the merchants themselves, and free from Government control, is more in accord with British sentiment and practice. The question of native membership is then left for their own decision. An Economic Board such as I suggest would in no way interfere with the local Chamber, though its unofficial members would no doubt be drawn from the Chambers of Commerce

[1] Report, *loc. cit.*, pp. 23, 24.

and of Mines. Its merit would lie in the fact that both officials and unofficials would be better able to tender useful advice to Government after hearing each other's views.

The report of the East African Economic Commission recommends that the proposed trade commissioner for East Africa should have a corresponding agency in London.[1] So far as the requirements of the European settlers are concerned, it is perhaps open to question whether an agency under private control—which might possibly include the function of disposing of produce for individual shippers—might not prove more useful, and less likely to give rise to controversy, than one under the control either of the Board of Trade or the local Government. The need for commercial intelligence would to some extent be met by the suggestions made in chapter ix. (pp. 188-89).

So far as West Africa is concerned, the annual report of the London Chamber of Commerce states that "it was unanimously agreed that owing to the totally different methods employed in the carrying on of business by merchants in the British West African colonies, as compared with other dominions and colonies, the appointment of a trade commissioner for those colonies is unnecessary, and would be of no advantage."[2] The Sudan Government maintains an agency in London, but the business requirements of all African dependencies under the control of the Colonial Office are transacted by the Crown agents.

The work of the Crown Agents' Department is not directly concerned with colonial trade, but I will digress for a moment to discuss the subject, since it has some bearing on the question of overseas agency and the market which the dependencies afford to the manufacturers of the United Kingdom.

The system has been vigorously attacked both by Governors of colonies and by the colonial press.[3] Towards the close of

[1] Ibid., pp. 29, 30.

[2] Report of May 1921. The trade of West Africa differs from that of most other places, as pointed out by the Liverpool Merchants' Association (October 1921), in that manufacturers do not consign direct to local buyers. Probably 90 per cent of both import and export trade is conducted between British firms and their branch houses. There is very little if any c.i.f. sale of exported produce in West Africa.

[3] Sir H. Johnston writes that "the out-worn institution of the Crown agents must disappear" after the war.—'African World,' 17th August 1918. Mr Morel speaks of them as "an anomaly which ought to disappear," and quotes Sir

his administration of the Colonial Office, Mr Chamberlain circularised the Crown colonies asking for any specific complaints, and left it on record that in his view the number of these was small, and not serious in proportion to the number of colonies, and that "the existing system had beyond question worked well for the colonies," a view which his successor —Mr Lyttelton—endorsed, while at the same time introducing some modifications with the object of making the Crown agents more directly responsible to the colonial Governments.[1]

Criticism and complaint has not, however, been silenced, though it cannot, I think, be denied that in the course of years the agency has grown in efficiency, and the old complaints of delay, &c., have now little or no justification. The chief objections which are taken to the system may perhaps be summarised as follows :—

(1) That colonial Governments are compelled under colonial regulations to obtain all their requirements—whether they be materials costing millions for railway or harbour construction, or small articles costing only a few pounds—through the Crown agents, and are precluded from calling for local tenders, except for local produce. Some relaxation of this rule has been urged in the interests of private enterprise in the colonies, but the general principle undeniably has the advantage of placing in very competent and experienced hands the greater part of the capital expenditure of colonial revenues. It also ensures a preference to the home market, if it can supply the goods required—a matter of great importance to the United Kingdom.

(2) That though in the words of Mr Chamberlain "the able, upright, and single-minded service" rendered by the Crown agents—who are paid fixed salaries and have no pecuniary interest in the agency—is absolutely unquestioned and unquestionable, the system is not in accord with business principles. Colonial criticism of materials and stores purchased by the Crown agents can, it is said, only be directed to quality and not to price, since the colonial Government has no means of knowing the range of home and foreign

W. Macgregor in support of his views.—'Affairs of West Africa,' p. 31. On the other hand, Sir C. Bruce is enthusiastic in their praise.—'Broad Stone of Empire,' vol. ii. chap. xxi.

[1] Cd. 1944 of 1904. In view of the frequent questions in the House, Lord Crewe appointed a Committee in 1908 under the chairmanship of Colonel Seely to inquire into the allegations. Their report was entirely favourable.

prices, and does not see the tenders made. There is therefore, the critics allege, an inevitable and natural bias on the part of the Crown agents towards limiting the list of firms from whom tenders are invited to a comparatively few of the highest standing, with prices corresponding to their reputation (in some cases wholesale dealers and not manufacturers), and to incur unduly heavy charges for inspection, &c. One per cent commission is charged on all stores obtained through the Crown agents. It is asserted that the list of tenderers is too exclusive, that opportunities for purchasing bankrupt stock are not fully utilised, and that these methods do not make for economy.

(3) Another complaint is that if a mistake is made for which the supplying firm cannot be held responsible, or if the goods are not suitable, the colony must bear the loss, since the Crown agents accept no financial liability, and that such mistakes—though in my experience they are rare—might be minimised, were the services of expert officers of the requisitioning department more fully utilised. Indeed the remedy for both this and the last-mentioned complaint lies largely in the hands of the colonial Governments, which should direct their departmental officers to keep in closer touch with the Crown agents when in England. On the other hand, the extensive business of the Crown agents sometimes enables them to dispose of unsuitable stores elsewhere.

(4) That the colonies pay a substantial sum—in the assessment of which they have no voice—for the transaction of their business (apart from commission, inspecting charges, &c.), and may reasonably ask for a fuller statement of the way in which this amount is assessed, and the disposal of interest on current balances, including salaries of officers on leave.

Business agencies in the execution of contracts and orders, and the exercise of large patronage, are, it is argued, liable, in case of failure to give satisfaction, either to the termination of the agency, or to pecuniary liability, or to censure; but a colonial Government can exercise no option, and Parliament has no right of scrutiny, since the funds are not voted by it, unless a grant-in-aid is involved. The accounts are, however, audited by the Comptroller and Auditor-General, and in theory at any rate are passed by the Secretary of State.

To that section of the Crown agents' business which deals with railway construction, and has provoked the greatest criticism, I have referred in the last chapter.

Such are the criticisms to which the Crown Agents' Department as an institution of the Empire has been exposed. That it has been worked with singular ability, with unvarying courtesy, and with single-minded devotion by the Crown agents themselves, who are not responsible for any defects in the system they administer, no one will, I think, deny. In all banking, and operations connected with the issue of loans, they have earned universal approbation.

The Memo. of 1904 states that the Crown agents transact the business of forty-four colonies, exclusive of various military forces, &c. But the expenditure of single dependencies like Nigeria or Malaya (including loans) would to-day represent a very great part of the aggregate expenditure of twenty years ago, and their general business has proportionately increased. It would seem open to consideration whether in the case of the larger dependencies more latitude would not be advisable in the transaction of their business. The Indian Industrial Report criticises adversely the parallel system of the Stores Department of the India Office.[1]

[1] Cmd. 51 of 1919, pp. 126-130.

CHAPTER XXV.

ECONOMIC DEVELOPMENT.

Necessity for economic development—State-aided enterprise—Railways—Research and propaganda—Functions of the technical departments: (*a*) Laboratory research; (*b*) Experimental research; (*c*) Propaganda and instruction—The native staff—Practical application of research results—The Imperial Institute—Advantage of free native cultivation—Specialisation in dealing in products—The evolution of industrialism—The indictment against Indian policy—First steps in Africa: (*a*) Preparation and semi-manufacture of exports; (*b*) Local substitutes for imports; (*c*) New local manufactures—Employment of native capital—Industries not inimical to British trade.

It is not the purpose of this chapter to record the statistics of the phenomenal progress achieved by our tropical African dependencies in the last two decades,[1] but rather to offer with diffidence some few suggestions, which may or may not commend themselves to those who now guide imperial policy, whether officially or as magnates of commerce. I had hoped to inaugurate some of them in Nigeria had not the war rendered all such projects out of the question.

Writing after the war in a circular despatch to colonial Governors,[2] Lord Milner observed that "it is more than ever necessary that the economic resources of the Empire should be developed to the utmost," in view of the depletion of raw materials, and the financial burdens left by the war. Much of the existing deficiency, he adds, could be produced by the tropical colonies if their great potential resources were adequately developed.[3]

[1] The table and note on p. 45 shows that the total trade of British tropical Africa had increased in this twenty years nearly sevenfold, from under 11¼ to over 76½ millions sterling.

[2] Despatch of 11th June 1919.

[3] The potentialities of the African tropics for the supply of raw materials and food were, as I have pointed out in an earlier chapter, the chief cause of the partition of Africa among the nations of Europe. Other nations have proceeded in a more systematic way than England. When the United States assumed

The Indian Industrial Commission discusses the desirability of Government "pioneering" of industries—viz., "the inception by Government of an industry on a small commercial scale, in order to ascertain and overcome the initial difficulties, and discover if the industry can be worked at a profit, when private enterprise is not forthcoming."[1] In Jamaica we read that the principle of State aid for enterprises has been accepted "with the object of inculcating in the minds of the people the principle of co-operation in every phase of industry." Large areas of land have been acquired by the Government, divided into holdings, and sold to the peasantry, who are encouraged to improve them by facilities offered by agricultural loan banks. Such inducements may be needed in the new effort to develop industrial enterprise in India (*vide infra*), or they may be adapted to the conditions of the West Indies, where one of the objects in view is to check emigration (200,000, we are told, have gone from Jamaica to the United States and Cuba in the past two years). Moreover, the education afforded by the advanced system of agricultural colleges, &c., has presumably evolved a more scientific method of peasant cultivation than at present obtains in Africa.

As we have seen, however, in the chapter on land, there is no need for the State to acquire land for peasant proprietors in Africa, and the commercial banks are prepared to afford them such assistance as the conditions justify. In the larger operations of commerce, enterprising and wealthy companies with abundant capital are ready in West Africa to explore every avenue of trade and development, and ask for no State assistance other than the development of transport

control of the Philippines, the Chicago University commissioned Mr Alleyne Ireland to study British, Dutch, and French methods in the Far East. Governor-General Roume in French West Africa sent special missions to England to study the organisation of commercial ports, to America to study production and trade in oils, to Belgium and Holland to study commercial exhibitions, and to Indo-China to study political problems. The German Association of Merchants and Manufacturers (Kolonial Wirtschaftliches Komittee), with Government support, sent out botanical and agricultural expeditions to German and other colonies to report on economic possibilities, and how native industries could be improved and increased by scientific methods. The conference between British and French merchants in April 1920, at which every kind of subject of mutual interest was discussed, and standing Committees for preparing questions for future conferences appointed, was a new and practical departure. The usual British panacea is a Royal Commission of Enquiry, as advocated recently in Parliament (August 1919). The results of their immense labours, and the examination of a host of witnesses, are buried in the pages of a voluminous blue-book.

[1] Report, p. 135.

facilities; adequate educational establishments, both general and technical, for the training of native subordinates; efficient research departments in agriculture and forestry; an adequate currency; and co-operation in the normal sphere of Government functions. Private enterprise in all these branches, including banking and shipping,[1] is ready enough to provide capital or service if the prospects justify the venture, and where this is the case the less State interference—whether imperial or colonial—the better.

The participation by Government in commercial enterprise, whether justified in order to pioneer the way, or in such exceptional cases as those referred to on page 484 (coal-mines, water transport, &c.) is, however, an entirely different matter from the initiation by Government of development works such as railways, harbours, irrigation, and roads, which fall within its proper sphere. In the less wealthy dependencies—and even in augmentation of the resources of those whose financial position is strong—imperial guarantees for a limited number of years, of the interest on loans, will assist the mother country by enabling the colonies to undertake such remunerative development projects as would otherwise have been deferred, and the benefit of immediate construction will be reciprocal.[2] I shall therefore confine myself to those matters in which it is the undoubted function of the local Government to co-operate with private enterprise, and to suggestions by which on the one side or the other the co-operation, as I think, can be made most effective.

In the first place, I would reiterate that the foremost of all requirements for material development in Africa is rail-

[1] The Commissioners who presented the Economic Report of 1919 on East Africa ask that "the United Kingdom in her own interests should foster certain products by arranging . . . for improved shipping facilities." They propose the creation of a chartered bank with £2,000,000 capital, financed by and under Government control; and they ask that the capital required for the development of the main trunk system of railways should be provided from imperial funds free of interest for fifteen years. These proposals are individual to Kenya colony, and since they are fully described in the report, I do not propose to discuss them further here.—Report, pp. 26, 28, 35, 41, and 42.

[2] Since these pages went to the press, Mr Churchill, with the same foresight and imagination which guided his great predecessor at the Colonial Office—Mr J. Chamberlain—has urged the development of the Crown dependencies as the best way of meeting the present crisis in trade and industry. Loans to the amount of £20,000,000 will be floated on their own security, and the Prime Minister has announced (19th October 1921) that imperial guarantees will be given where needed for further loans. This policy, says the city editor of the 'Times,' meets with the cordial approval of commercial men.

ways. Everything else—even research—is subordinate to this prime necessity. Much progress has been made in these two decades, but even the arterial systems are still incomplete. A railway in Africa is bound to be remunerative, generally in a very short time—indeed, sometimes almost before it is completed. As the Under-Secretary observed in a debate on the Colonial Office vote, thousands of miles of railways are built in the Dominions through waste and unpopulated lands, but you cannot lay 100 miles of line in Africa but it pays in a few months. In the Dominions there is a mile of railway for every 220 of the population; in the Crown colonies and protectorates the ratio is only one for every 7700.[1]

The financial standing of most of our African protectorates is sufficient guarantee for large loans, the interest on which is a first charge on revenue. Wherever there is an objective, wherever there is population, railway construction will pay, though a main trunk line which crosses unpopulated regions or involves an exceptionally costly bridge may temporarily be unable to meet its full loan charges. One great difficulty is the supply of the necessary subordinate staff—a matter to which I have referred in the chapter on education. If railways are built, feeder roads with auxiliary transport will grow of themselves.

The second main line of development is by research—which shall "systematise experience and place it at the disposal of private enterprise"—and propaganda. These are functions of Government.[2] The agricultural, forestry, and veterinary departments need to be greatly strengthened and brought into closer and more fruitful co-operation with each other and with other departments—administrative and educational—on the one hand, and with commercial agencies on the other, so that they may increase results by combined effort instead of overlapping, and keep abreast of progress in the home institutions such as the Imperial Institute, and the bureaux of entomology and of mycology, and the home universities.[3]

[1] Colonel Amery in debate of August 1919.

[2] Colonel Amery, in a letter to the Liverpool Chamber of Commerce, suggested that they should supplement the work of Government by organising research work on their own account, and either endow chairs for agriculture, geology, &c., at the University, or form a Research Association under the Government Industrial Research Department.

[3] I have before me the reply of the Leeds University (dated 1st February 1921) to "Lord Milner's suggestion that fuller and more systematic use may be made of the scientific and technological departments of the British Universities in

The District Officer, in turn, should ever be collecting data as to the resources and possibilities of his province, submitting samples and instructing the people, not pressing the cultivation of any particular crop, but informing them of the demand and price, and assisting the technical departments in making known the elementary truths regarding bush fires, shifting cultivation, deforestation, isolation of disease and the like, and in outlying stations keeping a record of meteorological observations.

The objects in view are to increase the quantity and improve the quality of the products of the country by new discoveries, by raising the standard of cultivation, by scientific animal and plant breeding, and by preventing loss and destruction —whether by disease or by wasteful methods. The results obtained by research in India are stated to " have added enormously to the productive capacity of the country." To the three technical departments which I have named may be added the geological survey now being undertaken in most colonies for research in minerals.

The work of these departments falls into three more or less distinct spheres of activity, between which a somewhat greater discrimination may be advisable, as well as a clearer appreciation of the precise object in view, in the courses of instruction given to natives.

The first branch of work—laboratory research—is concerned, as Lord Milner says, with objects whose practical end is not immediately obvious; with the investigation of the chemical and bacteriological properties of different soils, and the means of increasing their fertility; with analysis of the qualities and possible uses of new products; with the assay of mineral ores; and, above all, with ascertaining the cause and checking the spread of disease both of animals and plants, " by which literally millions of pounds are lost each year."

carrying out researches for the benefit of the colonies and protectorates, and in recruiting the number of trained investigators required for that purpose, both in this country and abroad." In both directions the University promises its hearty co-operation. It is recommended that research studentships should be endowed, and that after completing a post-graduate course candidates for scientific posts in the colonies should be selected by a system of nomination rather than by competitive examination. "As years went on the departments of the University would accumulate a wider experience of the conditions of the various colonies . . . and an intimate connection would be maintained between scientific investigators in the colonies and those at the universities at home." The Imperial College of Agriculture in Trinidad will offer the highest technical training in tropical agriculture in a tropical environment.

In this task the Empire Cotton Corporation proposes to assist by adding to the local staff a few scientific investigators, who will specialise in their own particular line while remaining under the control of Government. Nothing could be better, and I trust that many large firms will follow their example. The supply of trained investigators is by no means too large, and their time should not be wasted in lecturing to boys, or merely in demonstrations from the practical utility standpoint. For this pure research work, the African dependencies do not, and will not in the near future, supply native candidates. Reference libraries and study-leave are matters of great moment to the branch.

The second sphere of activity in the technical departments is concerned with *experimental* research by means of plantations, where improved varieties, and types resistant to disease and suited to the climate and soil, may be tested over a series of years, indigenous types improved by selection and by hybridisation, and the best varieties converted into species which shall breed true to type and combine the various improvements; [1] or, on the other hand, by means of live-stock farms for experimental treatment of disease, culture of serums, improvement of stock, and so on.

The central institution, necessary alike for the pure research branch and for continuous supervision of experimental work, should be located where the greatest variation in soil and other conditions affecting agriculture and forestry are obtainable, and for live-stock where the best opportunities are available for the veterinary department.

The senior staff must consist of highly-trained specialists, working in collaboration with the laboratory investigators, and themselves conducting practical tests. The subordinate European staff need not have the same scientific knowledge, but they must be capable of recognising and diagnosing disease in animals and plants, of arranging and supervising experiments, of imparting instruction in practical agriculture, forestry, and the care of animals, and in the preparation of produce (whether of crops or of hides, &c.) for the market.

The third branch of work of these departments is intimately

[1] Excellent results have been obtained in Nigeria by the introduction of improved varieties of sugar-cane, tobacco, maize ("Hickory-King"), and cotton, and local crops have been improved by seed selection. There is an eager demand, and the native is learning no longer to reserve his worst produce for seed.

associated with the second, and consists in propaganda, and instruction—locally by means not only of the British staff (including the administrative and educational officers), but also by trained native instructors touring through the country, and by the preparation of leaflets dealing in simple language with each special subject; outside the colony by full and adequate reports for the information of private enterprise and commerce. This branch of the work utilises the experimental plantations and the live-stock farms as object-lessons, where the results obtained, and the lessons to be learnt from them, may be conveyed by demonstration in new methods and improved implements, in seed selection, preparation for the market, manuring, pruning, grafting, and drainage, on the one hand, and the management and improvement of stock and the practical treatment of diseases on the other.

Small "model farms" are maintained at various centres throughout the country, and visited periodically by the staff, for the like purpose, and as nurseries for the distribution of seeds and seedlings. Private estates conducted on scientific principles and under skilled European direction are hardly less valuable as models for natives, and private stock farms or ranches serve a like purpose.

It is particularly desirable to interest the native administrations in such matters, and to induce them to institute similar instructional farms for themselves. Indian experience attests the value of practical lectures and demonstrations—adapted to the particular district—but regards the effect as ephemeral. Plantations which show the actual results obtained by the methods advocated, and the increased money value realised by a successful neighbour, have a more lasting effect and produce a demand for seed distribution.[1]

Agricultural and stock shows also excite interest, and help to stimulate co-operation by organised bodies, such as the seed unions of Madras. Prizes can be given not only for the best exhibits, but for the best kept and equipped plantations.

This branch (viz., propaganda and instruction) should be supplemented by the largest possible number of Africans who have passed one of the higher school standards, and have specialised in the continuation classes—in one or the other line. At this stage they would be transferred to the department

[1] Report on agriculture in India, 1916, p. 66 *et seq.*; and Indian Industrial Commission, Cmd. 51 of 1919.

concerned for a three years' course as paid apprentices. The value of this class cannot, I think, be too highly estimated, either as subordinates in charge of model plantations (agricultural or forestry), and stock farms, or as instructors accompanying the British staff on tour, and imparting instruction in their own language, or as technical teachers in the schools.

The attempt to attach half-educated schoolboys, who have evinced no special aptitude or liking for the work, to those departments as "learners" has not, in my experience, proved a generally useful one. In many cases they resented manual work, and were too ill-educated to be able to benefit by instruction in theory. It is not until a youth has manifested some inclination towards the work, and has acquired an elementary knowledge of the subject, that it is worth while to pay him as an apprentice, or to spend the valuable time of the scientific staff on his instruction. A special class, lasting for a few days only, to a gathering of headmasters and teachers of schools during vacation, may have very useful results, and encouragement is afforded by granting certificates of proficiency which qualify the holder for a small increase of pay.

Continuity on these lines would, I hope, in course of time, by the creation of a demand for agricultural training of a more advanced type, render possible the formation of an agricultural college, but such an institution would at present be premature in most, if not in all, of our African dependencies. With the all-important question of elementary and practical teaching of agriculture, forestry, &c., in the primary and the village schools I have dealt briefly in the chapter on education. The subject should, I think, be a compulsory one in Government and aided schools alike.

Research and its practical application should between them include a systematic survey of natural resources, and their results should increase the diversity of the commercial products, so that a country may not risk disaster by being dependent on a single staple. By the expansion of the export of ever-improving raw materials, or by their utilisation in organised local industry, the prosperity of the people and the revenues of the State may be enhanced.[1] "The type of

[1] A good example of the results which may be obtained by organised scientific investigation, and its practical application, may be seen in the flax industry of East Africa: "In 1911 an expert in flax was appointed, and his work during the

mind best qualified to undertake scientific research is probably least adapted to deal with commercial matters," so that a link is required to connect research and successful commercial undertakings. This may probably be found in the suggested department of trade and industry (p. 492), whose rôle it would be to place the results of scientific investigation before the industrialist, and to secure for them the test of practical applications. The agricultural and the forestry economist, and agricultural and forestry engineers, are no less essential for practical development than the work of the laboratory or of the forest conservator.

In the Imperial Institute the tropical protectorates have an invaluable agency, which combines the functions of research with those of inquiry as to commercial utility, demand, and prices in the home markets. The scientific departments abroad can work in close collaboration with it, submit samples for analysis and report, and refer any special problem for concurrent or independent investigation.

Its able director would, however, be the first to insist on the vital necessity for research on the spot, where the conditions necessary for commercial success can be studied with abundant material. It is through the local department that samples should be submitted to the Institute, with carefully verified data, and to the local department should be submitted for local confirmation the results obtained in England before publication. India, the Commissioners consider, has outgrown the uses of the Imperial Institute, but the Institute can keep in touch with progress in India for the benefit of Africa.

"No sound policy has yet been formulated," says Dr Barker, echoing the dictum of Benjamin Kidd, "to ensure the development of tropical lands in the interest of Europe, while safeguarding the rights of the native." The formula we suggest in reply is: "Develop resources through the agency of the natives under European guidance, and not by direct European ownership of those tropical lands which are unsuited for European settlement." As in the sphere of political,

next three years clearly showed that flax culture could be made very profitable. Pre-war prices for British East African flax averaged about £50 a ton, but with improved knowledge on the part of growers, higher prices may be anticipated—in fact a recent consignment sent home realised £220 a ton, this being the current price for the higher-grade flax on the home market at the time."—East African Report, 1916-17.

so also in that of material progress—teach the native to manage his own affairs and better his own methods. "The tropics will never be developed by the natives themselves," says Mr Kidd, and he shows how the mistaken idea that the British tropics if left to themselves would begin to exploit their own resources, and develop into modern States, resulted in the decrease of trade in the West Indies and Guiana from fifteen to six million sterling.[1] The development must be under British guidance, without encroaching on native rights, or reducing the African to a state of serfage.

I said in chapter xiv. that as a cultivator of his own land the African will work harder and produce more than he will as a hired labourer, and the progress made will be the more rapid and permanent, and the output cheaper, while labour difficulties do not arise. There are, however, those who hold a contrary view. The late Mr Farquharson, Acting Director of Agriculture in Southern Nigeria, whose opinions I have already quoted as those of an able and original thinker, considered that the labour employed on native-owned cocoa estates was inadequate to maintain even an ordinary standard, and the soil was exploited and impoverished. Undue profits were made and spent on luxuries instead of on the land. Large blocks of land acquired by coast traders were left to the care of an ignorant headman, the labour was underpaid, and the owner was indifferent as to the quality of the produce. Cocoa-growing thus tended to become an industry in the hands of large owners, and not of peasant proprietors. The real remedy against "these greatest enemies of agriculture" was, in his view, the introduction of European enterprise, as proved by the higher prices which the cocoa of the Cameruns and San Thomé could command.[2] In his opinion education was useless, and only compulsion would effect reform.

The illustration supplies the answer. The methods of San Thome and the Cameruns are too well known to need description here. Large European estates cannot be worked

[1] 'Control of the Tropics,' pp. 35, 39, and 52, &c.

[2] It is stated that native-owned plantations of cocoa in the Cameruns are much better kept than those in British protectorates, and that the cocoa is of better quality, since the natives had at some time been compulsorily employed and taught on the German estates. The German policy is of course the reverse of that for which I contend (see notes, pp. 391 and 397). On the East Coast for miles inland, in the low-lying tropical belt, and in the West on the slopes of the Camerun mountain and in the coastal regions, permanent German-owned plantations were formed.

without recourse either to imported or to compulsory labour. Estates owned by native absentee landlords who have no interest in agriculture, and acquire them by foreclosing on mortgages, differ essentially from the principles of the free cultivator working for his own benefit on his own land. The evils of such a system as Mr Farquharson described are not, however, inherent in native-owned plantations of the type to which I have referred elsewhere, which are under the supervision of their native owners.

But no one will, I think, deny that small well-managed estates in European ownership are invaluable as object-lessons to supplement the efforts of Government; and it is, as Colonel Amery declared, to the advantage of Africa that they should be encouraged, in order to set a high standard in centres of native population. The European owner can often co-operate with and assist the small native cultivator by purchasing his crop, grading, packing, and preparing it for market, and transporting it with his own, thus affording a useful object-lesson to the native.

The advantage of specialisation in one or two commodities is worthy of the consideration of merchants. The specialist would select areas whose soil and climate favour a particular product, and confine his attention to them, to the exclusion of districts less favourable, buying all of the product which the area could produce, offering prices according to quality, and taking a personal interest in its improvement and the increase in the quantity offered for sale. The Cotton-growing Corporation will lead the way in this field of specialisation —an example which may prove invaluable to the economic progress of Africa. The same arguments for selection and specialisation apply to hides.

Turning from these questions of the improvement of the exports from Africa, let us consider the matter from the larger standpoint of African progress. Since we have accepted the task of guiding the people along that path, we must contemplate the time when they too will desire to manufacture for themselves, instead of remaining dependent on the factories of Europe, and we have seen that the African is capable of becoming an efficient and skilled mechanic.[1]

[1] The Industrial Commission says of India: "Her labour is inefficient, she relies almost entirely on foreign sources for foremen and supervisors, and her educated people have yet to develop a right tradition of industrialism" (p. 4.). The words apply with added force to Africa.

In the natural evolution of industrial progress a country begins by exporting raw materials in exchange for manufactured goods, later improving its exports by better preparation and semi-manufacture, and finally becoming itself a manufacturing community. The self-governing Dominions offer striking illustrations of this process, but India, of course, as a tropical dependency under British control, offers a closer parallel.

Whether the African races are capable, like Japan and other races of the East, of some day rivalling Europe and America in manufactures requiring the highest skill, it is for the distant future to determine, and we may safely leave posterity to deal with the problem, if and when it arises. Our present task is clear. It is to promote the commercial and industrial progress of Africa, without too careful a scrutiny of the material gains to ourselves, that we may not incur the accusation of having inflicted upon Africa " the grave economic wrong " for which our commercial policy in India is alleged to have been responsible in that country.

In the younger dependencies in Africa we are shaping policies for the future, and if in the material, no less than in the moral and political sphere, we have benefited from the experience of the past and enlarged our ideals, the principles upon which these policies are framed must accord with our larger horizons. Our reward may probably be misrepresentation and dislike, for though the individual benefactor may sometimes meet with gratitude, the national benefactor never does.

The indictment against British commercial policy in India is formulated by the Hon. Pundit Malaviya, a member of the Indian Industrial Commission, and supported by weighty arguments in his addendum to the report.[1] It has, he says, been our policy to encourage the export of raw materials, and to improve their quality, to promote trade and commerce, but not manufacture and industry. Instead of making India strong and self-supporting, we have in our own interests as a manufacturing nation retarded her industrial progress, which had already reached a high development when Europe was uncivilised.[2] We have made her dependent on ourselves

[1] Report of the Indian Industrial Commission, 1916-1918.—Cmd. 51 of 1919 pp. 245-300. This chapter will not be without utility if it avails to invite the attention of those who have not read it to this report, which the 'Times' (10th December 1919) describes as of "epoch-marking importance."

[2] It must be remembered that Kano in Nigeria has also for 1000 years been a manufacturing city trading its cloth, &c., for raw materials. Its sheep and goat

for manufactured goods, and unduly dependent on agriculture, with resulting famines, though we may claim to have ameliorated their severity by railways and a superb organisation.

The Commissioners deplore "the laissez-faire Government tradition in industrial matters, which has rendered India liable to foreign penetration in time of peace, and to serious dangers in time of war." This has been due in part to "the erroneous idea that tropical countries, with their naturally fertile lands and trying climate, were suited to the production of raw materials rather than to manufactures." [1]

But though we may admit that in the last century the industrial progress of India was not as rapid as it might have been, and that commerce prospered too well for Government to give proper thought to industry, recent years have seen considerable developments in her mills and power-plants,[2] and the output of manufactured goods, while the lessons of the war and the policy outlined for the future point to the opening of a new chapter.

In Africa the profits to be made by the production of raw materials and foodstuffs are so large, the majority of the people are so little advanced, and the means of transport and the fuel supplies for industrial undertakings so little developed, that we are not as yet called upon to consider the question from the Indian standpoint, and may regard the future of Africa for some decades to come as chiefly concerned with the development of her agricultural, pastoral, and mineral resources.

The time has, however, already arrived in some of the more prosperous protectorates to take the first steps, by seeing, as I said in the last chapter, that the raw materials are brought to the most finished state possible before export, with the object of increasing their value, avoiding waste in

skins, beautifully tanned and dyed red, had become famous under the name of "Morocco leather" (since they were exported by sea from that country), and had been an important article of trade for centuries. (Compare the "ram-skins dyed red" which Moses required for the tabernacle.—Exodus xxv. 5.)

[1] Ibid., p. 6.

[2] See the Indian Progress Report (No. 143 of 1919), pp. 22, 105, &c., and the Report for 1920 (No. 202), pp. 96, 97. The Tata Iron and Steel works alone produced in 1917-18 nearly ¾ million tons, and saved the situation in the war, exporting to Mesopotamia and Palestine 1800 miles of railway track, 13,000 ft. of bridging, 200 engines, and 6000 vehicles. Sir V. Chirol ('Times,' 19th March 1921) tells how the founders had to look to American assistance for the inauguration of this enterprise in the face of British apathy.

preparation, utilising by-products, and decreasing bulk and so saving cost in transport both by land and sea. With these objects in view mills have already been erected locally to crush palm-kernels, and so secure a better quality of oil, and a large saving in freight charges. Similar mills for dealing with ground-nuts would greatly decrease transport charges, both by railway from districts in the interior and by sea, while the oil-cake should find a local market not less remunerative than that in England. The oil should be transported in casks, or preferably in tank waggons and steamers.

Railways in Africa have to carry excessive loads going seawards, which necessitates empty or half-loaded up-trains, and so adds to freight charges. Labour would also be saved, for at present the nuts must be decorticated by hand, or shipped undecorticated, since they are broken by machinery, and deteriorate unless the oil is expressed at once. The value of the oil-cake for manure or fuel, and especially for cattle food, would be considerable, for in the tropics, towards the end of the dry season, the village herds are reduced almost to starvation, while the large nomad herds have to traverse great distances, and congregate in the marsh lands to find subsistence, with consequent increase of epizootic disease.

Ginneries for separating the lint from the seed cotton, and hydraulic presses for baling, have also been erected. Local tanneries for the partial preparation of hides, like the "East India Kips" from Madras, and similar treatment for skins, would decrease their bulk and freight charges. By the introduction of simple industrial processes, aided by machinery, almost all the raw produce exported from Africa could be improved in quality, and labour and transport charges reduced. Many products at present neglected could also be placed on the home market, especially from West Africa, which is only about half the distance of Calcutta or the Straits from England, and has no canal dues to pay.[1]

[1] To the African merchant, as to the old East India Company, it is not a matter of vital importance whether the goods he exports are raw materials or manufactured articles. Vested interests in England, however, declared that it was a mistaken policy on the part of the East India Company to export the latter. The new departure was inaugurated in 1905 by the creation of the Department of Commerce and Industry, but was again resented by the European community of Madras, as being an interference with private enterprise. The "Swadeshi" movement was directed to secure for India some of the profits accruing from the manufacture of her raw materials.

By the adoption of the same principles of self-help, these countries should be able to render themselves independent of many of the articles at present imported at great cost from overseas, thereby saving their revenue for internal development. Hitherto it has been a pernicious tradition to order everything from England. The mother country has no need to fear a diminution of her market by such a policy, as I shall presently endeavour to show. On the contrary, the consequent extension of railways, irrigation works, &c., increases it, and even the older markets merely change the nature of their demands.

I have in my report on Nigeria indicated a number of such local industries.[1] Cement—of which thousands of tons are imported annually, a demand which increases with the extension of ferro-concrete work for bridge-building, piers, houses, &c.—should be locally made, where, as in Nigeria, lime, clay, and coal are available. Brick and tile making in properly constructed kilns should save the importation of much building material, and improve the quality and permanency of the houses. Sawmills and carpenter shops, fitted with up-to-date power-driven machinery, should utilise the local timbers, and render unnecessary the import of shooks for oil-casks, doors, window-frames, and furniture, &c., while the export of sawn and seasoned timber should replace that of unwieldy logs. Simple machinery for the preparation of fibres should result in an enormous saving by the local manufacture of twine and of sacks, of which millions are at present imported.

It may even be that the time is ripe for inaugurating the local manufacture of some of the articles in demand by the natives. Experiments are already reported from Nigeria in the making of soap and candles from ground-nut oil. Already in 1914 Zanzibar was manufacturing 75,000 lbs. of soap a month, and exporting cocoa-nut oil to Madagascar.[2] Sugar in small quantities has been made in Nigeria by West Indians attached to the Missions. Improved varieties of cane have been introduced and done well.[3] Soda, fire-clay, and

[1] Cmd. 468 of 1920. App. vi. gives cost of local tiles in contrast with other roofing materials.

[2] Report for 1914, Cd. 7622 of 1915, p. 11.

[3] Indian reports say that sugar-beet yields 20 tons of white sugar as compared with 15 tons from cane, requires six months instead of nine to mature, needs only a fifth of the irrigation, and no manuring.

sand are all obtainable in abundance for the manufacture of glass bottles. It will not be till later, as in India, that the manufacture of cheap textiles, of paper from bamboo and other wood pulp, and even the production of "power-alcohol,"[1] will become practical propositions in the industrial development of Africa.

The encouragement of progress in manufacturing industry—when once a country has embarked on an industrial career—is the counterpart of free trade in commerce, and brings its own reward in extended markets for higher-class goods. The attempt to suppress local industries by excise duties or otherwise is, on the other hand (like a restricted market for exports of raw materials), a short-sighted policy, unjust to the people for whose development we have assumed responsibility, and one, moreover, which fails to achieve its selfish object.[2] The introduction into tropical Africa under European initiative and guidance[3] of such simple industries as

[1] The Committee which reported on this subject in June 1919 (see also the Report of the Australian Committee of 1917) arrived at the conclusion that the outstanding and fundamental attraction of alcohol as motor fuel lies in the fact that since some of its chief sources are found in the vegetable world the supplies are continuously renewed, and can be greatly expanded without encroaching on food supplies. These sources are products which contain (*a*) sugar, (*b*) starch, or (*c*) cellulose. Of the first, the flowers of the mahua tree (*Bassia latifolia*) yield 90 gallons of alcohol to the ton, as against 20 from potatoes. The tree grows all over India, and should do well in Africa. Of the second, the sweet potato (*Batatas edulis*) and yams (*Dioscorea*), maize (*Zea mays*) and casava (*Mainhot utilissima*), are all common African products, which can be grown in unlimited quantities. Of the third, the supply is illimitable, not only in the waste of the saw-mills, but in the scrub-growth of untilled lands. The Committee recorded its opinion that "so far as vegetable sources of raw material for the manufacture of power-alcohol are concerned, we must rely mainly, if not indeed entirely, on increased production in tropical and semi-tropical countries."

[2] The right of a local Government to impose such import duties as it may see fit in its own interests was in principle challenged by the opponents of the Indian cotton goods tariff. The British Government, they argue, refused to permit the Bombay manufacturers to establish the tariff for their own private benefit, in the belief that free trade would best promote India's prosperity, and Indian consumers thereby obtained their goods more cheaply. Their opponents maintain that though the Indian consumer may temporarily have to pay a higher price while Indian mills are in their infancy, he will eventually buy more cheaply; that the temporary enhancement in price is more than compensated by the encouragement afforded to Indian industry and employment; and that the tariff was undeniably imposed in the interest of Lancashire and not of India, as proved by the imposition of an excise on Indian-made goods, and the circumstances in which the tariff was imposed and maintained against Indian opinion.

[3] Owing to the difficulty of getting managing directors to reside in the country long enough to give the necessary continuous supervision, large "agency firms" grew up in India, consisting of several partners, who took turns in managing the business in India and in London.—Indian Report, pp. 12, 13. It would be advantageous if African merchants did the same.

those to which I have referred is, however, a very different matter from industrialism properly so called, with its factories and power-driven machinery employing thousands of hands under modern industrial conditions.

The replacement by local manufacture of goods in demand by the natives (*e.g.*, soap, sugar, &c.) does not, moreover, increase wealth as the better preparation of exports does, or save revenue and so lighten taxation and increase funds for development, as does the local manufacture of Government necessaries at present imported (*e.g.*, furniture, tiles, cement, &c.). Discrimination, moreover, must be exercised in order to avoid deflecting labour which would be more profitably employed in growing or collecting raw materials for export than in competing with the output of organised industry and power-driven machinery in civilised countries.

The development of industrialism in Africa would seem at first sight to deprive us of our markets, and to limit our supplies of raw materials, but experience has shown that the result has only been to change the character of the trade. The creation of cotton-mills in India deprived Lancashire of an enormous market for cheap calico, not only in India but in East Africa; but, as a leading Manchester merchant told me many years ago, the loss had been made good by the demand for textiles of a better quality and design, to the benefit of the trade.

When factories are established to manufacture the cheaper articles, which formed the staples of their earlier needs, our customers have required in their place the specialised tools, machinery and belting for these new factories, and the iron-work for buildings, &c. With increasing wealth, and an improved standard of comfort, they require fabrics of cotton and wool of a higher class than they can themselves produce. Imports of all kinds increase with prosperity and the growth of industrialism. Our trade with Japan is over eight times greater than it was twenty-eight years ago, and that with the United States is two and a half times its volume in 1880. In spite of the industrial progress of India, she still exports large quantities of raw materials to this country, and her trade with us to-day, though differing in kind, is greater than it has ever been.[1]

[1] In the half-century from 1865 to 1918 India's imports increased from about 25 to 110 millions sterling, and her exports from about 35 to 163 millions; her

In an age of industrialism a suzerain Power cannot deny the claim of a population for which it is trustee to share the supposed benefits which accrue from being industrially self-supporting and independent of foreign imports. But, in my judgment, a Government would not be wise to hasten the advent of the factory in Africa, for there is another side to the picture. The student of history contemplating the social effects of the industrial era in Europe, and in England in particular, may well view with misgiving the efforts of Indian reformers to industrialise a population 90 per cent of which is agricultural, with few wants and, on the whole, moderately contented.

First, there is a clamour for protective tariffs, with the result of high prices, a decline in foreign trade, and loss of prosperity. Crowded communities of factory workers, dependent on the prosperity of each industry, will demand higher wages to satisfy new wants and new tastes—it may be for liquor, cigarettes, and cinemas. When trade is slack, with consequent unemployment, discontent will be rife, and there will be no lack of labour leaders eager to organise agitation on the worst models of the West. "The factory worker soon loses respect for caste and faith in his religion. He has no guiding spirit to help him, and he becomes degraded, demoralised, and ultimately degenerate. This can be seen any day in the big mill and coal-mining centres." So writes "an influential and well-informed Anglo-Indian who is a prominent member of the Indian Legislative Assembly." [1] The picture applies equally to Africa or any other country whose population is almost entirely agricultural and pastoral.

total trade from about 60 millions to 273. The import of cotton piece goods in 1917-18 stood at 38 per cent of the total, the next largest being only 10 per cent. Of these, the pre-war average from the United Kingdom was 98 per cent in grey and white goods and 93½ per cent in coloured. Her exports to the United Kingdom were 26 per cent (to the Empire 53 per cent, pre-war average 42 per cent) in 1917-18.—[Progress Report 143 of 1919, pp. 99, 100.] The recently-issued Report for 1920 (No. 202) gives the latest figures. The import of cotton goods has fallen to 28 per cent (the lowest since 1866), but of these the United Kingdom supplied 89·8 per cent (an increase on 1919 of 12½ per cent), Japan coming second with 7 per cent only. The share of the United Kingdom in the total imports had increased from 45 per cent to 51 per cent (to whole Empire 61 per cent). The exports to the United Kingdom had increased to 30 per cent (to Empire 44 per cent)—(pp. 86-89).

[1] 'Times,' 22nd November 1922.

CHAPTER XXVI.

ECONOMIC DEVELOPMENT (*Continued*).

The economy of labour—Domestic animals—Mechanical appliances—Irrigation—Reclamation of desert—Natural power—Saving of waste—Staple products—Oil-nuts—Cotton—Cocoa—Hides—Timber—The task of the forest officer—Destruction of forests—Measures for protection—Reserves—Reasons for conservation—The object in view: co-operation—Other methods—Other products and possible products—Ranching and stock-raising—Tsetse-fly—Preservation of game.

I HAVE dealt in a previous chapter with the subject of the labour supply in Africa, and the means by which it can be augmented, and I propose in this chapter to make some few suggestions as to how the existing supply can be better utilised and economised, and how the produce of the tropics can be increased in quantity and value by the resources of science and the saving of waste. I will take a few of the principal staples as illustrative of these suggestions.

Agriculture is the most essential of industries, and increase of output means improvement of social conditions, and a larger demand for articles of comparative luxury. At present the yield of the staple crops of Africa is poor, and probably even less than the yield in India.[1]

In the economy of human labour the use of domestic animals stands foremost. I have already dwelt on the value of the ox for transport, but the people of tropical Africa have still to learn his value in agriculture. It is probably no exaggeration to say that half the population of the East would starve if deprived of the use of the ox in the operations of field culti-

[1] Sugar-cane in India 10 tons per acre; Java 40 tons. Ginned cotton in India 98 lbs. per acre; United States 200 lbs.; Egypt 450 lbs. Rice in India, half that of Japan. Wheat in India 814 lbs. per acre; England 1919 lbs.—Indian Industrial Report, p. 53.

vation. Since men alone tend oxen in Africa, the result, as I have elsewhere said, will be to replace female labour in the fields to a large extent. When the ox takes the place in Africa which he has occupied for centuries both in agriculture and transport in Asia, a very large number of men will be set free for productive work.

The utilisation of domestic animals for these purposes obviously depends upon the simultaneous introduction of simple appliances known for at least 3000 years in the East, but of which the primitive tribes, and even the advanced communities of Africa, are strangely ignorant.[1] Of these, the plough for earth work, the windmill and the Persian water-wheel (*sakia*) for lifting water for irrigation, are the most ancient and simple. They may be supplemented, and the latter perhaps superseded by more modern methods and appliances. The use of simple mechanical appliances can also be extended to other operations, such as grinding corn, cracking or decorticating nuts, expressing oil, and many other tasks, at present laboriously performed by hand.

Lord Leverhulme tells us that in civilised countries the capital invested in machinery represents more than 90 per cent of the cost of production, and human labour only 10 per cent. In Africa the proportions are reversed, and the problem of labour education is how to reduce this proportion, so as to make greater use of the labour supply.

Of imported mechanical appliances, the windmill (already largely used in European gardens) and pumps supplied on the hire-purchase system for testing before purchase, small sugar-mills, hand-gins for cotton, and continuously operated screw-presses for oil extraction, are all within the compass of the peasant's intelligence. The craftsman should in like manner benefit by the use of synthetic dyes, of mill-yarn, of sheet-metal, and of sewing-machines, and many other aids and appliances for his "cottage industries"; but I am here primarily concerned with the development of the exportable

[1] We read of the plough in Deuteronomy (xxii. 10), 1450 B.C. Though practically unknown in tropical Africa, it is in constant use by the Abyssinians. The "Meston" plough has been found the most useful type in India. Mr Lamb (Director of Agriculture, Northern Nigeria) is however sceptical as to the value of the plough in Nigeria—citing Egypt in illustration—and sees no great future for the use of European agricultural implements. The use of the plough (introduced by him) has become very popular in Uganda, and a ploughing school has been established.—(Annual Report, 1918-19.)

resources of the country, and these, so far as the native is concerned, are agricultural, and for this in the tropics the essential factor is the water-supply.

It is estimated that there are in India 3,000,000 irrigation wells, by which some 16,000,000 acres are brought under cultivation. But the African cultivator—elsewhere than in the Sudan, where he has to some extent copied the methods of Egypt—is singularly backward in this respect. With the exception of the weighted lever (*shaduf*), by which water is raised 5 or 6 ft., he is ignorant of any mechanical appliances for irrigation, the benefit of which in the arid regions subject to drought would be incalculable. By the use of animal power, with the Persian wheel or with rope and bucket as in India and China, by deepening existing wells and digging new ones, by imported pumps, by boring for artesian water, or by tube-wells (viz., pipes driven to water-level), the area of production might be greatly extended, the fertility of the land increased, and many a crop saved in the drought.[1]

Throughout Asia permanent irrigation channels, led by carefully-adjusted gradients from the higher reaches of a neighbouring stream, often many miles distant, traverse the cultivated lands, from which each field draws its supply when needed. They have existed from time immemorial, and often stand between the cultivator and famine. In Africa this system is almost entirely lacking, and needs to be introduced.[2]

The Governor of Sierra Leone lately intimated that funds had been provided for the purpose in the estimates of that colony for the current year, and the extremely sensible course of bringing two instructors from India "to teach the simple processes of irrigation in use by the peasantry in the East" had been adopted. "Later," he added, "it may be possible to make reservoirs and canals to bring large tracts under cultivation." [3] The Governor of Nigeria has also foreshadowed some possibility of expenditure on irrigation in the provinces of Sokoto and Bornu. I have already mentioned the keen

[1] See "Note on Well-boring," by W. M. Schutte, Bulletin (of Bombay) 68 of 1914, and "Well Waters of Western India," Mann, No. 74 of 1915.

[2] The tribes around Lake Baringo (East Africa) form an exception, and have a well-organised system of irrigation; there is also a simple form in the Taita and Voi districts.—Adm. Handbook, 'Kenya,' pp. 248 and 395.

[3] Speech to Legislative Council, 25th December 1920.

interest of the Sultan of Sokoto in artesian well-boring. There are immense possibilities.

The creation of storage reservoirs may in some cases also provide a piped water-supply of pure water for large cities, thereby not only adding greatly to the comfort of the people, and decreasing water-borne diseases, but also saving labour in the carrying of water.[1]

How even the arid desert itself may be reclaimed and converted into highly productive land has been illustrated by the canal colonies of the Punjab, and the extension of irrigated land in Egypt. The same results cannot be realised in the greater part of the desert tracts of Africa, which are not traversed by mighty snow-fed rivers like the five great streams from which the Punjab derives its name. But the Nile crosses the Eastern Sahara, and the northern bend of the Niger touches its southern fringe in the west, while the Okavango and Cunene may yet be employed to fertilise the Northern Kalahari. It is for such projects that the services of the agricultural engineer and irrigation officer are needed.

French schemes for impounding the flood-water of the Niger in Lake Fagabini and surrounding depressions near Timbuktu are estimated to result in a water surface of some 500 square miles, irrigating 750,000 hectares (2900 square miles) for cotton cultivation.[2] What may be done in a small way has been shown by the results achieved by an observant District Officer—Mr Edwardes—in the Sokoto province of Nigeria, which borders the Sahara desert.

He observed that the mouths of the various tributaries of

[1] Such a reservoir for supplying the city of Kano from the Chalowa river was planned before the war, but had to be deferred (p. 208).

[2] The scheme is stated to consist of "a barrage across the river and the digging of a canal on the right bank," at a cost of 250,000,000 francs. Such a scheme must necessarily have a very serious effect on the navigability of the lower Niger, which for the last 700 miles flows entirely through British territory, and forms an artery of communication by river steamers on which commercial firms have invested much capital. Great Britain was appointed custodian of the Niger navigation under the Berlin Act, and though that Act is abrogated by the new Convention of 10th September 1919 (except as regards Article 1 of that Convention, which establishes the principle of free trade within an area therein defined), the principles of the navigation clauses of the Berlin Act are re-enacted, with the general object of facilitating the navigation of the Niger and Congo.

One seems to recollect, at the time of the British conquest of the Sudan, that the French protested against the possibility of restrictions of the supply of the Nile water to Egypt, and were the position reversed there is little doubt that the French would take exception to the claim of a Power controlling the upper reaches of the Niger to construct a barrage, and deflect so large a volume of water.

the Sokoto river-bed had become blocked by detritus, and the resulting lakes had in turn become filled with sediment and finally dried up, so that the river level was higher than surrounding areas of land. By cutting a series of short channels only a few hundred yards long, he reflooded these depressions, creating reservoirs totalling 3000 acres, with a storage of 20,000,000 cubic yards of water, to the immense benefit of agriculture.[1]

The seriousness of this problem of irrigation is enhanced by the increasing desiccation of the continent, and the encroachment of the desert on the cultivated lands.[2] This disastrous retrogression from productive output is no doubt assisted by the ruthless destruction of forest trees, which has decreased the rainfall. Some years ago Mr Theodore Bent attributed the desiccation of the Eastern Sudan to "the Arab and his axe"—viz., the indiscriminate felling of trees for camel fodder.[3]

The utilisation of natural power belongs to a later stage of industrial progress, but it is not too soon, as Lord Milner has pointed out, for each Government to make a survey of its resources in water-power, and rough estimates of the cost of utilising such waterfalls, natural or artificial, as would supply power by electric transmission, especially for existing railway and other workshops.

In seeking to develop the economic resources of a country, the efforts of Government will be directed not only to increasing productivity, but to saving waste. The native cultivator will be taught the value of by-products, and the neces-

[1] 'Geographical Journal,' August 1918, March 1919, and December 1920.

[2] "The evidence is held to be incontestable that the Sahara desert within the historic period, and the Kalahari much more recently, were well watered and thickly populated."—Ibid., February 1919. I have myself witnessed the rapid encroachment of the desert in both cases. The Resident of Sokoto (Mr Arnett) writes: "Whether we consider merely what we have seen from year to year with our own eyes, or examine what has been happening during past decades or past centuries, there are the same processes in operation,—the drying up of rivers, streams, and lakes, the diminishing rainfall, the dying out of large forests and their replacement by poor scrub, the increase in area where crops will not grow, and the gradual decline in yield on the best-watered parts; lastly, the never-ceasing movement of races, tribes, families and individuals from north to south." There is ample evidence that all of the Central African lakes are shrinking, and traces of ancient beaches can be found far inland at much higher levels.—See Handbook, 'Kenya,' p. 122, &c.

[3] In Nigeria stringent regulations prohibit this practice. Forest reserves of over 1000 square miles have been created in the Sokoto province alone, and artesian boring is to be tried.

sity for conserving fuel supplies. I have in this connection referred to the destructive processes of "shifting cultivation" (p. 299), to the impoverishment of the soil by bush fires, to preventible diseases in live-stock (from which it is estimated that £1,000,000 is lost yearly in East Africa),[1] to plant diseases, to the waste in methods of preparation of produce for export, and to the neglect of by-products. All these and many others which affect the animal and vegetable products of Africa call for thought and remedial action, by education of the natives through Government agencies in co-operation with merchants, and especially by interesting and instructing the native administrations.

In the exploitation of minerals the terms of leases and licences must ensure that wasteful methods are not employed, by the exhaustion of the richest "pockets" of alluvial fields —"picking the eyes out of the country," as the phrase is— which ought to pay for the systematic working of the whole area, and that adequate development work is done by those whose profits are considerable. If properly qualified men are employed by the mining companies; if licences and leases are granted on short terms, renewable for good work; if short-term simple leases, unburdened by onerous conditions, are obtainable by the small capitalist; and if the Government Inspectorate Staff is adequate and capable—much will have been done to ensure the careful exploitation of an alluvial mine-field.

I have neither space nor am I competent to discuss in detail the chief products of tropical Africa and the means by which the quality of each might be improved. In this paragraph I will merely recapitulate, in illustration of the ways in which waste may be avoided and output increased, some of the suggestions already made regarding them.

Recent discoveries regarding the hardening of oil by hydrogenation, while increasing the value of certain vegetable oils by rendering them suitable for the manufacture of margarine, have accentuated the competition of inferior fish-oils for the same purpose. The fatty acids increase when unpurified oil is kept, and they reduce the glycerine content and the value of the oil. Only the oil extracted from the kernels ("kernel-oil") has hitherto been used for edible purposes, but recent processes of refining have rendered the oil from

[1] Economic Report, *loc. cit.*, p. 20.

the fruit itself ("palm-oil") available for margarine.[1] The world's competition for fresh oils for edible purposes, as well as for soap-making, candles, and lubricants, is likely to become increasingly keen, and Africa must adopt improved methods if she means to hold her own. Properly-organised plantations of oil-palms must replace the haphazard collection of the wild forests, as we have seen in the case of rubber. The Dutch are making a vast experiment in the intensive culture of the oil-palm in the East Indian Archipelago, and already claim to produce more cheaply than West Africa. Local mills for expressing the oil,[2] the use of hand appliances for cracking the nuts, and in districts distant from means of transport the use of hand-presses, should result in improved quality, in economy of labour, and of bulk and weight, while providing cake for feeding local stock and for manure. In the report of the Edible Nuts Committee will be found a very great deal of useful information on this subject.[3] Legislation, strictly enforced, is necessary to prevent the tapping of the stem for liquor—a more lucrative product than the oil when transport charges are heavy.[4] The value of this product is very great.[5]

Hardly less important than palm products—in the future if not in the present—is cotton. The bibliography of Empire-grown cotton is already becoming portentous, as a reference to the list of publications on p. 59 of the exhaustive report of the Empire Cotton Committee will show.[6] The main problem in the development of cotton-growing for export is to ensure that it shall be at least as lucrative a crop to the

[1] Mr Tingey, in a paper read at the Rubber Exhibition in June 1921, states that if the fatty acids exceed 10 per cent, palm-oil cannot be profitably used for edible purposes; at present they may be anything from 14 per cent to 70 per cent.

[2] The chief difficulty lies in getting adequate supplies of fresh fruit to keep a mill going. To supply 5 tons a day for 200 days in the year is estimated to require 30,000 trees, covering at least 400 acres, and a large and regular labour supply. Native methods only extract about 12 per cent of the 17 per cent to 20 per cent of oil contained in the fruit.—'Imperial Institute Bulletin,' September 1917, &c.

[3] Cd. 8248 of 1916. See also the many references given in the bulletin quoted.

[4] The process is known as "cabbage tapping," and is opposed to native law and custom. Tapping by an incision in the flower-stalk does not injure the tree.

[5] The quantity of palm-oil and kernels exported from Nigeria alone in 1919 was 318,000 tons, valued at £9,200,000. Between 1900 and 1913 exports increased from 1½ to 5 million sterling.—Foreign Office Handbook 94, p. 45.

[6] Cmd. 523 of 1920. See also Appendix B of the Indian Report (Cmd. 51, 1919). These two reports form landmarks in the history of Empire cotton-growing, and formulate a policy.

cultivator as ground-nuts and other exportable products which are attended with less risk of failure from climate or disease. This, as Mr M'Connell pointed out in his excellent paper at the Royal Colonial Institute,[1] can be achieved by growing the varieties which command the best price and yield the highest percentage of lint; by obtaining the largest possible output per acre; and by reducing charges in connection with transport and marketing. The two former are matters of research and experiment; the latter may be effected by the adoption of some of the suggestions I have already made regarding labour and transport. I add a few further tentative suggestions in regard to this particular crop.

In districts which offer every inducement for cotton-growing except population, a scheme of colonisation by immigration from congested districts might, under the auspices of a powerful organisation such as the Empire Cotton Corporation, prove of value, with the co-operation of the local Government. A deputation of village headmen having approved the site, free transport and temporary food supplies would be provided for the immigrants, with the requisite cotton-seed.

Ginneries and pressing machinery should be established in the centre of cotton-producing areas, and not on the railway, with a view to minimising transport, since the seed cotton is more than three times the weight, and perhaps a hundred times the bulk, of the pressed bales of lint. These can easily be carried by mechanical transport from the ginnery to the railway, thus saving time and cost to the cultivator, while the seed has not to be retransported back again. The ginnery should, if possible, be driven by water-power.

Imported cloth, if cheap and strong, decreases the demand for raw cotton for local weaving. New incentives to the cultivation of cotton would be afforded by facilities for insuring the crop against disease and drought, so as to reduce the risk to the cultivator. This might perhaps be effected through the local banks.

Risks from drought may be further reduced by the *partial* irrigation of rain-grown cotton—viz., by irrigation only in the driest weeks, to save the crop in case of prolonged drought. This can be done by the methods and appliances I have suggested, and the knowledge that he had such means at his

[1] See 'United Empire' for April 1921.

disposal for saving his crop would no doubt do much to popularise the cultivation of cotton with the peasant cultivator. Cotton already enjoys the advantage of being a later crop than the main staples, so that the cultivator is able to turn his attention to it when they are already harvested. Arrangements for collecting direct from the growers, so as to exclude the middleman's profit—for which he often renders little or no equivalent service—are advisable. For this purpose I think the hand-propelled ped-rail, which I have described in the chapter on transport, would be very useful—for its pressure when loaded is only 6 lbs. to the square inch, and it can be taken over growing crops without injuring them.

Since the peasant cultivator is more influenced by the success of his neighbour than by any amount of advice, it may be useful to guarantee a few selected planters against loss if they will grow improved varieties under prescribed conditions. In Nigeria the native administrations have been encouraged to pass by-laws prohibiting the sowing of any but the authorised seed in specified districts, in order to prevent hybridisation, and deterioration of a successful exotic variety.[1] It is most essential that the cultivator should be guaranteed a minimum price over a period of time,[2] and that he should be assured of a market at that price for all the cotton he can grow.[3]

[1] As regards Nigeria some suggestions will be found in my report (Cmd. 468, 1920). The Chad region offers great possibilities for irrigation. The Shuwa Arabs are very intelligent, and understand something of irrigation. Their higher standard of life is an incentive to earn money. Their ex-slaves are now casual labourers. The extension of the railway to Chad is under consideration. There are extensive areas in this district suitable and available for cotton, and a tolerably good labour supply. Zaria is the headquarters of the cotton industry. Irrigation from the Chalowa and Hadeija rivers should increase the yield. "Allen's" variety has been introduced, and the quantity exported has increased very rapidly. It should gradually supersede all native cotton. Sokoto cotton is mostly carried to Zaria, 246 miles. The completion of the main trunk road will render wheeled transport possible, and lorries can obtain a load both ways—thus greatly reducing cost—since there are large cities along the route. The provinces of Kontagora and Borgu afford large areas suitable for cotton, but the difficulty here is lack of population and labour owing to the slave-raiding of the past. The eradication of venereal disease, and a greater yield of foodstuffs per acre, by improved varieties and labour-saving methods, are, as I have said, the remedies.

[2] For lint cotton which commands a price of 5d. per lb. in Liverpool, 1d. per lb. (seed cotton) can be given in Nigeria, and so in proportion.

[3] Complaints are made that although the natives have been urged to grow cotton, Lancashire is not willing to purchase it if American cotton is plentiful. Sir H. Leggett states that out of 50,000 bales of the Uganda crop of 1920 only

With the important question of directing the crop to British markets I have dealt in chapter xiii. (pp. 271-72). The most promising solution seems to be that adopted in the Sudan with the Gezireh, Kassala, and Tokar cotton crops, where a system of tripartite profit-sharing has been introduced with success between the Government which provides the water for irrigation, private enterprise which furnishes the capital, and the natives who undertake the labour. Cotton-growing is essentially a native industry, and the best results have been obtained where this is recognised.[1] In Uganda the Cotton Ordinance prohibits the purchase of cotton in specified districts, except at the standard price and at licensed buying posts.[2] It has not been found necessary in Nigeria to interfere with the liberty of the individual to sell his produce to whom and at what price he prefers. The importance of encouraging this industry cannot be over-estimated.[3]

The gravamen of the remarks which I have made in chapter xix. in regard to the cocoa industry is, that greater attention on the part of the cultivator is needed in clearing the ground, removing diseased trees and stumps, which breed fungi—in short, more labour and care, if the yield and quality are to come up to a reasonable standard,[4] and plantations must not

8000 had been bought up to date, and asked that preference should be given to Empire-grown cotton at equal prices for equal quality. The Corporation will see to this.—'United Empire,' April 1921, p. 245.

[1] This is the case in Uganda (Coryndon, 'United Empire,' June 1920) and in Nigeria. In Nyasaland 76 per cent is grown on European estates, and only 24 per cent by natives.—Foreign Office Handbook 95, p. 49.

[2] In the Sudan ginneries and the importation of cotton-seed are subject to licence. A scheme is adopted for enclosing the warehouses in which cotton is stored with gauze netting, so as to catch and destroy the boll-worm moth when it emerges. All cotton is graded and sealed by Government.—Handbook 98, pp. 99, 100.

[3] Of the total export of manufactured goods from the United Kingdom, valued at £411,000,000 in 1913, £125,000,000 consisted of cotton goods. A capital of £500,000,000 is employed, and it is estimated that not fewer than 10,000,000 people in this country are directly or indirectly engaged in the industry. The total requirements of the United Kingdom are put at four million bales of 500 lbs. each per annum. Of this, 3,200,000 comes from the United States, leaving 800,000 to be found from other sources within and without the Empire. The Empire output is over 5½ millions, but 85 per cent is unsuitable for Lancashire. It is therefore very essential to increase the Empire-grown supply of long-staple varieties, since Mr M'Connel states that the United Kingdom is dependent at present for 75 per cent of its requirements on foreign countries.—Cotton Report, *loc. cit.*, appendix ii. and p. 54.

[4] It is asserted that the average yield per tree in native-owned plantations on the Gold Coast is under 1 lb. on the best land, while on Government plantations on inferior land it is 8 lbs.—Nigerian 'Pioneer,' 18th February 1918. Dr Unwin states that the Gold Coast cocoa is "the lowest grade put on the

be overcrowded. I have emphasised also the importance of paying a price according to quality. At present it is stated that the farmer who takes the trouble to prepare his beans properly can obtain no better price than his neighbour whose plantation is neglected.[1]

Since the cocoa must be fermented on the spot to avoid the necessity of carrying the bulky pods to a central fermenting and drying station, uniformity in fermentation can only be secured by educating the native to dry and ferment the beans himself, the merchant completing the process so as to ensure the cocoa reaching the European market without deterioration. Such a system is more consonant with the self-reliant traditions of British trade, and less "bureaucratic," than the demand that Government should employ expert cocoa samplers in every village, and prohibit purchase except of certificated cocoa. Model plantations run by Government as object-lessons are needed. This crop forms the main staple of the Gold Coast, and is rapidly increasing in importance in Nigeria.

As regards hides, freight charges may be reduced by decreasing bulk as the result of partial preparation. Natives may be instructed in better methods of flaying and of drying the hides, discarding offals, &c. The Indian report contains a useful appendix on tanneries.[2] Africa possesses many excellent tanning materials. The excellence of the tanned goatskins of Kano (see note, pp. 509-10) proves the high efficiency of native methods. I have myself furniture upholstered with this leather, which is almost as good to-day as when done twenty years ago.

The preservation and control of the forests of Africa is a matter of such vital economic importance that it demands more than the brief references which I have already made to it.[3] The forest officer is concerned both with the afforestation of areas denuded of forest and with the preservation or exist-

world's markets," and commands only half the price of better grades. He advocates a tax on each tree according to its healthiness.—'West Africa,' 25th December 1920.

[1] Foreign Office Handbook No. 93, p. 33.

[2] See Appendix D, Cmd. 51, 1919.

[3] It is to Mr H. N. Thompson, Director of Forests, Nigeria (late of the Indian Forestry Department), that West Africa owes the proper recognition of the importance of forestry, and these notes are compiled from his teaching. His report on the Gold Coast was published as a Blue-book (Cd. 4993 of 1910.)

ing forests and their "organisation," so that different age classes of trees are evenly graded, and occupy equal areas, and the forest may return its full annual interest on the timber-producing capital. To effect this the conservator regulates the number and girth of trees to be felled in the reserves, their removal without damage, and their replacement by saplings. For an effective forest administration, a continuous policy, to which the Government alone can give effect, is essential.[1] Native administrations cannot take a sufficiently far-sighted view, and are apt to sacrifice the interests of the future to present needs; but they can be associated with the Government in carrying out its policy, and entrusted with the largest possible share of responsibility and initiative, in accordance with the principles of native rule described in chapters x. and xi.

"Shifting cultivation," which I have fully described elsewhere (chapter xiv., p. 299), is the most potent agent in the destruction of forests. By this system the cultivator takes up from five to nine times (according to the period of rotation) the acreage annually cropped. Primeval forest is thus replaced by secondary and inferior growth, in which useless trees predominate, and eventually by grass, with consequent jungle fires, till the land is quite exhausted.

The chief measures for the preservation of forests are: (*a*) a better system of agriculture; (*b*) the creation of forest reserves (see chapter xv., p. 315); and (*c*) the protection in unreserved areas of the more valuable species, by prohibiting felling for sale, except by licence. All forests in the upper catchment areas of rivers should be reserved, and areas should be reserved for afforestation where forests do not exist. Mr Thompson states that the area placed under reserve in different countries varies from 15 per cent to 67 per cent, and he considers that 33 per cent, as in India, is the minimum in a well-populated tropical country, and the proportion should be greater in less-populated regions.

The objects of forestry reserves are:—

1. To supply forest produce continuously for local use (railways, buildings, and native requirements) and for export, and to add to revenue.

[1] This is recognised even in countries with the most advanced forestry organisation. In France and Germany, municipal and even private forests are under Government supervision.

2. To conserve the water-supply and control the "run-off" from the hills, thus regulating waterfalls for power, maintaining irrigation and the flow of springs, ensuring a higher level in the rivers in the dry season, and preventing floods, which deposit large quantities of barren soil in the valleys, and ruin them for agriculture.

3. To increase the humidity of the atmosphere, and so promote the growth of crops. Experiments in Europe prove that forests increase rainfall by 28 per cent.

4. To prevent landslides and erosion, silting of rivers, and shifting sands.

5. To act as barriers against the spread of insect and fungoid pests from one cultivated area to another.

6. To conserve and improve the qualities of the soil, until required for cultivation by the increase of the population.

7. To form a sanctuary for game, and provide grazing in time of famine.

The law should empower the Governor to create reserves compulsorily (if agreement with native communities claiming ownership is not possible) on lands "in respect of which it appears that the extinction of forests is diminishing, or likely to diminish, the water-supply, or injuring the agricultural conditions of neighbouring lands, or imperilling the continuous supply of forest produce to the village communities contiguous to such lands."

Where forests are recognised as tribal property, a "settlement" is made with the native grantors, in which all native rights (unless extinguished by purchase) are protected, including the right to take forest produce for domestic requirements. Produce for sale or export is controlled by Government, the tribal authorities receiving a royalty upon it. Except as regards the rights recorded in the "settlement" the reserve becomes an estate exclusively subject to forest law, on which trespass may be prohibited.

Advanced native communities have in some cases in Nigeria been entrusted with the entire charge of a reserve, under the supervision of the forest officer. In most cases they participate in its control, and share its profits. The forest officer looks after the planting and care of seedlings, the maintenance of fire-traces, the regulation of grazing, and other technical work in a reserve, instructs the natives, and sees that the law and the terms of the settlement are observed. In some cases it may be desirable to fire the reserve annually, early in the year, to prevent the occurrence of later fires at the end of the dry season, which destroy all young trees, especially if there is an accumulation of combustible material.

Partial protection in unreserved areas is afforded by prohibiting, except under licence, the felling of protected trees of special value, until such time as sufficient reserves have been created. Plantations are maintained for the supply of seedlings, including exotic trees of value such as teak, and also to provide fuel near large cities. Newly-afforested areas require much protection from fires and from cattle. The planting of economic trees, such as oil-palms, kolas, cocoanuts, and fruit-trees on cultivated lands is encouraged. Gum-bearing acacias are protected by special legislation in the Sudan.

Particular attention is needed to prevent the wholesale destruction of trees for steamer fuel, or in the vicinity of mines for pit-props and other purposes. The supply to natives at cost price of cheap angle-iron, or rod-iron, for hut-building will decrease the annual destruction of saplings. The example of Government in improved methods of exploiting a forest, and establishing a market for the less-known classes of timber, may afford a useful lesson.[1]

In the more arid regions, where extensive forests do not exist, the trees require protection against the axe of the nomad, who lops off the limbs to afford fodder to his camels, and leaves the stump to die. The afforestation of such regions in order to check the encroachments of the desert, to act as a break to dry and scorching winds, to increase rainfall, and to provide fuel and timber, is a work of immense benefit and importance.

The development of plantation rubber has of late years received so much attention that there is no need of any remarks on this head. In Africa the native must be better trained in methods of tapping and of coagulating the latex.

In making these brief and somewhat crude suggestions regarding some of the chief staples of tropical Africa, I have not attempted to discriminate between the share of the

[1] Such an experiment was undertaken in Nigeria under the able control of Mr Thompson, and an industry worth some £250,000 (including the forest) was built up in six years, "which was from every point of view a complete success.' It was estimated that 500,000 cubic feet of timber would be cut in 1920.—Dr Unwin, Forest Consultant, in 'West Africa,' 12th June 1920.

Government, the merchant, the native administration, or the individual native cultivator in giving effect to the object in view—the increase in quantity and quality of African exports. For it is essentially a task which invites and depends upon co-operation. The Government, by means of its technical departments, by improved transport, and in the other ways upon which I have dwelt elsewhere, leads the way and assists the efforts of others, and endeavours to awaken the interest and excite the emulation of the native administrations. The merchant has it in his power to prove to the natives the practical benefit of the methods suggested, by offering good prices for improved products, and in some cases by himself co-operating with Government in providing the object-lessons required. The native rulers can exert their influence, with immense benefit to the people, by popularising by example and precept the teaching of the new methods where they are opposed to the conservative customs of primitive cultivation. By such co-operation material prosperity will be assured.

The African tropics afford a vast and fascinating field for experiment in the acclimatisation of new products, with a view to broadening the basis of industry, and for the improvement of those products which are indigenous. The Indian agricultural, forestry, and veterinary publications are full of suggestion and experience for Africa.[1]

In the domain of vegetable products one may instance the need of investigation into the question of fodder grasses, and the storage of grass as hay or ensilage.[2] Fibres are chiefly important in the barren lands near the east coast, since they will not bear heavy transport charges from the interior; and as the Director of Agriculture on the Gold Coast observes, they cannot compete with "cocoa grown with the minimum expenditure of capital and energy and the maximum financial return." Sisal, ramie, and piassava [3] have received attention.

[1] See 'General Catalogue of Government of India Publications' (Government Printing Office, Calcutta).

[2] Guinea-grass and alfafa have both received some attention, and the former promises well. Bersem-grass and shaftal (*Trifolium alexandrium* and *resupinatum*), highly praised in India, merit experiment. ("Bersem as a new fodder crop," Bulletin No. 66 of 1916, Calcutta).

[3] The fibre of the common food-plant "okro" is said to be better than that of jute ('Board of Trade Journal,' 7th October 1909, p. 26). We read of a company being formed at the Cape to exploit the baobab tree (*Adansonia digitata*), and a leading commercial firm reports that "it is probably the finest paper-material without exception to be found in Nature."

It is reported that jute grows well, and flax (which, of course, stands in a class apart) has lately, as I have narrated, proved a valuable crop in East Africa.[1] In the interior, rope, string, and especially bags for produce may, as we found during the war, be profitably manufactured as "cottage industries" by primitive tribes.

Maize, if grown for export, requires bulk carriage by rail and sea, and storage and discharge by elevators. The Germans had prepared for a large ripe-banana export, the fruit being prepared in drying sheds. This industry should promise well. The dried fruit makes an excellent stew, and tastes like dried figs. Pine-apples of great size and very delicious flavour were grown in the Government gardens in Nigeria, and could be canned for export. Banana-flour, ginger, and limes offer possibilities. The latter grow and fruit most freely in West Africa; the juice or citric acid could be prepared from it locally. The cultivation of vegetables has been neglected in West Africa, though the French have set us an example.[2]

In favourable localities the curing and fermentation of high-class tobacco may offer a valuable export, as has been proved in Nyasaland. The sunflower yields a valuable oil and cake, which is largely exploited in Russia. The castor-oil plant gives good results in French Dahomey. Economic trees, such as the kola, the cocoa-nut (which is little liable to disease and easily harvested), the gum-bearing species, timber-trees like the teak, fruit-trees like the mango, all call for increased attention. It is worth remembering that South Africa, being in the southern hemisphere, offers particular advantages as a source from which to obtain young plants of fruit-trees and other economic species, since they can be transplanted at the most favourable season, and introduced into tropical Africa just before the rains.

The field for enterprise is no less in the animals and the animal products of Africa. Cattle, goats, sheep, and swine

[1] The Agricultural Department of Nyasaland reports on a wild product, "buaze" (*Securidaca longipedunculata*), as being in every way superior to flax. It is said, however, to be difficult to cultivate, and the gum it contains renders it hard to separate the fibre.—Handbook 95, p. 54.

[2] On the Bauchi plateau in Nigeria the cultivation of potatoes has been eagerly adopted by primitive tribes, and they can now be bought in the native markets. We read of vegetables, sun-dried and compressed into bricks, being exported from India to Mesopotamia, and found indistinguishable from fresh. — See 'The Sun-drying of Vegetables,' by G. Howard. Bulletin No. 8 of 1917, Calcutta.

can all be improved, whether for meat or hides, by crossing with imported stock, by castration of males, and provision of stud animals for service of females of approved standard. The possibilities of stall-feeding instead of or in addition to grazing, of cattle fodder and cake, invite fuller investigation. Ostrich-farming,[1] bee-keeping (a lucrative industry in India),[2] the domestication of the elephant, eland, and zebra,[3] and the breeding of zebroid mules—all these and a hundred other problems offer inducements to the scientific investigator.

Thousands of tons of dried fish are imported yearly to West Africa, though the sea teems with every variety, which, with the use of steam trawlers, proper curing establishments, and refrigerators, could be made available for food, and the offals for valuable manure.

The day of the nomad pastoral must before long pass in Africa as it has passed in other countries, and give place to village-owned herds. Already in Rhodesia movement beyond defined areas is prohibited without a veterinary officer's permit. The northern provinces of Nigeria and the northern territories of the Gold Coast have been said by experts to be at least as well suited for cattle-rearing as Rhodesia or North Australia, and they have the great advantage that their proximity to Europe enables the meat to be sent to the home market within the number of days for which "chilled" carcases will keep.

In those regions of British tropical Africa, however, where water and fodder are found, foreign enterprise in ranching is generally already forestalled by the indigenous population and its cattle. In such districts there is no room for the ranch properly so-called, but the European stock-breeder on a limited holding should not only be able to find profit, but by the object-lesson which his methods afford to the native, and by the purchase of surplus native stock, he may be of the greatest value to the country.

[1] In West Africa, the French have experimented largely in ostrich-farming and claim success. The cost is estimated at £4 per bird per annum (Revue Coloniale, 1901). In East Africa, the indigenous bird under proper care is reported to produce feathers almost equal to the South African.

[2] Calcutta Bulletin, No. 46 of 1915. The African bee (*Apis mellifica*) is (says Mr Lamb) much more promising than the Indian species (*Apis Indica*).

[3] The zebra is reported to have done well in harness in South Africa, and to be immune to horse-sickness. The experiments of Baron de Parana in Brazil in the breeding of zebra mules appear to be extremely successful.—'Times,' 13th November 1899.

If it be our aim to teach the natives how to develop the resources of their country themselves in the most efficient way, there is perhaps no sphere of industrial activity in which an object-lesson is more essential than in that of stock-raising. For there is no class more conservatively ignorant than the pastoral races of Africa, whose methods have not changed since the time of Abraham. To such people no means of education other than ocular demonstration is of any use whatever.

The educative value of an object-lesson in the treatment of the common diseases,[1] isolation against contagion, selection for breeding, the flaying of hides, and fattening for market, &c., cannot be overrated. But the application of modern science can do more than this. By artesian well-boring, and raising water by mechanical appliances and irrigation, by importing stock and cross-breeding, by introducing new fodder grasses and scientific methods of storing them, by utilising local oil-cake for fattening, and by creating a steady market, a trade of great value may be built up. The wild nomad pastorals of to-day may become the stock-raisers of to-morrow, and the yearly increment of the herds, instead of perishing by epizootic disease and the starvation of the dry season, may provide food for the industrial classes of Europe, who in turn will raise the standard of comfort of the natives by their manufactured goods. We have seen the process at work all over the world; it is no longer the fanciful picture of the enthusiast.

This form of enterprise seems indeed to offer such opportunities for genuine development as to merit every encouragement, even if the non-native lessee encroaches somewhat on the grazing lands of the pastorals. The area granted must, of course, depend on what is available, and will form an adequate inducement. A few square miles of ordinary grazing land with water might be attached to a larger block of 100 or even 200 square miles of land at present useless. The conditions of the lease should be liberal, for the task of the lessee is to convert arid waste into profitable pasture lands.[2]

[1] Rinderpest and East Coast fever, of which the germ is conveyed from animal to animal, and not like anthrax or tetanus contained in the soil, are preventible diseases comparatively easy to stamp out.—Tanganyika Report, 1921, p. 58.

[2] Land can be acquired in Rhodesia at a distance of 25 miles and upwards from the railway, for 5s. an acre and upwards; 5 per cent of the purchase price is paid on allotment, and the balance in nineteen instalments. —British South

Among the desiderata of the future few projects are of greater importance than the extirpation of the tsetse-fly, alike for the eradication of "sleeping-sickness" (of which it carries the bacillus), and the corresponding disease (trypanisomiasis) among cattle and other live-stock. The achievement of Colonel Gorgas in his campaign against the mosquito in Panama, and the methods successfully adopted in San Thomé Island, show that there is no reason to despair of success against the tsetse-fly.

The task, colossal though it be, is facilitated by the fact that the "fly-belts" are for the most part well defined, and often not extensive. The first step is to map these accurately—a task for which I collected material for many years in Nigeria. Guinea-fowl, which feed on the pupæ (as well as on grasshoppers, ticks, &c.), should be protected in fly-country. Incidentally the pea-fowl and the jungle-fowl, so common and so picturesque in the forests of India and Burmah, should be introduced into Africa.

The society for the preservation of the fauna of Africa (of which I have the honour to be an original member) has done much to preserve the big game of the continent, and has devoted special care to the elephant.[1] Viewed, however, from the economic standpoint, the wild elephant must share with monkeys and wild pigs the charge of being terribly destructive to native crops. He soon learns that he is immune from serious assault, and defies the peasants' efforts to drive him off. The wanton destruction wrought by a herd in a banana plantation or a young forest is terrible. The number of elephants in each herd should be known, and licences to shoot a proportionate number of mature males each year can be issued, so as to afford the cultivators some protection. The best means, on the other hand, of preventing the ruthless extermination of the elephant for ivory is to prohibit the export of all tusks under a minimum weight, and to make it

African Pamphlet, 'Rhodesia,' p. 22. The size of ranches in Australia (where areas of 1500 square miles have been granted) bears, of course, no comparison to Africa, for the country had no indigenous population.

[1] The massacre of elephants for ivory used to be very great indeed some years ago. Published figures of ivory exported from German East Africa and the Congo are as follows: in 1893-94 from German East Africa, 13,923 tusks weighing 242,494 lbs.; in 1894-95, 14,692 tusks weighing 317,777 lbs.—viz., 28,615 tusks or 14,300 elephants; average tusk under 20 lbs. In 1892 from the Congo 183½ tons, say 10,300 elephants. Total elephants killed in these two areas alone, 17,500 per annum.

an offence to attempt to export or to offer such tusks for sale.

The game laws of British dependencies in Africa now afford protection to the beautiful fauna—the main desiderata are to institute a close season, and for the larger game a sanctuary; to protect some of the rarer species, and the females and immature males of all; to prohibit the destruction of game by unfair means, such as nets, game-pits, poisoned arrows, and hunting with dogs; and to offer rewards, as in India, for hyenas and snakes.

CHAPTER XXVII.

THE LAW AND THE COURTS OF JUSTICE.

The law in African dependencies—Ordinances—Regulations—The courts—The Supreme Court—Merger of judicial and executive functions—Disadvantages of the Supreme Court as the sole tribunal—The provincial courts—Contrast between the two systems—Some advantages of provincial courts—Legal practitioners in courts—Special procedure *re* plea and oath—Collective punishment—Reconciliation—Native debts—Value of native courts—The objects in view—Native customary law—Constitution and powers of native courts—Supervision of native courts.

THE fundamental law, applicable alike to Europeans and natives in all our African tropical dependencies, is the common law and doctrines of equity, administered concurrently, and the statutes of general application which were in force in England at the time the administration was created.[1] This body of law is modified (*a*) by any law made by the Imperial Parliament which is declared to extend to any or all of these dependencies,[2] and by orders of His Majesty in Council; and (*b*) by local ordinances.

This fundamental law, in so far as it is applicable to natives, is modified by the proviso that British courts shall in civil cases affecting natives (and even non-natives in their contractual relations with natives) recognise native law, religion, and custom when not repugnant to natural justice and humanity, or incompatible with any local ordinance, especially in matters relating to land, marriage, and inheritance. The native courts administer native law. Thus in a Moslem State

[1] In some colonies, where a European code existed prior to the assumption of British rule, the fundamental law existing at the time was not changed—*e.g.*, part of Canada and Mauritius retain the Napoleonic code, and the Cape retains the Roman Dutch law.

[2] Parliament does not usually legislate direct for the colonies.—'Taring,' p. 407.

such as Zanzibar, or the Emirates of Nigeria, British courts recognise the Koranic law in dealing with natives, and it constitutes the fundamental law of the native courts, subject to the provisos mentioned.

It is one of the first preoccupations of a British Administration in newly-occupied territories to check with a strong hand the exercise of arbitrary powers, whether by Europeans, official or unofficial, or by native chiefs without the authority and safeguards provided by the courts of law.

Ordinances—except on certain subjects reserved in the Royal Instructions, which require prior reference to the Secretary of State—are enacted, after publication in the 'Gazette,' by the Legislative Councils of the Colonies, and when assented to by the Governor become law, subject to disallowance by His Majesty. Ordinances for the protectorates are enacted by the Governor-in-Council, and unless urgent must be published in the 'Gazette' for two months prior to enactment, so as to give ample time for any suggestions or criticisms. In some cases the Colonial Legislative Council is, or was, empowered to enact laws for the protectorates attached to the colony, as well as for the colony. The Executive Council considers all draft Bills. In order to simplify the criminal law, and to enable every person to know what are offences in law, and the degree of punishment attached, most dependencies have a criminal code, in which the English criminal law is codified with some minor local adaptations.[1]

Most ordinances empower the Governor-in-Council to make regulations with limited penalties, and also Orders-in-Council having the force of law. In some cases a municipality, or a native administration or other authority, is empowered to make rules or by-laws, subject to approval and publication in the 'Gazette.' Regulations can be made and altered without the formalities and delays, or the congestion of the Statute-book, involved by frequent amending ordinances. They can deal in great detail with complicated matters, which are unsuited for enactment in a statute, and which may be applicable only to a particular district.

A strong and effective Legislative Council is apt to chafe under this partial transfer of legislative power to the Governor and his Executive Council, and to demand that all regulations shall be submitted to it for final approval. This would to a

[1] In East Africa the Indian penal code is adopted with modifications.

large extent introduce delay and formality, and would overtax the time of the Legislative Council, the unofficial members of which have their own business to attend to, upon which attendance at the council makes no small inroads.

The Executive Council, consisting of the heads of the principal departments and the Attorney-General, is a body well constituted to scrutinise and amend regulations intended to give effect to a law, and members of the Legislative Council have always, of course, the power to criticise them by way of motion. The occasion for these protests, which one reads from time to time in the debates of all colonies, would, however, be decreased if the structural regulations under a skeleton ordinance (viz., one which does little more than empower the Governor to make regulations on the subject of the ordinance), together with other regulations of special importance, were submitted to the council before coming into operation, and if all other regulations and Orders-in-Council were laid on the table—as indeed they usually are.

It is of importance that amendments to regulations should convey a clear meaning without the necessity of reference. The busy man has no time to ascertain what is the purport of an announcement that "regulation . . . is amended by inserting (or omitting) the words . . ." It is also very desirable that all regulations and Orders-in-Council published during the year should be available in a bound volume (and issued to all who have to administer them), and that they should be reprinted as amended every three or four years. I have known a case in which no volume of regulations had been issued for a generation at least, and even the law officers were uncertain in regard to them.

The highest tribunal in an African dependency is the Supreme Court, which exercises all the local jurisdiction, civil and criminal, vested in His Majesty. It consists of a Chief Justice and Puisne Judges, including, it may be, those of a neighbouring colony. The full court, consisting of the Chief Justice and two or more judges, forms a Court of Appeal from the decisions of the Divisional Courts, and a further appeal lies to the Privy Council, in claims over £500 in value, or if a question of public importance is involved. The Royal prerogative of pardon or commutation is exercised by the Governor alone.

The area under the Supreme Court jurisdiction is usually

formed into divisions or circuits, and Assizes are held periodically in each division, and at any place the Chief Justice may appoint. Special courts are also held at the discretion of the divisional judge. The bulk of the work of the Supreme Court is, however, done by courts of limited jurisdiction, under magistrates or *ex officio* commissioners (viz., administrative or police officers), who deal with cases within the powers assigned to them, or commit them for trial to the Divisional Court.

In countries of great size, like the African dependencies and India, it is obviously unavoidable that judicial and executive powers should be exercised by the same officer, and that some of the officers who exercise small judicial powers should not possess recognised legal qualifications. The separation of these functions would seem unnatural to the primitive African, since they are combined in his own rulers, and a system which involved the delay caused by reference, even in minor cases, would be detested. The people like to bring such cases to a man whom they know, who can often effect settlement without litigation. He would usually have more experience of native motives, and hence of the degree of criminality—a point of view to which I shall refer again presently. As a judicial officer he can maintain closer touch with the native courts, which he has to supervise, and whose cases he occasionally transfers to his own court. Moreover, in a country recently brought under administration, and in times of political difficulty, occasions may arise when the strictly legal aspect must give way to expediency—as we have seen in the chapter on slavery. I am convinced that, even were it possible, the separation of the judicial and executive functions held by the District Officer would not be for the good of the country.[1]

[1] "I do not consider," says Chief Justice Osborne, "that the merger of judicial and executive functions in the same officer works badly in West Africa." Sir E. Speed, Chief Justice of Nigeria, points out that the law administered is largely native law, and with this and with the native language the Administrative Officer should be more familiar than the Assize Judge, who may be new to Africa or to the colony. The same inevitable exercise of dual functions obtains in India, and in other dependencies.

By Ordinance I. of 1st January 1902 of the Gold Coast Legislature (enforcing the Royal Order-in-Council of 26th September 1901) the Chief Commissioner of Ashanti—an executive (and legally unqualified) officer—was vested with the powers of a judge of the Supreme Court, except in matrimonial cases. Appeals lay to the Governor—not to the Supreme Court—by whom sentences exceeding five years were confirmed. District and Provincial Commissioners, not necessarily

Though the Supreme Court is well adapted for the needs of an old-established colony, and of those commercial centres where non-natives and educated natives chiefly reside, it labours under certain disadvantages as the sole British tribunal in a country like Africa, where distances are great and means of transport deficient, where the people are addicted to endless litigation regarding tribal boundaries and the possession of land, and where there is a multiplicity of languages. The restricted powers of the Commissioners, and the natural tendency to remand cases for trial at Assize, must in the circumstances cause delays, and result in cases being heard at great distances from the place where they originated, with hardship to witnesses, who must be forcibly detained, and in waste of time by the reopening of land disputes often long since settled by the executive officer. The subject is discussed at much length in the report on the amalgamation of Nigeria.[1]

"Delay," wrote the Chief Justice of Nigeria, discussing the judicial system of the Southern Nigeria Protectorate, "is the greatest enemy of efficient administration of criminal law, and delay is inherent in the Supreme Court system, . . . it has, in my opinion, proved a failure." Mr Osborne, late Chief Justice of Southern Nigeria, writes: "The Supreme Court is not the most suitable tribunal for new territories in the opening stages of civilisation. . . . It is not so much the establishment of the tribunal itself which is unsuitable as its inevitable consequences—viz., the influx of alien practitioners." He adds that the civil jurisdiction of the Supreme Court should not be extended to newly-administered districts until the people are thoroughly familiarised with British methods, and "only when the tribal and communal boundaries have been politically settled, so that they cannot form the subject of litigation."

Both Chief Justices, after long experience in West Africa, supported by a strong body of expert opinion, thus condemn

possessed of professional qualifications, exercised varying powers, with an appeal to the Chief Commissioner's Court. A circuit judge was appointed in 1919.—'A Vanished Dynasty,' Sir F. Fuller, pp. 214 and 221.

Mr F. H. Migeod, an officer of the Gold Coast Government, who recently visited the Congo in his journey across Africa, relates that he found warlike operations on a considerable scale in progress there. He attributes the outbreak partly to "the separation of judicial from administrative functions," for the judicial officers were apt to work against the political officers, whose power and influence has thus been undermined.—'West Africa,' 14th May 1921.

[1] Cmd. 468, 1920, pp. 20-25 and 75-78.

the extension of the Supreme Court jurisdiction to newly-acquired territories, on the grounds that it involves unnecessary delays and hardships on litigants, prisoners awaiting trial, and witnesses (with a consequent inducement to conceal crime); [1] because it introduces alien practitioners, who foment litigation for their own gain; does not effectively punish crime; and creates needless friction with the executive, whose carefully-adjudicated decisions in land cases may be called in question, with a consequent weakening of their influence and authority in the maintenance of law and order; while the work of the court becomes congested by the frequency of appeals. These are important conclusions, which no doubt have a wider application than Nigeria.

The alternative known as the "Provincial Court System" was set up by me in Northern Nigeria at a time when the Treasury grant admitted of only a single judge, who could not possibly have held Assizes throughout a country more than five times the size of England—putting aside other aspects of the question. Under the close supervision of the Governor and Chief Justice the system had worked well for fifteen years, and with the approval of the Chief Justices of both north and south it was extended to the whole of Nigeria on amalgamation.

The system has been criticised by some who have had no practical experience of it, and has been warmly praised by others who have seen it in operation. A full discussion of the matter may be found in the report referred to. I will endeavour briefly to indicate how it has dealt with the difficulties I have described, omitting minor controversial details—such as who should be confirming officer, or whether the powers of transfer to the Supreme Court should be exercised concurrently or solely by the Governor or Chief Justice, &c.

The jurisdiction of the Supreme Court is restricted territorially under this system to those "local limits" to which it is best adapted, and which are capable of indefinite expansion as the development of the territory proceeds and circumstances require, but it exercises full jurisdiction in all proceedings, civil and criminal in the country, to which a

[1] The peasant prefers to suffer oppression rather than leave his farm and his family for an indefinite time, for he is uncertain whether he will find them unharmed on his return. It becomes, therefore, almost impossible to procure witnesses, and the least that can be done is to maintain them, and to give liberal compensation for detention.

non-native is a party. In each province—there are twenty-one in Nigeria—a Provincial Court is set up, with unlimited powers and concurrent jurisdiction over non-natives, except in the local limits of the Supreme Court—within which District Officers or other magistrates become commissioners of that court. The Provincial Court is thus relieved of the bulk of judicial work which is not directly concerned with the native administration.

The Resident of the Province, as President, alone exercises full powers *ex officio*, and all administrative officers are Commissioners of the court, with powers varying according to their legal knowledge and proved capacity, irrespective of their rank. Judicial ability counts for promotion. Police officers and others may be appointed Commissioners by the Governor. All criminal cases in which a penalty of six months imprisonment or its equivalent is inflicted, and civil suits in which a judgment of £50 and upwards is awarded, require confirmation by the Governor, who in practice delegates his powers to the Chief Justice, or it may be to a Lieut.-Governor assisted by his legal adviser. It is usually sent by telegraph.

The returns of the cases tried, usually called the "Cause Lists" of the Resident, and through him those of the Commissioners, are transmitted to the Governor or his delegate, and they operate automatically as appeals, and ensure some uniformity in sentences. There is no other appeal in criminal cases, but an appeal lies to the Supreme Court in civil suits over £50. Capital sentences must be confirmed by the Chief Justice before final review by the Governor-in-Council. The confirming officer can, on judicial grounds, reduce or annul a sentence, or order a rehearing before the Supreme or Provincial Court.

It would at first sight seem as though there were little difference between the "Provincial Court system" and the "Supreme Court system," since the same law is administered by the same men in both cases, and there is the same obligation to take cognisance of native customary law. In the Provincial Court system, however, a larger initiative and more extended powers are conferred upon experienced officers. If fully qualified—and apart from practical experience (which is the best training) there are many barristers and solicitors among the administrative staff—a district officer may be allowed to exercise the full powers of the court, subject to the rules for confirmation. If without professional qualification, every administrative officer is required to pass a simple test in law and evidence, suited to the restricted powers he exercises.[1] The verdict of the judicial officers after a long experience in reviewing and confirming the sentences of these courts, has been that they have progressed steadily in efficiency, and the work has been carefully and satisfactorily done.

Under this system no cases come automatically before the Supreme Court, and the procedure is summary and simple. Any case, especially a technical or complicated civil suit, or a murder case where there is a conflict of evidence, can be transferred to the Supreme Court, either at the request of one of the parties, or by the Chief Justice, or by the Provincial Court with his consent. A British subject may originate proceedings in the Supreme Court, and if summoned by a Provincial Court may demand trial in the Supreme Court, though in practice few such demands have been made.

In order to cope with the work before provincial courts were created, very large powers were conferred in the Southern Nigeria Protectorate on native courts, which consisted of a large number (as many as sixty in some cases) of illiterate chiefs of the most primitive communities. Any District Officer, however junior, sat as President, and in this anomalous position could exercise larger powers than as a Commissioner of the Supreme Court.[2]

It is claimed for the Provincial Court system that it restricts the powers of the junior officer, and surrounds him with safeguards to prevent injustice. All minor cases pass through the hands of the Resident (who can transfer any case from a Commissioners' Court to his own), and are reviewed by the legal adviser. The Resident is the officer with the largest experience of native administration. Important cases,

[1] Memoranda on judicial procedure and points of law, noting any misconceptions or errors brought to light by the cause lists, have, since the creation of the system, been issued to administrative officers in Northern Nigeria. These officers at first attended the Supreme Court, and were personally instructed by the Chief Justice, but the courts have now their own tradition, and such methods are no longer necessary.

[2] Mr Chamberlain, 9th April 1900, replying to a question in the House, stated that a District Commissioner in Sierra Leone, sitting with native chiefs, could hear and determine capital cases. There was no right of appeal to the Supreme Court, but the death sentence requires the warrant of the Governor. Counsel were allowed to appear in a District Commissioner's Court, but they could not appear when he sat with native chiefs or assessors, except in capital cases or by leave of the District Commissioner. No test of legal knowledge was demanded from these officers.

on the other hand, are tried by qualified officers with a knowledge of native law and custom, and often of the native language also. Their judicial work adds to their store of knowledge regarding land tenure, fishing, hunting, and forestry rights, &c., while the Assize Judge is probably ignorant of local customs, and very much in the hands of his interpreter. Serious cases are tried on the spot with less delay, and less chance of suborning witnesses, and the sentence or judgment is subjected to the scrutiny of the confirming officer. The influence of the District Officer, which is of vital importance in the interest of good government, is increased instead of being lessened, and by putting an end to litigation regarding land, friction with the Supreme Court is abolished, and frivolous and costly litigation decreased.

There is a consensus of official opinion that the courts are popular with the people, since justice is brought within the reach of all and delay avoided, but they are unpopular with the educated natives. This class is almost entirely confined to the limits of the colony proper,[1] and large commercial centres, which remain under the Supreme Court jurisdiction, and they have therefore little or no personal experience of the Provincial Courts. Their ground of objection is that legal practitioners are excluded from these courts, and from appearing in appeals from them to the Supreme Court in civil suits, except by leave of the Chief Justice when a question of law is involved.

In Africa, as in India, the legal profession has a strong attraction for the native, and is overcrowded—in Nigeria largely by aliens from other colonies. Its members and their friends are very clamant; but both Chief Justices, and (according to Sir E. Speed) "every single officer, judicial or administrative, who has had any experience of districts recently brought under control, have emphatically pronounced against the right to be represented by counsel."[2] They state that the touts of native lawyers have constantly fomented litigation among the illiterate people of the interior, ever-

[1] The colony proper is 1/240th part of the area of Nigeria.

[2] Sir E. Speed adds that the Yorubas and Egbas—the most progressive tribes in the south—expressly stipulated that no lawyers should have audience in the courts in their territories—though usually speaking their language,—and this demand has, I believe, recently been reaffirmed by the latter. See also the reference to Sierra Leone practice in the last footnote (p. 543), and to Indian conditions at the end of this chapter.

ready to reopen land disputes—most of which were not *bona-fide* questions of individual or family ownership of land, but disputes as to tribal or other boundaries—which had been settled after thorough investigation by the District Officer. They point out that the native lawyer is probably a complete stranger to the country, and certainly has nothing in common with these tribes, of whose language and customs he is ignorant, and among whom he has only comparatively recently dared to penetrate under British protection for professional gain.

These charges were not denied by the native members of council—themselves barristers of high standing. But the opponents of the system appealed to the Secretary of State and to sympathetic societies in England, largely on the ground that a man accused on a capital charge had a right to be defended by counsel. The judges, however, affirm that native barristers rarely attended criminal trials, which were not sufficiently lucrative, and confined themselves chiefly to the recurrent appeals in land cases, from which, as Chief Justice Osborne observed, the "fat fees" accrue.

This specious argument might have been met (with little satisfaction to themselves) by allowing counsel to appear in capital trials, but Chief Justice Speed was averse to such a course, and held that existing safeguards (including the power of transfer to the Supreme Court) were ample, and it was the duty of the judge to watch the interests of the accused. For the rest, he showed that there was ample commercial business in which counsel could find legitimate employment. Thus Indian experience repeats itself in Nigeria, and doubtless in other African dependencies.[1]

[1] Sir Francis Fuller, in his book, 'A Vanished Dynasty' (chapter xii. p. 220), gives an account of present-day administration of justice in Ashanti: "The close touch and constant intercourse between commissioners and natives have engendered feelings of mutual regard and respect. Nor is it too much to add that this sympathy has, in many instances, amounted to real affection. Litigation is beloved by the Ashantis, and land disputes form a large proportion of court cases, owing to the accruing value of the soil for planting purposes. Litigants are only too ready to take their complaints to the Commissioners, who, they well realise, will mete out strict justice at but slight cost to the parties. Appeals lie from the Commissioner's decision to the Governor of the Gold Coast Colony, but this last procedure is seldom resorted to.

"By wise decree lawyers cannot plead in the dependency, for such a litigious people would fight to the bitter end and ruin themselves in payment of exorbitant fees. One of the secrets of their present contented state may be ascribed to this rule. . . . The penalties which may be inflicted by the Commissioners vary according to rank from a maximum of six months' imprisonment allowed to District Commissioners, to one year in the case of a Provincial

Nothing except education can compare in importance with the administration of justice in British colonies, and this must be my apology for so lengthy a discussion of this matter, for the issues are not confined to Nigeria. Sir Edwin Speed, lately Chief Justice of Nigeria, whose views are shared by his able successor, and others who have maintained these principles in the face of a very vocal and occasionally opprobrious agitation, deserve the gratitude of the silent and ignorant millions whose welfare is affected. I am indeed convinced that those native gentlemen who have espoused the cause of the native barrister have done so in ignorance of the real issues at stake.

Turning now to matters of procedure, a plea of not guilty is recorded on behalf of an illiterate accused, and in capital cases the evidence must, generally speaking, be sufficient for conviction irrespective of his own assertions. In other cases, if the accused adheres to his plea of guilty, he would be convicted unless the evidence was such as to throw strong doubt on his guilt. I recollect the surprise of a Chief Justice new to Africa, when an accused man pleaded guilty to having turned himself into a hyena by night and devoured children, because there was a consensus of village opinion that he had done so. Or when another, who manifestly could not have committed the murder of which he was accused, pleaded guilty because his friends had told him it would save trouble if he did so.

It is regarded as insulting by a Moslem, and as a misuse of the Koran, to be required to swear an oath that he will not give false evidence, or to statements of detail, though he is willing to swear if his evidence is challenged, or if the matter is one which is vital to the issue; for the rest he is willing to affirm. Pagans are sworn on the knife or bayonet.

There is a type of judicial inquiry, indispensable among primitive and barbarous communities, which we have of late

Commissioner, and finally five years in the Chief Commissioner's Court. All sentences exceeding five years must be confirmed by the Governor. Up to 1919 the Chief Commissioner heard all important cases, but in that year a Circuit Judge was appointed to relieve him of these duties."

The Nigerian system appears to differ from this only in that confirmation is required for every case over six months' imprisonment instead of five years; that the powers exercised by Commissioners are graduated according to legal knowledge and proved capacity instead of by rank alone, and that the duty of reviewing sentences is in practice delegated by the Governor to the Chief Justice. Ashanti is "annexed territory" enjoying the status of a "colony."

seen applied in principle in Ireland. When it is apparent that a community has taken part in, or connived at, an outrage—murder, riot, or arson—and voluntarily accepts responsibility for it, or refuses to give evidence, and knowingly harbours the criminals, possibly aggravating the offence by opposing the police or military forces, the Governor is empowered by special ordinance to cause a judicial inquiry to be held, at which the chiefs and notables are afforded an opportunity of exonerating themselves and their people. If they are recalcitrant, or if the charge is proved, a collective fine may, with the approval of the Governor, be imposed, and if not paid may be collected by distraint. It need not be collected in full, and the village can be "bound over," the balance standing as security, and being remitted unless the peace is again broken.[1] This procedure—"binding over" —is very useful in cases of "political" disturbance due to the assumption by a chief of powers which do not belong to him, or to the intrigues of one who has forfeited his position.

British courts are directed to promote reconciliation in avoidance of litigation when possible, and the administrative officer, in his dual judicial and executive capacity, is well able to give effect to this direction. District Officers are, of course, constantly occupied in hearing informal complaints and petitions, which can be settled advantageously without recourse to the courts. A debt by a native to a European may not be enforced, if it is reasonably probable that the debtor did not understand the nature of the obligation and the consequences of default.

The profound importance of the administration of British justice in British courts in our dependencies needs no emphasis by me, but in my view, if our aim be to raise the mass of the people of Africa to a higher plane of civilisation, and to devote thought to those matters which (though less picturesque than the construction of large public works, or a large surplus revenue) most intimately affect their daily life and happiness, there are few of greater importance than the constitution of the native courts. These must be based on a system which contains the elements of steady growth and evolution, *pari*

[1] Sir J. D. Rees, formerly British Resident in the native States of the Malabar coast, speaking of the Moplahs, says that similarly "special acts were passed in 1854 providing for penal fines in the district in which outrages are committed."—'Times,' 26th August 1921.

passu with the growth of village education. Among the most primitive of human communities, it is in the adjudication of tribal and family disputes, in the punishment by common consent of the violation of accepted rules of conduct, and in the authority vested in chosen members of the community to give effect to the popular will, that the germ of progress and evolution is to be found. This is the very "eye" of the seed whose spontaneous and natural growth means healthy development.

It may perhaps hardly seem worth while to set up a crude tribunal consisting of primitive pagans, who can hardly be called chiefs, and have but a limited control over a few families, but from such small beginnings alone is it possible to create the rudiments of law and order, to inculcate a sense of responsibility, and evolve among a primitive community some sense of discipline and respect for authority. A Resident in such cases will doubtless feel that it would be much less trouble to do the work himself than to place even the smallest reliance upon so ineffectual an instrument; but even though the judicial work be not so well done as it would be by himself, it is only by the patient training of such a court that better tribunals can be evolved and real progress achieved. The close supervision of such a court, and the personal education of its members, will involve more labour and personal effort than direct administration, but it is surely worth the effort.

If the native courts are to become an integral part of the machinery of Government—in which they will take an increasingly important share as they increase in efficiency—in accordance with the system of encouraging the native communities to manage their own affairs, to which I have alluded in a former chapter, then as it seems to me the following must be among the aims which the Resident will set before himself and his staff:—

(*a*) To provide for the Natives tribunals which fully understand their own customs and modes of thought, and command their confidence.

(*b*) To create an adequate number of courts, so that each unit may have its own, and complainants may be able to obtain redress without travelling prohibitive distances, and the difficulties of summoning witnesses may be reduced.

(*c*) To foster their influence, and to make them effective

instruments of justice, by teaching them, and by enforcing strict impartiality and integrity.

(*d*) To develop independence of judgment, initiative, and a sense of responsibility, while maintaining a close supervision, and avoiding unnecessary interference.

(*e*) To put a stop to the adjudication of cases elsewhere than in a duly constituted court.

(*f*) To promote co-operation between the native executive authority and the courts. In the more advanced communities the courts would look to the native officials to effect arrests, and to see that the sentence or judgment of the court was duly executed, including the payment of fines. They in turn would support the executive authority against the alien native middleman and other disintegrating influences, including that of fetish in pagan districts.

(*g*) To promote co-operation between the provincial and native courts as component parts of a single judicial system, and to relieve the former of work which can better be done by the natives themselves. With this object the native court can upon occasion undertake a preliminary investigation, or its members can sit as assessors in the Provincial Court to advise regarding native law and custom.

Such a system, in which the judges and members of a court receive adequate salaries but no personal share of the fines inflicted—which formerly constituted a large part of their income,—is an integral part of an organised native administration. The court receipts are paid into the native Treasury, from which the court officials, like all others, receive their salaries. Since the native staff is not necessarily so limited in numbers as the European, a gradual discrimination between those charged with judicial or with executive responsibility respectively becomes feasible, by the training of a body of selected native judges, distinct from the district headmen, and wholly independent of the earnings of the court for their emoluments.

The jurisdiction of native courts is limited to natives, and with the exception of a few specified ordinances which they are empowered to enforce—such as those relating to taxation and to native authority—they administer native law and custom only, modified or added to by such by-laws as may be made by the Native Authority to give effect to local ordinances. The native customary law must, of course, be admitted as such by competent spokesmen, and not the mere whim or *ipse dixit* of the chief, and it must be that of the tribe to which the accused or defendant belongs. It must also be consonant with the dictates of humanity and of natural justice.

Thus a native law which prescribes the destruction of twins would not only be unenforceable, but the court must regard the act as an offence; such a case would, however, as a matter of course, be tried in the Provincial Court. Or again, if an ordinance or regulation constitutes it an offence to tap the stem of the oil-palm for liquor, the native court, by means of a by-law, would recognise the act as punishable, even if not contrary to native law and custom.

Space precludes any attempt to review the system of native courts in the various British African dependencies, and I will confine myself to a few brief notes on those set up in Nigeria.[1] They vary both in constitution and powers, from the Moslem court presided over by a single judge (sitting with or without assessors), learned in law and apt in precedent, to those which I have described as the very germ of embryonic evolution. The former present some points of interest, but it is the latter which form the more difficult problem of administration.

The courts are set up by warrant (a version in the vernacular being printed in parallel columns for the Moslem courts) in which the powers they may exercise and the limits of their jurisdiction are defined, and the judges and members (if any) are named. These are settled by the Resident in consultation with the paramount chief if there is one.

The courts are chiefly engaged in settling questions which arise out of the domestic relations, such as matrimonial disputes, petty debts, trespass, assaults, and inheritance—where both parties are natives subject to its jurisdiction. Alien natives permanently residing in the jurisdiction would be amenable to the court, but those who are not so resident, or who are not ordinarily subject to native court jurisdiction —*e.g.*, British subjects born in the colony—are only amenable with their own consent. A similar exemption is extended to natives in the permanent service of Government, but they are encouraged to take their matrimonial and petty debt cases

[1] See note on page 199-200 regarding the constitution and powers of the native courts in Uganda.

to the native courts, to which, in fact, it is reported that they increasingly resort.

Powers are conferred upon the courts in proportion to the ability and integrity of its members. In criminal matters those of the lowest grade are naturally very small, for the members are too ignorant, and often too dominated by fetish, to use them wisely. But I regard it as essential that these courts should be genuine native courts, not hampered by formalities of procedure, or presided over by a District Officer with an interpreter, so that the members become mere dummies. To confer large powers on such primitive courts, to demand lists of cases (necessarily without adequate notes even in cases which would in a Provincial Court require confirmation) for review by an overworked judge of the Supreme Court, and to allow appeals to the Supreme Court, is in my view hopelessly to confuse the functions of a native court with those of the British Commissioner's Court—as I conceive them—and to reduce the former to a caricature of the latter They are no longer native courts in any proper sense of the term, they are no longer educative, and "abuses are so many and so grievous" that the country is better without them.[1]

It is essential that the courts should be open at all times to the District Officer, who can revise the sentence or judgment, or order a rehearing, or, if desirable (because there is a conflict of evidence, or for some reason it appears doubtful if justice would be done), re-try the case in his own court. This close supervision takes the place of appeals, which would

[1] The courts which formerly existed in Southern Nigeria (central and eastern provinces) were set up to remedy the state of chaos which is reported to have been brought about by the breakdown of tribal authority. This is said to have been due partly to the slave-trade, which was chiefly in the hands of middlemen traders, who thus usurped the power of the chiefs, partly to the growth of the wealth and power of the coast chiefs and middlemen at the expense of those in the interior, and partly by the increasing power of the Aros, a tribe of professional slave-dealers, who ruled by fetish and terror and destroyed the power of the tribal chiefs.

The object of the native courts was to re-establish the power of the chiefs after the Aros had been conquered. Tribal authority, except through the medium of the native courts, was however abolished, for clause 15 of the Ordinance (No. 15 of 1906) enacted that "no jurisdiction (other than that of the native court) shall be exercised in the district by any other native authority on any pretext whatever." A native council (viz., a native court other than a "subordinate court") could inflict a sentence of imprisonment for two years, with or without flogging, and determine personal suits up to £200 ('Southern Nigeria Laws,' ed. 1908, chap. 123). As a consequence of Supreme Court intervention, it was alleged that frequent acquittals on technical legal grounds of self-confessed murderers had destroyed confidence and induced the chiefs to take the law into their own hands.

merely foster the tendency to litigation, and destroy the influence of the court. This passion for litigation is not, however, wholly to be condemned, for it provides a safety-valve, and supersedes recourse to violence.

There can be no more important duty imposed upon an administrative officer than that of keeping the closest touch with the native courts—especially those of the lowest grade. —of seeing that the sentence or judgment is that of the court itself, uninfluenced by the clerk or by tribal partisanship, that the decisions are reasonable and just and within the powers of the court, and of verifying the disposal of fines and fees. This he can do by frequently attending the sittings, and by questioning the members, the clerk, and others.

He would impress on the court the necessity of granting a patient hearing, but avoid intervention himself during the proceedings, so as not to lower the prestige of the court, or appear to try the case himself. Even if the decision appears wrong on the facts, it is better to abstain from interference at the time, and to suggest modification later, since the court which heard the case is the best judge, and revision should be as unobtrusive as possible, in order to preserve its influence. The District Officer is not justified in overriding the genuine opinion of the court as to native law and custom, which alone it administers.

If, however, an unjust decision were given from corrupt or perverse motives, the Provincial Court would deal with the matter. If a complaint is preferred against a court, the investigation should be conducted on the spot, so that members can explain their action. Similarly, if a judgment or sentence is cancelled, the reason should be explained in open court. The review of their cases encourages the court by showing them that an interest is taken in their proceedings, and it is instructive to the District Officer. The efficiency of the native courts depends on the adequacy of the British staff.

CHAPTER XXVIII.

COURTS OF JUSTICE (*Continued*).

The evolution of native courts in primitive communities—Clerks of native courts — Higher - grade courts — Application of ordinances, &c., in native courts—Native courts and slavery—Punishments by native courts—Imprisonment—Corporal punishment—Other punishments—Capital sentences — Punishment of women — Differences in native punishments—Witchcraft—Respective functions of British and native courts—Results in Nigeria—Offences against natives—The judge's vacation—Magistrates—The Indian parallel—Appendix : The French system.

THE object of the lowest grade of native court in a very primitive community is to transfer the *patria potestas*, exercised by the head of a family, or of a village group, to a tribunal covering a wider area of jurisdiction, without destroying the authority of the village *panchayet* (Council of Elders) on the one hand, or the legitimate executive authority of a chief on the other hand. Thus the decision of a recognised tribunal is substituted for the arbitrary will of an individual (whether a chief or a fetish priest), or the operation of mob-law, and the power of the secret society. As the official explanation of the recent Native Jurisdiction Bill in the Gold Coast aptly expresses it, "the headman and the village chief will continue to exist, and their customary right to sit in arbitration for the settlement of small local disputes will not be interfered with. They will, however, have no power to enforce their decisions as a tribunal, and persons dissatisfied with such decisions must apply for redress to the tribunal of the superior chief. It is only at this stage that it becomes necessary to facilitate and regulate the administration of justice in the tribunals."

Each clan must have its court, or easy access to one, and since each unit desires representation, the number of members must at first be large, and the area of jurisdiction small. Only the principal members need perhaps hold warrants and receive sitting fees. As each court gains in self-confidence, competence, and prestige, and members learn that they are not mere partisans of the litigants of their own tribe, the number of members can be decreased, and the area of jurisdiction enlarged, or new courts created to deal with expanding work. In order to check frivolous and vexatious litigation, the complainant in any case dismissed by the court may with advantage be charged a fee.

As soon as may be, fixed salaries to members would be substituted for sitting fees. The members can if desired be elected by the community, subject to approval (so as to ensure that their election has not been due to any wrong influence, and that they are the best men), but the expedient of appointing an alien as judge is one I deprecate. Though an educated Moslem, or a Christian clerk, may secure more rapid progress, the principle of evolution on indigenous lines would be retarded. It may, however, in exceptionally difficult cases be necessary to adopt this method, with assessors from the tribe of each litigant.[1]

[1] My able successor (Sir H. Clifford), in his speech to the Nigerian Council in December 1920, remarks: "There is, I fear, only too much reason to apprehend that the wide judicial powers granted to a host of 'warrant chiefs'—few of whom have any extended or natural jurisdiction over more than a small fraction of the people upon whose affairs they adjudicate—are too often used as legalised instruments of oppression. In such localities I think we cannot hope to build up native administrations, because the collective or national instincts and sentiments which are their foundation are lacking. . . . It should be our object . . . while exercising a much closer supervision over the dispensation of justice by the native courts, to allot to the chiefs collectively a fairly substantial share of the revenues which those courts collect, for expenditure under the supervision of their Residents upon local works of visible utility. . . . I hope to see a return to the old system inaugurated, subject to such alterations in detail as changed conditions may render necessary."

The apprehension that wide judicial powers would be exercised oppressively is no doubt only too well founded. The new system curtailed these powers very drastically, and it was the aim of the administration (which was being effectively carried out) to reduce the host of "warrant chiefs" (as they had been called) as rapidly as circumstances would permit and to increase the supervision. The principle of distributing among very primitive chiefs a portion of the court receipts gives rise to a fear lest heavier fines may be imposed. It is true that among the most primitive tribes the foundations of organised administration are lacking, but I do not think that it is beyond the capacity of the British district officer gradually to create that foundation, through and by the tribal organisations, by which in some cases the tribes have unaided evolved a higher status.

It was intended that the system introduced should be in the nature of evolution and progress, and not such as would present to the native mind any idea of subversive change. The district officer no longer presides, the powers of the courts are curtailed, the number of members gradually reduced, a closer supervision is

In order to give effect to these principles, it is obvious that the procedure of a native court should not be modelled on that of a British court, or hampered by the observance of legal formalities. Some degree of formality is, however, desirable, in order to maintain its dignity and influence, such as assembly in a regular court-house, and the preservation of strict order and decorum. Whether the issue of a formal summons, or a warrant of arrest, may or may not be desirable, will depend upon the degree to which the community has become habituated to the procedure of the British courts.

But it is obviously necessary that every court should maintain a record of its cases—often a mere entry of the decision and date is enough—as a check on the receipt counterfoils for the fines and fees received. These entries act as a check on the members, who fear lest an unreported case should come to the knowledge of the district officer. In more important cases—especially land disputes—unless there is a record, cases would be brought up again and again. The provision of a reliable clerk or scribe for this purpose is one of the chief difficulties to be overcome in setting up tribunals among primitive and illiterate people, who dislike and fear court clerks.

In the lower-grade courts of the Northern Provinces of Nigeria, scribes capable of keeping simple records in the vernacular were generally available in the Moslem districts. Some pagan courts rendered an oral account weekly to the District Officer—a course preferable to employing a Mohamedan scribe, who would probably display a tendency to proselytise. In the south, half-educated youths from Mission schools could be obtained for low salaries; but efficient and reliable men were not available, and there was a danger lest the clerk should dominate the court (as investigation proved to be the case), and would use the glamour of his education, and his supposed influence with Government, to extort bribes and pervert justice.

The law administered under such conditions would no longer be native law and custom, which would gradually

enjoined, the receipts of the courts are paid into revenue, the influence of the court clerk is controlled, and appeals to the Supreme Court are abolished. We have seen that in the early conditions of the country the courts as established were a substantial advance, but in none of these directions, it is to be hoped, will the projected reversion to the "old system" be sanctioned by the Secretary of State.

be destroyed, but a hybrid based on English law as known to the clerk from some elementary text-book. The clerk was placed in a position of great temptation where there were no chiefs capable of exercising authority, and it is not surprising that many succumbed to it. It is essential that the members should learn that the clerk is the servant, not the master, of the court, and that he should not be allowed to interfere in any way with its judicial work. The only effective check on such malpractices is constant supervision by the District Officer (especially as regards the disposal of fines and fees), the gradual education of the members, and the periodical transfer of clerks from one court to another.

The powers of a native court of the highest grade in Nigeria may extend to capital sentences—a question to which I shall refer in a later paragraph. The court of the head chief may consist of his principal officers with a native judge, and be constituted as a "Judicial Council," empowered by the Governor to exercise executive functions. It would have concurrent jurisdiction with the native judge's court, but can best deal with such matters as offences or defaults by the officials of the native administration, land and boundary disputes which refer to ancient titles, quarrels between Moslems and pagans, sedition by fanatical preachers, breaches of by-laws made by the native authority, and cases in which the action or authority of the native judges are called in question. The Moslem ruler and his council are guided by equity, the native Kadi solely by "the Book." Much of the time of the latter is occupied in the administration of estates of deceased persons.

The court of the chief native judge in a province can be made an appellate court for the lesser Moslem courts, which would submit their reports through him for comment, and any recommendation to the Resident. The chief Kadi would call in any native judge, if he so desired, and discuss his cases with him.

Tribunals such as these are capable, like British courts, of modifying their fundamental law by giving due weight to native law and custom when dealing with pagans, and like them should sit with pagan assessors when dealing with tribal customs. The best Moslem judges are actuated by enlightened traditions as to the equality of all persons before the law. Some are averse from the infliction of fines, on the grounds that no revenue should accrue from the administration of justice. "Justice is of God, and no man should derive profit from dispensing it." In accordance with Mohamedan custom, the ruler must be acknowledged as supreme over the judiciary equally with the executive.

The advanced courts in non-Moslem countries have no written code of native law, with voluminous books of reference, such as the Mohamedan jurists possess. They administer the unwritten native customary law of their community, and the simple principles of English law. As opportunity permits, it would no doubt be desirable gradually to reduce this mixed and unwritten body of principles to a simple code, and to train judges on the parallel of the Moslem Kadis.

It is important that the advanced native communities, whether Christian or Moslem or pagan, should have an opportunity of becoming acquainted with the ordinances of Government which affect them, both with a view to their promulgating their main principles in the form of by-laws for observance by native courts, and in order to promote the feeling of solidarity with Government which it is so desirable to foster. For this purpose a transcription of such laws into the simplest possible language, and the rendering of it into the vernacular, for distribution and explanation by District Officers, is, I think, of great value, for ignorance of the law is a very valid excuse when it is enacted in an unknown language.

Such laws are those relating to slavery, vaccination, the possession of firearms or of imported spirits in prohibited districts, the forestry regulations, the adulteration of produce, the preservation of wild animals, and various clauses of the criminal code, among others. These higher courts can be encouraged to enforce by-laws based on these ordinances, and others dealing with such matters as sanitation, markets, the isolation of infected cattle, the control of middlemen touts, the checking of grass fires, and similar questions. The object of such a by-law is, on the one hand, to make the matter with which it deals cognisable by a native court—which, unless so empowered can only administer native law—and, on the other hand, to inform the people that a specified act, or failure to act, will, in accordance with the by-law, be dealt with as an offence by the native courts. As being the lawful orders of the ruler, such by-laws can be enforced with

Koranic sanction. Lower-grade courts can make useful by-laws against fetish ordeal, the worship of the smallpox fetish, shifting cultivation, grass fires, tapping palms for liquor, the use of poison, and concerning the occupation of land by strangers.

The attitude of a native court towards slavery questions has already been discussed in the chapter on slavery. Briefly, its authority cannot be invoked to the detriment of any person on the grounds that he or she is or was a slave—*e.g.*, to assist an owner in detaining or recovering a slave—nor can it discriminate as regards sentence or award between a slave and a free man, but its assistance can be invoked on behalf of the slave by certifying to liberation and ransom. A native court should, like a British court, view the relations between the master and a slave who of his own wish continues in that status as those between master and servant, and not between owner and slave.

Native customary law (even Koranic law), speaking generally, regards offences as having been committed against the individual rather than against the community, and punishment therefore takes the form of vengeance and reprisal. An African despot regarded rebellion as a crime against himself, and he resorted to burying or burning alive, to successive mutilations till the victim expired, or to impalement. Witnesses and prisoners were tortured to extort evidence, or a confession of guilt. Imprisonment was rare, and could only be inflicted in a capital city possessing a dungeon. I have described in chapter x. the dungeon at Kano.

The conception that the suppression of crime for the public benefit is the function of the State, and that it can be effected by punishments which are deterrent though humane, and by the reform of the criminal, while the individual aggrieved has his own remedy in a civil action for damages, is one which has to be instilled into the rulers and the courts. The punishments inflicted upon the African by his own rulers were sufficiently deterrent, but chiefs complain that wherever the white man comes crime increases, and they are not allowed to inflict punishments which will check it.

Imprisonment—a form of punishment which the unorganised community could with difficulty inflict—becomes under British rule the most common. It has an educative value, for the community on the one hand by showing that convict labour may be employed for the public benefit—in road-making, sanitation, &c.,—and, on the other hand, for the individual, who is taught a trade, such as brick-making, or the making of sacks, twine, rope, mats, or baskets. But the extent to which it is deterrent varies greatly. To some the regular work and good food is not distasteful. I have known a prisoner due for discharge prove triumphantly that he had still a day to serve. On the inauguration of the British administration in Northern Nigeria we had no gaols, or even houses other than the grass-mat shelters in which we all lived. Prisoners lived in the village, and reported themselves for work each morning. On one occasion a prisoner ran away. The single constable in charge ran after him, and failing to capture him and fearing the consequences, he laid down his rifle and equipment and bolted himself, whereupon a prisoner marched his fellow-convicts back to prison, bringing the constable's arms with them.

Such incidents would seem to indicate that prison life, so far from being deterrent, is even popular. That it is not looked on as degrading may be judged by the respectful salute paid by a warder to a prisoner of petty rank, and by the terms of fellowship and equality which often exist between the prisoners and their guardians.

Yet there are other tribes to whom even a short term of imprisonment means death. They simply pined away and died, or made desperate attempts to escape. I have known the hard-won confidence established with a primitive tribe destroyed in a moment by the transfer to prison of a convict whom they considered had been carried off as a slave. It is the District Officer who knows these things, and can best gauge the degree of criminality on the one hand, and the deterrent effect of the punishment on the other.[1]

Imprisonment can be inflicted by British courts, and the convict removed to prison; but unless native court prisoners are confined in British gaols—a course to which there is obviously strong objection—it can only be inflicted by native courts at those centres where a native administration prison exists under the close supervision of a District Officer, who

[1] I once spent some time among a tribe in North Nyasaland where apparently a thief or burglar was considered to be lawfully entitled to the property he had stolen—and would openly offer it for sale to its original owner—if he chose to take the risk of losing his life in its acquisition.

can see that the prisoners are properly fed and cared for, and that accused persons are not detained interminably without trial, and where a medical officer is available to attend the sick whom it is undesirable to release to spread disease in their villages.[1]

Since imprisonment is not always deterrent, and often difficult for a native administration to carry out, the native courts have to resort to corporal punishment—a common form of penalty in African communities. There are those in England who allow their anxiety for the gentle treatment of the criminal to outweigh the claims of the law-abiding for protection, who measure the deterrent effect on the African by what would be deterrent to themselves, and clamour to apply to Africa a code which it has taken us many years to reach.

That code should indeed be applicable to the non-negro races of Africa, and to the educated African, who, like the Asiatic, shares with the European an increased sensibility both to the moral degradation and the physical pain of corporal punishment, which the primitive African does not feel.[2] They forget that only about a hundred years ago sentences of 1000 lashes were inflicted for comparatively trivial offences in England: it was a capital offence to steal to the amount of 5s. from a shop, and a child could be hung for stealing 5s. worth of apples. The opposition to the repeal of this shockingly barbarous law was led by the English bishops! [3]

No English gentleman, least of all a lover of Africa, can do otherwise than regard with detestation the methods of Germany, or contemplate the revival in Africa of the barbarous traditions from which we ourselves have so recently emerged. I am glad to think that I may have assisted in directing Mr Chamberlain's attention to the question of arbitrary flogging—which led to the strict limitation of corporal

[1] It is somewhat curious how keen an interest the advanced native administrations in Nigeria take in these institutions in contrast with the horrors of their former dungeons. The native prisons are now surrounded by imposing walls, kept scrupulously clean, and elaborate prison books are kept by the official in charge.

[2] I could give some very striking experiences of the insensibility to physical pain of the African, but space does not permit.

[3] The date was 1811—within the lifetime of my own father. See 'Life of Sir S. Romilly,' vol. ii. pp. 331 and 380. At page 368 an instance is quoted of a soldier being flogged to death for being dirty on parade, and another of a veteran of sixty, who bore an exemplary character, being given 300 lashes for absence for a day. See also 'Thirty Years' Peace,' Martineau, vol. i. chap. vii. p. 98 *et seq.*

punishment by British courts—and to the abolition of the old " chain-gang," which disgraced British rule in East Africa in the early 'nineties.

But the law-abiding section of the community has a claim to consideration at least equal to that of the criminal, and punishment must therefore be deterrent. We are somewhat apt to run to extremes. There is nothing inhumane in consecutive floggings, inflicted at considerable intervals, with every formality and precaution (especially in the case of the African, whose inability to anticipate the future I have described), or in whipping (as opposed to flogging) for repeated offences of larceny. Native courts administering native law have more latitude in these matters, and their penalties may be greater or less severe than a British court would award for the same offence, provided they are not contrary to humanity. It is very desirable that summary punishments for crimes of violence should, when possible, be carried out at the scene of the crime.

Fines can be more easily imposed when currency has been introduced, and they are suited for offences other than crimes of violence, provided that care is taken that they are never the perquisite of the court. Punishments involving derision are particularly effective and deterrent in Africa, such as confinement in the stocks. I have heard of prisoners being ordered by a native court to march round the village proclaiming their sentence.

Native courts are often better able to get at the truth than a British court is, owing to their more intimate knowledge of native modes of thought. In pursuance of the policy of self-government in domestic affairs, the power of life and death has in Nigeria been allowed to some of the most advanced Moslem courts, presided over by judges learned in Mohamedan law. The sentence is pronounced by the ruler. Such powers are regarded as inherent in the ruler of a Moslem State. "Now we know that the Emir is Emir indeed since he has the power of life and death," the people of Illorin are reported to have exclaimed.

Such cases are very carefully reviewed by the Resident, who usually has some knowledge of Mohamedan law, and his report and recommendation must be submitted to the Governor when reviewing the sentence in council.[1] Owing to the admis-

[1] See note on p. 543 *re* capital powers of native courts in Sierra Leone.

sion of hearsay evidence, the weight attached to the Koranic oath, and a procedure which appears to us crude, it is often difficult to decide between the desire not to interfere with decisions which are in accord with the native law, and fully accepted by popular opinion on the one hand, and the fear of concurrence in the execution of a possibly innocent man on the other. The Secretary of State considered that "unless the capital sentence has been passed for an offence which is not punishable by death under English law, or unless the facts disclosed in the *Alkali's* report on the case, or in that of the Resident, are such that there is a serious likelihood of a miscarriage of justice if the sentence is carried out, the Governor and the Executive Council are justified in accepting the verdict and sentence of a native Mohamedan court which has passed a sentence within its powers, after a trial carried out in accordance with the procedure enjoined by the native law, and not obviously inequitable, even though that procedure is widely different from the practice of English criminal courts." Since the native courts are integral parts of the machinery of administration in a British protectorate, the Governor cannot evade responsibility for their action. Additional evidence is therefore called for when necessary, and the Resident goes fully into every case before recording his recommendation.

Difficulty arises in dealing with female criminals, for unless there are separate quarters in the prison, with female wardresses (and there may not be a native administration prison at all), it is manifestly impossible to confine them, even temporarily. Moslem judges in Africa are liberal in their treatment of women (who, under the Maliki law, may hold and bequeath real and personal property and contract debts, &c.), but since the Koran, like the Mosaic law, prescribes death by stoning for the offence of adultery, they maintain the necessity of substituting a light birching on the shoulders.

The person who inflicted the chastisement had to keep some cowrie-shells under his or her armpit, so as to prevent the raising of the arm to strike with force. If the cowries dropped the culprit was reprieved. It was, I believe, universally allowed to "buy the lashes," if preferred, by paying from 1s. to ½d. for each stroke. Repugnant as the infliction of corporal punishment on a woman must be to the mind of a British officer, it is questionable whether in the circumstances it could be said to be "repugnant to natural justice and humanity," which would justify intervention. But with the improvement of native prisons, and the provision of separate cells for women, it has been possible to prohibit the practice altogether. It has, of course, never been inflicted by a British court.[1]

In reviewing the findings of a native court a nice discrimination is often required between unnecessary interference with native custom on the one hand, and the violation of natural justice on the other. Thus the payment of blood-money in expiation of certain cases of homicide may not be repugnant to natural justice, and when admissible under Moslem law it has been ruled that interference is not necessary, though the penalty does not accord with our views. But to demand it from relations or fellow-villagers, where no connivance has been shown, would not be in accord with justice. Lifelong imprisonment for debt would be equally inadmissible.

Some even of the devout Moslems who interpret the Koranic law are not immune from a lingering belief in the power of the "Evil Eye," and in their endeavours to give due regard to pagan custom are found to differ considerably in their treatment of witchcraft cases, whether it be the complaint of the person bewitched or the murder of a person supposed to be a wizard. The same difficulty is presented in a British court, and confronts the Governor in his exercise of the prerogative.[2]

It may, for instance, be in evidence that the ordeal by poison was actuated by a profound belief that it would be harmless if the accused were innocent. The accuser may or may not have been actuated by malice, and those

[1] The present Governor of Nigeria says that he had caused exhaustive inquiry to be made on this subject, and was satisfied that the "floggings" are administered with the object of subjecting an adulteress "to acute humiliation rather than to any very severe bodily pain." He adds: "I see no reason actively to interfere with the practice of the Mohamedan courts. Of their own motion they have reduced the very severe punishments prescribed for adultery in the Koran to an actual and more or less publicly-inflicted humiliation, accompanied by corporal punishment of an almost nominal description. I have asked the Residents, however, to let it be generally known that the Government dislikes the idea of women being flogged, and would be glad to see the practice die out. To do more than this, however, would, in my opinion, be inexpedient at the present time."—Speech, 31st December 1920.

[2] Similar cases are not infrequent even in Great Britain. See the amazing story from the Channel Isles in the 'Times' of 8th October 1920.

who administered the ordeal may have had no option but to do so when it was demanded, or the accuser may have killed the supposed witch in defence, as he believed, of his own life. Or twins may have been murdered, or even human sacrifice perpetrated to avert, as they believed, disaster from the village.

The degree of criminality is lessened by the superstitious terror which prompted the crime, but the necessity for stamping out such practices compels recourse to deterrent penalties, and since fear of death was the motive, no less penalty than death will be deterrent. It appears to me, therefore, that the only course which an administration can follow is to see that it is thoroughly understood in every village that participation in such deeds will involve the death penalty, while exercising the prerogative in any case in which any extenuating circumstances can be shown, and discriminating between wizards who exercise their supposed powers beneficently, or for gain or revenge.

As a general rule, offences against the person are appropriately dealt with by a native court, while offences against public order would be tried in a British court. Competent authorities assert that it is more in accord with native modes of thought that the latter class should be regarded as private wrongs, and that actions for damages should be encouraged rather than trials for criminal offences.

A British court would, of course, deal with all offences which are not such under native law, or are not made justiciable by a native court, by virtue of a by-law. Even if thus brought within the purview of a native court, offences which we regard as serious may to them appear venial, and in such a case they would preferably be dealt with by a provincial court.

If important evidence is inadmissible in a Moslem court—such as that of a son against his father or a slave against his master—and its omission affected the issue of the trial, the case should obviously be transferred. Similarly, if a difference in religion was likely in any way to prejudice the chances of a litigant, or to cause favour or disfavour to be shown towards an accused person—as, for instance, if a Moslem murderer were leniently treated because his victim was a non-Moslem or a slave; or if the evidence of a Moslem was held to override that of a Christian or pagan; or if inheritance by will were denied to an "unbeliever"; or in cases among primitive tribes where superstition or the position of the accused might affect the course of justice.

On the other hand, in cases of quasi-religious rebellion, such as the frequent emergence of a "Mahdi" in the early days of British rule in Nigeria, the passing of sentence by the native ruler, who is also the religious head, may serve to convince the peasantry that they have been misled. But it is very necessary to see that vindictive sentences are not inflicted, or—such is the native mind—that the idea does not gain credence that Government fears to try the case, or desires excessive penalties.

A superior native court—especially the judicial council of a ruler—may be more competent to deal with a disputed land boundary where ancient rights are in question than a British court. It is of importance that such decisions should be recorded in its archives, especially in the cases of extra-territorial allegiance to which I have referred elsewhere.

The native courts of Nigeria which I have endeavoured to describe are still in their infancy, and the ideals regarding them, which the British staff hope some day to realise, are only as yet partially achieved. But there is a consensus of opinion both in the north and south that they command confidence, that their judgments are generally fair and just, and their returns passably accurate. That they serve a useful purpose is evident from the number of cases, almost entirely civil disputes, with which they deal.[1] It is interesting to learn that the by-laws promulgated by the chiefs are appreciated, and in Sokoto cattle-owners appeal to the courts against persons violating the rules against the isolation of diseased herds.

The illiterate African, when clothed with power, is like other people apt to misuse it, and for the better protection of the native population against illegal acts by the soldiery it is desirable that "civil offences" (viz., criminal offences by persons subject to military law against the ordinary law of the country) should be tried by the civil courts to which the people are accustomed to look for redress.

[1] The Lieutenant-Governor of the Northern Provinces, in his report for 1919, states that there were 407 native courts, which dealt with 148,255 cases. There were 69 prisons, and a daily average of 2512 prisoners in a population of nine millions.

One of the most difficult of all offences to deal with—as has also been found in India—is the crime of extortion in the name of Government, and of lying reports brought against those who have failed to satisfy the blackmailers, to which I have already referred (pp. 135 and 252). The ignorant peasantry are easily misled, especially if the impostor is wearing part of a soldier's uniform. Even if aware of the illegality of the demand, they may regard it as a lesser evil than having to go long distances to complain, or to defend themselves against his charges, involving detention as witnesses when their crops demand their care. They fear the plausible lies of the accused, and his greater familiarity with the ways of the white man.

Continual touring through the villages by the District Officers, the hearing of the complaint on the spot and the infliction of a flogging when the offender is convicted, and education, are the only methods of checking this hateful offence, which brings odium on the Government. As a measure of precaution, it is desirable that all *bona fide* messengers should carry a badge of office; that the sale of discarded uniforms should be prohibited; and that payment should never be made through a third person. The difficulty of finding honest subordinates is one of the greatest causes of anxiety in tropical administration. Forced presents to those in authority, though sanctioned by custom, cease to be legitimate when the recipient is a salaried officer of Government or of the native administration.

In the tropics there is stagnation during the season of the heavy rains. Crime and litigation both decrease, while travelling (on assize) is most difficult. This therefore is the period fixed for the court vacation; and in West Africa, where officials have four months' leave after completing a year in Africa, it is much to the advantage of public work, as well as more popular with the judges themselves, that they should take their leave annually during the court vacation.

One vacation judge can carry on the urgent work of the court, while the police magistrates in the larger commercial centres deal with minor crime and other business. These officers in Nigeria belong to the judicial and legal department, while the "station magistrates" in the smaller centres, who are engaged less with court work than with municipal affairs, are selected from the administrative staff.

The description of the constitution of the new frontier province in India (which was inaugurated by Lord Curzon in 1901 after over twenty years of discussion), given by the 'Times' correspondent, is in many respects so apposite to the conditions of Africa that I make no apology for quoting a few passages.[1]

"There is," says the writer, "a growing school of critics who condemn our present system of administration in India for . . . the complicated legal machinery of the courts of justice; who assert that . . . the executive officers are the slaves of clerical routine, and the judicial ones of legal technicalities; that both alike have lost their old touch with the people, and that the only classes which benefit by this development are the office babus, and the barristers and pleaders, parasitic growths alien to the soil of India, but thriving on the system we have introduced. With this condition of things is contrasted the golden age of personal contact and paternal Government, of rough justice and true sympathy between the white men and the natives of the soil. . . . The complicated land tenure in the Peshawar district gives unusual opportunities for disputes, and of these the *bona fide* ones can often be settled out of court, but those of a bogus nature are carried on in a spirit of gambling, from court to court, in the hope that victory may at last be achieved by the ingenuity of a pleader or the ignorance of a judge. . . . The *jirga* and the village organisation still exist (among the Baluchis) in their primitive vigour, and by taking these as their basis the authorities have been able to dispense with much of the judicial machinery of a larger province, and yet at the same time to keep down crime within much narrower bounds. In all cases, civil, criminal, and revenue, except serious offences committed by European British subjects, a single officer is the final appellate authority; he disposes of them with a minimum of legal formalities, and he prohibits pleaders except by special permission from practising in Baluchistan. The general principle is to put pressure on the people, through their natural leaders, to settle their own disputes, and to hold those leaders responsible for the good behaviour of their village or clan."

The results, says the writer, are admitted to be "wonderfully good," and he lays special emphasis on "the restriction

[1] 'Times,' 13th November 1901.

of the privileges of pleaders, and the curtailment of appeals." The reforms, he tells us, are not without their critics, and to their criticisms must be added the protests of the pleaders.

The judicial system adopted by the French in their African territories cannot fail to be of interest, and since it is tersely though comprehensively described in the Foreign Office Handbook, recently issued,[1] I have added as an appendix to this chapter the account which it gives.

APPENDIX.

THE JUDICIAL SYSTEM IN FRENCH TROPICAL AFRICA.

"The judicial system rests upon the decrees of November 10, 1903, and of August 16, 1912, the latter of which replaces the system of native courts provided for in the former enactment. A complete distinction is drawn between the sphere of authority of French and native courts. The former exercise jurisdiction exclusively in all cases where both parties are not natives of French West Africa or French Equatorial Africa, or of foreign possessions between these limits, and do not enjoy in their native places the rights of Europeans. The cases which affect natives are reserved for the native courts; but natives may agree to submit their civil actions to the French courts, in which case French law is applied in determining their rights. If either party is a European, French law is always applied to the exclusion of native law.

"The *French courts* form an elaborate hierarchy of (1) Justices of the Peace with very limited powers; (2) Justices of the Peace with extended powers at Kayes, Bamako, Kankan, and Bové, and Tribunals of First Instance at Konakry, Grand Bassam, Kotonou, Saint Louis, and Dakar, with full powers in civil and commercial matters, and considerable jurisdiction in less serious criminal offences; (3) Assize courts to deal with crimes proper; and (4) a Court of Appeal, which hears appeals from the Courts of First Instance and from Justices of the Peace with extended powers. Decisions in these colonial courts are subject to revision by the Courts of Cassation.

"The *native courts* are also arranged hierarchically. They comprise (1) village courts consisting of the chief, who may give decisions in civil and commercial matters if submitted to him, but whose decisions are not binding on the parties; (2) the courts of the subdivisions, composed of a native president and two native assessors with deliberative voices, selected by the head of the colony on the

[1] No. 100 of 1920, pp. 7-9 and 13.

recommendation of the head of the division: these courts have full civil and commercial jurisdiction, and criminal jurisdiction in such matters as are not reserved to the tribunals of the divisions, subject to appeal to these tribunals; (3) divisional tribunals, consisting of the chief civil officer, assisted by two native assessors with consultative voices only. The divisional tribunal hears appeals from the courts of the subdivision in all civil and commercial matters, and from decisions in criminal cases of a grave character, including murder, dangerous wounding, pillage, arson, kidnapping, poisoning of wells, and mutilations; it has also an exclusive criminal jurisdiction in respect of offences of slave-dealing, crimes committed by native Government agents or against them in the exercise of their duties, crimes committed by soldiers in union with non-soldiers, usurpation of Government authority, offences against regulations affecting matters specially assigned to these courts, and offences against the safety of the State; and (4) a special section of the Court of Appeal, composed of three councillors, two officials, and two natives, charged with the duties of homologation and annulment. Any decision of the inferior courts may be submitted to it by the Procurator-General; and it deals also with every sentence of over five years' imprisonment or in respect of a slave-trade offence, pronounced by the divisional tribunals, and with sentences exceeding six months' imprisonment or 500 francs fine imposed on native Government agents.

"The native courts apply native law; in cases where the parties are subject to different laws they follow the law of the place of conclusion in respect of contracts (including marriage), and in respect of questions of status that of the defendant's tribe. The penalties allowed are death, imprisonment for life or for a term not exceeding twenty years, banishment for the same period, and fines; penalties for breach of contract are permitted if in accord with native law. Europeans who have disputes with natives may submit themselves to the courts, in which case native law is applied. These rules are subject to modification both in Senegal and in certain portions of Upper Senegal and the Niger, in the Niger Territory, and in Mauretania. . . .

"Great progress has also been made in the application to the natives of regular administration; and, though the administrators necessarily retain special powers of taking repressive measures against natives without bringing them before the established courts, the Governor-General has laid it down (circular of September 28, 1913) that, since the enactment of the decree of August 12, 1912, the use of these reserved powers should be restricted to cases where political considerations render action by the ordinary courts dangerous, or at least highly undesirable."

CHAPTER XXIX.

SOME OTHER PROBLEMS.

A. *Municipal Self-Government.*—Disinclination to pay rates—Autonomy depends on financial solvency—Nomination or election of councillors—Varying types of municipalities—Constitution and powers in Nigeria—Distinctive features of townships.

B. *Armed Forces and their Employment.*—African races as soldiers—Points to be noted—Danger of discontent among troops—The application of force—Home critics—Methods of maintaining law and order—The attitude of primitive tribes—Mistaken methods—The avoidance of occasions of trouble—"Hill-top" pagans—Method of using force—Military operations—Enforcing the civil law—Measures to avoid conflict—Nature of penalty—Precautions.

(*a*) MUNICIPAL SELF-GOVERNMENT.

THROUGHOUT the foregoing chapters I have urged the wisdom of decentralisation on the one hand, and on the other hand of allowing the natives to manage their own domestic affairs, in proportion to their ability. In chapter x. I discussed the devolution of authority to "native administrations" for the control of executive duties, and in chapters xxvii. and xxviii. I described how the principles could be applied to judicial work by the creation of native courts administering native law and custom, and approved by-laws.

The third sphere to which this principle is applicable is that of municipal responsibility. The two former applied to the vast mass of the population, from the primitive savage to the "advanced community," but this form of devolution applies, as I have said in chapter iv., to the educated class of natives, and to the unofficial European community. Here is the opportunity for the educated African to show that he is in earnest in his desire for self-government, by hearty co-operation in the conduct of those affairs which most immediately concern his own interests. Nor will occasion be lacking to prove his ability to control the welfare of those illiterate classes who live under conditions more nearly resembling tribal life, for every municipality has its native town peopled by these folk.

How is it, then, that the strong movement towards municipal control, which is so marked a feature of social progress in Europe, finds so little corresponding expression in those large cities on the West African coast, where the educated African and the European unofficials are chiefly to be found? The reason is that since the fundamental basis of autonomy is financial independence, the funds at the disposal of a municipality must be derived (as in every civilised community) from local rates and taxes; and, with a few notable exceptions, the natives who clamour for the right to govern the millions of the interior are disinclined to make a contribution, however moderate, to municipal funds for the right to govern themselves. They content themselves with agitating by the press and platform that town councillors should be elected and not nominated by the Governor. It is a mere side-issue, with which I will presently deal.

Manifestly the Government, as trustee for the governed, is only justified in allocating such a sum of money, raised by taxation from the people of the interior (on whom falls the bulk of the customs and other taxes), as may seem to be reasonable and equitable for the maintenance of the port and other facilities in which the hinterland is interested. For the rest, the greater part of the cost of purely municipal services and amenities must be provided by those for whose benefit they are maintained.

So long, therefore, as the municipal funds are dependent on a grant from revenue, complete local control must be deferred, and it is the duty of the Governor to select for the proper supervision of those funds the councillors who in his judgment are best suited to discharge that responsibility.

These are nominated at the suggestion of those best able to advise. They are selected for their local influence, their experience of affairs, and their public spirit, nor do I recollect any instance where the nomination has given rise to popular dissatisfaction. It is also obviously desirable that any possible friction between unofficial members of the Legislative Council and the town councillors of the capital city should be avoided.

Subject to these provisos there can be no objection to the election of the members of the municipal body, but since the European, Asiatic, and native communities represent somewhat different though not antagonistic interests, it is desirable that each should elect its own members, and perhaps preferable that the functions of legislative and municipal councillor should be combined in the same individual. The European community has, I think, usually been satisfied with nomination by the Governor, nor has the native community shown any great eagerness to exercise the vote when granted.

As with the native administrations, and the native courts, and indeed any and every other institution in Africa, it is obvious that the constitution and the powers delegated to a town council must vary according to the circumstances, and the degree of its development. In some the education and intelligence of its native citizens may well fit them to bear an equal, and in native affairs a predominant, share with the European community, and the council can be entrusted with large powers of civic responsibility. Others may claim a large measure of autonomy on the grounds that they are financially self-supporting. In one, the policy of segregation may have simplified many questions, and differentiated the responsibilities of European and native members respectively. In another, a survival of tribal authority may co-exist with the progressive educated section, and claim its share of control.

The constitution and the powers of the municipal body must therefore vary according to the importance of the community, the measure of its ability to accept, and discharge satisfactorily, independent or semi-independent powers, and the degree to which it is able to provide its own financial requirements.

The township ordinances and the regulations made under them in the several African dependencies are very voluminous. In Nigeria the general principle has been adopted of including all matters directly connected with health and sanitation in a "Public Health Ordinance," for the proper enforcement of which the medical and sanitary departments, and their representatives on the town councils, are responsible, while all matters of internal control and finance, of roads, buildings, and lands, &c., are included in a "township's ordinance." The whole or any part of the regulations under these ordinances may be applied to any particular township, or varied in their application by special rules or by-laws.

Townships under the control of a "local authority," and duly defined as to area, are created by a 'Gazette' notice. They are in Nigeria of three classes. The local authority in the first class is a "town council" consisting of official and unofficial members—European and native,—the intention being that so soon as it becomes independent of a grant from revenue the unofficials should constitute an elected majority. It appoints its own officers and employees, and is charged with the administration within its area of specified ordinances (to the extent prescribed), such as those relating to motor traffic, liquor, dogs, water-works, auctions, markets, pawnbrokers, and public health, &c., and it receives as revenue the rates, fees, charges, and fines which accrue. It is also empowered to make by-laws (subject to approval) for giving effect to these laws, and for the good order and control of the township.

The local authority—usually a "station magistrate"—of a second-class township is appointed by the Governor, and exercises the ordinary powers of a corporation, assisted by an "advisory board" of nominated officials (including the health officer) and unofficials including natives. The chairman of the board may be senior in standing to the local authority, who is charged with the execution of routine duties, and the carrying out of the decisions of a majority of the board, subject to the concurrence of the Lieut.-Governor. Rules and by-laws are made by the Governor, and include authority to administer such laws, and impose such licences, &c., as may be desirable. The local authority, working in conjunction with the medical, public works, and other departments, deals with sanitation, housing, roads, markets, land leases, water-supply, public gardens, &c., and collects rates, rents, and licence fees.

The third class consists of such small centres as contain few European or educated native residents. It is an embryo, and the local authority—usually the District Officer—is without an advisory board or a township fund. The township estimates of revenue and expenditure are subject to the approval of the Lieut.-Governor.

The essential feature of a township is that it is an enclave outside the jurisdiction of the native authority and native courts, which are thus relieved of the difficult task (which is foreign to their functions) of controlling the alien natives and employees of the Government and Europeans, who, together with natives engaged in ministering to the requirements of the township, constitute the native residents. Persons properly belonging to the native jurisdiction are as far as possible excluded, and the local authority has power to eject undesirable persons and prostitutes, subject to appeal. Exceptions, of course, exist, as in many of the old coast towns.

Townships of the first and second class are placed in the Supreme Court jurisdiction, of which court the local authority in a second-class township is a commissioner. British law is administered, and no resident may own a slave. Recreation grounds and club-houses are encouraged for social intercourse. General principles are laid down as to the size and care of "compounds," the location of outhouses, the construction of roads and avenues, precautions against fires, the control of markets and hawkers, the overcrowding of native residential sites, offensive trades, and similar matters, including, in particular, the rules regarding segregation with which I have dealt in a former chapter. New townships should never be located close to a native city.

(*b*) ARMED FORCES AND THEIR EMPLOYMENT.

In my earliest African experience it fell to my task to engage levies of wild and undisciplined savages to withstand the slave-raiders in Nyasaland; later, to create the first nucleus of a disciplined force in Uganda; and finally, to raise the West African Frontier Force in Nigeria, which eventually became the model for the troops of the West African dependencies. I have therefore had some experience of the African as a fighting man. The typical African races may, as soldiers, be described as keen and courageous fighters, impulsive, obedient, and faithful, with implicit trust in their leaders. Under the best officers they are capable of becoming excellent troops in action. Their weak points are, that they lack a sense of responsibility, which makes them undependable in reporting crime and in exercising control as N.C.Os., and unreliable as sentries. These drawbacks are less manifest in the negroid than in the pure negro races, while the nilotic tribes—known as "Sudanese" and "Blacks"—though not intelligent, are more dependable in these respects, and the Hausas approximate to them.

The loyalty and gallantry of our native African troops in the war were the pride and the well-merited reward of the officers who had trained them, and who led them in action. It would, I think, be untrue to say that they gave their lives to uphold the British Empire, for that was a conception beyond their understanding. No doubt they hated what they knew of German rule, but their chief motives were, I think, personal love of their officers, the terms of pay offered, the decorations they hoped to win, ignorance of the conditions of warfare to which they would be exposed, and their natural courage and love of adventure.

There are a few points which I think it is worth while to note in connection with the military side of African administration, and I will put them very briefly :—

(*a*) Recruiting should not be restricted exclusively to Moslems, who may be susceptible to religious propaganda. Diversity of language is the chief difficulty in using pagan tribes, but they learn the *lingua franca* with surprising rapidity.

(*b*) The period of enlistment should be for as long as possible, and re-engagement should be encouraged in every way. The cost and labour of training men who are later discharged as unlikely to make good soldiers is thus saved, efficiency is increased, and, above all, the danger of flooding the country with men trained to arms and discipline and European methods of warfare is lessened. It is true that the material for reserves is *pro tanto* decreased—a matter which I do not personally regard as of much importance.

(*c*) The number of troops it is necessary to maintain depends partly on their mobility, partly on the proportion of Europeans to natives. It can be reduced as railways, roads, and mechanical transport add to mobility. The proportion of Europeans should not, I think, be less than 4 per cent in peace and 10 per cent or 12 per cent in action. I am strongly opposed to any form of conscription.[1]

[1] In the war Nigeria was able to recruit all, and more than all, the troops asked for, for service overseas, without any form of conscription, though the

(*d*) To promote fellow-feeling and concord, officers and men should, as far as is compatible with their own special duties, assist in civil work, and be identified in the general aims and policy of the administration. Officers and British N.C.Os. should be encouraged to learn the language, for an officer interested in the people acquires a better understanding of his own men, and his time is more fully employed.

(*e*) The employment of native levies in aid of the troops, and *a fortiori* the issue of arms to natives for the purpose of carrying out reprisals—a course, as we are informed in a consular report, which is occasionally adopted by the French—is, in my opinion, a policy which may lead to such grave abuses, and is so subversive of discipline among the troops, that it should, I think, be universally prohibited, unless the very existence of the administration is at stake.[1] No non-combatant natives other than necessary transport should accompany a force engaged to enforce the law.

(*f*) The arms of the force should be kept in an arms house, under the close supervision of the British N.C.Os., and issued only when required by the troops on duty or at drill.

(*g*) The system of deferred pay is, I think, a valuable one. It acts as a check on desertion, and provides a soldier on discharge with a lump sum to start life as a trader, thereby acting as a great incentive to enlistment.

(*h*) Soldiers should not be exempt from fatigue work, which is a valuable part of their discipline. With the diminution of purely military duties—especially of fighting—I should like to see a considerable part, if not the whole, of our African forces converted into engineer or pioneer corps, employed on railway and road construction, and similar work, made popular by a small extra working pay. Such attempts as I have seen in this direction have been wonderfully successful.

(*j*) Similarly the armed constabulary, known as "Civil

Sultans of Sokoto and Bornu asked permission to use compulsion. Conscription was established in the French Colonies in Africa by the decree of 7th February 1912. The terms were four years' service between the ages of twenty and twenty-eight, with liability for foreign service.—Handbook 100, p. 13. The 'Times' (16th April 1918) estimates that the contingents for the war, including labourers, numbered 700,000.

[1] In the 'Annual Report for East Africa, 1909-1910,' it is stated that "the system of issuing arms and ammunition to the rubber collectors (in Tanaland) has proved most successful, as the men have confidence that they will get all they make, instead of as formerly having to pay toll to the Somalis in food and produce."—Cd. 5467 of 1911. The system is, I think, one to be deprecated, if indeed it is not in violation of our obligations under the Brussels Act.

Police," should, I suggest, be employed in all townships and organised districts as an unarmed force, and trained in detective and purely police duties. Only those small detachments employed in out-stations to supply escorts, guard prisoners and prisons, or to relieve the military forces, should bear arms, so that the latter may be kept together in larger units under their own officers for drill and discipline.

Where a handful of white men are engaged in the difficult task of introducing peace and good government among a vast and ignorant population, the chief danger, as we have learnt to our cost in India, in Uganda, in the Sudan, Somaliland, the Gold Coast, and Sierra Leone, lies in possible disaffection among the troops. This has, I think, invariably been due to grievances of their own, and not to political causes. I have seen, alike among Indian troops in the Afghan war, and in Nigeria in the advance on Kano, how the native soldier identifies himself with the Government he serves, and will march against his co-religionists, and even against his own village. Mutinics may generally be ascribed to lack of touch and ignorance of causes of discontent.

It is impossible, therefore, to exaggerate the importance of selecting the right type of officer and British N.C.O. Men who have sympathy with and are proud of their soldiers will be followed with blind devotion, while the martinet who despises his men, loses his temper, and strikes or abuses them—happily an extremely rare phenomenon—should be got rid of as a public danger. I am not in favour of tribal companies, which lead to quarrels in barracks, but battalions or wings of battalions, composed of races which have no affinities with the population of the region in which they are serving, and even the introduction of an alien battalion may be a wise precaution.

There was a time—I am not sure that it has wholly passed—when it seemed the fashion for good folk in England to accuse the African administrator of partiality to "punitive expeditions," and to sneer at his explanations. The tone of the press and of questions in the House of Commons, and the accusations of certain societies, led the man on the spot to feel that he was regarded as a swashbuckler, ever ready to carry fire and sword into some peaceful African territory, that he might lay claim to having been the first to hoist the flag, or might gain some paltry decoration. Miss Kingsley led the way, in contrast to what she called "the honourable wars of conquest by the French," and even an African administrator was found to declare that "there would be fewer of these little wars if there were no decorations." [1]

Now the British military officer in tropical Africa is usually a public-school boy, with the traditions of fair-play common to that class. The use of modern rifles against antagonists armed only with archaic weapons is contrary to that sense of fair-play. He is, moreover, almost invariably very sympathetic to primitive races, and regards them as his own special protégés. Military officers, in my experience, when employed in administrative work, are perhaps especially apt to champion their own charges, and to shield them from the penalties which their acts may have merited.

The British officer is very sensitive to the charge of reckless disregard of native life, and resents it very bitterly. Not once but very many times I have known an officer, with an armed escort at his heels, expose his life recklessly to a shower of poisoned arrows, a scratch from one of which would probably mean death, rather than fire a shot, in the conviction that he would presently be able to settle matters without bloodshed. And I have sometimes wondered whether those who without knowledge accuse him of carelessness of human life would have stood the test themselves.

British officers engaged in African work appreciate the motives of those societies which have constituted themselves the protectors of subject races, whether from slavery, liquor, opium, or maladministration, for they are championing the causes which the administrative officer generally has most at heart. But he feels that they are sometimes too ready to believe evil of others, and to start with the hypothesis that there is something to conceal. During very many years of African administration it is my experience that it is more often necessary to warn the British officer against exposing his own life too freely than against needlessly sacrificing those of others.

The maintenance of law and order depends in every country on the power of coercion by force, and is supported by force if collectively defied. The ultimate sanction for recourse to the use of armed force to compel obedience to the law is derived from the same source as the right to inflict a judicial

[1] Sir Chas. Eliot, 'The East African Protectorate,' p. 200.

penalty. It is inherent in the right to govern, and that right entails the obligation of protecting all sections of the community from outrage and violence. The Government which is unable or unwilling to do this ceases to be worthy of the name. Though, as Mr Chamberlain finely said twenty-three years ago, the idea that colonies were paying dependencies had been replaced by the idea of kinship, and the sense of possession in the tropics had given place to that of obligation, for "our rule could never be justified unless it added to the happiness and prosperity of the people. Nevertheless (he added) you cannot have omelettes without breaking eggs, you cannot destroy the practices of barbarism, of slavery, of superstition which for centuries have desolated the interior of Africa without the use of force." [1]

Judicial powers are exercised in accordance with the strict interpretation of the law, which lays down the method by which law-breakers shall be brought to trial, and the maximum penalty for each class of offence; but when the law is defied and is temporarily in abeyance, and cannot be enforced by the ordinary processes, the methods by which recognition of the law must be restored are dictated by the Head of the executive, without appeal to judicial tribunals. It is therefore essential that his personal approval—or that of the Lieut.-Governor or other responsible officer to whom limited powers in this regard may have been delegated—should be given. Without such approval the employment of armed force, beyond the limits of legal sanction, except for self-defence, renders an officer liable to process of law.

In Africa you are dealing with tribes who, as a general rule, regard force as the sole arbiter, who are combative, and value life very lightly indeed. Let me put a case in illustration. The young bloods of a tribe, confident in their own weapons, and ignorant of the power of the rifle, think maybe that a "scrap" with the white man, who objects to their raids on less warlike neighbours, would not be unattractive. Conciliatory talks in such a case are obviously useless, and are only tolerated by the tribe in order to gain opportunity to count the number of the escort, or to provide a favourable occasion for a surprise attack. The British officer, hating to "mow down" the brave savages who expose themselves so

[1] 'Proceedings of Royal Colonial Institute,' vol. xxviii. pp. 236, 237 (1896 and 1897).

unknowingly, reserves his fire, and in the encounter only two or three are killed. For the moment they are cowed, and come in to hear the white man's terms. Probably he imposes a fine of a few goats, and insists that for the future they shall refrain from attacking their neighbours. They readily agree, and presently they are all chaffering with the soldiers on friendly terms.

After the next beer-drinking the young men propose to make a foray. The elders remind them of the compact with the British officer. "What is this white man," they retort, "that we should fear him? Had he not fifty soldiers, and he only killed three of us? These rifles which make such a terrible noise are not so deadly as our own poisoned arrows. But we will make an overwhelming combination this time, and be sure of success. Moreover, we will attack him unawares in a place of thick jungle." So messages are sent round the whole district—another fight takes place. This time the tribesmen, despising the rifle, charge recklessly. Their numbers are great, and the troops have to fire in earnest to avoid being overwhelmed. The casualties among the tribesmen are very heavy. They count them up, and decide that the rifle is stronger than the bow and arrow, and the game is not good enough. The officer's report perhaps reads—"Enemy's casualties, 50 killed; ours, 1 killed, 2 wounded." "Mere butchery!" cries the critic.

This hypothetical case suggests reflections. If in the first attack the officer had fired with more deadly effect, and demonstrated the power of the rifle beyond doubt, the ultimate loss of life would have been much less. The critic would perhaps have asked, "Could you not have beaten off the attack with less loss of life?" and receiving an affirmative reply, would suggest that here indeed was a case of ruthless slaughter for the mere love of killing.

I will take another case. A friendly tribe in the neighbourhood of a British trading depot welcomes the advent of the administration, and gladly pays the nominal tax, of perhaps 6d. a head per annum, as a token of its intention to keep the peace. Presently it is raided by a neighbour, and it appeals for the promised protection. Perhaps it is quite ready to undertake a vendetta of reprisals, including the carrying off of women, &c., but is restrained by the law of the white man.

The Government sends a message to the aggressive tribe, informing them that it is loath to resort to force, but if they will not desist from attacking peaceful neighbours, there will be no alternative. In one such case I received a reply that they had eaten every kind of man except a white man, and they invited me to come that they might see what I tasted like.

These are instances, which it were easy to multiply, of the occasions in which an African administrator finds himself compelled to resort to force. As the power of the Government to enforce its prohibition of inter-tribal war and the murder and looting of traders and enslaving of persons becomes known, and still more as the District Officer gets into closer and closer touch with the tribesmen, and relations of mutual liking and goodwill are formed, the necessity of resorting to force decreases, until it is only necessary in the case of bandit communities, with whom all other methods have failed. To avoid occasions of trouble, turbulent districts are declared to be "unsettled," and Europeans are forbidden to enter them. Government and native court messengers are not sent into districts where they are likely to be attacked, and armed natives are never sent to effect arrests by force.

Some corners of tropical Africa, however, resemble the condition of predatory warfare which is characteristic of animal life in the ocean's depths. Centuries of slave-raiding and of inter-tribal warfare had driven some of the pagan communities to build their villages among the boulders and caves, on or near the crests of the hills, where they were invulnerable to attack. A little precarious cultivation in the valley below—whence their women daily toil up the hillside with the day's supply of water—forms their livelihood, with the exception of the loot of passing traders.

It has been the aim of the Nigerian Government to induce these "hill-top pagans," as they are called, to build their villages in the plain below, and this has been a condition imposed whenever their lawless actions have necessitated coercive measures. It is a practical guarantee of the adoption of peaceful agriculture. Few now remain in such fastnesses.[1]

When, therefore, the law has been defied by the murder of a Government agent or others, or by the head-hunting propensities of a predatory tribe, recourse must be had to force,

[1] See note, p. 222.

if the community refuses to surrender the murderers, or to allow their arrest, and accepts collective responsibility for the crime—threatening the agents of Government with violence. The people of England have of late years had these conditions brought home to them in Ireland, and can realise them as they did not realise before.

The object which the party of police or soldiers has in view is the arrest of the original offenders and their abettors for trial by due process of law, and the imposition of some penalty on the community under the Collective Punishment Ordinance, to which I have referred in chapter xxvii. This object may sometimes be attained without bloodshed by the exhibition of a sufficiently imposing force.

In Nigeria, since the earliest days of the administration in the north, very explicit rules have been in operation regarding the conditions in which force, when unavoidable, may be applied, and the respective duties of the officer in command of the armed party on the one hand, and the civil officer on the other. Doubtless similar rules are in force in all our protectorates, and my reader who has not had personal experience of administration in Africa may be interested to know their nature.

In the first place, a clear distinction is drawn between military operations and the support of the civil power in enforcing obedience to the ordinary law. "Military operations" (now happily a thing almost entirely of the past) are undertaken when some widespread rising—due to the appearance of a local Mahdi, or the revival of the cult of some "Juju" or other cause—has taken place, accompanied perhaps by the murder of Europeans and Government employees, and there are possibilities of the disaffection spreading and assuming dangerous proportions.

The conduct of operations and the responsibility for the measures taken rest, in this case, primarily on the senior military officer, acting under the direct instructions of the Governor. A civil officer is attached to the force to carry out measures of pacification as they become possible.

At the present day, in Africa, the disciplined and well-armed forces at the disposal of Government are generally well able to carry out any necessary coercive measures without recourse to surprise attacks on villages by night, and fire should never be opened until the women—who are indistinguishable from the men even at a short distance—have been afforded time and a means of escape. Effective prohibition of looting, or indiscriminate burning of villages—which are demoralising to the troops and reminiscent of the slave-raider—is invariably enforced, and such acts are sternly repressed. It may generally be advisable to retain the troops for a time in a district in which military operations have been necessary, and their presence has a wholesome effect.

In all other cases the armed force is at the disposal of the civil officer for the enforcement of the civil law, and upon him rests the responsibility for its application, the officer in command of the armed party being responsible only for the actual conduct of the offensive and defensive measures, and the control of the constabulary or soldiers.

When, therefore, a community has committed serious crimes, and it is known that armed opposition will be offered to the administrative officer, an armed party accompanied by a medical officer is applied for by the Resident, who explains the reasons which necessitate intervention, unless extreme urgency compels him to accept responsibility for immediate action.

The officer in command of the " patrol "—who must always be a European—may not commence hostilities until required to do so by the civil officer, or extend the area of the operations, after the first resistance has been overcome, without his concurrence, and must justify his action if he continues them when the civil officer has intimated that in his opinion they should cease. On the other hand, it is for the officer in command to judge whether his force is adequate, to take proper precautions for their safety, and to control them in action.

On approaching the village the civil officer endeavours to get into touch with the people, informing them of his demands. If the threat is sufficient he proceeds with his escort to interview the chiefs, withdrawing again temporarily to give them time to comply with his terms, and surrender the criminals. If, however, the demands are ignored, he advances to occupy the village, after giving time for the non-combatants to clear out. Fire is not opened unless the force is attacked, or there is no possible doubt of the intention to attack. The object still is to occupy the empty village with as little loss of life as possible.

A fine of live-stock and grain is collected and supplies for the troops, and the civil officer again endeavours to get in touch with the chiefs and elders, informing them that they will not be seized if they come in to parley, but that if they do not, the principal huts will be fired—viz., those of the chiefs, and any which are known to belong to the criminals. If these pacific overtures have been unsuccessful, the troops remain in occupation until the chiefs make their submission, which would rarely be delayed beyond a day or two.

Thus extreme measures are only resorted to when the tribesmen refuse any other alternative. The punishments are not unduly severe, for in Africa the burning of a hut, which is built of reeds and grass, and rapidly reconstructed, is not so heavy a penalty as confiscation of live-stock and crops. Permanent crops (economic trees, &c.) are never destroyed, and it is preferable to seek out and inflict loss on the fighting men than to destroy food, thereby causing hunger to those who are not directly responsible.

A penalty is provisionally imposed after full inquiry under the Collective Punishment Ordinance, and is subject to the Governor's approval. If the casualties have been heavy, and if the criminals are surrendered, it is usually made as light as possible, especially if the tribe had not hitherto been under administrative control. It usually consists in the surrender of a number of arms or bows and arrows, a small fine, or a few days' work on road-making.

It is, of course, made clear to all officers, civil and military, that they have no authority to inflict any punishment whatever except by due process of law, or in such cases as those described by special authority from the head of the Government, and then only in conformity with the instructions.

Great care must be taken to ascertain that the alleged crimes have actually been committed, and also to ascertain whether they were perpetrated in reprisal for some outrage or crime done by the persons murdered or assaulted. Very full reports are required from both the civil and the military officer, with careful estimates of all casualties, and an account of the origin of the trouble and the measures taken to avert hostilities.

In the beginnings of African administration recourse to the use of force to restrain lawlessness and crime, and to stop inter-tribal disputes, was, as Mr Chamberlain said in the passage quoted, often unavoidable, but in my experience it has chiefly been due to the inadequacy in the numbers of the civil staff. The best officers hardly ever find it necessary, and the way in which turbulent and sometimes treacherous tribes have been converted into staunch friends—fairly law-abiding and progressive—by the sympathy and personal courage of the British District Officer, is nothing short of amazing.

CHAPTER XXX.

SOME OTHER PROBLEMS (*Continued*).

C. Missions.—The debt to Missions—Missions in East Africa—Missionaries and politics—Missions in West Africa—Evils of sectarian rivalry—Polygamy—Missions and European prestige—Social effects of Mission work—Missions in pagan districts—Missions to Moslems—Lord Salisbury's opinion—Restriction in Nigeria and the Sudan—Justification of restriction—The Moslem point of view—Concurrence of Government needed for establishment of Missions—Mission spheres—Religious ministrations.

D.—The Use of Intoxicants.—Import of spirits—Origin of movement for suppression—The position in West Africa—Measures of restriction—Prohibition by convention—The moral aspect of the traffic—The material aspect—The present position and policy—Native liquor—Control of native liquor—Distilleries.

(*c*) MISSIONS.

In the chapter on education I pointed out how great a debt the secular governments in tropical Africa owe to the efforts of the missionaries, by whom the bulk of the subordinate native staff has been trained, and I advocated a closer co-operation between the Government and Missions in their common task for the welfare of the people. It is to the devoted work of the missionary that the educated African owes his existence, for their schools preceded by many decades the comparatively recent Government educational establishments. If it has been said with some truth that trade preceded the flag in many parts of tropical Africa, it may be said with equal truth that missionary effort has generally preceded either, and opened the way for both. Missions have been the pioneers of our tropical Empire, and the wives of missionaries have done much by example, as well as by patient teaching.

To the eminently practical, unostentatious, and successful

work of Dr Laws and his colleagues of the Livingstone Mission, and to the other Scottish Missions in Nyasaland, it has already been my privilege to bear witness.[1] Though that country was, when I knew it, unappropriated by any European Power, and the scene of some of the worst barbarities of the slave-raider, the Missions, with remarkable restraint, refrained from using their influence to acquire secular power, or to precipitate the inevitable conflict with the aggressive forces of Islam, though they appreciated its aims (see p. 359).

In Uganda the circumstances were different. Here an isolated Mission had been established, 800 or 1000 miles in the interior, without any means of access by waterway, as the result of an outburst of enthusiasm evoked by Stanley's appeal. Protestant Missions were quickly followed by those of the Roman Church. Islam had already preceded the Christian Missions, and the adherents of the rival creeds fought out their differences in bloody battles. Great numbers of Christian converts were put to death, many of whom were burned alive. Twenty-two of them have recently been beatified as martyrs.[2]

The Christians won, and the Moslems were ousted from the country, till they were repatriated by me after a new defeat in 1891. With this common danger removed, the rival Christian sects (which, however, were perhaps more political than religious, and represented French and British influence respectively) could no longer be restrained from settling their mutual antagonism in the old way. In a pitched battle the Protestants were victorious, and Cardinal Lavigerie's vision of the revival of the temporal power of the Pope in an African State vanished away.[3] Uganda, like Nyasaland, became a British protectorate.

In these turbulent times it was difficult for the English (Protestant) Missions to refrain from participation in the politics of the country—the more so that their Roman Catholic (French) rivals frankly asserted their right to do so. Sir G. Portal stated that the respective missionaries were the veritable political leaders of the two factions. Later, however, when the head of the British Mission declared to the accredited representative of the secular power that he regarded this

[1] 'Rise of East African Empire,' vol. i. pp. 68-75.
[2] 'Times,' 7th June 1920.
[3] 'The British East African Company.' P. Macdermott, p. 129.

participation in political affairs as within the functions of the Missions, his view was discountenanced by the Home Committee of the Church Missionary Society.[1]

In the West, missionary effort was largely identified with the philanthropic impulses which, following the suppression of the overseas slave-trade, led to the founding of the Freetown settlement for liberated slaves at Sierra Leone. These Missions, with the exception of that to the Hausa Moslems, were chiefly confined to the coast and adjacent regions, and to the waterway of the Niger, until the extension of the administration to the interior, and the opening of railway communication, gave access to districts further afield.

The beneficial effect of Mission work in Africa is marred —no less than religious work in Christian countries—by sectarian rivalries and differences in teaching. The antagonism between the Protestants and Roman Catholics which so puzzled Mtesa of Uganda was no doubt accentuated by national rivalry, and resulted, as we have seen, in actual war. Elsewhere it is often disguised under a thin veneer.

The special dogmas of the "Memnonite Brothers in Christ," the "Pentecostal Missions," and many others, confuse the African, and have no doubt encouraged that secessional movement which in West Africa has led to the establishment of various African Churches in which polygamy is recognised, or some other departure from orthodoxy is introduced.

Church conferences have shown that there is a minority among those interested in Mission work who regard polygamy with tolerance, as an institution almost universal in the tropics from the earliest records of history. The early maturity of women, and the rapid evanescence of their sexual attractions in contrast with men; the postponement of the weaning of children (p. 66); the necessity for every woman to have a male protector in the conditions of African life; the practical impossibility of chastity among unattached women; the sanction of tradition and custom, are arguments brought forward in defence of the institution.

On the other hand, it is urged that it favours the wealthy and the powerful, and may even deprive some few of the poor of the possibility of finding a mate at all—though statistics show that in most African countries there is a preponderance —though not a large one—of females. Whether polygamy is

[1] 'Rise of East African Empire,' vol. ii. pp. 456-458.

responsible for an increase or decrease in the population appears to be in doubt, but it would certainly seem to decrease prostitution.

Some few Missions carry the ideal of the equality of man to a point which the intelligence of the primitive savage does not appreciate in its true significance. That a white man should come to Africa to do menial work in the furtherance of an altruistic ideal is not comprehensible to him, and the result is merely to destroy the missionary's own influence for good, and to lessen the prestige of Europeans, upon which the avoidance of bloodshed and the maintenance of law and order so largely depend in Africa.

The Colonial Office issued a regulation towards the close of the war that missionaries must obtain sanction before proceeding to West Africa. Its object, no doubt, was not primarily concerned with the financial position or the physical fitness of the applicant and his family for life in the tropics, but these things merit attention too. We read of the arrival of a ship with "several small children, being taken by their parents to stations many miles from medical aid, there to stay for two or three years"; of a missionary and his wife whose joint salary, in these times of excessive prices, was £160 per annum—too poor to buy meat.[1] I recollect a case of a missionary too poor to take his dying wife out of the country. These things do not promote the cause of the gospel. They do harm.

I have in chapter iv. discussed the influence of Christianity and of Islam respectively on the social life of their converts, remarking that the former has exerted a more denationalising effect than the latter—a result perhaps inevitable from the fact that Christianity has been promulgated by Europeans, and Islam by tribes naturalised in Africa. I am not, I hope, wrong in believing that Missions have of late years increasingly recognised the desirability of discouraging the adoption of European dress and habits by natives where they have not already become practically universal—as in the coast towns among the educated classes. The "black white-man" has been scornfully handled by his own press, and there seems now to be a growing tendency to a race-consciousness which deprecates the slavish imitation of European dress and customs.

[1] Letter from a "Tropical Resident for many Years."—'West Africa,' 23rd October 1920.

On the question of the advisability of the establishment of a Mission in a pagan region, a very natural divergence of opinion may arise between the missionary and the administrator who is charged with the maintenance of peace and good order. The latter fears that the advent of defenceless Europeans in turbulent districts, where as yet the machinery of Government has not been set up, or only partially introduced, and is unable to ensure adequate protection of life and property, may result in some untoward catastrophe which will necessitate a punitive expedition. In the gradual extension of the area of Government responsibility, as staff and finance permit, he cannot allow his hand to be forced. In most cases, therefore, an "Unsettled Districts" ordinance empowers the Governor to prohibit the entry of Europeans —whether missionaries, prospectors, or too adventurous traders—into such regions as may be notified in the 'Gazette.' The missionary, on his part, declares that he asks for no protection, and will accept the consequences of carrying out his Master's command to preach the gospel to every person, and he demands the right to do so in a British protectorate.

Every administrator would, I think, cordially welcome the establishment of Missions among pagan tribes—except, perhaps, that type of Mission to which I have alluded, whose actions, however well-intentioned, degrade the European in the eyes of the native. It would only be in extreme cases, where insulting treatment, or worse, might compel intervention, and so cause loss of life—not only of the missionaries—that temporary prohibition would be enforced.[1]

In some cases the adoption of a nominal profession of Christianity by a community has outrun the control of the heads of the Mission, and resulted in fracas with pagan neighbours. Traders who have become Christians carry their proselytising zeal with them no less than their Mohamedan compatriots, and (as Bishop Melville-Jones explained to me) the result is an automatic spread of nominal Christianity, in which the converts have not yet learned the principles of the faith they profess, and the supervising staff is insufficient to meet the needs. The administration on the other hand, of

[1] The late Lord Salisbury observed that formerly a missionary who courted martyrdom exposed only himself. To-day he exposes the people to reprisals, "because his position is closely mixed up with that of the secular Powers, who cannot in justice to their own subjects allow his death to go unavenged."

course, insists that the profession of any creed, whether it be Christian or Mohamedan, shall in no way absolve the convert from obedience to his rulers, or from the observance of native law and custom when not repugnant to his conscience.

The case is otherwise when the missionary desires access to an advanced Moslem State, where his presence would be resented, and might be regarded as a breach of the pledge of non-interference with the religion of the people, with consequent loss of confidence. "At present," wrote the Special Correspondent of the 'Times' in the Sudan in 1900, "all Englishmen are regarded as officers or representatives of the Government. The tourist is everywhere saluted in the streets of Omdurman. It would be impossible for any Englishman to establish a Mission without causing the belief that this was a department of Government. The Government could not disclaim responsibility. It would be accused of a breach of faith."[1] The correspondent of the same paper in Nigeria used almost identical language in 1911.[2]

And indeed the native ruler has some grounds for considering that exceptional protection is accorded to a European, or even to a native Christian. If a Moslem missionary were hustled out of a pagan village, it is probable that the Government would never hear of it, and would only intervene if murder or a grievous assault had been committed. But the native evangelist from the coast is unlikely to suffer in silence, and would receive the active support of the missionaries in his complaints. In a Moslem emirate in Nigeria, it is unlikely that violence would be offered, until smouldering discontent took fire in the preaching of a "Mahdi," hostile alike to Europeans and to the native rulers who had worked in harmony with them, and had tolerated the Christian propaganda.

On this subject Dr Blyden quotes an interesting pronouncement of the late Lord Salisbury, who was at the time Foreign Minister.[3] Speaking on 19th June 1900 at Exeter Hall of "the position which this country, and those who represent its moral and spiritual forces, occupy to those great Mohamedan populations which in so many parts of the world come into

[1] 'Times,' 16th April 1900.

[2] 'Times,' 5th and 14th September 1911. See also the letter from Sir Mackworth Young of 22nd September 1911, and a reply dated 28th September.

[3] 'West Africa before Europe,' p. 71.

close connection with our rule," he said, "I have pointed out to you how difficult it is to persuade other nations that the missionary is not an instrument of the secular Government. It is infinitely more difficult in the case of Mohamedans. He cannot believe that those who are preaching the Gospel against the religion of Mahomet are not incited thereto and protected therein, and governed in their action, by the secular Government of England, with which they are connected. . . . And remember that in these Mohamedan countries you are not dealing with men who are wholly evil. You are dealing with men who have a religion, erroneous in many respects, terribly mutilated in others, but a religion that has portions of our own embodied in its system. You are dealing with a force which a sincere though mistaken theism gives to a vast population. You will not convert them. I do not say that you will never do so—God knows, I hope that is far from our fears. But dealing with events of the moment, I think that your chances of the conversion of them, as proved by our experience, are infinitely small, and the danger of creating great perils and producing serious convulsions, and it may be of causing bloodshed, which shall be a serious and permanent obstacle to that Christian religion which we desire above all things to preach, is a danger that you must bear in mind."

The "man in the street" asks difficult questions. It costs, says he, an ascertainable sum to convert each native. If souls are of equal value in the sight of God, why establish a Mission in a district where, prior to the advent of the railway, the cost must be many times as great as in one more accessible, and consequently the number of souls saved in proportion to the subscriptions received from supporters must be so much fewer? In Uganda the experiment was perhaps justified, because the material upon which the Mission had to work was so eager. But is it justified, he would say, in the case of a Mission to Moslems, of whom Lord Salisbury said that experience proved that the chances of conversion are infinitely small? [1] Would not the money be better employed in Missions to pagans, where cannibalism, human sacrifice,

[1] The writer of the very interesting articles on the "Opening of the Sudan," to which I have referred, though sympathetic to the missionary view, says: "Missionaries have never obtained any great success in Mohamedan countries. It is sometimes alleged that a genuine conversion of a genuine Mussulman has never taken place. He has a traditional contempt for the dogmas of Christianity."

and the terror of fetish superstition exercise a sway which Islam has abolished where it has taken root?

Such discussions are outside the domain of the administrator, but for the reasons which concern his own responsibility it was found necessary, both by Lord Kitchener in the Sudan and by myself in Nigeria, to prohibit for the time being the establishment of Christian Missions in Moslem districts. The four Missions which hurried to Omdurman after the defeat of the Mahdi "all laboured under the heavy engagement laid upon them by the late Governor-General, of not attempting to convert a member of the Mohamedan religion," and were compelled to confine their energies to medical and educational work, and to propaganda among the pagans.

It was a particularly hard sentence in the Sudan, for the pagan tribes lay beyond, and not on the way to the Moslem centres, as in Nigeria. It was, moreover, to atone for the violence with which the death of Gordon had been avenged, "to heal the feud and to bear the reconciling Christian message to the Mahdists, that the missionaries sought to enter the Sudan. . . . They saw in the Arabs a people whose capacity of receiving the true faith may be measured by their capacity of dying for the false one."[1] Later the rule was relaxed, and Missions were allowed to enter the Sudan on condition that all members were unreservedly under the local laws and regulations, and that they should "act only with the approval and permission of the Governor-General, and with the concurrence of the local authorities of Government in the province," and that "each Mission is a separate body under the sole control of its local head in the country."[2]

Are these restrictions justified? "The value of missionaries to a State lies not in the number of proselytes whom they convert, but in the lives they lead." Are such men to be excluded and every petty trader allowed freedom to settle where he chooses? The reply of the administrator, however

[1] Ibid.

[2] Sir R. Wingate to Governor of Uganda, 30th November 1905. The Foreign Office Official Handbook No. 98, published in 1920, says: "The policy of the Sudan Government has always been and remains that of encouraging Islam in all its legitimate modes of expression. It has built and maintained many mosques all over the country. Christian churches and schools are allowed only in Khartum city. . . . Outside Khartum no Christian missionary is authorised to preach in any part of the Northern Sudan. . . . The early Government pledge of non-interference with any man in the exercise of his religion has been loyally kept" (p. 57).

reluctantly given, can only be what it has always been in Nigeria: that the Government will offer no objection if the ruling chief concurs; that in a matter solely concerned with religion the Government does not feel justified in compelling a Moslem ruler to grant permission which but for Government intervention he would refuse; that access to a Mission-field which is gained by such means is in doubtful accord with the principles of Christianity, and it lies with the missionaries of their own efforts in medical and educational work to win acceptance, and to change hostility into friendship—a change which will, moreover, be fostered by the general spread of education. This can perhaps be effected by the object-lesson of their work in neighbouring pagan districts, or in those regions not under Moslem rule, where Christian and Mohamedan teachers meet on neutral ground.

At present the ejection of Christian missionaries by a native ruler could only be regarded as an act hostile to the Government which had authorised their coming, and could not be tolerated by it. If a Moslem ruler, in reply to the question whether he had any objection to the presence of missionaries, says that he and his responsible chiefs do not desire them, unless the Government orders otherwise, there is no escaping from the conclusion that their presence depends on the secular force of the Government. The responsible spokesman of the Church Missionary Society in London repudiated the desire to introduce Missions on such terms.

It has sometimes been alleged that the Governments of the Sudan and Nigeria favour Mohamedanism. The attitude which British Governments have endeavoured to assume is that of strict neutrality, impartiality, and tolerance in all religious matters—that "every man should be free to worship God as he chooses." If, however, any particular form of religion sanctions or enforces acts which are contrary to humanity or good order, the Government intervenes regardless of religious sanctions. Thus in the case of Islam, slave-raiding and slave-dealing and any exclusive privilege of Moslems in the Courts of Justice; in the case of fetish creeds, human sacrifice, ordeals, and twin-murder; and among Christian converts, any attempt to repudiate the authority of chiefs, or forcibly to interfere with the religious observances of their neighbours—or of Moslems to interfere with Christians—are all alike prohibited.

The attitude of the native Moslem ruler is very natural. He commands allegiance as the "Head of the Faith." The Koran enjoins implicit obedience to his commands. A widespread desertion to Christianity would undermine his secular no less than his religious power. The English missionary, and even the native pastor from the coast in European coat and trousers (whom he dislikes), would rob him of authority. His own devout followers would regard him as a traitor, who had opened the gate to the enemy.

Moreover, the Mohamedan law which regulates the conduct of a Moslem as a citizen, is so bound up with that which prescribes his religious obligations, that to separate the one from the other is a new and difficult conception to his mind. The itinerating missionary preacher who tells his hearers that the claim of their chiefs to be their rulers and guides equally in spiritual as in the material relations of life is founded on heresy, seems to him to differ little from the preaching of sedition. The attitude of Mohamedans towards the Christian Government which has deprived them of their dominant position, and made their favourite pastime of slave-raiding a criminal offence, has on the whole been one of tolerance and acquiescence.

That the Moslems of Northern Nigeria, cut off from access to Tripoli and the Mediterranean coast, have maintained so high a standard of competence in Mohamedan jurisprudence and literary ability in Arabic; that while retaining a dignity of deportment and courtesy of manners they have resisted denationalising tendencies; that their influence over the lower classes and neighbouring tribes has increased now that their rule has been purged of its excesses; and that the better classes have consistently maintained their hostility to intoxicating liquor, speaks well for the hold which Mohamedan culture, within its limits, had obtained over these northern races.

For the reasons I have given it is necessary that the prior concurrence of Government should be sought before a Mission is established in either a Moslem or a pagan district. There can be no fear that a British administrator would withhold consent unless for some very cogent reason. If his reasons appeared insufficient, there is probably no class which commands a wider means of influencing public opinion through the press and Parliament, and can more effectively bring any decision which it regards as unjust to the bar of public opinion in England, than the missionaries and their supporters.

But these reasons do not stand alone. Cases have been known where the sole apparent motive for the extension of a Mission was to compete with an earlier arrival. This rivalry, as the story of Uganda and many a minor field has shown, is greatly to be deprecated, and justifies an administrator in withholding his sanction.

It is much to be desired that spheres of Mission influence should be mapped out, within which each particular sect should be free to teach according to its own dogmas, without aggression from others. In Uganda I carried out this principle after the fighting, and it is more or less in operation in Northern Nigeria. But in the complicated network of Mission activities which I found existing in Southern Nigeria it was difficult to effect an agreement. If the heads of the various Missions could come to terms on this matter, nothing but good would result. It has been reported to me by administrative officers that the spectacle of the jealousy between rival Missions has a very bad effect on the people, and increases the tendency towards indiscipline.[1]

There is no Established Church in our African dependencies, though bishops—European and African—are appointed to dioceses, which parcel out British tropical Africa between them. In Southern Nigeria the salary of a chaplain was provided from revenue, but the Colonial Office has directed that he shall not be replaced when he retires. That the cost of building churches and the maintenance of a minister should fall on the very small group of Europeans and Christian natives who can count with any degree of certainty on being permanently resident at any place, is to ask more than the none too large salaries at their disposal can provide.

Missionaries, when asked to undertake religious services, have in some cases replied that their duties did not extend to such work; in others, they have generously responded. Whether some satisfactory arrangement could be made is a matter which seems to deserve the consideration of the societies. The absence of the outward observances of religion

[1] In the Sudan among the pagan tribes in the south "the Government encourages Christian missions, and has allotted strict geographical limits or 'reservations' to the different churches."—'Foreign Office Handbook,' p. 58.

among European Christians is, I believe, a matter of comment among Mohamedans, whose creed is so insistent on such public observances.

(*d*) THE USE OF INTOXICANTS.

The horrors of the overseas slave-trade from West Africa were succeeded by the steady growth of a trade in cheap spirits for sale to the natives. The facts, brought to light by the Colonial Congress of the Temperance League in 1886, and the data recorded in a pamphlet by Rev. H. Waller, reinforced the startling reports of Burton, Thomson, and other eminent African explorers regarding the demoralisation of the native races by the liquor traffic. Public opinion was considerably stirred, and on 30th March 1887 a very influential meeting was held in London, followed on 1st April by another in the conference-room of the House of Commons; and on 27th April a Committee was formed under the presidency of the Duke of Westminster and the chairmanship of the Bishop of London, on which a large number of Mission and other societies were officially represented, for the prevention of the traffic. The Committee published quarterly papers, and an annual report. A debate in the Commons took place in March 1888, and an influential deputation to the Foreign Minister (Lord Salisbury) was organised in December 1888, and elicited his strong support. A further debate took place in May 1889 in the House of Lords. As a result of these efforts, the subject was included in the work of the Brussels Conference of 1889.

By the Brussels Act—ratified in 1892—the Powers agreed (Articles 91-94) that total prohibition, except for non-natives, should be enforced in that part of Africa lying between N. lat. 20° and S. lat. 22°, in which the use of distilled liquor did not exist or had not been developed, and that elsewhere a specified duty should be imposed as a minimum, subject to revision after six years. Holland, who has no African possessions, and was the chief exporter of trade gin, jeopardised the Act by her long delay in ratifying.

In that year the total quantity of trade spirits imported into British West Africa was about 3,400,000 gallons. The average duty imposed by the different British colonies stood at 1s. 8d. per gallon, and the aggregate revenue realised was

£236,724. In 1894 half the revenue and 94·8 per cent of the customs of the Niger Coast Protectorate were derived from spirits, and in 1895 the 'Times' observed that half the produce exported from West Africa was purchased with spirits. The duties in the French and German colonies were much lower.

Twenty-one years after the ratification of the Brussels Act in 1892—the year before the war—the duties had been more than trebled (average, 5s. 9d.), but the quantity imported had nevertheless more than doubled (7,144,549 gallons), while the revenue derived from duties had increased eight-fold (£1,832,420). This immense increase in the imports was probably attributable rather to the expansion of trade in the interior than to an increase of consumption in the older markets near the coast.

At the stipulated revisions of the duties, in 1899 and 1906, Great Britain was willing to raise them to any level, but France and Germany would only consent to follow her lead to a very limited extent; and since the colonies of all three Powers alternate with each other with common frontiers, any increase in British duties, in excess of those in a neighbouring foreign colony, involved the maintenance of a costly preventive service.

These figures show that the policy of *gradually* raising the duty had so far failed to effect any decrease in the import. When I assumed the governments of Southern and Northern Nigeria in 1912, the former colony was by far the largest importer, though the quantity in proportion to its population was only about half that of the Gold Coast. The duties were *rapidly* raised each year from 5s. 6d. to 10s. a gallon in 1918, with the intention of crushing the trade. But the war proved an even more effective agent by closing the export from Hamburg and Rotterdam, and in 1917 the import had fallen to about one-twentieth of the pre-war total.[1] The Gold Coast, however, which obtained nearly three-fifths of her spirits from the United States, continued to increase her imports, and actually reached her highest record in 1916.[2] The Governor of Sierra Leone also reported that the United States was rapidly taking the place of Germany in the traffic.[3]

[1] Cmd. 468 of 1920, pp. 55-59, in which a full account is given.

[2] The Gold Coast imported double as much rum as gin, while Nigeria consumed eight times as much gin as rum ('Times,' 8th April 1919).

[3] 'Sierra Leone Annual Report, 1917,' Cd. 8434, p. 5.

The belief hitherto held by the merchants that the native would not produce raw materials for export except in exchange for spirits was abundantly disproved by the facts in Nigeria, for the value of native produce exported in 1917 was actually the highest recorded. The loss of revenue, amounting to over £1,000,000, had been made good by other means, and the theory that no single Government could act independently for fear of smuggling had been shown to be without foundation. The merchants were quick to respond, and now pressed for the gradual extinction of the trade.

On 10th September 1919 a Convention [1] was signed between the United States, France, Italy, Japan, Belgium, Portugal, and the British Empire prohibiting throughout the territories of tropical Africa under their respective control "the importation, distribution, sale, and possession of trade spirits of every kind, and of beverages mixed with these spirits," together with certain other "distilled beverages injurious to health." A minimum duty upon all other distilled beverages was fixed, and distillation in tropical areas was wholly prohibited. Article 22 of the Treaty of Versailles had already pledged its signatories to the "prohibition of abuses such as . . . the liquor traffic" in mandated territories.

Early in the same year prohibition of "trade spirits" was enforced in all the British West African dependencies, in anticipation of the Convention, which was to come into force from date of ratification. The French Government (which had made a step forward by abolishing the sale of absinthe in November 1914) followed on 8th July 1919 with a similar decree, but made it applicable only to *foreign*—viz., non-French—spirits. This action was severely condemned by the 'Temps,' and the eminent French publicist, M. Emile Baillaud (in 'Les Cahiers Coloniaux'), observed that "the errors—not to use a stronger term—verge on the violation by the French Government of international agreements signed by itself. . . . France seemed to be using the great principles, to which she had appealed for the protection of native interests, merely to protect her national spirit trade against foreign competition." [2]

The British Foreign Office, at the instance of the Liverpool and Manchester Chambers of Commerce, protested,[3] on the

[1] Cmd. 478 of 1919. [2] June 1920, quoted by 'West Africa,' 3rd July 1920.
[3] 'Manchester Chamber of Commerce Monthly Record,' January 1921, p. 15.

grounds that discrimination between British and French imports in the territories to which the Convention of June 1898 applied was a contravention of that agreement, and as regards French Equatorial Africa an infringement of the Berlin Act. The Union Coloniale, representing all the French West African trading firms, had advocated even more drastic measures of suppression than the British merchants were prepared to support, and it now appealed to M. Simon, but were informed on 18th December 1919—viz., after the signature of the Convention—that the decree was applicable to all French colonies, and he could not consent to alter it.[1]

In view, however, of the protest of the British Government, the prohibition was withdrawn by decree of 23rd March 1920, and alcohol, whether French or other, was no longer prohibited. Effect was eventually given to the Convention by the arrête of the Governor-General of French West Africa, dated 24th December 1921, and by the decrees of 2nd September and 24th October 1922, which were promulgated for French Togo on 30th November 1922 and 31st January 1923.

Now that this consummation has thus happily been reached, there is no occasion to go into any detail regarding the moral objections to this trade, which Mr Chamberlain summed up by saying that he held it as a matter of deep conviction that it was discreditable to the British name and disastrous to trade. But since, as we shall see, there are still loopholes, of which the powerful vested interests concerned may take advantage, I will very briefly summarise some of the arguments.

A Committee appointed by Lord Crewe in 1909 took a great deal of evidence on the spot.[2] They negatived the view that the traffic was responsible for physical deterioration, or a decrease in the birth-rate, which I am myself inclined to attribute chiefly to venereal disease.[3] · "But however this

[1] Dépêche Coloniale quoted by 'West Africa,' 6th November 1920.

[2] Cd. 4906, October 1909.

[3] Dr Bedford, I.M.S., Director of the Central Excise Laboratory in India, stated that there was nothing physiologically injurious in the trade spirit. The Committee reported that the almost unanimous medical opinion was that it was not responsible for physical deterioration. This verdict, of course, applies to the liquor sold in West Africa, and not to that sold in South Africa or elsewhere. The conflict of evidence with the earlier reports of wholesale race deterioration (which may be found in the first two or three reports of the "United Committee") may perhaps be explained in part by an improvement in the quality of the liquor between the date of those reports (1887) and the sitting of the Committee (1909).

may be," I wrote, "no one can deny that it is a sterile import, upon which the natives (of Southern Nigeria) wasted over 1½ millions sterling annually without securing any improvement in their standard of comfort, or increasing their productive output, and that it is a disgrace to an administration that nearly half its revenue should be derived from such a source."[1] It was calculated that the consumption in Southern Nigeria was about one gallon (at 50° Tralles[2]) per head per annum; but the calculation is quite unreliable. In Nigeria railway rates on spirits increased rapidly with the distance from the coast, with the object of making them not less than the cost of head-carriage.

From the commercial point of view, the spirit trade was a disastrous policy—as I pointed out in the 'Nineteenth Century' as long ago as 1897.[3] Not only was it a foreign manufacture, carried in foreign vessels—and *pro tanto* opposed to British trade—but since it supplied German vessels with outward cargoes, it enabled Germany to secure the practical monopoly of the homeward palm-kernel trade.[4] The Comptroller of Customs in Nigeria states that "Continental trade spirits were the mainstay of German outward cargoes, and Germany's African trade was built up on them." The spirit trade was indeed synonymous with German influence in West Africa. It is a traffic which not only usurps the place of more legitimate trade, but kills it.

The prohibition of "trade spirits" presupposes a definition of the article, but it is by no means easy to define, as may be seen by the varying definitions of the different Govern-

[1] See report on Nigeria (Cmd. 468 of 1920).

[2] This is the strength at which the duty has been calculated since 1909—viz., 12½ u.p. by English standards (English proof is 37° absolute alcohol). This reform made it no longer profitable to import over-proof spirit for local manipulation. The further the spirit travels up-country the more diluted it becomes.

[3] "Liquor Traffic in Africa," November 1897. The article contained a review of the evidence as to both the moral and material aspects of this question. See also 'Proceedings of the Royal Colonial Institute,' vol. xxvii. p. 31.

[4] The Committee state that 90 per cent of the spirits imported into Nigeria come from Holland and Germany. Mr T. Welsh (a member of the Committee), writing to the 'Times' (28th January 1919), states that seventy-one German vessels with an aggregate tonnage of 329,000 tons were mainly engaged in supplying West Africa with intoxicants. The manifest of one ship—the *Degama*—which he says is typical, showed 169,288 gallons (approximately) of liquor. The German Woermann Line was created by the spirit trade, for though the bulk of the spirits came from Holland they were shipped in German vessels.

ments.[1] Mr Welsh argues that quality and price should be the determining factors, and states that Cuban rum is admitted to Sierra Leone, while West Indian, French, Spanish, and English liquors are being offered at moderate prices.[2] Another correspondent states that he has seen quotations of Scotch whisky at 4s. 6d. a case f.o.b. Glasgow and Leith.

At the conference between British and French merchants in April 1920 the spirit trade was the subject of prolonged discussion. The views expressed by Mr Holt and other British merchants were moderate and practical. It was finally unanimously resolved to advocate the restriction and regulation of imported alcoholic liquor, but that since fermented liquors have been used by the natives from time immemorial, absolute prohibition would be an interference with personal liberty; that the import of wines and beers free from noxious constituents and impurities should be permitted, except to prohibited areas; and that, without expressing an opinion as to the importation of properly-rectified spirits, they should, if imported, be reduced in alcoholic strength, and consumption restricted by a duty of 15s. or more per liquid gallon at the fixed maximum strength.

The alternatives seem to be either total prohibition of distilled liquor, while admitting fermented beverages—for to prohibit the import of these while native-made intoxicants are beyond control would be absurd and unjust to non-natives,—or some method (which I should prefer) of imposing a duty which will increase in severity as the spirits fall below a given standard of quality and price, so that it would no longer pay to import any spirits below that standard.

The attempt to deprive a people entirely of a stimulant or sedative to which they have become accustomed, has usually done much more harm than good to the classes on whose behalf the legislation was initiated, while interfering

[1] The Colonial Office, in a letter to the Liverpool Chamber of Commerce dated 24th April 1919, quoted the following definitions: "In Nigeria, 'spirits imported for sale to natives, and not generally consumed by Europeans.' In Sierra Leone, 'spirits commonly known as trade or common gin, and trade or common rum.' In the Gambia, 'spirits of a low-grade value, which in the Receiver-General's opinion, subject to any direction of the Governor, are imported mainly for native consumption.' In the Gold Coast no definition of the term 'trade spirits' has been adopted, but . . . no difficulty in restricting licences to other than trade spirits is anticipated in practice." The Chambers' own definition reads: "Spirits which are contained in bottles of less than one-sixth of an imperial gallon, or being contained in such bottles have not been in warehouse in the country of manufacture for at least three years."

[2] 'Times,' 11th March 1920.

with the liberty of those who use it in moderation, and creating new offences. The arbitrary prohibition of opium, used in moderation, to which a smoker had become habituated, has in some places in the East resulted in the increased use of morphine and cocaine, with far worse results. In the case of spirits there is the alternative of fermented beverages —wines, beer, and native-made intoxicants—as a safety-valve, but there seems no good reason why natives, other than inhabitants of a prohibition zone, should be debarred from purchasing high-priced spirits of good quality equally with Europeans. Delivery from the customs warehouse might, however, be made contingent on dilution to a fixed maximum strength, and sale in excess of that strength forbidden by law.

I have advocated a light beer, prepared in local breweries, which is likely to be popular among natives of West Africa, who have a great liking for the bitter kola-nut.

The use of fermented liquor is universal throughout Africa. It is usually made from grain (a fermented gruel), or from the sap of various palms, especially the raphia (*vinifera*) and the wild date. The oil-palm is also tapped, though the stem incision, which destroys the tree, is in Nigeria prohibited by law, and enforced by native court by-laws. It would, if resorted to on a large scale, threaten the staple industry of Southern Nigeria, but tapping by means of an incision in the flower-stem does not seriously injure the tree. I am told that the maximum strength which it is possible for palm-wine to reach is 7 per cent absolute alcohol, as against 44·86 per cent in trade spirit as ordinarily sold. The result of some tests showed ordinary palm-wine to contain about 4·69 per cent absolute alcohol (8·2 per cent of proof spirit).

In East Africa the beverage made by fermenting the liquid contained in the green cocoanut (*Madafu*) produces a most potent drink (*tembo*), which the Moslem owners of the plantations, though abstaining themselves, allowed their slaves to prepare and sell in great quantities to the neighbouring pagan tribes (Giryama), among whom I have seen more drunkenness than elsewhere in Africa.[1] The banana-wine of Uganda is very like cider, and though consumed in large quantities is not a violent intoxicant. Reports from the grain-producing districts of the Northern Provinces of Nigeria speak of constant orgies held by primitive tribes. Whole villages, in-

[1] Drunkenness is said to be increasing, in spite of a tax on tembo.—Handbook, 'Kenya,' p. 324.

cluding women and children, indulge in continued intoxication, with crime and bloodshed as a result.[1] Restriction of drunkenness among primitive tribes can only be effected by gradual administrative progress and educational reform, and by the introduction of palatable and less noxious beverages.

It is possible to exercise some control over the preparation and sale of native-made intoxicants through the native administration in Moslem districts, where their use is contrary to Koranic law.[2] But Moslems are often indifferent to the use of intoxicants by pagans under their control, as shown by the Arabs on the east coast, and the Committee of 1909 reported that the Moslem communities of Southern Nigeria traded in spirits, and were averse to prohibition.

In townships and mining areas, and in proximity to the railways, where direct control is feasible, a check can be instituted, but among pagan tribes it is at present impracticable to introduce any form of licence or excise on native-made intoxicants. The Congo State is reported to have forbidden the manufacture of liquor over 8° in strength, but such a rule would be extremely difficult to enforce. It seems desirable that a system of licences for the sale of imported intoxicants should be instituted wherever feasible, and gradually extended to sale of native liquor, as the administrative machine permits of effective control.

The really serious danger lies in the acquisition by the natives of knowledge of the simple process of distillation. In the conditions of Africa pot-stills would be impossible to detect or control. Sir Samuel Baker relates how he amused himself by teaching the natives of Unyoro how to distil spirit from sweet potatoes. I found in 1890 that the Sudanese had not forgotten the art. The introduction of sugar-refining in Africa is to be feared for the same reason.

Distilleries, at one time common in Portuguese Africa, are now prohibited.[3] President King states that they are rapidly

[1] 'Native Races and their Rulers,' C. L. Temple, p. 173.

[2] By the Native Liquor Regulation decree of 1914 total prohibition was enforced in Zanzibar (a Moslem State).—Cd. 7622 of 1917, p. 17 (annual report).

[3] By the decrees of 27th May 1911, and 675 of 1913, not only was distillation entirely prohibited in Angola, but also the cultivation of sugar-cane, sweet potatoes, "and other plants especially useful in the manufacture of alcohol," involving heavy compensation to growers—stated by the Portuguese Minister to have exceeded £2,000,000; according to the 'Daily Telegraph' (22/1/23), £666,000. The importation or local manufacture of all kinds of intoxicants, whether for Europeans or natives, appears to have been prohibited by a later decree (No. 200 of 26th October 1922), in accordance with the declarations of Senor d'Andrade at the Paris Conference.

increasing in Liberia. There are many in Abyssinia, chiefly in Greek ownership, but we hear that a Belgian company has lately acquired the Alcohol Regie in that country. Italy alone of the signatory Powers reserves in her African colonies the right to manufacture distilled beverages other than "trade spirits" and certain specified "injurious spirits," subject to an excise duty equal to the prescribed import duty. With this exception, distillation for purposes of consumption or sale is now absolutely prohibited by Article 5 of the Convention of September of 1919. It is to be hoped that the League of Nations, under whose control the Central International Office is placed, will take special care to ensure the observance of this important article.

Since this chapter was written, it has been repeatedly stated that the financial difficulties from which Nigeria is at present suffering are due in large part to the decrease in revenue derived from the sale of spirits to natives, and the sudden prohibition of "trade spirits" by the Convention of September 1919 without due regard to its economic effects.[1]

The Nigerian annual reports, 1914-1919, show that the maximum revenue derived from this source was £1,138,000 in 1913, when the value of spirit imports was 6·28 per cent of the whole inward trade, including specie. (This percentage was even higher in previous years—viz., 7·79 per cent in 1910.) From 1913 the revenue from spirits declined steadily each year till 1919, when only £74,700 was realised (·83 per cent of the total inward trade). In the following year the revenue from spirits was trebled (£242,565), and the estimate for 1921 was £216,000.[2] These figures appear to demonstrate that the effect on the revenue was not sudden or unexpected, and the revenue from spirits shows a substantial increase in the two years following the Convention—the last for which figures are available.

But, however this may be, it seems pertinent to ask why these West African dependencies, whose natural resources in palm oil and kernels, in cocoa, ground-nuts, tin, and gold, &c., render them by universal consent among the wealthiest of our tropical colonies, should claim that a revenue from trade spirits, which is possessed by no other colonies, should be indispensable to balance their budgets.

[1] See 'Report on Trade and Taxation in British West Africa,' Cmd. 1600 of 1922, p. 23, *et seq.*

[2] Ibid., pp. 34 and 67.

CHAPTER XXXI.

CONCLUSION—THE VALUE OF BRITISH RULE IN THE TROPICS TO BRITISH DEMOCRACY AND THE NATIVE RACES.

The nature of the task—The views of the "Labour Research Department"—The cost to the British taxpayer—The benefits to the democracy—Food and defence—Trade and employment—Openings for personal enterprise—Formation of national character—Motives for acquisition—Some moral incentives—Pressure of population—The right of mankind to tropical products—The verdict of democracy—Accusations in regard to treatment of native races—Benefit to Africa—England's mission.

THREE decades have passed since England assumed effective occupation and administration of those portions of the interior of tropical Africa for which she had accepted responsibility when the nations of Europe partitioned the continent between them. How has her task as trustee, on the one hand, for the advancement of the subject races, and on the other hand, for the development of its material resources for the benefit of mankind, been fulfilled? There is no one, I think, who has been privileged to bear a share in the task, with its immeasurable opportunities, who, looking back, would not echo Mr Rhodes' dying words, "So much to do—so little done!"

In the foregoing chapters I have endeavoured to describe some of the problems which confront the administrator, and with diffidence to indicate the path by which, as it seems to me, the best solution may in the course of time be found.

Viceroys and Governors of the older dependencies, of Colonies and of Dominions, occupy posts of greater titular importance than those who are entrusted with the charge of these tropical dependencies in Africa, but their own personal initiative is circumscribed and controlled by Ministers, by effective assemblies and councils, by a local press which reflects public opinion and criticism, and to a greater or less extent by the Parliament and press of England. The Governors in Africa are to-day gradually being brought under the same guiding and controlling influences, but in the earlier beginnings of our rule these influences hardly existed. Neither the Foreign Office nor the Colonial Office had any experience of Central African conditions and administration, when, at the close of the nineteenth century, the summons for effective occupation compelled this country to administer the hinterlands of the West African colonies, and to assume control of vast areas on the Nile, the Niger, the Zambesi, and the great lakes in the heart of Africa.

The self-governing Dominions grew by slow stages from small municipalities to the status of United Nations. In India and the Eastern colonies, territorial expansion was the slow increment of many decades. But in Africa it was not a matter of *expansion* from existing nuclei of administration, but of sudden creation and improvisation. Perhaps it was well that Great Britain, following the tradition of the Empire, did not (as she might have been expected to do) select from her most experienced servants, trained in the school of Indian administration, those who should grapple with this sudden emergency, but trusted to the men on the spot. The pioneers of African administration came to their task with minds unbiassed by traditions unsuited to the races and conditions of Africa, and more ready to attempt to make bricks without straw. The perspective of history will perhaps show more clearly the magnitude of that task, and the opportunity it gave for initiative, almost unprecedented in the annals of the Empire.

It was for these pioneers to cope with the internal slave-trade, the very existence of which was hardly known in England, to devise their own laws, to set up their courts of justice, to deal with foreign aggression, to create an administration, and bring order out of chaos. The funds at their disposal were wholly inadequate, the staff poorly paid, painfully insufficient, and recruited somewhat at haphazard, whether for chartered companies or for Crown dependencies. The areas to be controlled were most of them many times the size of England, with populations numbered in millions, seething with internal strife, and wholly without roads or means of communication.

The nation is justified in demanding how, in such circumstances, the administrative officers and their colleagues in the judicial and educational departments on the one hand, and the engineers, the medical, agricultural, and forestry officers, and the rest of the technical staff on the other hand, have acquitted themselves in their respective responsibilities towards the native races, and the material progress of these countries.

We are all familiar with the creed of the "Little Englander." At each fresh access of responsibility and expansion of the Empire he has warned us that "the white man's burden" was already growing too heavy for this country to bear, that the British taxpayer was being called on to support the ambitions of chauvinists, and that the native races were misgoverned and robbed of their lands and their proper profits by the greed of exploiters.

Of late, since the war, it would almost seem as if an organised attempt was being made to promulgate these doctrines among the Labour Party, and to persuade them that the existence of the Empire is antagonistic alike to their own interests and to those of the subject races. That Party has not as yet had experience of overseas problems. Its "Research Department" for the investigation of these subjects appears to have fallen under the influence of those who hold these narrow views. They would persuade the British democracy that it is better to shirk Imperial responsibility, and relegate it to international committees; that material development benefits only the capitalist profiteer; and that British rule over subject races stands for spoliation and self-interest. Guided by these advisers—some of the more prominent of whom are apparently not of British race—the Labour Party has not hesitated to put forward its own thesis of Government of tropical dependencies under the Mandates. To these views I hope that I have already in some measure offered a reply, and I will endeavour briefly to summarise in these concluding pages.

"Nothing," says Sir C. Lucas, "should appeal so strongly as the Empire to democracy, for it is the greatest engine of democracy the world has ever known. . . . It has infected the whole world with liberty and democracy."[1] There is no doubt that the control of the tropics, so far from being a charge on the British taxpayer, is to him a source of very

[1] 'United Empire,' March 1919.

great gain. I have in a previous chapter shown how the products of the tropics have raised the standard of comfort of the working man, added to the amenities of his life, and provided alike the raw materials on which the industry and wealth of the community depend, and the market for manufactures which ensure employment.

So keenly do other nations value the assured possession of these sources of supply and these markets, that they have been willing to expend enormous sums for their acquisition and development,[1] and (unlike Great Britain) have built tariff walls around them to exclude other nations from participation. "Never in the world's history was there an Empire which in proportion to its size encroached so little upon the public time and the public cost." [2]

The temporary subsidies which have been paid to some of these tropical possessions in their earlier years, as "grants-in-aid," have decreased yearly until the countries became self-supporting, since which time they have not cost the taxpayer a penny, and the temporary grants have been indirectly much more than repaid.

Prior to the war Nigeria was the latest addition to the Empire, and if against the original payment to the Chartered Company and all subsequent grants, be set the profit derived by the British Exchequer on the import of silver coin, and the contributions offered by Nigeria to the war, it will be found that the debit is on the other side, and the country, with all its potentialities and expanding markets, has cost the British taxpayer nothing. Its trade—already £42,000,000—the greater part of which is with the United Kingdom, is of the kind which is the most valuable possible to the workers of this country—raw materials and foodstuffs in exchange for textiles and hardware.

Democracy has learnt by the war how absolutely dependent it is on the supply of these vital necessities from overseas, and even for the material for munitions in time of war. We have realised that the import can only be maintained by command of the seas. Some of these tropical dependencies are essential as naval bases, as cable and wireless stations, and as aerodromes, for that command of sea and air and of

[1] Herr Dernburg stated that Algeria had cost France £343,720,000 up to 1906 —'Times,' 23rd November 1906.

[2] Lucas, *loc. cit.*

world communications upon which these islands depend for their existence. Without them we could only survive on such terms as the powerful nations might choose to dictate.

Before the war the Little Englander was wont to argue that these world-wide outposts were a source of weakness, and in time of war their defence would be a burden which we could not sustain. But when Armageddon came, we required no additional garrisons to hold these vast territories in check; on the contrary, thousands of volunteers were ready to fight the Empire's battles. The West African colonies (relying, of course, on British supremacy at sea) were able, with the French, to capture the German Cameruns and Togoland, and to send thousands to fight or serve as transport units in German East Africa, and if need be in Palestine. These colonies asked for no financial assistance to help them through the crisis; indeed, they subscribed largely to the cost of the war and to war charities.

But let us return to the more normal conditions of peace and commerce. It is alleged that we could do an equally lucrative trade in the possessions of other Powers, instead of incurring the cost and responsibility of maintaining possessions of our own. But I have shown that foreign colonies are increasingly exclusive, and do not welcome British competition; that the cost of maintenance is borne by the revenues of the colonies themselves, and not by the British taxpayer; and, finally, it were easy to demonstrate that the largest proportion of their trade is done with the United Kingdom and not with foreign nations.

The fallacies put forward by these critics have long since been disproved, though the Labour Party may not be familiar with the statistics. It suffices here to point out that the trade of the single dependency of Nigeria for 1920 stood at over £42,200,000 in value, which, however, was probably abnormal and due to the "boom" of that year. Of this 96·74 per cent of the imports and 97·35 per cent of the exports were carried in British vessels—mainly, of course, to British ports.[1] For East Africa and Uganda the latest figures (1918-1919) show 84·3 per cent of imports and 91·1 per cent of exports from and to the Empire (United Kingdom 61 per

[1] Governor's address to Nigerian Council, December 1920. The destination is not stated, but in 1918 92·4 per cent of exports, and 87 per cent of imports, were to and from the Empire.—Cmd. 508/14 of 1919.

cent and 53·5 per cent).[1] How rapidly the trade of these colonies is expanding may be judged from the fact that the trade of Nigeria in 1913 (pre-war) was under 13½ million.

As to the assertion that we do just as good trade with countries in tropical Africa which are not under the British flag, I find in the 'Statistical Abstract for the British Empire'[2] that the trade of the United Kingdom with all French possessions (including those in India and the Far East) was, in 1913, £6,730,244, while our trade with the single dependency of Nigeria for the same year stood at £8,278,813, in spite of the fact that in that year Germany had monopolised nearly half the Nigerian trade, which has since reverted to the United Kingdom.[3]

The critics quote statistics showing the proportion that the trade of this or that tropical dependency bears to the whole volume of our foreign trade, as though any comparison could be instituted between our commerce with wealthy, populous, and highly industrialised countries like the United States, Germany, or France, and that of new and undeveloped markets in the tropics, whose present output or demands are no measure whatever of their future potentialities.

And though our markets are free to all the world, British merchants have no small advantage in the first-hand and early knowledge of the conditions and resources of each country, available in their own language. They can and do bring their influence to bear in order to secure as far as possible that the conditions of trade shall be made to suit their own convenience. The home market, provided it can hold its own as to quality, price, and rapidity of delivery, has the first opportunity of supplying colonial demands.

These are indeed matters of such common knowledge that I refrain from dilating further upon them, and will content myself with referring to one or two other aspects which have

[1] East African Report, 1918-19, No. 1073 of 1921.

[2] Cd. 7827 of 1915. It is to be regretted that no later edition has yet appeared.

[3] The war has, of course, exercised a great influence on the origin of imports and the destination of exports of the African dependencies. In Nigeria prior to the war Germany by importing trade spirits had, as we have seen, been able to monopolise the export of palm-kernels, and so to secure 44 per cent of the exports. This has been almost completely absorbed by British merchants. In other West African colonies, however, the place of Germany has been largely taken by the United States. The pre-war proportion of the East African trade with the Empire is given by the Economic Commission (p. 11) as 62½ per cent of imports and 54½ per cent of exports.

perhaps received less recognition. The abounding progress of our tropical dependencies calls not only for millions of pounds worth of railway and other construction material, but for men to construct and to maintain the railways and other works. The expansion of administration equally demands officers for every branch—administrative, medical, educational, &c. The development of commerce requires local agents. The opening of mine-fields calls for expert workers.

In all these fields of activity openings are afforded for every class of the youth of England, whether from the universities, the technical schools, or the workshop. It is difficult to realise how severe would be the blow to the life of the nation if these thousands of avenues to independent initiative and individual enterprise and ambition were closed, as Germany has largely closed them to her people by her crime against the world.

I have already pointed out that this large field of opportunity and of responsibility must undoubtedly have contributed very greatly to the formation of the national character, which the late Lord Salisbury described in memorable words: "Our people, when they go into the possession of a new territory, carry with them such a power of initiative, such an extraordinary courage and resource in the solving of new problems and the facing of new difficulties, that if they are pitted against an equal number—I care not what race it is, or what the part of the world is—and if you keep politics and negotiations off them, it will be our people that will be masters, it will be our commerce that will prevail, it will be our capital that will rule, though not a sword has been unsheathed, and though not a blow has been struck in their defence." [1] He did but echo the words of Adam Smith, which I have quoted elsewhere, that the debt of the colonies to the motherland consists in the fact that "it bred and formed the men who were capable of achieving such great actions, and of laying the foundations of so great an Empire."

The British working man is told that the exploitation of Africa was undertaken by groups of financiers and capitalists, who desired to profiteer at the expense of the nation and of the native races alike. "Common greed," says the reviewer of the Labour Research Committee's report, summing up the

[1] Debate, House of Lords, 14th February 1895.

gist of the argument, " came to be avowed openly as the most respectable of reasons for establishing colonies or protectorates anywhere and everywhere," [1] in contrast with the nobler motives which prompted the bold adventurers of the spacious Elizabethan days.

I will not digress to discuss those motives here, or the navigation laws which treated the colonies merely as sources of profit, or the fortunes which Macaulay's " Nabobs " brought from India, or the quest for an " El Dorado." The partition of Africa was, as we all recognise, due primarily to the economic necessity of increasing the supplies of raw materials and food to meet the needs of the industrialised nations of Europe. It is a cheap form of rhetoric which stigmatises as " common greed " the honourable work by which men and nations earn their bread and improve their standard of life.[2]

But while admitting this we must not lose sight of the fact that several of our West African colonies had been acquired solely as depots to assist in the suppression of the overseas slave-trade, others in support of missionary endeavours which were certainly not prompted by greed for profit. Others again, as I have shown, were necessary for the maintenance of our sea-power. In all these cases a higher civilisation was brought into contact with barbarism, with the inevitable result, as history teaches, that boundaries were enlarged in the effort to protect the weak from the tyranny of the strong, to extend the rule of justice and liberty, to protect traders, settlers, and missions, and to check anarchy and bloodshed on our frontiers, even though territorial expansion was not desired.[3] Nor must we ignore the very real desire of the people of this country to assist in the suppression of slavery and barbarous practices. These are matters in which I am convinced that the British democracy has a deep interest, deeper perhaps than its political leaders credit it with. They cannot be disposed of with a sneer. But I return to the economic question, since this argument of " capitalist exploi-

[1] 'The New Statesman,' 19th June 1920.

[2] Carlyle, describing all that work has done for England, and what it has made England, says: "The English are a dumb people. They can do great acts but not describe them. . . . Their epic is written on the earth's surface: England her mark."—'Past and Present,' p. 135.

[3] As Bacon says: "It was not the Romans who spread themselves upon the world, but the world which spread itself upon the Romans.' — 'Essays,' p. 44.

tation" appears to be a favourite one with which to capture the ear of Labour.

In the introductory chapter I cited statistics to show that, at the time of the first impulse of Imperial expansion in the reign of Queen Elizabeth, the small and chiefly agricultural population of these islands was able to supply its own essential needs in food and materials; that when the second impulse came 240 years later, after the Napoleonic wars, the population had quadrupled, while in the next seventy-five years of the nineteenth century, 1816-91 (when the partition of Africa began in earnest), it again nearly doubled itself. The congestion of the population, assisted by the discovery of the application of steam to industrial uses, led to the replacement of agriculture by manufacturing industry, with the consequent necessity for new markets for the product of the factory, and the importation of raw materials for industry, and of food to supplement the decreased home production, and feed the increased population. The same phenomenon was to be seen in Germany and elsewhere in Europe.[1] I recapitulate these figures because their importance in this connection can hardly be over-estimated.

But mere increase in population alone, prodigious though it was, does not represent the full measure of the pressure on the Governments of the industrial nations of Europe. The standard of comfort, and what had come to be regarded as the absolute necessities of life by the mass of the population, had, during the nineteenth century, advanced in an even greater ratio. I cannot here attempt to depict the contrast. It is enough to recall the fact that 100 years ago a labourer's wage was 4s. to 6s. a week. He rarely tasted white bread, for the quartern loaf stood at 11d., and had been double that price a few years before. Still less could he afford to eat beef or mutton. Towards the close of the nineteenth century, tea, coffee, and cocoa, previously unknown luxuries, were his daily beverages and white bread his daily food. Sugar

[1] The population of the United Kingdom in 1816 was about 19,890,000, and in 1891 it had increased to 38,104,000. That of Germany was respectively 24,831,000 and about 50,000,000, and of France about 29,000,000 and 38,342,000. The pressure of population was thus not so great a factor in France, who was foremost in the scramble for Africa. Her motives, as I have said, were chiefly due to the belief that it was by expansion in Africa alone that she could hope to find means to recover from the effects of the war with Germany in 1870.—See note 1, p. 3.

was cheap, and rice, sago, and other tropical products were in daily use. If my reader will turn to the pages of Miss Martineau's history,[1] or to those of Carlyle, and contrast the condition of squalor and misery in which the bulk of the people of these islands lived in 1816 with the conditions prevailing in 1891, he will realise how insistent had become the demand alike for the food-supplies and for the raw materials which were the product of the tropics.

These products lay wasted and ungarnered in Africa because the natives did not know their use and value. Millions of tons of oil-nuts, for instance, grew wild without the labour of man, and lay rotting in the forests. Who can deny the right of the hungry people of Europe to utilise the wasted bounties of nature, or that the task of developing these resources was, as Mr Chamberlain expressed it, a "trust for civilisation" and for the benefit of mankind? Europe benefited by the wonderful increase in the amenities of life for the mass of her people which followed the opening up of Africa at the end of the nineteenth century. Africa benefited by the influx of manufactured goods, and the substitution of law and order for the methods of barbarism.

Thus Europe was impelled to the development of Africa primarily by the necessities of her people, and not by the greed of the capitalist. Keen competition assured the maximum prices to the producer. It is only where monopolies are granted that it can be argued that profits are restricted to the few, and British policy has long been averse to monopolies in every form. The brains, the research, the capital, and the enterprise of the merchant, the miner, and the planter have discovered and utilised the surplus products of Africa. The profits have been divided among the shareholders representing all classes of the people,[2] and no small share of them has gone to the native African merchant and the middleman as well as to the producer. It is true to say that "a vast area of activity has been opened up to the British workman, in which he shares with the capitalist the profits of the development of tropical resources." [3]

[1] 'The Thirty Years' Peace,' vol. i. chapters 4, 7, &c.

[2] Lord Leverhulme lately stated that in his Company alone—which is largely concerned in the development of the African tropics—there were no less than 127,000 shareholders.

[3] Bruce, *loc. cit.*, p. 4. In view of all these facts I read with amazement the verdict of the Labour Research Committee, that "it is doubtful whether the

In accepting responsibility for the control of these new lands, England obeyed the tradition of her race. British Africa was acquired not by groups of financiers, nor yet (as I have related in chapter i.) by the efforts of her statesmen, but in spite of them. It was the instinct of the British democracy which compelled us to take our share. When Mr Gladstone's Cabinet in 1893 had decided to evacuate Uganda, he was told by his Scottish agent that if he did so he would have to evacuate Downing Street too. Even were it true—and I have shown that it is not—that we could do as lucrative a trade in the tropical possessions of other nations, there can be no doubt that the verdict of the British people has been emphatic that we will not ask the foreigner to open markets for our use, or leave to him the responsibility and its reward. Nor will tariff walls, like those of Jericho, fall flat at the sound of the trumpet of the new Labour leaders.

"The general effects of European policy in Africa have been almost wholly evil," says the Labour reporter, yet he admits that "experience and temperament have made the rule of the British over non-adult races an example of everything that is best in modern imperialism." The verdict of another of the prophets of Labour is to the same effect. The fundamental character of British official policy in West Africa, he says, has primarily been influenced by a desire to promote the welfare and advancement of the native races. England, he points out, led the way in the suppression of the overseas slave-trade, paying enormous sums in compensation to slave-owners in the West Indies, and at the Cape, and to Spain and Portugal, and in patrolling the seas. She espoused the cause of Congo reform, and of the indentured labour in Portuguese West Africa. The extension of British control in the Gold Coast hinterland was (he adds) to secure protection of the natives, and in Southern Nigeria to suppress war and human sacrifice.

The indictment against European misrule in Africa appears therefore to lack consistency, and to be directed chiefly against foreign Powers, though bitter charges, as we have seen, are made against some of the Eastern British dependencies in Africa, which have been fully discussed in these pages. In

acquisition of territory in Africa has added to the power of the European States who have assumed it. It is certain that it has not added to their wealth."—'Empire and Commerce,' p. 317.

so far as they concern the territories of other Powers, this attitude of what Mr Rhodes called "unctuous righteousness," which has the appearance of assuming that others are actuated by less generous motives than our own, is more likely to promote resentment than reform. That the aims of these critics are good will not be denied, but they write without actual experience, and they create prejudice where sympathy and appreciation would be more promising of results.

Let it be admitted at the outset that European brains, capital, and energy have not been, and never will be, expended in developing the resources of Africa from motives of pure philanthropy; that Europe is in Africa for the mutual benefit of her own industrial classes, and of the native races in their progress to a higher plane; that the benefit can be made reciprocal, and that it is the aim and desire of civilised administration to fulfil this dual mandate.

By railways and roads, by reclamation of swamps and irrigation of deserts, and by a system of fair trade and competition, we have added to the prosperity and wealth of these lands, and checked famine and disease. We have put an end to the awful misery of the slave-trade and inter-tribal war, to human sacrifice and the ordeals of the witch-doctor. Where these things survive they are severely suppressed. We are endeavouring to teach the native races to conduct their own affairs with justice and humanity, and to educate them alike in letters and in industry.

When I recall the state of Uganda at the time I made the treaty in 1890 which brought it under British control, or the state of Nigeria ten years later, and contrast them with the conditions of to-day, I feel that British effort—apart from benefits to British trade—has not been in vain. In Uganda a triangular civil war was raging—Protestants, Roman Catholics, and Moslems, representing the rival political factions of British, French, and Arabs, were murdering each other. Only a short time previously triumphant paganism had burnt Christians at the stake and revelled in holocausts of victims. To-day there is an ordered Government with its own native parliament. Liberty and justice have replaced chaos, bloodshed, and war. The wealth of the country steadily increases.[1]

[1] The last report, 1918-19, shows an export of cotton alone valued at close on a million sterling.—Cmd. 508/37, 1920.

The slave-raids and tyranny of the neighbouring kingdom of Unyoro have given place to similar progress and peace.

In Nigeria in 1902 slave-raiding armies of 10,000 or 15,000 men laid waste the country, and wiped out its population annually in the quest for slaves. Hundreds of square miles of rich well-watered land were depopulated. Barth bore witness to a similar condition of things fifty years ago. Men were impaled in the market-place of Kano. I have described its dungeon (p. 199). Nowhere was there security for life and property. To-day the native Emirs vie with each other in the progress of their schools; the native courts administer justice, and themselves have liberated over 50,000 slaves. The Sultan of Sokoto and the other Emirs are keenly interested in such questions as afforestation, artesian well-boring, and vaccination. The native prisons have been pronounced by the medical authority to be a model for Government to imitate; the leper settlement in Bornu under purely native control is the most successful I know of.

I refer to these two countries because I happen to have personally witnessed their condition prior to the advent of British control, but similar results may be seen in every other British dependency in tropical Africa.

As Roman imperialism laid the foundations of modern civilisation, and led the wild barbarians of these islands along the path of progress, so in Africa to-day we are repaying the debt, and bringing to the dark places of the earth, the abode of barbarism and cruelty, the torch of culture and progress, while ministering to the material needs of our own civilisation. In this task the nations of Europe have pledged themselves to co-operation by a solemn covenant. Towards the common goal each will advance by the methods most consonant with its national genius. British methods have not perhaps in all cases produced ideal results, but I am profoundly convinced that there can be no question but that British rule has promoted the happiness and welfare of the primitive races. Let those who question it examine the results impartially. If there is unrest, and a desire for independence, as in India and Egypt, it is because we have taught the value of liberty and freedom, which for centuries these peoples had not known. Their very discontent is a measure of their progress.

We hold these countries because it is the genius of our race to colonise, to trade, and to govern. The task in which England is engaged in the tropics—alike in Africa and in the East—has become part of her tradition, and she has ever given of her best in the cause of liberty and civilisation.[1] There will always be those who cry aloud that the task is being badly done, that it does not need doing, that we can get more profit by leaving others to do it, that it brings evil to subject races and breeds profiteers at home. These were not the principles which prompted our forefathers, and secured for us the place we hold in the world to-day in trust for those who shall come after us.

[1] "I believe," says Sir C. Lucas, "that to our people has been given the work of carrying justice and freedom throughout the world. I do not claim for them any immunity from wrong-doing. Like other people, they have sought and found gain. But I find the weak peoples of the world looking to and trusting England. I find British justice a proverb among nations. . . . I believe the world to be a better world for the fact that the British have peopled some lands with their own race, and taken the rule of others into their own hands."

"We of West Africa ought from our heart of hearts to thank Almighty God that we have been born into the British Empire," says a Lagos paper on Empire Day 1920; while a Gold Coast journal observed that "to us of West Africa Empire means a relation of goodwill between the Imperial unit and its links, harmonising all interests irrespective of race and colour." West Africa, it adds, looks to Imperial Britain to lead the nations to a just recognition of Africa's claims.

Beaulieu pays a very generous tribute to England's success. "La nation qui tient le premier rang dans la colonisation, celle qui donne à tous l'exemples de vastes empire fondés au dela des mers, c'est l'Angleterre. . . . Mais le temps le grand maître et ce juge impartial, qui met enfin de compte chaque peuple à la place que ses qualités ou ses défauts lui assignent sédormé à l'Angleterre pour ne plus le lui reprendre le premier rang parmi les nations colonisatrices."—*Loc. cit.*, vol. ii. p. 246. See also vol. i. p. 92.

FINIS.

INDEX.